This book belongs to

Naacy Wheeler

For my very flavorite
teacher (Nancy Wheeler)

Mathematics UNLIMITED

 Harcourt Brace Jovanovich, Inc.

Holt, Rinehart and Winston, Inc.

Orlando • Austin • San Diego • Chicago • Dallas • Toronto

AUTHORS

Francis "Skip" Fennell
Associate Professor of Education
Western Maryland College
Westminster, Maryland

Barbara J. Reys
Assistant Professor of Curriculum
and Instruction
University of Missouri, Columbia, Missouri
Formerly Junior High Mathematics Teacher
Oakland Junior High, Columbia, Missouri

Robert E. Reys
Professor of Mathematics Education
University of Missouri
Columbia, Missouri

Arnold W. Webb
Senior Research Associate
Research for Better Schools
Philadelphia, Pennsylvania
Formerly Asst. Commissioner of Education
New Jersey State Education Department

ILLUSTRATION

Alex Bloch: pp. 8, 9, 191, 256, 257, 370, 371 • Janet Bohn: pp. 76, 77, 140, 141, 176, 177, 198, 238, 239, 288, 289, 302 • Jack Davis: pp. 38, 39, 50, 51, 62, 63, 346, 347 • Nancy Didion: pp. 11, 146, 391 • Ivan Dieruf: pp. 22, 23, 74, 75, 244, 245, 262 • Creston Ely: pp. 6, 7, 132, 152, 153, 329, 350, 366, 404, 405 • Simon Galkin: pp. 46, 47, 78, 79, 94, 95, 144, 160, 220, 221, 227, 254, 255, 278, 279, 290, 291, 376, 377 • Mark Giglio: pp. 286, 287 • Fred Harsh: pp. 82, 108, 109, 161 • Kristina Juzaitis: pp.147, 276, 280, 281 • John Killgrew: pp. 36, 37, 138, 139, 246, 247, 252, 294, 295, 401, 406 • Elliot Kreloff: pp. 4, 5, 92, 93, 129, 142 • Diana Magnuson: p. 114 • Laurie Marks: p. 218 • Roland Moch: p. 99 • Jan Palmer: p. 89 • Beverly Pardee-Rich: pp. 78, 179, 265, 363 • Tom Powers: pp. 18, 19, 120, 121 • Jan Pyk: p. 104 • David Reinbold: p. 135 • Karen Ryan: p. 226 • Claudia Sargent: pp. 27, 264, 292, 293, 310, 312, 325, 337, 382, 402, 403 • Dorothea Sierra: pp. 116, 117, 128 • N. Jo Smith: pp. 48, 49, 58 • Judith Sutton: p. 188 • Debbie Tilley: pp. 54, 61, 180, 181 • George Ulrich: p. 110 • Vera Vullo: pp. 168, 205 • Nina Wallace: pp. 26, 248 • Jack Wallen: pp. 186, 187 • Fred Winkowski: pp. 200, 201, 242, 243, 378 • Nina Winters: pp. 84, 90, 122, 123, 216, 217 • Lane Yerkes: pp. 14, 271, 284, 333, 339 • Clare Sup: pp. H181, H182, H183, H184, H185, H187, H189, H191, H192, H193, H194, H197, H198, H200, H201, H202, H203, H204. **Chapter Opener Illustrations:** Tom Powers: pp. 1, 35, 73, 107, 137, 167, 197, 235, 273, 305, 345, 369. **Cover Illustration:** Jeannette Adams.

PHOTOGRAPHY

Alpha/P. Gridley: p. 238 • Bruce Coleman, Inc./Eric Crichton: p. 80 • DPI/Wil Blanche: p. 360 • DRK Photo/Stephen J. Krasemann: p. 97 • Duomo/David Madison: pp. 356, 357, 373 • Esto Photographics, Inc./Dan Cornish: p. 314 • Focus on Sports: p. 349 • FPG/Jack Zehrt: p. 336 • Granger Collection: p. 42 • Tino Hammid: p. 284 • Michal Heron: pp. 183, 198 • HRW Photo/Russell Dian: p. 270; Richard Haynes: pp. 2, 3, 44, 45, 86, 154, 155, 169, 202, 203, 205, 236, 237, 258, 260, 331, 338, 352, 353, 374, 375; Ken Karp: pp. 174, 209; Yoav Levy: p. 232 • Image Bank/Bill Carter: p. 322; Andy Caulfield: p. 159; Don Klumpp: pp. 380, 381 • International Stock Photo/Wayne Sproul: p. 212 • Ken Karp: p. 189 • Lawrence Migdale: pp. 20, 21, 71, 124, 125, 296, 297 • Monkmeyer Press/Mimi Forsyth: p. 33 • NASA: pp. 12, 13, 25 • Marvin E. Newman: p. 316 right • Omni-Photo Communications, Inc./Ken Karp: pp. 20, 21, 71, 124, 125, 170, 171, 206, 207, 209, 250, 251, 252, 306, 354, 386, 387; John Lei: pp. 10, 40, 41, 56, 57, 110, 111, 185, 210, 222, 223, 274, 275, 358 • Peabody Museum: p. 156 • Photo Researchs, Inc./Robert Borneman: p. 88; Rob Gray: pp. 90, 91; George Holton: p. 328; George J. Joines III: pp. 118-119; Sven-Olof Lindblad: p. 96; R. Rowan: p. 385 • Jim Pickerell: p. 318 • Private Collection: p. 60 • Chuck Solomon: p. 348 • Stock Market/Paul Barton: p. 299; Claudia Parks: p. 52; Lewis Portnoy: p. 65 • Taurus Photos/Ellis Herwig: p. 16 • Wheeler Pictures/Joe McNally: p. 175 • Woodfin Camp & Associates/Jim Anderson: p. 150; Robert Frerck: pp. 326, 327; George Hall: p. 283; Michal Heron: pp. 12, 113; Loren McIntyre: p. 172; Sepp Seitz: pp. 316 left, 389; Homer Sykes: p. 149. Page H186tr, Tony Freeman/PhotoEdit; H186cl, HBJ Photo/b.b.Steel; H196, Bob Rashid/TSW-Click/Chicago; H203, Gabe Palmer/The Stock Market.

Printed in the United States of America

ISBN 0-15-351565-1

CONTENTS

1 BASIC FACTS, PLACE VALUE

2 How Big Is a Thousand?
4 Thousands
6 **Problem Solving:** Four-Step Plan
8 Comparing and Ordering Whole Numbers
10 Money
12 Millions
14 Rounding Numbers

16 **Problem Solving:** Using Outside Sources Including the Infobank
18 Addition Facts
20 Subtraction Facts
22 Fact Families
24 **Problem Solving:** Choosing the Operation
26 **Math Communication**
27 **Group Project**
28 Chapter Test
30 Reteaching
31 Enrichment: Roman Numerals
32 Technology
34 Cumulative Review

2 ADDITION AND SUBTRACTION

36 Adding 2-Digit Numbers
38 More Adding 2-Digit Numbers
40 Number Sense
41 Estimating Sums
42 **Problem Solving:** Identifying Needed Information
44 Adding Larger Numbers
46 Working with Money
48 Column Addition
50 Estimating Sums by Rounding

52 **Problem Solving:** Estimation
54 Subtracting 2-Digit Numbers
56 Estimating Differences
58 Subtracting 3-Digit Numbers
60 Subtracting Larger Numbers
62 Subtracting with Zeros
64 **Problem Solving:** Writing a Number Sentence
66 Calculator
67 **Group Project**
68 Chapter Test
70 Reteaching
71 Enrichment: Making and Counting Change
72 Cumulative Review

3 MULTIPLICATION FACTS, TIME

74 Multiplying with 2 and 3
76 Multiplying with 4 and 5
78 Properties of Multiplication
80 **Problem Solving:** Choosing the Operation
82 Multiplying with 6 and 7
84 Multiplying with 8 and 9
86 Multiples

88 **Problem Solving:** Solving Two-Step Problems/Making a Plan
90 Units of Time
92 Telling Time
94 More Units of Time
96 **Problem Solving:** Using a Bar Graph
98 Calculator
99 **Group Project**
100 Chapter Test
102 Reteaching
103 Enrichment: Even and Odd Sums, Differences, and Products
104 Technology
106 Cumulative Review

DIVISION FACTS

108 Dividing by 2 and 3
110 Dividing by 4 and 5
112 Problem Solving: Making a Line Graph
114 Families of Facts
116 0 and 1 in Division
118 Problem Solving: Making a Table to
    Find a Pattern

120 Dividing by 6 and 7
122 Dividing by 8 and 9
124 Factors
126 Problem Solving: Choosing Strategies
128 **Math Communication**
129 Group Project
130 Chapter Test
132 Reteaching
133 Enrichment: Factor Trees
134 Technology
136 Cumulative Review

 **MULTIPLICATION: 1-DIGIT MULTIPLIERS**

138 Multiples of 10; 100; and 1,000
140 Estimating Products
142 Multiplying 2-Digit Numbers
144 More Multiplying 2-Digit Numbers
146 Problem Solving: Estimation
148 Multiplying 3-Digit Numbers
150 More Multiplying 3-Digit Numbers

152 Multiplying 4-Digit Numbers
154 Multiplying Money
156 Problem Solving: Identifying Extra
    Information
158 Problem Solving: Choosing the
    Operation
160 Logical Reasoning
161 Group Project
162 Chapter Test
164 Reteaching
165 Enrichment: Order of Operations
166 Cumulative Review

 **DIVISION: 1-DIGIT DIVISORS**

168 Dividing with Remainders
170 Estimating Quotients
172 Two-Step Division
174 Problem Solving: Interpreting the
    Quotient and the Remainder
176 More Two-Step Division
178 Three-Step Division

180 Finding Averages
182 Problem Solving: Choosing Strategies
184 Zero in the Quotient
186 Dividing with Money
188 Problem Solving: Writing a Number
    Sentence
190 Calculator
191 Group Project
192 Chapter Test
194 Reteaching
195 Enrichment: Divisibility
196 Cumulative Review

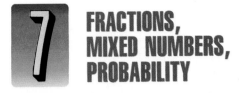

FRACTIONS, MIXED NUMBERS, PROBABILITY

198 Fractions: Part of a Whole
200 Fractions: Part of a Set
202 Finding Part of a Set
204 Equivalent Fractions
206 More Equivalent Fractions
208 **Problem Solving:** Using a Circle Graph
210 Mixed Numbers
212 Comparing Fractions and Mixed Numbers

214 **Problem Solving:** Working Backward
216 Probability
218 More Probability
220 Ratio
222 **Problem Solving:** Making a Diagram
224 **Problem Solving:** Choosing/Writing a Sensible Question
226 **Math Communication**
227 **Group Project**
228 Chapter Test
230 Reteaching
231 Enrichment: United States Time Zones
232 Technology
234 Cumulative Review

FRACTIONS, MIXED NUMBERS, DECIMALS

236 Adding Fractions
238 Adding Fractions with Unlike Denominators
240 **Problem Solving:** Choosing Strategies
242 Subtracting Fractions
244 Subtracting Fractions with Unlike Denominators
246 Adding and Subtracting Mixed Numbers
248 **Problem Solving:** Making an Organized List

250 Tenths
252 Hundredths
254 Comparing and Ordering Decimals
256 Rounding/Estimating
258 Adding Decimals
260 Subtracting Decimals
262 **Problem Solving:** Writing a Simpler Problem
264 Logical Reasoning
265 **Group Project**
266 Chapter Test
268 Reteaching
269 Enrichment: Percent
270 Technology
272 Cumulative Review

MEASUREMENT

274 Centimeter
276 Meter and Kilometer
278 Liter and Milliliter
280 Gram and Kilogram
282 **Problem Solving:** Drawing a Picture/ Making a Model
284 **Problem Solving:** Guessing and Checking
286 Inch

288 Foot, Yard, and Mile
290 Ounce, Pound, and Ton
292 Cup, Pint, Quart, and Gallon
294 Temperature: Fahrenheit
295 Temperature: Celsius
296 **Problem Solving:** Identifying Needed Information
298 Calculator
299 **Group Project**
300 Chapter Test
302 Reteaching
303 Enrichment: Reading a Recipe
304 Cumulative Review

GEOMETRY

306 Lines and Line Segments
308 Rays and Angles
310 Polygons
312 Circles
314 **Problem Solving:** Checking That the Solution Answers the Question
316 Congruence, Enlarging Drawings
318 Symmetry
320 Ordered Pairs
322 Perimeter

324 Area
326 **Problem Solving:** Looking for a Pattern
328 Solid Figures
330 Volume
332 **Problem Solving:** Using Advertisements
334 Making a Bar Graph
336 Making a Pictograph
338 Calculator
339 **Group Project**
340 Chapter Test
342 Reteaching
343 Enrichment: Flips, Slides, and Turns
344 Cumulative Review

MULTIPLICATION: 2-DIGIT MULTIPLIERS

346 Multiplying Multiples of 10; 100; and 1,000
348 Estimating Products
350 **Problem Solving:** Choosing Strategies
352 Multiplying Two 2-Digit Factors

354 More Multiplying Two 2-Digit Factors
356 **Problem Solving:** Estimation
358 Multiplying a 3-Digit Factor
360 **Problem Solving:** Checking for a Reasonable Answer
362 Logical Reasoning
363 **Group Project**
364 Chapter Test
366 Reteaching
367 Enrichment: Casting Out Nines
368 Cumulative Review

DIVISION: 2-DIGIT DIVISORS

370 Mental Computation: Dividing Tens and Hundreds
372 **Problem Solving:** Writing a Number Sentence
374 Dividing by Multiples of 10
376 Dividing with 2-Digit Divisors
378 Correcting Estimates

380 **Problem Solving:** Choosing Strategies
382 1-Digit Quotients
384 2-Digit Quotients
386 Dividing Money
388 **Problem Solving:** Estimation
390 Calculator
391 **Group Project**
392 Chapter Test
394 Reteaching
395 Enrichment: Time Cards
396 Cumulative Review
397 **Connecting Math Ideas**
401 Infobank

STUDENT HANDBOOK

H1 Classwork/Homework
H157 More Practice
H181 Math Reasoning
H205 Table of Measures and Symbols
H207 Glossary

Index
Learning Resources

Earth is one of nine known planets in our solar system. We already have sent spacecraft to take photographs of some of the other eight. If you could visit one of the other eight planets, which would it be? How would you decide which planet most of your classmates would like to visit?

1 BASIC FACTS, PLACE VALUE

How Big Is a Thousand?

A. It is sometimes hard to imagine large numbers. In this lesson, you will explore what 1,000 is.

Step 1: Take 10 counters and stack them.

- How tall is the stack? How can you show this with your fingers?

- How many stacks of 10 counters would you need to make 100 counters?

- How many counters would there be in 100 stacks of 10 counters each?

- How high would a stack of 1,000 counters be? How could you figure this out?

Step 2: Put 100 X's on a piece of paper.

- How long did it take you to make the marks?

- Work with your classmates to put 10 of these pieces of paper together so that you will have 1,000 marks. How much space do these marks take? Could you fit 1,000 marks on a single sheet of paper? How?

- How long would it take one person to make 1,000 X's?

Thinking as a Team

1. How big is one thousand? How many hundreds are in one thousand? How many tens? How many ones?

2. Which things in your classroom do you think there are a thousand of?

3. If 1,000 children gathered in one place, how much space would they take? Which rooms in your school can hold 1,000 children?

Record your answers, and discuss them with the class.

B. Discuss each question or group of questions listed below. Pick 2 of them. Work with your team to find ways to answer the questions you chose.

- How big a container would you need to hold 1,000 pencils?

- How thick is a notebook containing 1,000 pieces of paper?

- Could you stand on one leg for 1,000 seconds? How could you time yourself?

- How long would it take to count to 1,000 by ones? by twos? by fives?

- If you were given $1,000 in $1 bills, would they fit in a shoebox?

- What could you buy with $1,000? with 1,000 pennies? with 1,000 dimes? How would you carry 1,000 pennies or 1,000 dimes to the store?

Record your choices, methods, and answers. Discuss your results with the class.

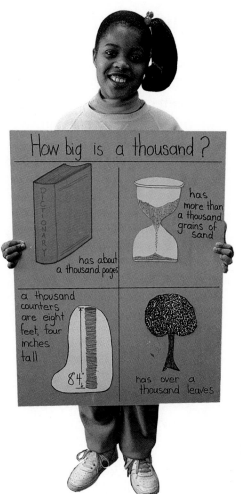

C. Here are some statements about 1,000. Some are true and some are not. Work with your team to find out which are true. Base your answers on what seems reasonable.

- There are more than 1,000 books in your classroom.

- The population of your town is less than 1,000.

- You can stay awake for at least 1,000 minutes.

- There are fewer than 1,000 words in most books.

Record your answers and your reasons for choosing them. Discuss them with the class.

D. How could you and your team describe 1,000 to someone who had no idea of the size of this number? Come up with a way to do this. Then take turns with other teams and describe 1,000 to the class.

Thousands

A. One group of space campers visited the planetarium. They learned that the distance across the center of the sun is eight hundred sixty-four thousand miles. How would you write this number?

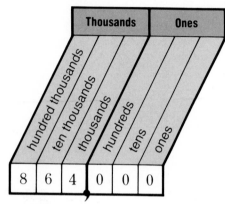

Read: 864 thousand.
Write: 864,000.

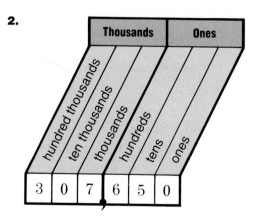

A comma helps you read large numbers.

In 864,000:
the value of the digit 8 in the hundred thousands place is 800,000.
the value of the digit 6 in the ten thousands place is 60,000.
the value of the digit 4 in the thousands place is 4,000.

B. You can write numbers in standard form or in expanded form.

Standard form	**Expanded form**
6,927	6,000 + 900 + 20 + 7
3,027	3,000 + 20 + 7

Write each in standard form.

1.

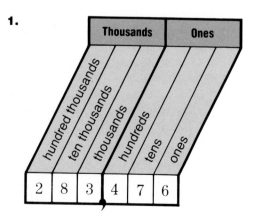

2.

4

Write each in standard form.

3. one thousand, three hundred fifty-five

4. seventy-six thousand, two hundred twelve

Write each number in expanded form.

5. 6,713   **6.** 856   **7.** 4,983   **8.** 6,491   **9.** 8,921

10. 984   **11.** 5,921   **12.** 8,641   **13.** 9,432   **14.** 371

Write the value of the blue digit.

15. 783   **16.** 4,789   **17.** 8,799   **18.** 321   **19.** 4,235

20. 3,984   **21.** 6,600   **22.** 62,329   **23.** 44,822   **24.** 55,897

25. 76,491   **26.** 78,255   **27.** 45,455   **28.** 34,999   **29.** 34,444

30. 234,678   **31.** 457,897   **32.** 897,655   **33.** 256,789   **34.** 156,789

For each number, write the digit that is in the given place.

35. 6,289 (hundreds place)   **36.** 579 (ones place)

37. 68,910 (tens place)   **38.** 49,286 (thousands place)

39. 457,892 (ten thousands place)   **40.** 298,675 (hundred thousands place)

Write each number in words.

41. 8,349   **42.** 896   **43.** 34,897   **44.** 45,789   **45.** 34,789

46. 234,467   **47.** 568,006   **48.** 190,609   **49.** 333,330   **50.** 222,006

NUMBER SENSE

Look at the numbers in the box. Choose three that are close to 10; three that are close to 100; and three that are close to 1,000. What numbers have you chosen for each group?

9	1,002	7
45	629	98
104	1,009	3
991	12	94

Problem Solving
A Four-Step Plan

One day the Searcher space probe traveled nearly four hundred thousand miles. Which day was it?

Mark used a four-step plan to solve the problem. You can use this method whenever you are solving a problem.

JOURNEY OF THE SEARCHER

Day	Distance (mi)
Monday	157,624
Tuesday	460,533
Wednesday	398,721
Thursday	574,009
Friday	513,218

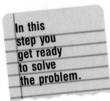

In this step you get ready to solve the problem.

1. QUESTIONS
First, he read the problem carefully. He made sure he understood the *question*. Then he stated the problem in his own words.

I need to find the number in the table that is close to four hundred thousand.

In this step you plan your solution.

2. TOOLS
Next, he chose the *tools* he needed. Tools are the skills you use to solve problems.

I can use what I know about place value and the standard form of numbers to solve the problem.

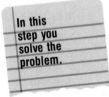

In this step you solve the problem.

3. SOLUTIONS
Mark found the *solution* by applying the tools he had chosen.

I can write four hundred thousand as 400,000. The number in the table that is close to 400,000 is 398,721. The day must have been Wednesday.

In this step you check your answer.

4. CHECKS
Finally, he *checked* his solution to be sure it made sense.

None of the other numbers in the table is close to 400,000. My answer makes sense.

Do not solve the problem. Name a tool you can use to solve the problem. Use the table on page 6.

1. How far did the Searcher space probe travel altogether on Thursday and Friday?

2. How much farther did the Searcher travel on Wednesday than it traveled on Monday?

3. The Searcher traveled 214,811 miles per day for 8 days in a row. How many miles did the Searcher travel in all during the 8 days?

4. The Searcher weighed 8,403 pounds. Suppose each of the 3 sections of the probe weighed the same. How much did each section weigh?

Use the 4-step problem solving plan. Solve.

5. One day the Searcher traveled about five hundred ten thousand miles. Which day was it?

6. One day the digit in the ten thousands place of the distance that the Searcher traveled was a 7. How far did the Searcher travel the following day?

7. The Quest satellite traveled 163,024 miles on a certain day. That same day the Searcher's distance showed the same hundreds digit as the Quest's. Which day was it?

8. On which day or days did the Searcher's distance show a tens digit that is greater than its thousands digit?

Comparing and Ordering Whole Numbers

A. Jack wants to explore our solar system. He read that Venus is about the same size as Earth. Earth is 7,926 miles through its center. Venus is 7,524 miles through its center. Which planet is larger?

You can use a number line to compare 7,926 and 7,524.

7,926 is to the right of 7,524.
7,926 is greater than 7,524.
$7,926 > 7,524$

7,524 is to the left of 7,926.
7,524 is less than 7,926.
$7,524 < 7,926$

Earth is larger than Venus.

> means **is greater than.**	< means **is less than.**
= means **is equal to.**	≠ means **is not equal to.**

B. You can compare numbers by comparing digits. Line up the digits that are in the ones place.

Compare 6,592 and 6,587.
Begin at the left. Check each place until the digits differ.

Compare the thousands.
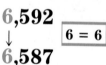

Compare the hundreds.
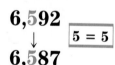

Compare the tens.
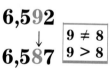

So, $6,592 > 6,587$.

C. Write 2,650; 255; and 2,429 in order from the least to the greatest.

Compare the first two numbers.

$255 < 2,650$

Compare the first two numbers to the third number.

$255 < 2,429$
$2,429 < 2,650$

So, the order from the least to the greatest is: 255; 2,429; 2,650.
The order of the numbers from the greatest to the least is: 2,650; 2,429; 255.

Math Reasoning, page H181

Compare. Write = or ≠ for ⬤.

1. 869 ⬤ 895 **2.** 1,321 ⬤ 1,321 **3.** 25,652 ⬤ 2,592 **4.** 329 ⬤ 3,291

Compare. Write >, <, or = for ⬤.

5. 2,429 ⬤ 2,567 **6.** 6,415 ⬤ 645 **7.** 987 ⬤ 999 **8.** 425 ⬤ 4,250

9. 32,067 ⬤ 32,141 **10.** 98,104 ⬤ 9,804 **11.** 62,011 ⬤ 63,110 **12.** 27,123 ⬤ 27,123

13. 9,999 ⬤ 1,000 **14.** 4,561 ⬤ 5,416 **15.** 1,001 ⬤ 2,000 **16.** 845 ⬤ 849

17. 12,005 ⬤ 12,050 **18.** 8,799 ⬤ 6,777 **19.** 71,234 ⬤ 23,209 **20.** 8,765 ⬤ 975

21. 1,090 ⬤ 1,009 **22.** 56,756 ⬤ 57,999 **23.** 44,876 ⬤ 44,876 **24.** 546 ⬤ 399

25. 8,009 ⬤ 8,090 **26.** 4,758 ⬤ 4,777 **27.** 797 ⬤ 979 **28.** 90,876 ⬤ 98,076

Write in order from the least to the greatest.

29. 392; 3,129; 3,912; 3,219 **30.** 140; 4,104; 418; 4,186

31. 3,257; 5,237; 3,132; 5,312 **32.** 213; 1,203; 203; 1,313

33. 798; 9,877; 9,789; 897 **34.** 4,217; 217; 7,241; 4,172

Write in order from the greatest to the least.

35. 6,799; 9,799; 799; 677 **36.** 341; 457; 9,711; 497

37. 3,218; 832; 2,931; 3,918 **38.** 2,918; 918; 892; 9,892

NUMBER SENSE

For the number 25,641, write the number that is

1 more.   10 more.   100 more.   1,000 more.

For the number 32,112, write the number that is

1 less.   10 less.   100 less.   1,000 less.

Money

A. Marta collects rocket stickers. She bought 5 stickers. Each sticker cost 1 nickel. How much did Marta spend?

You can count nickels by skip-counting by fives.

| **5** | **10** | **15** | **20** | **25** |

5 nickels are worth 25¢, or $0.25.
Read: twenty-five cents.

Marta spent 25¢.

B. You can count dimes by skip-counting by tens.

10   **20**   **30**   **40**   **50**

5 dimes are worth 50¢, or $0.50.
Read: fifty cents.

C. You can count bills and coins. Start with the bills that are worth the most.

$10.00 + $1.00 + $0.50 + $0.25 + $0.10 + $0.10 + $0.05 + $0.01
$10.00 ⟶ $11.00 ⟶ $11.50 ⟶ $11.75 ⟶ $11.85 ⟶ $11.95 ⟶ $12.00 ⟶ $12.01
Read: twelve dollars and one cent.

Count the money. Write each total. Use the dollar sign and the cents point.

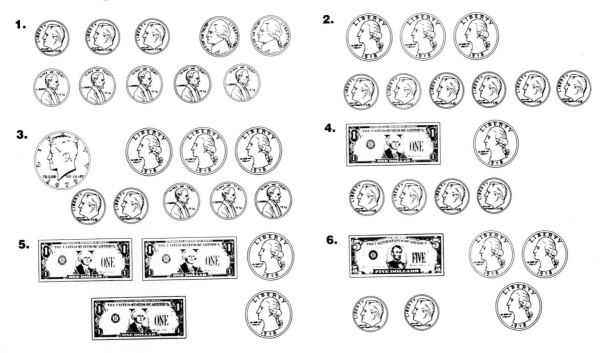

Write each amount. Use the dollar sign and the cents point.

7. seven dollars and eighty cents

8. eight dollars and twenty-three cents

9. fifteen dollars and seventy-five cents

10. fourteen dollars and eighty cents

11. five dollars and twenty cents

12. sixteen dollars and three cents

13. eight dimes

14. four nickels

15. six quarters

16. three quarters, two dimes, and one nickel

17. five nickels and four pennies

18. one half-dollar, four dimes, and three pennies

CHALLENGE

May bought a book about careers in the aerospace industry for six dollars and ninety-two cents. Which bills and coins should she have used if she wanted to use the least number possible?

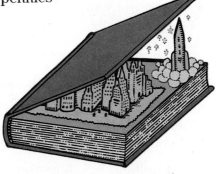

Millions

One day, Saturn's orbit had taken the planet eight hundred thirty-five million, one hundred forty-two thousand, sixty-seven miles away from the sun.

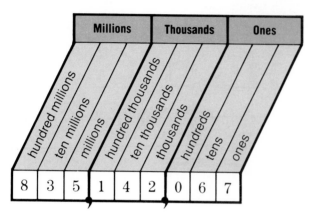

Read: 835 million, 142 thousand, 67.
Write: 835,142,067.

In 835,142,067:

the value of the digit 8 in the hundred millions place is 800,000,000.
the value of the digit 3 in the ten millions place is 30,000,000.
the value of the digit 5 in the millions place is 5,000,000.

Write each in standard form.

1.

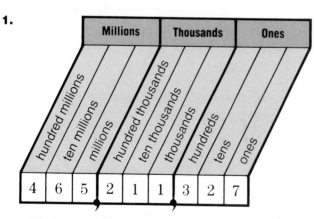

2. ninety-two million, six hundred fifty thousand, one hundred

3. one hundred five million, forty thousand, two hundred forty-eight

4. 934 million, 723 thousand, 412

Write the digit that is in the ten millions place.

5. 742,355,648   6. 305,679,122   7. 944,325,493   8. 654,269,077

9. 856,599,033   10. 955,321,756   11. 688,000,476   12. 999,857,444

Write the digit that is in the hundred millions place.

13. 971,459,632   14. 109,254,188   15. 435,297,031   16. 216,441,621

17. 795,320,364   18. 733,918,000   19. 410,746,037   20. 603,888,579

Write the digit that is in the millions place.

21. 431,622,987   22. 327,216,918   23. 248,802,468   24. 500,317,464

25. 733,955,364   26. 694,739,122   27. 836,089,755   28. 921,635,888

Write the value of the blue digit.

29. 564,095,866   30. 922,617,346   31. 129,500,981   32. 475,239,688

33. 104,692,387   34. 679,615,227   35. 450,821,607   36. 317,122,511

Solve. For Problem 38, use the Infobank.

37. Hal studied the solar system for a space project. He found that Mercury is sometimes one hundred thirty-eight million miles away from Earth. Write this distance in standard form.

38. Use the information on page 401 to solve. Which distance from the planets to the sun has the greatest digit in the ten millions place? Which distance has a 6 in the ten millions place? Which has a distance from the sun to Mars in the millions place?

CALCULATOR

Enter the largest number you can on your calculator. What is the number?

Now enter a number that is 100,000 less than that number. What is the number?

Now enter a number that is 100 less than the largest number. What is the number?

Rounding Numbers

A. Stan's model rocket traveled to an altitude of 481 feet. Estimate the altitude by rounding the number to the nearest hundred. To the nearest hundred feet, how high did the rocket travel?

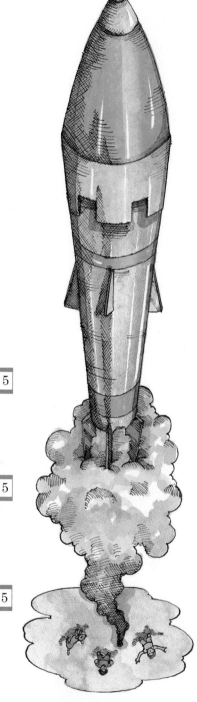

```
       481
←——•———————•———————•———————•—•———————•——→
  400     425     450     475  481    500
```

481 is between 400 and 500.
481 is closer to 500 than it is to 400. Round up to 500.
481 rounded to the nearest hundred is 500.

To the nearest hundred feet, the rocket traveled to an altitude of 500 feet.

B. You can round numbers to different places.
Round 36 to the nearest ten.
Find the digit that is in the ones place.
If the digit is 5 or greater, round up.   36   6 > 5
If the digit is less than 5, round down.

36 rounded to the nearest ten is 40.

Round 8,249 to the nearest hundred.
Find the digit that is in the tens place.   8,249   4 < 5
Since the digit is less than 5, round down.

8,249 rounded to the nearest hundred is 8,200.

Round 64,529 to the nearest thousand.
Find the digit that is in the hundreds place.   64,529   5 = 5
Since the digit is 5, round up.

64,529 rounded to the nearest thousand is 65,000.

C. Round money in the same way.

Round to the nearest ten cents.	Round to the nearest dollar.	Round to the nearest ten dollars.
77¢ ⟶ 80¢	$6.25 ⟶ $6.00	$37.65 ⟶ $40.00
$5.42 ⟶ $5.40	$25.53 ⟶ $26.00	$181.14 ⟶ $180.00

Round to the nearest ten or to the nearest ten cents.

1. 58   **2.** 62   **3.** 27   **4.** 79¢   **5.** 65¢   **6.** 33¢

7. 156   **8.** 179   **9.** 388   **10.** 491   **11.** 826   **12.** 565

13. $6.43   **14.** $5.43   **15.** $7.91   **16.** $6.33   **17.** $7.45   **18.** $9.11

Round to the nearest hundred or to the nearest dollar.

19. 361   **20.** 429   **21.** 750   **22.** $5.47   **23.** $9.71

24. 5,392   **25.** 7,501   **26.** 1,991   **27.** 9,950   **28.** 4,499

29. $16.34   **30.** $95.17   **31.** $34.99   **32.** $35.46   **33.** $83.12

Round to the nearest thousand.

34. 3,500   **35.** 4,500   **36.** 7,531   **37.** 3,899   **38.** 4,981

39. 11,927   **40.** 49,899   **41.** 38,466   **42.** 93,294   **43.** 77,123

Round to the nearest ten dollars.

44. $14.75   **45.** $13.96   **46.** $15.75   **47.** $17.15   **48.** $24.99

49. $14.65   **50.** $13.99   **51.** $27.86   **52.** $39.84   **53.** $52.88

54. $62.28   **55.** $75.86   **56.** $88.95   **57.** $466.85   **58.** $717.84

MIDCHAPTER REVIEW

Compare. Write >, <, or = for ●.

1. 348 ● 483   **2.** 6,724 ● 6,714   **3.** 10,594 ● 10,595

Write the value of the blue digit.

4. 32,895,051   **5.** 415,623,988   **6.** 2,755,894   **7.** 747,935

Write each amount. Use the dollar sign and the cents point.

8. thirty-six cents   **9.** three dollars and ten cents

Round each number to the nearest hundred.

10. 426   **11.** 397   **12.** 7,865   **13.** 8,225   **14.** 6,241

PROBLEM SOLVING
Using Outside Sources Including the Infobank

You don't always have all the information you need to answer the question in a problem. To find the information you need, you may have to go to outside sources.

You can use books, magazines, or newspapers. You can also obtain information from museums, government agencies, or other sources.

> The students at Witte School are planning a "Space Race." They want the racecourse to be as long as possible. Some students want to set up the race on the ice-hockey rink. Other students want to use the football field. Which playing area is longer?

To answer this question, you need to know the length of each playing area. You could find the information in an encyclopedia or an almanac.

Follow these steps.

Step 1: Look in the table of contents or in the index under *sports*.
Step 2: Find the page you need.
Step 3: Read carefully to find the information.

To practice finding information in an outside source, use the Infobank on page 406 of this book.

After you have found the length of each playing area, compare the two numbers.

A football field	(is longer than)	an ice-hockey rink.
360 feet	>	200 feet

The football field is longer.

Would you need an outside source to answer each question? Write *yes* or *no*.

1. Jeb wants to use the soccer field for the "Space Race." Is the soccer field longer than the football field?

2. Students collected 6 car tires, 8 truck tires, and 12 bicycle tires for the race. How many tires did they collect?

Solve. Use the Infobank that begins on page 401 if you need additional facts.

3. Did the Mudville baseball team score more runs or make more errors in the last four-game series?

4. Mudville scored 20 runs in a five-game series. Is this more or less than the number of runs it scored in the last four-game series?

5. Four magazines are sold at newsstands in one city. Which magazine is sold at the greatest number of newsstands?

6. Round the number of copies of *Nature* magazine to the nearest ten and to the nearest hundred.

7. At a clambake in Maine, Jerry served 2,738 lobsters. Is this more or less than the number of lobsters Jerry served in Rhode Island?

8. Was the least number of clams served on Fire Island, on Rhode Island, or on Nantucket? Where was the greatest number of lobsters served?

9. For which two kinds of motion does Jane shoot an equal number of frames for her movie?

10. One of Fay's mobiles is made up of 1,534 different parts. Round this number to the nearest thousand.

11. Write in words the number of miles that Jupiter is from the sun.

★12. Suppose you want to find the distance from Saturn to the sun. First, check the Infobank on page 401. If the information isn't there, what books might contain it? What people could help you find the books you need?

Addition Facts

A. Lynn's space-camp team worked for 2 hours in the model shuttle cockpit and for 4 hours learning how to operate mission control instruments. What was the total number of hours they worked?

You can add to find the total. Add 2 + 4.

$$
\begin{array}{l}
2 \longleftarrow \textbf{addend} \\
\underline{+\ 4} \longleftarrow \textbf{addend} \\
6 \longleftarrow \textbf{sum}
\end{array}
\qquad
\underset{\underset{\textbf{addend}}{\uparrow}}{2} + \underset{\underset{\textbf{addend}}{\uparrow}}{4} = \underset{\underset{\textbf{sum}}{\uparrow}}{6}
$$

They worked for a total of 6 hours.

B. The properties of addition can help you find sums.

Order Property If you change the order of the addends, the sum is always the same.	$3 + 6 = 9$ $\quad\begin{array}{r}3\\+6\\\hline9\end{array}\ \begin{array}{r}6\\+3\\\hline9\end{array}$ $6 + 3 = 9$
Zero Property If one addend is 0, the sum is equal to the other addend.	$5 + 0 = 5$ $\quad\begin{array}{r}5\\+0\\\hline5\end{array}\ \begin{array}{r}0\\+5\\\hline5\end{array}$ $0 + 5 = 5$
Grouping Property If you change the way addends are grouped, the sum is always the same. $(1 + 3) + 4 \qquad\qquad 1 + (3 + 4)$ $\quad\ \ \downarrow \qquad\qquad\qquad\qquad\quad \downarrow$ $\quad 4\ \ + 4 = 8 \qquad\ 1 +\ \ 7\ \ = 8$	

Add.

1. 5 + 6
6 + 5

2. 8 + 2
2 + 8

3. 7 + 5
5 + 7

4. 2 + 1
1 + 2

5. 4 + 5
5 + 4

6. 8 + 3
3 + 8

7. 4 + 2
2 + 4

8. 6 + 4
4 + 6

9. 9 + 8
8 + 9

10. 1 + 7
7 + 1

11. 5 + 3
3 + 5

12. 3 + 7
7 + 3

13. 8 + 5
5 + 8

14. 9 + 6
6 + 9

15. 6 + 8
8 + 6

16. 7
+ 8

17. 7
+ 6

18. 3
+ 4

19. 9
+ 8

20. 8
+ 6

21. 9
+ 9

22. 2
+ 4

23. 8
+ 8

24. 6
+ 3

25. 7
+ 7

26. 4
+ 9

27. 9
+ 2

28. 8
+ 7

29. 5
+ 7

30. 5
+ 5

31. 4
+ 7

32. 1
+ 6

33. 5
+ 2

34. 3
+ 9

35. 4
+ 0

36. 8
+ 5

37. (5 + 3) + 2
5 + (3 + 2)

38. 2 + (4 + 4)
(2 + 4) + 4

39. (7 + 2) + 5
7 + (2 + 5)

40. (1 + 2) + 3
1 + (2 + 3)

Solve.

41. Katherine drove the moon buggy for 5 miles. Then Lewis drove it for 6 miles. How many miles did they travel?

42. The space campers used 2 robot arms to lift boxes into the shuttle's cargo bay and 3 robot arms to stack the boxes. How many robot arms did they use?

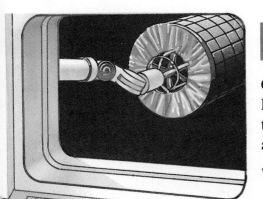

CHALLENGE

Copy the circles.
Place 1, 2, 3, 4, 5, and 6 in the circles so that the sum of the numbers that appear along each side is the same.

What is the sum?

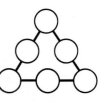

Subtraction Facts

A. Lucy collected 15 space-flight decals from NASA.
She gave Ted 6 decals. How many decals did Lucy have left?

You can subtract to find how many are left.
Subtract 15 − 6.

$$\begin{array}{r} 15 \\ -\ 6 \\ \hline 9 \end{array}$$ 15 − 6 = 9

9 ⟵ **difference**

Lucy had 9 decals left.

B. You can also use subtraction to compare and to find how many more are needed.

Compare.

How many more decals does Lucy have than Ted?

$$9 - 6 = 3$$

Lucy has 3 more decals than Ted.

How many more are needed?

How many more decals does Ted need to have as many as Lucy?

6 + ■ = 9   Since 9 − 6 = 3, then 6 + 3 = 9.

Ted needs 3 more decals.

C. The rule for zero can help you find differences.

If you subtract 0 from a number, the difference is equal to that number.	7 − 0 = 7	$\begin{array}{r} 7 \\ -\ 0 \\ \hline 7 \end{array}$
If you subtract a number from itself, the difference is 0.	7 − 7 = 0	$\begin{array}{r} 7 \\ -\ 7 \\ \hline 0 \end{array}$

Subtract.

1.	2.	3.	4.	5.	6.	7.
$\begin{array}{r} 7 \\ -\ 4 \\ \hline \end{array}$	$\begin{array}{r} 9 \\ -\ 5 \\ \hline \end{array}$	$\begin{array}{r} 6 \\ -\ 3 \\ \hline \end{array}$	$\begin{array}{r} 12 \\ -\ 7 \\ \hline \end{array}$	$\begin{array}{r} 15 \\ -\ 9 \\ \hline \end{array}$	$\begin{array}{r} 17 \\ -\ 9 \\ \hline \end{array}$	$\begin{array}{r} 14 \\ -\ 6 \\ \hline \end{array}$

Subtract.

| 8. 8
− 8 | 9. 18
− 9 | 10. 5
− 5 | 11. 12
− 5 | 12. 3
− 0 | 13. 14
− 9 | 14. 6
− 0 |

| 15. 15
− 8 | 16. 10
− 0 | 17. 11
− 5 | 18. 8
− 6 | 19. 10
− 4 | 20. 10
− 3 | 21. 11
− 8 |

22. $12 − 4$ 23. $13 − 9$ 24. $10 − 8$ 25. $8 − 4$ 26. $12 − 9$

27. $14 − 8$ 28. $13 − 5$ 29. $7 − 7$ 30. $11 − 4$ 31. $17 − 8$

32. $9 − 0$ 33. $13 − 6$ 34. $15 − 7$ 35. $4 − 0$ 36. $11 − 3$

Solve.

37. John stands 14 miles away from Cape Canaveral to watch lift-offs. Sue stands 7 miles away. How much farther away from Cape Canaveral is John than Sue?

38. At the end of the week, campers launched their own model rockets. Alpha Group launched 4 *Mercury* rockets. Beta Group launched 7 *Apollo* rockets. How many rockets were launched altogether?

★39. At space camp, the children simulate space missions. Use the chart at the right to write and solve your own word problems.

Simulated space missions	Mission- crew size
Space walk	2
Lunar landing	3
Skylab	3
Space shuttle	4

CHALLENGE

The sum of two numbers is 15. The difference of the two numbers is 3. What are the two numbers?

Fact Families

A. After a visit to the Kennedy Space Center, Dan and Julie built 15 model spaceships. Dan built 8 models, and Julie built 7.

The numbers 15, 8, and 7 make up a **family of facts**. You can write four number sentences for this family of facts.

$$8 + 7 = 15 \qquad 15 - 7 = 8$$
$$7 + 8 = 15 \qquad 15 - 8 = 7$$

Knowing one fact can help you find related sums and differences.

B. You can use families of facts to find missing addends. Find the number that is equal to ■ in the number sentence $3 + ■ = 5$.

Think: $3 + ■ = 5$.
You know that $5 - 3 = 2$
So, $3 + 2 = 5$.

The missing addend is 2.

Write each sum and each difference.

1. $5 + 6$
$6 + 5$
$11 - 6$
$11 - 5$

2. $7 + 2$
$2 + 7$
$9 - 2$
$9 - 7$

3. $4 + 3$
$3 + 4$
$7 - 3$
$7 - 4$

4. $9 + 9$
$18 - 9$

5. $7 + 6$
$6 + 7$
$13 - 6$
$13 - 7$

Complete each family of facts.

6. $6 + 9 = 15$ **7.** $12 - 8 = 4$ **8.** $3 + 8 = 11$ **9.** $8 + 8 = 16$

10. $2 + 4 = 6$ **11.** $5 + 3 = 8$ **12.** $9 - 3 = 6$ **13.** $14 - 7 = 7$

Write a family of facts for each group.

14. 6, 8, 14 **15.** 5, 2, 7 **16.** 6, 12, 6 **17.** 13, 8, 5

18. 9, 4, 5 **19.** 10, 6, 4 **20.** 1, 3, 4 **21.** 4, 11, 7

Write the missing addend.

22. $8 + \blacksquare = 15$ **23.** $9 + \blacksquare = 12$ **24.** $2 + \blacksquare = 3$ **25.** $7 + \blacksquare = 12$

26. $\blacksquare + 9 = 17$ **27.** $4 + \blacksquare = 12$ **28.** $\blacksquare + 6 = 8$ **29.** $1 + \blacksquare = 8$

30. $6 + \blacksquare = 13$ **31.** $\blacksquare + 3 = 12$ **32.** $2 + \blacksquare = 11$ **33.** $\blacksquare + 4 = 8$

34. $\blacksquare + 3 = 8$ **35.** $2 + \blacksquare = 5$ **36.** $\blacksquare + 4 = 13$ **37.** $5 + \blacksquare = 5$

Solve.

38. Kim interviewed 8 people at the space center. She met 3 astronauts and 5 members of the ground crew. Use these numbers to write a family of facts.

39. Use the information given in the table to write three families of facts.

SPACE CLUB (WEEKLY HOURS)

	Computers	Rockets
Jane	2	1
Eva	2	3
Paul	1	4

FOCUS: REASONING

There are 5 red rockets. There are 3 more blue rockets than red rockets. There are 9 more green rockets than blue rockets.

1. How many blue rockets are there?
2. How many green rockets are there?

PROBLEM SOLVING
Choosing the Operation

Here are hints to help you decide whether you should add or subtract to solve a problem.

A. In 1975, 2 Soviet cosmonauts and 3 American astronauts met in space. How many people met in space?

$2 + 3 = 5$ people

You know	how many in each of two or more groups.
You want to find	how many in all.
You can	ADD.

B. For a test, 5 astronauts reported in the morning and 4 reported in the afternoon. How many astronauts reported for the test?

$5 + 4 = 9$ astronauts

You know	how many in one group. how many join the group.
You want to find	how many in all.
You can	ADD.

C. The first spaceflight to the moon carried 3 astronauts. Only 2 of the astronauts landed. How many astronauts did not land on the moon?

$3 - 2 = 1$ astronaut

You know	how many in all. how many taken away.
You want to find	how many are left.
You can	SUBTRACT.

D. One year, 7 rockets were launched. The next year, 3 rockets were launched. How many more rockets were launched in the first year?

$7 - 3 = 4$ rockets

You know	how many in each of two groups.
You want to find	how many more in one group than in the other.
You can	SUBTRACT.

E. In a parade, there were 9 astronauts who had walked on the moon. Of these, 7 had been on the moon once. How many had been on the moon more than once?

$9 - 7 = 2$ astronauts

You know	how many in all. how many in part of the group.
You want to find	how many in the rest of the group.
You can	SUBTRACT.

Which operation would you choose? Write the letter of the correct answer.

1. Galileo discovered 4 moons of Jupiter. Other astronomers discovered 8 other moons of Jupiter. How many moons of Jupiter did they discover altogether?

   a. addition   **b.** subtraction

2. The *Gemini* spacecraft carried 2 astronauts. The *Mercury* spacecraft carried 1 astronaut. How many more astronauts did the *Gemini* carry than the *Mercury*?

   a. addition   **b.** subtraction

Solve.

3. The *Gemini 3* spacecraft orbited the earth 7 times. The *Gemini 8* orbited the earth 3 times. How many more times did the *Gemini 3* orbit the earth?

4. Of the 3 women astronauts at a meeting, 1 was from the United States. The other women were from the Soviet Union. How many women astronauts were from the Soviet Union?

5. In 1860, scientists believed that there were 5 planets in our solar system. We now know that there are 4 more planets. How many planets are there in our solar system?

6. Estrella plans to be an astronaut. She knows that she will have to go to college for 4 years and then train to fly rockets for 6 years. How many years will it take Estrella to become an astronaut?

7. Beth has pictures of 15 Apollo astronauts. Of all the astronauts in her pictures, 7 have landed on the moon. How many of the pictured astronauts have not landed on the moon?

MATH COMMUNICATION

$$\begin{array}{r} 3 \\ + \ 9 \\ \hline 12 \end{array} \begin{array}{l} \text{addend} \\ \text{addend} \\ \text{sum} \end{array}$$

$$\begin{array}{r} 14 \\ - \ 6 \\ \hline 8 \end{array} \begin{array}{l} \\ \\ \text{difference} \end{array}$$

Math has its own vocabulary. There are words that have certain meanings in math.

When you add numbers, each number that you add is called an *addend.*

When you add numbers, the answer is called the *sum.*

When you subtract one number from another, the answer is called the *difference.*

Read each problem. Write the letter of the correct answer.

1. The constellation called the *Big Dipper* has 7 stars. There are 6 stars in the constellation Cassiopeia. How many stars are in both constellations?

   In this problem, what is the number 7 called?

   a. *sum* **b.** *addend*
   c. *plus* **d.** *difference*

   When you solve the problem, what will you find?

   a. *sum* **b.** *addend*
   c. *plus* **d.** *difference*

2. Paulo took photographs of 10 different stars. Only 7 of the photographs were clear. The others were too dark. How many of the photographs were too dark?

   When you solve this problem, what will you find?

   a. *sum* **b.** *addend*
   c. *plus* **d.** *difference*

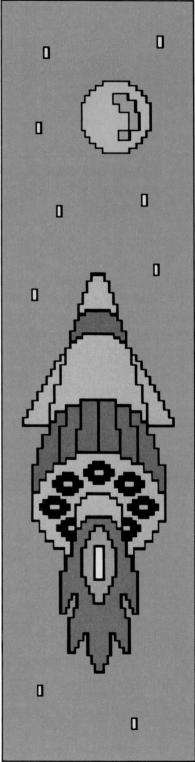

GROUP PROJECT

A Time Capsule for the Future

The problem: At the library, your class saw a time capsule that was put together by fourth graders in 1940. They filled a box with items that showed what life was like at that time. Then the capsule was sealed for 50 years.

You and your classmates decide to make a time capsule. It will tell people in the future about your lives today. The same library said that they would store yours for 50 years if it was no bigger than a shoe box. You can fit up to 20 items into the box.

Key Questions

- How would your class go about choosing the items to be put into the time capsule?
- Would the class vote on each item?
- What would you want people in the future to know about your life?
- What could you include that would explain the jobs people have?
- How could you show how people of your age spend a typical day? What could you show about the typical day of adults?
- Will your 20 items fit into a shoe box? If not, what would you remove from your list?

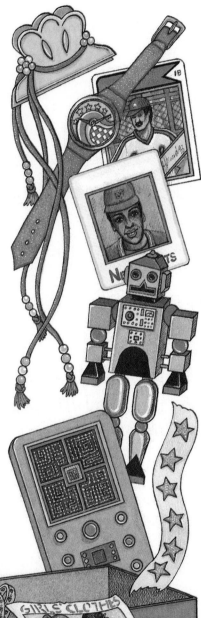

CHAPTER TEST

Write each in standard form. (pages 2, 4, and 12)

1. seventy-eight million, two hundred five thousand, sixty-one

2. 162 million, 434 thousand, 12

3. 495 thousand, 102

4. 400 + 50 + 7

5. 1,000 + 700 + 30 + 8

Write the digit that is in the given place. (pages 2, 4, and 12)

6. 186,753,291 (millions place)

7. 204,853,176 (ten thousands place)

Write the value of the blue digit. (pages 2, 4, and 12)

8. 186,553,251

9. 99,940,257

10. 89,368

11. 379,108,426

Compare. Write >, <, or = for ●. (page 8)

12. 5,726 ● 5,762

13. 429 ● 429

14. 91,851 ● 18,159

15. 2,107 ● 2,107

16. 8,830 ● 8,530

17. 35,551 ● 35,552

18. 6,965 ● 60,965

19. 485 ● 4,580

20. 98,741 ● 8,974

Write in order from the greatest to the least. (page 8)

21. 6,214; 12; 11,421; 997

22. 495; 4,852; 635; 8,128

Write in order from the least to the greatest. (page 8)

23. 5,171; 1,717; 7,173; 7,316

24. 5,660; 5,600; 6,000; 6,603

Write each amount. Use the dollar sign and the cents point. (page 10)

25. twelve dollars and nine cents

26. three quarters and two pennies

27. eight dimes, seven nickels, and thirteen pennies

28. eighteen dollars and forty-two cents

Round to the nearest thousand or to the nearest ten dollars. (page 14)

29. $17.85

30. 7,368

31. 2,750

32. $264.95

33. 46,739

34. $91.54

Add. (page 18)

35. $2 + 4$ **36.** $6 + 3$ **37.** $8 + 7$ **38.** $7 + 6$ **39.** $9 + 9$

Subtract. (page 20)

40. $12 - 5$ **41.** $17 - 8$ **42.** $7 - 3$ **43.** $13 - 8$ **44.** $5 - 2$

Find the missing addend. (page 22)

45. $2 + \blacksquare = 8$ **46.** $\blacksquare + 4 = 13$ **47.** $5 + \blacksquare = 11$ **48.** $9 + \blacksquare = 16$

Solve. (page 24)

49. Lester built 7 model ships last year. Torian built 6 more ships than Lester. How many ships did Torian build?

50. There are 12 pairs of socks in Ida's drawer. If 3 pairs of socks are blue, how many pairs of socks are other colors?

BONUS

Look at each circle below. For each circle, find two numbers that make the greatest sum and two other numbers that make the least sum.

1.

8
1   7
5
3   2
9
6   4

2.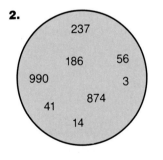

237
186   56
990   3
874
41
14

3.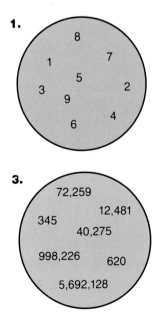

72,259
12,481
345
40,275
998,226   620
5,692,128

RETEACHING

A. Compare 7,219 and 7,217.

Compare thousands.
7,219
7,217
$\boxed{7 = 7}$

Compare hundreds.
7,219
7,217
$\boxed{2 = 2}$

Compare tens.
7,219
7,217
$\boxed{1 = 1}$

Compare ones.
7,219
7,217
$\boxed{9 > 7}$

So, 7,219 > 7,217.

You can see this on a number line.

```
◄──┼────────┼────────┼────────┼────────┼────────┼──►
 7,215    7,216    7,217    7,218    7,219    7,220
```

B. Write 2,729; 3,729; and 2,792 in order from the greatest to the least.

Compare the first two numbers.

3,729 > 2,729

Compare the first two numbers to the third number.

3,729 > 2,792
2,792 > 2,729

So, the order from the greatest to the least is 3,729; 2,792; 2,729.

The order of these numbers from the least to the greatest is 2,729; 2,792; 3,729.

Compare. Write >, <, or = for each ●.

1. 2,345 ● 244

2. 8,921 ● 8,912

3. 7,617 ● 7,620

4. 4,638 ● 4,638

5. 5,025 ● 5,022

6. 52,168 ● 52,178

Write in order from the greatest to the least.

7. 1,243; 2,934; 1,943

8. 2,919; 3,929; 2,909

9. 7,004; 7,505; 7,654

10. 8,509; 8,905; 8,095; 8,950

Write in order from the least to the greatest.

11. 1,835; 1,548; 1,854

12. 3,295; 3,529; 3,025

13. 6,603; 6,306; 6,006

14. 8,690; 9,860; 896; 8,906

ENRICHMENT

Roman Numerals

The ancient Romans used letters as symbols to name numbers. Look at these Roman numerals for 1, 5, 10, 50, 100, 500, and 1,000.

I	V	X	L	C	D	M
1	5	10	50	100	500	1,000

To find what number a Roman numeral names, add or subtract.

When symbols for greater values are to the left of the symbols for lesser values, add.

XVIII
↓
$10 + 5 + 1 + 1 + 1 = 18$

CLVI
↓
$100 + 50 + 5 + 1 = 156$

When the symbol for a lesser value is to the left of the symbol for a greater value, subtract.

IV
↓
$5 - 1 = 4$

XC
↓
$100 - 10 = 90$

XXXIX
↓
$10 + 10 + 10 + (10 - 1) = 39$

Write the number.

1. VIII
2. LXI
3. XCIII
4. CLX
5. XLVII
6. CCXVI
7. LXXIII
8. CCCLXXXV
9. CIV
10. LXXXVII
11. DCCXI
12. MCDLXIV

Write the Roman numeral.

13. 7
14. 22
15. 58
16. 61
17. 97
18. 106
19. 1,222
20. 329
21. the current year
22. your age plus 4

TECHNOLOGY

Here are some LOGO commands.

FD   This makes the turtle move forward the number of steps shown.

BK   This moves the turtle backward the number of steps shown.

RT   This makes the turtle turn to the right. RT 90 turns the turtle this far.

LT   This makes the turtle turn to the left. LT 45 turns the turtle this far.

To move the turtle without drawing a line, use the command PENUP, or PU. Then tell the turtle where to move. It will not draw another line until you use the command PENDOWN, or PD. Use PU and PD to draw shapes that are not connected to each other. Always remember to use PD after PU.

A LOGO program is called a **procedure.** When you type a procedure's name, the turtle follows all the commands in the procedure. Two or more commands can be on a line. The last command in a procedure must be END.

1. Rewrite this procedure so that it draws a rectangle instead of a square.

   TO FOURSIDE
   FD 50   RT 90   FD 50   RT 90
   FD 50   RT 90   FD 50
   END

2. Write a procedure to draw the figure that is shown in the box.

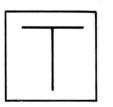

3. This procedure should draw this figure. Find five mistakes, or "bugs." Write the commands correctly.

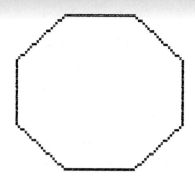

```
TO OCTAGON
FD 40   RT 45   FD 80   RT 45   FD 40
LT 45   FD 40   RT 45   BK 40   RT 45
FD 40   RT 90   FD 40   RT 45   FD 4
END
```

4. Write a procedure to draw this figure. Each side is 50 steps long, and each turn should be marked 72.

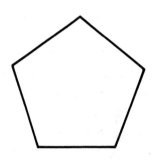

★5. What would this procedure draw? Draw the picture.

```
TO BROKEN
FD 20   RT 90   FD 20   PU   FD 20   PD   FD 20
RT 90   FD 20   PU   FD 20   PD   FD 20   RT 90
FD 20   PU   FD 20   PD   FD 20   RT 90   FD 20
END
```

CUMULATIVE REVIEW

Write the letter of the correct answer.

1. What is three thousand, four hundred seventy-two written in standard form?

   a. 3,472
   b. 340,072
   c. 3,000,472
   d. not given

2. What is the place value of 4 in 875,403,621?

   a. hundreds
   b. ten thousands
   c. hundred thousands
   d. not given

3. What is the value of the digit 1 in 93,681,244?

   a. 100
   b. 1,000
   c. 10,000
   d. not given

4. What is $2,000 + 500 + 4$ in standard form?

   a. 2,054
   b. 2,504
   c. 20,005,004
   d. not given

5. Order 3,695; 3,569; and 3,965 from the greatest to the least.

   a. 3,569; 3,695; 3,965
   b. 3,695; 3,965; 3,569
   c. 3,965; 3,569; 3,695
   d. not given

6. Which is seventy-eight cents?

   a. $0.708
   b. $0.78
   c. $78
   d. not given

7. Round 8,479 to the nearest thousand.

   a. 8,000
   b. 8,500
   c. 9,000
   d. not given

8. Round $26.52 to the nearest dollar.

   a. $26.00
   b. $27.00
   c. $30.00
   d. not given

9. $\begin{array}{r} 8 \\ +\ 7 \\ \hline \end{array}$

   a. 1
   b. 15
   c. 78
   d. not given

10. $\begin{array}{r} 9 \\ -\ 5 \\ \hline \end{array}$

    a. 4
    b. 5
    c. 14
    d. not given

11. What is the value of ■ in $5 + ■ = 11$?

    a. 6
    b. 15
    c. 16
    d. not given

12. John has 7 marbles. Laverne has 16 marbles. How many more marbles does Laverne have than John?

    a. 9 marbles
    b. 11 marbles
    c. 23 marbles
    d. not given

13. Jo and Lee collect rocks together. Jo finds 5 rocks, and Lee finds 8 rocks. How many rocks do they find?

    a. 3 rocks
    b. 15 rocks
    c. 58 rocks
    d. not given

34

You have just won $1,000 for a trip. You and one adult are going to Frontier Days, a giant rodeo in Cheyenne, Wyoming. Now all you have to do is plan the trip. What kind of transportation will you use? How much will it cost? Where will you stay? How much money do you have left for food, gifts, or souvenirs?

2 ADDITION AND SUBTRACTION

Adding 2-Digit Numbers

A. Andy earned 37 points in the bull-riding event at the rodeo. He earned 46 points in the saddle-bronc-riding event. How many points did Andy earn in both events?

To find how many points in all, you can add. Sometimes you regroup ones to add.

Add 37 + 46.

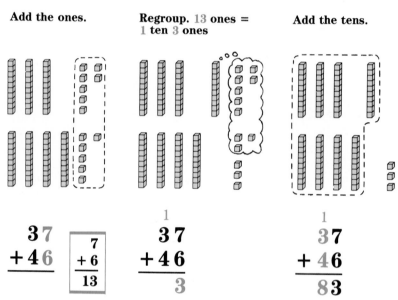

Add the ones.	Regroup. 13 ones = 1 ten 3 ones	Add the tens.

$$\begin{array}{r} 3\,7 \\ +\,4\,6 \\ \hline \end{array} \quad \boxed{\begin{array}{r} 7 \\ +\,6 \\ \hline 13 \end{array}} \qquad \begin{array}{r} \overset{1}{3}\,7 \\ +\,4\,6 \\ \hline 3 \end{array} \qquad \begin{array}{r} \overset{1}{3}\,7 \\ +\,4\,6 \\ \hline 8\,3 \end{array}$$

Andy earned 83 points in both events.

B. You can add amounts of money the same way you add whole numbers. Place the dollar sign and the cents point in the answer. Add $0.21 + $0.67.

$$\begin{array}{r} \$0.2\,1 \\ +\ \ 0.6\,7 \\ \hline 8 \end{array} \quad \boxed{\begin{array}{r} 1 \\ +\,7 \\ \hline 8 \end{array}} \qquad \begin{array}{r} \$0.2\,1 \\ +\ \ 0.6\,7 \\ \hline \$0.8\,8 \end{array}$$

Checkpoint   Write the letter of the correct answer.

Add.

1. $46 + 9$ **a.** 55   **b.** 45   **c.** 19   **d.** 145
2. $\$0.37 + \$0.15$ **a.** $0.42   **b.** $4.12   **c.** $0.52   **d.** 52

Add.

1. 51
    + 4

2. 15
    + 63

3. 14
    + 44

4. 63
    + 12

5. 41
    + 4

6. 25
    + 72

7. $0.41
    + 0.34

8. $0.23
    + 0.22

9. $0.09
    + 0.60

10. $0.56
    + 0.03

11. $0.62
    + 0.33

12. $0.75
    + 0.14

13. 13
    + 28

14. 48
    + 17

15. 18
    + 74

16. 65
    + 7

17. 19
    + 42

18. 23
    + 8

19. $0.47 + $0.26

20. $0.27 + $0.19

21. $0.35 + $0.39

22. $0.48 + $0.24

23. 72 + 19

24. 66 + 28

25. 21 + 35

26. 36 + 7

27. $0.29 + $0.32

Solve.

28. At the rodeo, the steer-wrestling event lasted 34 minutes. The bull-riding event lasted 23 minutes. How long did the two events last in all?

29. There were 25 cowhands in the bareback-bronc-riding event. There were 67 in the bull-riding event. How many cowhands entered the two events?

30. Use the information at the right to find how much Sandy spent on a rodeo button and a plastic ring.

Rodeo buttons	$0.25 each
Lassos	$3.50 each
Cowhand dolls	$0.98 each
Plastic rings	$0.57 each
Souvenir pennants	$1.50 each

ANOTHER LOOK

Write the number that is 1,000 more.

1. 3,721

2. 6,899

3. 7,405

4. 33,600

5. 56,975

6. 47,680

7. 5,657

8. 78,985

9. 1,200

10. 36,770

11. 25,643

12. 19,999

More Adding 2-Digit Numbers

The Barn Dance Boys play music at square dances. They played at 57 dances last year and 64 dances this year. At how many dances have the Barn Dance Boys played in the two years?

To find out at how many dances they have played in the two years, you can add. Add 57 + 64.

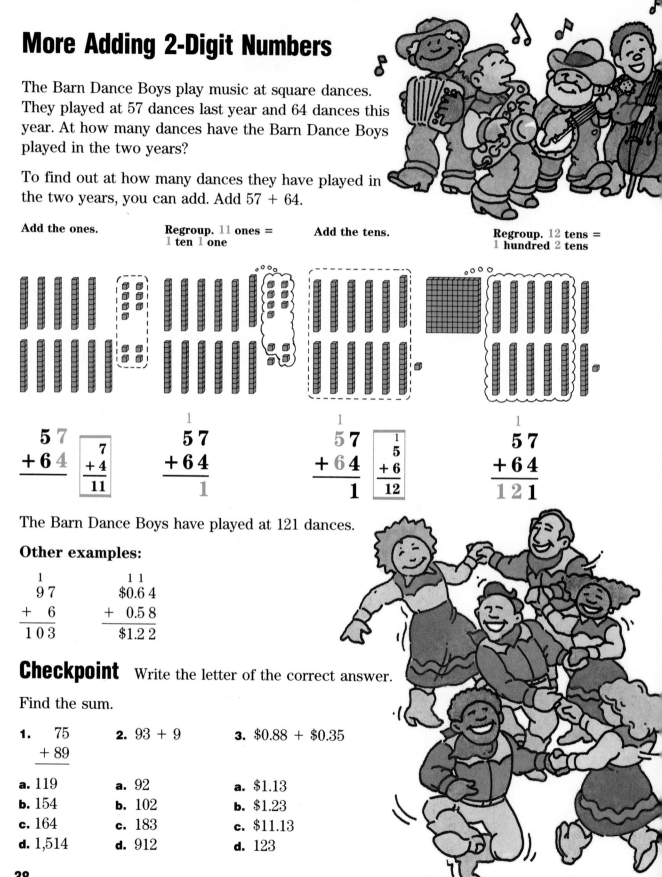

Add the ones.	Regroup. 11 ones = 1 ten 1 one	Add the tens.	Regroup. 12 tens = 1 hundred 2 tens

$$\begin{array}{r} 5\,7 \\ +\,6\,4 \\ \hline \end{array} \quad \begin{array}{r} 7 \\ +\,4 \\ \hline 11 \end{array}$$

$$\begin{array}{r} 1 \\ 5\,7 \\ +\,6\,4 \\ \hline 1 \end{array}$$

$$\begin{array}{r} 1 \\ 5\,7 \\ +\,6\,4 \\ \hline 1 \end{array} \quad \begin{array}{r} 1 \\ 5 \\ +\,6 \\ \hline 12 \end{array}$$

$$\begin{array}{r} 1 \\ 5\,7 \\ +\,6\,4 \\ \hline 1\,2\,1 \end{array}$$

The Barn Dance Boys have played at 121 dances.

Other examples:

$$\begin{array}{r} 1 \\ 9\,7 \\ +\ \ 6 \\ \hline 1\,0\,3 \end{array} \qquad \begin{array}{r} 1\ 1 \\ \$0.6\,4 \\ +\ \ 0.5\,8 \\ \hline \$1.2\,2 \end{array}$$

Checkpoint Write the letter of the correct answer.

Find the sum.

1.   75
      + 89

2. 93 + 9

3. $0.88 + $0.35

a. 119	**a.** 92	**a.** $1.13
b. 154	**b.** 102	**b.** $1.23
c. 164	**c.** 183	**c.** $11.13
d. 1,514	**d.** 912	**d.** 123

Add.

1. 8
   + 98

2. 97
   + 7

3. 94
   + 6

4. 7
   + 98

5. 99
   + 9

6. 69
   + 97

7. 99
   + 52

8. 98
   + 78

9. 75
   + 37

10. 88
    + 44

11. $0.93
    + 0.08

12. $0.99
    + 0.02

13. $0.96
    + 0.05

14. $0.09
    + 0.95

15. $0.08
    + 0.97

16. $0.62
    + 0.59

17. $0.37
    + 0.94

18. $0.49
    + 0.89

19. $0.99
    + 0.13

20. $0.22
    + 0.78

21. 68
    + 34

22. 49
    + 15

23. $0.57
    + 0.55

24. 82
    + 28

25. $0.29
    + 0.75

26. 92 + 9

27. $0.47 + $0.84

28. 97 + 38

★29. 93 + 5 + 2

Solve.

30. There are two square-dance clubs in Plainville. The Do-Si-Dos have 68 members, and the Promenade Rights have 54 members. How many people belong to the two clubs?

31. The McKenneys have been to 9 dances. The Ballins have been to 5 dances. How many more dances have the McKenneys attended?

32. Look at the chart. How many members in all belong to the two Fairview square-dance clubs?

CHALLENGE

Dance clubs/ Fairview		Dance clubs/ Springfield	
Rounders	88	Jollys	64
Clogs	72	Barn Kids	58

Compare. Write >, <, or = for ●.

1. 3 + 6 ● 5 + 5

2. 6 + 7 ● 13 − 5

3. 18 − 5 ● 13 + 8

4. 4 + 2 + 7 ● 6 + 1 + 5

5. 3 + 9 + 5 ● 4 + 1 + 6

6. 10 + 5 − 9 ● 13 − 8 + 1

7. 1 + 8 − 4 ● 15 − 9 + 3 − 2

Number Sense

A. Sometimes you can find number pairs that add together to about 100.

The sum of 65 + 38 is about 100.

| 6 tens + 3 tens = 9 tens, or 90 |

90 is close to 100.

The sum of 91 + 13 is about 100.

| 9 tens + 1 ten = 10 tens, or 100 |

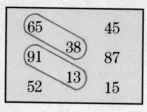

B. Sometimes you can find number pairs that add to about 1,000.

The sum of 127 + 839 is about 1,000.

| 1 hundred + 8 hundreds = 9 hundreds, or 900 |

900 is close to 1,000.

The sum of 289 + 839 is about 1,000.

| 2 hundreds + 8 hundreds = 10 hundreds, or 1,000 |

Find and list number pairs that add together to about 100.

1.

72		15
56	36	48
90	38	61

2.

57		54
25	83	49
66	79	33

Find and list number pairs that add together to about 1,000.

3.

634		712
316	851	178
437	905	599

4.

901		141
762	342	826
675	244	481

Estimating Sums

A. At the Lenawee County Fair, there were 478 students from Stark School, 216 students from Central School, and 193 students from Kaye School. About how many students from the three schools came to the fair?

To find about how many, you estimate.
Estimate 478 + 216 + 193.

Add the front digits.	Write zeros for the other digits.
$$\begin{array}{r} 478 \\ 216 \\ +193 \\ \hline 7 \end{array}$$	$$\begin{array}{r} 478 \\ 216 \\ +193 \\ \hline \text{about } 700 \end{array}$$

Rough estimate: 700
About 700 students from the three schools came to the fair.

B. You can adjust your estimate by looking at the other digits. Look for number pairs that add together to about 100.

4̲78   +   2̲16   +   1̲93

> These add together to about 100.

> This is about 100.

100 + 100 = 200

Adjusted estimate: 700 + 200 = 900
About 900 students from the three schools came to the fair.

Estimate. Add the front digits. Then adjust.

1. 436 + 269   **2.** 137 + 378   **3.** 294 + 327   **4.** 365 + 517

5. 136 + 219 + 353   **6.** 416 + 198 + 389   **7.** 214 + 288 + 196

8. $$\begin{array}{r} 4,326 \\ +1,747 \\ \hline \end{array}$$ **9.** $$\begin{array}{r} 3,284 \\ +1,623 \\ \hline \end{array}$$ **10.** $$\begin{array}{r} 2,896 \\ 3,427 \\ +4,529 \\ \hline \end{array}$$ **11.** $$\begin{array}{r} 1,888 \\ 4,219 \\ +2,756 \\ \hline \end{array}$$

PROBLEM SOLVING
Identifying Needed Information

You may need information to solve a problem that is not given in the problem.

> In 1851, Queen Victoria visited the Crystal Palace Exhibition. For how many years had she been queen of England when the exhibition opened?

What information is needed?

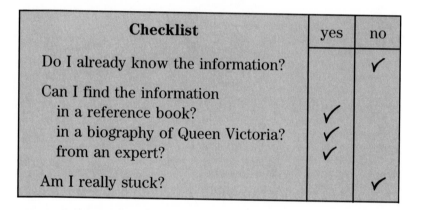

Checklist	yes	no
Do I already know the information?		✓
Can I find the information in a reference book?	✓	
in a biography of Queen Victoria?	✓	
from an expert?	✓	
Am I really stuck?		✓

Once you find the information, the problem can be solved.

> Of the 6,039,195 visitors to the Crystal Palace Exhibition, how many were British?

What information is needed?

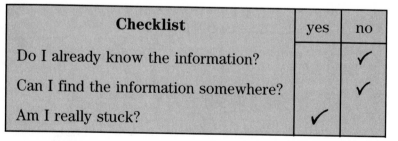

Checklist	yes	no
Do I already know the information?		✓
Can I find the information somewhere?		✓
Am I really stuck?	✓	

You cannot solve this problem, because there is no record of how many visitors were British. To answer, you could write *There is not enough information.*

Choose the information you would need to be able to solve each problem. Write the letter of the correct answer.

1. Many world's fairs have been held in the United States. New York has had 3, San Francisco has had 3, and Philadelphia has had 2. How many world's fairs were held in the United States in all?

   a. how many world's fairs have been held in other United States cities
   b. when the first world's fair was held
   c. how many United States cities have held world's fairs more than once

2. In 1853, a world's fair was held in New York. It was named the Crystal Palace Exhibition after the fair in London. How many more people attended the Crystal Palace Exhibition in London than the one in New York?

   a. the number of days the fairs were open
   b. the number of people who attended each fair
   c. the populations of the United States and Great Britain in the 1850's

Write what information you would need to be able to solve each problem.

3. People in the United States first ate bananas at the Centennial Exposition in Philadelphia in 1876. These bananas sold for $0.10 each. How much money was earned from selling bananas during the first 3 days of the exposition?

4. The first Ferris wheel was built in 1893. A larger Ferris wheel was later built in England. It had 10 first-class cars and 30 second-class cars. How many more people could ride on the English Ferris wheel than on the first Ferris wheel?

5. On May 1, 1893, the Columbian Exposition opened in Chicago. When it closed, more than 27 million people had visited the fair. About how many people visited the fair each month during the time it was open?

6. According to the rules of the Bureau of International Expositions, only one major fair can be held every ten years. How many fairs could have been held before 1980?

Adding Larger Numbers

A. You can use number sense and estimation to tell whether a calculator answer is reasonable.

Step 1: From the numbers in the box, choose 2 numbers that add to about 10,000. Record the numbers. Use your calculator to add the numbers.

3,674	8,139	3,850
4,762	5,403	2,599
6,213	7,325	6,634
1,915	4,123	9,348

- How close is your calculator answer to 10,000?

- Is your calculator answer reasonable?

Choose other pairs of numbers that add to about 10,000. Use your calculator to add the numbers. Then determine whether your calculator answer is reasonable.

Step 2: Choose any 3 numbers from the box in Step 1. Estimate the sum. Then add the numbers on your calculator.

- Is your calculator answer reasonable?

Try estimating and adding other sets of 3 numbers. Use your calculator. Then determine whether your calculator answer is reasonable.

Thinking as a Team _____

1. Why would you want to be able to tell whether a calculator answer is reasonable?

2. What would you do if your calculator answer was not close to your estimate?

3. How could you check an answer to see whether it is correct?

44

B. You can work in pairs to play "Target Sums." The winner of the game is the first player to hit the Target Sum exactly.

Rules

1. The first player chooses an addend from the list below, enters it on a calculator, and then enters ⊞. The next player enters an addend and ⊞ on another calculator.

2. Take turns entering a second addend from the list and ⊞. Remember: *You are trying to hit the target sum exactly.*

3. If no one hits the target sum after entering two addends, continue to play in the same way until the target sum is reached.

4. If any player's sum is greater than the target sum, that player must clear the calculator and begin again.

5. Start with Game 1. Then go on to play the other games in order.

GAME 1	GAME 2	GAME 3	GAME 4	GAME 5
125	**875**	**1,370**	**5,796**	**$107.48**
95	525	872	3,126	$76.88
72	487	848	3,012	$65.50
53	314	522	2,342	$38.98
20	220	300	1,799	$25.50
10	89	170	871	$ 5.00
	79	28	401	$ 3.00
	36		41	$ 0.10

Thinking as a Team

1. Did you choose your addends at random, or did you use a strategy to choose addends?

2. If you used a strategy, explain it to your team.

Working with Money

A. Your team is in charge of choosing a computer system for your class. A local computer store is having a sale on three different systems. Your team must decide which system costs the least to run the educational software you need.

Here is some information about the systems on sale.

System 1	System 2	System 3
Handy 400	Plum IIId	JCN ST
192K RAM	256K RAM	256K RAM
$479	$778	$898
B & W monitor	B & W monitor	B & W monitor
$248	$207	$217
Disk drive	Disk drive	Disk drive
$129	$148	$176
Printer	Printer	Printer
$249	$213	$267
Educational programs (256K needed)	Educational programs (256K needed)	Educational programs (256K needed)
$435	$435	$435

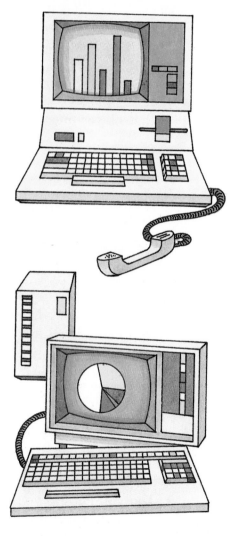

The store also offers these special deals.

- $100 off the price of System 1 if all of the parts are purchased together.

- $150 off the price of the educational programs if you buy a 64K RAM chip that costs $314 for System 1.

- The educational programs are included free with System 2 if a color monitor is purchased instead of a B & W monitor. The color monitor sells for $324.

- $200 off the price of System 3 if a second disk drive is purchased.

- The store offers 2 years of free service for System 3. The service contract usually costs $59 a year.

Math Reasoning, page H183

Working as a Team

1. Can you quickly find which system is the most expensive? Which is the least? Tell why or why not.
2. Which system is the most expensive? Which is the least? How can you be sure your answers were reasonable?
3. What other things besides cost should you think about before you decide which system to buy? How could you find this information?

Report to the class on your choice of systems and the reasons for your choice.

B. Your team has been given $200 to buy 5 programs for the new computer. You need to buy one program in each of the following subject areas:

Mathematics   History   Science   English   Art

Working as a Team

1. As you select the programs, can you quickly estimate which group of 5 programs is the most expensive? Which is the least? How?

2. Which 5 programs would you buy if you wanted to spend as much of the $200 as possible? Could you buy any other programs? Which ones?

3. Which is the least expensive group of 5 programs? How much does it cost?

4. If you bought the least expensive group of 5 programs, what other programs would you buy? Explain why.

5. What is the greatest number of programs you could buy if you only had $100? Which programs are they? Each program must be for a different subject.

Compare your answers and methods with those of other teams.

Programs	
Mathematics	
Calc Kids	$17.49
Math Mavens	$23.33
Number Wiz	$26.78
History	
History Buffs	$27.75
Pastfinders	$34.50
Were You There?	$38.78
Science	
Bio Busters	$25.50
Hi! Sci!	$35.65
Sci Lab	$43.95
English	
Words R Us	$49.95
Write Right	$52.75
Plum Write	$56.75
Art	
Plum Paint	$24.65
Easy Easel	$36.25
Spray Can	$38.76

Column Addition

Jerry Lawson spent one summer catering clambakes. There were 476 people at the clambake in New York; 185 at the clambake in Massachusetts; and 257 at the clambake in Rhode Island. How many people went to the three clambakes?

You can add to find how many people went to the three clambakes. Add 476 + 185 + 257.

Add the ones. Regroup the 18 ones.	Add the tens. Regroup the 21 tens.	Add the hundreds.
$\begin{array}{r} 1 \\ 476 \\ 185 \\ +257 \\ \hline 8 \end{array}$	$\begin{array}{r} 21 \\ 476 \\ 185 \\ +257 \\ \hline 18 \end{array}$	$\begin{array}{r} 21 \\ 476 \\ 185 \\ +257 \\ \hline 918 \end{array}$

There were 918 people who went to the three clambakes.

Other examples:

$$\begin{array}{r} 1\,1\,2\,1 \\ \$1\,3\,2.6\,6 \\ 3\,6\,1.7\,5 \\ +\ \ 2\,1\,9.9\,4 \\ \hline \$7\,1\,4.3\,5 \end{array} \qquad \begin{array}{r} 1\,2 \\ 3,2\,9\,5 \\ 1,7\,6\,0 \\ +\,2,4\,5\,1 \\ \hline 7,5\,0\,6 \end{array} \qquad \begin{array}{r} 1\,2\,2 \\ 4\,8\,9 \\ 4,1\,0\,8 \\ 3\,8\,2 \\ +\ \ \ \ 9\,1 \\ \hline 5,0\,7\,0 \end{array} \qquad \begin{array}{r} 1\,2 \\ 3,1\,2\,3 \\ 1,2\,3\,9 \\ 2,3\,8\,4 \\ +\,2,1\,4\,6 \\ \hline 8,8\,9\,2 \end{array}$$

Checkpoint   Write the letter of the correct answer.
Add.

1. $\begin{array}{r} 246 \\ 43 \\ +\ 435 \\ \hline \end{array}$ **2.** $\begin{array}{r} \$726.35 \\ 51.62 \\ +\ \ 141.28 \\ \hline \end{array}$ **3.** $\begin{array}{r} \$\ 0.76 \\ 92.90 \\ 1.90 \\ +\ \ 65.85 \\ \hline \end{array}$ **4.** 7,491 + 86 + 195

1.	2.	3.	4.
a. 614	**a.** $819.25	**a.** $16,141	**a.** 7,772
b. 624	**b.** $819.216	**b.** $159.41	**b.** 7,672
c. 724	**c.** $919.25	**c.** $161.41	**c.** 7,562
d. 814	**d.** $929.15	**d.** $158.31	**d.** 8,772

Math Reasoning, page H184

Add.

1.	2.	3.	4.	5.
20 75 + 89	$0.65 0.09 + 0.73	687 829 + 305	292 83 + 107	876 9 + 23

6.	7.	8.	9.	10.
3,681 4,925 + 1,303	$16.65 7.32 + 28.43	27,425 32,919 + 40,617	$ 32.84 127.00 + 689.77	83,622 25,814 + 32,771

11.	12.	13.	14.	15.
26 80 5 + 49	381 26 492 + 674	357 489 123 + 987	$8.94 6.20 1.50 + 7.65	$6.92 0.09 3.42 + 2.86

16.	17.	18.	19.	20.
8,756 4,321 3,222 + 3,559	7,305 862 2,001 + 4,105	$32.15 65.60 29.83 + 38.75	$44.27 6.48 17.35 + 29.02	8,091 3,368 4,805 + 693

21. 253 + 782 + 50

22. 7,609 + 8,321 + 4,166 + 1,767

23. 12,017 + 64,615 + 21,141

24. $121.19 + $64.52 + $368.00

25. $859.03 + $37.50 + $56.06

26. 5,433 + 76,098 + 679

Solve. Use the Infobank.

27. Use the information on page 401 to solve. Find how many clams were eaten at the three clambakes on Nantucket and Fire Island and in Rhode Island.

NUMBER SENSE

You can mentally add 240 + 36.

$$\begin{array}{r} 240 \\ + \ 36 \\ \hline 276 \end{array}$$

Think:

$$\begin{array}{r} 24 \text{ tens} \\ + \ 3 \text{ tens} \\ \hline 27 \text{ tens} \end{array}$$

Compute mentally.

1. 250 + 27   2. 380 + 14   3. 540 + 27   4. 370 + 18

Estimating Sums By Rounding

A. There were 7,465 people who visited the Topsfield Fair on opening day; 6,519 on the second day; and 8,792 on the third day. About how many people visited the fair during the three days?

To find about how many, you can estimate. Estimate 7,465 + 6,519 + 8,792 by rounding each number. Then add.

Round each number to the largest place.	Then add.
$7,465 \longrightarrow 7,000$	$7,000$
$6,519 \longrightarrow 7,000$	$7,000$
$+8,792 \longrightarrow 9,000$	$+9,000$
	$23,000$

About 23,000 people visited the fair during the three days.

Other examples:

$$48 + 62 + 37$$
$$\downarrow \quad \downarrow \quad \downarrow$$
$$50 + 60 + 40 = 150$$

$$173 \longrightarrow 200$$
$$+265 \longrightarrow +300$$
$$\overline{500}$$

B. You can estimate sums of money in the same way. Write the dollar sign and the cents point in the answer.

Round to the nearest $0.10.

$$\$0.85 \longrightarrow \$0.90$$
$$0.29 \longrightarrow 0.30$$
$$+ \ 0.53 \longrightarrow + \ 0.50$$
$$\overline{\$1.70}$$

Round to the nearest $1.00.

$$\$8.39 \longrightarrow \$8.00$$
$$+ \ 2.75 \longrightarrow + \ 3.00$$
$$\overline{\$11.00}$$

Round to the nearest $10.00.

$$\$34.60 + \$47.30$$
$$\downarrow \qquad \downarrow$$
$$\$30.00 + \$50.00 = \$80.00$$

Estimate the sums by rounding each addend to the largest place.

1. $25 + 16 + 42$

2. $38 + 12 + 45$

3. $\$0.88 + \$0.21 + \$0.65$

4. $89 + 48 + 35$

5. $17 + 49 + 22$

6. $\$0.46 + \$0.43 + \$0.27$

50

Estimate by rounding to the largest place.

7. 456
449
+ 313

8. 567
+ 309

9. 871
234
+ 198

10. $7.68
+ 8.19

11. $2.36
3.98
+ 1.96

12. 4,987
+ 1,276

13. 1,573
3,468
+ 5,796

14. 4,441
3,909
+ 6,008

15. $31.12
+ 15.96

16. $38.74
29.07
+ 56.86

17. 824 + 854 + 129

18. 2,357 + 1,977

19. $6.82 + $8.75 + $9.21

20. 6,421 + 3,166 + 1,001

21. 563 + 205 + 911

22. $54.98 + $26.13 + $32.50

Estimate. Write the letter of the best answer.

23. 63 + 29 + 45   **a.** 120   **b.** 140   **c.** 150

24. $0.21 + $0.63 + $0.92   **a.** $1.70   **b.** $1.80   **c.** $11.00

25. 567 + 558 + 417   **a.** 1,400   **b.** 1,600   **c.** 1,700

26. $6.59 + $8.25   **a.** $14.00   **b.** $15.00   **c.** $20.00

27. 8,352 + 7,581   **a.** 14,000   **b.** 16,000   **c.** 17,000

28. $24.98 + $83.75   **a.** $12.00   **b.** $100.00   **c.** $120.00

MIDCHAPTER REVIEW

Add.

1. 25 + 14

2. 18 + 76

3. $0.53 + $0.28

4. 743 + 7

5. $2.54
+ 5.48

6. $7.81
+ 2.30

7. 7,326
+ 8,954

8. 64,593
+ 92,478

9. $629.95
+ 79.89

10. 30
26
+ 58

11. 828
49
+ 731

12. 6,329
451
62
+ 4,190

13. $18.25
14.45
+ 6.56

14. $49.64
26.05
9.98
+ 73.02

PROBLEM SOLVING
Estimation

Sometimes you can estimate to solve a problem. But if your estimate does not give you enough information, you should find the exact answer.

David Schaffer wants to hold a horse show in Ponoma County. If at least 150 horse owners sign up, he will hold the horse show. Mr. Schaffer makes a list of owners who will bring their horses to the show.

$$
\begin{array}{lcr}
39 \text{ owners} & \longrightarrow & 40 \\
29 \text{ owners} & \longrightarrow & 30 \\
58 \text{ owners} & \longrightarrow & 60 \\
37 \text{ owners} & \longrightarrow & + 40 \\
\hline
& & 170
\end{array}
$$

David Schaffer rounds the numbers and adds them in his head. Without finding the exact sum, he knows that there are enough interested owners.

Mr. Schaffer has to decide whether to hold the horse show for 1 day or 2 days. If at least 365 horses are entered, he will hold a 2-day show.

Here is a list of   Here is Mr. Schaffer's
horses entered.   estimate.

64 palominos	60
49 Morgans	50
58 Clydesdales	60
69 pintos	70
48 Arabians	50
53 Tennessee Walking Horses	50
24 Appaloosa	+ 20
	360

The estimate of 360 is under the 365 horses needed to have a 2-day show. But 360 is very close to 365. So, Mr. Schaffer decides to find the exact sum. The exact sum is 365. Mr. Schaffer decides to hold a 2-day show.

Write the letter of the better way to solve each problem.

1. Tickets for a horse show cost $4.50 for adults, $3.60 for senior citizens, and $2.95 for children. Jenna wants to buy one of each kind of ticket. She has $10.85. Does she have enough money?

    a. Estimate the cost.
    b. Find the exact cost.

2. At a rodeo, each rider tries 3 times to ride a bronco. Jed stayed on a bronco for 11 seconds, 21 seconds, and 12 seconds. In all 3 tries, did Jed stay on the bronco for at least 60 seconds?

    a. Estimate the time.
    b. Find the exact time.

Solve. Find an estimate or an exact answer as needed.

3. Terry will win a prize if she sells 1,000 tickets. She sold 258 tickets on Monday, 314 tickets on Tuesday, and 491 tickets on Wednesday. Has she sold enough tickets to win a prize?

4. Shelly wants a rodeo program that sells for $1.75. She also wants a pennant for $2.98 and 2 rodeo hats for $3.29 each. She has $10. Does she have enough to pay for the items she wants?

5. Carol goes to a refreshment booth. She wants to buy one sandwich for $1.25 and another for $2.65. She also wants to buy juice for $1.10 and milk for $1.25. Does she have enough money?

6. A school rents a bus to drive students to the rodeo. The bus seats 105 people. There are 32 students in one class, 28 in another, and 29 in the third. Will the 3 classes fit on the bus?

7. Paul scored 43 points in bronco riding, 32 points in calf roping, and 38 points in steer wrestling. Did Paul score more than 100 points?

★8. A rodeo rider earns $495 per show. A trainer is paid $685, and an announcer is paid $275. The rodeo committee hires 2 people for each job. Is $3,000 enough money to pay all these people?

Subtracting 2-Digit Numbers

A. The town library has 35 books about square dancing. People have checked out 21 of the books. How many books about square dancing remain in the library?

To find how many remain, you can subtract. Subtract 35 − 21.

Subtract the ones.	Subtract the tens.
$\begin{array}{r} 3\,5 \\ -\,2\,1 \\ \hline 4 \end{array}$	$\begin{array}{r} 3\,5 \\ -\,2\,1 \\ \hline 1\,4 \end{array}$

In the library, 14 books about square dancing remain.

B. Sometimes you may need to regroup to subtract. Subtract 90 − 63.

Not enough ones.	Regroup. 1 ten 0 ones = 10 ones.	Subtract the ones.	Subtract the tens.
$\begin{array}{r} 9\,0 \\ -\,6\,3 \\ \hline \end{array}$	$\begin{array}{r} {}^{8}\;{}^{10} \\ \cancel{9}\,\cancel{0} \\ -\,6\,3 \\ \hline \end{array}$	$\begin{array}{r} {}^{8}\;{}^{10} \\ \cancel{9}\,\cancel{0} \\ -\,6\,3 \\ \hline 7 \end{array}$	$\begin{array}{r} {}^{8}\;{}^{10} \\ \cancel{9}\,\cancel{0} \\ -\,6\,3 \\ \hline 2\,7 \end{array}$

C. You can check subtraction by adding.

	Check:		Check:
$\begin{array}{r} {}^{8}\;{}^{13} \\ \$0.\cancel{9}\,\cancel{3} \\ -\;\;\;0.5\,4 \\ \hline \$0.3\,9 \end{array}$	$\begin{array}{r} \$0.54 \\ +\;\;0.39 \\ \hline \$0.93 \end{array}$	$\begin{array}{r} {}^{7}\;{}^{15} \\ \cancel{8}\,\cancel{5} \\ -\;\;\;8 \\ \hline 7\,7 \end{array}$	$\begin{array}{r} 8 \\ +\;77 \\ \hline 85 \end{array}$

Subtract.

1. 78 − 61	**2.** 87 − 54	**3.** 69 − 32	**4.** 48 − 32	**5.** 38 − 15	**6.** 39 − 11
7. $0.83 − 0.71	**8.** $0.78 − 0.31	**9.** $0.67 − 0.36	**10.** $0.77 − 0.15	**11.** $0.96 − 0.32	**12.** $0.48 − 0.27
13. 60 − 38	**14.** 72 − 64	**15.** 40 − 26	**16.** 80 − 69	**17.** 84 − 37	**18.** 93 − 15
19. $0.45 − 0.37	**20.** 71 − 42	**21.** $0.73 − 0.37	**22.** 94 − 58	**23.** $0.88 − 0.49	**24.** 79 − 51
25. 28 − 15	**26.** $0.57 − 0.22	**27.** 61 − 47	**28.** $0.76 − 0.38	**29.** 82 − 53	**30.** $0.50 − 0.46

31. 82 − 60

32. $0.62 − $0.47

★**33.** 73 − (29 − 8)

Solve.

34. Mike Jones baked 49 pies for the Lone Star square dance. Dancers ate 31 of the pies. How many pies were left?

35. One bus carried 35 people to the square dance. A second bus carried only 27. How many people attended the square dance?

NUMBER SENSE

You can use front-end subtraction to check that the difference is a reasonable answer. To estimate 416 − 239, follow these steps.

Find the digit in the largest place.	Subtract the digits in the largest place.	Write zeros for the other digits.

416
− 239
	416
	− 239
	——
	2 **Think: 4**
	             − 2
	              2
		416
		− 239
		about 200

Estimate by front-end subtraction.

1. 529 − 467

2. 437 − 295

3. 9,837 − 6,165

4. 7,718 − 4,657

Estimating Differences

A. On Monday, 393 people saw a demonstration of weaving at the Eastern States Exposition. On Tuesday, 755 people saw the demonstration. About how many more people saw the demonstration on Tuesday?

To find about how many more, you need to estimate 755 − 393. Round each number. Then subtract.

Round each number to the nearest 100.

Then subtract.

$$755 \longrightarrow 800$$
$$-393 \longrightarrow 400$$

$$800$$
$$-400$$
$$\overline{400}$$

About 400 more people saw the demonstration on Tuesday.

Another example:

$$7,423 \longrightarrow 7,000$$
$$-5,918 \longrightarrow -6,000$$
$$\overline{1,000}$$

B. Estimate differences in money in the same way. Write the dollar sign and the cents point in the answer.

Round to the nearest $10.00.

$$\$26.75 \longrightarrow \$30.00$$
$$- 19.83 \longrightarrow - 20.00$$
$$\overline{\$10.00}$$

Round to the nearest $1.00.

$$\$6.32 \longrightarrow \$6.00$$
$$- 4.21 \longrightarrow - 4.00$$
$$\overline{\$2.00}$$

C. You can estimate when there is more than one operation. Estimate 53 + 29 − 42.

$$53 + 29 - 42$$
$$\downarrow \quad \downarrow \quad \downarrow$$
$$50 + 30 - 40 = 40$$

Estimate by rounding to the largest place.

1. 885 − 269

2. 535 − 219

3. $7.74 − $5.46

4. $2.43 − $1.15

5.   472
     − 315

6.   621
     − 439

7.   527
     − 358

8. $3.32
     − 1.74

9. $3.50
     − 2.52

10.   5,142
      − 3,297

11.   6,163
      − 1,745

12.   3,828
      − 1,546

13. $66.57
      − 10.98

14. $29.02
      − 11.50

15. 930 − 432

16. 781 − 433

17. 7,954 − 1,228

18. $4.41 − $1.27

19. 8,678 − 3,281

20. 726 − 372

21. 838 − 619

22. $45.78 − $26.09

23. 5,160 − 2,059

24. 335 − 129

25. $9.45 − $1.63

26. $8.24 − $1.65

27. 72 + 85 − 26

28. 38 + 42 − 17

29. $0.65 + $0.56 − $0.33

Solve.

30. There were 52 buses in the exposition's parking lot at nine o'clock. By three o'clock, about 30 buses had left. About how many school buses remained in the parking lot?

31. One day, 6,943 people visited the Vermont building. The next day, 8,254 visited it. How many people visited the Vermont building during the two days?

★32. Frank spent $17.95 at the exposition. Dennis spent $21.32. Estimate how much more Dennis spent. Then estimate how much they spent in all.

33. There were about 250 children from Hamden School who attended the exposition. There were nearly 200 children from Kirby School who also attended. Use this information to write and solve your own word problem.

CALCULATOR

Use a calculator.
Use the numbers 15, 22, 25, 33, 38, 45, 60, and 68 to find the addends.

1. ▨ + ▨ = 105

2. ▨ + ▨ = 60

3. ▨ + ▨ = 83

4. ▨ + ▨ = 58

Subtracting 3-Digit Numbers

At the Buchanan County Fair, the 4-H club entered 233 sheep and 159 hogs in the livestock competition. How many more sheep than hogs did the club enter?

To compare the numbers of animals, you need to subtract $233 - 159$.

Regroup. Subtract the ones.	Regroup. Subtract the tens.	Subtract the hundreds.
2 13 2 3 3̶ −1 5 9 —— 4	12 1 2̶ 13 2 3̶ 3̶ −1 5 9 —— 7 4	12 1 2̶ 13 2 3̶ 3̶ −1 5 9 —— 7 4

The club entered 74 more sheep than hogs.

Other examples:

$$\begin{array}{r} 467 \\ -314 \\ \hline 153 \end{array} \qquad \begin{array}{r} {\scriptstyle 8\ 12} \\ 9\!\!\!/\, 2\!\!\!/\, 4 \\ -532 \\ \hline 392 \end{array} \qquad \begin{array}{r} {\scriptstyle 10} \\ {\scriptstyle 5\ \cancel{0}\ 15} \\ \$6.1\!\!\!/\, 5\!\!\!/ \\ -\ 4.66 \\ \hline \$1.49 \end{array} \qquad \begin{array}{r} {\scriptstyle 6\ 11} \\ 8\, 7\!\!\!/\, 1\!\!\!/ \\ -\ 69 \\ \hline 802 \end{array}$$

Checkpoint   Write the letter of the correct answer.

Subtract.

1. $\begin{array}{r} 849 \\ -\ 31 \\ \hline \end{array}$ **2.** $\begin{array}{r} 571 \\ -228 \\ \hline \end{array}$ **3.** $628 - 169$ **4.** $\$5.46 - \$2.37$

a. 18	a. 343	a. 369	a. $3.19
b. 518	b. 359	b. 459	b. $3.09
c. 718	c. 799	c. 541	c. $3.11
d. 818	d. 853	d. 569	d. $7.83

58

Subtract.

1. 857 − 233	**2.** 879 − 156	**3.** 796 − 612	**4.** 839 − 126	**5.** $4.89 − 1.52	**6.** $6.19 − 3.03
7. 998 − 419	**8.** 642 − 219	**9.** 761 − 414	**10.** 981 − 364	**11.** $5.81 − 3.69	**12.** $4.27 − 3.19
13. 124 − 119	**14.** 467 − 42	**15.** 829 − 327	**16.** 729 − 68	**17.** $3.91 − 2.85	**18.** $8.51 − 6.30
19. 565 − 352	**20.** $8.51 − 2.84	**21.** 729 − 716	**22.** $4.75 − 0.79	**23.** 513 − 37	**24.** $2.85 − 2.41

25. $9.82 − $4.45   **26.** 961 − 352   **27.** $6.62 − $4.89   **28.** 515 − 69

29. 319 − 299   **30.** $8.21 − $7.95   **31.** 428 − 219   **32.** $5.17 − $2.88

★**33.** 945 − (26 − 8)   ★**34.** 383 − (80 − 11)   ★**35.** 838 − (295 − 9)

Solve.

36. Boys and girls all over the country belong to 4-H clubs. In Buchanan County, 988 boys and 892 girls are members. How many more boys than girls belong to the club?

37. Louie is a livestock judge at the fair. On Tuesday he judged 314 animals, and on Wednesday he judged 139. How many more animals did Louie judge on Tuesday than on Wednesday?

★**38.** Sandy went to the fair with $5.27 in her pocket. She wanted to buy a balloon for $0.85 and a T-shirt for $4.38. Could she afford both items with the amount of money she had in her pocket?

★**39.** Louie judged a total of 566 calves, hogs, and sheep. Of this total, 229 were hogs and 89 were sheep. How many calves did Louie judge?

NUMBER SENSE

Compute mentally.

1. 63 − 21	**2.** 163 − 21	**3.** 763 − 121	**4.** 463 − 221	**5.** 963 − 121

Subtracting Larger Numbers

The first local fair in the United States took place in 1644 in Connecticut. The first state fair was held in 1841 in New York. How many years passed between the two fairs?

To find differences in time, you need to subtract.
Subtract 1,841 − 1,644.

Regroup. Subtract the ones.	Regroup. Subtract the tens.	Subtract the hundreds.	Subtract the thousands.
$\begin{array}{r} \scriptstyle 3\ 11 \\ 1,84\cancel{1} \\ -1,644 \\ \hline 7 \end{array}$	$\begin{array}{r} \scriptstyle 13 \\ \scriptstyle 7\ 3\ 11 \\ 1,8\cancel{4}\cancel{1} \\ -1,644 \\ \hline 97 \end{array}$	$\begin{array}{r} \scriptstyle 13 \\ \scriptstyle 7\ 3\ 11 \\ 1,8\cancel{4}\cancel{1} \\ -1,644 \\ \hline 197 \end{array}$	$\begin{array}{r} \scriptstyle 13 \\ \scriptstyle 7\ 3\ 11 \\ 1,8\cancel{4}\cancel{1} \\ -1,644 \\ \hline 197 \end{array}$

Between the two fairs, 197 years passed.

Other examples:

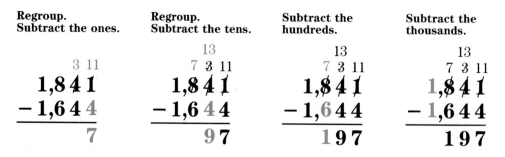

$$\begin{array}{r} \scriptstyle 5\ 15 \\ 37,1\cancel{6}\cancel{5} \\ -22,148 \\ \hline 15,017 \end{array} \qquad \begin{array}{r} \scriptstyle 13\ 10 \\ \scriptstyle 8\ 3\ 0\ 11 \\ \$8\cancel{9}\cancel{4}.\cancel{1}\cancel{1} \\ -\ \ 88.32 \\ \hline \$805.79 \end{array}$$

$$\begin{array}{r} 4,797 \\ -3,125 \\ \hline 1,672 \end{array} \qquad \begin{array}{r} \scriptstyle 111 \\ 85,4\cancel{2}\cancel{1} \\ -\ \ 4,319 \\ \hline 81,102 \end{array}$$

Checkpoint   Write the letter of the correct answer.

Subtract.

1. $\begin{array}{r} 7,758 \\ -2,983 \\ \hline \end{array}$ **2.** $\begin{array}{r} 86,921 \\ -1,176 \\ \hline \end{array}$ **3.** $575.41 - 286.99$ **4.** $2,553 - 2,314$

a. 5,235	**a.** 5,745	**a.** $2.8842	**a.** 139
b. 4,775	**b.** 74,745	**b.** $288.42	**b.** 241
c. 3,875	**c.** 85,745	**c.** $399.52	**c.** 239
d. 10,741	**d.** 75,745	**d.** $28,842	**d.** 249

Subtract.

1. 5,217 − 3,681	**2.** 8,134 − 1,297	**3.** 7,422 − 6,679	**4.** 9,966 − 7,511	**5.** 6,898 − 379
6. 73,121 − 31,105	**7.** 83,832 − 15,625	**8.** 91,355 − 47,859	**9.** 56,128 − 37,028	**10.** 63,125 − 2,689
11. $33.12 − 12.09	**12.** $64.95 − 27.57	**13.** $85.96 − 36.92	**14.** $564.99 − 162.91	**15.** $424.71 − 140.03
16. 6,743 − 1,758	**17.** $92.89 − 27.06	**18.** 5,638 − 1,758	**19.** $321.27 − 143.95	**20.** 9,479 − 8,471
21. $54.02 − 32.21	**22.** 3,847 − 42	**23.** $219.37 − 149.29	**24.** 4,116 − 3,027	**25.** $51.83 − 28.46

26. 8,384 − 3,518

27. $173.14 − $123.34

28. 16,387 − 992

Solve.

29. Last year, Wilma earned $413.29 by selling her prize-winning carrot bread at the Nebraska State Fair. This year she earned $592.56. How much more did Wilma earn this year?

★**31.** Use the information in the table to find how many more people attended the Danbury Fair in 1990 than in 1989.

30. The table below shows the number of people who attended the state fair in Danbury in 1989 and in 1990. How many people attended in 1990?

WEEKLY ATTENDANCE AT THE DANBURY FAIR

Year	Week 1	Week 2
1989	16,972	31,112
1990	38,415	66,970

Use your calculator to solve.

1. 8,976,541 + 3,784,687	**2.** 39,468,792 + 4,874,586	**3.** 8,756,487 − 4,988,076	**4.** 7,250,641 − 6,576,429

Subtracting with Zeros

Burgoo is a stew served at some festivals in the United States. For a fair in Kentucky, it was made in a huge pot that holds 500 gallons. By the end of one day, 456 gallons had been eaten. How many gallons were left?

To find the amount that was not eaten, you need to subtract. Subtract 500 − 456.

Regroup the hundreds.	Regroup the tens. Subtract the ones.	Subtract the tens.	Subtract the hundreds.
$\begin{array}{r} 4\ 10 \\ \cancel{5}\ \cancel{0}\ 0 \\ -\ 4\ 5\ 6 \\ \hline \end{array}$	$\begin{array}{r} 9 \\ 4\ \cancel{10}\ 10 \\ \cancel{5}\ \cancel{0}\ \cancel{0} \\ -\ 4\ 5\ 6 \\ \hline 4 \end{array}$	$\begin{array}{r} 9 \\ 4\ \cancel{10}\ 10 \\ \cancel{5}\ \cancel{0}\ \cancel{0} \\ -\ 4\ 5\ 6 \\ \hline 4\ 4 \end{array}$	$\begin{array}{r} 9 \\ 4\ \cancel{10}\ 10 \\ \cancel{5}\ \cancel{0}\ \cancel{0} \\ -\ 4\ 5\ 6 \\ \hline 4\ 4 \end{array}$

There were 44 gallons left.

Other examples:

$$\begin{array}{r} 9\ 9 \\ 3\ \cancel{10}\cancel{10}17 \\ \cancel{4},\cancel{0}\ \cancel{0}\ 7 \\ -\ 1,3\ 9\ 8 \\ \hline 2,6\ 0\ 9 \end{array} \qquad \begin{array}{r} 9\ 9\ 9 \\ 5\ \cancel{10}\cancel{10}\cancel{10}10 \\ \$\cancel{6}\ \cancel{0}\ \cancel{0}.\cancel{0}\ \cancel{0} \\ -\quad 6\ 7.9\ 4 \\ \hline \$5\ 3\ 2.0\ 6 \end{array} \qquad \begin{array}{r} 9 \\ 6\ \cancel{10}13 \\ 5\ 6,7\ \cancel{0}\ \cancel{3} \\ -\ 4\ 5,4\ 3\ 9 \\ \hline 1\ 1,2\ 6\ 4 \end{array} \qquad \begin{array}{r} 9\ 9 \\ 6\ \cancel{10}\cancel{10}10 \\ 7,\cancel{0}\ \cancel{0}\ \cancel{0} \\ -\ 5,2\ 8\ 7 \\ \hline 1,7\ 1\ 3 \end{array}$$

Checkpoint   Write the letter of the correct answer.

Find the difference.

1. $\begin{array}{r} 803 \\ -\ 176 \\ \hline \end{array}$ **2.** $4.07 − $3.09   **3.** $\begin{array}{r} 9,100 \\ -\quad 463 \\ \hline \end{array}$ **4.** 50,030 − 8,659

a. 627	**a.** $0.0098	**a.** 8,637	**a.** 1,371
b. 727	**b.** $0.89	**b.** 8,737	**b.** 42,481
c. 637	**c.** $0.98	**c.** 8,747	**c.** 41,371
d. 979	**d.** $98	**d.** 6,747	**d.** 58,689

Subtract.

1. 903 − 745	**2.** 306 − 129	**3.** 401 − 212	**4.** $7.10 − 6.59	**5.** $8.00 − 0.77
6. 5,803 − 3,516	**7.** 6,400 − 2,217	**8.** 7,003 − 2,512	**9.** 8,009 − 732	**10.** $70.50 − 12.37
11. 85,000 − 34,421	**12.** 98,000 − 17,261	**13.** 81,009 − 56,321	**14.** $700.04 − 93.42	**15.** 30,200 − 27,639
16. $1.00 − 0.15	**17.** 702 − 263	**18.** 8,001 − 3,592	**19.** $600.65 − 305.32	**20.** 90,002 − 8,461
21. 30,408 − 13,267	**22.** $505.05 − 46.39	**23.** 2,000 − 1,821	**24.** 70,000 − 39,542	**25.** $908.00 − 7.59

26. 3,006 − 465   **27.** 90,050 − 12,637   **28.** 70,000 − 2,940

Solve.

29. This burgoo recipe was printed in a Kentucky newspaper. The recipe serves 5,000 people. If 3,295 people are served in the morning, how many people can be served in the afternoon?

30. The cook added 112 pounds of spices to the burgoo while it was cooking. Afterward, the cook added 43 more pounds of spices. How many pounds of spices were added to the burgoo?

31. The Louisville Fair committee uses the recipe for burgoo. The Prairie Beef Company donates 325 pounds of beef. Use the table to find how much more beef the committee should purchase in order to feed 5,000 people.

Burgoo for 5,000

800 pounds beef
200 pounds fowl
168 gallons tomatoes
350 pounds cabbage
24 gallons carrots
1,800 pounds potatoes

Write each in words.

1. 3,000   **2.** 124,005   **3.** 5,775,008   **4.** 535,229   **5.** 6,003

PROBLEM SOLVING
Writing a Number Sentence

A number sentence can show you how to use the numbers you know to find the number you need. Read the problem below. Then follow the three steps to write a number sentence for the problem.

For 200 years, a small town in Mexico has held a Festival of the Radishes. These vegetables are carved into fantastic shapes by local artists. If one artist carved 35 human faces and 26 animal shapes, how many radishes did she carve in all?

1. List what you know and what you need to find.

> Know She carved 35 human faces.
> She carved 26 animal shapes.

> Find How many radishes did she carve in all?

2. What does your list tell you about whether to + or −? Write a number sentence about this problem. Use n to stand for the number you need to find.

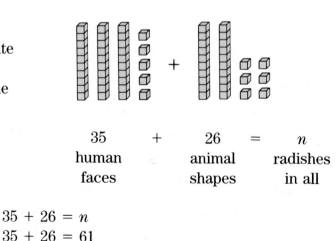

$$35 \quad + \quad 26 \quad = \quad n$$

human   animal   radishes
faces   shapes   in all

3. Solve. Write the answer.

$$35 + 26 = n$$
$$35 + 26 = 61$$
$$n = 61$$

She carved 61 radishes in all.

Write the letter of the correct number sentence.

1. A dog mart has been held in Fredericksburg, Virginia, every year since 1698. The first settlers arrived in Virginia in 1607. How long after the settlers arrived did the dog mart begin?

   a. $1607 + 1698 = n$
   b. $1698 - 1607 = n$
   c. $1607 - 98 = n$

2. On September 23, 1897, the first Cheyenne Frontier Day was held in Wyoming. The festival includes rodeos, dancing, and games. In which year was the festival 25 years old?

   a. $1897 - 25 = n$
   b. $1985 + 1897 = n$
   c. $1897 + 25 = n$

Write a number sentence. Then solve.

3. Glenbrook's first annual Festival of the Arts lasted two days. On the first day, 138 paintings were sold, and 207 paintings were sold on the second day. How many paintings were sold at the festival?

4. There was a corn-eating contest at the Harvest Fair in Brookfield. Zeke ate 17 ears of corn. Amos ate 23 ears of corn. How many more ears of corn did Amos eat than Zeke?

5. On Founder's Day in Hawaii, a hotel gave a luau for 2,745 guests. Of the guests, 1,628 watched the canoe races. How many guests did not watch the canoe races?

6. Eve sold jars of home-canned tomatoes at the fair. She sold 78 jars the first day and 97 jars the second day. How many jars of tomatoes did she sell?

7. Gary spent $4.75 on lunch at the fair. He spent $3.17 on a souvenir hat. How much more did he spend on lunch than on the hat?

★8. Rosemary went to the county fair. She spent $5.75 for souvenirs, $4.50 for rides, and $3.15 for lunch. How much did Rosemary spend at the fair?

CALCULATOR

It is easy and fast to add or subtract with a calculator. But sometimes it is just as fast to compute mentally or use paper and pencil.

Example: Find. 8 + 7 = ■

You should mentally compute 8 + 7 = 15.

To press: $\boxed{8}$ $\boxed{+}$ $\boxed{7}$ $\boxed{=}$ 15 takes more time than doing the exercise in your head.

The following exercises will allow you to compare how fast you can compute mentally (or use paper-pencil) versus using a calculator.

For each of the three sets of exercises do the following:

1. Copy the exercise.

2. Compute the answers mentally (or use paper-pencil). Write them and record your time.

3. Use the calculator to compute each answer. Write the answer and record your time.

Row A:

1. 9 + 8	**2.** 8 + 7	**3.** 6 + 5	**4.** 4 + 3	**5.** 7 + 4

Row B:

6. 24 + 15	**7.** 36 + 12	**8.** 43 + 15	**9.** 22 + 17	**10.** 56 + 22

Row C:

11. 1,249 +2,137	**12.** 9,056 +4,193	**13.** 10,671 +25,063	**14.** 21,592 + 879	**15.** 72,609 +15,293

Which row(s) could you solve faster in your head (or with paper-pencil)?

Which row(s) could you solve faster on the calculator?

GROUP PROJECT

Lambs or Chickens

The problem: You are studying in your social studies class about farm life. Your class must decide on a project. The choice has been narrowed down to raising lambs or raising chickens. Discuss the two projects with your classmates. Use the Key Facts to make a decision.

Key Facts

Lambs

- Lambs will need more room.
- You will need to provide food for the lambs.
- In early spring, you will cut the lambs' wool.
- Wool does not spoil. It can be easily shipped to a buyer.
- You can play with the lamb.

Chickens

- You will need chicken feed.
- The chicks will begin to lay eggs in twenty-two weeks.
- You will need to refrigerate the eggs.
- You can sell the eggs to parents.
- You will have eggs to sell every day.

CHAPTER TEST

Add. (pages 36, 38, 44, 46, and 48)

1. 12 + 16

2. 99 + 77

3. 189 + 410

4. 4,596 + 1,221

5. $0.17 + $0.46

6. $0.95 + $0.79

7. $4.36 + $5.62

8. $61.50 + $9.46

9. 43 + 50 + 19

10. 1,765 + 2,107 + 3,096 + 1,824

11.
```
   450
 + 531
```

12.
```
   1,247
 +   356
```

13.
```
   1,056
 +    38
```

14.
```
   25,406
 + 13,942
```

15.
```
   4,026
     874
     419
 +    27
```

16.
```
   $351.75
     90.06
 +   86.50
```

17.
```
   43,092
   12,856
 + 36,317
```

18.
```
   $35.25
     3.76
    16.18
 + 20.80
```

Subtract. (pages 54, 58, 60, and 62)

19. 67 − 9

20. 432 − 185

21. 480 − 390

22. 4,452 − 1,121

23. $0.39 − $0.23

24. $1.11 − $0.99

25. $45.67 − $0.78

26. $5.06 − $4.41

27.
```
   56
 − 49
```

28.
```
   314
 − 195
```

29.
```
   56,751
 − 18,673
```

30.
```
   18,001
 −  6,352
```

31.
```
   $5.11
 − 0.55
```

32.
```
   $24.39
 −  4.13
```

33.
```
   $893.14
 −  59.87
```

34.
```
   $700.00
 −  55.44
```

Estimate by rounding to the largest place. (pages 50 and 56)

35. 578 − 356

36. 449 + 443

37. $7.67 − $2.09

38. 649 + 122

39. 568 − 249

40. $5.79 + $4.66

41.
```
   4,941
 − 1,678
```

42.
```
   4,495
   1,249
 + 6,611
```

43.
```
   $68.13
 − 13.40
```

44.
```
   $61.56
    19.99
 + 56.42
```

Solve. (pages 42, 52, and 64)

45. At the county fair, Jim spent $2.25 on games, $2.50 on rides, $2.75 on food, and $1.50 on admission. Did he spend more than $10?

46. Ellen spent $1.50 on admission and $3.75 on rides. What do you need to know to find how much money she had when she left the fair?

47. There were 78 hogs on show at the fair. There were 56 female hogs. Write and solve a number sentence to find the number of male hogs at the show.

BONUS

Add or subtract.

1. 354,478 + 152,521	**2.** 555,201 − 333,101	**3.** 39,384,860 + 213,129	**4.** 5,728,916 − 2,116,803

5. 4,305,934 − 1,203,935	**6.** 67,458 + 17,341	**7.** 125,475,296 − 22,286,296	**8.** 33,534 + 86,568

9. 548,226 30,142 + 412,612	**10.** 35,784 123,404 + 740,812	**11.** 1,287,345 2,400 + 3,610,124	**12.** 497,210 111,529 + 500,351

RETEACHING

You may need to regroup more than once when you subtract across zeros.

Subtract 6,004 − 3,927.

Regroup the thousands.

$$\begin{array}{r} \overset{5\ \ 10}{\cancel{6},\cancel{0}\,0\,4} \\ -\ 3,9\,2\,7 \end{array}$$

Regroup the hundreds.

$$\begin{array}{r} \overset{\ \ \ \ 9}{\overset{5\ 10\,10}{\cancel{6},\cancel{0}\,\cancel{0}\,4}} \\ -\ 3,9\,2\,7 \end{array}$$

Regroup the tens.

$$\begin{array}{r} \overset{\ \ \ 9\ 9}{\overset{5\ 10\,10\,14}{\cancel{6},\cancel{0}\,\cancel{0}\,\cancel{4}}} \\ -\ 3,9\,2\,7 \end{array}$$

Subtract.

$$\begin{array}{r} \overset{\ \ \ 9\ 9}{\overset{5\ 10\,10\,14}{\cancel{6},\cancel{0}\,\cancel{0}\,\cancel{4}}} \\ -\ 3,9\,2\,7 \\ \hline 2,0\,7\,7 \end{array}$$

Other examples:

$$\begin{array}{r} \overset{\ \ \ 9}{\overset{6\,10\,13}{\$\cancel{7}.\cancel{0}\,\cancel{3}}} \\ -\ 2.7\,9 \\ \hline \$4.2\,4 \end{array}$$

$$\begin{array}{r} \overset{\ \ 9}{\overset{5\,10\,10}{\cancel{6}\,\cancel{0}\,\cancel{0}}} \\ -\ 2\,3\,9 \\ \hline 3\,6\,1 \end{array}$$

$$\begin{array}{r} \overset{\ \ \ \ 9\,10}{\overset{1\,10\ 0\,13}{\$\cancel{2}\cancel{0}.1\,\cancel{3}}} \\ -\ 1\,7.3\,5 \\ \hline \$2.7\,8 \end{array}$$

$$\begin{array}{r} \overset{\ \ \ 9\ 9}{\overset{4\,10\,10\,10}{\cancel{5},\cancel{0}\,\cancel{0}\,\cancel{0}}} \\ -\ 2,6\,3\,5 \\ \hline 2,3\,6\,5 \end{array}$$

Subtract.

1. 303 − 145	**2.** 601 − 283	**3.** 707 − 159	**4.** $5.06 − 4.87	**5.** $8.05 − 4.56
6. 300 − 248	**7.** 800 − 572	**8.** 900 − 433	**9.** $6.00 − 3.97	**10.** $5.00 − 2.63
11. 6,043 − 3,758	**12.** 8,502 − 2,899	**13.** 4,604 − 1,975	**14.** $80.71 − 38.93	**15.** $55.02 − 18.67
16. 4,006 − 3,158	**17.** 2,002 − 969	**18.** 5,008 − 3,219	**19.** $90.02 − 57.24	**20.** $80.01 − 47.95
21. 8,000 − 3,068	**22.** 7,000 − 2,656	**23.** 4,000 − 1,428	**24.** $90.00 − 61.95	**25.** $30.00 − 27.35

ENRICHMENT

Making and Counting Change

Ed buys a clipboard that costs $2.48. He pays for the clipboard with a $5 bill. What coins and bills does he receive as change? What is the total amount of his change?

To make or count change, begin with the cost of the item or items bought. Then use the least amount of coins and bills to count up to the amount given.

Cost   Amount given

$2.48 $\longrightarrow$ $2.49 $\longrightarrow$ $2.50 $\longrightarrow$ $3.00 $\longrightarrow$ $4.00 $\longrightarrow$ $5.00

= $2.52

Ed receives 2 pennies, 1 half-dollar, and 2 $1 bills as change. The total amount of his change is $2.52.

Write what change you should receive. Then write the total amount of the change.

1. Cost: $0.32
Amount given: $0.50

2. Cost: $0.27
Amount given: $0.50

3. Cost: $0.66
Amount given: $0.75

4. Cost: $1.29
Amount given: $2.00

5. Cost: $6.26
Amount given: $7.00

6. Cost: $2.33
Amount given: $3.00

7. Cost: $3.75
Amount given: $5.00

8. Cost: $4.41
Amount given: $5.00

9. Cost: $2.99
Amount given: $5.00

10. Cost: $8.28
Amount given: $10.00

11. Cost: $6.57
Amount given: $10.00

12. Cost: $3.94
Amount given: $10.00

13. Cost: $1.73
Amount given: $5.00

14. Cost: $2.13
Amount given: $2.25

★15. Cost: $8.24
Amount given: $20.00

CUMULATIVE REVIEW

Write the letter of the correct answer.

1. What is six hundred forty-two thousand, ninety-five written in standard form?

   a. 64,295
   b. 642,095
   c. 642,950
   d. not given

2. What is the place value of 6 in 26,472,391?

   a. hundred thousands
   b. millions
   c. ten millions
   d. not given

3. What is the value of the digit 3 in 29,075,360?

   a. 30
   b. 300
   c. 3,000
   d. not given

4. What is $900 + 40 + 1$ written in standard form?

   a. 941
   b. 90,041
   c. 900,401
   d. not given

5. Which number sentence is true?

   a. $4,685 > 4,687$
   b. $5,221 < 5,210$
   c. $26,725 = 26,735$
   d. not given

6. Which is five dollars and five cents?

   a. $5.005
   b. $5.05
   c. $55.00
   d. not given

7. Round 4,841 to the nearest hundred.

   a. 4,800
   b. 4,900
   c. 5,000
   d. not given

8. $8 - 4$
   a. 4
   b. 5
   c. 12
   d. not given

9. $6 + 2$
   a. 4
   b. 8
   c. 62
   d. not given

10. What is the value of ■ in $13 - ■ = 6$?

    a. 7
    b. 8
    c. 19
    d. not given

11. Barry has 4 pennants on the wall of his room. Jack has 6 more pennants than Barry. How many pennants does Jack have?

    a. 2 pennants
    b. 6 pennants
    c. 10 pennants
    d. not given

12. Sally has 8 oranges. She shares 3 oranges with her friends. How many oranges does Sally have left?

    a. 5 oranges
    b. 8 oranges
    c. 11 oranges
    d. not given

Your class has been invited to help run a farm for a week. The farm has 200 chickens, 100 cows, a very big garden, and a few cats and dogs. Which chores would need to be done every day? Which chores could be done less frequently? How would you organize a schedule for your week-long visit?

3 MULTIPLICATION FACTS, TIME

Multiplying with 2 and 3

A. Amanda saw 4 pairs of owls on a branch. How many owls did she see?

You can count and add the number of owls on the branch.

$$2 + 2 + 2 + 2 = 8$$

You can multiply because the groups have the same number.

$$4 \times 2 = 8$$

factor   factor   product   **OR**

$$\begin{array}{r} 2 \\ \times 4 \\ \hline 8 \end{array}$$ ← factor
← factor
← product

Amanda saw 8 owls.

B. You can multiply 2's.

$$\begin{array}{r} 2 \\ \times 1 \\ \hline 2 \end{array} \quad \begin{array}{r} 2 \\ \times 2 \\ \hline 4 \end{array} \quad \begin{array}{r} 2 \\ \times 3 \\ \hline 6 \end{array} \quad \begin{array}{r} 2 \\ \times 4 \\ \hline 8 \end{array} \quad \begin{array}{r} 2 \\ \times 5 \\ \hline 10 \end{array} \quad \begin{array}{r} 2 \\ \times 6 \\ \hline 12 \end{array} \quad \begin{array}{r} 2 \\ \times 7 \\ \hline 14 \end{array} \quad \begin{array}{r} 2 \\ \times 8 \\ \hline 16 \end{array} \quad \begin{array}{r} 2 \\ \times 9 \\ \hline 18 \end{array}$$

You can also multiply 3's.

$$\begin{array}{r} 3 \\ \times 1 \\ \hline 3 \end{array} \quad \begin{array}{r} 3 \\ \times 2 \\ \hline 6 \end{array} \quad \begin{array}{r} 3 \\ \times 3 \\ \hline 9 \end{array} \quad \begin{array}{r} 3 \\ \times 4 \\ \hline 12 \end{array} \quad \begin{array}{r} 3 \\ \times 5 \\ \hline 15 \end{array} \quad \begin{array}{r} 3 \\ \times 6 \\ \hline 18 \end{array} \quad \begin{array}{r} 3 \\ \times 7 \\ \hline 21 \end{array} \quad \begin{array}{r} 3 \\ \times 8 \\ \hline 24 \end{array} \quad \begin{array}{r} 3 \\ \times 9 \\ \hline 27 \end{array}$$

Multiply.

1.	2.	3.	4.	5.	6.	7.
3 $\times 1$	2 $\times 4$	2 $\times 7$	2 $\times 3$	2 $\times 8$	2 $\times 9$	3 $\times 5$

8.	9.	10.	11.	12.	13.	14.
3 $\times 4$	2 $\times 5$	2 $\times 6$	3 $\times 3$	2 $\times 2$	3 $\times 7$	3 $\times 8$

15. 9×2 16. 7×3 17. 9×3 18. 7×2 19. 6×2
20. 4×3 21. 5×2 22. 6×3 23. 8×2 24. 2×3
25. 9×2 26. 8×3 27. 7×2 28. 6×3 29. 5×3
30. 4×2 31. 9×3 32. 6×2 33. 7×3 34. 8×2
★35. $(6 + 1) \times 2$ ★36. $(3 - 2) \times 2$ ★37. $(3 + 3) \times 2$ ★38. $(2 + 2) \times 3$

Solve.

39. Amanda collects pictures of owls. She has 2 pictures of great horned owls, 2 of barn owls, and 2 of snowy owls. How many pictures of owls does she have?

40. During the summer bird-count, spotters counted 16 owls at Haven Woods, 24 owls at the reservation, and 12 owls at the nature preserve. How many owls did the spotters count altogether?

41. Amanda and her father keep a chart that shows where they find nests of owls. Look at the chart. How many nests did they find in the 3 trees? How many nests did they find in the 4 barns?

PLACES WHERE OWL NESTS ARE FOUND

Location	Number of Nests
3 trees	2 nests each
4 barns	3 nests each
2 logs	1 nest each

CHALLENGE

Andy, Bill, Carl, and Dave are standing in line in the cafeteria. Dave is between Andy and Bill. Andy is not first in line. Carl is standing next to Andy. Bill is not second in line. Carl is last in line. In what order are the boys standing in line?

Multiplying with 4 and 5

A. Gary has 7 iris plants. There are 4 blossoms on each plant. How many blossoms are there?

To find how many blossoms there are on the plants, you can multiply 7 × 4.

$$7 \times 4 = 28 \qquad \text{OR} \qquad \begin{array}{r} 4 \\ \times\, 7 \\ \hline 28 \end{array}$$

There are 28 blossoms on Gary's plants.

B. You can multiply 4's.

| $\begin{array}{r}4\\\times 1\\\hline 4\end{array}$ | $\begin{array}{r}4\\\times 2\\\hline 8\end{array}$ | $\begin{array}{r}4\\\times 3\\\hline 12\end{array}$ | $\begin{array}{r}4\\\times 4\\\hline 16\end{array}$ | $\begin{array}{r}4\\\times 5\\\hline 20\end{array}$ | $\begin{array}{r}4\\\times 6\\\hline 24\end{array}$ | $\begin{array}{r}4\\\times 7\\\hline 28\end{array}$ | $\begin{array}{r}4\\\times 8\\\hline 32\end{array}$ | $\begin{array}{r}4\\\times 9\\\hline 36\end{array}$ |

You can also multiply 5's.

| $\begin{array}{r}5\\\times 1\\\hline 5\end{array}$ | $\begin{array}{r}5\\\times 2\\\hline 10\end{array}$ | $\begin{array}{r}5\\\times 3\\\hline 15\end{array}$ | $\begin{array}{r}5\\\times 4\\\hline 20\end{array}$ | $\begin{array}{r}5\\\times 5\\\hline 25\end{array}$ | $\begin{array}{r}5\\\times 6\\\hline 30\end{array}$ | $\begin{array}{r}5\\\times 7\\\hline 35\end{array}$ | $\begin{array}{r}5\\\times 8\\\hline 40\end{array}$ | $\begin{array}{r}5\\\times 9\\\hline 45\end{array}$ |

Math Reasoning, page H185

Multiply.

1. 4
   × 3

2. 5
   × 6

3. 4
   × 7

4. 4
   × 2

5. 5
   × 2

6. 5
   × 9

7. 4
   × 4

8. 4
   × 1

9. 4
   × 8

10. 5
    × 8

11. 5
    × 7

12. 4
    × 5

13. 5
    × 1

14. 4
    × 9

15. 3×4

16. 4×5

17. 5×4

18. 6×5

19. 7×4

20. 8×5

21. 9×4

22. 1×4

23. 3×5

24. 5×5

25. 8×4

26. 4×4

27. 1×5

28. 9×5

29. 2×5

★30. $(3 \times 2) \times 5$

★31. $(3 \times 3) \times 4$

★32. $(4 \times 1) \times 4$

★33. $(2 \times 2) \times 4$

Solve. For Problem 37, use the Infobank.

34. Kay plants 7 Golden Charm tulip bulbs. There will be 5 tulips that grow from each bulb. How many tulips will bloom in Kay's garden?

35. Gino spends $15.40 for tulip bulbs, $9.75 for crocus bulbs, $12.62 for daffodil bulbs, and $3.49 for a bulb planter. How much does Gino spend?

★36. In Vera's garden, there are 5 pink lilies in each of 3 rows and 4 white lilies in each of 2 rows. How many lilies are there in Vera's garden?

37. Use the information on page 402 to solve. Joe's grandmother keeps a planting diary. Find how many yellow daylilies she planted from 1987 through 1989.

NUMBER SENSE

You can use a shortcut to add two numbers that end in 5. Add 45 + 35.

Think: 40 + 30 = 70.   70 + 10 = 80
            5 + 5 = 10

So, 45 + 35 = 80.

Use the shortcut to add.

1. 25 + 35

2. 45 + 15

3. 25 + 65

4. 55 + 15

5. 75 + 45

Properties of Multiplication

A. During a nature hike, Art saw 4 goldfinches in each of 2 trees. In his backyard, he saw 2 goldfinches in each of 4 trees.

The properties of multiplication can help you find products.

2 sets of 4   4 sets of 2

$2 \times 4 = 8$
$$\begin{array}{r} 4 \\ \times 2 \\ \hline 8 \end{array}$$

$4 \times 2 = 8$
$$\begin{array}{r} 2 \\ \times 4 \\ \hline 8 \end{array}$$

Order Property
If the order of the factors is changed, the product remains the same.

B. There are other properties of multiplication.

Property of One
If one factor is 1, the product is always the other factor.

$7 \times 1 = 7$
$1 \times 7 = 7$
$$\begin{array}{r} 1 \\ \times 7 \\ \hline 7 \end{array} \qquad \begin{array}{r} 7 \\ \times 1 \\ \hline 7 \end{array}$$

Property of Zero
If a factor is 0, the product is always 0.

$5 \times 0 = 0$
$0 \times 5 = 0$
$$\begin{array}{r} 0 \\ \times 5 \\ \hline 0 \end{array} \qquad \begin{array}{r} 5 \\ \times 0 \\ \hline 0 \end{array}$$

Grouping Property
If the grouping of the factors is changed, the product remains the same.

$(2 \times 3) \times 1 \qquad 2 \times (3 \times 1)$
$\quad\downarrow \qquad\qquad\qquad\quad \downarrow$
$\quad 6 \quad \times 1 = 6 \qquad 2 \times \quad 3 \quad = 6$

Multiply.

1. 1×0 2. 1×3 3. 5×0 4. 1×2 5. 1×9 6. 0×8

7. 6×1 8. 1×4 9. 7×1 10. 0×4 11. 1×8 12. 1×1

13. 1×5 14. 8×1 15. 7×0 16. 0×0 17. 3×0 18. 2×0

19. $\begin{array}{r} 4 \\ \times 1 \\ \hline \end{array}$ 20. $\begin{array}{r} 0 \\ \times 7 \\ \hline \end{array}$ 21. $\begin{array}{r} 1 \\ \times 5 \\ \hline \end{array}$ 22. $\begin{array}{r} 9 \\ \times 1 \\ \hline \end{array}$ 23. $\begin{array}{r} 8 \\ \times 0 \\ \hline \end{array}$ 24. $\begin{array}{r} 6 \\ \times 0 \\ \hline \end{array}$

Write the missing factor. Then write the product.

25. $4 \times 8 = \blacksquare \times 4$ 26. $7 \times 5 = 5 \times \blacksquare$ 27. $9 \times 3 = \blacksquare \times 9$

28. $1 \times 5 = 5 \times \blacksquare$ 29. $4 \times 9 = \blacksquare \times 4$ 30. $5 \times 8 = 8 \times \blacksquare$

31. $3 \times 2 = \blacksquare \times 3$ 32. $4 \times 5 = 5 \times \blacksquare$ 33. $3 \times 7 = 7 \times \blacksquare$

34. $6 \times 2 = 2 \times \blacksquare$ 35. $9 \times 2 = \blacksquare \times 9$ 36. $5 \times 3 = \blacksquare \times 5$

Group the factors another way and multiply.

37. $1 \times (2 \times 1)$ 38. $(7 \times 2) \times 2$ 39. $(1 \times 6) \times 1$

40. $1 \times (5 \times 1)$ 41. $(7 \times 1) \times 2$ 42. $2 \times (3 \times 3)$

★43. $8 \times (2 \times 2)$ ★44. $7 \times (5 \times 1)$ ★45. $(4 \times 2) \times 6$

Solve.

46. Use the chart. How many birds were found in the barns? How many birds were found in the trees?

Place	Birds in each
4 barns	0
1 pond	8
6 trees	1

47. The people at the winter bird-count spotted 876 grackles last year. They spotted 1,207 grackles this year. How many more grackles did they spot this year?

★48. Margie found 23 bird nests. Each nest contained 1 egg. How many eggs did Margie find?

 **CHALLENGE** Patterns, Relations, and Functions

Complete the pattern. Write the rule used in each.

1. 2, 3, 6, 7, $\blacksquare$, $\blacksquare$, $\blacksquare$, $\blacksquare$

2. 3, 6, 12, 15, 30, $\blacksquare$, $\blacksquare$

3. 2, 4, 5, 10, 11, 22, $\blacksquare$, $\blacksquare$, $\blacksquare$

PROBLEM SOLVING
Choosing the Operation

When solving a problem in which two or more groups
are to be joined together, you can add to find the total.
Sometimes you can multiply.

A. Koalas from Australia eat the leaves of eucalyptus
trees. One zoo feeds 2 pounds of eucalyptus leaves
each day to each of its koalas. There are 4 koalas in
the zoo. How many pounds of eucalyptus leaves are fed
to the koalas each day?

You know	You want to find	You can
how many groups, how many in each group, and that the number in each group is the same.	how many in all.	MULTIPLY or ADD.

You can multiply. $4 \times 2 = 8$ pounds
You can add. $2 + 2 + 2 + 2 = 8$ pounds

B. One koala ate 3 pounds of eucalyptus leaves.
Another ate 2 pounds of leaves. A third koala ate 1
pound of leaves, and the fourth ate 3 pounds of leaves.
How many pounds of leaves did the koalas eat
altogether?

You know	You want to find	You can
how many in each group and that the groups are not the same size.	how many in all.	ADD.

You can add. $3 + 2 + 1 + 3 = 9$ pounds
You cannot multiply.

Decide whether you can multiply to solve these problems. Write the letter of the correct answer.

1. There are 4 monkeys in each of 3 monkey cages at the zoo. How many monkeys are there in the 3 cages?

   a. you can multiply
   b. you cannot multiply

2. One zoo has 3 elephants from Kenya, 4 elephants from India, and 2 elephants from Malaysia. How many elephants are there in the zoo?

   a. you can multiply
   b. you cannot multiply

Solve.

3. Each of 5 leopard cubs is fed 2 pounds of food per day. How many pounds of food do all the leopard cubs eat?

4. There are 8 black bears and 2 Kodiak bears in the bear house at the zoo. How many bears are there in all?

5. In the Africa World section of the zoo, there are 3 mother lions. Each mother lion has 4 cubs. How many cubs are there?

6. At the zoo, 5 otters are sunning themselves on a rock. There are 9 more otters swimming in the stream. How many otters are there?

7. Marty petted 6 goats, 3 lambs, 4 rabbits, and 2 calves at the petting zoo. How many animals did Marty pet?

8. There are 4 zebra corrals at the zoo. There are 6 zebras in each corral. How many zebras are there in all the corrals?

9. In the American Exhibit live 3 mother opossums. Each opossum carries 7 babies on her back. How many baby opossums are there in the American Exhibit?

10. Of the deer in Forest World, 2 are stags, 7 are does, and 6 are fawns. How many deer are there in Forest World?

11. There are 5 different houses for birds at the zoo. Each house holds 5 different types of birds. How many types of birds are there at the zoo?

12. In the Winter Exhibit there are 3 snow leopards, 4 Siberian tigers, and 2 yaks. How many animals are there in the Winter Exhibit?

Multiplying with 6 and 7

A. A forest ranger sees 6 raccoons in each of 5 different parts of the forest. How many raccoons does the ranger see?

You can multiply to find how many raccoons the ranger sees. Multiply 5×6.

$$5 \times 6 = 30 \qquad \text{OR} \qquad \begin{array}{r} 6 \\ \times\, 5 \\ \hline 30 \end{array}$$

The ranger sees 30 raccoons.

B. You can multiply 6's.

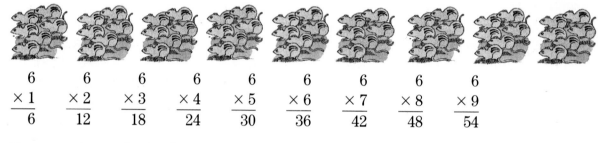

$$\begin{array}{ccccccccc} 6 & 6 & 6 & 6 & 6 & 6 & 6 & 6 & 6 \\ \times\,1 & \times\,2 & \times\,3 & \times\,4 & \times\,5 & \times\,6 & \times\,7 & \times\,8 & \times\,9 \\ \hline 6 & 12 & 18 & 24 & 30 & 36 & 42 & 48 & 54 \end{array}$$

You can also multiply 7's.

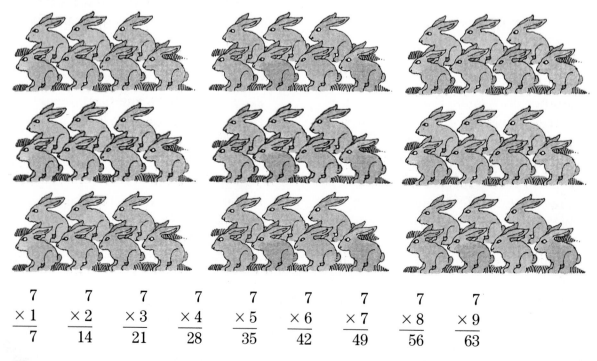

$$\begin{array}{ccccccccc} 7 & 7 & 7 & 7 & 7 & 7 & 7 & 7 & 7 \\ \times\,1 & \times\,2 & \times\,3 & \times\,4 & \times\,5 & \times\,6 & \times\,7 & \times\,8 & \times\,9 \\ \hline 7 & 14 & 21 & 28 & 35 & 42 & 49 & 56 & 63 \end{array}$$

Math Reasoning, page H186

Multiply.

1. 6×3
2. 7×2
3. 6×4
4. 7×5
5. 6×5
6. 7×8
7. 7×9

8. 7×1
9. 6×0
10. 6×6
11. 7×0
12. 6×9
13. 6×2
14. 6×7

15. 1×6
16. 3×7
17. 4×7
18. 5×7
19. 6×6

20. 8×6
21. 6×7
22. 0×7
23. 5×6
24. 3×6

25. 0×6
26. 1×7
27. 8×7
28. 4×6
29. 9×7

30. $(1 \times 3) \times 7$
31. $(2 \times 2) \times 6$
32. $(4 \times 2) \times 7$
33. $(9 \times 0) \times 6$

Solve.

34. In the forest, there are 7 white-tailed deer at each of 2 ponds. How many white-tailed deer are at both ponds?

35. There are two hundred seventy-six different kinds of mammals and birds that live in the forest. Write this number in standard form.

★36. In one part of the stream, 3 otters caught 6 fish each. In another part of the stream, 5 otters caught 7 fish each. How many fish did all the otters catch?

37. In the spring, there are 6 beaver lodges on the stream. There are 4 beavers living in each lodge. Use this information to write and solve your own word problem.

ANOTHER LOOK

Add or subtract.

1. $25,679 + 3,825$
2. $\$80.09 - 41.75$
3. $68,325 - 32,873$
4. $\$32.75 + 94.88$
5. $4,522 + 7,883$

6. $8,699 - 7,780$
7. $52,644 + 18,975$
8. $\$29.65 - 8.99$
9. $\$481.00 + 36.75$
10. $9,006 - 8,894$

Multiplying with 8 and 9

A. Mr. Clark's class is doing a project on honeybees. There are 4 groups of students in the class. Each group has to report on a different aspect of honeybees. If there are 8 students in each group, how many students are there in the class?

$$4 \times 8 = 32 \qquad \text{OR} \qquad \begin{array}{r} 8 \\ \times 4 \\ \hline 32 \end{array}$$

There are 32 students in the class.

B.

You can multiply 8's.

| $\begin{array}{r}8\\ \times 1\\ \hline 8\end{array}$ | $\begin{array}{r}8\\ \times 2\\ \hline 16\end{array}$ | $\begin{array}{r}8\\ \times 3\\ \hline 24\end{array}$ | $\begin{array}{r}8\\ \times 4\\ \hline 32\end{array}$ | $\begin{array}{r}8\\ \times 5\\ \hline 40\end{array}$ | $\begin{array}{r}8\\ \times 6\\ \hline 48\end{array}$ | $\begin{array}{r}8\\ \times 7\\ \hline 56\end{array}$ | $\begin{array}{r}8\\ \times 8\\ \hline 64\end{array}$ | $\begin{array}{r}8\\ \times 9\\ \hline 72\end{array}$ |

You can also multiply 9's.

| $\begin{array}{r}9\\ \times 1\\ \hline 9\end{array}$ | $\begin{array}{r}9\\ \times 2\\ \hline 18\end{array}$ | $\begin{array}{r}9\\ \times 3\\ \hline 27\end{array}$ | $\begin{array}{r}9\\ \times 4\\ \hline 36\end{array}$ | $\begin{array}{r}9\\ \times 5\\ \hline 45\end{array}$ | $\begin{array}{r}9\\ \times 6\\ \hline 54\end{array}$ | $\begin{array}{r}9\\ \times 7\\ \hline 63\end{array}$ | $\begin{array}{r}9\\ \times 8\\ \hline 72\end{array}$ | $\begin{array}{r}9\\ \times 9\\ \hline 81\end{array}$ |

Multiply.

1. $\begin{array}{r} 8 \\ \times 5 \\ \hline \end{array}$	**2.** $\begin{array}{r} 9 \\ \times 3 \\ \hline \end{array}$	**3.** $\begin{array}{r} 8 \\ \times 6 \\ \hline \end{array}$	**4.** $\begin{array}{r} 9 \\ \times 6 \\ \hline \end{array}$	**5.** $\begin{array}{r} 9 \\ \times 2 \\ \hline \end{array}$	**6.** $\begin{array}{r} 8 \\ \times 1 \\ \hline \end{array}$	**7.** $\begin{array}{r} 9 \\ \times 7 \\ \hline \end{array}$
8. $\begin{array}{r} 9 \\ \times 5 \\ \hline \end{array}$	**9.** $\begin{array}{r} 8 \\ \times 7 \\ \hline \end{array}$	**10.** $\begin{array}{r} 8 \\ \times 9 \\ \hline \end{array}$	**11.** $\begin{array}{r} 9 \\ \times 8 \\ \hline \end{array}$	**12.** $\begin{array}{r} 9 \\ \times 4 \\ \hline \end{array}$	**13.** $\begin{array}{r} 8 \\ \times 2 \\ \hline \end{array}$	**14.** $\begin{array}{r} 9 \\ \times 9 \\ \hline \end{array}$
15. $\begin{array}{r} 0 \\ \times 9 \\ \hline \end{array}$	**16.** $\begin{array}{r} 6 \\ \times 6 \\ \hline \end{array}$	**17.** $\begin{array}{r} 5 \\ \times 3 \\ \hline \end{array}$	**18.** $\begin{array}{r} 8 \\ \times 7 \\ \hline \end{array}$	**19.** $\begin{array}{r} 6 \\ \times 8 \\ \hline \end{array}$	**20.** $\begin{array}{r} 9 \\ \times 4 \\ \hline \end{array}$	**21.** $\begin{array}{r} 7 \\ \times 4 \\ \hline \end{array}$
22. $\begin{array}{r} 2 \\ \times 7 \\ \hline \end{array}$	**23.** $\begin{array}{r} 4 \\ \times 3 \\ \hline \end{array}$	**24.** $\begin{array}{r} 7 \\ \times 0 \\ \hline \end{array}$	**25.** $\begin{array}{r} 6 \\ \times 1 \\ \hline \end{array}$	**26.** $\begin{array}{r} 7 \\ \times 5 \\ \hline \end{array}$	**27.** $\begin{array}{r} 0 \\ \times 1 \\ \hline \end{array}$	**28.** $\begin{array}{r} 6 \\ \times 2 \\ \hline \end{array}$

29. 4×8 **30.** 5×8 **31.** 6×9 **32.** 1×9 **33.** 0×8

34. 9×1 **35.** 3×8 **36.** 5×9 **37.** 0×9 **38.** 8×8

39. 4×7 **40.** 7×7 **41.** 5×4 **42.** 4×4 **43.** 9×8

44. 7×2 **45.** 5×5 **46.** 6×3 **47.** 7×1 **48.** 6×7

49. 8×4 **50.** 3×0 **51.** 9×2 **52.** 6×6 **53.** 2×5

54. $(3 \times 3) \times 4$ **55.** $(5 \times 1) \times 8$ **56.** $(3 \times 2) \times 3$ **57.** $(4 \times 2) \times 6$

58. $(3 \times 1) \times 9$ **59.** $(3 \times 2) \times 7$ **60.** $(3 \times 3) \times 9$ **61.** $(8 \times 0) \times 9$

Solve.

62. A beekeeper has 4 hives. If each hive has 9 worker bees on guard at its entrance, how many worker bees are there on guard?

63. In one year, 4 hives produce 127 pounds of honey. The next year, the same hives produce 152 pounds of honey. How much honey is produced in these two years?

64. Harry Harwood ships bees to honey producers. Use the table of shipments to write and solve three word problems of your own.

SHIPMENTS

Client	Pounds of bees in 1 package	Packages
Honey & Co.	2	8
Sweet Stuff	3	9
Nectar, Inc.	5	8

Multiples

A. You can discover the multiples of a number.

Step 1: List all the whole numbers from 0 to 50. You may wish to draw a number line. Draw a circle around 0. Then circle every second number.

- What numbers did you circle? These are some **multiples** of 2. They are also known as **even** numbers.

- What do you notice about multiples of 2 and multiplication facts for 2?

- Can you find a pattern for the ones digits of the even numbers? What is the pattern?

- The numbers you have not circled are **odd** numbers. What is the pattern for the ones digit of the odd numbers?

Step 2: Pick a number from 3 to 9. Underline all of the numbers on the list that are multiples of the number you picked.

- Is the number you picked even or odd?

- Are its multiples even or odd?

- Can you find a pattern for the ones digits of the multiples of the number you picked? What is the pattern?

- Use this pattern to find the next multiple. How can you check your answer?

Step 3: Compare your list to those of your teammates.

- Is the number you picked a multiple of any other numbers? Which numbers?

- Are any of the multiples of the number you picked also multiples of any other numbers? Which numbers?

Thinking as a Team _____

1. What number is a multiple of every number?

2. Do even numbers have multiples that are odd or even? What about odd numbers?

3. If a number is a multiple of another number, are all of the multiples of the first number also multiples of the second number?

4. Are all of the multiples of the second number also multiples of the first number?

5. Is the sum of two multiples of a number also a multiple of that number? Is the difference? Is the product?

6. What other patterns can you find?

List what you have discovered about the multiples of numbers. Discuss your list with other teams.

B. You can use your calculator to find multiples.

Press any number on your calculator. Then press $+$ $=$. Keep on pressing $=$.

Record the multiples of each number you try. Do you notice any patterns? Describe them. Think of other ways you could find multiples on your calculator.

Working as a Team _____

Play *Bing, Bang, Boom* with your team or class. Pick any two numbers from 2 to 9. Begin to count, starting with 1.

For each multiple of the first number, say *Bing*.
For each multiple of the second number, say *Bang*.
For each multiple of both numbers, say *Boom*.
If someone makes a mistake, begin again at 1.
Try to reach 100. Make your own multiples game.

For a related activity, see **Connecting Math Ideas,** p. 397

PROBLEM SOLVING
Solving Two-Step Problems/Making a Plan

You may need to use more than one step to solve a problem. Making a plan can help you solve such a problem.

> Josh raises chickens as a hobby. He raises White Leghorns and Rhode Island Reds. He has 8 White Leghorns and 6 times as many Rhode Island Reds. How many chickens does he have?

Needed Data: the total number of Rhode Island Reds

Plan

Step 1: Find the total number of Rhode Island Reds.

Step 2: Find the sum of the number of White Leghorns and the number of Rhode Island Reds.

Step 1: Multiply to find the number of Rhode Island Reds.

$$\begin{array}{r} 8 \text{ (White Leghorns)} \\ \times 6 \\ \hline 48 \text{ (Rhode Island Reds)} \end{array}$$

Step 2: Add to find the sum.

$$\begin{array}{r} 48 \text{ (number of Rhode Island Reds)} \\ + \ 8 \text{ (number of White Leghorns)} \\ \hline 56 \text{ (total number of chickens)} \end{array}$$

Josh has 56 chickens.

Complete the plan by writing the missing step.

1. A certain porpoise guided ships through an ocean channel near New Zealand. The porpoise was first seen in 1871. It was wounded 32 years later, but it still guided ships safely for 9 more years. Then the porpoise disappeared. In which year did it disappear?

   Step 1: Find the year in which the porpoise was wounded.

   Step 2:

Complete the plan by writing the missing step.

2. Alice's neighbors planted a community garden. They wanted to plant 51 trees. There were 5 people who planted 6 trees each. How many trees remained to be planted?

Step 1:

Step 2: Find the difference between the total number of trees to be planted and the number of trees that were actually planted.

Make a plan for each problem. Solve.

3. In the summer, Jason works on his uncle's farm. He spends 2 hours per day caring for the animals and 3 hours per day weeding the gardens. For how many hours does Jason work in 5 days?

4. Penny is a scientist who studies ants. She began a study of ants in 1980 and finished it in 1990. She spent 7 of those years at a college. The rest of the time, she studied ants in the desert. For how many years did Penny study ants in the desert?

5. Eric studies a family of monkeys to see how they behave. He spends 3 hours per day at the zoo watching one family of monkeys. Eric goes to the zoo 3 days per week. In 4 weeks, how many hours will he spend studying monkeys?

★**6.** Shepherds must pay tolls to take their sheep across a bridge. One shepherd has 5 sheep. Look at the price list. How much change will he receive from a 100-drina bill?

★**7.** Another shepherd wants to take his 7 sheep across the bridge. He has already paid 100 drinas. How many more drinas does he need to pay before he can cross the bridge?

1st — 50 drinas
2nd — 25 drinas
3rd — 12 drinas
additional — 5 drinas

Units of Time

A. Margaret likes to watch the robins that have nested in a tree outside her window. Every morning at 11:40, the mother robin flies from the nest to collect food for the baby robins.

11:40

Read: eleven-forty, or
         20 minutes to 12.
Write: 11:40.

B. A.M. is the time between 12:00 midnight and 12:00 noon.
Write eleven-forty in the morning as 11:40 A.M.

P.M. is the time between 12:00 noon and 12:00 midnight.
Write nine o'clock in the evening as 9:00 P.M.

C. Time is measured in different units.

    60 seconds (s) = 1 minute (min)
    60 minutes (min) = 1 hour (h)
    24 hours (h) = 1 day (d)

To know which unit to use, you have to think about how much time is to be measured.

taking a drink	feeding babies	sleeping	nest building
seconds	minutes	hours	days

90

Write the time for each.

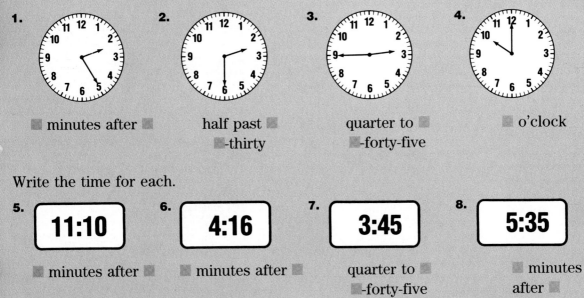

1. ▨ minutes after ▨

2. half past ▨
   ▨-thirty

3. quarter to ▨
   ▨-forty-five

4. ▨ o'clock

Write the time for each.

5. **11:10**   ▨ minutes after ▨

6. **4:16**   ▨ minutes after ▨

7. **3:45**   quarter to ▨
   ▨-forty-five

8. **5:35**   ▨ minutes after ▨

Complete. Write *seconds*, *minutes*, *hours*, or *days* for each ▨.

9. There are 24 ▨ in a day.

10. There are 60 ▨ in a minute.

11. The students are allowed about 25 ▨ for lunch.

12. A movie lasts for about 2 ▨.

Complete. Write *A.M.* or *P.M.* for each ▨.

13. The rooster wakes up at 6:00 ▨.

14. The nightly news begins at 6:00 ▨.

15. Ed eats supper at 5:00 ▨.

16. Sue's morning class starts at 8:45 ▨.

Use the colon (:) and *A.M.* or *P.M.* to write each time.

17. three o'clock in the afternoon

18. seven o'clock in the morning

19. ten o'clock in the morning

20. eight o'clock at night

MIDCHAPTER REVIEW

Multiply.

1. $\begin{array}{r} 2 \\ \times 6 \end{array}$

2. $\begin{array}{r} 2 \\ \times 9 \end{array}$

3. $\begin{array}{r} 3 \\ \times 7 \end{array}$

4. $\begin{array}{r} 3 \\ \times 3 \end{array}$

5. $\begin{array}{r} 4 \\ \times 8 \end{array}$

6. $\begin{array}{r} 4 \\ \times 2 \end{array}$

7. $\begin{array}{r} 5 \\ \times 4 \end{array}$

8. 5×0

9. 1×3

10. $(3 \times 2) \times 2$

11. $4 \times (5 \times 1)$

12. 6×6

13. 8×6

14. 9×7

15. 5×7

16. 3×8

17. 7×8

18. 6×9

19. 9×9

Telling Time

A. Jake hiked on the Appalachian Trail. He left his home at 7:15 A.M. and reached the trail at 7:45 A.M. How many minutes did it take Jake to reach the trail from his home?

7:15   7:45

One way to find how many minutes it took Jake to reach the trail is to count by fives.

It took Jake 30 minutes to reach the trail from his home.

B. Suppose Jake had left his house at 6:10 A.M. and reached the trail at 6:37 A.M.

Count by fives. Then count by ones.

$$25 + 2 = 27$$

Jake would have taken 27 minutes to reach the trail.

C. Suppose Jake started his hike at 10:30 A.M. and completed his hike at 2:15 P.M.

To find how many hours and minutes have passed, first count the hours.
Then count the minutes.

From 10:30 A.M. to 1:30 P.M. is 3 hours.
From 1:30 P.M. to 2:15 P.M. is 45 minutes.

Jake would have hiked for 3 hours 45 minutes.

Write the amount of time that has passed.

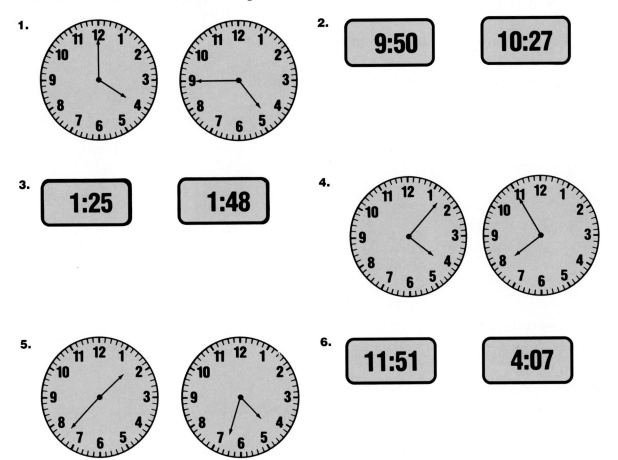

1.

2. 9:50   10:27

3. 1:25   1:48

4.

5.

6. 11:51   4:07

7. from 6:15 to 6:50

8. from 1:05 to 1:35

9. from 3:20 to 3:47

10. from 4:30 to 4:52

11. from 7:00 to 11:30

12. from 3:00 to 7:25

13. from 6:00 to 8:37

14. from 5:00 to 7:17

15. from 8:15 to 10:35

16. from 9:25 to 10:48

17. from 3:12 to 4:35

18. from 9:58 to 12:00

19. from eleven-thirty A.M. to two P.M.

20. from noon to three-forty-seven P.M.

21. from midnight to one-fifteen A.M.

22. from eight-forty-five P.M. to two-ten A.M.

23. from a quarter to five A.M. to one P.M.

24. from three-fifteen P.M. to seven-twenty-eight P.M.

25. from ten-twenty-five P.M. to five-thirty A.M.

More Units of Time

A. A robin built its nest in a tree in Jennifer's yard. The robin began its nest on April 21. It finished the nest 4 days later. On what date did the robin finish building its nest?

JANUARY	FEBRUARY	MARCH	APRIL
S M T W T F S	S M T W T F S	S M T W T F S	S M T W T F S
1 2	1 2 3 4 5 6	1 2 3 4 5	1 2
3 4 5 6 7 8 9	7 8 9 10 11 12 13	6 7 8 9 10 11 12	3 4 5 6 7 8 9
10 11 12 13 14 15 16	14 15 16 17 18 19 20	13 14 15 16 17 18 19	10 11 12 13 14 15 16
17 18 19 20 21 22 23	21 22 23 24 25 26 27	20 21 22 23 24 25 26	17 18 19 20 21 22 23
24 25 26 27 28 29 30	28 29	27 28 29 30 31	24 25 26 27 28 29 30
31			

MAY	JUNE	JULY	AUGUST
S M T W T F S	S M T W T F S	S M T W T F S	S M T W T F S
1 2 3 4 5 6 7	1 2 3 4	1 2	1 2 3 4 5 6
8 9 10 11 12 13 14	5 6 7 8 9 10 11	3 4 5 6 7 8 9	7 8 9 10 11 12 13
15 16 17 18 19 20 21	12 13 14 15 16 17 18	10 11 12 13 14 15 16	14 15 16 17 18 19 20
22 23 24 25 26 27 28	19 20 21 22 23 24 25	17 18 19 20 21 22 23	21 22 23 24 25 26 27
29 30 31	26 27 28 29 30	24 25 26 27 28 29 30	28 29 30 31
		31	

SEPTEMBER	OCTOBER	NOVEMBER	DECEMBER
S M T W T F S	S M T W T F S	S M T W T F S	S M T W T F S
1 2 3	1	1 2 3 4 5	1 2 3
4 5 6 7 8 9 10	2 3 4 5 6 7 8	6 7 8 9 10 11 12	4 5 6 7 8 9 10
11 12 13 14 15 16 17	9 10 11 12 13 14 15	13 14 15 16 17 18 19	11 12 13 14 15 16 17
18 19 20 21 22 23 24	16 17 18 19 20 21 22	20 21 22 23 24 25 26	18 19 20 21 22 23 24
25 26 27 28 29 30	23 24 25 26 27 28 29	27 28 29 30	25 26 27 28 29 30 31
	30 31		

Begin with the date the robin began its nest. Count 4 more days. You have counted to April 25. The robin finished its nest on April 25.

B. A sparrow finished its nest on April 29. It began the nest 3 days earlier. When was the nest begun? What day of the week was this?

Begin with April 29. Count back 3 days. You have counted to April 26. This is a Tuesday. The sparrow began its nest on April 26.

C. There are 12 months in a year. You can count forward to find the month that is 3 months after April. You can count backward to find the month that is 3 months before April.

3 months after April is July. 3 months before April is January.

94

Use the calendar to answer the questions.

1. How many days have passed between May 3 and May 14?

2. How many weeks have passed between May 2 and May 16?

3. What is the date 1 week before May 21?

4. What is the date 16 days before May 30?

5. What is the next Tuesday after May 9?

6. What is the nearest Thursday before May 22?

7. How many Sundays are there in May?

8. What month is 4 months after May?

9. What month is 2 months before May?

10. What date is 12 days before May 9?

JANUARY						
S	M	T	W	T	F	S
					1	2
3	4	5	6	7	8	9
10	11	12	13	14	15	16
17	18	19	20	21	22	23
24	25	26	27	28	29	30
31						

FEBRUARY						
S	M	T	W	T	F	S
	1	2	3	4	5	6
7	8	9	10	11	12	13
14	15	16	17	18	19	20
21	22	23	24	25	26	27
28	29					

MARCH						
S	M	T	W	T	F	S
		1	2	3	4	5
6	7	8	9	10	11	12
13	14	15	16	17	18	19
20	21	22	23	24	25	26
27	28	29	30	31		

APRIL						
S	M	T	W	T	F	S
					1	2
3	4	5	6	7	8	9
10	11	12	13	14	15	16
17	18	19	20	21	22	23
24	25	26	27	28	29	30

MAY						
S	M	T	W	T	F	S
1	2	3	4	5	6	7
8	9	10	11	12	13	14
15	16	17	18	19	20	21
22	23	24	25	26	27	28
29	30	31				

JUNE						
S	M	T	W	T	F	S
			1	2	3	4
5	6	7	8	9	10	11
12	13	14	15	16	17	18
19	20	21	22	23	24	25
26	27	28	29	30		

JULY						
S	M	T	W	T	F	S
					1	2
3	4	5	6	7	8	9
10	11	12	13	14	15	16
17	18	19	20	21	22	23
24	25	26	27	28	29	30
31						

AUGUST						
S	M	T	W	T	F	S
	1	2	3	4	5	6
7	8	9	10	11	12	13
14	15	16	17	18	19	20
21	22	23	24	25	26	27
28	29	30	31			

SEPTEMBER						
S	M	T	W	T	F	S
				1	2	3
4	5	6	7	8	9	10
11	12	13	14	15	16	17
18	19	20	21	22	23	24
25	26	27	28	29	30	

OCTOBER						
S	M	T	W	T	F	S
						1
2	3	4	5	6	7	8
9	10	11	12	13	14	15
16	17	18	19	20	21	22
23	24	25	26	27	28	29
30	31					

NOVEMBER						
S	M	T	W	T	F	S
		1	2	3	4	5
6	7	8	9	10	11	12
13	14	15	16	17	18	19
20	21	22	23	24	25	26
27	28	29	30			

DECEMBER						
S	M	T	W	T	F	S
				1	2	3
4	5	6	7	8	9	10
11	12	13	14	15	16	17
18	19	20	21	22	23	24
25	26	27	28	29	30	31

Solve. Use the calendar to answer the questions.

11. The Bird-Watching Club meets on the third Thursday of each month. On what date will they meet in June?

12. Tom and Laura are planning a bird-watching outing. The outing is planned for the second Sunday in August. What date is that outing?

13. Margaret is planning a trip to a bird museum. She is leaving 2 months and 5 days after August 2. What day and date will she go on her trip?

14. Use the calendar above to write and solve your own word problem.

For a related activity, see **Connecting Math Ideas,** p. 397

PROBLEM SOLVING
Using a Bar Graph

Information that is shown in a bar graph is easy to compare. This bar graph can help you compare the average life spans of some mammals.

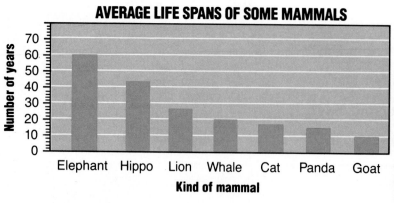

AVERAGE LIFE SPANS OF SOME MAMMALS

The labels on the bar graph tell you what kind of information is being compared in the graph.

There is a bar for each mammal. You can use the numbers on the side of the graph to tell how many years each bar stands for.

For example, the bar labeled *Whale* goes to the line marked 20. This means that whales live for about 20 years.

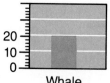

Whale

- Does this mean that all whales live for 20 years? No, this bar graph shows about how long a whale lives. Some whales live for more than 20 years. Some whales live for less than 20 years.

- Find the bar labeled *Lion*. It goes to a point partway between the line for 20 and the line for 30. Look at the four small marks between 20 and 30 at the left of the graph. These marks stand for the numbers *22, 24, 26,* and *28.* The number *26* shows where the bar labeled *Lion* ends.

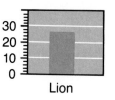

Lion

Use the information on the bar graph on page 96 to solve.

1. Which animal has the shortest life span of the mammals shown on the graph?

2. Which mammal has the longest life span? What is the life span of this mammal?

3. Find the life span of the whale. Which mammal shown on this graph has a life span that is about 40 years longer than a whale's?

4. Which mammal has a life span that is about 30 years longer than the goat's?

5. Suppose you have just been given a kitten as a pet. Can you use the information on this bar graph to predict how long your cat will live? Explain your answer.

6. One panda lived to be 21 years old. How much longer did it live than a panda would be expected to live?

7. A scientist studied the life span of 100 goats. Would you expect the life span of most of those goats to be about 10 years? Explain your answer.

8. Would you expect that the life spans of 100 goats would be longer or shorter than the life spans of 100 pandas? Explain your answer.

9. A horse lives for about 30 years. Between which two mammals would you place it on the graph?

★10. The life spans of seven mammals are given on this bar graph. Could you use the information on this bar graph to predict the life spans of different mammals that are not shown on this graph? Explain.

CALCULATOR

You can use a calculator to count by twos.

Press: [0] [+] [2] [=] [=] [=]

Each time you press the [=], the calculator adds 2 more to the total. The calculator display should show 2, 4, then 6.
Continue to press [=] to find the first ten multiples of 2: 2, 4, 6, 8, 10, 12, 14, 16, 18, 20. You can use your calculator to count by any number by pressing [0] [+], then the number, then [=].

Use your calculator to find ten multiples of each number. Then determine the common multiples of each pair.

	Numbers	First Ten Multiples	Common Multiples
Example	2	2, 4, 6, 8, 10, 12, 14, 16, 18, 20	6, 12, 18
	3	3, 6, 9, 12, 15, 18, 21, 24, 27, 30	
1.	2		
	5		
2.	8		
	12		
3.	15		
	9		
4.	35		
	25		
5.	75		
	30		

GROUP PROJECT

Mapping the Neighborhood

The problem: You and your classmates are going to draw a map of the area around your school. You must decide how the map should be made. Should each student make a map, or should you have teams who will draw certain parts of the map? Is there another way to complete the map? How will you make a fair decision?

Your map should meet the following requirements.

- It should show an area at least a block long on each side.
- It should include your school, streets, buildings, houses, benches, traffic lights, fields, ponds, plants, animals, and other things you can find.
- It should be labeled so that it is easy to understand what each item on the map is.

CHAPTER TEST

Multiply. (pages 74, 76, 78, 82, and 84)

1. 4×5 **2.** 7×6 **3.** 8×2 **4.** 9×4 **5.** 3×1

6. 3×8 **7.** 5×5 **8.** 5×7 **9.** 8×4 **10.** 7×4

11. 6×2 **12.** 3×9 **13.** 4×3 **14.** 6×6 **15.** 5×6

16. 8×9 **17.** 1×4 **18.** 2×5 **19.** 3×7 **20.** 6×7

21. $\begin{array}{r} 6 \\ \times 9 \\ \hline \end{array}$ **22.** $\begin{array}{r} 5 \\ \times 8 \\ \hline \end{array}$ **23.** $\begin{array}{r} 7 \\ \times 1 \\ \hline \end{array}$ **24.** $\begin{array}{r} 6 \\ \times 4 \\ \hline \end{array}$ **25.** $\begin{array}{r} 3 \\ \times 5 \\ \hline \end{array}$

26. $\begin{array}{r} 1 \\ \times 7 \\ \hline \end{array}$ **27.** $\begin{array}{r} 8 \\ \times 8 \\ \hline \end{array}$ **28.** $\begin{array}{r} 1 \\ \times 0 \\ \hline \end{array}$ **29.** $\begin{array}{r} 2 \\ \times 5 \\ \hline \end{array}$ **30.** $\begin{array}{r} 7 \\ \times 7 \\ \hline \end{array}$

Write *even* or *odd* for each number. (page 86)

31. 18   **32.** 427   **33.** 91   **34.** 34   **35.** 556   **36.** 9

Write the time for each. (page 90)

37.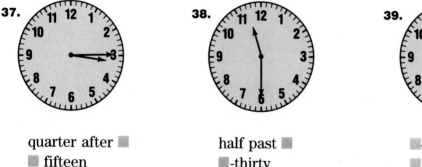

quarter after ▪
▪ fifteen

38.

half past ▪
▪-thirty

39.

▪-eight past ▪
▪ ▪-eight

Write the amount of time that has passed. (pages 92 and 94)

40. from two-seventeen P.M. to four-forty-five P.M.

41. from nine-forty A.M. to nine-fifty-two A.M.

42. from five-forty-one A.M. to four-forty-six P.M.

43. from May 1 to May 19

44. from September 4 to September 14

Use the information on the bar graph to solve. (page 96)

AVERAGE YEARLY RAINFALL

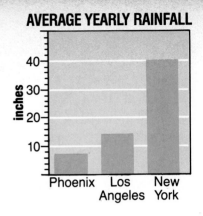

45. The graph shows average yearly rainfall in three cities. Write the cities in order, from the one with the least rainfall to the one with the most rainfall.

46. How many more inches does it rain in Los Angeles each year than in Phoenix?

Solve. (pages 80 and 88)

47. Jermaine puts 3 decals on his toy tractor, 3 on his toy plow, and 3 on his toy boat. How many decals does he put on his toys in all?

48. Anita's 2 sisters each bought 2 flowers for Mother's Day. Then Anita and her brother each bought 2 flowers. How many flowers did Anita and her brother and sisters buy in all?

BONUS

You can use slashes to write a date in a short way.

September 3, 1989 = 9/3/89
month day year

June 21, 1962 = 6/21/62
month day year

The chart shows the months of the year and the number to use for each month. Use the chart and slashes to write each date.

Month	Number	Month	Number
January	1	July	7
February	2	August	8
March	3	September	9
April	4	October	10
May	5	November	11
June	6	December	12

1. October 29, 1961

2. April 1, 1988

3. February 12, 1999

4. November 3, 1909

5. July 4, 1990

6. August 31, 1978

7. 3 days before January 6, 1987

8. 7 months after March 30, 1971

9. 5 years before May 20, 1908

RETEACHING

A. You can find how many minutes have passed from 3:45 to 4:07.

There are 5 minutes between each of the numbers.

So, first count by fives.

Then count by ones.

From 3:45 to 4:07, 22 minutes have passed.

B. You can find how many hours and minutes have passed from 11:25 A.M. to 2:03 P.M.

First count the hours.

> From 11:25 A.M. to 1:25 P.M. is 2 hours.

Then count the minutes.

> From 1:25 P.M. to 2:03 P.M. is 38 minutes.

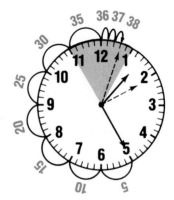

From 11:25 A.M. to 2:03 P.M., 2 hours 38 minutes have passed.

Write how much time has passed

1. from 1:15 to 2:00.

2. from 12:20 to 12:47.

3. from 5:30 to 5:45.

4. from 3:30 to 3:48.

5. from 5:10 to 5:35.

6. from 1:50 to 2:17.

7. from 9:25 to 9:56.

8. from 8:20 to 9:00.

9. from 7:30 to 8:26.

10. from 5:47 P.M. to 9:35 P.M.

11. from 6:25 A.M. to 11:10 A.M.

12. from 10:00 A.M. to 1:25 P.M.

13. from 8:35 A.M. to 12:02 P.M.

14. from 11:35 P.M. to 2:36 A.M.

15. from 10:17 P.M. to 3:05 A.M.

ENRICHMENT

Even and Odd Sums, Differences, and Products

You can check your answers for addition, subtraction,
and multiplication. You look for even or odd sums,
differences, or products.

The sum of two even numbers or of two odd numbers is even.	EVEN + EVEN = EVEN ODD + ODD = EVEN
The sum of an even number and an odd number is odd.	EVEN + ODD = ODD ODD + EVEN = ODD
The difference of two even numbers or of two odd numbers is even.	EVEN − EVEN = EVEN ODD − ODD = EVEN
The difference of an even number and an odd number is odd.	EVEN − ODD = ODD ODD − EVEN = ODD
The product of two even numbers or of an even number and an odd number is even.	EVEN × EVEN = EVEN EVEN × ODD = EVEN ODD × EVEN = EVEN
The product of two odd numbers is odd.	ODD × ODD = ODD

Write *even* or *odd* for each sum, difference, or product.

Solve to check your answer.

1. 9
   $+3$

2. 7
   -2

3. 4
   $\times 5$

4. 6
   $\times 3$

5. 8
   -5

6. 9
   -5

7. 3
   -1

8. 6
   -2

9. 8
   $+2$

10. 5
   $+4$

11. 4
   $\times 6$

12. 7
   $\times 3$

13. 9
   $\times 7$

14. 8
   $\times 3$

15. 10
   -8

16. 4
   $+9$

17. 7
   $+5$

18. 3
   $\times 5$

19. $9 - 8$

20. 5×2

21. $7 + 7$

22. $6 + 5$

23. 2×7

TECHNOLOGY

Here are two LOGO procedures that draw exactly the same square.

TO SQUARE
FD 40   RT 90   FD 40   RT 90   FD 40   RT 90   FD 40   RT 90
END

TO SQUARE
REPEAT 4   [FD 40   RT 90]

Compare the two procedures. REPEAT 4 is used instead of repeating the same commands four times. REPEAT 4 tells the turtle to repeat a command or group of commands four times. The commands to be repeated must have brackets around them. You can use any number with REPEAT.

1. Write commands to tell the turtle to repeat these commands six times.

RT 90   FD 30   LT 90   FD 30

2. Read this procedure. What does it tell the turtle to draw? Draw the picture.

TO FOURTIMES
REPEAT 4   [FD 20   RT 90]
PU   RT 90   FD 20   LT 90   PD
REPEAT 4   [FD 20   RT 90]
PU   BK 20   PD
REPEAT 4   [FD 20   RT 90]
PU   LT 90   FD 20   RT 90   PD
REPEAT 4   [FD 20   RT 90]
END

104

3. Change this procedure so that it draws three triangles in a row. (HINT: You must do more than just add a REPEAT command!)

```
TO TRIANGLE
RT 30   FD 40   RT 120   FD 40   RT 120   FD 40
END
```

4. The procedure below should draw the figure that is shown in the box. Find five mistakes in the procedure. Write the procedure correctly.

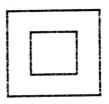

```
TO DOUBLESQUARE
REPEAT 6   [FD 40   RT 90]
PU   BK 10   RT 90   FD 10   PU
REPEAT 4   [FD 20   RT 45]
END
```

★**5.** Write a procedure to draw this shape. All the lines in the shape are 40 steps long. The angles in the triangles each measure 60.

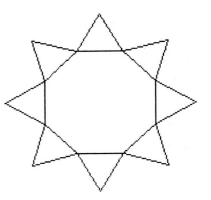

★**6.** Write a procedure to draw this house.

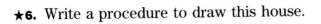

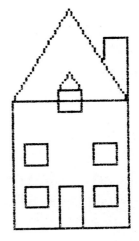

105

CUMULATIVE REVIEW

Write the letter of the correct answer.

1. 245 + 39
   a. 84
   b. 274
   c. 284
   d. not given

2. 3,465
   + 8,379
   a. 11,734
   b. 11,844
   c. 13,734
   d. not given

3. 25
   143
   2,625
   + 739
   a. 1,532
   b. 3,522
   c. 3,532
   d. not given

4. $6.02 + $0.99 + $12.75
   a. $9.76
   b. $19.76
   c. $82.85
   d. not given

5. 4,124
   − 1,935
   a. 2,179
   b. 2,189
   c. 3,299
   d. not given

6. $30.07 − $8.98
   a. $21.09
   b. $22.19
   c. $32.19
   d. not given

7. Estimate by rounding.
   435 + 289 + 851
   a. 1,400
   b. 1,600
   c. 1,700
   d. 435,289,851

8. Which number sentence is true?
   a. 28,201 = 28,301
   b. 64,905 > 64,925
   c. 52,166 < 52,366
   d. not given

9. Round 432 to the nearest hundred.
   a. 400
   b. 430
   c. 500
   d. not given

10. Round $26.65 to the nearest ten dollars.
    a. $26.00
    b. $26.70
    c. $27.00
    d. not given

11. 8 − 0
    a. 0
    b. 1
    c. 8
    d. not given

12. There are 16 dolls in the Dolls of the World collection. Lori has 9 of the dolls. How many more dolls does she need to complete her collection?
    a. 7 dolls
    b. 9 dolls
    c. 25 dolls
    d. not given

13. Estimate how much Gary will spend if he buys a book for $3.15, a box of crayons for $1.29, and construction paper for $2.07.
    a. $6.00
    b. $7.00
    c. $8.00
    d. $9.00

Plan a party for 24 people. You have collected a total of $96 from all the people who will attend the party. What will you need to buy for the party?

4 DIVISION FACTS

Dividing by 2 and 3

A. There are 8 members of the band who need sheet music. The music is sold in packets of 2 copies each. How many packets should the bandleader buy?

You can divide to find how many groups of 2 there are in 8. Find the quotient of 8 ÷ 2.

Think: ■ × 2 = 8.

4 × 2 = 8   **So,**   8   ÷   2   =   4.
                      ↑   ↑   ↑
              dividend **divisor** **quotient**

The bandleader should buy 4 packets.

B. There are 12 tickets left for the glee club concert. The box office sells these tickets to 3 students. If each student buys the same number of tickets, how many tickets does each student buy?

Because each student buys the same number of tickets, you can divide to find how many tickets each student buys. Divide $3\overline{)12}$.

Think: 3 × ■ = 12.

3 × 4 = 12   **So,** $\overset{4}{3\overline{)12}}$.   ⟵ **quotient**
                                                    ⟵ **dividend**
                                    ↑
                               divisor

Each student buys 4 tickets.

Math Reasoning, page H187

Divide.

1. $2\overline{)8}$ 2. $2\overline{)14}$ 3. $3\overline{)9}$ 4. $2\overline{)18}$ 5. $3\overline{)6}$

6. $3\overline{)21}$ 7. $2\overline{)12}$ 8. $2\overline{)16}$ 9. $3\overline{)15}$ 10. $3\overline{)18}$

11. $2\overline{)4}$ 12. $3\overline{)27}$ 13. $2\overline{)10}$ 14. $2\overline{)6}$ 15. $3\overline{)24}$

16. $24 \div 3$ 17. $10 \div 2$ 18. $18 \div 3$ 19. $6 \div 2$ 20. $18 \div 2$

21. $8 \div 2$ 22. $9 \div 3$ 23. $15 \div 3$ 24. $12 \div 2$ 25. $6 \div 3$

26. $21 \div 3$ 27. $14 \div 2$ 28. $4 \div 2$ 29. $12 \div 3$ 30. $16 \div 2$

31. $18 \div 3$ 32. $12 \div 2$ 33. $21 \div 3$ 34. $4 \div 2$ 35. $12 \div 3$

36. $18 \div 2$ 37. $15 \div 3$ 38. $8 \div 2$ 39. $9 \div 3$ 40. $6 \div 3$

Solve.

41. There is 1 music stand for every 2 flutists in the band. How many stands are needed for 10 flutists?

42. Students set up rows of 3 chairs each for their special guests. They expect 18 special guests. Use this information to write and solve a word problem of your own.

FOCUS: REASONING

1. The rule is: Divide by 3. What is the output?

Input	3	6	9	12	15	18
Output	■	■	■	■	■	■

★2. What is the rule?

Input	4	8	10	14	16	18
Output	2	4	5	7	8	9

Dividing by 4 and 5

Mr. Mack's class of 28 students is going to a baseball game. Each of 4 adults chaperons an equal number of students. How many students does each adult chaperon?

Because each adult chaperons an equal number of students, you can divide. Divide $4\overline{)28}$.

Think: $4 \times \blacksquare = 28$.
$4 \times 7 = 28$ So, $4\overline{)28}^{\,7}$.

Each adult chaperons 7 students.

Another example:

Find the quotient of $30 \div 5$.

Think: $\blacksquare \times 5 = 30$.
$6 \times 5 = 30$ So, $30 \div 5 = 6$.

Find the quotient.

1. $4\overline{)16}$ **2.** $4\overline{)20}$ **3.** $5\overline{)20}$ **4.** $5\overline{)30}$ **5.** $5\overline{)45}$

6. $4\overline{)24}$ **7.** $5\overline{)40}$ **8.** $4\overline{)32}$ **9.** $4\overline{)36}$ **10.** $5\overline{)25}$

11. $4\overline{)8}$ **12.** $5\overline{)25}$ **13.** $5\overline{)15}$ **14.** $4\overline{)12}$ **15.** $5\overline{)10}$

16. $35 \div 5$ **17.** $24 \div 4$ **18.** $32 \div 4$ **19.** $40 \div 5$ **20.** $20 \div 4$

Divide.

21. $5\overline{)10}$ **22.** $4\overline{)12}$ **23.** $5\overline{)30}$ **24.** $4\overline{)28}$ **25.** $4\overline{)36}$

26. $32 \div 4$ **27.** $15 \div 5$ **28.** $16 \div 4$ **29.** $28 \div 4$ **30.** $10 \div 5$

31. $20 \div 4$ **32.** $8 \div 4$ **33.** $35 \div 5$ **34.** $45 \div 5$ **35.** $12 \div 4$

36. $24 \div 4$ **37.** $40 \div 5$ **38.** $25 \div 5$ **39.** $35 \div 5$ **40.** $20 \div 5$

Solve. For Problem 44, use the Infobank.

41. The 4 best batters on the home team hit 8 singles altogether. Each has the same number of singles. How many singles does each hit?

42. The home team scores 1 run in each of the first 4 innings; the visiting team remains scoreless. What is the score at the end of the fourth inning?

43. Toward the end of the game, a new pitcher is brought in. He throws 20 pitches. If he throws 5 pitches to each batter, how many batters does he face?

44. Use the information on page 402 to solve. How many runs per game did Mudville score if it scored the same number in each game? how many hits?

NUMBER SENSE

Which is the better buy:
5 apples for 25¢ or 4 apples for 16¢?

Divide $25 \div 5$.   Divide $16 \div 4$.

$25 \div 5 = 5$, or 5¢ $16 \div 4 = 4$, or 4¢

Compare: 5¢ > 4¢.
So, 4 apples for 16¢ is the better buy.

Find the better buy.

1. 3 plums for 27¢ or 5 plums for 35¢

2. 4 pencils for 20¢ or 2 pencils for 8¢

3. 5 peaches for 20¢ or 3 peaches for 15¢

★**4.** 8 pens for 40¢ or 6 pens for 36¢

More Practice, page H163

PROBLEM SOLVING
Using and Making Line Graphs

A line graph shows how something changes over a period of time. This line graph shows how sales of single records in the United States changed from 1981 to 1988.

Use the line graph to find how many records were sold in 1983.

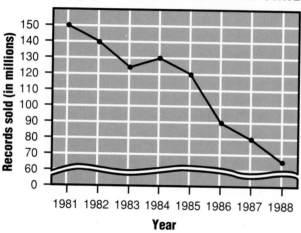

SALE OF SINGLE RECORDS IN THE UNITED STATES

- The title tells you that this line graph shows sales of single records in the United States.

- The labels at the left tell you how many millions of single records were sold.

- The labels at the bottom of the graph tell you the years the graph covers.

- Each point on this graph shows you the number of records sold in one particular year. In 1983, 125 million single records were sold.

Use the line graph on page 112 to answer each question.

1. In which of these years was the greatest number of single records sold in the United States?

2. In which year was the least number of single records sold in the United States?

Use the line graph on page 112 to solve.

3. About how many single records were sold in 1985?

4. About how many single records were sold in 1982?

5. What was the difference in record sales between 1982 and 1985?

6. What happened to record sales from 1983 to 1984? Did they rise or did they fall?

7. During which one-year period did record sales show the greatest drop?

8. In general, were record sales rising or falling from 1981 to 1988?

9. Can you tell whether one particular record company's sales were going up or going down from 1981 to 1988?

10. Suppose you are the manager of an audio equipment store. Will you keep more or fewer record players in stock in the 1990s than you did in the 1980s?

11. Make a line graph that shows how many pages you read in one week. Show the number of pages you read along the left side of the graph. Show the days of the week along the bottom of your graph.

12. Make up two questions that can be answered by looking at your graph. Exchange with a classmate and solve.

For a related activity, see *Connecting Math Ideas,* p. 397

Families of Facts

A. There are 24 children in Andrea's class. When the class saw a play, the teacher had the children sit in 4 rows, with 6 children in each row.

You can write two multiplication sentences and two division sentences with the numbers 24, 4, and 6. All the number sentences make up a family of facts.

Multiplication	**Division**
4 rows; 6 chairs per row	24 chairs; 4 rows
$4 \times 6 = 24$	$24 \div 4 = 6$
6 rows; 4 chairs per row	24 rows; 6 chairs per row
$6 \times 4 = 24$	$24 \div 6 = 4$

B. You can use multiplication facts to help you find quotients. Find the quotient of $12 \div 4$.

Think: $4 \times \blacksquare = 12$.

$4 \times 3 = 12$ So, $12 \div 4 = 3$.

C. You can use division facts to help you find missing factors. Find the value of $\blacksquare$ in $\blacksquare \times 5 = 10$.

Think: $\blacksquare \times 5 = 10$ is the same as $10 \div 5 = \blacksquare$.

$10 \div 5 = 2$

So, the missing factor is 2.

114

Copy and complete each family of facts.

1. $5 \times 3 = \blacksquare$ 2. $2 \times 9 = \blacksquare$ 3. $4 \times 5 = \blacksquare$ 4. $3 \times 2 = \blacksquare$ 5. $5 \times 7 = \blacksquare$

   $3 \times 5 = \blacksquare$ $9 \times 2 = \blacksquare$ $5 \times 4 = \blacksquare$ $2 \times 3 = \blacksquare$ $7 \times 5 = \blacksquare$

   $15 \div 3 = \blacksquare$ $18 \div 9 = \blacksquare$ $20 \div 5 = \blacksquare$ $6 \div 2 = \blacksquare$ $35 \div 7 = \blacksquare$

   $15 \div 5 = \blacksquare$ $18 \div 2 = \blacksquare$ $20 \div 4 = \blacksquare$ $6 \div 3 = \blacksquare$ $35 \div 5 = \blacksquare$

Write a family of facts for each set of numbers.

6. 2, 4, 8   7. 6, 3, 18   8. 25, 5, 5   9. 5, 30, 6   10. 12, 2, 6

Write the value of $\blacksquare$ for each.

11. $3 \times \blacksquare = 15$ 12. $4 \times \blacksquare = 24$ 13. $2 \times \blacksquare = 16$ 14. $2 \times \blacksquare = 12$

15. $5 \times \blacksquare = 30$ 16. $3 \times \blacksquare = 21$ 17. $4 \times \blacksquare = 16$ 18. $6 \times \blacksquare = 18$

19. $\blacksquare \times 3 = 9$ 20. $\blacksquare \times 5 = 25$ 21. $\blacksquare \times 2 = 14$ 22. $\blacksquare \times 4 = 32$

23. $24 \div \blacksquare = 8$ 24. $35 \div \blacksquare = 7$ 25. $12 \div \blacksquare = 4$ 26. $10 \div \blacksquare = 5$

27. $40 \div \blacksquare = 8$ 28. $20 \div \blacksquare = 5$ 29. $30 \div \blacksquare = 6$ 30. $32 \div \blacksquare = 8$

★31. $\blacksquare \div 5 = 6$ ★32. $\blacksquare \div 2 = 7$ ★33. $\blacksquare \div 3 = 8$ ★34. $\blacksquare \div 9 = 4$

Solve.

35. A group of 21 children went to the play. An equal number of children rode in each mini-van. If there were 3 mini-vans, how many children rode in each?

★36. During June, July, and August, Lois and her daughter went to 12 plays. They saw the same number of plays each month. Write two multiplication sentences and two division sentences for this family of facts.

NUMBER SENSE

Estimate.

1. $\begin{array}{r} 452 \\ 903 \\ + 326 \end{array}$ 2. $\begin{array}{r} 321 \\ - 195 \end{array}$ 3. $\begin{array}{r} 679 \\ 849 \\ + 648 \end{array}$ 4. $\begin{array}{r} 771 \\ - 152 \end{array}$ 5. $\begin{array}{r} 507 \\ + 764 \end{array}$

0 and 1 in Division

A. Josh has 6 different posters of rock stars. He bought an equal number of each at 6 different concerts. How many posters did Josh buy at each concert?

You can divide to find how many posters Josh bought at each concert. Find the quotient of $6 \div 6$.

$$6 \div 6 = 1 \quad \text{OR} \quad 6\overline{)6} \; ^{1}$$

Josh bought 1 poster at each concert.

B. These rules of division can help you divide.

If a number other than 0 is divided by itself, the quotient is 1.	$4 \div 4 = 1$	$4\overline{)4} \; ^{1}$
If a number is divided by 1, the quotient is always that number.	$8 \div 1 = 8$	$1\overline{)8} \; ^{8}$
If 0 is divided by any number except 0, the quotient is always 0.	$0 \div 7 = 0$	$7\overline{)0} \; ^{0}$
A number cannot be divided by 0.	$2 \div 0$	$0\overline{)2}$
	There is no answer.	

Find the quotient.

1. $9\overline{)9}$ **2.** $1\overline{)4}$ **3.** $2\overline{)2}$ **4.** $4\overline{)0}$ **5.** $1\overline{)3}$ **6.** $8\overline{)0}$

7. $3 \div 1$ **8.** $0 \div 9$ **9.** $3 \div 3$ **10.** $0 \div 5$ **11.** $5 \div 1$

12. $6 \div 1$ **13.** $8 \div 8$ **14.** $0 \div 3$ **15.** $2 \div 1$ **16.** $9 \div 9$

Math Reasoning, page H188

Divide.

17. $1\overline{)8}$ **18.** $4\overline{)4}$ **19.** $6\overline{)0}$ **20.** $1\overline{)2}$ **21.** $5\overline{)5}$ **22.** $3\overline{)3}$

23. $6\overline{)6}$ **24.** $1\overline{)0}$ **25.** $1\overline{)1}$ **26.** $1\overline{)8}$ **27.** $2\overline{)2}$ **28.** $1\overline{)7}$

29. $5 \div 5$ **30.** $0 \div 7$ **31.** $5 \div 1$ **32.** $7 \div 7$ **33.** $2 \div 2$

Is there a quotient? Write the quotient or write *no*.

34. $6 \div 1$ **35.** $0 \div 7$ **36.** $8 \div 0$ **37.** $5 \div 5$ **38.** $9 \div 9$

39. $3\overline{)0}$ **40.** $0\overline{)4}$ **41.** $1\overline{)2}$ **42.** $7\overline{)7}$ **43.** $0\overline{)2}$ **44.** $1\overline{)1}$

Solve.

45. As a favor, Jane buys 4 concert tickets and gives 1 ticket to each of her friends. How many friends receive tickets?

★46. Ted has 25 record albums. He keeps them in boxes that hold 5 albums each. If Ted buys 5 more albums, how many more boxes does he need to hold his new albums?

★47. The chart shows the number of hours per 7-day week that four friends spend listening to music. Each listens to a certain type of music for the same number of hours each day. For how many hours each day does Mary listen to classical music? For how many hours each day does Mel listen to rock music?

WEEKLY LISTENING TIME			
Name	**Jazz**	**Rock**	**Classical**
Mary	14	7	7
Barb	21	7	0
Mel	0	0	14
Jorge	7	7	0

MIDCHAPTER REVIEW

Divide.

1. $2\overline{)16}$ **2.** $2\overline{)12}$ **3.** $3\overline{)18}$ **4.** $3\overline{)27}$ **5.** $4\overline{)28}$

6. $36 \div 4$ **7.** $12 \div 4$ **8.** $25 \div 5$ **9.** $40 \div 5$ **10.** $15 \div 5$

11. $21 \div \blacksquare = 7$ **12.** $10 \div \blacksquare = 5$ **13.** $5 \div 5$ **14.** $4 \div 1$

PROBLEM SOLVING
Making a Table To Find a Pattern

Sometimes you can use a table to find a pattern that will help you solve a problem.

> Corey's class went on a field trip to the tallest building in his city. It is 60 stories high. A nonstop elevator went from the first floor to the tenth floor in 11 seconds. From the first floor, it reached the twentieth floor in 22 seconds and the thirtieth floor in 33 seconds. How many seconds did the elevator take to reach the sixtieth floor?

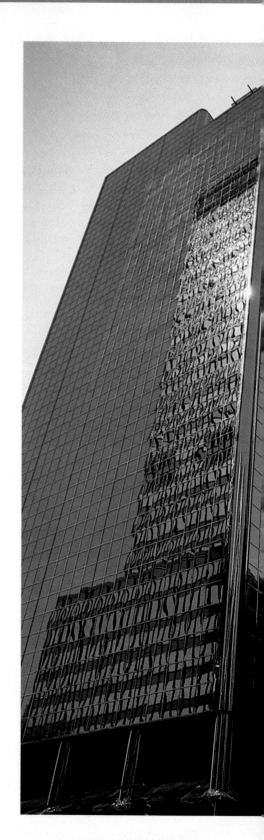

You can make a table to find a pattern that will help you solve this problem.

Floor	10	20	30	■
Seconds	11	22	33	■

You can see that the increase in the number of floors shows a pattern. It increases by 10 each time. So, the next floor number will be 40.

You can see that there is a pattern in the way the number of seconds increases by 11 each time. So, the next number of seconds will be 44.

You can use these patterns to fill in the table until you reach the sixtieth floor.

Floor	10	20	30	40	50	60
Seconds	11	22	33	44	55	66

The elevator took 66 seconds to reach the sixtieth floor.

Copy and complete the table to help you find the pattern. Then solve.

1. Abe's class is going to a concert. There will be 3 chaperons for every 15 students. There will be 18 chaperons in all. How many students are going to the concert?

Chaperons	3	6	9					
Students	15	30	45					

2. If there were going to be 24 chaperons, how many students would be going to the concert?

Make a table. Solve.

3. There is a special sale of 2 concert tickets for $3. How much does Anne-Marie pay for 6 tickets?

4. Russ has $15. How many concert tickets can he buy at the sale price of 2 tickets for $3?

5. After a movie, members of the audience were asked whether they liked or disliked the movie. For every 4 people who disliked the movie, 10 people liked it. If 90 people liked the movie, how many people disliked it?

6. If 32 people disliked the movie, how many people liked it?

7. Rob is saving money for a field trip to a baseball game. His mother will give him $0.25 for every $0.50 that he saves from his allowance. How much will Rob's mother give him if he saves $2.00? If Rob saves $7.50, how much will his mother give him?

8. Rob's mother gives him $8.00 for the field trip. How much did he save from his allowance?

Dividing by 6 and 7

There are 48 people who play in a hockey league. Each ice-hockey team has 6 skaters. How many teams are there in the league?

Because each team has the same number of skaters, you can divide.

Divide $6\overline{)48}$.

Think: ■ × 6 = 48.

8 × 6 = 48   So, $6\overline{)48}$. ^{8}

There are 8 teams in the league.

Another example:

Find the quotient of 42 ÷ 7.

Think: ■ × 7 = 42.

6 × 7 = 42   So, 42 ÷ 7 = 6.

Divide.

1. $7\overline{)0}$	**2.** $6\overline{)12}$	**3.** $6\overline{)42}$	**4.** $7\overline{)63}$	**5.** $7\overline{)35}$
6. 6 ÷ 6	**7.** 21 ÷ 7	**8.** 36 ÷ 6	**9.** 56 ÷ 7	**10.** 0 ÷ 6
11. 30 ÷ 6	**12.** 7 ÷ 7	**13.** 18 ÷ 6	**14.** 28 ÷ 7	**15.** 24 ÷ 6
16. 14 ÷ 7	**17.** 12 ÷ 6	**18.** 48 ÷ 6	**19.** 54 ÷ 6	**20.** 49 ÷ 7

Find the quotient.

21. $7\overline{)56}$ **22.** $7\overline{)14}$ **23.** $6\overline{)48}$ **24.** $7\overline{)28}$ **25.** $7\overline{)21}$

26. $48 \div 6$ **27.** $18 \div 6$ **28.** $7 \div 7$ **29.** $35 \div 7$ **30.** $54 \div 6$

31. $63 \div 7$ **32.** $12 \div 6$ **33.** $14 \div 7$ **34.** $42 \div 7$ **35.** $42 \div 6$

36. $21 \div 7$ **37.** $36 \div 6$ **38.** $49 \div 7$ **39.** $6 \div 6$ **40.** $0 \div 7$

Solve.

41. The 36 members of Marlene's hiking club decided to form a hockey league for the winter months. They formed teams of 6 players each. How many teams were there?

42. The Ridgewood Community Center had 63 hockey sticks to distribute evenly among 7 teams. How many hockey sticks did each team receive?

★43. The Speed Demons hockey team played 48 games over 6 consecutive years. Each year, they played the same number of games. Copy the chart, and use this information to complete it.

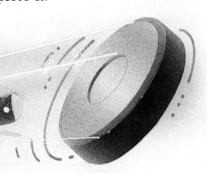

Year	Games played at home	Games played away
1980	4	
1981	5	
1982		6
1983		5
1984	1	
1985		4

ANOTHER LOOK

What time is shown on each clock?

1.

2.

3.

4.

Dividing by 8 and 9

There are 56 people who enter a relay race. The contestants are divided into 8 teams, with the same number of runners on each team. How many runners are there on each team?

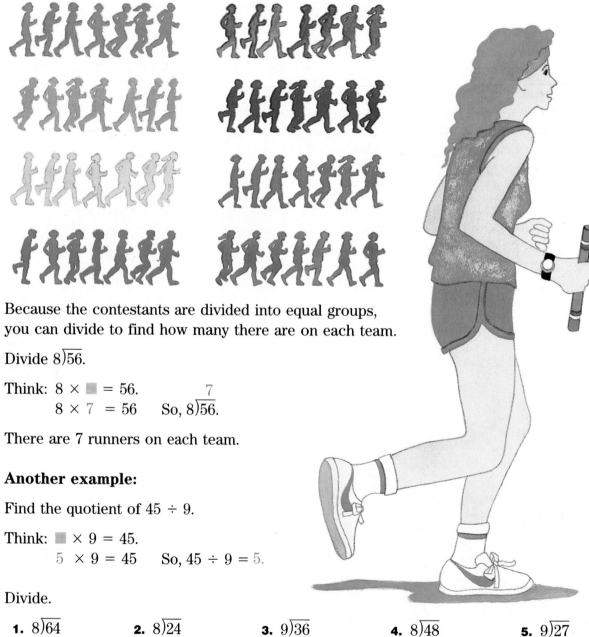

Because the contestants are divided into equal groups, you can divide to find how many there are on each team.

Divide $8\overline{)56}$.

Think: $8 \times \blacksquare = 56$.
$8 \times 7 = 56$ So, $8\overline{)56}^{\,7}$.

There are 7 runners on each team.

Another example:

Find the quotient of $45 \div 9$.

Think: $\blacksquare \times 9 = 45$.
$5 \times 9 = 45$ So, $45 \div 9 = 5$.

Divide.

1. $8\overline{)64}$ 2. $8\overline{)24}$ 3. $9\overline{)36}$ 4. $8\overline{)48}$ 5. $9\overline{)27}$

6. $8 \div 8$ 7. $0 \div 9$ 8. $40 \div 8$ 9. $81 \div 9$ 10. $72 \div 9$

11. $9 \div 9$ 12. $16 \div 8$ 13. $18 \div 9$ 14. $32 \div 8$ 15. $64 \div 8$

122   **Math Reasoning, page H188**

Find the quotient.

16. $8\overline{)8}$ **17.** $8\overline{)24}$ **18.** $9\overline{)36}$ **19.** $8\overline{)56}$ **20.** $9\overline{)54}$

21. $9\overline{)63}$ **22.** $9\overline{)72}$ **23.** $8\overline{)48}$ **24.** $8\overline{)16}$ **25.** $9\overline{)45}$

26. $8\overline{)32}$ **27.** $8\overline{)40}$ **28.** $8\overline{)0}$ **29.** $9\overline{)9}$ **30.** $8\overline{)72}$

31. $81 \div 9$ **32.** $64 \div 8$ **33.** $8 \div 8$ **34.** $9 \div 9$ **35.** $24 \div 8$

36. $27 \div 9$ **37.** $63 \div 9$ **38.** $45 \div 9$ **39.** $48 \div 8$ **40.** $36 \div 9$

Solve.

41. The runners are ready to warm up for the race. Each of the 8 teams receives the same number of batons. There are 32 batons in all. How many batons are there for each team?

42. There are 54 people who have volunteered to work at the refreshment stand. They work in shifts of 9 people each. Use this information to write and solve a word problem of your own.

CHALLENGE

Copy and complete. Write $+$, $-$, $\times$, or $\div$ for each ●.
Do the operations in parentheses first.

1. $3 ● 3 ● 4 = 5 ● 2$

2. $(6 ● 2) ● 3 = 2 ● 2$

3. $3 ● 2 = (3 ● 2) ● 1$

4. $10 ● 2 ● 2 ● 2 = 20 ● 5$

5. $63 ● (3 ● 3) = 1 ● 7$

6. $(8 ● 4) ● (2 ● 3) = (6 ● 2) ● 4$

Factors

A. You can use multiplication facts to help you find all the factors of 8.

The factors of 8 are all the numbers from 1 through 8 that have 8 as a multiple.

$1 \times 8 = 8$
$2 \times 4 = 8$

The factors of 8 are 1, 2, 4, and 8.

B. You can find **common factors** of two or more numbers. Find the common factors of 6 and 12.

List the factors of 6.

$1 \times 6 = 6$
$2 \times 3 = 6$

List the factors of 12.

$1 \times 12 = 12$
$2 \times 6 = 12$
$3 \times 4 = 12$

The factors of 6 are 1, 2, 3, and 6.

The factors of 12 are 1, 2, 3, 4, 6, and 12.

The common factors of 6 and 12 are 1, 2, 3, and 6.

Find all the factors of 16.

1. $1 \times \blacksquare = 16$ **2.** $2 \times \blacksquare = 16$ **3.** $4 \times \blacksquare = 16$

4. The factors of 16 are 1, 2, ■, ■, and 16.

Find all the factors of 25.

5. $1 \times \blacksquare = 25$ **6.** $5 \times \blacksquare = 25$

7. The factors of 25 are $\blacksquare$, $\blacksquare$, and 25.

Find all the factors of 18.

8. $1 \times \blacksquare = 18$ **9.** $2 \times \blacksquare = 18$ **10.** $3 \times \blacksquare = 18$

11. The factors of 18 are 1, 2, 3, $\blacksquare$, $\blacksquare$, and $\blacksquare$.

List the factors of each number.

12. 3   **13.** 5   **14.** 12   **15.** 7   **16.** 15   **17.** 6

18. 14   **19.** 10   **20.** 9   **21.** 20   **22.** 11   **23.** 24

Find the common factors of each set of numbers.

24. 4, 6   **25.** 10, 8   **26.** 16, 10   **27.** 9, 15   **28.** 8, 4

29. 18, 15   **30.** 2, 10   **31.** 15, 12   **32.** 8, 12   **33.** 6, 18

34. 7, 14   **35.** 9, 8   **36.** 10, 20   **37.** 8, 16   **38.** 25, 35

★39. 4, 12, 16   **★40.** 9, 12, 18   **★41.** 10, 12, 20   **★42.** 4, 20, 25

FOCUS: REASONING

Write whether each statement is *true* or *false*.

1. All of the factors of 4 are factors of 8.

2. None of the factors of 3 are factors of 7.

3. Some of the factors of 36 are factors of 12.

4. All of the factors of 9 are factors of 3.

5. Some of the factors of 5 are not factors of 20.

PROBLEM SOLVING
Choosing a Strategy or Method

Choose a strategy or method and solve.

| Solving Two-Step Problems |
| Writing a Number Sentence |
| Using a Bar Graph |
| Identifying Needed Information |
| Using a Line Graph |

1. Rita Moreno has won awards in four areas of entertainment. She won a Tony for a play, an Oscar for a movie, a Grammy for a recording, and 2 Emmys for television work. How many awards has she won in all?

2. Anthony was given 35 tickets to sell for the school band concert. On one day, he sold all but 5 of the tickets. How many tickets did Anthony sell that day?

3. Anna Neagle missed 140 of the 2,002 performances of the play *Charlie Girl*. Marian Seldes played all 1,793 performances of *Deathtrap*. In how many more performances did Anna Neagle play than Marian Seldes?

4. Amy, Katy, and Rusty collect pictures of movie stars. Amy has 158 pictures. Katy has 47 fewer pictures than Amy. Rusty has 23 more pictures than Katy. How many pictures of movie stars does Rusty have?

5. In which year did the greatest number of people attend the Wilson School Band Concert?

6. How many people attended the band concert in 1990?

7. In which year were there 100 fewer people attending than in 1980?

8. How many more people attended the concert in 1975 than in 1985?

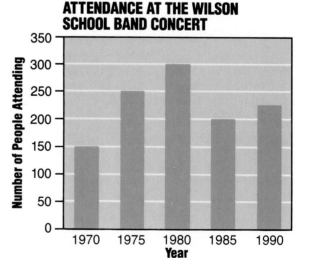

ATTENDANCE AT THE WILSON SCHOOL BAND CONCERT

Choose a strategy or method and solve.

9. In which month were the fewest tickets sold?

10. How many tickets were sold in February?

11. In which two months were the ticket sales the same?

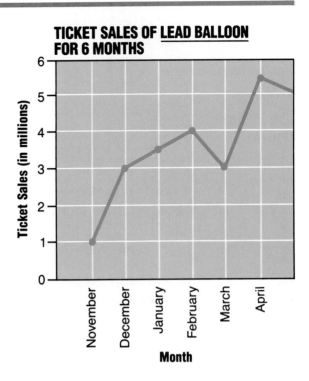

TICKET SALES OF LEAD BALLOON FOR 6 MONTHS

Ticket Sales (in millions)

Month

Solve.

12. Shakespeare's play *Richard III* contains 28,309 words. His play *Hamlet* contains 1,242 more words than *Richard III*. The actor who plays Hamlet has to speak 11,610 words. How many of the words in *Hamlet* are spoken by actors other than Hamlet?

13. For the World Peace Jubilee in 1872, there were 20,000 people in the choir and 1,600 people in the orchestra. There were another 400 first violins. The concert was conducted by its composer, Johann Strauss. How many people took part in the concert?

14. Howard Hughes of Fort Worth, Texas, saw 5,512 theatrical performances. An Englishman, Edward Sutro, saw 3,000 first-night performances and 2,000 regular performances. How many more performances did Mr. Hughes see than Mr. Sutro?

15. Georg Philipp Telemann wrote 40 operas, 600 suites, 44 chorales, 12 complete sets of church music, and 78 other musical pieces for special occasions. How many musical pieces did he write?

16. Look back at your answers to the problems you have solved. Are the answers reasonable? Have you answered the questions that were asked in the problems?

MATH COMMUNICATION

Read this poem.

A bird on the wing
Is a beautiful thing.
When I watch one fly,
I feel *I'm* in the sky.

What is the first word you read? What is the fourth word? What are the last three words?

How do you read a poem? Your eyes follow a path.

- You start at the top of the page.
- You read from left to right across to the end of each line.
- Then you go back to the left and move down one line.
- Then you read from left to right again.

You don't always read from left to right in math. How would you solve this problem? Which number would you write first? second? third? fourth? fifth?

$$
\begin{array}{r} 238 \\ -\ \ 43 \\ \hline \end{array}
\qquad
\begin{array}{r} 238 \\ -\ \ 43 \\ \hline 5 \end{array}
\qquad
\begin{array}{r} ^{1}\!\overset{13}{2}\overset{}{\cancel{3}}8 \\ -\ \ 43 \\ \hline 5 \end{array}
\qquad
\begin{array}{r} ^{1}\!\overset{13}{2}\overset{}{\cancel{3}}8 \\ -\ \ 43 \\ \hline 95 \end{array}
\qquad
\begin{array}{r} ^{1}\!\overset{13}{2}\overset{}{\cancel{3}}8 \\ -\ \ 43 \\ \hline 195 \end{array}
$$

To subtract numbers that have more than one digit, you work from top to bottom and move from right to left. You work from right to left when you regroup.

Copy the problem below on a separate sheet of paper. Solve. Notice the direction in which you read the numbers. Notice the direction in which you write them.

$$
\begin{array}{r} 481 \\ -\ \ 36 \\ \hline \end{array}
$$

GROUP PROJECT

Radio Play

The problem: Your class has been asked to put on a radio play. Work together as a group to plan the play. Discuss all the activities that should be included in your plan. Decide who should be responsible for each activity. Determine how you will make decisions.

Key Facts

- Everyone in the class should be involved in planning the play. Make a decision about whether everyone should act in the play.
- All the parts of the show must add up to exactly one hour. Every minute must be scheduled.
- You will choose your own play.
- You will want to include an introduction, music, and a closing.
- Decide whether you'll need any money to do the show. If you will, figure out how you will obtain it.
- Old radio shows had advertisements. You will need to decide whether you want to include any and how long they will be.
- You will have to create your own sound effects, such as doors opening and closing, people walking, horses galloping, and so on.

CHAPTER TEST

Find the quotient. (pages 108, 110, 116, 120, and 122)

1. $7\overline{)21}$ **2.** $5\overline{)20}$ **3.** $2\overline{)14}$ **4.** $4\overline{)32}$

5. $3\overline{)12}$ **6.** $2\overline{)0}$ **7.** $8\overline{)48}$ **8.** $9\overline{)81}$

9. $5\overline{)35}$ **10.** $3\overline{)3}$ **11.** $3\overline{)18}$ **12.** $9\overline{)36}$

13. $1\overline{)6}$ **14.** $6\overline{)12}$ **15.** $3\overline{)27}$ **16.** $8\overline{)40}$

17. $2\overline{)8}$ **18.** $6\overline{)24}$ **19.** $4\overline{)16}$ **20.** $5\overline{)10}$

21. $3 \div 1$ **22.** $30 \div 5$ **23.** $56 \div 7$ **24.** $72 \div 8$

25. $4 \div 2$ **26.** $42 \div 6$ **27.** $24 \div 3$ **28.** $36 \div 6$

29. $63 \div 9$ **30.** $24 \div 8$ **31.** $49 \div 7$ **32.** $64 \div 8$

List the factors of each number. (page 124)

33. 18 **34.** 25 **35.** 12 **36.** 35

Find the common factors of each set of numbers. (page 124)

37. 12, 16 **38.** 10, 30 **39.** 3, 9 **40.** 11, 4

Write the value of ■ for each. (page 114)

41. $8 \times ■ = 56$ **42.** $2 \times ■ = 0$ **43.** $4 \times ■ = 36$ **44.** $9 \times ■ = 27$

45. $15 \div ■ = 3$ **46.** $48 \div ■ = 8$ **47.** $24 \div ■ = 6$ **48.** $63 \div ■ = 9$

Solve. (page 112)

49. In which month did the Bester Ballet Company sell the most tickets? How many tickets were sold in that month?

50. Did the Bester Ballet Company sell more or fewer tickets in March than in August?

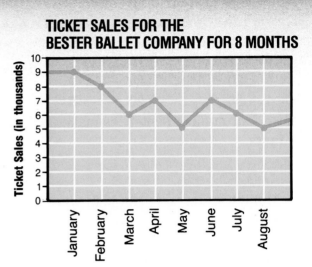

TICKET SALES FOR THE BESTER BALLET COMPANY FOR 8 MONTHS

BONUS

Compare. Write >, <, or = for ●.

1. $40 \div 8$ ● $32 \div 4$

2. $35 \div 5$ ● $27 \div 3$

3. $15 \div 3$ ● $16 \div 4$

4. $12 \div 2$ ● $18 \div 6$

5. $42 \div 7$ ● $54 \div 9$

6. $24 \div 6$ ● $63 \div 7$

Find the value of ■ for each. Then order your answers from the greatest to the least.

7. $24 \div 4 = ■$; $9 \div 3 = ■$; $14 \div 2 = ■$; $72 \div 9 = ■$

Find the value of ■ for each. Then order your answers from the least to the greatest.

8. $8 \div 4 = ■$; $45 \div 5 = ■$; $42 \div 7 = ■$; $24 \div 3 = ■$

131

RETEACHING

A. You can write two multiplication sentences and two division sentences with the numbers 20, 5, and 4.

Multiplication   *Division*
4 × 5 = 20   20 ÷ 5 = 4
5 × 4 = 20   20 ÷ 4 = 5

These four number sentences make up a **family of facts.**

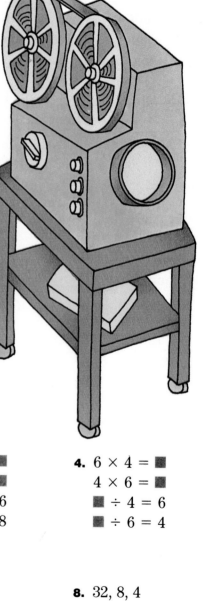

B. Multiplication facts can help you find quotients. Find the quotient of 28 ÷ 7.
Think: ■ × 7 = 28.
        4 × 7 = 28   So, 28 ÷ 7 = 4.

C. Division facts can help you find missing factors. What is the missing factor in 5 × ■ = 45?

Think: 5 × ■ = 45 is the same as 45 ÷ 5 = ■.

45 ÷ 5 = 9

So, the missing factor is 9.

Copy and complete each family of facts.

1. 3 × 9 = ■
        9 × 3 = ■
        27 ÷ 9 = ■
        27 ÷ 3 = ■

2. 7 × 5 = ■
        5 × 7 = ■
        35 ÷ 5 = ■
        35 ÷ 7 = ■

3. 6 × 8 = ■
        8 × 6 = ■
        ■ ÷ 8 = 6
        ■ ÷ 6 = 8

4. 6 × 4 = ■
        4 × 6 = ■
        ■ ÷ 4 = 6
        ■ ÷ 6 = 4

Write a family of facts for each set of numbers.

5. 5, 40, 8   **6.** 6, 2, 12   **7.** 9, 7, 63   **8.** 32, 8, 4

Write the value of ■ for each.

9. 4 × ■ = 16   **10.** ■ × 3 = 18   **11.** 8 × ■ = 24   **12.** ■ × 6 = 36

13. 20 ÷ ■ = 4   **14.** 36 ÷ ■ = 9   **15.** 72 ÷ ■ = 8   **16.** ■ ÷ 2 = 5

ENRICHMENT

Factor Trees

A prime number has exactly two factors, itself and 1. Some prime numbers are 3, 19, and 59. A composite number has more than two factors. Some composite numbers are 6, 8, and 25.

A prime factor is a prime number that is a factor of another number.

A factor tree can help you find all the prime factors of 36. The number 1 is neither prime nor composite. It has only one factor: itself.

Find two factors whose product is 36. List them as the first two branches of the factor tree.

Next, find factors whose products are 9 and 4. List them as the next four branches of the factor tree.

$$36$$
$$9 \times 4$$

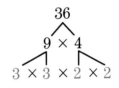

$$36$$
$$9 \times 4$$
$$3 \times 3 \times 2 \times 2$$

The prime factorization of 36 is $3 \times 3 \times 2 \times 2$.

Here is another factor tree for 36.

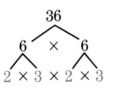

$$36$$
$$6 \times 6$$
$$2 \times 3 \times 2 \times 3$$

The prime factors of a number are always the same.

Copy and complete the factor trees.

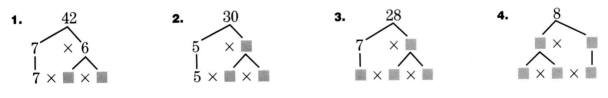

1. 42
7 × 6
7 × ▩ × ▩

2. 30
5 × ▩
5 × ▩ × ▩

3. 28
7 × ▩
▩ × ▩ × ▩

4. 8
▩ × ▩
▩ × ▩ × ▩

Find the prime factors of each. Draw a factor tree to help you.

5. 12   **6.** 18   **7.** 20   **8.** 32   **9.** 24   **10.** 54

TECHNOLOGY

Your computer speaks a language called BASIC. The PRINT statement is an instruction in BASIC that your computer understands.

You type this.
PRINT "HI THERE"

The computer prints this.
HI THERE

You type this.
PRINT "BLUE CAT"

The computer prints this.
BLUE CAT

When you use the PRINT statement with quotation marks, the computer prints whatever is between the quotation marks.

You can also use the PRINT statement as a calculator.

You type this.
PRINT 12 + 3

The computer prints this.
15

You type this.
PRINT 12 − 3

The computer prints this.
9

Use the PRINT statement without quotation marks to compute.

There are two symbols used in arithmetic that are written differently in BASIC. The * symbol stands for multiplication and the / symbol stands for division.

PRINT 10 * 2   means print the product of 10 multiplied by 2.

PRINT 10 / 2   means print the quotient of 10 divided by 2.

1. Write down what the computer prints.

   PRINT 12 / 4

   PRINT 6 * 3

   PRINT 1 * 2 * 3

The PRINT statement can also be used in a program.

A **program** is a group of computer instructions. Each instruction has a **line number** in front of it. You type RUN to make the computer follow the instructions one right after the other and in the order of the line numbers.

Here is a program.

10 PRINT "A BAKER'S DOZEN"
20 PRINT "6 + 7"
30 PRINT 6 + 7

2. What is printed when this program is RUN?

3. Change lines 20 and 30. Use a division problem. The answer should still be 13.

You can use parentheses in a PRINT statement. The computer will calculate the number inside the parentheses first and then go on and finish the equation.

If you type: the computer will print:
PRINT 5 * (1 + 6)   35

The computer first added 1 and 6 to find 7; then it multiplied 5 times 7 to produce 35.

4. Write what the computer prints when this program is RUN.

10 PRINT "MY UNCLE HAS"
20 PRINT 32 / (2 + 2)
30 PRINT "COWS AND"
40 PRINT (5 − 2) * 4
50 PRINT "CHICKENS"

CUMULATIVE REVIEW

Write the letter of the correct answer.

1. 9
$\times 2$

    a. 7
    b. 11
    c. 18
    d. not given

2. 6×3

    a. 9   **b.** 18
    c. 63   **d.** not given

3. 8
$\times 7$

    a. 1
    b. 15
    c. 56
    d. not given

4. Which are all odd numbers?

    a. 22, 23, 28, 31
    b. 73, 79, 81, 85
    c. 81, 82, 87, 90
    d. not given

5. Which is quarter past seven in the morning?

    a. 7:15 A.M.   **b.** 7:30 A.M.
    c. 7:15 P.M.   **d.** not given

6. How much time has passed between 6:35 and 10:27?

    a. 3 h 27 min   **b.** 3 h 52 min
    c. 4 h 52 min   **d.** not given

7. $1.25 + $4.82 + $13.66

    a. $9.73   **b.** $18.63
    c. $74.36   **d.** not given

8. $0.84 − $0.29

    a. $0.55   **b.** $0.65
    c. $1.13   **d.** not given

9. 17,001 − 9,875

    a. 7,126   **b.** 7,226
    c. 17,126   **d.** not given

10. What is the value of the digit 5 in 452,376,238?

    a. 500,000   **b.** 5,000,000
    c. 50,000,000   **d.** not given

11. 8
$+ 4$

    a. 12
    b. 32
    c. 84
    d. not given

12. Jane is 5 years old. Bo is 3 years older than Jane. Max is 4 times as old as Bo. How old is Max?

    a. 12 years old   **b.** 20 years old
    c. 32 years old   **d.** not given

13. In Ludlow, there are 9,725 children in elementary schools and 6,987 children in high schools. How many more children are there in elementary schools?

    a. 2,738 children
    b. 9,725 children
    c. 16,712 children
    d. not given

Think of something you could make and sell for a holiday of your choice. What would it be? How many could you make in time for the holiday? Plan a schedule for making and selling your holiday items.

5 MULTIPLICATION: 1-DIGIT MULTIPLIERS

Multiples of 10; 100; and 1,000

A. On Student Day, 4 art classes from Bellow School visit the art museum. There are 20 students in each class. How many students visit the museum?

You can multiply mentally when you multiply tens.

Multiply 4×20.

$$\begin{array}{r} 20 \\ \times\ 4 \\ \hline 80 \end{array}$$

Think: $4 \times 2 = 8$.
$4 \times 20 = 80$

There are 80 students who visit the museum.

B. You can see a pattern when you multiply with multiples of 10; 100; and 1,000.

$7 \times 5 = 35$
$7 \times 50 = 350$
$7 \times 500 = 3,500$
$7 \times 5,000 = 35,000$

Checkpoint   Write the letter of the correct answer.
Multiply.

1. $\begin{array}{r} 40 \\ \times\ 5 \\ \hline \end{array}$

2. $\begin{array}{r} 700 \\ \times\ 2 \\ \hline \end{array}$

3. $8 \times 2,000$

a. 90	**a.** 140	**a.** 1,600
b. 95	**b.** 702	**b.** 10,000
c. 200	**c.** 922	**c.** 10,222
d. 2,000	**d.** 1,400	**d.** 16,000

Multiply.

1. $\begin{array}{r} 30 \\ \times\ 9 \\ \hline \end{array}$

2. $\begin{array}{r} 50 \\ \times\ 6 \\ \hline \end{array}$

3. $\begin{array}{r} 40 \\ \times\ 8 \\ \hline \end{array}$

4. $\begin{array}{r} 20 \\ \times\ 3 \\ \hline \end{array}$

5. $\begin{array}{r} 60 \\ \times\ 5 \\ \hline \end{array}$

6. $\begin{array}{r} 600 \\ \times\ 9 \\ \hline \end{array}$

7. $\begin{array}{r} 200 \\ \times\ 5 \\ \hline \end{array}$

8. $\begin{array}{r} 400 \\ \times\ 6 \\ \hline \end{array}$

9. $\begin{array}{r} 700 \\ \times\ 7 \\ \hline \end{array}$

10. $\begin{array}{r} 800 \\ \times\ 9 \\ \hline \end{array}$

Multiply.

11.	4,000 $\times$ 6	12.	6,000 $\times$ 8	13.	8,000 $\times$ 3	14.	2,000 $\times$ 7	15.	5,000 $\times$ 5
16.	70 $\times$ 3	17.	8,000 $\times$ 7	18.	600 $\times$ 8	19.	900 $\times$ 9	20.	20 $\times$ 4
21.	700 $\times$ 4	22.	90 $\times$ 5	23.	1,000 $\times$ 8	24.	6,000 $\times$ 7	25.	500 $\times$ 9
26.	4,000 $\times$ 5	27.	300 $\times$ 8	28.	60 $\times$ 6	29.	400 $\times$ 9	30.	8,000 $\times$ 5

31. $5 \times 3,000$ 32. 4×80 33. $8 \times 9,000$ 34. $9 \times 2,000$

35. 6×90 36. $2 \times 5,000$ 37. 3×700 38. 6×400

39. 9×90 40. $7 \times 4,000$ 41. $8 \times 8,000$ 42. $5 \times 7,000$

Solve.

43. Selene makes greeting cards for the museum shop. She had 50 boxes. For each box she made 8 cards. How many cards did Selene make?

44. There are 963 people who visit the Egyptian show on Saturday and 875 people who visit it on Thursday. How many more people visited the Egyptian show on Saturday?

★45. The museum displays children's paintings. For the display, 2 schools send 20 paintings each, and 2 other schools send 30 paintings each. How many children's paintings are on display?

46. About 300 people visit the Native American Art Museum every hour. The museum is open for 6 hours each day. Use this information to write and solve your own word problem.

ANOTHER LOOK

Add.

1. $21 + 456 + 33$

2. $389 + 1,243 + 78$

3. $992 + 3 + 25 + 2,816$

Estimating Products

A. Ms. Ferar's art classes are making sculptures from pipe cleaners. Last year, one art class used 1,890 pipe cleaners. About how many pipe cleaners does Ms. Ferar need for 8 classes?

To find about how many, you can estimate. Round 1,890 to the nearest thousand. Then multiply.

$8 \times 1,890$
$8 \times 2,000 = 16,000$

Ms. Ferar needs about 16,000 pipe cleaners for 8 classes.

Other examples:

Round to the nearest ten.

4×35
$4 \times 40 = 160$

Round to the nearest hundred.

6×823
$6 \times 800 = 4,800$

B. You can estimate with money in the same way you estimate with whole numbers. Write the dollar sign and the cents point in the product.

Round to the nearest ten dollars.

$4 \times \$16.21$
$4 \times \$20.00 = \$80.00$

Round to the nearest dollar.

$5 \times \$7.53$
$5 \times \$8.00 = \$40.00$

Round to the nearest ten cents.

$6 \times \$0.72$
$6 \times \$0.70 = \$4.20$

C. There may be more than one way to estimate a product.

A paintbrush costs $1.48. Rusty wants to buy 3 paintbrushes. About how much will they cost?

Since Rusty wants to be sure he has enough money to buy the paintbrushes, he might estimate using $2.

$3 \times \$2 = \$6$

$6 will be enough money to buy 3 paintbrushes.

Estimate by rounding.

1. 6×74 **2.** 5×57 **3.** $5 \times \$0.96$ **4.** $9 \times \$0.56$

5. 4×323 **6.** 9×242 **7.** $8 \times \$7.28$ **8.** $6 \times \$3.61$

9. $\begin{array}{r} 9,484 \\ \times\ \ \ \ 6 \\ \hline \end{array}$ **10.** $\begin{array}{r} 5,726 \\ \times\ \ \ \ 7 \\ \hline \end{array}$ **11.** $\begin{array}{r} 3,897 \\ \times\ \ \ \ 5 \\ \hline \end{array}$ **12.** $\begin{array}{r} \$40.24 \\ \times\ \ \ \ 5 \\ \hline \end{array}$ **★13.** $\begin{array}{r} \$25.39 \\ \times\ \ \ \ 8 \\ \hline \end{array}$

Estimate.

14. 9×649 **15.** 3×728 **16.** $6 \times \$3.77$ **17.** $7 \times \$6.13$

18. $6 \times 2,174$ **19.** $4 \times 9,503$ **20.** $9 \times 7,778$ **21.** $4 \times 8,721$

22. $5 \times \$28.16$ **23.** $7 \times \$45.49$ **24.** $5 \times \$36.13$ **25.** $9 \times \$98.74$

Solve.

26. Mr. Ray teaches art in high school. If he orders $77.50 worth of supplies each month for 3 months, about how much does he spend?

27. The 20 fourth graders who are making a mural for the school share 4 staplers equally among them. How many students share each stapler?

28. The table lists the amount of art supplies Mrs. Greenberg needs for 1 month. Estimate how many supplies she will need for 9 months.

Supply	Amount for 1 month	Estimated amount for 9 months
Paper	1,250 sheets	
Glue	24 bottles	
Tape	25 rolls	
Paint	197 jars	

ANOTHER LOOK

Divide.

1. $48 \div 6$ **2.** $72 \div 9$ **3.** $54 \div 9$ **4.** $25 \div 5$ **5.** $35 \div 5$

6. $28 \div 7$ **7.** $18 \div 3$ **8.** $40 \div 8$ **9.** $36 \div 4$ **10.** $56 \div 7$

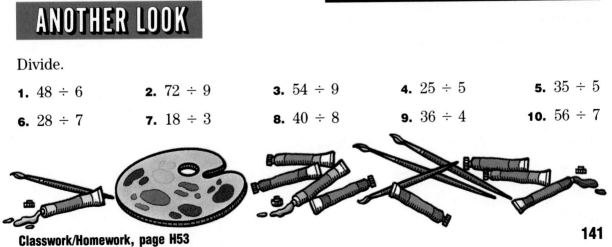

Multiplying 2-Digit Numbers

A. Len uses drying racks to dry his silk-screen prints. Each rack holds 23 prints. If he fills 2 racks with prints, how many prints did Len make?

Since there are an equal number of prints on each rack, you can multiply 2 × 23.

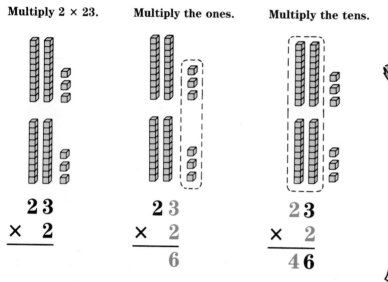

Multiply 2 × 23.

$$\begin{array}{r} 2\,3 \\ \times\ 2 \\ \hline \end{array}$$

Multiply the ones.

$$\begin{array}{r} 2\,3 \\ \times\ 2 \\ \hline 6 \end{array}$$

Multiply the tens.

$$\begin{array}{r} 2\,3 \\ \times\ 2 \\ \hline 4\,6 \end{array}$$

Len made 46 prints.

B. Sometimes you need to regroup when you multiply.

Multiply 3 × 25.

Multiply the ones.
Regroup the 15 ones.

$$\begin{array}{r} \overset{1}{2}\,5 \\ \times\ \ 3 \\ \hline 5 \end{array} \qquad \begin{array}{r} 5 \\ \times\ 3 \\ \hline 15 \end{array}$$

Multiply the tens.
Then add the 1 ten.

$$\begin{array}{r} \overset{1}{2}\,5 \\ \times\ \ 3 \\ \hline 7\,5 \end{array} \qquad \begin{array}{r} 2 \\ \times 3 \\ \hline 6 \\ +1 \\ \hline 7 \end{array}$$

Checkpoint Write the letter of the correct answer.

Multiply.

1. $\begin{array}{r} 31 \\ \times\ 3 \end{array}$ **a.** 33   **b.** 34   **c.** 91   **d.** 93

2. 5 × 16   **a.** 21   **b.** 56   **c.** 61   **d.** 80

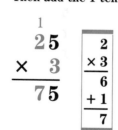

Math Reasoning, page H189

Multiply.

1.	34	2.	22	3.	43	4.	21	5.	11	6.	31
	× 2		× 4		× 2		× 3		× 7		× 3

7.	24	8.	12	9.	14	10.	45	11.	26	12.	18
	× 3		× 6		× 5		× 2		× 3		× 5

13.	33	14.	12	15.	10	16.	47	17.	21	18.	19
	× 3		× 8		× 9		× 2		× 4		× 5

19. 2×17　　20. 4×20　　21. 1×38　　22. 6×15　　23. 2×24

24. 9×11　　25. 2×26　　26. 4×23　　27. 3×29　　28. 3×25

29. 4×17　　30. 2×22　　31. 3×32　　32. 6×13　　33. 7×13

34. 2×19　　35. 6×14　　36. 2×49　　37. 4×16　　38. 3×16

Solve.

39. The members of the Young Artists Club carve designs on 2 blocks of wood. Then they use each woodblock to make 47 prints. How many prints are made?

40. An art dealer buys two sets of prints from a famous artist. One set has 39 prints. The other set has 22 prints. How many prints does the dealer buy?

41. Chester uses a silk screen to print banners. For each banner, he prints 11 pieces of cloth and sews them together. How many pieces of cloth would he print to make 9 banners?

★42. To make a potato-stamp picture, Ms. Lempke carves a different design on each of 17 potatoes. She stamps 4 blue prints and 3 yellow prints with each potato. How many prints does Ms. Lempke stamp?

CHALLENGE

Copy. Write $+$, $-$, $\times$, or $\div$ for ●.

1. 42 ● 2 ● $7 = 77$

2. 2 ● 2 ● $17 = 21$

3. 15 ● 5 ● $41 = 51$

4. 65 ● 8 ● $12 = 85$

5. $(30$ ● $2)$ ● $4 = 8$

6. $(48$ ● $6)$ ● $6 = 7$

More Multiplying 2-Digit Numbers

A. Lara sculpts tiny clay animals for nature scenes. If she sculpts 38 animals for each of 4 scenes, how many animals does she sculpt?

Since she sculpts the same number of animals for each nature scene, you can multiply 4×38.

Multiply the ones.
Regroup the 32 ones.

$$\begin{array}{r} \overset{3}{3}8 \\ \times\ 4 \\ \hline 2 \end{array} \qquad \begin{array}{r} 8 \\ \times\ 4 \\ \hline 32 \end{array}$$

Multiply the tens.
Then add the 3 tens.
Regroup.

$$\begin{array}{r} \overset{3}{3}8 \\ \times\ 4 \\ \hline 15\,2 \end{array} \qquad \begin{array}{r} 3 \\ \times 4 \\ \hline 12 \\ +\ 3 \\ \hline 15 \end{array}$$

Lara sculpts 152 animals.

B. You can multiply three 1-digit factors.

Multiply $8 \times (4 \times 7)$.

First multiply the numbers inside the parentheses.

$$8 \times (4 \times 7)$$
$$\downarrow$$
$$28$$

Then multiply by the other factor. $8 \times 28 = 224$

Checkpoint   Write the letter of the correct answer.

Multiply.

1. $\begin{array}{r}84\\ \times\ 6\end{array}$	2. $\begin{array}{r}67\\ \times\ 3\end{array}$	3. $(6 \times 6) \times 5$	4. $5 \times (9 \times 8)$
a. 164	**a.** 181	**a.** 36	**a.** 77
b. 484	**b.** 201	**b.** 41	**b.** 350
c. 504	**c.** 241	**c.** 150	**c.** 360
d. 604	**d.** 1,821	**d.** 180	**d.** 3,510

Find the product.

1. 98 × 2	**2.** 36 × 4	**3.** 44 × 6	**4.** 59 × 7	**5.** 38 × 8	**6.** 34 × 5

7. 72 × 5	**8.** 19 × 9	**9.** 44 × 7	**10.** 15 × 8	**11.** 96 × 3	**12.** 82 × 5

13. 8 × 32   **14.** 6 × 66   **15.** 7 × 38   **16.** 5 × 84   **17.** 4 × 76

18. 3 × 53   **19.** 5 × 57   **20.** 3 × 69   **21.** 9 × 38   **22.** 8 × 19

23. 7 × 67   **24.** 9 × 21   **25.** 5 × 35   **26.** 8 × 70   **27.** 7 × 15

28. 4 × 29   **29.** 6 × 22   **30.** 4 × 45   **31.** 8 × 17   **32.** 6 × 49

33. (7 × 3) × 8   **34.** (4 × 6) × 9   **35.** 5 × (7 × 6)   **36.** 7 × (2 × 6)

37. 5 × (8 × 7)   **38.** (9 × 9) × 2   ★**39.** 9 × (12 × 3)   ★**40.** 7 × (2 × 11)

Solve. For Problem 42, use the Infobank.

41. Lina makes 3 molds that she uses to cast tiny bronze statues. If she casts 45 statues from each mold, how many statues does she cast?

42. Use the information on page 403 to solve. There are 9 people who want to buy Fay's "Flying Birds" mobile. How many metal rods does Fay need to make the 9 mobiles?

MIDCHAPTER REVIEW

Multiply.

1. 4 × 30   **2.** 5 × 20   **3.** 7 × 600   **4.** 3 × 9,000

Estimate by rounding.

5. 3 × 62   **6.** 6 × 954   **7.** 4 × $71.83

Find the product.

8. 12 × 3	**9.** 46 × 2	**10.** 24 × 4	**11.** 71 × 8	**12.** 64 × 6	**13.** 93 × 5

PROBLEM SOLVING
Estimation

Often, you can estimate to solve problems. Sometimes it makes sense to round the numbers up to make an overestimate. At other times, it is better to round the numbers down to make an underestimate.

The students at Macon Elementary School are planning an art fair. Lee has been given $100 to buy supplies. This is his shopping list.

plaster: 15 pounds
paint: 10 tubes
art paper: 5 pads

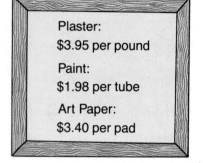

Plaster:
$3.95 per pound

Paint:
$1.98 per tube

Art Paper:
$3.40 per pad

To be sure he has enough money, Lee overestimates the price of each item.

$3.95 ⟶ $4
$1.98 ⟶ $2
$3.40 ⟶ $4

Then he multiplies each estimate by the number of items he needs.

$15 × 4 = $60
$10 × 2 = $20
$5 × 4 = + $20
Total _____ $100 overestimated amount

Lee can be sure he has enough money.

Sancha does a quick mental tally of ticket sales to see whether she has reached her goal of selling 100 tickets. She sold 53 tickets on Monday, 31 tickets on Tuesday, and 36 tickets on Wednesday.

Sancha underestimates each day's sales.

53 ⟶ 50
31 ⟶ 30
36 ⟶ + 30
_____ 110 underestimated amount

Because she underestimated, Sancha can be sure she has reached her goal.

Decide whether you should overestimate or underestimate to solve each problem. Write *overestimate* or *underestimate*.

1. Ted wants to rent a booth at the art fair, which will begin in 3 weeks. He earns between $2 and $4.75 per week. A booth at the fair rents for $5.75. Will Ted earn enough to pay for the booth? Should Ted underestimate or overestimate his earnings?

2. Ann has $8.71. She wants to buy 3 candles, an animal magnet, and a pair of mittens. Does she have enough money? Should Ann underestimate or overestimate the prices?

Solve.

3. Joann wants to buy 2 candles, a keyholder, and a mug. She has $10. Does she have enough money?

4. Terry has $4.57. She has bought a pair of mittens. Can she also buy an animal magnet?

5. Jeff has sold 4 animal magnets and 9 mugs. He wants to sell at least $30 worth of goods. Has he reached his goal?

6. Lee sold 2 pairs of mittens. With the money she earned from the sale, can she buy a mug and 2 magnetic animals?

7. Luis wants to buy key holders for himself, his brother, and his parents. He has $10. Can he buy 4 key holders?

★8. The sellers told Jem she could buy 2 mugs for the price of one. She has 2 one-dollar bills and 6 quarters. Can she buy the 2 mugs?

Multiplying 3-Digit Numbers

At a recent art fair, 3 art collectors each bought 132 drawings. Together, they bought all the drawings at the fair. How many drawings were there at the fair?

To find how many drawings there were at the fair, you can multiply 3 × 132.

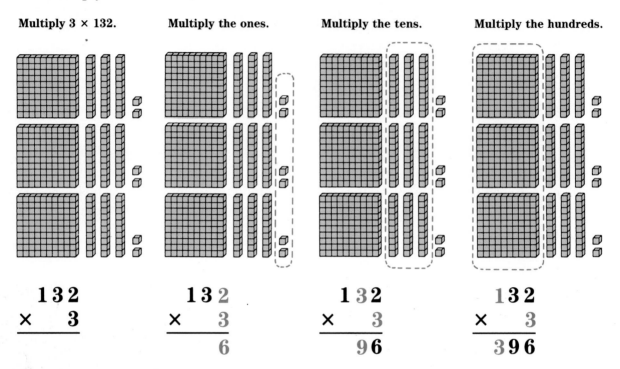

Multiply 3 × 132.	Multiply the ones.	Multiply the tens.	Multiply the hundreds.
132 × 3	132 × 3 —— 6	132 × 3 —— 96	132 × 3 —— 396

There were 396 drawings at the fair.

Other examples:

240	300	133
× 2	× 3	× 3
———	———	———
480	900	399

Checkpoint   Write the letter of the correct answer.
Multiply.

1. 221
    × 3

a. 223 b. 224
c. 553 d. 663

2. 200
    × 4

a. 200 b. 204
c. 800 d. 844

3. 2 × 103

a. 106 b. 205
c. 206 d. 325

4. 3 × 123

a. 126 b. 129
c. 169 d. 369

Find the product.

1. 232 × 3	**2.** 421 × 2	**3.** 312 × 3	**4.** 101 × 6	**5.** 111 × 9
6. 800 × 1	**7.** 211 × 3	**8.** 144 × 2	**9.** 100 × 7	**10.** 203 × 3
11. 300 × 3	**12.** 109 × 1	**13.** 193 × 1	**14.** 202 × 4	**15.** 311 × 2
16. 509 × 1	**17.** 112 × 3	**18.** 400 × 2	**19.** 420 × 2	**20.** 987 × 1

21. 8×111 **22.** 1×900 **23.** 2×303 **24.** 6×110 **25.** 2×444

26. 2×103 **27.** 2×404 **28.** 2×300 **29.** 3×113 **30.** 1×578

31. 8×101 **32.** 1×666 **33.** 2×204 **34.** 1×990 **35.** 2×314

Solve.

36. An art dealer received a large shipment of paintings. He sold them all at 2 shows. If he sold 124 of the paintings at each show, how many paintings were there in the shipment?

★**37.** A gallery owner held five open-house parties. She invited 110 guests to each of 3 parties and 104 guests to each of the other 2 parties. How many guests did she invite in all?

Find the missing number.

1. $(4 \times 202) - \blacksquare = 287$ **2.** $(3 \times 312) + \blacksquare = 1,404$ **3.** $(4 \times 102) - \blacksquare = 352$

4. $(\blacksquare \times 113) - 106 = 233$ **5.** $(\blacksquare \times 222) + 23 = 689$ **6.** $(\blacksquare \times 194) + 124 = 318$

More Multiplying 3-Digit Numbers

An art school has work space for 125 students in each of 4 subjects: painting, sculpture, design, and printmaking. For how many art students does the school have space?

To find how many, you can multiply 4 × 125.

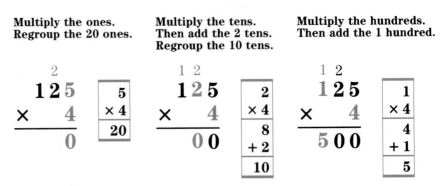

Multiply the ones.
Regroup the 20 ones.

$$\begin{array}{r} 2 \\ 125 \\ \times4 \\ \hline 0 \end{array}$$

5
× 4
20

Multiply the tens.
Then add the 2 tens.
Regroup the 10 tens.

$$\begin{array}{r} 1\ 2 \\ 125 \\ \times4 \\ \hline 00 \end{array}$$

2
× 4
8
+ 2
10

Multiply the hundreds.
Then add the 1 hundred.

$$\begin{array}{r} 1\ 2 \\ 125 \\ \times4 \\ \hline 500 \end{array}$$

1
× 4
4
+ 1
5

The school has space for 500 art students.

Other examples:

$$\begin{array}{r} 1\ 3 \\ 436 \\ \times5 \\ \hline 2{,}180 \end{array} \qquad \begin{array}{r} 5 \\ 307 \\ \times8 \\ \hline 2{,}456 \end{array} \qquad \begin{array}{r} 7 \\ 680 \\ \times9 \\ \hline 6{,}120 \end{array} \qquad \begin{array}{r} 700 \\ \times4 \\ \hline 2{,}800 \end{array}$$

Checkpoint Write the letter of the correct answer.
Multiply.

1. $\begin{array}{r} 147 \\ \times4 \\ \hline \end{array}$ **a.** 468 **b.** 488 **c.** 588 **d.** 1,248

2. 7 × 234   **a.** 1,418 **b.** 1,438 **c.** 1,638 **d.** 3,558

Find the product.

1. 4 × 412	**2.** 3 × 511	**3.** 3 × 632
4. 5 × 301	**5.** 8 × 200	**6.** 2 × 154
7. 5 × 131	**8.** 2 × 260	**9.** 2 × 374
10. 4 × 181	**11.** 3 × 214	**12.** 2 × 419
13. 6 × 107	**14.** 5 × 119	**15.** 2 × 327

Math Reasoning, page H190

Multiply.

16. 493 × 8	17. 243 × 7	18. 896 × 5	19. 634 × 4	20. 989 × 3
21. 264 × 6	**22.** 629 × 9	**23.** 375 × 8	**24.** 467 × 5	**25.** 388 × 7
26. 301 × 6	**27.** 252 × 3	**28.** 611 × 7	**29.** 141 × 7	**30.** 450 × 2
31. 237 × 4	**32.** 300 × 4	**33.** 803 × 6	**34.** 914 × 5	**35.** 219 × 6

36. 5×277 **37.** 6×321 **38.** 9×209 **39.** 2×713 **40.** 5×171

41. 3×487 **42.** 7×640 **43.** 6×861 **44.** 3×559 **45.** 4×208

Solve.

46. The art-history professor teaches 3 courses each term. There are 175 students in each course. How many students does he teach each term?

★47. Donna is a printmaker. For her senior art show, she published 5 folders of 105 prints each and 2 folders of 75 prints each. How many prints did she publish?

NUMBER SENSE

You can multiply a 2-digit number mentally.

Multiply 7×52.   Think: $7 \times 52 = (7 \times 50) + (7 \times 2)$.
$$350 \quad + \quad 14$$
So, $7 \times 52 = 350 + 14 = 364$.

Compute mentally.

1. 6×53 **2.** 5×46 **3.** 4×28 **4.** 7×82 **5.** 3×44

6. 5×24 **7.** 4×77 **8.** 3×94 **9.** 6×73 **10.** 4×57

Multiplying 4-Digit Numbers

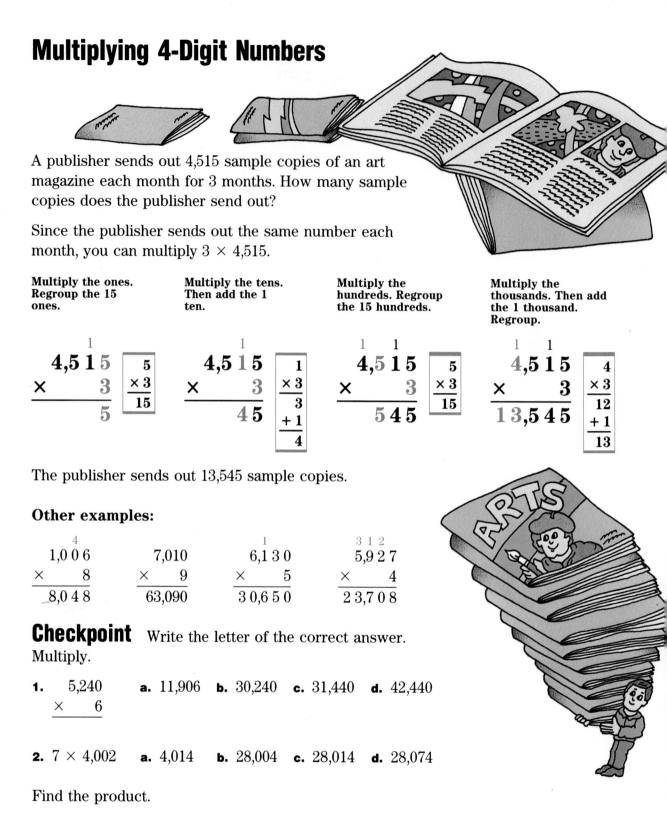

A publisher sends out 4,515 sample copies of an art magazine each month for 3 months. How many sample copies does the publisher send out?

Since the publisher sends out the same number each month, you can multiply 3 × 4,515.

Multiply the ones. Regroup the 15 ones.

$$\begin{array}{r} 1 \\ 4{,}5\,1\,5 \\ \times 3 \\ \hline 5 \end{array}$$

$$\begin{array}{r} 5 \\ \times 3 \\ \hline 15 \end{array}$$

Multiply the tens. Then add the 1 ten.

$$\begin{array}{r} 1 \\ 4{,}5\,1\,5 \\ \times 3 \\ \hline 4\,5 \end{array}$$

$$\begin{array}{r} 1 \\ \times 3 \\ \hline 3 \\ +1 \\ \hline 4 \end{array}$$

Multiply the hundreds. Regroup the 15 hundreds.

$$\begin{array}{r} 11 \\ 4{,}5\,1\,5 \\ \times 3 \\ \hline 5\,4\,5 \end{array}$$

$$\begin{array}{r} 5 \\ \times 3 \\ \hline 15 \end{array}$$

Multiply the thousands. Then add the 1 thousand. Regroup.

$$\begin{array}{r} 11 \\ 4{,}5\,1\,5 \\ \times 3 \\ \hline 1\,3{,}5\,4\,5 \end{array}$$

$$\begin{array}{r} 4 \\ \times 3 \\ \hline 12 \\ +1 \\ \hline 13 \end{array}$$

The publisher sends out 13,545 sample copies.

Other examples:

$$\begin{array}{r} 4 \\ 1{,}0\,0\,6 \\ \times 8 \\ \hline 8{,}0\,4\,8 \end{array} \qquad \begin{array}{r} 7{,}010 \\ \times 9 \\ \hline 63{,}090 \end{array} \qquad \begin{array}{r} 1 \\ 6{,}1\,3\,0 \\ \times 5 \\ \hline 3\,0{,}6\,5\,0 \end{array} \qquad \begin{array}{r} 3\;1\;2 \\ 5{,}9\,2\,7 \\ \times 4 \\ \hline 2\,3{,}7\,0\,8 \end{array}$$

Checkpoint Write the letter of the correct answer.
Multiply.

1. $\begin{array}{r} 5{,}240 \\ \times 6 \end{array}$ **a.** 11,906   **b.** 30,240   **c.** 31,440   **d.** 42,440

2. 7 × 4,002   **a.** 4,014   **b.** 28,004   **c.** 28,014   **d.** 28,074

Find the product.

1. $\begin{array}{r} 1{,}011 \\ \times 8 \end{array}$ **2.** $\begin{array}{r} 1{,}324 \\ \times 2 \end{array}$ **3.** $\begin{array}{r} 3{,}214 \\ \times 2 \end{array}$ **4.** $\begin{array}{r} 3{,}002 \\ \times 2 \end{array}$ **5.** $\begin{array}{r} 3{,}322 \\ \times 3 \end{array}$

Multiply.

6. 9,601 × 7	**7.** 1,313 × 4	**8.** 2,604 × 2	**9.** 5,218 × 4	**10.** 4,271 × 3

11. 8 × 3,671 **12.** 4 × 8,037 **13.** 2 × 6,725 **14.** 5 × 1,285

15. 5 × 4,836 **16.** 8 × 3,972 **17.** 7 × 6,467 **18.** 6 × 8,295

19. 4 × 6,556 **20.** 7 × 4,004 **21.** 7 × 9,532 **22.** 8 × 4,354

23. 2 × 9,407 **24.** 3 × 2,455 **25.** 2 × 2,301 **26.** 2 × 8,679

27. 2 × 3,144 **28.** 4 × 2,159 **29.** 5 × 3,756 **30.** 6 × 6,050

31. 4 × 8,799 **32.** 4 × 5,988 **33.** 6 × 1,010 **34.** 2 × 4,023

35. 6 × 8,799 **36.** 7 × 4,549 **37.** 4 × 3,024 **38.** 2 × 6,509

Solve.

39. In its first year in print, an art magazine had 1,809 readers. Five years later, it had 8 times as many readers. How many readers did it have after five years?

40. An art magazine prints 873 photos one year, 635 the next year, and 792 photos the year after that. Order these numbers from the least to the greatest.

★41. A design magazine took a poll to find its readers' occupations. It found that there were 2,463 photographers. There were 4 times as many designers, and 3 times as many illustrators as photographers. Copy the chart. Use this information to complete it.

Readers' occupations	Number of readers
Photographers	2,463
Designers	▨
Illustrators	▨
Total	▨

CHALLENGE

From the ten numbers below, find five pairs of factors whose product is 120.

5, 60, 15, 6, 24, 30, 8, 4, 2, 20

Multiplying Money

Your class wants to raise money to buy toys for children in your local hospital. You vote to hold a Read-A-Thon. In a Read-A-Thon, students form teams and read a certain number of books. For each book read, outside sponsors will donate a certain amount of money. Each team is responsible for computing how much money its members have raised.

After you receive the money raised by the Read-A-Thon, your team will visit a toy store to buy as many toys as you can.

This is how your Read-A-Thon will work.

- Each team member will promise to read from 1 to 3 books per week for 3 weeks.

- For each book read, each sponsor will pay the reader from $0.15 to $0.25.

- Each reader will have from 2 to 5 sponsors.

Use this information to decide what your team will do. Then use the decisions to find out how much money your team will raise in all.

Here is a price list for some toys you may want to buy with the money you will raise. If you wish, you may use catalogs and ads to find other toys and other prices.

Racing Car	$1.59
Tool Kit	$4.20
Jigsaw Puzzle	$1.99
Action Figure	$7.99
Paint Box	$3.29
Paper Dolls	$2.79
Boardgame	$2.95
Teddy Bear	$3.98

Working as a Team _____

Before your team decides which toys to buy, think about the following:

- how much money you can spend
- which toys you will buy, and the cost of each
- how you can be sure that you have enough money to buy the toys you choose
- what you will do with the money you have left

Some tools that can help you are graph paper, pencil and paper, and a calculator.

Report your team's decisions to the class. Compare your report to those of other teams.

- What kinds of problems did your team have? How did you try to solve them?

- Which tools did you use? Why did you choose those tools?

- How can you be sure that your answers are reasonable?

- Discuss your results with other teams. Which team can buy the most toys? Why?

- If all the teams combined the money they raised, could the class buy more toys? Why or why not?

- If all of the teams combined their money, do you think the choice of toys would be different? Why or why not?

- Suppose the price of the jigsaw puzzle was $3.00 for 2. Would the better buy be 4 jigsaw puzzles or 3 jigsaw puzzles? Explain your answer.

- Which other kinds of money-raising activities would your team plan if you wanted to raise more money?

PROBLEM SOLVING
Identifying Extra Information

> There is an unusual carving at the Peabody
> Museum in Salem, Massachusetts. The carving is
> made of 2 halves of a necklace bead. Neither
> half is more than 2 inches in size. Yet each half
> contains 50 carved human figures. How many
> carved figures do both halves contain?

A problem may contain more information than you
need to answer the question that is asked. If the
problem you are reading seems to contain extra
information, follow these steps.

1. Study the question.
How many carved figures do both halves contain?

2. List the information in the problem.
  a. The location is Massachusetts.
  b. Each bead is made of 2 halves.
  c. Each half is smaller than 2 inches.
  d. Each half contains 50 figures.

3. Cross out the information that will not help you
answer the question. (Cross out choices **a.** and **c.**)

4. Use the information that is left to solve the
problem.

Solve:
$$\begin{array}{r} 50 \text{ carved figures} \\ \times\ \ 2 \text{ halves} \\ \hline 100 \text{ carved figures in both halves} \end{array}$$

Both halves contain 100 carved figures.

Write the letter of the fact that is not needed in order
to solve the problem.

1. John Banvard painted the world's
   largest picture in 1846. The
   16,000-foot-long painting is of
   Mississippi River scenery. How old
   was the painting when Banvard died
   in 1891?

   a. The painting was finished in 1846.
   b. Banvard died in 1891.
   c. The painting is 16,000 feet long.

2. It took 3 years for the artist
   Tintoretto and his son to paint their
   largest painting. They painted 24 feet
   of the picture each year. It shows
   more than 350 human figures. How
   long was the finished painting?

   a. They painted a 24-foot portion
      each year.
   b. It contains more than 350 figures.
   c. It took 3 years to paint.

Use only the needed facts to solve.

3. The jeweler Fabergé created jeweled
   eggs for the last Russian emperor.
   One egg showed a picture of his 5
   children. Fabergé created 2 eggs per
   year for 21 years. How many eggs
   did he create for the emperor?

4. The Winter Palace is the world's
   largest art museum. It contains 322
   art galleries. Walking at 3 miles per
   hour, it would take you 5 hours to
   walk all the hallways. How many
   miles of hallways does the Winter
   Palace have?

5. The Woolworth Building in New
   York City was built in 1913. It was
   the tallest building in the world for
   16 years. Woolworth's first
   five-and-ten store opened in 1879.
   How many years later was the
   Woolworth Building built?

6. The Fine Arts School has 35
   sculpting students and 5 teachers.
   Prince Art School has 50 sculpting
   students and 7 teachers. How many
   more students than the Fine Arts
   School does Prince Art School
   have?

7. One artist makes silk-screen prints.
   She makes 24 prints at a time and
   charges $35 for each print. How
   much does she earn from the sale of
   8 prints?

★8. A painting hung upside down in a
   museum for 47 days, beginning on
   October 18, 1961. More than 100,000
   people saw it before it was rehung
   correctly. On what date was it
   rehung right side up?

PROBLEM SOLVING
Choosing the Operation

Dividing and multiplying can help you solve certain problems. Here are some hints to help you.

A. An art show is being held in Pineville. There are 63 works of art entered in 7 categories. Each category has the same number of works of art. How many works are there in each category?

You know	You want to find	You can
how many in all, how many groups, and each group is the same size.	how many in each group.	DIVIDE.

total   number of groups   number in each group
 63 ÷   7   =   9 works of art

B. At the end of the show, 12 works of art had not been sold. There were 3 works of art left in each category that did not sell out. How many categories did not sell out?

You know	You want to find	You can
how many in all, how many in each group, and each group is the same size.	how many groups.	DIVIDE.

total   number in each group   number of groups
 12 ÷   3   =   4 categories

C. One artist entered 3 works of art in each of 4 categories. How many works of art did she enter?

You know	You want to find	You can
how many groups, how many in each group, and each group is the same size.	how many in all.	MULTIPLY.

number in each group   number of groups   total
     3   ×   4   = 12 works of art

Decide whether to add, subtract, multiply, or divide to solve. Write the letter of the correct answer.

1. All 28 oil paintings were displayed on tables. There were an equal number of oil paintings on each of 4 tables. How many oil paintings were there on each table?

   a. add   **b.** subtract   **c.** multiply   **d.** divide

2. One artist made separate drawings of 12 animals. He made 2 drawings of each animal. How many drawings did he make?

   a. add   **b.** subtract   **c.** multiply   **d.** divide

Solve.

3. There were 35 artists who entered their works in the art show. The artists separated into groups so that an equal number of them could display their works in each of 7 tents. How many artists displayed their works in 1 tent?

4. Chairs were set aside for the art-show committee and their guests. Each committee member was given tickets for 4 chairs. There were 32 chairs in all. How many committee members were there?

5. One statue was a grizzly bear carved from a block of wood. The block weighed 45 pounds before the artist began. She carved away 17 pounds of wood to create the bear. How much did the bear weigh?

6. In one tent, there was an artist who cut out silhouettes of children. She cut out 12 silhouettes per hour. How many silhouettes did she cut out in 5 hours?

7. One artist created a mobile that had 9 arms. From each arm he hung 235 pieces of sparkling glass. How many pieces of glass did he hang?

LOGICAL REASONING

On Thursday, Ramon decided to go swimming and to stop at the hobby store. Here is what happened.

- Ramon walked home without his jacket.
- When Ramon left home, his watch read 12:00.
- Ramon left his watch in his jacket while he was swimming.
- When Ramon left the hobby store, his watch read 2:30.

Did Ramon swim before 2:30?

Sometimes you need to put numbers or events in order to solve a problem. Make a list that shows which events came before others.

1. Left home (12:00)
2. Visited hobby store (2:30) ←— Ramon still had his watch.
3. Put watch in jacket
4. Swam
5. Walked home without jacket

So, Ramon swam after 2:30.

Solve.

Lisa bought a book in the bookstore.
She bought a record in the record store at 9:30.
Lisa left her book at the roller rink.
The bookstore opened at 10:00.

1. Did Lisa have her book in the record store?

2. Did Lisa have her record at the roller rink?

3. Did Lisa reach the roller rink before or after 9:30?

GROUP PROJECT

Fabulous Fruit Salad

The problem: Your class wants to be entered into the record books for creating the world's largest fruit salad. Discuss with your classmates how you will do it. Make a plan.

Key Questions

- How large must your fruit salad be to break the record? Where can you find this information?
- What kinds of fruits will you use?
- How much will the salad cost?
- Where will you obtain the money to buy the fruit?
- Where will you find a container large enough to hold the salad? How large a container must it be?
- How many hours will it take to make the salad?
- How many people will you need to prepare the salad?
- What are all the tasks that will have to be done? Who will do each job?
- How will you keep the fruit fresh?
- How will you have your accomplishment entered in the record books?
- What will you do with the salad when you've finished making it?

CHAPTER TEST

Multiply. (pages 142, 144, 148, 150, 152, and 154)

1. 2×24

2. 7×35

3. 7×111

4. 3×185

5. $4 \times 2,900$

6. $6 \times 5,505$

7. $6 \times \$8.21$

8. $6 \times \$23.45$

9.
$$\begin{array}{r} 12 \\ \times\ 3 \\ \hline \end{array}$$

10.
$$\begin{array}{r} 32 \\ \times\ 4 \\ \hline \end{array}$$

11.
$$\begin{array}{r} 26 \\ \times\ 3 \\ \hline \end{array}$$

12.
$$\begin{array}{r} 99 \\ \times\ 3 \\ \hline \end{array}$$

13.
$$\begin{array}{r} 66 \\ \times\ 5 \\ \hline \end{array}$$

14.
$$\begin{array}{r} 38 \\ \times\ 8 \\ \hline \end{array}$$

15.
$$\begin{array}{r} 210 \\ \times\ 4 \\ \hline \end{array}$$

16.
$$\begin{array}{r} 600 \\ \times\ 7 \\ \hline \end{array}$$

17.
$$\begin{array}{r} 608 \\ \times\ 7 \\ \hline \end{array}$$

18.
$$\begin{array}{r} 300 \\ \times\ 2 \\ \hline \end{array}$$

19.
$$\begin{array}{r} 697 \\ \times\ 7 \\ \hline \end{array}$$

20.
$$\begin{array}{r} 432 \\ \times\ 9 \\ \hline \end{array}$$

21.
$$\begin{array}{r} 2,146 \\ \times\ 2 \\ \hline \end{array}$$

22.
$$\begin{array}{r} 2,975 \\ \times\ 8 \\ \hline \end{array}$$

23.
$$\begin{array}{r} \$0.76 \\ \times\ 7 \\ \hline \end{array}$$

24.
$$\begin{array}{r} \$39.05 \\ \times\ 9 \\ \hline \end{array}$$

Estimate by rounding. (page 140)

25. $3 \times 4,216$

26. $6 \times \$57.30$

27. 5×689

28. $9 \times \$0.31$

Solve. Find an estimate or an exact answer as needed. (page 146)

29. Ira plans to buy a paint set that costs $10.75. He receives $3.50 allowance each week. If he saves his allowance for 4 weeks, will he have enough money to buy the paint set?

30. Gregory wants to buy an easel that costs $18. To earn enough money, he plans to sell some of his drawings. If he sells 5 of his drawings for $2.99 each, will he have enough money to buy the easel?

Use only the needed facts to solve. (page 156)

31. Billie uses fabric, stuffing, and fabric paint to make stuffed animals. He uses 2 yards of fabric and 2 packages of stuffing for each animal. How many yards of fabric would Billie need to make a stuffed animal for each of his 17 relatives?

32. In Janna's Art Gallery, there are 210 paintings, 35 photographs, 67 drawings, and 11 sculptures. Of the 4 art galleries in her city, Janna's is the largest. How many works of art are there in Janna's Art Gallery?

Solve. (page 158)

33. Ms. Concepción's 6 art classes made decorations for School Open House. There are 24 students in each art class. How many students in all are there in Ms. Concepción's art classes?

BONUS

Find the product.

1. $34,672 \times 2$	**2.** $68,017 \times 5$	**3.** $27,894 \times 7$	**4.** $44,275 \times 6$
5. $\$293.85 \times 3$	**6.** $\$875.09 \times 8$	**7.** $\$921.37 \times 4$	**8.** $\$408.32 \times 9$
9. $192,837 \times 2$	**10.** $465,322 \times 5$	**11.** $394,166 \times 4$	

RETEACHING

You may need to regroup more than once when you multiply.

Find the product of 8 × 864.

Multiply the ones.
Regroup the 32 ones.

$$\begin{array}{r} \overset{3}{8\,6\,4} \\ \times\ \ 8 \\ \hline 2 \end{array}$$

$$\begin{array}{r} 4 \\ \times\ 8 \\ \hline 32 \end{array}$$

Multiply the tens.
Add the 3 tens.
Regroup the 51 tens.

$$\begin{array}{r} \overset{5\ 3}{8\,6\,4} \\ \times\ \ 8 \\ \hline 1\,2 \end{array}$$

$$\begin{array}{r} 6 \\ \times\ 8 \\ \hline 48 \\ +\ 3 \\ \hline 51 \end{array}$$

Multiply the hundreds.
Add the 5 hundreds.
Regroup.

$$\begin{array}{r} \overset{5\ 3}{8\,6\,4} \\ \times\ \ 8 \\ \hline 6,9\,1\,2 \end{array}$$

$$\begin{array}{r} 8 \\ \times\ 8 \\ \hline 64 \\ +\ 5 \\ \hline 69 \end{array}$$

Other examples:

$$\begin{array}{r} \overset{5}{97} \\ \times\ 8 \\ \hline 776 \end{array} \qquad \begin{array}{r} \overset{2\ 1}{\$0.85} \\ \times\ \ 3 \\ \hline \$2.55 \end{array} \qquad \begin{array}{r} \overset{6\,8}{4,069} \\ \times\ \ 9 \\ \hline 36,621 \end{array} \qquad \begin{array}{r} \overset{1\,4\,2}{\$32.63} \\ \times\ \ 7 \\ \hline \$228.41 \end{array}$$

Multiply.

1. 6×86 2. 5×49 3. 3×66 4. 8×78 5. 9×34

6. 5×873 7. 7×492 8. 4×673 9. 6×909 10. 3×588

11. $\begin{array}{r} 3,963 \\ \times\ \ \ 5 \\ \hline \end{array}$ 12. $\begin{array}{r} 4,855 \\ \times\ \ \ 8 \\ \hline \end{array}$ 13. $\begin{array}{r} 3,919 \\ \times\ \ \ 4 \\ \hline \end{array}$ 14. $\begin{array}{r} 2,494 \\ \times\ \ \ 9 \\ \hline \end{array}$ 15. $\begin{array}{r} 5,729 \\ \times\ \ \ 6 \\ \hline \end{array}$

16. $\begin{array}{r} \$0.76 \\ \times\ \ \ 5 \\ \hline \end{array}$ 17. $\begin{array}{r} \$0.99 \\ \times\ \ \ 3 \\ \hline \end{array}$ 18. $\begin{array}{r} \$0.64 \\ \times\ \ \ 8 \\ \hline \end{array}$ 19. $\begin{array}{r} \$0.96 \\ \times\ \ \ 2 \\ \hline \end{array}$ 20. $\begin{array}{r} \$0.74 \\ \times\ \ \ 6 \\ \hline \end{array}$

21. $\begin{array}{r} \$3.47 \\ \times\ \ \ 7 \\ \hline \end{array}$ 22. $\begin{array}{r} \$6.92 \\ \times\ \ \ 2 \\ \hline \end{array}$ 23. $\begin{array}{r} \$39.81 \\ \times\ \ \ 7 \\ \hline \end{array}$ 24. $\begin{array}{r} \$99.99 \\ \times\ \ \ 4 \\ \hline \end{array}$ 25. $\begin{array}{r} \$68.45 \\ \times\ \ \ 9 \\ \hline \end{array}$

ENRICHMENT

Order of Operations

Nicole and Grace were given this problem to solve.

$$28 - 4 \times 5 + 6$$

Grace answered 126.
She subtracted $28 - 4 = 24$.
Then she multiplied $24 \times 5 = 120$.
Then she added $120 + 6 = 126$.

Nicole answered 14.
She multiplied $4 \times 5 = 20$.
Then she subtracted $28 - 20 = 8$.
Then she added $8 + 6 = 14$.

Which student had the correct answer?

To decide which answer is correct, work from left to right, and follow this order of operations:

1. Do all multiplications and divisions in order from left to right.
2. Do all additions and subtractions from left to right.

So, Nicole had the correct answer.

If there are parentheses in a problem, always do the operation in parentheses first. Then follow the order of operations.

$$
\begin{array}{l}
(7 - 3) \times 4 + 2 \\
\quad 4 \quad \times 4 + 2 \\
\qquad 16 \quad + 2 = 18
\end{array}
$$

Solve.

1. $7 + 3 - 4$ **2.** $6 - 1 + 4$ **3.** $8 + 4 \div 2$

4. $4 \times 7 - 6$ **5.** $8 - 6 \div 2$ **6.** $11 - 5 \times 2$

7. $8 \div 4 + 5 \times 2$ **8.** $8 - 4 \div 2 + 1$ **9.** $6 \times 5 + 10 \div 5$

10. $4 \times 3 + 6 \div 3$ **11.** $8 \div 4 + 7 - 2$ **12.** $26 - 5 + 9 \div 3$

13. $3 + (4 \times 7) - 6$ **14.** $(48 - 8) \div 5 + 2$ **15.** $6 + (6 \times 3) \div 9$

16. $12 + 4 \div (2 + 2)$ **17.** $8 \times 3 + (6 - 3)$ **18.** $6 \times (7 - 2) + 1$

19. $8 + (1 \times 9) - 2$ **20.** $6 \div (3 \times 1) + 18$ **21.** $45 \div (5 + 4) - 4$

22. $8 + (16 \div 2) + 8$ **23.** $18 + (8 - 4) \div 2$ **24.** $12 + (6 \div 2) + 1$

CUMULATIVE REVIEW

Write the letter of the correct answer.

1. $7\overline{)42}$
 a. 6
 b. 7
 c. 60
 d. not given

2. $36 \div 4$
 a. 9
 b. 32
 c. 40
 d. not given

3. $6 \div 1$
 a. 0
 b. 1
 c. 6
 d. not given

4. Which are the factors of 8?
 a. 1, 2, 3, 4
 b. 1, 2, 4, 8
 c. 1, 2, 8, 12
 d. not given

5. What is the value of ▧ in $24 \div ▧ = 6$?
 a. 4
 b. 18
 c. 30
 d. not given

6. What is the value of ▧ in $▧ \times 5 = 30$?
 a. 6
 b. 25
 c. 35
 d. not given

7. $\begin{array}{r} 7 \\ \times\ 9 \\ \hline \end{array}$
 a. 56
 b. 63
 c. 79
 d. not given

8. 6×8
 a. 14
 b. 40
 c. 68
 d. not given

9. $672 + 325$
 a. 347
 b. 997
 c. 1,107
 d. not given

10. $9,148 - 2,029$
 a. 6,129
 b. 7,119
 c. 7,129
 d. not given

11. Round 688 to the nearest ten.
 a. 600
 b. 680
 c. 700
 d. not given

12.

STUDENT WALKING TIMES

The bar graph shows how much time each child takes to walk to school. Who takes 3 times as much time as Dee to walk to school?
 a. Al
 b. Ed
 c. Moe
 d. not given

13. In a classroom, there are 25 chairs in 5 equal rows. How many chairs are there in each row?
 a. 5 chairs
 b. 20 chairs
 c. 30 chairs
 d. not given

Your school is planning a parade. Traffic laws state that the parade can take up only 150 yards from the first marcher to the last marcher. Your parade will include floats, marching bands, and giant balloons of different lengths. How would you go about organizing the parade?

6 DIVISION: 1-DIGIT DIVISORS

Dividing with Remainders

A. When you try to separate a set of objects into groups of equal size, you sometimes have a number left over. That number is called a **remainder.** This activity will help you to explore remainders.

Step 1: Copy the table. Put 14 paper clips on your desk. Separate the paper clips into groups of 6. The remainder is shown in the table for you. Try making groups of 6 from 15 paper clips. Now try making groups of 6 from 16, 17, 18, 19, and 20 paper clips. Record the remainders in your table.

- Do you see any pattern in the remainders?

- What do you notice about the size of the remainders?

Number of Counters

	14	15	16	17	18	19	20
6	2						
5							
4							
3							
2							
1							

Size of Groups

Step 2: Try making groups of 5 from 14 paper clips. Do the same with 15, 16, 17, 18, 19, and 20 paper clips. Record the remainders in your table.

- Predict any patterns for the rest of your table.

- Check to see whether your predictions are correct.

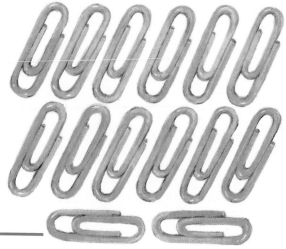

Thinking as a Team

1. What can you say about the size of a remainder in comparison to the size of the divisor?

2. Can you use subtraction to help you find the remainder in a division problem? How?

3. Can you use multiplication to help you find the remainder in a division problem? How?

B. A local TV station has a program called "What Do Children Collect?" The station has decided to make a traveling exhibit of some of the collections. Your team is in charge of selecting the collections and arranging them in display cases for the shows.

The station gives your team some rules to follow.

- You may choose any 6 collections from this list:

38 shells	76 striped marbles	22 dried flowers
87 foreign coins	63 United States coins	75 old keys
60 comic books	94 postcards	41 glass animals
26 pictures of rock stars	39 combs	54 fancy boxes

- There are 40 display cases in all. You must use all of the cases.

- Your team must decide how many cases to use for each collection, but you cannot use more than 9 cases for any one collection. You do not need to use all of a collection.

- Each collection must be evenly divided among the cases in which you choose to display it.

Working as a Team

Choose the collections for the exhibit.

1. Does the size of the object affect the number of cases you choose? Why or why not?

Decide how many items in each collection you will display in each case. Then find how many items in each collection will be left.

2. Does the size of the object affect the number in each case? Why or why not?

You have these tools to help you: a box of paper clips, a calculator, and a pencil and paper.

Describe your exhibit to the class. Discuss the reasons for your choices, the tools you used, any problems you might have had, and how you solved them.

Estimating Quotients

Linda has 7,495 stamps and 9 stamp albums. She puts about the same number of stamps in each album. About how many stamps are there in each album?

To find about how many stamps there are in each album, you can estimate 7,495 ÷ 9.
Divide the thousands.   Think: $9\overline{)7}$.
Not enough thousands.
Divide the hundreds.   Think: $9\overline{)74}$.
Enough hundreds.

So, the quotient begins in the hundreds place. $9\overline{)7,495}$
It will have 3 digits.

Think: $8 \times 9 = 72$.   Write zeros for the
         $9 \times 9 = 81$ other digits.
Too great. So, use 8.

$$9\overline{)7,495}^{\ 8} \qquad\qquad 9\overline{)7,495} \rightarrow \underline{8}00$$

There are about 800 stamps in each album.

Checkpoint   Write the letter of the correct answer.

How many digits will be in the quotient?

1. $4\overline{)436}$ **a.** 1   **b.** 2   **c.** 3   **d.** 4

2. $7\overline{)3,973}$ **a.** 1   **b.** 2   **c.** 3   **d.** 4

Estimate the quotient.

3. $6\overline{)269}$ **a.** 4   **b.** 40   **c.** 300   **d.** 400

4. $5\overline{)6,059}$ **a.** 10   **b.** 100   **c.** 1,000   **d.** 2,000

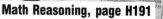

Write how many digits the quotient will contain.

1. $2\overline{)347}$ 2. $4\overline{)983}$ 3. $4\overline{)546}$ 4. $6\overline{)197}$ 5. $3\overline{)984}$

6. $6\overline{)3,146}$ 7. $4\overline{)3,872}$ 8. $7\overline{)8,126}$ 9. $5\overline{)5,643}$ 10. $9\overline{)8,046}$

Estimate. Write the letter of the correct answer.

11. $7\overline{)368}$ **a.** 5   **b.** 50   **c.** 500   12. $3\overline{)128}$ **a.** 4   **b.** 40   **c.** 400

13. $5\overline{)2,146}$ **a.** 4   **b.** 40   **c.** 400   14. $7\overline{)3,678}$ **a.** 5   **b.** 50   **c.** 500

15. $9\overline{)9,143}$ **a.** 10   **b.** 100   **c.** 1,000

Estimate.

16. $3\overline{)279}$ 17. $9\overline{)296}$ 18. $5\overline{)387}$ 19. $6\overline{)505}$ 20. $8\overline{)463}$

21. $9\overline{)4,942}$ 22. $7\overline{)2,254}$ 23. $8\overline{)4,851}$ 24. $6\overline{)1,527}$ 25. $2\overline{)1,119}$

26. $678 \div 2$ 27. $3,468 \div 5$ 28. $925 \div 2$ 29. $9,473 \div 9$ 30. $937 \div 3$

31. $3,074 \div 7$ 32. $401 \div 9$ 33. $658 \div 9$ 34. $845 \div 3$ 35. $5,251 \div 7$

Solve.

36. Terry has 1,606 stamps from 6 countries. He has the same number from each country. About how many stamps does he have from each country?

37. Helen buys 6 stamp albums. Each album holds 950 stamps. Estimate how many stamps Helen will need in order to fill all the albums.

CHALLENGE

1. What two numbers have a quotient of 6 and a difference of 20?

2. What two numbers have a quotient of 9 and a difference of 56?

Two-Step Division

Greg likes to photograph his friends' pets and give the pictures away as presents. Last week, he took 36 pictures of pet birds. If he took 2 pictures of each bird, how many birds did he photograph?

You need to find the quotient of 36 ÷ 2.

Divide the tens.
Think: 2)3̄
Write 1.

$$\begin{array}{r} 1 \\ 2\overline{)3\ 6} \\ 2 \\ \hline 1 \end{array}$$

Multiply. 1 × 2 = 2
Subtract. 3 − 2 = 1
Compare. 1 < 2

Divide the ones.
Bring down the 6.
Think: 2)1̄6̄
Write 8.

$$\begin{array}{r} 1\,8 \\ 2\overline{)3\ 6} \\ 2\downarrow \\ \hline 1\,6 \\ 1\,6 \\ \hline 0 \end{array}$$

Multiply. 8 × 2 = 16
Subtract. 16 − 16 = 0
So, there is no remainder.

Greg photographed 18 birds.

Another example:

$$\begin{array}{r} 1\,4\ \text{R1} \\ 5\overline{)7\,1} \\ 5\downarrow \\ \hline 2\,1 \\ 2\,0 \\ \hline 1 \end{array}$$

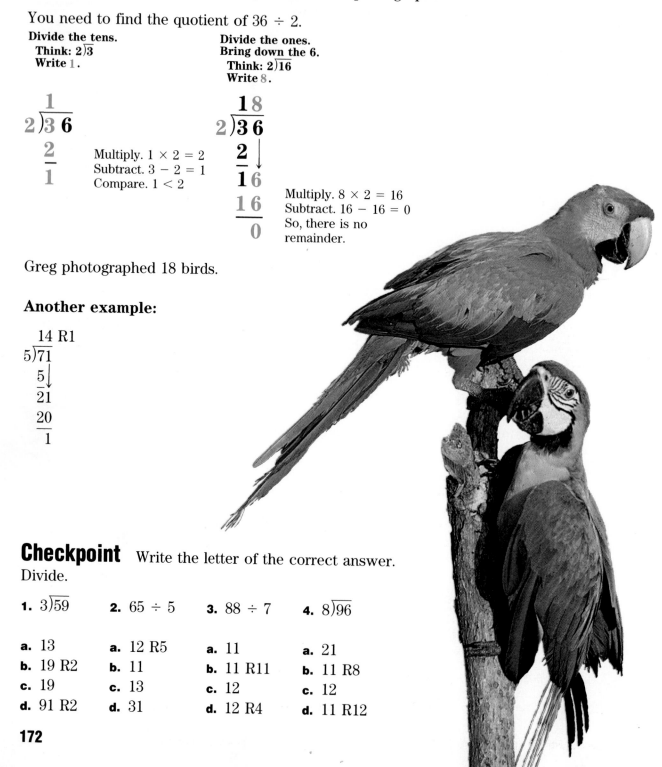

Checkpoint   Write the letter of the correct answer.
Divide.

1. 3)59

a. 13
b. 19 R2
c. 19
d. 91 R2

2. 65 ÷ 5

a. 12 R5
b. 11
c. 13
d. 31

3. 88 ÷ 7

a. 11
b. 11 R11
c. 12
d. 12 R4

4. 8)96

a. 21
b. 11 R8
c. 12
d. 11 R12

Divide.

1. $4\overline{)44}$ 2. $6\overline{)72}$ 3. $2\overline{)70}$ 4. $5\overline{)55}$ 5. $7\overline{)84}$

6. $3\overline{)99}$ 7. $5\overline{)95}$ 8. $6\overline{)78}$ 9. $2\overline{)90}$ 10. $4\overline{)64}$

11. $2\overline{)57}$ 12. $7\overline{)90}$ 13. $3\overline{)76}$ 14. $6\overline{)67}$ 15. $7\overline{)97}$

16. $4\overline{)89}$ 17. $3\overline{)50}$ 18. $4\overline{)57}$ 19. $6\overline{)73}$ 20. $5\overline{)39}$

21. $7\overline{)81}$ 22. $3\overline{)36}$ 23. $5\overline{)65}$ 24. $8\overline{)92}$ 25. $6\overline{)84}$

26. $56 \div 4$ 27. $99 \div 9$ 28. $40 \div 3$ 29. $90 \div 5$ 30. $56 \div 3$

31. $48 \div 4$ 32. $79 \div 7$ 33. $78 \div 3$ 34. $96 \div 8$ 35. $76 \div 5$

36. $66 \div 5$ 37. $82 \div 2$ 38. $66 \div 3$ 39. $83 \div 6$ 40. $94 \div 8$

Solve. For Problem 42, use the Infobank.

41. Pat takes a class picture of 51 fourth graders. She wants them to stand in 4 equal rows. She will seat the remaining children. How many children will stand in each row? How many will be seated?

42. Use the information on page 403 to solve. Jane's movie has superslow-, slow-, normal-, and fast-motion effects. For each kind of motion, how many frames of film can be shot in one second?

NUMBER SENSE

You can use a shortcut to divide when both the dividend and the divisor are multiples of 10. Divide $30\overline{)150}$.

Cross out the same number of zeros in both the dividend and the divisor.

$$3\cancel{0}\overline{)15\cancel{0}}$$

Divide:

$$3\overline{)15}^{\,5}. \quad \text{So, } 30\overline{)150}^{\,5}.$$

Use the shortcut to divide.

1. $40\overline{)160}$ 2. $60\overline{)360}$ 3. $20\overline{)120}$ 4. $50\overline{)250}$ 5. $80\overline{)240}$

PROBLEM SOLVING
Interpreting the Quotient and the Remainder

Sometimes when you divide to solve a problem, the answer is not a whole number. If the answer is a quotient with a remainder, read the question again. Be sure that the answer you write really answers the question.

You may need to:

1. drop the remainder

2. round the quotient to the next-greater whole number.

> Coin collecting is a popular hobby. One company packs sets of coins in boxes for collectors. The company packs 6 coins in each box. There are 57 coins to be put into boxes.

Divide.

$$6 \overline{)57} \quad \begin{array}{r} 9\ \text{R3} \\ \end{array}$$

$$\begin{array}{r} 54 \\ \hline 3 \end{array}$$

Read each question below. Think about how the answers differ for each question.

Question	Action	Answer
1. How many boxes can be filled with coins?	Drop the remainder from the quotient. 9 R3 ⟶ 9	9 boxes can be filled with coins.
2. How many boxes would be needed to hold all the coins?	Round the quotient to the next-greater whole number. 9 R3 ⟶ 10	10 boxes would be needed. (9 boxes would be full, and 1 box would hold the extra coins.)

Read the following tale. Use it to solve each problem.

> Once upon a time, there was a wealthy merchant.
> He had 2 sons and 1 daughter. He had 29 gold
> coins. He gave a bag of coins to each child. Each
> bag contained the same number of coins.

Write the letter of the correct answer.

1. How many coins were there in each
bag?

   a. 9 coins

   b. 9 R2 coins

   c. 10 coins

2. How many bags did he need to put
all his coins into bags?

   a. 3 bags

   b. 3 R2 bags

   c. 4 bags

Write how to use the remainder, and then solve.

3. The merchant's oldest child wanted to see the
world. He spent all his money on travel. Traveling 9
miles per day, he went to a town 87 miles away
from his home. How many days did it take him to
reach the town?

4. The second child loved music. She saw a merchant
who sold silver flutes. The flutes cost 2 gold coins
each. How many flutes could she buy with her
coins?

5. The third child loved parties. He spent all his coins
on a dinner for 58 guests. Each table at the dinner
could seat 8 guests. How many tables did he
need?

6. Of the 3 children, 2 had spent all their money. The
third child felt sorry for them. He traded his gold
coins for 47 silver coins and divided them equally
among himself and his brother and sister. He kept
the coins that were left. How many coins did he give
to his brother?

More Two-Step Division

Emily has 139 tulip bulbs. She wants to plant an equal number of each in 3 sections of her garden. How many should she plant in each section? How many will be left?

To find how many tulip bulbs should be planted, you can divide $3\overline{)139}$.

Divide the hundreds.

Think: $3\overline{)1}$. Not enough hundreds.

Divide the tens.
 Think: $3\overline{)13}$.
 Write 4.

Divide the ones.
 Bring down the 9.
 Think: $3\overline{)19}$.
 Write 6.

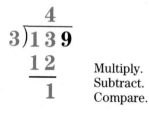

Multiply.
Subtract.
Compare.

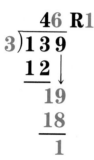

Multiply.
Subtract.
Compare.
Write the remainder.

Emily should plant 46 bulbs in each section. There will be 1 bulb left.

Check.

```
   46
 ×  3
 ----
  138
 +  1
 ----
  139
```

Checkpoint   Write the letter of the correct answer.

Divide.

1. $145 \div 2$

2. $5\overline{)445}$

3. $647 \div 7$

a. 7   **b.** 22 R1
c. 70 R5   **d.** 72 R1

a. 19   **b.** 81
c. 80 R4   **d.** 89

a. 91   **b.** 92
c. 92 R3   **d.** 29 R3

176

Math Reasoning, page H191

Divide.

1. $5\overline{)285}$ 2. $9\overline{)855}$ 3. $4\overline{)312}$ 4. $3\overline{)297}$ 5. $6\overline{)582}$

6. $3\overline{)195}$ 7. $9\overline{)117}$ 8. $8\overline{)688}$ 9. $6\overline{)396}$ 10. $6\overline{)522}$

11. $5\overline{)213}$ 12. $7\overline{)254}$ 13. $6\overline{)578}$ 14. $8\overline{)151}$ 15. $3\overline{)157}$

16. $6\overline{)489}$ 17. $4\overline{)143}$ 18. $7\overline{)297}$ 19. $9\overline{)526}$ 20. $8\overline{)267}$

21. $9\overline{)487}$ 22. $4\overline{)212}$ 23. $9\overline{)771}$ 24. $6\overline{)294}$ 25. $5\overline{)391}$

26. $255 \div 3$ 27. $165 \div 9$ 28. $247 \div 3$ 29. $432 \div 6$

30. $481 \div 7$ 31. $675 \div 9$ 32. $342 \div 7$ 33. $731 \div 9$

34. $513 \div 9$ 35. $718 \div 8$ 36. $335 \div 6$ 37. $666 \div 9$

Solve.

38. Alan has 227 daisies to put in bouquets for the flower shop. If there are 9 daisies in each bouquet, how many bouquets can he make? How many daisies will be left?

39. Cara grows 9 different kinds of plants in her greenhouse. She has 215 plants in all. Use this information to write and solve your own word problem.

CALCULATOR

You can use a calculator to check the answer to a division problem.
Check $539 \div 8 = 67$ R3.

Enter the quotient. Press ⑥ ⑦.
Multiply the quotient by the divisor. Press ✕ ⑧. Then press ＝.
The display reads ⑤ ③ ⑥.
Add the remainder. Press ＋ ③.
The display reads ⑤ ③ ⑨. This is the dividend.

Use a calculator to check each answer. Correct those answers that are wrong.

1. 80 R1 $4\overline{)321}$ 2. 66 R5 $6\overline{)407}$ 3. 34 R6 $8\overline{)274}$ 4. 45 R2 $3\overline{)137}$ 5. 86 R4 $5\overline{)436}$

Three-Step Division

Last year, Jane used 3,664 patches to sew quilts for 4 friends. If she used an equal number of patches for each quilt, how many patches did she use for each?

Divide 3,664 ÷ 4.

Divide the thousands. Think: 4)3. Not enough thousands.

Divide the hundreds.
 Think: 4)36.
 Write 9.

$$
\begin{array}{r}
9 \\
4)\overline{3,664} \\
3\,6 \\
\hline
0
\end{array}
$$

Multiply.
Subtract.
Compare.

Divide the tens.
 Bring down the 6.
 Think: 4)6.
 Write 1.

$$
\begin{array}{r}
9\,1 \\
4)\overline{3,664} \\
3\,6\downarrow \\
\hline
0\,6 \\
4 \\
\hline
2
\end{array}
$$

Multiply.
Subtract.
Compare.

Divide the ones.
 Bring down the 4.
 Think: 4)24.
 Write 6.

$$
\begin{array}{r}
9\,1\,6 \\
4)\overline{3,664} \\
3\,6 \\
\hline
0\,6\downarrow \\
4\downarrow \\
\hline
2\,4 \\
2\,4 \\
\hline
0
\end{array}
$$

Multiply.
Subtract.
Compare.
So, there is
no remainder.

Jan used 916 patches for each quilt.

Another example:

$$
\begin{array}{r}
143\ \mathrm{R1} \\
6)\overline{859} \\
6\downarrow \\
\hline
25 \\
24\downarrow \\
\hline
19 \\
18 \\
\hline
1
\end{array}
$$

Checkpoint   Write the letter of the correct answer.

Divide.

1. 4)504   **a.** 101   **b.** 121   **c.** 125 R4   **d.** 126

2. 1,964 ÷ 3   **a.** 354 R2   **b.** 621 R1   **c.** 653 R5   **d.** 654 R2

Divide.

1. $3\overline{)369}$ 2. $2\overline{)568}$ 3. $5\overline{)985}$ 4. $6\overline{)846}$ 5. $3\overline{)741}$

6. $2\overline{)1,128}$ 7. $3\overline{)2,229}$ 8. $4\overline{)3,812}$ 9. $5\overline{)3,125}$ 10. $7\overline{)5,992}$

11. $4\overline{)866}$ 12. $5\overline{)916}$ 13. $3\overline{)463}$ 14. $7\overline{)789}$ 15. $2\overline{)563}$

16. $9\overline{)3,166}$ 17. $9\overline{)8,924}$ 18. $6\overline{)4,273}$ 19. $5\overline{)4,687}$ 20. $4\overline{)2,234}$

21. $423 \div 2$ 22. $6,641 \div 7$ 23. $613 \div 5$ 24. $775 \div 6$ 25. $2,226 \div 6$

26. $7,344 \div 8$ 27. $6,201 \div 8$ 28. $763 \div 3$ 29. $4,125 \div 5$ 30. $525 \div 3$

31. $733 \div 5$ 32. $1,451 \div 2$ 33. $988 \div 8$ 34. $6,713 \div 7$ 35. $744 \div 3$

36. $2,568 \div 4$ 37. $577 \div 5$ 38. $5,867 \div 6$ 39. $489 \div 3$ 40. $1,285 \div 7$

Solve.

41. There are 1,255 patches in Peter's patchwork box. He plans to use the patches to make 7 quilts, each containing the same number of patches. How many patches will he use in each? How many patches will be left?

42. For their town's birthday, 8 friends work for 1,368 hours on a presentation quilt. If each friend works for an equal number of hours, for how many hours does each work?

NUMBER SENSE

Estimate to check if the answer is reasonable. Write *yes* or *no*.

1.
$$\begin{array}{r} 8,761 \\ \times\ \ \ \ 8 \\ \hline 70,088 \end{array}$$

2. $3\overline{)168}$ with quotient 56

3.
$$\begin{array}{r} 8,214 \\ \times\ \ \ \ 6 \\ \hline 75,712 \end{array}$$

4. $4\overline{)3,936}$ with quotient 98

Finding Averages

Lewis likes to read good books. In the winter, he reads in front of the fireplace. In January, Lewis read 13 books; in February, he read 10; in March, he read 16. What is the average number of books he read per month?

To find the average, you add the number of books he read each month. Then divide the sum by the number of addends.

Add the numbers.	Divide by the number of addends.	The average is the quotient.
13 10 + 16 —— 39	$\begin{array}{r} 13 \\ 3\overline{)39} \\ \underline{3}\downarrow \\ 9 \\ \underline{9} \\ 0 \end{array}$	13

Lewis read an average of 13 books per month.

Another example:

$$\begin{array}{r} 134 \\ 362 \\ 429 \\ + 235 \\ \hline 1{,}160 \end{array} \qquad \begin{array}{r} 290 \\ 4\overline{)1{,}160} \\ \underline{8}\downarrow \\ 36 \\ \underline{36}\downarrow \\ 0 \end{array}$$

Since there are 4 addends, you divide by 4.

Checkpoint Write the letter of the correct answer.

Find the average.

1. 65, 14, 36, 49   **a.** 36   **b.** 41   **c.** 14   **d.** 31

2. 213, 135, 462   **a.** 203 R1   **b.** 233 R1   **c.** 27   **d.** 270

Find the average.

1. 28, 52

2. 56, 34

3. 28, 38, 48

4. 897, 211

5. 177, 213, 189

6. 123, 769, 470

7. 195, 726, 324

8. 25, 16, 82, 33

9. 12, 13, 16, 19

10. 14, 18, 20, 24

11. 313, 543, 495, 901

12. 864, 671, 443, 334

13. 19, 346, 68, 579

14. 1,112; 598; 864

15. 1,455; 107

Use the chart to solve.

Month	April	May	June	July	August
Books read by Jules	9	5	6	3	2
Books read by Jim	6	2	8	9	5

16. What is the average number of books Jules reads per month?

17. What is the average number of books Jim reads per month?

18. In which month does Jules read the same number of books as his monthly average?

19. In which month does Jim read the same number of books as his monthly average?

MIDCHAPTER REVIEW

Divide.

1. $27 \div 4$

2. $36 \div 5$

3. $66 \div 7$

4. $59 \div 8$

5. $75 \div 9$

6. $6\overline{)99}$

7. $5\overline{)88}$

8. $3\overline{)74}$

9. $7\overline{)99}$

10. $4\overline{)87}$

11. $4\overline{)296}$

12. $6\overline{)291}$

13. $8\overline{)153}$

14. $9\overline{)845}$

15. $7\overline{)359}$

16. $6\overline{)874}$

17. $7\overline{)891}$

18. $9\overline{)4,689}$

19. $8\overline{)5,095}$

20. $4\overline{)2,466}$

PROBLEM SOLVING
Choosing a Strategy or Method

Choose a strategy or method and solve.

1. Ralph has a coin album that is 36 pages long. There are 9 Mercury-head dimes on each page. How many dimes are there in the album?

2. Jo can put 5 silver dollars on each page of her coin album. Her album has places for 60 silver dollars. How many pages are there in the album?

> Choosing the Operation
> Identifying Extra Information
> Estimation
> Solving Two-Step Problems
> Drawing a Picture
> Identifying Needed Information

3. Lila sews stuffed toy animals. She sews an average of 3 animals per week. About how many animals does she sew in 52 weeks?

4. Model-airplane kits cost $5.25 each. Teddy has saved $10. Is this enough to buy 2 model-airplane kits?

5. Bob has 537 stamps from 35 countries. The same number of stamps are in each of 3 albums. How many stamps are there in each album?

6. Cara had 176 baseball cards in her collection. Andy gave her 195 more cards. Of these, 124 were of National League players. How many baseball cards does Cara have?

7. Inez has 234 seashells from Maine, Florida, and Georgia. Of these, 98 are from Maine. What do you need to know to find how many shells are from Florida?

8. Jim builds 4 model cars each month. What other fact will you need to find how many model cars he builds in 1 year?

9. Linda keeps her miniature-doll collection on 3 shelves in her room. There are 21 dolls on each shelf. How many dolls are there in Linda's collection?

10. Eric took 4 pictures of each animal in the petting zoo. He took 144 pictures in all. How many animals were there in the petting zoo?

Choose a strategy or method and solve.

11. Eileen bought a crewel kit for $7.25, yarn for $3.18, and a how-to booklet for $4.07. About how much did Eileen spend?

12. John videotaped 258 minutes of 6 school sporting events. He taped each event for the same amount of time. About how many minutes of each event did he tape?

13. A bird-watching magazine costs $1.75 per issue. It is sent to 954 people 8 times per year. What is the cost of a subscription to the magazine for one year?

14. Meg has 134 rocks in her rock collection. Ann has 59 more rocks than Meg. Jean has 272 rocks in her collection. How many more rocks does Jean have than Meg?

15. Both Ron and Chris collect postcards. Ron has 3 times as many postcards as Chris. How many postcards does Ron have?

16. Look back at the problems you have solved. Talk about the ones that seemed difficult. What method did you use? Is there more than one way to think about these problems? Share ideas with classmates.

Zero in the Quotient

Sarah is making beaded necklaces for her friends. She has 738 beads to make 7 necklaces. If she uses the same number of beads in each necklace, how many does she use in each? How many beads are left?

You can divide $7\overline{)738}$.

Divide the hundreds.
 Think: $7\overline{)7}$.
 Write 1.

$$
\begin{array}{r}
1 \\
7\overline{)738} \\
7 \\
\hline
0
\end{array}
$$
Multiply.
Subtract.
Compare.

Divide the tens.
 Bring down the 3.
 Think: $7\overline{)3}$. Not enough tens.
 Write 0 in the quotient.

$$
\begin{array}{r}
10 \\
7\overline{)738} \\
7 \\
\hline
03 \\
0 \\
\hline
3
\end{array}
$$
Multiply.
Subtract.
Compare.

Divide the ones.
 Bring down the 8.
 Think: $7\overline{)38}$.
 Write 5.

$$
\begin{array}{r}
105\ \text{R3} \\
7\overline{)738} \\
7 \\
\hline
03 \\
0 \\
\hline
38 \\
35 \\
\hline
3
\end{array}
$$
Multiply.
Subtract.
Compare.
Write the remainder.

Sarah uses 105 beads in each necklace. There are 3 beads left.

Other examples:

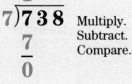

$$
\begin{array}{r}
10\ \text{R3} \\
5\overline{)53} \\
5 \\
\hline
03 \\
0 \\
\hline
3
\end{array}
\qquad
\begin{array}{r}
670 \\
3\overline{)2{,}010} \\
18 \\
\hline
21 \\
21 \\
\hline
0
\end{array}
$$

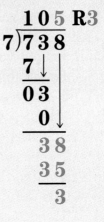

Checkpoint   Write the letter of the correct answer.
Divide.

1. $6\overline{)2{,}412}$ **a.** 204   **b.** 400 R12   **c.** 402   **d.** 420

2. $508 \div 5$ **a.** 100 R8   **b.** 101 R3   **c.** 301 R3   **d.** 151 R3

Divide.

1. $3\overline{)30}$ 2. $6\overline{)60}$ 3. $5\overline{)250}$ 4. $5\overline{)100}$ 5. $4\overline{)120}$

6. $4\overline{)83}$ 7. $2\overline{)61}$ 8. $8\overline{)87}$ 9. $2\overline{)121}$ 10. $6\overline{)302}$

11. $8\overline{)864}$ 12. $2\overline{)520}$ 13. $5\overline{)1,545}$ 14. $3\overline{)1,209}$ 15. $2\overline{)1,060}$

16. $7\overline{)764}$ 17. $4\overline{)826}$ 18. $3\overline{)902}$ 19. $3\overline{)1,828}$ 20. $6\overline{)3,005}$

21. $1,210 \div 3$ 22. $5,656 \div 7$ 23. $2,114 \div 7$ 24. $510 \div 5$ 25. $821 \div 2$

26. $92 \div 3$ 27. $929 \div 3$ 28. $4,567 \div 9$ 29. $1,530 \div 5$ 30. $704 \div 7$

31. $1,421 \div 2$ 32. $303 \div 5$ 33. $61 \div 3$ 34. $4,340 \div 7$ 35. $2,000 \div 4$

36. $626 \div 6$ 37. $545 \div 5$ 38. $5,421 \div 9$ 39. $401 \div 8$ 40. $2,042 \div 4$

Solve.

41. Charlie has 431 beads to make 4 headbands. If he uses an equal number of beads on each, how many does he use on each headband? How many are left?

★42. Jane worked on a beaded purse for three weeks. The first week she beaded 75 rows, and the next week she beaded 95 rows. If 298 rows are now done, how many rows did she bead the third week?

★43. Sue has 9 packets of beads. There are 48 beads in each packet. She uses an equal number of beads for each belt and decorates 4 belts. How many beads does she use for 1 belt?

44. Stan needs 1,640 inches of string to make 8 beaded bracelets. Use this information to write and solve your own word problem.

 **Patterns, Relations, and Functions**

Write = or ≠ for ● to make the sentence true.

1. $5,000 \div 5$ ● 10×100 2. $2,100 \div 7$ ● 10×300 3. $410 \div 2$ ● 1×200

4. $1,600 \div 4$ ● 40×40 5. $900 \div 9$ ● 10×9 6. $8,000 \div 8$ ● 4×250

Dividing with Money

For family picnics, Sam's father makes a special clam chowder. To make it, he buys 3 pounds of clams for $8.97. How much does he pay for 1 pound of clams?

To divide amounts of money, think of the amounts as whole numbers.

$3\overline{)\$8.97}$ Think: $3\overline{)897}$.

$$
\begin{array}{r}
\$2.99 \\
3\overline{)\$8.97} \\
6 \downarrow \\
\hline
2\ 9 \\
2\ 7 \downarrow \\
\hline
27 \\
27 \\
\hline
0
\end{array}
$$

> Remember to write the dollar sign and the cents point in the quotient.

Sam's father pays $2.99 for 1 pound of clams.

Other examples:

$$
\begin{array}{r}
\$0.71 \\
9\overline{)\$6.39} \\
6\ 3 \downarrow \\
\hline
09 \\
9 \\
\hline
0
\end{array}
\qquad
\begin{array}{r}
\$\ 4.81 \\
6\overline{)\$28.86} \\
24 \downarrow \\
\hline
4\ 8 \\
4\ 8 \downarrow \\
\hline
06 \\
6 \\
\hline
0
\end{array}
\qquad
\begin{array}{r}
\$0.07 \\
7\overline{)\$0.49} \\
49 \\
\hline
0
\end{array}
$$

> This 0 must be written.

Checkpoint   Write the letter of the correct answer.
Divide.

1. $4\overline{)\$6.28}$ | **2.** $\$3.52 \div 4$ | **3.** $\$10.32 \div 2$ | **4.** $8\overline{)\$0.64}$

a. $1.07	**a.** $0.80	**a.** $5.11	**a.** 8
b. $1.56	**b.** $0.88	**b.** 516	**b.** $0.08
c. $1.57	**c.** $8.80	**c.** $5.16	**c.** $.08
d. $1.70	**d.** 88	**d.** $50.16	**d.** $0.80

Find the quotient.

1. $7)\overline{\$9.66}$ 2. $5)\overline{\$7.90}$ 3. $3)\overline{\$4.74}$ 4. $7)\overline{\$8.61}$ 5. $2)\overline{\$5.46}$

6. $9)\overline{\$18.18}$ 7. $3)\overline{\$21.24}$ 8. $5)\overline{\$30.45}$ 9. $6)\overline{\$36.42}$ 10. $7)\overline{\$49.28}$

11. $5)\overline{\$1.25}$ 12. $4)\overline{\$2.32}$ 13. $9)\overline{\$8.19}$ 14. $3)\overline{\$2.61}$ 15. $8)\overline{\$5.92}$

16. $6)\overline{\$0.36}$ 17. $9)\overline{\$0.72}$ 18. $7)\overline{\$0.56}$ 19. $5)\overline{\$0.45}$ 20. $8)\overline{\$0.48}$

21. $7)\overline{\$32.76}$ 22. $5)\overline{\$40.60}$ 23. $5)\overline{\$8.90}$ 24. $9)\overline{\$0.81}$ 25. $2)\overline{\$1.88}$

26. $\$2.73 \div 7$ 27. $\$0.75 \div 5$ 28. $\$18.24 \div 6$ 29. $\$16.62 \div 6$ 30. $\$1.68 \div 4$

31. $\$8.47 \div 7$ 32. $\$12.36 \div 4$ 33. $\$0.96 \div 6$ ★34. $\$71.24 \div 4$ ★35. $\$75.15 \div 3$

Solve.

36. For a Sunday dinner for 3, Judy's mother buys a roast for $9.35, string beans for $1.51, and salad fixings for $3.00. What is the total cost of the meal? What is the cost per serving?

37. The *Blanch Gazette* ran this advertisement for a cooking-supplies sale at the general store. Look at the prices in the ad to find how much it costs for 1 of each item.

GENERAL STORE SALE

4 bowls for $16.48
6 spice jars for $12.54
2 spatulas for $2.40
3 dish towels for $3.75

Decide whether you would use mental math, pencil and paper, or a calculator to solve each. Explain your answer, then solve.

1. $\begin{array}{r} 9,876 \\ + 4,595 \\ \hline \end{array}$

2. $\begin{array}{r} 1,000 \\ - 975 \\ \hline \end{array}$

3. $\begin{array}{r} 5,110 \\ \times \quad 5 \\ \hline \end{array}$

4. $4)\overline{1,232}$

5. $\begin{array}{r} 425 \\ \times 25 \\ \hline \end{array}$

6. $9)\overline{888}$

PROBLEM SOLVING
Writing a Number Sentence

Writing a number sentence can help you figure out how the numbers you know relate to the number you need to find.

George's hobby is building model sailing ships. He displays an equal number of the finished models on 5 shelves in his workroom. George has 50 finished models. How many model sailing ships are there on each shelf?

1. List what you know and what you need to find.

Know — There are 50 finished models. Each shelf holds the same number of models.
There are 5 shelves.

Find — How many models are there on each shelf?

2. What does your list tell you about whether to × or ÷? Write a number sentence about this problem. Use n to stand for the number you need to find.

$$50 \div 5 = n$$
model ships   shelves   models on each shelf

3. Solve. Write the answer.

$$50 \div 5 = n$$
$$50 \div 5 = 10$$
$$n = 10$$

So, there are 10 model ships on each shelf.

Write the letter of the correct number sentence.

1. Lila likes to read mystery stories. She reads an average of 5 mystery stories per month. On the average, how many mystery stories does Lila read in 12 months?

   a. $5 \times 12 = n$
   b. $12 \div 5 = n$
   c. $5 + 12 = n$

2. Abner's hobby is raising tropical fish. He has 96 fish and 4 aquariums. The same number of fish are in each aquarium. How many fish are there in each aquarium?

   a. $4 \times 96 = n$
   b. $96 \div 4 = n$
   c. $96 - 4 = n$

Write a number sentence. Then solve.

3. Nan collects coins from other lands. She has 38 coins from England. She has 3 times as many coins from France. How many coins from France does Nan have?

4. Pete's hobby is photography. He took 60 pictures of the 4 other members of his family. If he took an equal number of pictures of each, how many pictures of each person did he take?

5. The kite-flying club mails 6 newsletters per year to each member of the club. There are 257 club members. How many newsletters does the club mail each year?

6. Robbie has a seashell collection. He decides to give 156 shells to 4 friends. He gives an equal number of shells to each friend. How many seashells does each friend receive?

7. Billy's grandmother made a patchwork quilt. The quilt is made up of 9 large squares. There is an equal number of red patches in each square. There are 324 red patches in all. How many red patches are there in each large square?

CALCULATOR

To solve a division problem on your calculator, you must use the  ÷ key. To find $4\overline{)92}$, think of $4\overline{)92}$ as $92 \div 4$.

Press: 9 2 ÷ 4 =

The display should show 23.
The quotient is 23.

Find $3\overline{)197}$

Press: 1 9 7 ÷ 3 =

The display should show 65.666666.

65 is the quotient. The .666666 means that there is a remainder. To find the remainder:

Multiply: $65 \times 3 = 195$.
Subtract: $197 - 195 = 2$.

The remainder is 2

So, $3\overline{)197}$ $\overset{65\ R2}{}$

Use estimation to find the exercise in each row that has the largest quotient. Then use your calculator to find each quotient.

Row A: **1.** $5\overline{)68}$ **2.** $4\overline{)85}$ **3.** $4\overline{)53}$

Row B: **4.** $6\overline{)545}$ **5.** $9\overline{)803}$ **6.** $7\overline{)620}$

Row C: **7.** $8\overline{)4,756}$ **8.** $6\overline{)2,479}$ **9.** $5\overline{)2,439}$

Row D: **10.** $3\overline{)\$4.77}$ **11.** $4\overline{)\$8.60}$ **12.** $5\overline{)\$8.75}$

Row E: **13.** $5\overline{)\$2.25}$ **14.** $9\overline{)\$3.15}$ **15.** $8\overline{)\$3.28}$

GROUP PROJECT

Using a Mileage Chart

The problem: Suppose Lena lives in Grey Slope. She wants to go to a crafts fair in Redville. How many miles will she travel?

Look at the chart. A **mileage chart** shows the distance between two places. Put your finger on Grey Slope. Move it to the right until it is under Redville. The distance in miles between the two cities is shown in the square.

MILEAGE CHART	Redville	Low Town	Little Stone	Grey Slope	High Ridge
Redville		9	11	27	49
Low Town	9		7	21	36
Little Stone	11	7		3	43
Grey Slope	27	21	3		14
High Ridge	49	36	43	14	

Lena will travel 27 miles.

Solve.

1. Lena averages 9 miles per hour on her bike. If she has to be at the crafts fair at noon, at what time should she leave Grey Slope?

2. Rosario has to travel from Little Stone to High Ridge for his birdwatcher's club meeting. How many miles will he travel?

3. José must walk from Redville to Low Town. If he leaves Redville at 6:00 A.M. and averages 3 miles per hour, will he reach Low Town by 11:30 A.M.?

CHAPTER TEST

Divide. (pages 168, 172, 176, 178, 184, and 186)

1. $46 \div 8$ **2.** $72 \div 6$ **3.** $464 \div 8$ **4.** $307 \div 3$

5. $822 \div 2$ **6.** $5{,}226 \div 6$ **7.** $\$1.12 \div 8$ **8.** $\$2.88 \div 4$

9. $3\overline{)29}$ **10.** $7\overline{)60}$ **11.** $8\overline{)94}$ **12.** $5\overline{)367}$

13. $3\overline{)396}$ **14.** $8\overline{)996}$ **15.** $6\overline{)2{,}712}$ **16.** $8\overline{)4{,}699}$

17. $9\overline{)95}$ **18.** $8\overline{)480}$ **19.** $7\overline{)633}$ **20.** $7\overline{)4{,}907}$

21. $6\overline{)\$0.54}$ **22.** $6\overline{)\$7.44}$ **23.** $9\overline{)\$20.79}$ **24.** $6\overline{)\$31.38}$

Find the average. (page 180)

25. 64, 174, 87, 295

26. 123, 396, 723

27. 35, 72, 40, 83, 95

28. 124, 864, 360, 492

Estimate. Write the letter of the correct answer. (page 170)

29. 6)$\overline{721}$ **a.** 10   **b.** 20   **c.** 100   **d.** 200

30. 9)$\overline{7,243}$ **a.** 8   **b.** 80   **c.** 800   **d.** 8,000

31. 3)$\overline{2,975}$ **a.** 9   **b.** 90   **c.** 900   **d.** 9,000

Write a number sentence. Then solve. (page 188)

32. Louise went to the hobby shop. She bought 3 needlepoint kits for $12.75. Each kit cost the same amount of money. How much did each kit cost?

Write how to use the remainder, and then solve. (page 174)

33. Mr. Anderson carved 74 small wooden toys to give as presents to his 8 grandchildren. He wanted to give the same number of toys to each grandchild. How many toys did each of Mr. Anderson's grandchildren receive?

BONUS

Divide.

1. 4)$\overline{8,974}$ **2.** 6)$\overline{9,541}$ **3.** 8)$\overline{9,637}$ **4.** 3)$\overline{9,816}$

RETEACHING

You may need to write one or more zeros in the quotient when you divide.

Divide $2,429 \div 4$.

Divide the thousands. Think: $4\overline{)2}$. Not enough thousands.

Divide the hundreds.
  Think: $4\overline{)24}$.
  Write 6.

$$\begin{array}{r} 6 \\ 4\overline{)2,4\,2\,9} \\ \underline{2\,4} \\ 0 \end{array}$$

Multiply.
Subtract.
Compare.

Divide the tens.
  Bring down the 2.
  Think: $4\overline{)2}$.
  Not enough tens.
  Write 0 in the quotient.

$$\begin{array}{r} 6\,0 \\ 4\overline{)2,4\,2\,9} \\ \underline{2\,4}\downarrow \\ 0\,2 \\ \underline{0} \\ 2 \end{array}$$

Multiply.
Subtract.
Compare.

Divide the ones.
  Bring down the 9.
  Think: $4\overline{)29}$.
  Write 7.

$$\begin{array}{r} 6\,0\,7 \text{ R1} \\ 4\overline{)2,4\,2\,9} \\ \underline{2\,4}\downarrow \\ 0\,2 \\ \underline{0}\downarrow \\ 2\,9 \\ \underline{2\,8} \\ 1 \end{array}$$

Multiply.
Subtract.
Compare

Write the
remainder.

Other examples:

$$\begin{array}{r} 10 \text{ R4} \\ 6\overline{)64} \\ \underline{6}\downarrow \\ 04 \\ \underline{0} \\ 4 \end{array}$$

$$\begin{array}{r} 50 \text{ R3} \\ 4\overline{)203} \\ \underline{20}\downarrow \\ 03 \\ \underline{0} \\ 3 \end{array}$$

$$\begin{array}{r} 205 \\ 3\overline{)615} \\ \underline{6}\downarrow \\ 01 \\ \underline{0}\downarrow \\ 15 \\ \underline{15} \\ 0 \end{array}$$

$$\begin{array}{r} 300 \text{ R2} \\ 4\overline{)1,202} \\ \underline{1\,2}\downarrow \\ 00 \\ \underline{0}\downarrow \\ 02 \\ \underline{0} \\ 2 \end{array}$$

Divide.

1. $4\overline{)42}$ **2.** $7\overline{)76}$ **3.** $5\overline{)53}$ **4.** $8\overline{)86}$ **5.** $3\overline{)32}$

6. $8\overline{)322}$ **7.** $3\overline{)271}$ **8.** $7\overline{)425}$ **9.** $5\overline{)201}$ **10.** $8\overline{)164}$

11. $5\overline{)533}$ **12.** $4\overline{)801}$ **13.** $6\overline{)656}$ **14.** $4\overline{)812}$ **15.** $2\overline{)415}$

16. $8\overline{)4,840}$ **17.** $7\overline{)3,504}$ **18.** $6\overline{)5,446}$ **19.** $3\overline{)2,413}$ **20.** $9\overline{)6,320}$

ENRICHMENT

Divisibility

If there is no remainder when you divide one whole number by another, the first number is divisible by the second.

$$\begin{array}{r} 46 \\ 4\overline{)184} \end{array}$$ 184 is divisible by 4.

Rules of divisibility can help you find whether one number can be evenly divided by another number.

All even numbers are divisible by 2.	398 is an even number. So, 398 is divisible by 2.
If the sum of the digits of a number is a multiple of 3, the number is divisible by 3.	342 $\longrightarrow$ 3 + 4 + 2 = 9 9 is a multiple of 3. So, 342 is divisible by 3.
If the digit in the ones place is either 0 or 5, the number is divisible by 5.	760 is divisible by 5. 1,395 is divisible by 5.
If the digit in the ones place is 0, the number is divisible by 10.	890 is divisible by 10.

Is each divisible by 2? Write *yes* or *no*.

1. 10 **2.** 173 **3.** 206 **4.** 454 **5.** 899 **6.** 6,371

Is each divisible by 3? Write *yes* or *no*.

7. 31 **8.** 822 **9.** 123 **10.** 195 **11.** 196 **12.** 3,215

Is each divisible by 5? Write *yes* or *no*.

13. 52 **14.** 670 **15.** 445 **16.** 736 **17.** 720 **18.** 6,125

Is each divisible by 10? Write *yes* or *no*.

19. 75 **20.** 360 **21.** 747 **22.** 990 **23.** 670 **24.** 4,525

CUMULATIVE REVIEW

Write the letter of the correct answer.

1. 8×200

    a. 160   **b.** 1,600
    c. 16,000   **d.** not given

2. 4×23

    a. 27   **b.** 82
    c. 92   **d.** not given

3. 9×716

    a. 6,344   **b.** 6,444
    c. 63,954   **d.** not given

4. $\begin{array}{r} 9,119 \\ \times \quad\quad 8 \\ \hline \end{array}$

    a. 72,882
    b. 72,952
    c. 77,642
    d. not given

5. $6 \times \$56.93$

    a. $306.48   **b.** $341.58
    c. 34,158   **d.** not given

6. $(4 \times 9) \times 5$

    a. 150   **b.** 245
    c. 1,530   **d.** not given

7. $9 \div 9$

    a. 0   **b.** 1
    c. 9   **d.** not given

8. $48 \div 8$

    a. 6   **b.** 8
    c. 40   **d.** not given

9. 7×5

    a. 12
    b. 35
    c. 75
    d. not given

10. $\begin{array}{r} 3,175 \\ 14,916 \\ + 29,053 \\ \hline \end{array}$

    a. 46,034
    b. 47,144
    c. 77,144
    d. not given

11. Estimate $5.98 − $3.07 by rounding to the nearest dollar.

    a. $1.00   **b.** $2.00
    c. $3.00   **d.** $9.00

12. Which number sentence is true?

    a. $35,684 < 35,683$
    b. $48,921 < 48,291$
    c. $62,608 < 62,806$
    d. not given

13. Lief runs 4 miles per day for 24 days to train for a race. How many miles does he run in training?

    a. 6 miles   **b.** 86 miles
    c. 96 miles   **d.** not given

14. In the pet shop, there are 54 fish and 18 turtles. Mr. Guy puts 6 fish in each tank. How many tanks are needed?

    a. 3 tanks   **b.** 9 tanks
    c. 12 tanks   **d.** not given

Your family is planning a winter trip to a remote mountain cabin. The 2-mile trail is covered with snow and ice. All your supplies must be carried in your backpacks. The amount of weight you can carry depends on your size. What would you take?

7 FRACTIONS, MIXED NUMBERS, PROBABILITY

Fractions: Part of a Whole

Marsha's vegetable stand is divided into 4 equal parts. She places fresh carrots in one part. What part of her stand contains carrots?

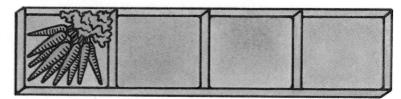

You can write a fraction to show the part of Marsha's stand that contains carrots.

numerator ⟶ **1 (number of parts with carrots)**
denominator ⟶ **4 (number of equal parts)**

Read: one fourth.
Write: $\frac{1}{4}$.

$\frac{1}{4}$ of her stand contains carrots.

You can also write a fraction for the part of Marsha's vegetable stand that is empty.

numerator ⟶ **3 (number of empty parts)**
denominator ⟶ **4 (number of equal parts)**

Read: three fourths.
Write: $\frac{3}{4}$.

$\frac{3}{4}$ of her stand is empty.

Checkpoint   Write the letter of the correct answer.

What is the fraction for the shaded part?

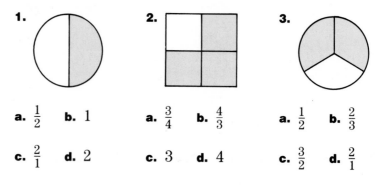

1.
a. $\frac{1}{2}$ b. 1

c. $\frac{2}{1}$ d. 2

2.
a. $\frac{3}{4}$ b. $\frac{4}{3}$

c. 3   d. 4

3.
a. $\frac{1}{2}$ b. $\frac{2}{3}$

c. $\frac{3}{2}$ d. $\frac{2}{1}$

Math Reasoning, page H193

Write a fraction for the shaded part.

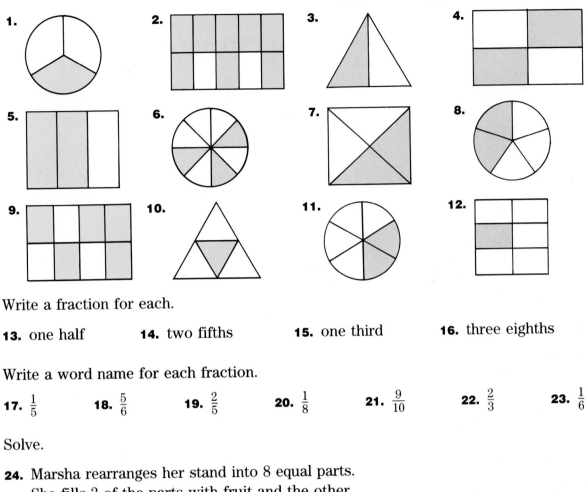

1.　　　　　　　　**2.**　　　　　　　　**3.**　　　　　　　　**4.**

5.　　　　　　　　**6.**　　　　　　　　**7.**　　　　　　　　**8.**

9.　　　　　　　　**10.**　　　　　　　　**11.**　　　　　　　　**12.**

Write a fraction for each.

13. one half　　　　**14.** two fifths　　　　**15.** one third　　　　**16.** three eighths

Write a word name for each fraction.

17. $\frac{1}{5}$　　　**18.** $\frac{5}{6}$　　　**19.** $\frac{2}{5}$　　　**20.** $\frac{1}{8}$　　　**21.** $\frac{9}{10}$　　　**22.** $\frac{2}{3}$　　　**23.** $\frac{1}{6}$

Solve.

24. Marsha rearranges her stand into 8 equal parts.
She fills 3 of the parts with fruit and the other
5 parts with vegetables. What fraction does she
fill with vegetables?

25. Look at the vegetable stand.
Is it divided into fifths?
Why or why not?

CHALLENGE Patterns, Relations, and Functions

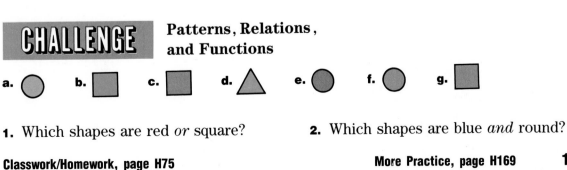

a. ○　**b.** □　**c.** □　**d.** △　**e.** ○　**f.** ○　**g.** □

1. Which shapes are red *or* square?　　　　**2.** Which shapes are blue *and* round?

Fractions: Part of a Set

Sally is carrying 5 apples in a basket. Of the 5 apples, 1 is green. What fraction of the set of apples is green?

You can write a fraction to show the part of the set of apples that is green.

1 (number of green apples)
5 (number of apples in all)

Read: one fifth.
Write: $\frac{1}{5}$.

$\frac{1}{5}$ of the set of apples is green.

You can write a fraction for the part of the set of apples that is red.

4 (number of red apples)
5 (number of apples in all)

Read: four fifths.
Write: $\frac{4}{5}$.

Checkpoint   Write the letter of the correct answer.

What fraction of each set is circled?

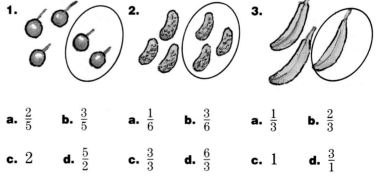

1.
a. $\frac{2}{5}$ b. $\frac{3}{5}$
c. 2   d. $\frac{5}{2}$

2.
a. $\frac{1}{6}$ b. $\frac{3}{6}$
c. $\frac{3}{3}$ d. $\frac{6}{3}$

3.
a. $\frac{1}{3}$ b. $\frac{2}{3}$
c. 1   d. $\frac{3}{1}$

Write a fraction for the shaded part of each set.

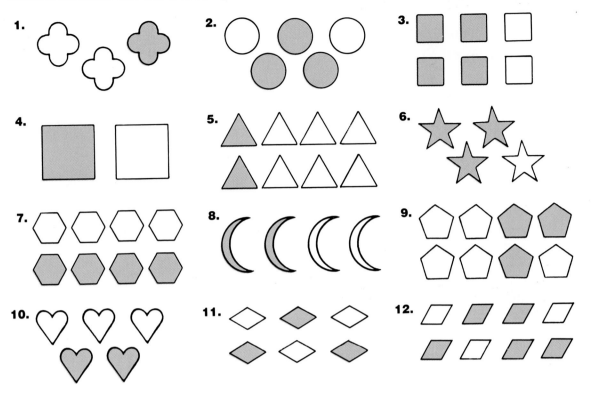

1. 2. 3.

4. 5. 6.

7. 8. 9.

10. 11. 12.

Solve.

13. Franco uses 5 slices of cheese to make a cheese sandwich. If 2 of the slices are swiss cheese, what part of the cheese is swiss cheese?

14. Yoshi buys 36 ounces of fresh tuna to make sushi, a Japanese dish of raw fish and rice. If Yoshi needs 3 ounces of tuna for each serving of sushi, how many servings can he make?

★15. Mr. and Mrs. Rosman serve a stew so that they and each of their 6 guests receive equal portions. What fraction of the stew do the Rosmans receive?

CHALLENGE

Draw a picture that shows each fraction.

1. $\frac{1}{2}$ 2. $\frac{3}{4}$ 3. $\frac{2}{3}$ 4. $\frac{1}{6}$ 5. $\frac{5}{8}$

Finding Part of a Set

Work with your team to explore how fractions can help describe part of a set.

Step 1: Place 12 counters on your desk. To show one third $\left(\frac{1}{3}\right)$ of the counters, separate them into 3 groups of equal size. How many counters are in each group? One third of the whole group is the number of counters in 1 group. Now count the number of counters in 1 group. This is $\frac{1}{3}$ of 12.

- How would you show $\frac{1}{4}$ of 12? Describe it to a teammate.

- Show $\frac{1}{6}$ of 12. Show $\frac{1}{2}$ of 12.

- How can you use division to find $\frac{1}{6}$ of 12? to find $\frac{1}{2}$ of 12?

- Can you show $\frac{1}{5}$ of 12 with the counters? Tell a teammate why or why not.

Step 2: In Step 1 you showed $\frac{1}{3}$ of 12. Here you will explore the relationship between $\frac{1}{3}$ of 12 and $\frac{2}{3}$ of 12.

Separate the 12 counters into 3 groups of equal size. One third of 12 would be one of these groups.

- How can you show $\frac{2}{3}$ of 12?

- How can you use division and multiplication to find $\frac{2}{3}$ of 12?

- What relationship is there between $\frac{1}{3}$ and $\frac{2}{3}$?

Step 3: Draw pictures of 24 counters on a piece of paper. Then ring them to show 6 groups of equal size. How many counters are there in each group?

Find each part of the set. Use your drawing to help.

What is

$\frac{1}{6}$ of 24?

$\frac{2}{6}$ of 24?

$\frac{3}{6}$ of 24?

$\frac{4}{6}$ of 24?

$\frac{5}{6}$ of 24?

$\frac{6}{6}$ of 24?

Describe a pattern in the answers. How could you show $\frac{0}{6}$ of 24?

Decide which of the following is the greatest number. Discuss the method you used with the rest of the class.

$\frac{1}{5}$ of 15 $\qquad$ $\frac{2}{3}$ of 12 $\qquad$ $\frac{1}{8}$ of 32 $\qquad$ $\frac{3}{4}$ of 8

Thinking as a Team

1. What have you learned about finding part of a set? List your conclusions, and discuss them with the class.

2. Can you think of a situation in which you would have to find part of a set? Write a problem using this situation. Share your problem with other students, and solve the problem together. Discuss different methods that you can use to solve the problem.

Equivalent Fractions

A. Do you have a friend named Elizabeth? Sometimes she may be called Liz, sometimes Beth, and sometimes Betty. These are all names for the same person. Fractions can have different names too but still name the same part. These are called **equivalent fractions.**

Work with the other members of your team to explore equivalent fractions.

Step 1: Make a set of fraction pieces. Cut out 6 pieces of paper that are each 12 inches long. Fold and mark the pieces as shown below. Then cut out each fraction piece.

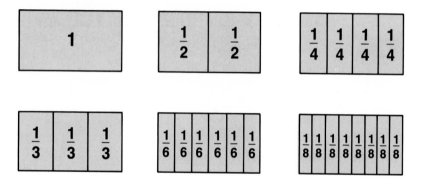

Step 2: Look at a piece marked $\frac{1}{2}$. Compare it to the other pieces.

- Name a fraction piece less than $\frac{1}{2}$.

- Name a fraction greater than $\frac{1}{2}$.

- How many eighths does it take to make $\frac{1}{2}$? How would you write this as a fraction?

- Why are they equivalent fractions?

- How many fourths does it take to make $\frac{1}{2}$? Can you name the same part as $\frac{1}{2}$ using fourths? How?

- Can you name the same part as $\frac{1}{2}$ using sixths? How?

- Can you name the same part as $\frac{1}{2}$ using thirds?

- List all the fractions you found that are equivalent to $\frac{1}{2}$.

B. You can use your fraction pieces to explore other equivalent fractions.

Show $\frac{3}{4}$ with the pieces. Find other fraction pieces that name the same part. Write the fraction.

Use your fraction pieces to find a fraction that is equivalent to $\frac{1}{3}$. Then find one equivalent to $\frac{1}{4}$.

C. Here are several fractions that are equivalent to $\frac{1}{5}$.

$$\frac{1}{5} \qquad \frac{2}{10} \qquad \frac{3}{15} \qquad \frac{4}{20} \qquad \frac{5}{25}$$

Thinking as a Team

1. Can you see a pattern? Describe it to your team. Use the pattern to name 2 more fractions equivalent to $\frac{1}{5}$.

2. Write a rule for finding fractions equivalent to any given fraction.

3. Write a fraction. Challenge the other members of your team to find equivalent fractions by using their rules.

4. Use what you have discovered to solve this problem.

Jerry, Alice, and Ted are having an argument. They are looking at this case of fruit juice. Some of the bottles are empty. The rest are full.

Jerry says that $\frac{1}{4}$ of the bottles are empty.

Alice says that $\frac{3}{8}$ of the bottles are empty.

Ted says that $\frac{1}{3}$ of the bottles are empty.

Who is correct? Why?

More Equivalent Fractions

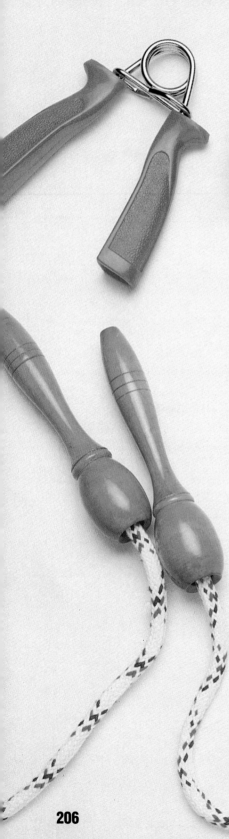

A. In Betty's Bookshop, 6 of every 10 health books are about physical fitness. How many fifths is this?

To find how many fifths are equivalent to $\frac{6}{10}$, you divide the numerator and the denominator by the same number.

$\frac{6}{10} = \frac{\blacksquare}{5}$ Think: $10 \div 5 = \blacksquare$.   **So,** $\frac{6}{10} = \frac{6 \div 2}{10 \div 2} = \frac{3}{5}$.

$10 \div 5 = 2$

Another example:

$\frac{4}{12} = \frac{1}{\blacksquare}$ Think: $4 \div 1 = \blacksquare$.   So, $\frac{4}{12} = \frac{4 \div 4}{12 \div 4} = \frac{1}{3}$.

$4 \div 1 = 4$

B. Sometimes you can continue dividing to find other equivalent fractions.

$\frac{8}{12} = \frac{8 \div 2}{12 \div 2} = \frac{4}{6}$ $\frac{4}{6} = \frac{4 \div 2}{6 \div 2} = \frac{2}{3}$ | 2 and 3 cannot be divided by a common factor other than 1.

$\frac{2}{3}$ is a fraction in **simplest form**. Its numerator and its denominator have no common factor greater than 1.

Checkpoint   Write the letter of the correct answer.

1. Find the fraction that is equivalent to $\frac{10}{12}$.

   a. 2   **b.** $\frac{5}{12}$ **c.** $\frac{5}{6}$ **d.** $\frac{8}{10}$

2. What is $\frac{16}{32}$ in simplest form?

   a. $\frac{2}{32}$ **b.** $\frac{8}{16}$ **c.** $\frac{1}{2}$ **d.** 2

Copy and complete.

1. $\frac{4}{8} = \frac{4 \div 4}{8 \div 4} = \blacksquare$

2. $\frac{12}{18} = \frac{12 \div 6}{18 \div 6} = \blacksquare$

3. $\frac{8}{20} = \frac{8 \div 4}{20 \div 4} = \blacksquare$

Write the equivalent fraction for each. Use models to check your work.

4. $\frac{6}{10} = \frac{\blacksquare}{5}$

5. $\frac{4}{6} = \frac{\blacksquare}{3}$

6. $\frac{6}{8} = \frac{\blacksquare}{4}$

7. $\frac{14}{18} = \frac{\blacksquare}{9}$

8. $\frac{15}{20} = \frac{3}{\blacksquare}$

9. $\frac{3}{9} = \frac{1}{\blacksquare}$

10. $\frac{12}{16} = \frac{3}{\blacksquare}$

11. $\frac{18}{20} = \frac{9}{\blacksquare}$

Is each fraction in simplest form? Write *yes* or *no*.

12. $\frac{6}{10}$

13. $\frac{3}{4}$

14. $\frac{5}{6}$

15. $\frac{2}{8}$

16. $\frac{4}{12}$

17. $\frac{1}{2}$

18. $\frac{1}{5}$

Write each fraction in simplest form.

19. $\frac{3}{6}$

20. $\frac{4}{10}$

21. $\frac{12}{20}$

22. $\frac{3}{9}$

23. $\frac{5}{10}$

24. $\frac{2}{6}$

25. $\frac{4}{8}$

26. $\frac{10}{22}$

27. $\frac{8}{16}$

28. $\frac{8}{10}$

29. $\frac{14}{20}$

30. $\frac{15}{25}$

31. $\frac{8}{14}$

32. $\frac{12}{15}$

Solve.

33. This morning in Betty's Bookshop, 9 out of 12 customers bought books. Write this as a fraction in simplest form.

★34. Of 25 books about nutrition in the bookshop, 10 are vegetable cookbooks and 5 are fish cookbooks. In simplest form, what fraction of the nutrition books are cookbooks?

NUMBER SENSE

If the numerator and the denominator of a fraction less than one are very different in value, the fraction is closer to 0 than to 1.
Example: $\frac{3}{21}$ is closer to 0.

If the numerator and the denominator of a fraction are about the same value, the fraction is closer to 1 than to 0.
Example: $\frac{9}{11}$ is closer to 1.

Write whether each fraction is *closer to 0* or *closer to 1*.

1. $\frac{1}{7}$

2. $\frac{7}{8}$

3. $\frac{5}{6}$

4. $\frac{3}{4}$

5. $\frac{8}{11}$

6. $\frac{1}{10}$

7. $\frac{3}{12}$

PROBLEM SOLVING
Using a Circle Graph

A circle graph shows how a total amount is divided into parts. This circle graph shows all the ingredients that there are in a breakfast cereal called Nature Flakes. The amount of each ingredient is shown by the size of its section of the circle graph.

Use the circle graph to answer this question.

What is the main ingredient in Nature Flakes?

INGREDIENTS IN NATURE FLAKES

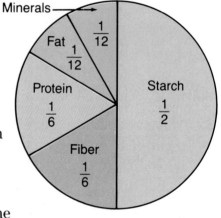

- The title tells you that this graph shows the ingredients in Nature Flakes cereal.

- Count the number of sections. There are 5 ingredients in Nature Flakes.

- Look at the size of each section. The largest section is starch. Starch is the main ingredient in Nature Flakes.

Use the circle graph to answer each question. Write the letter of the correct answer.

1. What fraction of Nature Flakes is starch?

    a. $\frac{1}{2}$ **b.** $\frac{1}{3}$ **c.** $\frac{1}{4}$

2. Which is not an ingredient in Nature Flakes?

    a. fiber   **b.** salt   **c.** minerals

3. Of which ingredient listed below does Nature Flakes contain the smallest amount?

    a. fiber   **b.** protein   **c.** minerals

4. If Eric eats 6 oz of Nature Flakes, how many ounces of protein does he eat?

    a. 1 oz   **b.** 6 oz   **c.** 36 oz

Circle graphs can also be used to compare information. Use the circle graphs on pages 208 and 209 to answer each question on this page.

INGREDIENTS IN FRUIT SHOTS CEREAL

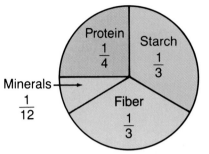

5. How many ingredients are there in Fruit Shots?

6. What fraction of Fruit Shots is starch?

7. Which ingredient makes up the same fraction in both Fruit Shots and Nature Flakes?

8. Which ingredient is found in Nature Flakes but not in Fruit Shots?

9. If you want to add more fiber to your diet, which cereal would you choose?

10. Which cereal would have more protein in a 1-ounce serving? in a 2-ounce serving?

11. How many minerals does each cereal contain?

12. If you prefer a cereal that has a high protein and mineral content, would you choose Nature Flakes or Fruit Shots?

★13. If the makers of Nature Flakes replaced $\frac{1}{2}$ of the cereal's fat with protein, what would be the main ingredient of Nature Flakes?

Mixed Numbers

A. Becky is making bran muffins for the school health fair. She fills 6 of the 6 cups of her muffin tin with batter. What part of the muffin tin does she fill with batter?

Becky filled $\frac{6}{6}$ of her muffin tin with batter.

You can write $\frac{6}{6}$ as a whole number. You divide the numerator by the denominator.

$6\overline{)6}$ with quotient 1 **So, $\frac{6}{6} = 1$.**

B. How many sixths are filled?

1                             $\frac{4}{6}$

$\frac{10}{6}$, or $1\frac{4}{6}$ are filled.

A **mixed number** is made up of a whole number and a fraction. You can rename $\frac{10}{6}$ with a mixed number by dividing.

Divide the numerator by the denominator.	Write the quotient as a whole number.	Write the remainder as a fraction in simplest form.
$\frac{10}{6} \longrightarrow 6\overline{)10}$ with quotient $1\text{ R}4$	1	remainder $\longrightarrow$ $\frac{4}{6} = \frac{2}{3}$ So, $1\frac{4}{6} = 1\frac{2}{3}$.

Checkpoint   Write the letter of the correct answer.

What is the whole number or the mixed number?

1. $\frac{4}{3}$ **a.** $\frac{1}{3}$ **b.** 1   **c.** $1\frac{1}{3}$ **d.** $1\frac{4}{3}$ **2.** $\frac{5}{4}$ **a.** $\frac{1}{4}$ **b.** 1   **c.** $1\frac{1}{4}$ **d.** $1\frac{5}{4}$

3. $\frac{12}{4}$ **a.** $\frac{1}{3}$ **b.** 12   **c.** $\frac{3}{4}$ **d.** 3

Write a whole number or a mixed number in simplest
form for each shaded part.

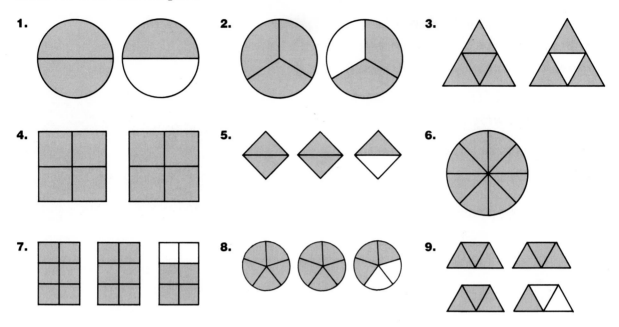

1. **2.** **3.**

4. **5.** **6.**

7. **8.** **9.**

Write a whole number or a mixed number for each
fraction.

10. $\frac{9}{3}$ **11.** $\frac{18}{9}$ **12.** $\frac{8}{5}$ **13.** $\frac{10}{10}$ **14.** $\frac{3}{2}$ **15.** $\frac{10}{5}$ **16.** $\frac{7}{6}$

17. $\frac{8}{8}$ **18.** $\frac{11}{7}$ **19.** $\frac{15}{9}$ **20.** $\frac{8}{4}$ **21.** $\frac{5}{5}$ **22.** $\frac{12}{8}$ **23.** $\frac{8}{3}$

24. $\frac{9}{6}$ **25.** $\frac{12}{10}$ **26.** $\frac{10}{8}$ **27.** $\frac{13}{3}$ **28.** $\frac{14}{6}$ **29.** $\frac{6}{4}$ **30.** $\frac{19}{7}$

Solve.

31. Martin spent $\frac{8}{6}$ hours at the school
health fair on Tuesday. Write this
as a mixed number in simplest
form.

★32. Jane brought 6 spinach pies to the
fair. She cut them into 8 pieces
each. At the end of the day, 16
pieces were left. How many pies
were eaten?

ANOTHER LOOK

Multiply.

1. 3,765
   $\times$ 8

2. 1,095
   $\times$ 4

3. 6,360
   $\times$ 6

4. 8,433
   $\times$ 7

5. 2,775
   $\times$ 9

Comparing Fractions and Mixed Numbers

A. Every day, Sarah exercises for $\frac{3}{4}$ hour. Joan exercises for $\frac{1}{4}$ hour. Who exercises for the longer time?

To find who exercises for the longer time, you can compare $\frac{3}{4}$ and $\frac{1}{4}$.

You can compare the fractions on a number line.

$$\overset{\longleftrightarrow}{\underset{0 \quad \frac{1}{4} \quad \frac{2}{4} \quad \frac{3}{4} \quad 1}{\bullet \quad \bullet \quad \bullet \quad \bullet \quad \bullet}}$$

$\frac{3}{4}$ is to the right of $\frac{1}{4}$. So, $\frac{3}{4} > \frac{1}{4}$.

Since $\frac{3}{4}$ and $\frac{1}{4}$ have like denominators, you can compare the numerators.

$$\frac{3}{4} \bullet \frac{1}{4} \qquad \text{Compare the numerators.} \qquad \text{So, } \frac{3}{4} > \frac{1}{4}.$$
$$3 > 1$$

Sarah exercises for the longer time.

B. When you compare mixed numbers, compare the whole numbers first. Compare $3\frac{1}{2}$ and $3\frac{3}{4}$.

Compare the whole numbers.	Check the denominators.	Rename as equivalent fractions.	Compare the numerators.
$3\frac{1}{2}$ $\boxed{3 = 3}$ $3\frac{3}{4}$	$3\frac{1}{2}$ $\boxed{\text{The denominators are unlike.}}$ $3\frac{3}{4}$	$\frac{1}{2} = \frac{1 \times 2}{2 \times 2} = \frac{2}{4}$ $\frac{3}{4}$	$3\frac{2}{4} \bullet 3\frac{3}{4}$ $3\frac{2}{4} < 3\frac{3}{4}$ So, $3\frac{1}{2} < 3\frac{3}{4}$.

Other examples:

$$1\frac{2}{3} \bullet 2\frac{1}{3} \qquad\qquad \frac{5}{6} \bullet \frac{2}{3} \qquad \boxed{\frac{2}{3} = \frac{2 \times 2}{3 \times 2} = \frac{4}{6}}$$
$$1 < 2 \qquad\qquad\qquad \frac{5}{6} > \frac{4}{6}$$
$$\text{So, } 1\frac{2}{3} < 2\frac{1}{3}. \qquad \text{So, } \frac{5}{6} > \frac{2}{3}.$$

Compare. Write >, <, or = for ⬤. Use models to check your work.

1. $\frac{1}{3}$ ⬤ $\frac{2}{3}$ **2.** $\frac{4}{5}$ ⬤ $\frac{3}{5}$ **3.** $\frac{3}{8}$ ⬤ $\frac{5}{8}$ **4.** $\frac{7}{10}$ ⬤ $\frac{7}{10}$ **5.** $\frac{3}{4}$ ⬤ $\frac{2}{4}$

6. $2\frac{3}{4}$ ⬤ $2\frac{2}{4}$ **7.** $4\frac{1}{8}$ ⬤ $4\frac{2}{8}$ **8.** $1\frac{3}{5}$ ⬤ $1\frac{3}{5}$ **9.** $2\frac{3}{6}$ ⬤ $2\frac{5}{6}$ **10.** $2\frac{7}{10}$ ⬤ $3\frac{6}{10}$

11. $\frac{3}{4}$ ⬤ $\frac{1}{2}$ **12.** $\frac{1}{2}$ ⬤ $\frac{3}{8}$ **13.** $\frac{3}{4}$ ⬤ $\frac{7}{8}$ **14.** $\frac{2}{3}$ ⬤ $\frac{9}{12}$ **15.** $\frac{3}{15}$ ⬤ $\frac{1}{5}$

16. $2\frac{2}{9}$ ⬤ $2\frac{1}{3}$ **17.** $8\frac{1}{8}$ ⬤ $8\frac{1}{4}$ **18.** $3\frac{1}{2}$ ⬤ $3\frac{4}{8}$ **19.** $6\frac{5}{8}$ ⬤ $5\frac{2}{4}$ **20.** $4\frac{1}{16}$ ⬤ $6\frac{7}{8}$

21. $1\frac{2}{8}$ ⬤ $1\frac{1}{4}$ **22.** $\frac{7}{9}$ ⬤ $\frac{2}{3}$ **23.** $\frac{5}{10}$ ⬤ $\frac{1}{2}$ **24.** $4\frac{1}{3}$ ⬤ $3\frac{2}{6}$ **25.** $\frac{9}{2}$ ⬤ $\frac{18}{4}$

26. $\frac{2}{6}$ ⬤ $\frac{5}{6}$ **27.** $9\frac{7}{8}$ ⬤ $9\frac{6}{8}$ **28.** $\frac{1}{2}$ ⬤ $\frac{3}{8}$ **★29.** $2\frac{3}{5}$ ⬤ $\frac{13}{10}$ **★30.** $5\frac{1}{2}$ ⬤ $\frac{21}{4}$

Solve.

31. Whitney can swim $\frac{5}{8}$ of the length of the pool underwater. Joy can swim $\frac{7}{8}$ of the length of the pool underwater. Who can swim the greater distance underwater?

★32. On a hike, Rosy walks $\frac{1}{2}$ mile, Ted walks $\frac{5}{10}$ mile, and Kay walks $\frac{3}{4}$ mile. Who walks the greatest distance?

MIDCHAPTER REVIEW

Find the part of each set.

1. $\frac{1}{4}$ of 16 **2.** $\frac{3}{6}$ of 18 **3.** $\frac{2}{3}$ of 21 **4.** $\frac{5}{10}$ of 20

Find the equivalent fraction.

5. $\frac{1}{5} = \frac{■}{10}$ **6.** $\frac{7}{8} = \frac{14}{■}$ **7.** $\frac{6}{9} = \frac{■}{3}$ **8.** $\frac{8}{18} = \frac{4}{■}$ **9.** $\frac{3}{12} = \frac{1}{■}$

Write each in simplest form.

10. $\frac{4}{6}$ **11.** $\frac{6}{9}$ **12.** $\frac{22}{33}$ **13.** $\frac{18}{21}$ **14.** $\frac{2}{14}$ **15.** $\frac{5}{20}$

Write a whole number or a mixed number for each.

16. $\frac{10}{2}$ **17.** $\frac{27}{5}$ **18.** $\frac{16}{4}$ **19.** $\frac{20}{6}$ **20.** $\frac{32}{16}$ **21.** $\frac{13}{9}$

PROBLEM SOLVING
Working Backward

Sometimes you have to work backward in order to solve a problem.

Denise, Greta, and Gina are on a bowling team. Denise scored 18 points more than Greta. Greta scored 5 points less than Gina. Gina scored 83 points. How many points did Denise score? How many points did Greta score?

Draw a flowchart. Work backward to solve the problem.

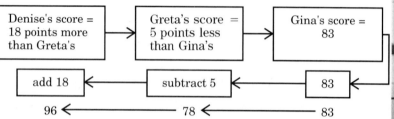

Denise scored 96 points and Greta scored 78 points.

Work backward to solve each problem.

1. Donna plans to enter the Triathlon competition. Each week she swims, runs, and bikes to prepare for the competition. She swims 2 hours more than she runs. She runs 1 hour more than she bikes. She bikes 2 hours a week.
   a. How many hours does she run each week?
   b. How many hours does she swim each week?

2. Gene bought a new jogging outfit. The shirt cost $2.10 less than the pants. The pants cost $8.79 more than the matching headband. The headband cost $3.99.
   a. What was the cost of the pants?
   b. What was the cost of the shirt?

3. John, Rick, and Billy are brothers. John weighs 3 times as much as Rick. Rick weighs $\frac{1}{2}$ as much as Billy. Billy weighs 40 pounds.
   a. How many pounds does Rick weigh?
   b. How many pounds does John weigh?

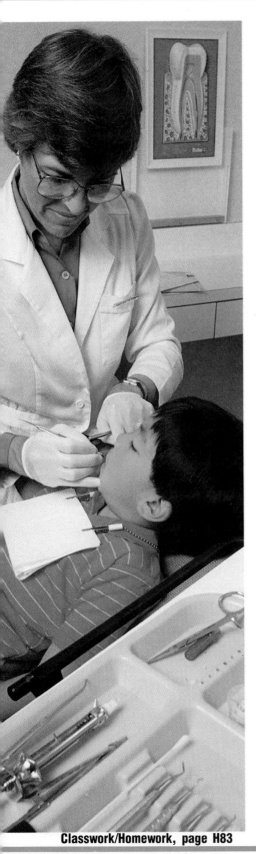

4. Lars bought a pair of running shoes, a package of socks, and a cap at the sports shop. The running shoes cost $23.00 more than the cap, which was $2.70 more than the socks. The socks cost $4.25.
   a. What was the cost of the cap?
   b. What was the cost of the running shoes?

5. Mrs. Miller bought an exercise video, a book on nutrition, and a health magazine. The price of the video was 3 times the price of the book. The price of the book was 5 times the price of the magazine. The price of the magazine was $1.95.
   a. What was the price of the book?
   b. What was the price of the video?

6. Jim's dentist told him he was eating too many sweets. So, instead of buying sweets, Jim bought an apple, milk, and a sandwich for lunch. The milk was $\frac{1}{4}$ the cost of the sandwich. The sandwich cost $1.20. Jim spent a total of $1.85.
   a. How much did the milk cost?
   b. How much did the apple cost?

7. The bowling team uses balls in three different weights. The medium-weight ball is $\frac{2}{3}$ the weight of the heaviest ball. The heaviest ball is 9 times heavier than the lightest ball. The lightest ball weighs 6 pounds.
   a. How much does the heaviest ball weigh?
   b. How much does the medium-weight ball weigh?

8. Mimi swims laps at the pool for exercise. She swam three times last week. The first time, she swam $\frac{1}{2}$ as many laps as the second time. The second time, she swam $\frac{4}{5}$ as many laps as the third time. She swam 15 laps the third time.
   a. How many laps did she swim the second time?
   b. How many laps did she swim the first time?

Probability

A. Liza is planting a garden. She has 2 packets of seeds in a bag. 1 packet contains lettuce seeds, the other packet contains carrot seeds. Without looking, Liza picks 1 packet. What is the probability that she will pick the packet of carrot seeds?

There is 1 chance out of 2 that she will pick the packet of carrot seeds.

You can show **probability** as a fraction.

$$\frac{1}{2} \quad \substack{\longleftarrow \textbf{ packet of carrot seeds} \\ \longleftarrow \textbf{ packets in the bag}}$$

The probability that Liza will pick the packet of carrot seeds is 1 out of 2, or $\frac{1}{2}$.

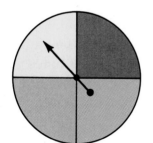

B. What is the probability that this spinner will land on red?

There are 4 colors on the spinner.
It is **equally likely** that the spinner will land on any one of the colors.
The probability of landing on red is 1 out of 4, or $\frac{1}{4}$.

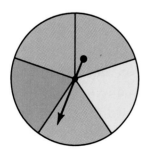

C. What is the probability that this spinner will land on green?

$$\frac{3}{5} \quad \substack{\longleftarrow \textbf{ green sections} \\ \longleftarrow \textbf{ total number of sections}}$$

3 parts of the spinner are green. 1 part of the spinner is yellow. 1 part of the spinner is blue. The outcomes are **not equally likely.**

Suppose you spin the spinner.
What is the probability of landing on

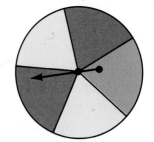

1. red?   **2.** blue?   **3.** yellow?

★**4.** red or yellow?   ★**5.** red or blue?   ★**6.** any color?

What is the probability of picking

7. a black marble?   **8.** a yellow marble?

9. a blue marble?   **10.** an orange marble?

★**11.** an orange or black marble?   ★**12.** any color but blue?

Solve.

Liza has a box filled with seeds for her vegetable garden. Suppose she picks 1 packet of seeds without looking. What is the probability that she will select

13. lettuce?   **14.** squash?

15. tomatoes?   ★**16.** corn or squash?

★**17.** a vegetable beginning with the letter *C*?

Seeds	Number of packets
Cabbage	3
Carrots	1
Corn	4
Lettuce	2
Squash	1
Tomatoes	2

CHALLENGE

There are always 100 names entered in the raffle. Chuck entered his name one time; so, his chances of winning were 1 in 100, or $\frac{1}{100}$.

How many times would he have to enter his name in the raffle to increase his chances of winning to

1. $\frac{1}{25}$?   **2.** $\frac{1}{10}$?   **3.** $\frac{1}{5}$?   **4.** $\frac{1}{4}$?

More Probability

A. Rita could not decide which category to enter in her school's Fitness Day. She wrote the names of the 7 events on a slip of paper; then she put all the slips in a jar. Predict the category it is most likely she will pick.

To make a prediction, you need to compare the probabilities for each category.

Swimming has 2 events, the backstroke and the crawl. The probability of Rita picking a swimming event is $\frac{2}{7}$.

Running has 4 events; so, the probability of her picking a running event is $\frac{4}{7}$.

Throwing has 1 event; so, the probability of her picking a throwing event is $\frac{1}{7}$.

$\frac{4}{7} > \frac{2}{7}$ and $\frac{4}{7} > \frac{1}{7}$

So, you can predict that it is most likely Rita will pick a running event.

B. The other 21 students in Rita's class decide to pick their category in the same way that Rita did. Rita predicts that most of them will pick a running event. She keeps a tally to see if her prediction is correct.

Category	Tally	Total
Swimming	IIII	5
Running	IIII IIII IIII	14
Throwing	II	2

Think: IIII equals 5.

A **tally** is a way to record data.

$14 > 5$ and $14 > 2$

So, Rita's prediction is correct.

FITNESS DAY EVENTS

Category	Event
Swimming	backstroke crawl
Running	50-m dash 100-m dash 440-m race 10-km run
Throwing	50-m throw

Solve. For Problem 4, use the Infobank.

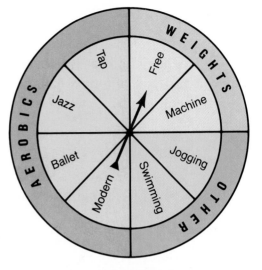

1. Paulo joined the fitness club at his school. The club offers different kinds of exercise programs. To choose a program, Paulo writes each kind of program on a spinner. Predict the kind of program on which the spinner is most likely to stop.

2. Paulo talked 10 of his friends into joining the fitness club. Each of his friends chooses a program the same way Paulo did. Paulo predicted that most of his friends would join one of the aerobics programs. He kept a tally of their choices. Complete the table to find out whether Paulo's prediction was correct.

Program	Tally	Total
Aerobics	卌 I	
Weights	III	
Other	I	

3. Jan likes to vary the kind of exercises she does each day. She gives each kind of exercise a number between 1 and 6. She rolls a number cube to choose which kind of exercise she will do. Predict the kind of exercise Jan is most likely to do.

★4. Use the information on page 404 to solve. Deana predicted that at least 50 new members would join her health club in one week. Was her prediction correct?

Exercise	Number
Leg lifts	1
Knee bends	2
Running	3
Sit-ups	4
Touch toes	5
Push-ups	6

FOCUS: REASONING

It is more likely for a certain spinner to land on green than on red. It is less likely to land on blue than on red. The spinner is divided into 6 equal sections. Describe the spinner.

Ratio

A. Caleb teaches tennis at the local health club. Each day he brings 1 can of tennis balls with him. The can contains 3 tennis balls.

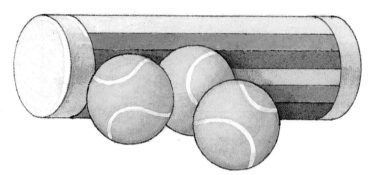

You can compare the number of tennis cans to tennis balls by using a **ratio.**

The ratio of the tennis can to tennis balls is 1 to 3.

You can write this as a fraction: $\frac{1}{3}$.

B. Caleb has a total of 12 tennis students: 5 boys and 7 girls. You can compare the number of boy students to the number of girl students.

> When you compare numbers in a ratio, be careful to write them in the correct order.

The ratio of boy students to girl students is 5 to 7, or $\frac{5}{7}$.

The ratio of girl students to boy students is 7 to 5, or $\frac{7}{5}$.

Checkpoint Write the letter of the correct answer.

Find the fraction for each ratio.

1. 4 to 9

a. $\frac{4}{9}$

b. $\frac{9}{4}$

c. 5

d. 13

2. 6 to 3

a. $\frac{1}{2}$

b. $\frac{3}{6}$

c. $\frac{6}{3}$

d. $\frac{2}{3}$

3. 1 to 3

a. $\frac{1}{3}$

b. $\frac{3}{1}$

c. 3

d. 2

Write the fraction to show each ratio.

1. 4 tennis balls to 2 tennis rackets

2. 3 children to 1 adult

3. 2 tennis players to 1 tennis net

4. 1 baseball to 5 bats

5. 3 hockey sticks to 6 skates

6. 11 football players to 1 football

7. 4 bowling balls to 6 bowlers

8. 6 badminton rackets to 3 birdies

9. 9 billiard balls to 2 billiard cues

10. 7 to 12

11. 4 to 9

12. 3 to 2

13. 5 to 4

14. 8 to 6

15. 15 to 1

16. 6 to 8

17. 10 to 10

Solve.

18. Yuri did 12 push-ups and 15 sit-ups before playing a game of tennis. What is the ratio of push-ups to sit-ups?

★19. In a tennis game, Gina had 9 good serves and 5 serves that were out of bounds. What is the ratio of good serves to all the serves?

CHALLENGE

Choose one of the following three projects. Use a tally to record the information. Then write a fraction showing the ratio of the first category to the second category.

1. The number of times your favorite baseball player was up at bat in one week; the number of hits he made

2. The number of meals you eat in one day; the number of meals you eat in one week

3. The number of people you see jogging in one week; the number of people you see riding bicycles in one week

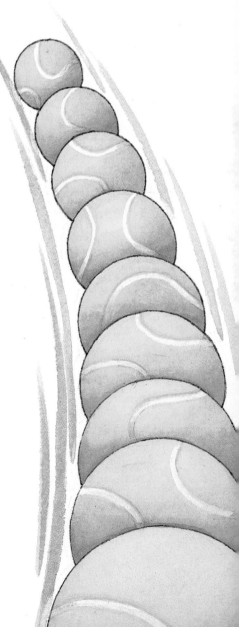

PROBLEM SOLVING
Making a Diagram

Making a diagram can help you solve certain problems. One kind of diagram is a tree diagram. A tree diagram looks like the branches of a tree.

> The fourth grade at the Edison School is planning a field day. The students decide that they will wear shorts and shirts in their school colors. The Edison School colors are red, yellow, and green. How many color combinations of shorts and shirts can each student make?

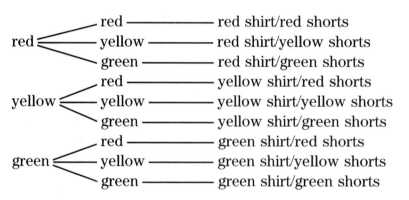

Shirt color   Shorts color   Combinations

red
- red ——————— red shirt/red shorts
- yellow ——————— red shirt/yellow shorts
- green ——————— red shirt/green shorts

yellow
- red ——————— yellow shirt/red shorts
- yellow ——————— yellow shirt/yellow shorts
- green ——————— yellow shirt/green shorts

green
- red ——————— green shirt/red shorts
- yellow ——————— green shirt/yellow shorts
- green ——————— green shirt/green shorts

Each student can make 9 color combinations of shirts and shorts.

Another way to find the number of possible color combinations is to multiply the number of shirt colors by the number of shorts colors.

shirt colors   short colors   combinations
$$3 \times 3 = 9$$

How many choices would each student have if Edison School had only 2 school colors? $2 \times 2 = 4$ choices

How many choices would each student have if Edison School had 4 school colors? $4 \times 4 = 16$ choices

Copy and complete each tree diagram.

1. Each member of a team plans to wear red, white, or blue socks and white or black sneakers. How many color combinations of sneakers and socks can each member of the team make?

Sneaker color   *Sock color*   *Combinations*
black —————— red ——— black sneaker/
                                     red socks

2. Frozen fruit ices will be served during field day. Strawberry ices and banana ices will be served. Each flavor can be bought in small, medium, or large cups. How many choices will each child have?

Flavor   *Size*   *Choices*
strawberry —— small ———— small strawberry ice

Make a tree diagram for each problem. Use the diagram to solve each problem.

3. Each team will carry a flag. The center circle of each flag is white, blue, orange, or black. The rest of the flag is red, yellow, or green. How many combinations of flag colors are there?

4. First-place, second-place, and third-place ribbons will be awarded in 5 different events. How many ribbons can each class win?

5. Each member of the winning class receives a T-shirt. The shirts come in red, yellow, or green. Names are imprinted in black or white. The shirt sizes are medium or large. How many possible combinations of shirt color and shirt size are there?

PROBLEM SOLVING
Choosing/Writing a Sensible Question

Asking the right questions can help you organize information and make good decisions.

The students at Sudley School are planning a Health Fair. They want to serve a dinner at which nutritious and healthful foods will be served. The students know that tickets have to be sold. They also know they will have to pay for the food they serve. They want to raise enough money so that they can make a donation to the school library.

The students have to decide how much to charge for each ticket. Which of these questions will help them decide on a ticket price?

- What is the date of the dinner?
  It is not important to know the date. It will not change the price of the ticket.

- How much will it cost to feed each person?
  Figuring out how much it will cost to feed each person is very important. The students have to set a ticket price that will cover the cost of the food and the library donation.

- How many tickets can they sell?
  Figuring out how many tickets they can sell is also important. If they cannot sell enough tickets to make the profit they need, their plan will not suceed.

- What are the names of the people who have agreed to buy tickets?
  It is not important to know the names of the ticket buyers. This information will not change the price.

Read each statement. For each statement, write two questions that the committee should answer before making a decision.

1. The students have to plan the meal. They have to decide which foods to serve.

2. The students have to decide when to have the dinner.

3. The students have to be sure that enough people can help make and serve the dinner.

4. The students have to decide how to advertise the dinner.

5. The students have to decide where to have the tickets printed.

6. The students have to decide how to keep track of ticket sales.

7. The students have selected the meal. Now they must decide how to obtain the things they need in order to make the dinner.

8. The students want to have music and a show during the dinner.

9. The students have to see to it that everything is cleaned afterward.

10. The students want to be sure that their donation is large enough to buy something the library really needs.

★11. The students want to think about other ways of raising money for the library. They want to decide whether the dinner is the best choice.

MATH COMMUNICATION

Look at the symbols below.

Symbols such as a stop sign, a dollar sign, and a gasoline sign give people needed information. Symbols also save space. We use symbols in math every day. Look at the symbols below. Write the meaning of each symbol.

1. ÷

2. ×

3. >

4. +

5. <

6. =

Rewrite the following examples. Fill in each missing symbol.

7. 3 ▧ 7 ▧ 3 = 63

8. 4 ▧ 7 ▧ 3 = 14

9. 235 ▧ 672

10. 600 × 6 ▧ 3,600

Use symbols to write a number sentence for each problem. Then solve the problem.

11. Lydia is a gymnast. After 7 days, she had practiced for a total of 21 hours in the gym. She spent the same amount of time practicing each day. For how many hours did she practice per day?

12. The city swimming team had 48 members. During the year, 22 new members joined. How many people are there on the team now?

13. At one meet, each diver made 8 dives. There were 14 divers. How many dives were made?

14. Teddy spent $4.98 on sport socks and $2.50 on a sweatband. How much did he spend in all?

GROUP PROJECT

To Have or Not To Have

The problem: Some of us have green eyes; others have blue eyes or brown eyes. Such traits as eye color and foot size differ from person to person. Here are some other traits that differ.

the shape of your ears

Earlobes attached

Earlobes free

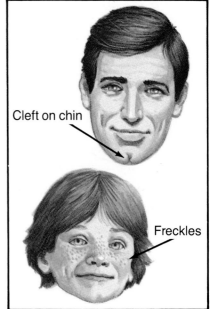

Cleft on chin

Freckles

Take a survey of the class. See the traits that each of you has. Make a chart like this one.

	Trait	Cheek dimples	Dimple or cleft on chin	Earlobes free	Can roll tongue
N	Brian	yes	no	yes	yes
A	Seth	no	no	yes	yes
M	Andrea	no	no	yes	yes
E	Leila	yes	no	yes	no
	Total	2	0	4	3

Here are some traits you might want to use for your chart.

- cheek dimples (seen when smiling)
- a dimple or cleft in the chin
- free or attached earlobes
- the ability to wiggle the ears
- straight, wavy, or curly hair
- blonde, red, brown, or black hair
- left-handedness or right-handedness
- freckles

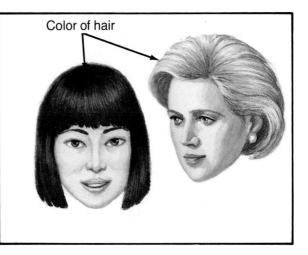

Color of hair

CHAPTER TEST

Write a fraction for the shaded or circled part. (pages 198 and 200)

1. **2.** **3.**

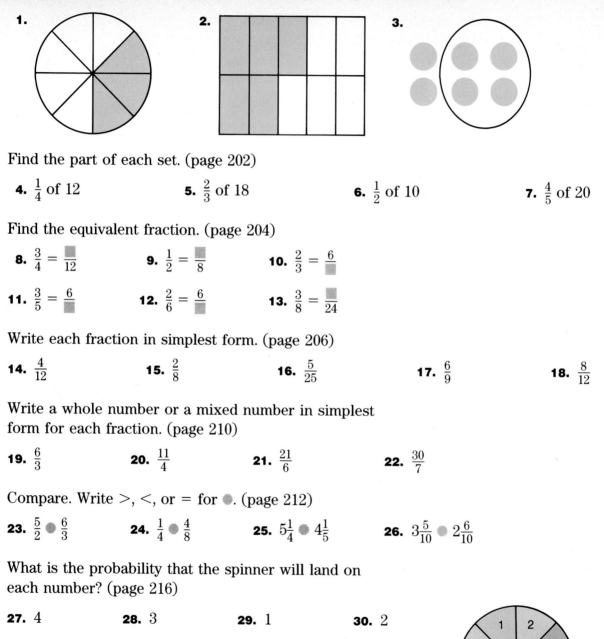

Find the part of each set. (page 202)

4. $\frac{1}{4}$ of 12 **5.** $\frac{2}{3}$ of 18 **6.** $\frac{1}{2}$ of 10 **7.** $\frac{4}{5}$ of 20

Find the equivalent fraction. (page 204)

8. $\frac{3}{4} = \frac{\blacksquare}{12}$ **9.** $\frac{1}{2} = \frac{\blacksquare}{8}$ **10.** $\frac{2}{3} = \frac{6}{\blacksquare}$

11. $\frac{3}{5} = \frac{6}{\blacksquare}$ **12.** $\frac{2}{6} = \frac{6}{\blacksquare}$ **13.** $\frac{3}{8} = \frac{\blacksquare}{24}$

Write each fraction in simplest form. (page 206)

14. $\frac{4}{12}$ **15.** $\frac{2}{8}$ **16.** $\frac{5}{25}$ **17.** $\frac{6}{9}$ **18.** $\frac{8}{12}$

Write a whole number or a mixed number in simplest form for each fraction. (page 210)

19. $\frac{6}{3}$ **20.** $\frac{11}{4}$ **21.** $\frac{21}{6}$ **22.** $\frac{30}{7}$

Compare. Write >, <, or = for ●. (page 212)

23. $\frac{5}{2}$ ● $\frac{6}{3}$ **24.** $\frac{1}{4}$ ● $\frac{4}{8}$ **25.** $5\frac{1}{4}$ ● $4\frac{1}{5}$ **26.** $3\frac{5}{10}$ ● $2\frac{6}{10}$

What is the probability that the spinner will land on each number? (page 216)

27. 4 **28.** 3 **29.** 1 **30.** 2

228

Solve. (page 208)

31. The circle graph shows the favorite health foods of Beth's class. Which is the most popular health food?

32. There are 24 students in Beth's class. How many students prefer raisins?

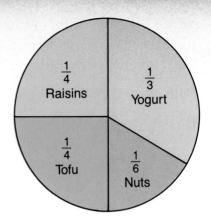

Choose the most sensible question. Write the letter of the correct answer. (page 224)

33. Jay wants to be physically fit. He decides to jog 21 miles per week. He wants to jog the same number of miles per day. There are 7 days in one week.

   a. How many weeks are there in one month?
   b. How many miles does he jog in 7 weeks?
   c. How many miles does he jog per day?

BONUS

There are 2 green marbles and 2 red marbles in a jar. The probability of picking a red or a green marble is $\frac{4}{4}$, or 1. An event with a probability of 1 is a *certain* event. The probability of picking a blue marble is $\frac{0}{4}$, or 0. An event with a probability of 0 is an *impossible* event.

Look at the letters in the word *IMPOSSIBLE*. If each letter were written on a card and the cards were turned down and mixed up, what would be the probability of picking

1. a vowel?   **2.** a consonant?   **3.** a *W*?   **4.** an *M* or a *B*?

5. a *T*?   **6.** a *C* or a *D*?   **7.** the ninth letter of the alphabet?

RETEACHING

A. To find a fraction of a number, first divide the number by the denominator. Then multiply the quotient by the numerator.

Find $\boxed{\frac{2}{3}}$ of 12.

Divide 12 by the denominator.	Multiply 4 by the numerator.
$12 \div 3 = 4$	$\boxed{2} \times 4 = 8$

So, $\frac{2}{3}$ of 12 = 8.

Find the part of each set.

1. $\frac{3}{4}$ of 12
2. $\frac{2}{5}$ of 10
3. $\frac{5}{6}$ of 12
4. $\frac{1}{2}$ of 8
5. $\frac{2}{3}$ of 6

6. $\frac{1}{5}$ of 15
7. $\frac{2}{3}$ of 9
8. $\frac{3}{4}$ of 16
9. $\frac{3}{8}$ of 24
10. $\frac{1}{4}$ of 20

11. $\frac{3}{5}$ of 20
12. $\frac{1}{8}$ of 32
13. $\frac{4}{5}$ of 25
14. $\frac{2}{7}$ of 14
15. $\frac{9}{10}$ of 20

16. $\frac{5}{8}$ of 24
17. $\frac{2}{3}$ of 18
18. $\frac{1}{6}$ of 18
19. $\frac{7}{8}$ of 8
20. $\frac{3}{7}$ of 21

B. If the numerator and the denominator of a fraction have no common factor greater than 1, the fraction is in **simplest form.**

Find the simplest form of $\frac{9}{12}$.

$\frac{9}{12} = \frac{9 \div 3}{12 \div 3} = \frac{3}{4}$ | 3 and 4 have no common factor greater than 1. |

Is each fraction in simplest form? Write *yes*, or write in simplest form.

21. $\frac{1}{2}$
22. $\frac{6}{8}$
23. $\frac{4}{12}$
24. $\frac{5}{6}$
25. $\frac{2}{3}$
26. $\frac{4}{8}$
27. $\frac{2}{6}$

28. $\frac{3}{9}$
29. $\frac{1}{2}$
30. $\frac{5}{10}$
31. $\frac{5}{8}$
32. $\frac{3}{7}$
33. $\frac{6}{9}$
34. $\frac{6}{10}$

ENRICHMENT

United States Time Zones

The continental United States is divided into four time zones. The clocks tell you what time it is in each zone when it is 12:00 noon Pacific time.

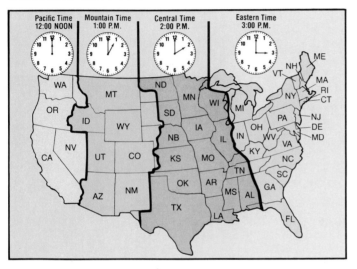

Solve.

How many hours difference is there between

1. Pacific time and Eastern time?

2. Mountain time and Central time?

3. If you live in Colorado and want to reach someone in Oklahoma by phone at 12:15 P.M. Central time, what time will it be in Colorado when you call?

4. If you live in Maine and want to reach someone in Illinois at 6:00 P.M. Central time, what time will it be in Maine when you call?

5. If you leave Vermont at 4:00 P.M. Eastern time and arrive in Oregon at 6:45 P.M. Pacific time, how long will the trip take?

6. It takes 7 hours to fly from New Jersey to Seattle, Washington. If you leave New Jersey at 12:00 noon Eastern time, what time will it be when you arrive in Washington?

★7. If you leave Kansas at 3:00 P.M. Central time and arrive in New Mexico at 2:50 P.M. Mountain time, how long did the trip take?

TECHNOLOGY

In BASIC, you can use parentheses to tell the computer the order in which to do operations.

1. Add parentheses to this program. When this program is RUN, the equations should be correct.

   10 PRINT "6 + 2 IS"
   20 PRINT 40 / 7 − 2
   30 PRINT "13 − 5 IS"
   40 PRINT 2 + 2 * 2

   Here is a short program.

   10 PRINT "THE AIR"
   20 PRINT "IS COLD"

2. Change one line so that this program prints this.

   THE WATER
   IS COLD

   Which line did you change?

3. Add a line so that this program will print this.

   THE WATER
   IN THE TUB
   IS COLD

   Which line did you add?

4. Copy the whole program.
   (HINT: Line 20 should still be 20 PRINT "IS COLD".)

5. Write a program that prints:

   14 DIVIDED BY 2 IS
   7

   One PRINT statement should use quotation marks; the other should not.

Here is a new program.

```
10 LET A = 15
20 PRINT A
```

When this program is RUN, it will print the number 15 on the screen. The LET statement in line 10 stores the number 15 in a **variable** called A. Variables are places in which the computer can store numbers. But you can't see the variables in the computer's memory or what's in them. If you want to see what is in variable A, you have to tell the computer to print it. That's what line 20 does.

Use the LET statement to store a number in a variable.
Use the PRINT statement to show the value of a variable.

6. Rewrite line 10 to store 12 in variable A.

Variable A is only one of many variables that you can use to store numbers in your program. You can make up your own variables. Here are some rules for naming variables.

The name of a variable can be a single letter.
A   S   N   X

The name of a variable can be any two letters.
NV   AB   XY

The name of a variable can be one letter and one number.
A2   V4   P1

But the name of a variable cannot start with a number.
5S   14   6T

7. Write the variables that you can use to store numbers.

A1	1A	P4	ZP	X
5	G5	6	1Y	HI
UR	R2	72	7A	LF

8. Write a program that stores the number 20 in the variable N, then prints out the value of N.

CUMULATIVE REVIEW

Write the letter of the correct answer.

1. $65 \div 8$

   a. 7 R9   **b.** 8

   c. 8 R1   **d.** not given

2. $8\overline{)428}$

   a. 52 R12   **b.** 53

   c. 53 R4   **d.** not given

3. $367 \div 3$

   a. 122   **b.** 122 R1

   c. 123   **d.** not given

4. $7\overline{)4,491}$

   a. 64 R1   **b.** 639 R18

   c. 641   **d.** not given

5. Find the average of 913, 152, and 489.

   a. 489   **b.** 518

   c. 1,554   **d.** not given

6. $\$13.26 \div 3$

   a. \$4.02   **b.** \$4.40 R6

   c. \$4.42   **d.** not given

7. $8 \times \$0.76$

   a. \$5.68   **b.** \$6.08

   c. \$56.48   **d.** not given

8. $6 \times 4,205$

   a. 24,200   **b.** 24,230

   c. 25,230   **d.** not given

9. Which are the common factors of 9 and 27?

   a. 1, 2, 3, 9

   b. 1, 3, 9

   c. 1, 3, 9, 27

   d. not given

10. $40 \div 8$

   a. 5

   b. 8

   c. 40

   d. not given

11. 8×3

   a. 5

   b. 24

   c. 83

   d. not given

12. $\begin{array}{r} 78 \\ + 99 \\ \hline \end{array}$

   a. 167

   b. 177

   c. 1,617

   d. not given

13. Fran earns \$4.75 per week on her paper route. Estimate how much she earns in 6 weeks.

   a. \$20.00   **b.** \$25.00

   c. \$30.00   **d.** \$35.00

14. Joe has a set of 137 baseball cards to divide evenly among 6 friends. How many baseball cards does Joe give to each friend?

   a. 22 cards   **b.** 22 R5 cards

   c. 23 cards   **d.** not given

Some inventions, such as a watch, are complicated. Others, such as a ruler, are simple. Can you describe a ruler without saying what it is? Find out whether a friend can draw the ruler from your description.

8 FRACTIONS, MIXED NUMBERS, DECIMALS

Adding Fractions

A. You can explore how fractions between 0 and 1 can be added. You can also explore whether the answer will be less than 1, equal to 1, or greater than 1.

Step 1: Work with your team. Cut 7 strips of paper. Make each 2 inches wide and 8 inches long. On one of the strips, mark off 4 inches. What is the fraction shown by each piece of this strip? Label each piece by its fraction name. Cut the pieces apart. Do the same thing with another strip.

Take another strip. Mark off every 2 inches. How many pieces of equal size do you have? What is the fraction shown by each piece? Label and cut apart the pieces. Do the same thing with another strip.

Take 2 more strips. Mark off every inch on each. Label and cut apart the pieces.

Step 2: Place the remaining whole strip on your desk. Lay a $\frac{1}{4}$ piece along the left edge of the whole. Now place 2 more $\frac{1}{4}$ pieces next to the first. You can use a number sentence to show what you did.

$$\frac{1}{4} + \frac{2}{4}$$

Thinking as a Team

1. How many fourths do you have altogether?

2. Is the sum greater than the whole, equal to the whole, or less than the whole?

3. Look at the numerators of both addends. What do you notice?

4. Look at the denominators of both addends. What do you notice?

Step 3: Use your fraction pieces to show each of these number sentences.

$$\frac{3}{8} + \frac{2}{8} \qquad\qquad \frac{3}{4} + \frac{1}{4}$$

$$\frac{1}{2} + \frac{1}{2} \qquad\qquad \frac{1}{8} + \frac{6}{8}$$

$$\frac{3}{4} + \frac{2}{4} \qquad\qquad \frac{1}{4} + \frac{1}{4}$$

- For each problem, give the fraction that names each sum.

- Is each answer greater than a whole, equal to a whole, or less than a whole?

Thinking as a Team ───────

1. Write a rule for adding any two fractions that have the same denominator. Test your rule by finding the sum of other fraction problems.

2. How can you check your answers to see that they are reasonable?

───────────────────────────

B. You can explore adding fractions with different denominators. Use the fraction pieces you made to help you think about the answers.

Place three $\frac{1}{8}$ pieces along the edge of the whole.

Now place a $\frac{1}{4}$ piece next to it.

Write a number sentence to show what you did.

Is the sum less than a whole, equal to a whole, or greater than a whole?

Use your fraction pieces to show each problem. Is the sum less than a whole, equal to a whole, or greater than a whole?

$$\frac{5}{8} + \frac{1}{4} \qquad\qquad \frac{2}{4} + \frac{1}{2}$$

$$\frac{7}{8} + \frac{1}{2} \qquad\qquad \frac{1}{2} + \frac{3}{4}$$

Adding Fractions with Unlike Denominators

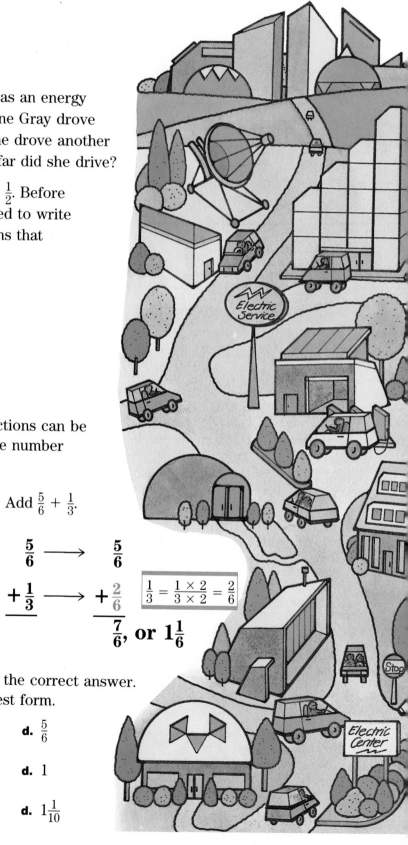

A. The electric car was invented as an energy saver. It does not use gasoline. Jane Gray drove her electric car $\frac{1}{4}$ mile to work. She drove another $\frac{1}{2}$ mile to the movie theater. How far did she drive?

You need to add the fractions $\frac{1}{4} + \frac{1}{2}$. Before you can add the fractions, you need to write the fractions as equivalent fractions that have like denominators.

$$\frac{1}{4} + \frac{1}{2} \qquad \boxed{\frac{1}{2} = \frac{1 \times 2}{2 \times 2} = \frac{2}{4}}$$

$$\frac{1}{4} + \frac{2}{4} = \frac{1 + 2}{4} = \frac{3}{4}$$

She drove $\frac{3}{4}$ mile.

B. Sometimes the sum of two fractions can be written in simplest form as a whole number or as a mixed number.

Add $\frac{3}{4} + \frac{2}{8}$.

$$\frac{3}{4} \longrightarrow \frac{6}{8} \qquad \boxed{\frac{3}{4} = \frac{3 \times 2}{4 \times 2} = \frac{6}{8}}$$

$$+\frac{2}{8} \longrightarrow +\frac{2}{8}$$

$$\frac{8}{8}, \text{ or } 1$$

Add $\frac{5}{6} + \frac{1}{3}$.

$$\frac{5}{6} \longrightarrow \frac{5}{6}$$

$$+\frac{1}{3} \longrightarrow +\frac{2}{6} \qquad \boxed{\frac{1}{3} = \frac{1 \times 2}{3 \times 2} = \frac{2}{6}}$$

$$\frac{7}{6}, \text{ or } 1\frac{1}{6}$$

Checkpoint   Write the letter of the correct answer.
Add. The answer must be in simplest form.

1. $\frac{2}{3} + \frac{1}{6}$ **a.** $\frac{3}{9}$ **b.** $\frac{3}{6}$ **c.** $\frac{5}{12}$ **d.** $\frac{5}{6}$

2. $\frac{6}{8} + \frac{1}{4}$ **a.** $\frac{8}{16}$ **b.** $\frac{7}{12}$ **c.** $\frac{7}{8}$ **d.** 1

3. $\frac{9}{10} + \frac{1}{5}$ **a.** $\frac{11}{20}$ **b.** $\frac{10}{15}$ **c.** 1 **d.** $1\frac{1}{10}$

Add. Write the sum in simplest form.

1. $\frac{1}{6} + \frac{1}{3}$ **2.** $\frac{2}{5} + \frac{3}{10}$ **3.** $\frac{1}{8} + \frac{2}{4}$ **4.** $\frac{1}{2} + \frac{2}{6}$ **5.** $\frac{1}{2} + \frac{3}{8}$

6. $\frac{1}{4} + \frac{6}{8}$ **7.** $\frac{4}{5} + \frac{2}{10}$ **8.** $\frac{2}{3} + \frac{2}{6}$ **9.** $\frac{3}{9} + \frac{2}{3}$ **10.** $\frac{1}{2} + \frac{2}{4}$

11. $\frac{3}{10} + \frac{4}{5}$ **12.** $\frac{7}{8} + \frac{3}{4}$ **13.** $\frac{6}{9} + \frac{2}{3}$ **14.** $\frac{5}{6} + \frac{2}{3}$ **15.** $\frac{1}{3} + \frac{8}{9}$

16. $\begin{array}{r} \frac{2}{9} \\ + \frac{1}{9} \\ \hline \end{array}$ **17.** $\begin{array}{r} \frac{1}{2} \\ + \frac{5}{6} \\ \hline \end{array}$ **18.** $\begin{array}{r} \frac{2}{3} \\ + \frac{1}{9} \\ \hline \end{array}$ **19.** $\begin{array}{r} \frac{4}{5} \\ + \frac{4}{10} \\ \hline \end{array}$ **20.** $\begin{array}{r} \frac{2}{10} \\ + \frac{8}{10} \\ \hline \end{array}$ **21.** $\begin{array}{r} \frac{3}{9} \\ + \frac{1}{6} \\ \hline \end{array}$ **22.** $\begin{array}{r} \frac{5}{10} \\ + \frac{1}{5} \\ \hline \end{array}$

23. $\begin{array}{r} \frac{4}{8} \\ + \frac{1}{2} \\ \hline \end{array}$ **24.** $\begin{array}{r} \frac{3}{6} \\ + \frac{1}{2} \\ \hline \end{array}$ **25.** $\begin{array}{r} \frac{8}{9} \\ + \frac{2}{3} \\ \hline \end{array}$ **26.** $\begin{array}{r} \frac{4}{5} \\ + \frac{9}{10} \\ \hline \end{array}$ **27.** $\begin{array}{r} \frac{4}{8} \\ + \frac{3}{6} \\ \hline \end{array}$ **28.** $\begin{array}{r} \frac{2}{3} \\ + \frac{4}{6} \\ \hline \end{array}$ **29.** $\begin{array}{r} \frac{2}{10} \\ + \frac{6}{10} \\ \hline \end{array}$

30. $\begin{array}{r} \frac{1}{3} \\ + \frac{6}{9} \\ \hline \end{array}$ **31.** $\begin{array}{r} \frac{1}{2} \\ + \frac{3}{4} \\ \hline \end{array}$ **32.** $\begin{array}{r} \frac{5}{9} \\ + \frac{2}{3} \\ \hline \end{array}$ **33.** $\begin{array}{r} \frac{3}{6} \\ + \frac{1}{3} \\ \hline \end{array}$ **34.** $\begin{array}{r} \frac{6}{8} \\ + \frac{5}{8} \\ \hline \end{array}$ **35.** $\begin{array}{r} \frac{3}{9} \\ + \frac{5}{6} \\ \hline \end{array}$ **36.** $\begin{array}{r} \frac{3}{5} \\ + \frac{6}{10} \\ \hline \end{array}$

Solve. For Problem 38, use the Infobank.

37. Every night, Jane recharges the battery in her electric car. It takes $\frac{1}{12}$ hour to connect the battery cables and $\frac{3}{4}$ hour to recharge. How long does it take Jane to recharge the battery?

38. Use the map on page 404 to solve. Find how far Carla traveled if she first drove from her home to the office and then to the store.

ANOTHER LOOK

Compare. Write $>$, $<$, or $=$ for each ⬤.

1. $3\frac{2}{4}$ ⬤ $3\frac{1}{2}$ **2.** $4\frac{1}{3}$ ⬤ $4\frac{1}{6}$ **3.** $1\frac{1}{4}$ ⬤ $1\frac{2}{4}$ **4.** $5\frac{3}{6}$ ⬤ $5\frac{6}{12}$

5. $3\frac{5}{8}$ ⬤ $1\frac{5}{8}$ **6.** $1\frac{3}{9}$ ⬤ $3\frac{1}{3}$ **7.** $6\frac{8}{10}$ ⬤ $6\frac{4}{5}$ **8.** $7\frac{1}{3}$ ⬤ $3\frac{2}{3}$

PROBLEM SOLVING
Choosing a Strategy or Method

Choose a strategy or method and solve.

1. The first bicycle invented had no pedals. The bicycle could go 20 miles in 2 hours. How many miles per hour did it go?

2. In 1974, an electric bicycle was tested. It ran on a battery or by a person pedalling. The cost to run it was $0.01 per 5 miles. How far could you travel for $0.05?

3. In the year 2000, the computer bike was invented. Was it the best-selling bike that year?

4. What fraction of the bikes sold were electric?

5. Sales of computer bikes increased by half a million every 2 years from the year 2000 to the year 2010. In 2010, 3 million computer bikes were sold. How many were sold in the year 2000?

6. One factory makes both electric and computer bikes. They offer the bikes in a choice of red, black, or silver. How many possible combinations of bike and color can a store order?

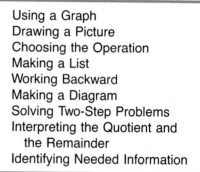

Using a Graph
Drawing a Picture
Choosing the Operation
Making a List
Working Backward
Making a Diagram
Solving Two-Step Problems
Interpreting the Quotient and
  the Remainder
Identifying Needed Information

BICYCLES SOLD IN THE YEAR 2000

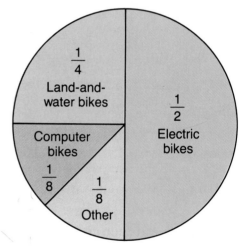

7. The factory that makes land-and-water bikes offers them with or without sails. They come in blue, red, or yellow. How many possible combinations do they offer?

Choose a strategy or method and solve.

8. Bikeworld needs 39 computer bikes. The factory's trucks carry 9 bikes at a time. How many trucks are needed to make the delivery?

9. The Pedal Store orders 14 computer bikes. How many trucks will the factory need if they deliver to both Bikeworld and the Pedal Store?

10. Kirkpatrick Macmillan invented the first pedal bicycle. It had wooden wheels and iron tires, making it 3 times heavier than a modern bike. A lightweight bike today weighs 22 pounds. How much did Kirkpatrick's bike weigh?

11. In 1861, Pierre Lallement invented a better pedal bike. It was called the boneshaker. The first year after he invented the bike, he made 142 boneshakers. By 1865, he was making 3 times that many. How many boneshakers did Lallement make in 1865?

12. Use the circle graph on page 240 to answer this question. What fraction of bikes sold in the year 2000 were land-and-water bikes?

13. Can you use the circle graph to find how many bikes were sold in the year 2000?

14. Mr. Tom is ordering material for the school library. He sees the titles *Inventions on Wheels* and *Bicycling Through the Ages* in a catalog. Both books come in both hardback and paperback. How many combinations can Mr. Tom order?

15. Felicia, Carol, Ross, Dylan, and Blake sit in the same row. Dylan sits between Felicia and Carol. Ross sits behind Blake and in front of Carol. Who sits in the last seat on the row?

16. Dr. James L. Plimpton invented roller skates in 1863. He put 4 small wooden wheels on each skate. If he had 29 wheels, how many roller skates could he make?

17. If Dr. Plimpton had 4 children, could he make enough skates, using the 29 wheels, to give each child a pair?

18. A Dutch sailboat traveled on land in about 1600. It was set on wheels. It could carry 28 people. Could it carry 4 groups of 8 people?

19. One day, 73 people wanted to travel on the land boat. If the boat made 3 trips that day, would all 73 people be able to ride?

Subtracting Fractions

Nan and Ted are building the frame for a dog-washing machine. They cut off $\frac{1}{4}$ yard from a board $\frac{3}{4}$ yard long. How long is the board now?

To find the length of the board, subtract $\frac{3}{4} - \frac{1}{4}$. To subtract fractions that have like denominators, subtract the numerators. Use the same denominator.

$$\frac{3}{4} - \frac{1}{4} = \frac{3-1}{4} = \frac{2}{4}, \text{ or } \frac{1}{2}$$

$\frac{2}{4}$ can be written in simplest form as $\frac{1}{2}$.

The board is $\frac{1}{2}$ yard long.

Other examples:

Subtract $\frac{4}{6} - \frac{3}{6}$.

$$\begin{array}{r} \frac{4}{6} \\ -\frac{3}{6} \\ \hline \frac{1}{6} \end{array}$$

Subtract $\frac{7}{8} - \frac{7}{8}$.

$$\begin{array}{r} \frac{7}{8} \\ -\frac{7}{8} \\ \hline \frac{0}{8} = 0 \end{array}$$

When zero is the numerator, the fraction equals 0.

Checkpoint Write the letter of the correct answer.

Subtract. The answer must be in simplest form.

1. $\frac{2}{4} - \frac{1}{4}$

a. $\frac{1}{4}$

b. $\frac{3}{8}$

c. $\frac{3}{4}$

d. $\frac{1}{0}$

2. $\frac{7}{10} - \frac{3}{10}$

a. $\frac{2}{5}$

b. 1

c. $\frac{4}{10}$

d. $\frac{4}{0}$

3. $\frac{4}{5} - \frac{4}{5}$

a. 0

b. $\frac{0}{0}$

c. $\frac{8}{10}$

d. $\frac{8}{5}$

Subtract. Write the answer in simplest form.

1. $\frac{5}{5} - \frac{4}{5}$

2. $\frac{7}{8} - \frac{7}{8}$

3. $\frac{2}{3} - \frac{1}{3}$

4. $\frac{5}{7} - \frac{2}{7}$

5. $\frac{3}{9} - \frac{2}{9}$

6. $\frac{7}{10} - \frac{2}{10}$

7. $\frac{7}{8} - \frac{1}{8}$

8. $\frac{8}{9} - \frac{5}{9}$

9. $\frac{4}{6} - \frac{2}{6}$

10. $\frac{8}{10} - \frac{6}{10}$

Subtract. Write the difference in simplest form.

11. $\frac{3}{4} - \frac{2}{4}$ **12.** $\frac{2}{3} - \frac{1}{3}$ **13.** $\frac{6}{7} - \frac{4}{7}$ **14.** $\frac{4}{9} - \frac{2}{9}$ **15.** $\frac{5}{6} - \frac{4}{6}$

16. $\frac{4}{6} - \frac{1}{6}$ **17.** $\frac{6}{8} - \frac{3}{8}$ **18.** $\frac{3}{12} - \frac{2}{12}$ **19.** $\frac{5}{6} - \frac{3}{6}$ **20.** $\frac{4}{5} - \frac{1}{5}$

21. $\frac{4}{5} - \frac{2}{5}$ **22.** $\frac{6}{7} - \frac{5}{7}$ **23.** $\frac{8}{10} - \frac{3}{10}$ **24.** $\frac{7}{9} - \frac{5}{9}$ **25.** $\frac{7}{8} - \frac{3}{8}$

26. $\begin{array}{r} \frac{1}{2} \\ -\frac{1}{2} \\ \hline \end{array}$ **27.** $\begin{array}{r} \frac{6}{9} \\ -\frac{5}{9} \\ \hline \end{array}$ **28.** $\begin{array}{r} \frac{3}{8} \\ -\frac{2}{8} \\ \hline \end{array}$ **29.** $\begin{array}{r} \frac{4}{5} \\ -\frac{3}{5} \\ \hline \end{array}$ **30.** $\begin{array}{r} \frac{7}{12} \\ -\frac{3}{12} \\ \hline \end{array}$ **31.** $\begin{array}{r} \frac{9}{10} \\ -\frac{2}{10} \\ \hline \end{array}$ **32.** $\begin{array}{r} \frac{2}{7} \\ -\frac{1}{7} \\ \hline \end{array}$

33. $\begin{array}{r} \frac{5}{8} \\ -\frac{1}{8} \\ \hline \end{array}$ **34.** $\begin{array}{r} \frac{6}{9} \\ -\frac{2}{9} \\ \hline \end{array}$ **35.** $\begin{array}{r} \frac{3}{4} \\ -\frac{3}{4} \\ \hline \end{array}$ **36.** $\begin{array}{r} \frac{7}{8} \\ -\frac{5}{8} \\ \hline \end{array}$ **37.** $\begin{array}{r} \frac{9}{10} \\ -\frac{8}{10} \\ \hline \end{array}$ **38.** $\begin{array}{r} \frac{3}{8} \\ -\frac{3}{8} \\ \hline \end{array}$ **39.** $\begin{array}{r} \frac{5}{6} \\ -\frac{1}{6} \\ \hline \end{array}$

Solve.

40. Nan fills the machine's water tank with $\frac{7}{8}$ gallon of water. There is a hole in the tank, and $\frac{1}{8}$ gallon leaks out. How much water is there in the tank now?

41. It takes the machine $\frac{3}{4}$ hour to wash Prince. It takes the machine another $\frac{1}{4}$ hour to wash Hobo. How long does it take to wash both dogs?

CHALLENGE

A prime number has exactly two different factors: itself and 1.
5 is a prime number. Its factors are 5 and 1.
6 is not a prime number. Its factors are 1, 2, 3, and 6.

1. List all the prime numbers between 2 and 25.

2. List all the prime numbers between 50 and 100.
For a related activity, see **Connecting Math Ideas**, p. 398

Subtracting Fractions with Unlike Denominators

Arnold designed a robot named Chance to tend his garden. It takes Chance $\frac{1}{2}$ hour to mow the lawn and $\frac{3}{4}$ hour to mow the lawn and trim the hedges. How long does it take Chance to trim the hedges?

To find how long it takes him, subtract $\frac{3}{4} - \frac{1}{2}$. Before you can subtract, you need to write the fractions as equivalent fractions that have like denominators.

$$\frac{3}{4} - \frac{1}{2} \qquad \boxed{\frac{1}{2} = \frac{1 \times 2}{2 \times 2} = \frac{2}{4}}$$

$$\frac{3}{4} - \frac{2}{4} = \frac{3-2}{4} = \frac{1}{4}$$

It takes Chance $\frac{1}{4}$ hour to trim the hedges.

Another example:

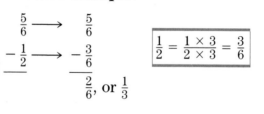

$$\boxed{\frac{1}{2} = \frac{1 \times 3}{2 \times 3} = \frac{3}{6}}$$

Checkpoint
Write the letter of the correct answer. Subtract. The answer must be in simplest form.

1. $\frac{5}{6} - \frac{2}{3}$ **a.** $\frac{1}{6}$ **b.** $\frac{3}{6}$ **c.** 1 **d.** $1\frac{1}{2}$

2. $\frac{7}{8} - \frac{3}{4}$ **a.** $\frac{1}{8}$ **b.** $\frac{4}{8}$ **c.** $\frac{10}{12}$ **d.** 1

3. $\frac{3}{6} - \frac{1}{2}$ **a.** 0 **b.** $\frac{0}{6}$ **c.** $\frac{1}{2}$ **d.** 1

Subtract. Write the difference in simplest form.

1. $\frac{3}{4}$
$-\frac{3}{8}$

2. $\frac{6}{10}$
$-\frac{1}{2}$

3. $\frac{3}{6}$
$-\frac{1}{3}$

4. $\frac{5}{8}$
$-\frac{1}{4}$

5. $\frac{5}{6}$
$-\frac{1}{2}$

6. $\frac{7}{8}$
$-\frac{1}{4}$

7. $\frac{1}{2}$
$-\frac{2}{10}$

Subtract. Write the difference in simplest form.

8. $\dfrac{4}{6}$ $-\dfrac{1}{2}$ 9. $\dfrac{5}{9}$ $-\dfrac{1}{3}$ 10. $\dfrac{7}{8}$ $-\dfrac{2}{4}$ 11. $\dfrac{9}{10}$ $-\dfrac{3}{5}$ 12. $\dfrac{5}{8}$ $-\dfrac{1}{2}$ 13. $\dfrac{2}{3}$ $-\dfrac{2}{6}$ 14. $\dfrac{7}{10}$ $-\dfrac{2}{5}$

15. $\dfrac{1}{2}$ $-\dfrac{5}{10}$ 16. $\dfrac{4}{6}$ $-\dfrac{2}{3}$ 17. $\dfrac{7}{10}$ $-\dfrac{1}{2}$ 18. $\dfrac{6}{9}$ $-\dfrac{1}{3}$ 19. $\dfrac{1}{2}$ $-\dfrac{3}{12}$ 20. $\dfrac{8}{10}$ $-\dfrac{1}{2}$ 21. $\dfrac{2}{3}$ $-\dfrac{4}{6}$

22. $\dfrac{5}{6} - \dfrac{1}{3}$ 23. $\dfrac{9}{10} - \dfrac{1}{2}$ 24. $\dfrac{6}{9} - \dfrac{1}{3}$ 25. $\dfrac{6}{8} - \dfrac{1}{4}$ 26. $\dfrac{4}{6} - \dfrac{1}{3}$

27. $\dfrac{7}{10} - \dfrac{1}{2}$ 28. $\dfrac{6}{8} - \dfrac{1}{2}$ 29. $\dfrac{4}{8} - \dfrac{1}{4}$ 30. $\dfrac{6}{10} - \dfrac{2}{5}$ 31. $\dfrac{8}{10} - \dfrac{2}{5}$

32. $\dfrac{3}{4} - \dfrac{2}{8}$ 33. $\dfrac{4}{6} - \dfrac{1}{2}$ 34. $\dfrac{7}{10} - \dfrac{3}{5}$ 35. $\dfrac{1}{2} - \dfrac{3}{10}$ 36. $\dfrac{5}{8} - \dfrac{1}{2}$

37. $\dfrac{5}{8} - \dfrac{2}{4}$ 38. $\dfrac{5}{12} - \dfrac{1}{4}$ 39. $\dfrac{4}{9} - \dfrac{1}{3}$ 40. $\dfrac{8}{10} - \dfrac{1}{5}$ 41. $\dfrac{2}{3} - \dfrac{1}{9}$

Solve.

42. It takes Chance a morning to weed $\dfrac{2}{3}$ of Arnold's flower beds. It takes Arnold a morning to weed $\dfrac{2}{6}$ of the flower beds. How much more can Chance do than Arnold does in a morning?

★43. Arnold can buy 3 rosebushes for $37.35 or 5 rosebushes for $59.95. Which do you think is the better buy? Why?

NUMBER SENSE

Add mentally.

1. $\dfrac{1}{4} + \dfrac{1}{4} + \dfrac{1}{4}$ 2. $\dfrac{3}{6} + \dfrac{1}{6} + \dfrac{1}{6}$ 3. $\dfrac{2}{10} + \dfrac{3}{10} + \dfrac{1}{10}$

4. $\dfrac{2}{7} + \dfrac{1}{7} + \dfrac{2}{7}$ 5. $\dfrac{5}{8} + \dfrac{1}{8} + \dfrac{1}{8}$ 6. $\dfrac{1}{9} + \dfrac{3}{9} + \dfrac{2}{9}$

Adding and Subtracting Mixed Numbers

A. Cynthia buys a portable pool. The pool part weighs $5\frac{1}{4}$ pounds. The hoses weigh $2\frac{2}{4}$ pounds. How much does Cynthia's portable pool weigh?

To find how much, you can add. Find the sum of $5\frac{1}{4} + 2\frac{2}{4}$.

Add the fractions. | Add the whole numbers.

$$\begin{array}{r} 5\frac{1}{4} \\ + 2\frac{2}{4} \\ \hline \frac{3}{4} \end{array} \qquad \begin{array}{r} 5\frac{1}{4} \\ + 2\frac{2}{4} \\ \hline 7\frac{3}{4} \end{array}$$

Cynthia's portable pool weighs $7\frac{3}{4}$ pounds.

B. Sometimes you need to rename when you add fractions.

Add $3\frac{1}{2} + 5\frac{1}{2}$.

Add the fractions.   Add the whole numbers.   Rename in simplest form.

$$\begin{array}{r} 3\frac{1}{2} \\ + 5\frac{1}{2} \\ \hline \frac{2}{2} \end{array} \qquad \begin{array}{r} 3\frac{1}{2} \\ + 5\frac{1}{2} \\ \hline 8\frac{2}{2} \end{array} \qquad 8\frac{2}{2} = 8 + 1 = 9$$

$$\boxed{\frac{2}{2} = 1}$$

C. In subtracting mixed numbers, subtract the fractional parts first.

Subtract $8\frac{5}{6} - 3\frac{1}{6}$.

Subtract the fractions.   Subtract the whole numbers.

$$\begin{array}{r} 8\frac{5}{6} \\ - 3\frac{1}{6} \\ \hline \frac{4}{6} \end{array} \qquad \begin{array}{r} 8\frac{5}{6} \\ - 3\frac{1}{6} \\ \hline 5\frac{4}{6} = 5\frac{2}{3} \end{array}$$

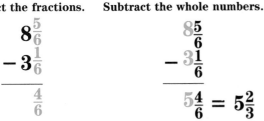

246

Add or subtract. Write the answer in simplest form.

1. $3\frac{3}{8}$
$+ 2\frac{2}{8}$

2. $1\frac{4}{6}$
$+ 3\frac{1}{6}$

3. $3\frac{2}{4}$
$+ 1\frac{1}{4}$

4. $5\frac{2}{5}$
$+ 1\frac{2}{5}$

5. $4\frac{1}{10}$
$+ 3\frac{6}{10}$

6. $7\frac{3}{5}$
$+ 2\frac{1}{5}$

7. $6\frac{5}{8}$
$+ 3\frac{3}{8}$

8. $3\frac{5}{6}$
$+ 2\frac{5}{6}$

9. $4\frac{3}{4}$
$+ 3\frac{1}{4}$

10. $10\frac{2}{3}$
$+ 7\frac{1}{3}$

11. $3\frac{7}{8}$
$+ 2\frac{1}{8}$

12. $2\frac{7}{10}$
$+ 4\frac{5}{10}$

13. $4\frac{1}{2} - 3\frac{1}{2}$

14. $6\frac{2}{6} - 2\frac{1}{6}$

15. $8\frac{7}{8} - 3\frac{2}{8}$

16. $5\frac{3}{6} - 2\frac{2}{6}$

17. $3\frac{2}{3} - 2\frac{1}{3}$

18. $2\frac{9}{10} - 1\frac{7}{10}$

19. $6\frac{3}{5} - 3\frac{2}{5}$

20. $8\frac{4}{8} - 6\frac{4}{8}$

21. $7\frac{5}{6} - 5\frac{3}{6}$

22. $5\frac{6}{10} - 4\frac{3}{10}$

23. $7\frac{1}{6} + 1\frac{1}{6}$

24. $8\frac{2}{3} + 1\frac{1}{3}$

25. $1\frac{4}{8} + 1\frac{2}{8}$

26. $4\frac{1}{6} + 5\frac{5}{6}$

27. $14\frac{1}{2} + 1\frac{1}{2}$

28. $4\frac{3}{8} - 3\frac{2}{8}$

29. $3\frac{4}{5} - 2\frac{4}{5}$

30. $5\frac{4}{9} - 3\frac{3}{9}$

31. $6\frac{3}{4} - 2\frac{1}{4}$

32. $9\frac{2}{3} - 3\frac{1}{3}$

33. $6\frac{2}{6} + 2\frac{3}{6}$

34. $4\frac{7}{10} - 1\frac{2}{10}$

35. $5\frac{1}{4} + 2\frac{1}{4}$

36. $3\frac{4}{8} - 1\frac{2}{8}$

37. $10\frac{3}{5} + 1\frac{2}{5}$

Solve.

38. Cynthia can attach her portable pool to her faucet in $2\frac{1}{2}$ minutes and then fill the pool in $4\frac{1}{2}$ minutes. How long does it take Cynthia to prepare her pool?

39. Cynthia fills her portable pool with $9\frac{3}{8}$ gallons of water. Of this, $5\frac{1}{8}$ gallons are hot water. How much cold water does Cynthia use?

For a related activity, see *Connecting Math Ideas,* p. 398

MIDCHAPTER REVIEW

Add or subtract. Write the answer in simplest form.

1. $\frac{3}{6} + \frac{2}{6}$

2. $\frac{5}{8} + \frac{1}{8}$

3. $\frac{2}{5} + \frac{4}{10}$

4. $\frac{1}{3} + \frac{4}{6}$

5. $\frac{3}{4} + \frac{3}{8}$

6. $\frac{7}{8} - \frac{4}{8}$

7. $\frac{8}{10} - \frac{2}{10}$

8. $\frac{1}{2} - \frac{1}{2}$

9. $\frac{7}{8} - \frac{1}{2}$

10. $\frac{4}{6} - \frac{1}{3}$

11. $2\frac{2}{6} + 3\frac{3}{6}$

12. $7\frac{4}{5} + 1\frac{3}{5}$

13. $10\frac{1}{8} + 4\frac{7}{8}$

14. $6\frac{8}{10} - 3\frac{1}{10}$

15. $13\frac{3}{4} - 5\frac{1}{4}$

PROBLEM SOLVING
Making an Organized List

Making an organized list can help you solve certain problems.

> Karen invented 5 video games called *Flytrap*, *Moonrock*, *Crickball*, *Lineup*, and *Possum*. Her nephew can choose to have any 2 of the games. From how many combinations of games can Karen's nephew choose?

Begin the list with *Flytrap*. List all the combinations that can be made with this game.

Then list all the combinations that can be made with *Moonrock*. Since you have already paired *Moonrock* with *Flytrap*, you cannot use that combination again.

Next, list all the combinations that can be made with *Crickball* and then those that can be made with *Lineup*. Remember not to repeat pairs you have listed before.

The only remaining game is *Possum*. You have already listed all the combinations that can be made with *Possum*.

Now, count the number of combinations.

Karen's nephew can choose from 10 combinations of video games.

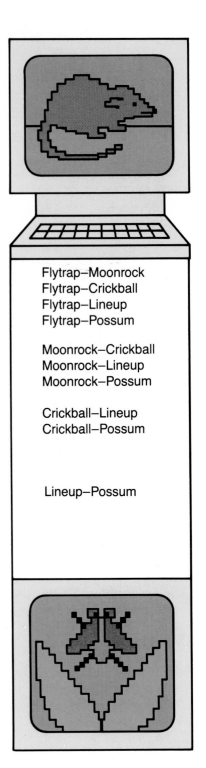

Flytrap–Moonrock
Flytrap–Crickball
Flytrap–Lineup
Flytrap–Possum

Moonrock–Crickball
Moonrock–Lineup
Moonrock–Possum

Crickball–Lineup
Crickball–Possum

Lineup–Possum

Solve.

1. David invented a talking wristwatch. Customers can buy the watch with a red, white, or blue case. They can also choose to have a green, yellow, or black wristband. From how many combinations can a customer choose?

2. Jo Ann invented a magnetic key holder. She makes it in 4 animal shapes: a whale, an elephant, a giraffe, and a rhinoceros. Claude wants 2 key holders in different shapes. From how many combinations can he choose?

3. Anyone who buys a video recorder from Alice's Appliances can choose 2 free videos. If the store offers 6 different videos, how many pairs of videos are possible?

4. Wally invents a circular picture frame that holds 3 pictures. Jessica has 5 pictures that she wants to display in the frame. From how many combinations can she select pictures to put into the frame?

5. There are 5 inventors at an inventor's meeting. Each inventor will work with one other inventor during each day of the meeting, and each inventor will work with every other inventor. How many pairs of inventors will there be?

6. Tom has created so many inventions that he has had to code them by 2-digit numbers. He uses only the digits 1, 3, 5, and 7. How many inventions has Tom created?

7. Annie's music machine plays 3 songs. It is programmed to play the songs in as many different orders as possible. In how many different orders can the music machine play the songs?

8. Barry and Josh play Pathfinder. They can each choose to be 1 out of 5 different characters in the game. How many pairs of characters are possible?

9. Val designs 2 new characters for her video game. She wants each to be a different color. If she has 6 colors to choose from, how many different colored pairs are possible?

★10. Danny invented a checkers machine. He plays in a league that has 7 other players. Each player plays each of the others twice in a season. How many games are played in a season?

Tenths

A. An odometer measures the number of miles a car or bicycle has traveled. The odometer measures distance in tenths of a mile.

Greta rode her bicycle three tenths of a mile. You can write three tenths as a fraction or as a decimal.

The drawing is divided into 10 equal parts, and 3 of the 10 parts are shaded.

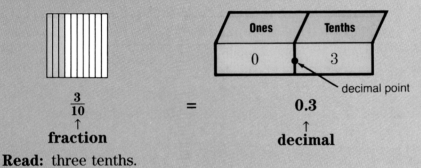

$$\frac{3}{10} = 0.3$$

fraction = decimal

Read: three tenths.

B. You can write a decimal for a number greater than 1.

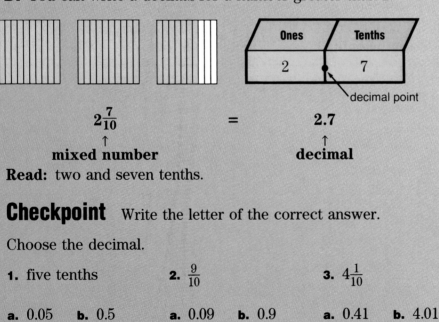

$$2\frac{7}{10} = 2.7$$

mixed number = decimal

Read: two and seven tenths.

Checkpoint Write the letter of the correct answer.

Choose the decimal.

1. five tenths

2. $\frac{9}{10}$

3. $4\frac{1}{10}$

a. 0.05   **b.** 0.5

a. 0.09   **b.** 0.9

a. 0.41   **b.** 4.01

c. $\frac{5}{10}$ **d.** 50.0

c. 9.0   **d.** 9.9

c. 4.1   **d.** 41

Write a decimal for the picture.

1. 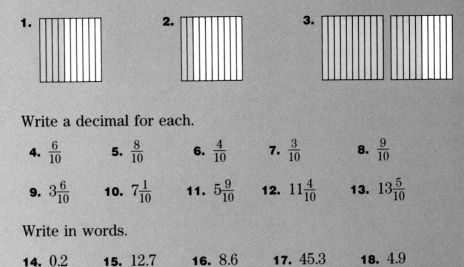 **2.** **3.**

Write a decimal for each.

4. $\frac{6}{10}$ **5.** $\frac{8}{10}$ **6.** $\frac{4}{10}$ **7.** $\frac{3}{10}$ **8.** $\frac{9}{10}$

9. $3\frac{6}{10}$ **10.** $7\frac{1}{10}$ **11.** $5\frac{9}{10}$ **12.** $11\frac{4}{10}$ **13.** $13\frac{5}{10}$

Write in words.

14. 0.2   **15.** 12.7   **16.** 8.6   **17.** 45.3   **18.** 4.9

Solve.

19. Vicki rode her bicycle $5\frac{7}{10}$ miles during a bike-a-thon. Marty rode his bicycle $5\frac{8}{10}$ miles. Write these mixed numbers as they would appear on an odometer.

20. The first car was built in 1770. It ran on steam power and could travel $2\frac{1}{4}$ miles per hour. A healthy person can walk $3\frac{3}{4}$ miles per hour. How much faster can a healthy person walk than the first car could travel?

21. In 1970, a car driven at Wood River, Illinois, set a world record by traveling $145\frac{5}{10}$ miles on 1 gallon of gas. Write this distance as a decimal.

★22. Centerville is $176\frac{8}{10}$ miles from Newport. Southside is one hundred twenty-five and seven tenths miles from Newport. Write these distances as decimals.

ANOTHER LOOK

Compare. Write >, <, or = for ●.

1. 132 ● 130   **2.** 6,743 ● 6,743   **3.** 2,887 ● 2,886

4. 798 ● 897   **5.** 5,422 ● 5,422   **6.** 6,375 ● 6,376

7. 4,948 ● 2,947   **8.** 3,486 ● 4,386   **9.** 689 ● 698

Hundredths

A. A pedometer measures the distance a person walks. The pedometer measures distances in hundredths of a mile.

Keith walked two and twenty-three hundredths miles on his way home from band practice. Two and twenty-three hundredths can be written as a mixed number or as a decimal.

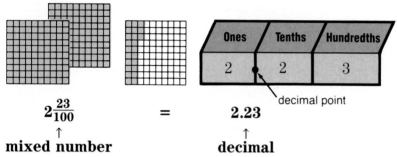

decimal point

$2\frac{23}{100}$ = **2.23**

↑
mixed number

↑
decimal

Read: two and twenty-three hundredths.

B. You can think of cents as hundredths of a dollar.

 = $0.01

one hundredth of a dollar

= $0.07

seven hundredths of a dollar

= $5.12

five and twelve hundredths dollars

Checkpoint   Write the letter of the correct answer.

Choose the decimal.

1. thirty-seven hundredths

 a. 0.037
 b. 0.37
 c. 3.07
 d. 30.07

2. $\frac{19}{100}$

 a. 0.019
 b. 0.19
 c. 1.9
 d. 19.00

3. $5\frac{3}{100}$

 a. 5.003
 b. 0.53
 c. 5.03
 d. 5.3

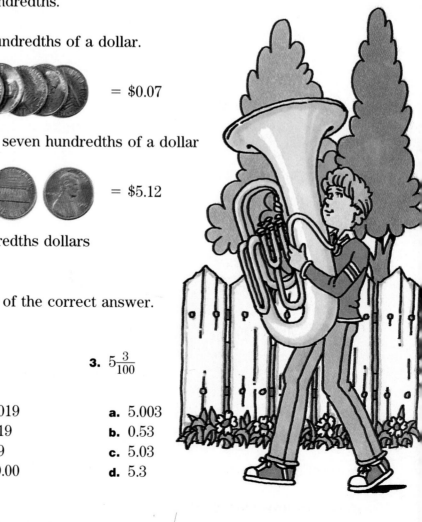

Write a decimal for the picture.

1.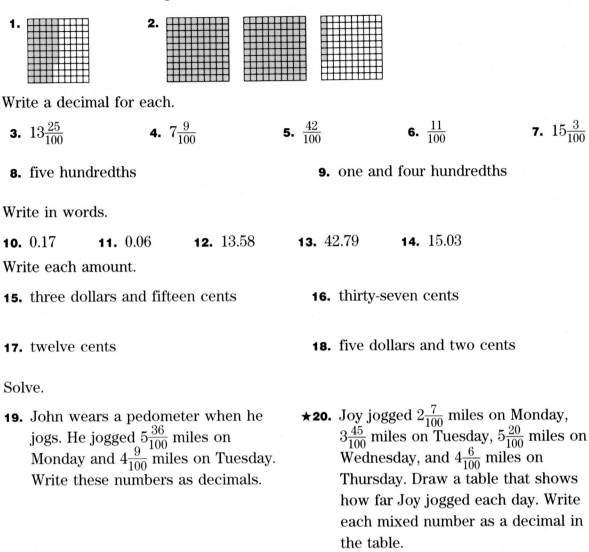

2.

Write a decimal for each.

3. $13\frac{25}{100}$ **4.** $7\frac{9}{100}$ **5.** $\frac{42}{100}$ **6.** $\frac{11}{100}$ **7.** $15\frac{3}{100}$

8. five hundredths   **9.** one and four hundredths

Write in words.

10. 0.17   **11.** 0.06   **12.** 13.58   **13.** 42.79   **14.** 15.03

Write each amount.

15. three dollars and fifteen cents   **16.** thirty-seven cents

17. twelve cents   **18.** five dollars and two cents

Solve.

19. John wears a pedometer when he jogs. He jogged $5\frac{36}{100}$ miles on Monday and $4\frac{9}{100}$ miles on Tuesday. Write these numbers as decimals.

★**20.** Joy jogged $2\frac{7}{100}$ miles on Monday, $3\frac{45}{100}$ miles on Tuesday, $5\frac{20}{100}$ miles on Wednesday, and $4\frac{6}{100}$ miles on Thursday. Draw a table that shows how far Joy jogged each day. Write each mixed number as a decimal in the table.

CHALLENGE

You can multiply a decimal by a whole number. Multiply as you would with whole numbers.

$$\begin{array}{r} 3.7 \\ \times\ \ 4 \\ \hline 148 \end{array}$$

Count the number of decimal places.

$$\begin{array}{r} 3.7 \\ \times\ \ 4 \\ \hline 148 \end{array}$$ **Think:** tenths

Write the decimal point in the same place in the product.

$$\begin{array}{r} 3.7 \\ \times\ \ 4 \\ \hline 14.8 \end{array}$$ tenths

Multiply.

1. 6×2.8 **2.** 5×3.09 **3.** 4×8.3 **4.** 3×6.25

Comparing and Ordering Decimals

A. Max wears a pedometer when he jogs. One week, Max jogged 25.38 miles. The next week, he jogged 25.09 miles. Which was the greater distance?

You can compare decimals by using a number line.

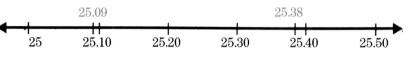

The greater distance was 25.38 miles.

B. Compare 37.62 and 37.41. Use <, >, or =.

Line up the decimal points.	Begin comparing digits at the left.	Continue comparing.	Continue comparing.
	3 = 3	7 = 7	6 > 4
37.62	37.62	37.62	37.62
37.41	37.41	37.41	37.41

So, 37.62 > 37.41.

C. Some decimals are equal. Compare 0.5 and 0.50.

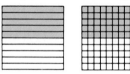

Line up the decimal points.	Write a zero to line up the digits.
0.5	0.50 $\boxed{0.5 = 0.50}$
0.50	0.50

D. You can order decimals by comparing two decimals at a time. Write 3.4, 3.29, and 3.65 in order from the greatest to the least.

Line up the decimal points. Write zeros if you need them.	Find the greatest number.	Find the next greatest number.
3.40	3.40 > 3.29	3.40 > 3.29
3.29	3.65 > 3.40	
3.65	So, 3.65 is the greatest	

So, the order from the greatest to the least is 3.65, 3.4, 3.29.

The order from the least to the greatest is 3.29, 3.4, 3.65.

Compare. Write >, <, or = for ●.

1. 7.9 ● 7.41

2. 16.5 ● 16.50

3. 9.53 ● 10.59

4. 12.6 ● 12.7

5. 9.30 ● 9.3

6. 0.3 ● 0.03

7. 2.03 ● 2.63

8. 14.5 ● 145

Write in order from the greatest to the least.

9. 7.8, 7.79, 8.7

10. 0.1, 0.01, 1.0

11. 62.74, 2.74, 26.4

12. 3.89, 3.68, 36.9

13. 0.74, 7.40, 4.07

14. 4.0, 3.88, 0.07

Write in order from the least to the greatest.

15. 4.56, 45.5, 0.46

16. 3.18, 3.1, 3.08

17. 8.9, 7.6, 8.5

18. 21.1, 2.01, 20.1

19. 9.13, 9.23, 8.32

20. 0.5, 0.05, 5.5

Compare. Write = or ≠ for ●.

★21. 3.4 ● 3.40

★22. 3.5 ● 3.05

★23. 0.4 ● 0.04

★24. 5.7 ● 5.27

Solve.

25. Three cars were driven as far as they could go on one gallon of gasoline. Car 1 traveled 28.6 miles, Car 2 traveled 26.68 miles, and Car 3 traveled 26.88 miles. Write these numbers in order from the least to the greatest.

26. Jill lives 2.65 miles from school, Ed lives 2.5 miles from school, and Bess lives 2.06 miles from school. Use this information to write and solve your own word problem.

CHALLENGE   Patterns, Relations, and Functions

Which figures are identical?
HINT: You may turn the figures around.

1.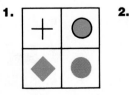

2.

3.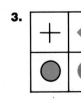

4.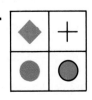

5.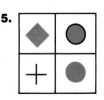

Rounding/Estimating

A. The world's longest bridge-tunnel system carries traffic across Chesapeake Bay in Virginia. It is 17.7 miles long. To the nearest mile, how long is the bridge-tunnel?

You can use a number line to round the decimal.

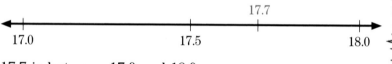

17.7 is between 17.0 and 18.0.
17.7 is closer to 18.0; so, round up.
17.7 rounds to 18.

To the nearest mile, the bridge-tunnel is 18 miles long.

Other examples:

$3.3 \longrightarrow 3$ $16.5 \longrightarrow 17$ $\$0.92 \longrightarrow \$1.00$

B. You can estimate sums and differences with decimals by rounding.

Estimate $16.25 + 7.89$.
Round each decimal to the nearest whole number. Then add.

$$
\begin{array}{r}
16.25 \longrightarrow 16 \\
+\ 7.89 \longrightarrow +\ 8 \\
\hline
24
\end{array}
$$

Estimate $4.37 - 0.58$.
Round each decimal to the nearest whole number. Then subtract.

$$
\begin{array}{r}
4.37 \longrightarrow 4 \\
-\ 0.58 \longrightarrow -\ 1 \\
\hline
3
\end{array}
$$

Round to the nearest whole number or to the nearest dollar.

1. 0.7 **2.** 0.95 **3.** 0.8 **4.** 0.67 **5.** $0.55 **6.** $0.81

7. 3.41 **8.** 6.9 **9.** 41.75 **10.** 4.2 **11.** $15.08 **12.** $9.53

13. 10.07 **14.** 65.1 **15.** 9.05 **16.** 37.4 **17.** $10.72 **18.** $1.25

Write the letter of the correct estimate.

19. $13.7 + 8.9$

    a. 5   **b.** 21   **c.** 23   **d.** 93

20. $75.8 - 42.01$

    a. 30   **b.** 34   **c.** 40   **d.** 120

21. $65.03 + 0.77$

    a. 65   **b.** 66   **c.** 70   **d.** 73

22. $83.45 - 9.1$

    a. 74   **b.** 82   **c.** 83   **d.** 94

Estimate.

23.	**24.**	**25.**	**26.**	**27.**
43.85 + 19.68	5.67 + 1.29	32.74 + 17.89	$9.47 + 1.59	$17.57 + 26.39

28.	**29.**	**30.**	**31.**	**32.**
52.75 − 41.89	87.85 − 15.96	8.75 − 3.41	$6.75 − 2.36	$89.65 − 32.70

Solve.

33. The Suez Canal in Egypt is 100.6 miles long. The Panama Canal is 50.7 miles long. Estimate the difference in length between the two canals.

34. The Canadian Sault Ste. Marie Canal is 1.4 miles long. The American canal is 1.6 miles long. Estimate the total length of both canals.

35. The Simplon II Tunnel in France is about $12\frac{1}{100}$ miles long. Write this distance as a decimal.

★36. Mr. Ray set his car's odometer to zero on entering a 13.7-mile-long tunnel. He looked at the odometer when he had gone 9.2 miles. About how far must he travel to the end of the tunnel?

NUMBER SENSE

You can estimate the sum of two fractions by rounding each to 0, or 1.

Estimate. $\frac{7}{9} + \frac{1}{16}$ Round $\frac{7}{9}$ to 1.   Round $\frac{1}{16}$ to 0. $1 + 0 = 1$

Estimate. **1.** $\frac{7}{8} + \frac{2}{13}$ **2.** $\frac{1}{9} + \frac{5}{6}$ **3.** $\frac{1}{99} + \frac{2}{123}$ **★4.** $\frac{2}{5} + \frac{3}{8}$

Adding Decimals

A. You can use what you have already learned about the addition of whole numbers to add decimals.

Step 1: Cut out a 10-by-10 square of graph paper.

- How many hundredths does the square contain?

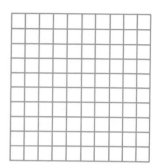

Step 2: Color 25 hundredths red.
Color 15 hundredths green.

- How many hundredths have you colored in all?

- How would you write an addition sentence for what you have just modeled?

Step 3: Cut out two 10-by-10 squares of graph paper. Color 0.75 of one square blue. Try to color 0.82 more of the square yellow.

- How many hundredths have you colored yellow so far? Complete coloring the second square yellow until you have 0.82 yellow in all.

- How many hundredths of the second square did you color? How would you write what you have modeled as an addition example, with one addend above the other?

Step 4: Choose pairs of decimals between 0.01 and 0.99. Add the decimals. Model the addition with graph paper if you need to.

Thinking as a Team _____

Use the numbers you picked in Step 4 to answer these questions.

1. Name the decimals that are less than $\frac{1}{2}$.

2. Name the decimals that are between $\frac{1}{2}$ and 1.

3. Will the sum of two decimals, each of which is less than $\frac{1}{2}$, be greater or less than 1?

4. Will the sum of two decimals, each of which is between $\frac{1}{2}$ and 1, be greater or less than 1?

B. Estimation can help you check calculator results.

Choose a decimal addend from the tenths column and another from the hundredths column from the chart at the right.

- Which whole number will your sum be closest to?

- Estimate your sum.

- Add the decimals on your calculator.

- Use your estimate to check your calculator sum.

Discuss how you used estimation to check your sum.

Tenths	Hundredths
9.3	0.74
0.7	25.21
14.2	0.06
87.4	2.07
0.2	13.89

Thinking as a Team _____

Look at the decimals in the hundredths column in the table above.

1. Which pairs of decimals have sums that can be expressed as tenths? What are their sums?

2. What happens on the calculator when there is a 0 in the written sum?

Subtracting Decimals

These activities will help you explore subtracting decimals.

Step 1: On a piece of paper, make a chart with headings like the one at the right.

Use base-10 blocks to model 2.45 on the chart.

- How many ones are there in this decimal? How many tenths? How many hundredths?

Ones	Tenths	Hundredths

Step 2: Take away 0.58 from your model.

- How many hundredths are there in 0.58?
- Do you have enough hundredths to take away? What do you have to do? Model this.
- How many hundredths are left?
- How many tenths do you have now? How many tenths are there in 0.58? Do you have enough tenths to take away? If not, what will you do? How many tenths are left?
- How many ones are left?
- What decimal does your model show now?

Step 3: Write a number sentence to show what you did.

- How do you know where to put the decimal point in the answer?
- How can you tell if your answer is reasonable?
- How can you check that your answer is correct?

Thinking as a Team

1. How is subtracting decimals like subtracting whole numbers? How is it different?

2. Suppose you had to subtract 5.72 from 7.5. How would you subtract hundredths? tenths? Model this subtraction with base-10 blocks. Write a number sentence to show what you did.

Working as a Team

Coach Timmons is timing qualifying races for the paired relay race. Each pair of students who completes the race in a combined time of 35 seconds or less will compete in the relay race on field day.

Jan completes her part of the race in 18.24 seconds. Her partner, Mark, asks the coach the slowest time he can run and still be able to compete on field day. Look at the notebook to see how Coach Timmons finds this time.

- What is the slowest time that Mark can run yet still be able to compete with Jan on field day?

- Why did Coach Timmons write a decimal point and zeros to the right of 35?

Andy and Chris have times of 17.09 and 17.64 seconds. Coach Timmons finds their combined time in her notebook.

- Will Andy and Chris be able to compete in the relay race on field day?

Pretend you and your partner are a team competing in another event. The combined qualifying time for this event is 33.8 seconds. Write each decimal from the list on a slip of paper and place the slips in a box.

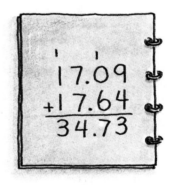

| 14.07 | 15.40 | 16.64 | 14.29 | 15.54 | 16.68 | 17.57 | 16.52 | 18.04 |
| 16.86 | 14.58 | 17.08 | 15.85 | 17.33 | 14.75 | 16.06 | 17.33 | 15.00 |

One partner picks a decimal from the box, then finds the time that the other partner must equal or beat in order to qualify. Next, the other partner picks a decimal. Compare the times. Does your team qualify? Now find the exact combined time.

- Compare all of the teams' times. If the qualifying teams compete in order from slowest to fastest, in what order will the teams compete?

PROBLEM SOLVING
Writing a Simpler Problem

Some problems contain fractions, decimals, or large numbers. These problems may seem difficult. Try solving problems such as these with simpler numbers. Then solve them with the actual numbers.

An invention convention will be held in California. An inventor who lives in Georgia wants to attend. A plane ticket from Georgia to California costs $548.17. The inventor has saved $312.92 for the trip. How much more money does she need?

Use simpler numbers.	Now use the actual numbers.
$5 (cost of plane ticket) − 3 (money saved) $2 (money needed)	$548.17 (cost of plane ticket) − 312.92 (money saved) $235.25 (money needed)

Choose the number sentence that uses the correct operation. Write the letter of the correct answer.

1. An inventor and his brother made display buttons that light up when people talk. He filled $2\frac{1}{2}$ baskets with buttons. His brother filled $1\frac{1}{4}$ baskets with buttons. Who made more buttons?

    a. $1 < 2$
    b. $2 + 1 = n$

2. One inventor gave away 8,709 pamphlets about his invention in 3 days. How many pamphlets did he give away during an average day?

    a. $8 \times 3 = n$
    b. $8 \div 3 = n$

Use simpler numbers to write a number sentence for each problem. Then solve.

3. One person invented two portable computers. The Zax had a mass of 0.75 kg. The Nix had a mass of 1.8 kg. How much greater a mass did the Nix have than the Zax?

4. James drove 1,213.6 km to the convention in California. Then he drove 2,672.63 km to another convention in Nevada. How far did James drive?

5. Jay worked for $3\frac{1}{2}$ hours at the solar music-box booth. His sister, Kay, worked for $2\frac{3}{4}$ hours. Which child worked for a longer time?

6. Sylvia learned that radio was invented in 1895. Television was not invented until 1927. How many years after the invention of radio was television invented?

7. Ned sold 3,978 combination pen-and-pencils during the first day. He sold 2,415 the next day, 5,618 the third day, and 7,312 the last day. How many combination pen-and-pencils did Ned sell?

8. Ann invented a water-powered motor. When full, its tank held $5\frac{3}{4}$ gallons of water. Ann poured $2\frac{1}{4}$ gallons of water into the tank. How much more water did she need to fill the tank?

9. Jay and Jon are passing out badges to the inventors. Jay has $3\frac{1}{4}$ bags of badges left. Jon has $4\frac{1}{3}$ bags left. How many bags of badges are left altogether?

10. Pat's invention cost $674.79 to build. He sold it at the convention for $935.25. How much profit did Pat make on the sale?

★11. The Edison family decides to visit the convention. Tickets to the convention cost $3.95 per adult and $2.35 per child. There are 3 adults and 4 children in the Edison family. How much will it cost the family to buy tickets to the convention?

★12. A new Power Punch is served at the convention. Each of the 7 members of the Edison family decides to buy a carton of punch. Each carton costs $1.85. Will $20 be enough to pay for punch for the Edisons? If so, how much change will Tom Edison receive from a $20 bill?

LOGICAL REASONING

Sometimes you can solve a problem by eliminating other possible answers.

Sammy, Cindy, and Kate each have a different kind of animal for a pet. Kate has a big red parrot. Sammy doesn't like snakes. Who owns the lizard?

Make a table to answer the question. Write *no* for every answer you can eliminate.

	Parrot	Snake	Lizard
Kate	yes	no	no
Sammy	no		
Cindy	no		

Kate owns the parrot. So, Sammy and Cindy do not have parrots. Kate does not have a snake or a lizard.

	Parrot	Snake	Lizard
Kate	yes	no	no
Sammy	no	no	yes
Cindy	no	yes	no

Sammy doesn't like snakes. So, Cindy owns the snake. Sammy owns the lizard.

Sammy owns the lizard.

Solve. Make a table to answer the questions.

Joe, Kelly, Lee, and Diane are playing hide-and-seek. Joe is afraid to hide in the basement. Kelly's friend is hiding in the closet. Lee is behind the couch, giggling. Kelly is looking for the others.

1. Who is hiding in the basement?

2. Who is hiding in the closet?

GROUP PROJECT

Broken Bicycle Blues

The problem: Your bicycle has two flat tires and the brakes don't work. You need it every day to go to school and to visit your friend's house afterward.

The Options: You can take it to a repair shop or fix it yourself.

After you look at the Key Facts, discuss the options with your classmates. Which option would you choose?

Key Facts

Repair Shop

- The repair shop charges $5.00 for a brake adjustment.
- A broken cable in the brake costs $6.00 to repair. That includes the adjustment.
- It costs $7.00 to install a front and $8.00 to install a rear tire.
- You will have to take the bike to the shop and then pick it up.
- The repair shop can fix it in 24 hours.

Self-Repair

- You will need tools.
- You may need a new brake cable. The cost of a brake cable is $1.00.
- A tire-patch kit costs $3.50.
- You don't know much about bike repair. You can buy a book for $4.95.
- You may have to find someone who can help you.
- It may take you a long time to do the repairs yourself.

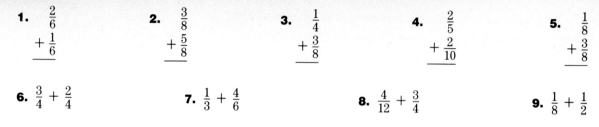

CHAPTER TEST

Add. Write the sum in simplest form. (pages 236 and 238)

1. $\frac{2}{6}$
$+\frac{1}{6}$

2. $\frac{3}{8}$
$+\frac{5}{8}$

3. $\frac{1}{4}$
$+\frac{3}{8}$

4. $\frac{2}{5}$
$+\frac{2}{10}$

5. $\frac{1}{8}$
$+\frac{3}{8}$

6. $\frac{3}{4} + \frac{2}{4}$

7. $\frac{1}{3} + \frac{4}{6}$

8. $\frac{4}{12} + \frac{3}{4}$

9. $\frac{1}{8} + \frac{1}{2}$

Subtract. Write the difference in simplest form. (pages 242 and 244)

10. $\frac{5}{8}$
$-\frac{3}{8}$

11. $\frac{3}{4}$
$-\frac{1}{4}$

12. $\frac{8}{10}$
$-\frac{3}{5}$

13. $\frac{5}{6}$
$-\frac{1}{3}$

14. $\frac{5}{6}$
$-\frac{5}{6}$

15. $\frac{5}{6} - \frac{1}{6}$

16. $\frac{3}{4} - \frac{9}{12}$

17. $\frac{7}{8} - \frac{3}{4}$

18. $\frac{1}{2} - \frac{1}{6}$

Add or subtract. Write the answer in simplest form. (page 246)

19. $8\frac{2}{3}$
$-7\frac{1}{3}$

20. $4\frac{3}{5}$
$+2\frac{1}{5}$

21. $3\frac{1}{2}$
$+2\frac{1}{2}$

22. $8\frac{3}{4}$
$-5\frac{1}{4}$

Write as a decimal. (pages 250 and 252)

23. three hundredths

24. twenty-seven and nine tenths

25. $\frac{7}{10}$

26. $7\frac{62}{100}$

27. $91\frac{8}{10}$

Compare. Write >, <, or = for ●. (page 254)

28. 25.9 ● 29.5

29. 0.7 ● 0.07

30. 127.5 ● 127.50

Write in order from the greatest to the least. (page 254)

31. 99.05; 99.5; 9.95

32. 27.9; 29.07; 29.70

Write in order from the least to the greatest. (page 254)

33. 6.79; 9.76; 7.96

34. 3.03; 0.03; 0.33

Add. (page 258)

35. 7.5
       + 8.9

36. 29.05
       + 31.2

37. 84.5
       + 6.09

38.   2.17
       + 12.58

Subtract. (page 260)

39. 45.6
       − 38.9

40. 55.05
       − 21.99

41. 63.5
       − 2.9

42. 8.7
       − 6.08

43. 21.63 − 5.8

44. 18.1 − 7.36

45. 95.3 − 0.08

46. 44.7 − 2.01

Estimate. (page 256)

47. 73.49 + 18.31

48. 32.91 − 20.35

49. 75.2 + 23.5

50. 97.1 − 64.8

BONUS

Compare. Write >, <, or = for ●.

1. $0.50 ● $5.00

2. $4.32 ● $3.42

3. $0.75 ● $0.75

Write in order from the greatest to the least.

4. $7.20; $72.20; $0.72

5. $0.25; $0.52; $0.27

6. $9.86; $90.68; $90.86

7. $4.00; $40.00; $400.00

RETEACHING

Before you can add or subtract fractions that have different denominators, you need to write the fractions as equivalent fractions that have like denominators.

Add $\frac{1}{3} + \frac{1}{6}$.

$\frac{1}{3} + \frac{1}{6}$ $\boxed{\frac{1}{3} = \frac{1 \times 2}{3 \times 2} = \frac{2}{6}}$

$\frac{2}{6} + \frac{1}{6} = \frac{2 + 1}{6} = \frac{3}{6}$, or $\frac{1}{2}$

Subtract $\frac{6}{12} - \frac{1}{4}$.

$\frac{6}{12} - \frac{1}{4}$ $\boxed{\frac{1}{4} = \frac{1 \times 3}{4 \times 3} = \frac{3}{12}}$

$\frac{6}{12} - \frac{3}{12} = \frac{6 - 3}{12} = \frac{3}{12}$, or $\frac{1}{4}$

Other examples:

$\frac{2}{3} \longrightarrow \frac{4}{6}$

$+\frac{5}{6} \longrightarrow +\frac{5}{6}$

$\frac{9}{6} = 1\frac{3}{6}$, or $1\frac{1}{2}$

$\frac{4}{5} \longrightarrow \frac{8}{10}$

$+\frac{2}{10} \longrightarrow +\frac{2}{10}$

$\frac{10}{10}$, or 1

$\frac{6}{8} \longrightarrow \frac{6}{8}$

$-\frac{3}{4} \longrightarrow -\frac{6}{8}$

$\frac{0}{8}$, or 0

Add or subtract. Write the answer in simplest form.

1. $\frac{1}{3}$
$+\frac{1}{9}$

2. $\frac{7}{8}$
$-\frac{2}{4}$

3. $\frac{1}{4}$
$+\frac{2}{12}$

4. $\frac{2}{3}$
$-\frac{1}{6}$

5. $\frac{3}{4}$
$+\frac{1}{8}$

6. $\frac{5}{6}$
$-\frac{1}{3}$

7. $\frac{3}{5}$
$+\frac{2}{10}$

8. $\frac{3}{4}$
$-\frac{1}{2}$

9. $\frac{2}{8}$
$+\frac{1}{4}$

10. $\frac{5}{8}$
$-\frac{1}{4}$

11. $\frac{4}{8}$
$+\frac{1}{4}$

12. $\frac{9}{10}$
$-\frac{2}{5}$

13. $\frac{2}{4}$
$+\frac{1}{8}$

14. $\frac{6}{8}$
$-\frac{2}{4}$

15. $\frac{2}{8} + \frac{3}{4}$

16. $\frac{3}{6} + \frac{1}{2}$

17. $\frac{5}{8} - \frac{1}{2}$

18. $\frac{1}{5} + \frac{8}{10}$

19. $\frac{7}{10} - \frac{1}{5}$

20. $\frac{2}{4} + \frac{4}{8}$

21. $\frac{2}{6} + \frac{2}{3}$

22. $\frac{3}{9} - \frac{1}{3}$

23. $\frac{3}{4} + \frac{1}{2}$

24. $\frac{2}{3} + \frac{4}{6}$

25. $\frac{1}{2} - \frac{6}{12}$

26. $\frac{6}{10} + \frac{3}{5}$

27. $\frac{7}{8} + \frac{1}{2}$

28. $\frac{7}{10} - \frac{1}{2}$

29. $\frac{8}{12} + \frac{2}{3}$

ENRICHMENT

Percent

You can write a ratio as a fraction.

Ratio	6 to 100	42 to 100	100 to 100
Fraction	$\frac{6}{100}$	$\frac{42}{100}$	$\frac{100}{100}$

If the denominator of the fraction is 100, you can write the ratio as a **percent (%)**. *Percent* means "per hundred."

Ratio	6 to 100	42 to 100	100 to 100
Fraction	$\frac{6}{100}$	$\frac{42}{100}$ ·	$\frac{100}{100}$
Percent	6%	42%	100%

Write each ratio as a fraction and as a percent.

1. 7 to 100   **2.** 9 to 100   **3.** 65 to 100   **4.** 1 to 100

5. 25 to 100   **6.** 13 to 100   **7.** 41 to 100   **8.** 99 to 100

Write each fraction as a percent.

9. $\frac{5}{100}$ **10.** $\frac{2}{100}$ **11.** $\frac{15}{100}$ **12.** $\frac{75}{100}$ **13.** $\frac{66}{100}$

14. $\frac{9}{100}$ **15.** $\frac{1}{100}$ **16.** $\frac{55}{100}$ **17.** $\frac{80}{100}$ **18.** $\frac{95}{100}$

Write each percent as a fraction.

19. 9%   **20.** 3%   **21.** 5%   **22.** 8%   **23.** 4%

24. 63%   **25.** 28%   **26.** 18%   **27.** 44%   **28.** 97%

TECHNOLOGY

You can write a LOGO procedure to draw a picture that has many different parts. First, write a procedure that tells the turtle to draw the different parts, one after another. Then write procedures to draw the different parts.

Here is an example.

The procedure TO FLAGPOLE tells the turtle to draw a flagpole. The procedure TO POLE draws the pole. The procedure TO FLAG draws the flag.

```
TO FLAGPOLE
POLE   FLAG
END

TO POLE
REPEAT 2   [FD 80   LT 90   FD 2   LT 90]   FD 80
END

TO FLAG
REPEAT 2   [RT 90   FD 60   RT 90   FD 30]
END
```

Here is what the flagpole looks like.

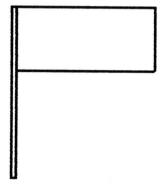

1. What does FLOWER draw? Draw the picture.

```
TO FLOWER
STEM
PETAL
END

TO STEM
PU   RT 90   FD 1   PD
REPEAT 2   [RT 90   FD 40   RT 90   FD 2]
RT 90   FD 40   LT 120   FD 20   LT 120   FD 10
LT 90   FD 17   RT 60   FD 2   RT 30   FD 20
RT 120   FD 10   RT 90   FD 17   LT 150   FD 40
RT 90   FD 1   LT 90
END

TO PETAL
LT 120   REPEAT 3   [FD 15   RT 120]
LT 120   REPEAT 3   [FD 15   LT 120]
LT 150   REPEAT 3   [FD 15   RT 120]
END
```

2. Write a line to add another petal to the flower.

★3. Use what you have learned about using one procedure to draw a picture that has many parts to write a procedure for drawing four flowers in a row.

CUMULATIVE REVIEW

Write the letter of the correct answer.

1. Which is the fraction for four fifths?

   a. $\frac{1}{5}$ **b.** $\frac{4}{5}$

   c. $\frac{5}{4}$ **d.** not given

2. Find $\frac{3}{8}$ of 24.   **a.** 3

                         b. 8

                         c. 9

                         d. not given

3. $\frac{2}{3} = \frac{\blacksquare}{12}$

   a. 6   **b.** 8

   c. 9   **d.** not given

4. $\frac{16}{24} = \frac{\blacksquare}{6}$

   a. 2   **b.** 3

   c. 4   **d.** not given

5. What is $\frac{10}{12}$ in simplest form?

   a. $\frac{2}{6}$ **b.** $\frac{5}{12}$

   c. $\frac{5}{6}$ **d.** not given

6. What is $\frac{21}{7}$ in simplest form?

   a. $\frac{1}{3}$ **b.** $\frac{3}{7}$

   c. 3   **d.** not given

7. $4\overline{)784}$

   a. 195   **b.** 195 R4

   c. 196   **d.** not given

8. 9×623

   a. 5,487   **b.** 5,587

   c. 541,827   **d.** not given

9. $35 \div 7$

   a. 5   **b.** 28

   c. 42   **d.** not given

10. 0×5

   a. 0   **b.** 1

   c. 5   **d.** not given

11. $879 + 8 + 3{,}926$

   a. 4,803   **b.** 4,813

   c. 20,716   **d.** not given

12.

Look at the circle graph to find how much of Amy's allowance she budgets for savings.

   a. $\frac{1}{8}$ **b.** $\frac{1}{2}$

   c. $\frac{1}{4}$ **d.** not given

13. There are 216 people on the minitrain at the zoo, and 8 people in each train car. How many cars are there?

   a. 27 cars   **b.** 208 cars

   c. 1,728 cars   **d.** not given

Your class is working on a science experiment. Make 5 paper airplanes of different lengths and widths. Then test each plane to see how far it flies. Compare the results, and decide how the size of an airplane affects the distance it flies.

9 MEASUREMENT

Centimeter

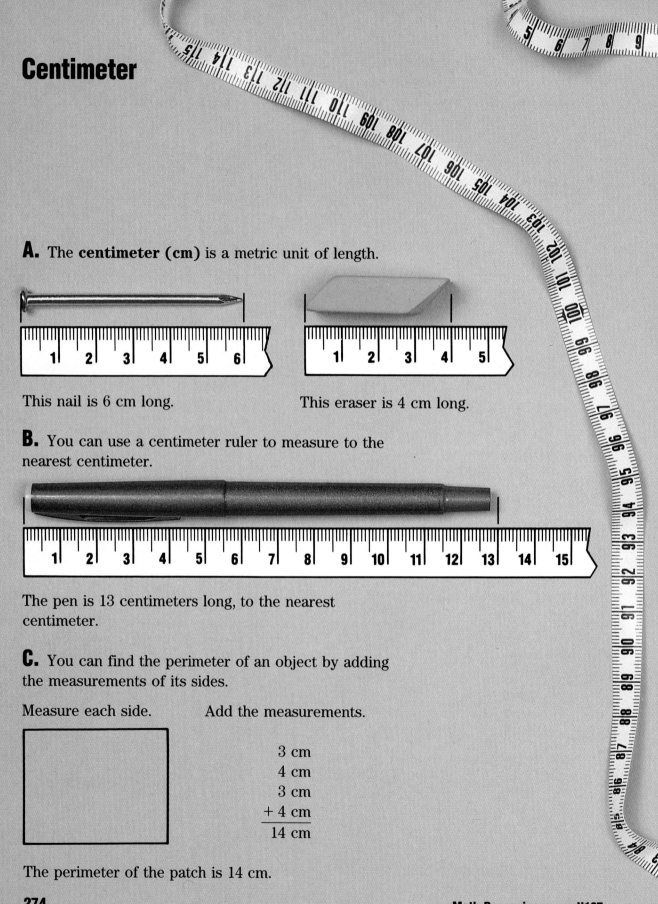

A. The **centimeter (cm)** is a metric unit of length.

This nail is 6 cm long.

This eraser is 4 cm long.

B. You can use a centimeter ruler to measure to the nearest centimeter.

The pen is 13 centimeters long, to the nearest centimeter.

C. You can find the perimeter of an object by adding the measurements of its sides.

Measure each side.

Add the measurements.

$$
\begin{array}{r}
3 \text{ cm} \\
4 \text{ cm} \\
3 \text{ cm} \\
+\ 4 \text{ cm} \\
\hline
14 \text{ cm}
\end{array}
$$

The perimeter of the patch is 14 cm.

Math Reasoning, page H197

Measure to the nearest centimeter.

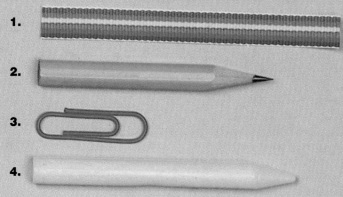

1.

2.

3.

4.

Find the perimeter of each shape.

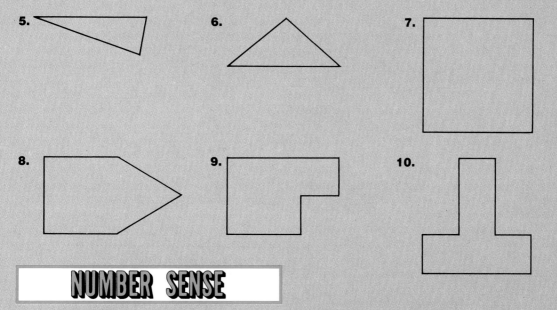

5.

6.

7.

8.

9.

10.

NUMBER SENSE

Copy and complete the table. Estimate in centimeters the length of different objects in your classroom. Then use a centimeter ruler to measure each object to the nearest centimeter.

Object	Estimate	Actual measure
Your shoe		
Your index finger		
A chalkboard eraser		
A pencil		

Meter and Kilometer

A. The **meter (m)** and the **kilometer (km)** are other metric units of length.

A golf club is about 1 m long.

You can walk 1 km in about 10 min.

> 1 meter (m) = 100 centimeters (cm)
> 1 kilometer (km) = 1,000 meters (m)

B. You can rename measurements by using a pattern.

You can rename a larger unit with a smaller unit.

6 m = ▧ cm
6 m = 600 cm

> 1 m = 100 cm
> So, 6 m = 600 cm.

m	1	2	3	4	5	6
cm	100	200	300	400	500	600

You can rename a smaller unit with a larger unit.

5,000 m = ▧ km
5,000 m = 5 km

> 1,000 m = 1 km
> So, 5,000 m = 5 km.

m	1,000	2,000	3,000	4,000	5,000
km	1	2	3	4	5

C. To choose a unit of length for measurement, think of the sizes of the units. Choose the unit that is appropriate.

To measure short distances, use centimeters.

20 cm

To measure longer distances, use meters.

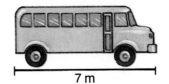

7 m

To measure very long distances, use kilometers.

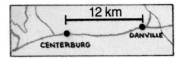

12 km

CENTERBURG DANVILLE

Copy and complete.

1. 3 m = ▨ cm
2. 8,000 m = ▨ km
3. 12 m = ▨ cm

4. 900 cm = ▨ m
5. 4 m = ▨ cm
6. 7 m = ▨ cm

7. 46 m = ▨ cm
8. 99,000 m = ▨ km
9. 26 km = ▨ m

Write *cm*, *m*, or *km* for the unit you would use to measure each.

10. the width of a book
11. the height of a house

12. the distance between two cities
13. the length of a pen

14. the height of a tree
15. the length of a shoelace

16. the length of a river
17. the width of a sidewalk

Solve.

18. Joyce learns that a diving bell can descend 3 kilometers into the ocean. How many meters is this?

19. Jane is growing vegetables for a school project. In her garden, she weeds a row that is 4 meters long. How many centimeters is this?

20. Zeke is building a fence for a model farm. The fence encloses a garden that has sides that are 15 cm, 10 cm, 15 cm, and 10 cm long. How many centimeters long must the fence be?

21. Keith uses binoculars for bird watching. He spots a bird at the top of a very tall tree. Estimate the height of the tree. Write the letter of the correct answer.

    a. 2 m   b. 20 m   c. 2 km

For a related activity, see *Connecting Math Ideas*, p. 398

ANOTHER LOOK

Multiply.

1. $2.16 × 6	2. $7.78 × 9	3. $1.21 × 4	4. $3.13 × 2	5. $4.65 × 7
6. $0.73 × 3	7. $15.95 × 2	8. $2.98 × 7	9. $1.59 × 4	10. $3.50 × 8
11. $8.75 × 9	12. $0.45 × 3	13. $9.35 × 4	14. $0.06 × 5	15. $34.95 × 2

Liter and Milliliter

A. The **milliliter (mL)** and the **liter (L)** are metric units of capacity.

10 drops from a medicine dropper is about 1 milliliter.

This container of milk holds 1 liter.

$$1 \text{ liter (L)} = 1{,}000 \text{ milliliters (mL)}$$

B. You can rename measurements by using a pattern.

You can rename a larger unit with a smaller unit.

3 L = ▥ mL
3 L = 3,000 mL

> 1 L = 1,000 mL
> So, 3 L = 3,000 mL.

L	1	2	3	4	5
mL	1,000	2,000	3,000	4,000	5,000

You can rename a smaller unit with a larger unit.

8,000 mL = ▥ L
8,000 mL = 8 L

> 1,000 mL = 1 L
> So, 8,000 mL = 8 L.

mL	1,000	2,000	3,000	4,000	5,000
L	1	2	3	4	5

C. To choose a unit of capacity for measurement, think of the sizes of the units. Choose the unit that is appropriate.

To measure small amounts of fluids, use milliliters.

To measure large amounts of fluids, use liters.

Checkpoint   Write the letter of the correct answer.

Complete.

1. 2 L = ▥ mL

a. 2   **b.** 20
c. 1,002   **d.** 2,000

2. 5,000 mL = ▥ L

a. 5,000,000   **b.** 5
c. 1,000   **d.** 50

3. The capacity of a bathtub is about 106 ▥.

a. kg   **b.** mL   **c.** L   **d.** cm

Copy and complete.

1. 5 L = ☐ mL

2. 6,000 mL = ☐ L

3. 9 L = ☐ mL

4. 4,000 mL = ☐ L

5. 8 L = ☐ mL

6. 7,000 mL = ☐ L

7. 16 L = ☐ mL

8. 27,000 mL = ☐ L

9. 92 L = ☐ mL

Write *mL* or *L* for the unit you would use to measure each.

10.

11.

12.

13.

14.

15.

Solve.

16. There are 19.8 liters of water in Sue's aquarium and 17.72 liters of water in Steve's aquarium. How many more liters of water are there in Sue's aquarium?

17. Craig's aquarium holds 30 liters of water. There are 22 liters of water in it. How many more liters does he need to fill the aquarium? How many milliliters is this?

MIDCHAPTER REVIEW

Copy and complete.

1. 7 m = ☐ cm

2. 4,000 m = ☐ km

3. 6 L = ☐ mL

4. 8,000 cm = ☐ m

5. 9 km = ☐ m

6. 2,000 mL = ☐ L

Use your ruler to find the perimeter.

7.

8.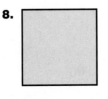

9.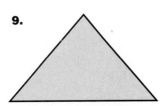

Gram and Kilogram

A. The **gram (g)** and the **kilogram (kg)** are metric units of mass.

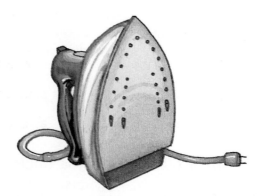

A pin has a mass of about 1 gram.

An iron has a mass of about 1 kilogram.

> 1 kilogram (kg) = 1,000 grams (g)

B. You can rename measurements by using a pattern.

You can rename a larger unit with a smaller unit.

kg	1	2	3	4	5
g	1,000	2,000	3,000	4,000	5,000

4 kg = ▨ g
4 kg = 4,000 g

> 1 kg = 1,000 g
> So, 4 kg = 4,000 g.

You can rename a smaller unit with a larger unit.

g	1,000	2,000	3,000	4,000	5,000
kg	1	2	3	4	5

7,000 g = ▨ kg
7,000 g = 7 kg

> 1,000 g = 1 kg
> So, 7,000 g = 7 kg.

C. To choose a unit of mass for measurement, think of the sizes of the units. Choose the unit that is appropriate.

To measure objects that have smaller masses, use grams.

To measure objects that have larger masses, use kilograms.

Checkpoint Write the letter of the correct answer.

Complete.

1. 5 kg = ▨ g

a. 5   **b.** 1,005
c. 50   **d.** 5,000

2. 6,000 g = ▨ kg

a. 6,000,000   **b.** 1,000
c. 6   **d.** 60

3. The mass of a glass measuring cup is about 100 ▨.

a. m   **b.** g   **c.** kg   **d.** km

Copy and complete.

1. 7,000 g = ▓ kg   **2.** 2 kg = ▓ g   **3.** 1,000 g = ▓ kg

4. 8 kg = ▓ g   **5.** 15,000 g = ▓ kg   **6.** 13 kg = ▓ g

7. 9,000 g = ▓ kg   **8.** 5 kg = ▓ g   **9.** 3,000 g = ▓ kg

Write *g* or *kg* for the unit you would use to measure each.

10.   **11.**   **12.**

13.   **14.**   **15.**

16.   **17.**   **18.**

Solve.

19. The self-winding wristwatch was invented in 1929. If you wanted to measure its mass, would you use grams or kilograms?

20. A portable alarm clock was built in 1550. Its mass was about 4 kilograms. How many grams is this?

21. The stem of a self-winding wristwatch has a mass of 1.4 grams. The crystal has a mass of 1.7 grams. What is the total mass of both watch parts?

★22. Estimate the mass of the following objects: a grapefruit, a feather, a football player, an alarm clock, an elephant, a bowling ball, and a wristwatch. Then order the objects by mass from the least to the greatest.

PROBLEM SOLVING
Drawing a Picture/Making a Model

Drawing a picture or making a model can sometimes help you understand a problem and plan a solution.

Ashley and her dad plan to put carpet squares on the floor of her playhouse. The playhouse is 8 feet long and 6 feet wide. Each carpet square is 1 foot long and 1 foot wide. Draw a picture on graph paper to find how many carpet squares Ashley and her dad will need.

1 square on the graph paper stands for 1 carpet square.

Count the squares on your drawing to solve the problem.

Ashley and her dad will need 48 carpet squares to cover the floor of her playhouse.

Suppose you cut squares of equal size from construction paper.

- How could you make a model to solve the problem?

Draw a picture or make a model to solve each problem.

1. Joshua told his class how the bus takes him home. The bus starts at the school, travels 4 blocks straight ahead, and turns left. It travels 8 blocks and turns left again. Finally, it travels 4 blocks and he reaches home. How many blocks does Joshua live from school? HINT: Use graph paper to help you.

2. Blue Lake School has a soccer competition at their Annual Field Day. This year the Red Team won more games than the Blue Team. The Green Team won more games than the Red Team but fewer games than the Yellow Team. Which team won the most games?

3. Look at the figures. How many dots will there be in the next figure?

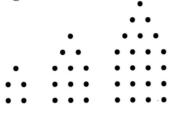

4. William is fencing his back yard. The yard is 54 feet long and 36 feet wide. If he puts a fence post every 6 feet, how many fence posts will he need? You may wish to use toothpicks to make a model.

5. Three of Kevin's classmates live in his apartment building. Yolanda lives 4 floors above Kevin. Kevin lives on the third floor, which is 2 floors below Sherry's floor. Alex lives four floors above Sherry. On which floor does Alex live?

6. Six cheerleaders line up in order from the shortest to the tallest for a team photograph. Sara is taller than Joan. Kim is shorter than Joan but taller than Sabrina. Sabrina is taller than Joy. Maria is the tallest of the team. Who is the shortest cheerleader on the team?

7. Jerry and his coach want to mark off sections of the playground for field-day events. The relay-race section is five times longer than the tug-of-war section, but only $\frac{1}{2}$ as wide as the sack-race section. The tug of war section is 10 yards long and the sack-race section is 20 yards wide. How long and wide is the relay-race section?

★8. Draw a picture to show the next figure.

PROBLEM SOLVING
Guessing and Checking

Sometimes guessing can help you solve problems. Guess at the answer by using the clues given. Check against the clues to see if your answer is correct.

> Kevin reported on 98 birds from North and South America. He studied 14 more birds from North America than from South America. On how many birds from each continent did he report?

What do you know about the 2 numbers you must find? $\longrightarrow$ Their sum is 98. Their difference is 14.

Make a guess. Since you know that the sum of the numbers is 98, begin your guess with two numbers that add to 98. $\longrightarrow$ $76 + 22 = 98$
$76 - 22 = 54 \qquad 54 \neq 14$

Your first guess was not correct. Think about 56 and 42. $\longrightarrow$ $56 + 42 = 98$
$56 - 42 = 14$

The second guess, 56 and 42, works.

Kevin reported on 56 birds from North America and 42 birds from South America.

This is Mystery Week at the library. Here is the mystery:

Find the missing Verne jewels. They were in 2 boxes that were loaded onto a train at Amethyst Station. They were supposed to be unloaded at Ruby, the last stop. But they were unloaded at 2 other stations by mistake.

Use the clues on the next page. You will be comparing the number of items unloaded at each station with the number that should have been unloaded at that station.

At which 2 stations were the jewels unloaded?

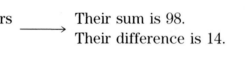

Solve.

1. There were 12 boxes and crates unloaded at Crystal Station. There should have been 2 more boxes than crates in this batch. Is there a pair of numbers whose sum is 12 and whose difference is 2?

Try 9 and 3. $9 + 3 = 12$; $9 - 3 = 6$ NO
Try 7 and 5. $7 + 5 = 12$; $7 - 5 = 2$ YES

There were 7 boxes and 5 crates unloaded here. Neither of the jewel boxes was unloaded at Crystal Station by mistake.

Look at each set of clues below. If the 2 clues match correctly, write how many boxes and crates were unloaded. If they don't match, write *jewels*. This shows that one of the jewel boxes has been found.

REMEMBER: You are trying to find 2 jewel boxes.

2. 12 boxes and crates were unloaded at Diamond. There should have been 6 more boxes than crates.

3. 25 boxes and crates were unloaded at Emerald. There should have been 11 more boxes than crates.

4. 17 boxes and crates were unloaded at Topaz. There should have been 2 more boxes than crates.

5. At Garnet, 23 items were unloaded. There should have been 7 more boxes than crates.

6. At Pearl, 22 items were unloaded. There should have been 6 more boxes than crates.

7. 19 items were unloaded at Jade. There should have been 8 more boxes than crates.

8. At which 2 stations were the jewel boxes mistakenly unloaded?

Inch

A. The **inch (in.)** is a customary unit of length.

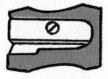

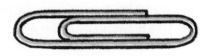

This pencil sharpener is 1 in. long.   This paper clip is 2 in. long.

B. You can use a ruler to measure to the nearest inch, half inch, or quarter inch.

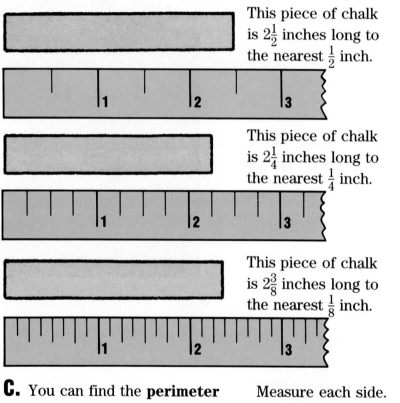

This piece of chalk is $2\frac{1}{2}$ inches long to the nearest $\frac{1}{2}$ inch.

This piece of chalk is $2\frac{1}{4}$ inches long to the nearest $\frac{1}{4}$ inch.

This piece of chalk is $2\frac{3}{8}$ inches long to the nearest $\frac{1}{8}$ inch.

C. You can find the **perimeter** of an object by adding the measurements of its sides.

Measure each side.

Add the measurements.

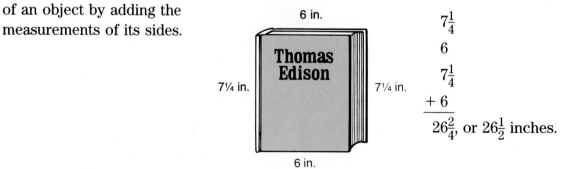

6 in.

Thomas Edison

7¼ in.   7¼ in.

6 in.

$$7\frac{1}{4}$$
$$6$$
$$7\frac{1}{4}$$
$$+\ 6$$

$26\frac{2}{4}$, or $26\frac{1}{2}$ inches.

Measure each length.

1.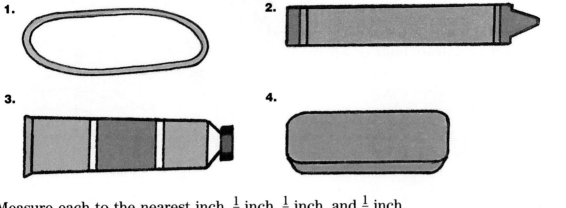

2.

3.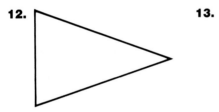

4.

Measure each to the nearest inch, $\frac{1}{2}$ inch, $\frac{1}{4}$ inch, and $\frac{1}{8}$ inch.

5.

6.

Use your ruler to draw each line.

7. $2\frac{1}{4}$ in.   **8.** 3 in.   **9.** $1\frac{1}{2}$ in.   **10.** $4\frac{3}{4}$ in.   **11.** $2\frac{1}{8}$ in.

Find the perimeter of each shape.

12. 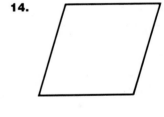   **13.**   **14.**

NUMBER SENSE

You can multiply a number by 10; 100; or 1,000.

Multiply 6×100.

Step 1: Write the first factor.   6

Step 2: Write the same number of zeros as   600   So, $6 \times 100 = 600$.
        in the second factor.

Multiply.

1. 6×10 **2.** 5×100 **3.** $4 \times 1,000$ **4.** 9×100

5. $8 \times 1,000$ **6.** 3×100 **7.** 25×100 **8.** 27×10

Foot, Yard, and Mile

A. The **foot (ft)**, the **yard (yd)**, and the **mile (mi)** are customary units of length.

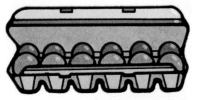

An egg carton is about 1 ft long.

A window is about 1 yd wide.

You can walk about 1 mi in 20 min.

B. You can rename units of length by following a pattern.

12 inches (in.) = 1 foot (ft)	36 inches (in.) = 1 yard (yd)
3 feet (ft) = 1 yard (yd)	5,280 feet (ft) = 1 mile (mi)
1,760 yards (yd) = 1 mile (mi)	

You can rename a larger unit with a smaller unit.

ft	1	2	3	4	5	6
in.	12	24	36	48	60	72

3 ft = ▓ in.

3 ft = 36 in.

Since 1 ft = 12 in.,
3 ft = 36 in.

You can rename a smaller unit with a larger unit.

ft	3	6	9	12	15	18
yd	1	2	3	4	5	6

12 ft = ▓ yd

12 ft = 4 yd

Since 3 ft = 1 yd,
12 ft = 4 yd

Math Reasoning, page H198

Write *in.*, *ft*, *yd*, or *mi* for the unit you would use to measure each.

1. the length of a football field

2. the height of a cup

3. the depth of a pond

4. the distance across California

5. the width of a door

6. the height of a man

7. the length of a pencil

8. the length of your classroom

Copy and complete.

9. 6 ft = ▨ yd

10. 5 yd = ▨ ft

11. 48 in. = ▨ ft

12. 3 yd = ▨ ft

13. 5 ft = ▨ in.

14. 12 ft = ▨ yd

15. 3 mi = ▨ yd

16. 84 in. = ▨ ft

17. 3,520 yd = ▨ mi

★18. 3 yd = ▨ in.

★19. 2 mi = ▨ ft

★20. 1 mi = ▨ in.

Solve.

21. Emmy needs 2 yd of twine for a science project. How many feet of twine is this?

22. Christine is making a diorama. She uses 16 in. of yellow string and 8 in. of blue string. How many feet of string does she use altogether?

23. Warren is building a flower box that is 36 inches long. How many feet or yards is this? Use this information to write and solve your own word problem.

CHALLENGE

Complete the magic square. The sum of the numbers in each row will be 21, whether added across, down, or diagonally.

8	3	▨
▨	▨	▨
▨	11	6

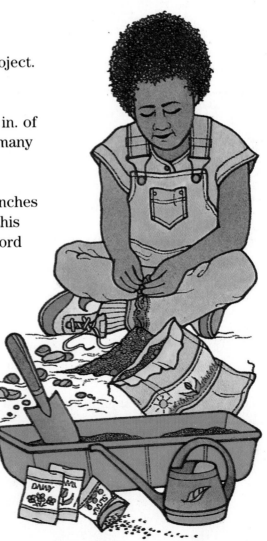

Ounce, Pound, and Ton

A. The **ounce (oz)**, the **pound (lb)**, and the **ton (T)** are customary units of weight.

A pencil weighs about 1 oz.

A telephone weighs about 1 lb.

A draft horse weighs about 1 T.

> 16 ounces (oz) = 1 pound (lb)
> 2,000 pounds (lb) = 1 ton (T)

B. You can rename units of weight by using a pattern.

You can rename a larger unit with a smaller unit.

lb	1	2	3	4	5	6
oz	16	32	48	64	80	96

4 lb = ▧ oz
4 lb = 64 oz

> Since 1 lb = 16 oz,
> 4 lb = 64 oz.

You can rename a smaller unit with a larger unit.

lb	2,000	4,000	6,000	8,000	10,000
T	1	2	3	4	5

6,000 lb = ▧ T
6,000 lb = 3 T

> Since 2,000 lb = 1 T,
> 6,000 lb = 3 T.

Write *oz*, *lb*, or *T* for the unit you would use to measure each.

1.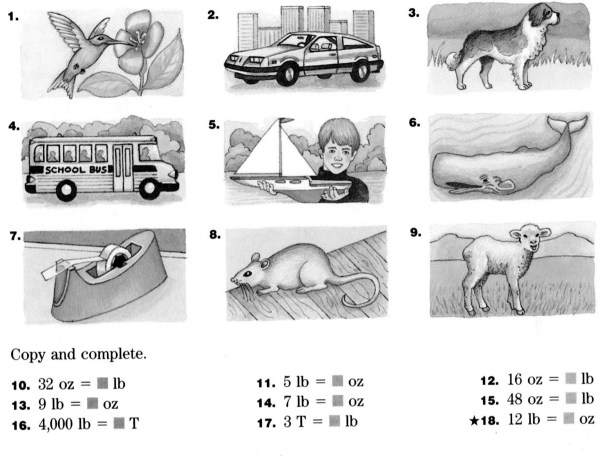

2.

3.

4.

5.

6.

7.

8.

9.

Copy and complete.

10. 32 oz = ▧ lb

11. 5 lb = ▧ oz

12. 16 oz = ▧ lb

13. 9 lb = ▧ oz

14. 7 lb = ▧ oz

15. 48 oz = ▧ lb

16. 4,000 lb = ▧ T

17. 3 T = ▧ lb

★18. 12 lb = ▧ oz

Solve. For Problem 20, use the Infobank.

19. LaDonna is keeping track of her turtle's growth. The turtle has gained 32 oz since LaDonna found it. How many pounds is this?

20. Use the information on page 405 to solve. The table shows Ray's growth over the last four years. Find how many ounces Ray gained between fourth grade and fifth grade.

CHALLENGE Patterns, Relations, and Functions

Find the missing unit of measurement.

1. 6,000 ▲ = 3 ●

2. 1 ● ÷ 10 = 200 ▲

3. 8,000 ▧ = 500 ▲

4. 160 ▧ = 10 ▲

5. 2 ● = 4,000 ▲

6. 32 ▧ = 2 ▲

Cup, Pint, Quart, and Gallon

A. The **cup (c)**, the **pint (pt)**, the **quart (qt)**, and the **gallon (gal)** are customary units of liquid capacity.

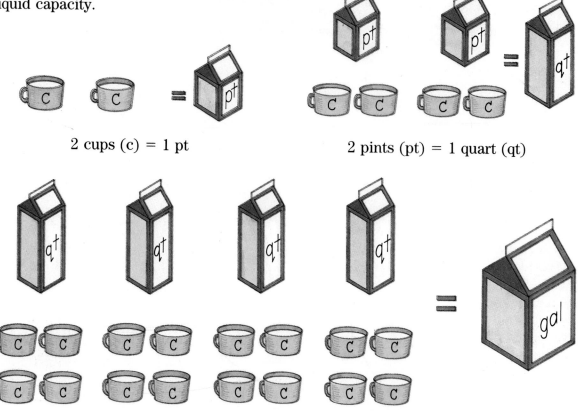

2 cups (c) = 1 pt

2 pints (pt) = 1 quart (qt)

4 quarts (qt) = 1 gallon (gal)

B. You can rename units of liquid measurement by following a pattern.

You can rename a larger unit with a smaller unit.

gal	1	2	3	4	5	6
qt	4	8	12	16	20	24

6 gal = ■ qt
6 gal = 24 qt

Since 1 gal = 4 qt,
6 gal = 24 qt.

You can rename a smaller unit with a larger unit.

c	2	4	6	8	10	12
pt	1	2	3	4	5	6

4 c = ■ pt
4 c = 2 pt

Since 2 c = 1 pt,
4 c = 2 pt.

Write *c*, *pt*, *qt*, or *gal* for the unit you would use to measure each.

1. juice in a drinking glass

2. water in a bathtub

3. a can of oil for your car

4. a jar of tomato sauce

Copy and complete.

5. 6 qt = ▨ pt

6. 8 c = ▨ pt

7. 12 pt = ▨ qt

8. 3 gal = ▨ qt

9. 5 pt = ▨ c

10. 20 pt = ▨ qt

11. 32 qt = ▨ gal

12. 16 pt = ▨ qt

13. 2 gal = ▨ qt

14. 16 qt = ▨ gal

15. 32 c = ▨ pt

16. 4 qt = ▨ pt

17. 9 qt = ▨ pt

★18. 3 gal = ▨ c

★19. 64 c = ▨ gal

Solve.

20. Jerry created a miniature waterfall for the annual science fair. At the end of every hour, he added a quart of water to his waterfall. After 4 hours, how many gallons had he added?

21. To fill her aquarium to the brim, Leslie used 4 gallons of water. How many quarts did she use?

★22. Mrs. Samson brought 2 gal of juice for the class trip to the zoo. How many quarts did she bring? If she used all the juice she brought in order to give each of her students 1 c of juice, how many students does she have?

★23. Scott needed a total of 3 gal of water to operate the water-powered mill he made for the science fair. He used 3 pt of hot water and 5 pt of lukewarm water. How much cold water did Scott add to complete the 3 gal?

For a related activity, see *Connecting Math Ideas,* p. 399

CHALLENGE

Which contains the greater number of units? Write the numbers and solve.

1. cups in 3 quarts   or   pints in 2 gallons

2. feet in 9 yards   or   inches in 1 yard

3. days in 3 weeks   or   weeks in 2 months

Temperature: Fahrenheit

A. A customary unit of temperature measurement is the **degree Fahrenheit (°F).**

The Fahrenheit thermometer shows normal body temperature, 98.6°F.

B. You write the below-zero temperatures with a minus sign.

⁻5°F is five degrees below zero.

Choose the most likely temperature for each.

1. hot soup

70°F   145°F

2. body temperature of a dog

100°F   0°F

3. sledding weather

22°F   56°F

4. an oven while baking bread

350°F   90°F

Write the temperature in degrees Fahrenheit.

5. twelve degrees below zero

6. six degrees below zero

230°
220°
212°F   Water boils
210°

140°
136°F   Highest weather
130°   temperature ever
         recorded
120°
110°
100°   98.6°F   Normal body
         temperature
90°
86°F   A warm day
80°
70°
68°F   Normal room
60°   temperature
50°← 50°F   A cool day
40°
32°F   Water freezes
30°
20°
10°← 10°F   A cold day
0°
-10°
-20°

Temperature: Celsius

A. The metric unit of temperature measurement is the **degree Celsius (°C).**

The Celsius thermometer shows normal body temperature, 37°C.

B. You write below-zero temperatures with a minus sign.

⁻10°C is ten degrees below zero.

Choose the most likely temperature for each.

1. beach weather

27°C   70°C

2. ice-skating weather

⁻2°C   40°C

3. inside a refrigerator

45°C   5°C

4. picnic weather

79°C   20°C

5. hot water from a faucet

60°C   90°C

Write the temperature in degrees Celsius.

6. seven degrees below zero

7. twenty degrees below zero

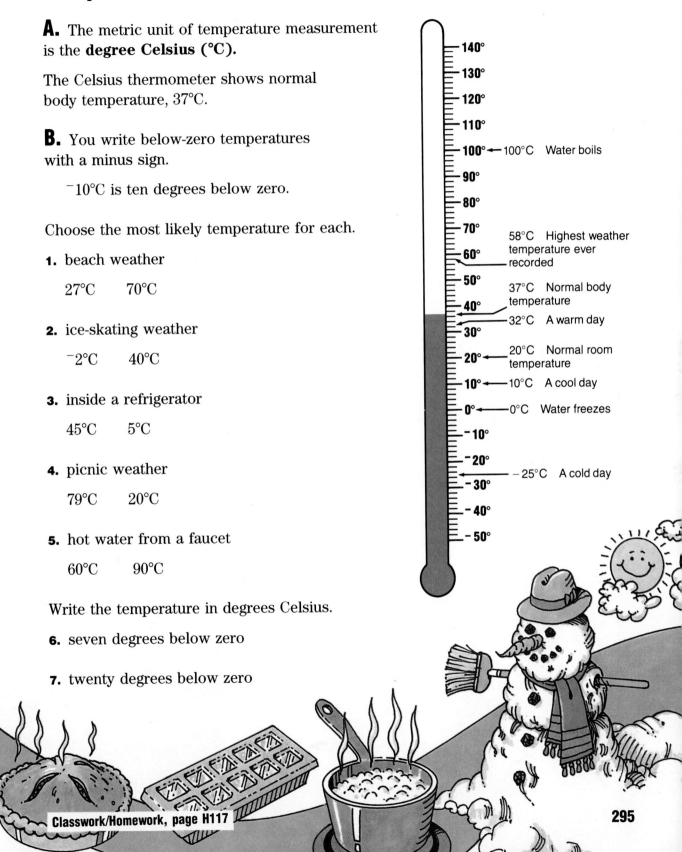

140°
130°
120°
110°
100° ← 100°C   Water boils
90°
80°
70°
60°   58°C   Highest weather temperature ever recorded
50°
40°   37°C   Normal body temperature
           32°C   A warm day
30°
20° ←   20°C   Normal room temperature
10° ←   10°C   A cool day
0° ←   0°C   Water freezes
⁻10°
⁻20°
           ⁻25°C   A cold day
⁻30°
⁻40°
⁻50°

PROBLEM SOLVING
Identifying Needed Information

Some problems do not contain all the information needed to solve them.

The Cranby School holds a science fair in the school gym each May. One row of display booths is 12 yards long. Each display booth is 6 feet long. The students want to know how many booths will fit into each row.

Use the checklist to help you find the needed information.

What information is needed?
   how many feet there are in a yard

Checklist	Yes	No
Do I already know the information?	✔	
Can I find the information		
in a magazine article?		✔
in a reference book?	✔	
from another person?	✔	
Am I really stuck?		✔

Because you know or can find the information, you can solve the problem. There are 3 feet in 1 yard.

So, there are 12 × 3 feet in 12 yards.
$$12 \times 3 = 36$$

There are 36 feet in 12 yards. You can divide 36 feet by 6 feet to find the number of booths.

$$36 \div 6 = 6$$

Each row can contain 6 booths.

Use the chart. Write the letter of the information you need to be able to solve each problem.

1. One booth has charts of the constellations. The class needed 100 stars to complete the charts. Mr. Ruiz bought 8 dozen stars. Did he buy enough for all the charts?

2. One class made nature-study kits. The kits were packed into 8-inch-high boxes. The boxes were stacked on top of one another at the back of a booth. The stack was 6 boxes high. How many feet high was the stack?

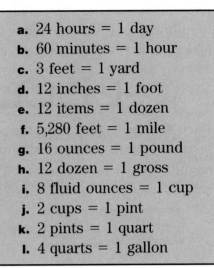

a. 24 hours = 1 day
b. 60 minutes = 1 hour
c. 3 feet = 1 yard
d. 12 inches = 1 foot
e. 12 items = 1 dozen
f. 5,280 feet = 1 mile
g. 16 ounces = 1 pound
h. 12 dozen = 1 gross
i. 8 fluid ounces = 1 cup
j. 2 cups = 1 pint
k. 2 pints = 1 quart
l. 4 quarts = 1 gallon

Write what information you need to solve each problem. Then solve.

3. Ms. Kowal's class built a model house in order to show different ways to save energy. The length of the house was 4 feet. What was the length of the house in inches?

4. The students in Mrs. Syman's class baked bread for the fair. Their recipe called for 8 cups of milk. How many pints of milk did they use?

5. The students in Mr. Kelly's class gave out 6 dozen pamphlets about garden pests. How many pamphlets did they give out?

6. The students served 5 gallons of apple punch at the science fair. How many quarts of punch did they serve? How many cups of punch did they serve?

CALCULATOR

Sometimes numbers less than 0 are used to represent temperatures. Your calculator will also show numbers less than 0. Press these keys on your calculator.

Each time you subtract 1, the answer is 1 less than the previous number. The final answer is 1 less than 0. You should see a 1 on the screen. You'll also see a minus sign. It may look like either of these screens:

| $-$ 1 | OR | $1-$ |

The minus sign on the screen does not show subtraction. It shows that the number on the screen is less than 0. This kind of number is called a **negative number.**

If you want to enter a negative number into the calculator, press the minus sign before the number. Try these additions on your calculator.

$^-3 + 1 + 1 + 1 + 1 =$ ▓ $^-3 + 4 =$ ▓

The sum for both is 1.

Use your calculator to compute these temperature changes in degrees Celsius. (Remember to clear the calculator between exercises.)

	Starting Temperature	Temperature Change	Calculator Keys	Final Temperature
Example	$^-3°$ C	up 5° C	$[-]\ [3]\ [+]\ [5]\ [=]$	2° C
1.	$^-4°$ C	up 7° C		
2.	$^-5°$ C	up 9° C		
3.	$^-7°$ C	up 5° C		
4.	$^-5°$ C	up 2° C		
5.	$^-8°$ C	up 8° C		

298

GROUP PROJECT

A Burning Question

The problem: Walking, running, dancing—all these activities burn Calories. How many Calories do you burn walking to school or riding a bike? Use the Key Facts to figure out how many Calories you burn per day while doing each of the activities.

Key Facts

- Walking burns 4 Calories per minute.
- Running burns 9 Calories per minute.
- Swimming burns 8 Calories per minute.
- Bicycling burns 6 Calories per minute.
- Dancing burns 7 Calories per minute.

Make a chart like this one for your class for one day.

Student	Activities	Calories burned per minute	Total minutes	Total calories burned
		Total for the class		

CHAPTER TEST

Measure to the nearest centimeter. (page 274)

1. ▬▬▬▬▬   **2.** ▬▬▬   **3.** ▬▬▬

Write *cm*, *m*, or *km* for the unit you would use to measure each. (page 276)

4. a TV screen

5. the distance between two towns

6. the length of an airplane

Write *L* or *mL* for the unit you would use to measure each. (page 278)

7. water in a vase

8. rain in a barrel

9. dew on a blade of grass

Write *g* or *kg* for the unit you would use to measure each. (page 280)

10. a snail

11. a watermelon

12. an apple

Copy and complete. (pages 276, 278, and 280)

13. 900 cm = ▨ m

14. 5,000 mL = ▨ L

15. 3,000 m = ▨ km

16. 4 L = ▨ mL

17. 9,000 g = ▨ kg

18. 5 kg = ▨ g

19. 8 m = ▨ cm

20. 9 km = ▨ m

21. 12,000 mL = ▨ L

Measure to the nearest $\frac{1}{8}$ inch. (page 286)

22. ▬▬▬▬▬▬   **23.** ▬▬▬▬   **24.** ▬▬▬▬

Write *in.*, *ft*, *yd*, or *mi* for the unit you would use to measure each. (page 288)

25. the length of a car

26. the length of a stapler

27. the distance to Mexico

Write *oz*, *lb*, or *T* for the unit you would use to measure each. (page 290)

28. a typewriter

29. a butterfly

30. a truck

Write *c*, *pt*, *qt*, or *gal* for the unit you would use to measure each. (page 292)

31. hot chocolate in a mug

32. gasoline for a car

33. milk in a pitcher

34. a bottle of cooking oil

Copy and complete. (pages 288, 290, and 292)

35. 4 lb = ■ oz

36. 6 yd = ■ ft

37. 8 qt = ■ pt

38. 48 oz = ■ lb

39. 72 in. = ■ ft

40. 4 gal = ■ qt

41. 8,000 lb = ■ T

42. 12 ft = ■ yd

43. 5 yd = ■ ft

44. 20 qt = ■ gal

45. 12 c = ■ pt

Choose the most appropriate temperature. (pages 294–295)

46. daytime in the desert

a. 15°F **b.** 105°F

47. a warm bath

a. 40°C **b.** 99°C

48. an ice cube

a. $^-$4°C **b.** 40°C

Write what information you need to solve each problem. Then solve. (page 296)

49. David's soup recipe calls for 2 qt water. David has only a 1-cup measure. How many cups water should he use for the soup?

Use the map to solve. (page 282)

50. By road, how many miles is it from Avon to Daley?

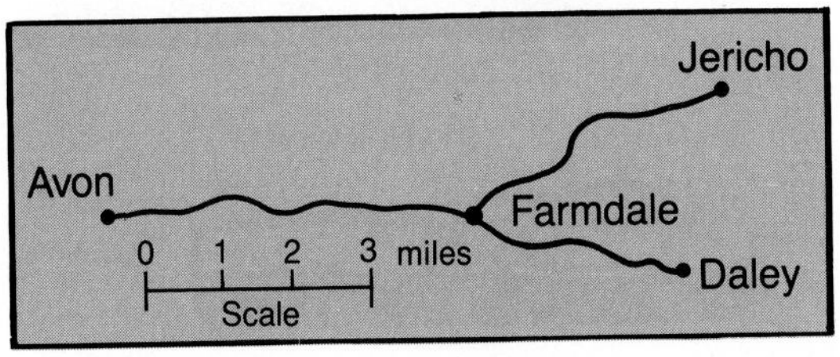

BONUS

Write the correct unit of customary measurement for ■.

Claude hikes 25 ■ on the Wilderness Trail. He brings everything he needs for 5 ■ of hiking. He carries maps that show 30 ■ of paths. The nights are sometimes as cold as 40°■; so, he brings a warm sleeping bag that is 50 ■ long.

RETEACHING

You can use a ruler to measure to the nearest half inch, quarter inch, or eighth inch.

This ruler is divided into one-eighth-inch units.

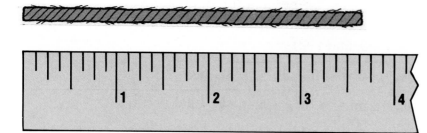

To the nearest half inch, the piece of yarn is $3\frac{1}{2}$ inches long.

To the nearest quarter inch, the piece of yarn is $3\frac{3}{4}$ inches long.

To the nearest eighth inch, the piece of yarn is $3\frac{5}{8}$ inches long.

Measure each to the nearest half inch, quarter inch, and eighth inch.

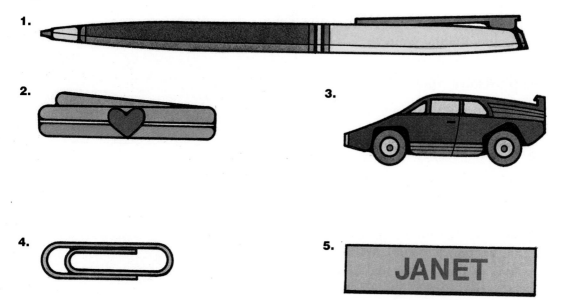

1.

2.

3.

4.

5. JANET

ENRICHMENT

Following a Recipe

Each year Amos bakes his famous old-fashioned pumpkin biscuits for the annual bake fair in his town. Here is the recipe he follows to bake 16 biscuits.

AMOS'S OLD-FASHIONED PUMPKIN BISCUITS

2 cups flour	$\frac{1}{2}$ teaspoon nutmeg
6 tablespoons butter	1 tablespoon sugar
1 cup milk	$\frac{1}{2}$ tablespoon salt
$\frac{3}{4}$ cup mashed pumpkin	4 teaspoons baking powder

---

1. If 1 bag of flour holds 8 cups flour, what fraction of the bag will Amos use to make 16 biscuits?

2. Amos's grandson, Jeb, wants to make pumpkin biscuits, but he cannot find a tablespoon. He knows that there are 3 teaspoons in 1 tablespoon. How many teaspoons of sugar should he use to make 16 biscuits?

3. If Jeb wants to make 8 biscuits, how many teaspoons of baking powder should he use?

4. How many cups of flour should Jeb use if he wants to make 32 biscuits? how many cups of mashed pumpkin?

★5. Amos knows there are 8 tablespoons in a $\frac{1}{4}$-pound stick of butter. How much of the stick should he use for his biscuits?

★6. Jeb's sister follows this recipe to make 24 biscuits for a party. How many tablespoons of butter should she use? how much flour?

CUMULATIVE REVIEW

Write the letter of the correct answer.

1. $\frac{7}{8} + \frac{3}{8}$

   a. $\frac{1}{2}$ **b.** $\frac{10}{16}$

   c. $1\frac{1}{4}$ **d.** not given

2. $\frac{6}{8} - \frac{1}{2}$

   a. $\frac{1}{4}$ **b.** $\frac{5}{6}$

   c. $\frac{7}{10}$ **d.** not given

3. $3\frac{5}{8} + 3\frac{3}{8}$

   a. $\frac{1}{4}$ **b.** $6\frac{1}{2}$

   c. 7 **d.** not given

4. Which is the decimal for $\frac{5}{10}$?

   a. 0.05   **b.** 0.5

   c. 5.10   **d.** not given

5. Which number sentence is true?

   a. 0.03 > 0.30   **b.** 4.08 > 4.8

   c. 7.57 > 7.75   **d.** not given

6. 25.4 − 1.18

   a. 13.6   **b.** 24.22

   c. 24.38   **d.** not given

7. Which number sentence is true?

   a. $\frac{3}{4} < \frac{5}{8}$ **b.** $1\frac{2}{3} < 1\frac{4}{6}$

   c. $2\frac{1}{5} < 2\frac{7}{10}$ **d.** not given

8. What is $\frac{25}{4}$ in simplest form?

   a. $\frac{4}{25}$ **b.** 6

   c. $6\frac{1}{4}$ **d.** not given

9. $35.05 ÷ 5

   a. $7.00   **b.** $7.01
   c. $71   **d.** not given

10. How much time passed from May 11 to May 17?

   a. 6 days   **b.** 7 days
   c. 17 days   **d.** not given

11. Amy does $\frac{2}{5}$ of a jigsaw puzzle. Leo does $\frac{1}{10}$ of the puzzle. How much of the puzzle is done?

   a. $\frac{3}{15}$ of the puzzle

   b. $\frac{3}{10}$ of the puzzle

   c. $\frac{1}{2}$ of the puzzle

   d. not given

12. Ed brings 6 favors to a party. May brings 8 favors. If 2 favors are given to each person at the party, how many people are there at the party?

   a. 2 people
   b. 4 people
   c. 7 people
   d. not given

Plan a trip to Washington, D.C. Since your visit will be a short one, you want to see and do as much as possible. You have three hours to see some of the city's famous buildings and monuments. Plan a route, and figure out what you can see in that period of time.

10 GEOMETRY

Lines and Line Segments

A. The many beautiful buildings and monuments in the United States were designed by architects and engineers. To design a monument, they needed to know about lines and line segments, as well as the rules of geometry.

A **line segment** is a figure from which many other shapes are formed. A line segment is straight. It has two endpoints.

D ●————————————————● E

Read: line segment *DE* or line segment *ED*.

Write: $\overline{DE}$ or $\overline{ED}$.
Points *E* and *D* are the endpoints.

B. A **line** goes on forever in both directions.

←——●————————————●——→
     A   B

Read: line *AB* or line *BA*.
Write: $\overleftrightarrow{AB}$ or $\overleftrightarrow{BA}$.
A and *B* are points on $\overleftrightarrow{AB}$ or $\overleftrightarrow{BA}$.

Intersecting lines are lines that meet at a common point.

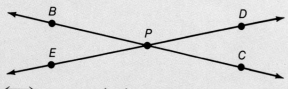

$\overleftrightarrow{BC}$ intersects $\overleftrightarrow{DE}$ at point *P*.

Parallel lines do not intersect.

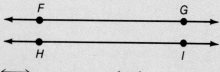

$\overleftrightarrow{FG}$ is parallel to $\overleftrightarrow{HI}$.

Write *line* or *line segment* for each.

1.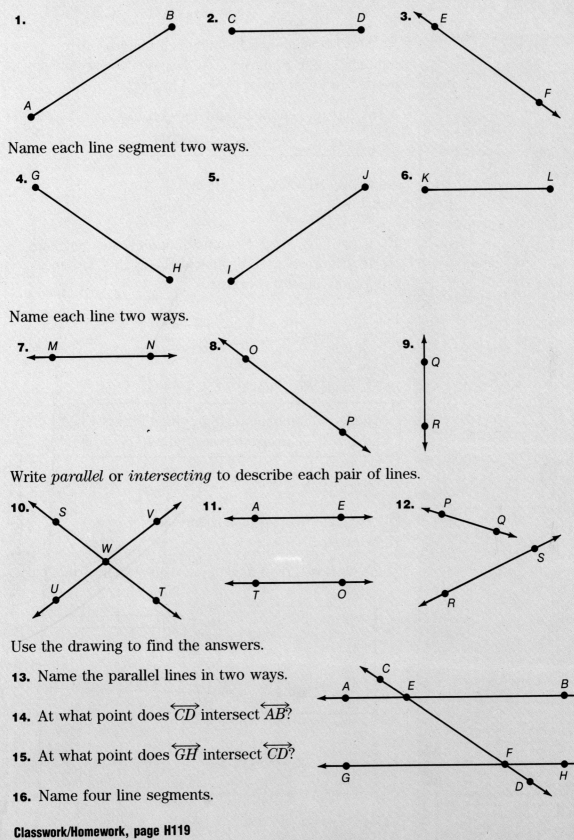

B

A

2. C   D

3. E

F

Name each line segment two ways.

4. G

H

5. J

I

6. K   L

Name each line two ways.

7. M   N

8. O

P

9. Q

R

Write *parallel* or *intersecting* to describe each pair of lines.

10. S   V

W

U   T

11. A   E

T   O

12. P

Q

S

R

Use the drawing to find the answers.

13. Name the parallel lines in two ways.

14. At what point does $\overleftrightarrow{CD}$ intersect $\overleftrightarrow{AB}$?

15. At what point does $\overleftrightarrow{GH}$ intersect $\overleftrightarrow{CD}$?

16. Name four line segments.

C

A   E   B

F

G   H

D

Rays and Angles

A. The Transamerica Building is a famous office building in San Francisco. To design it, the architects needed to know about rays and angles.

A **ray** has one endpoint and goes on forever.

A •————————————• B

Read: ray *AB*.
Write: $\overrightarrow{AB}$.

B. If two rays have the same endpoint, they form an **angle.** The rays are the sides of the angle. They meet at a point called the **vertex.**

vertex C

E

D

Read: angle *ECD*, angle *DCE*, or angle *C*.

> When you name an angle by three letters, the vertex is always the second letter.

Write: ∠*ECD*, ∠*DCE*, or ∠*C*.

C. An angle that forms a square corner is a **right angle.**

Angle *CAB* is a right angle.

C

A •————————————• B

The corner of this page forms a right angle.

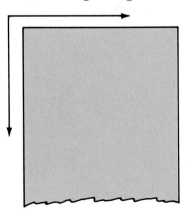

Write the name of each ray.

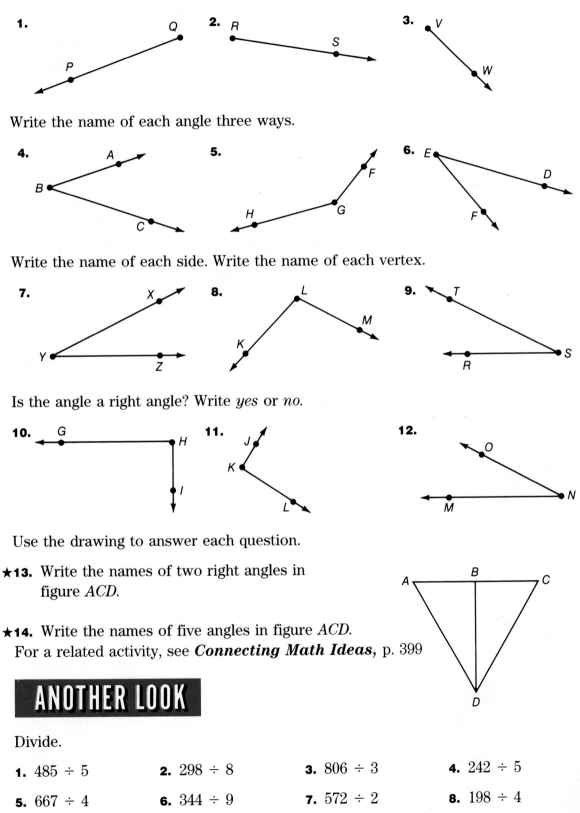

1.

Q

P

2. R

S

3. V

W

Write the name of each angle three ways.

4.

A

B

C

5.

F

H

G

6. E

D

F

Write the name of each side. Write the name of each vertex.

7.

X

Y

Z

8.

L

K

M

9.

T

R

S

Is the angle a right angle? Write *yes* or *no*.

10.

G

H

I

11.

J

K

L

12.

O

M

N

Use the drawing to answer each question.

★**13.** Write the names of two right angles in figure *ACD*.

★**14.** Write the names of five angles in figure *ACD*.
For a related activity, see **Connecting Math Ideas,** p. 399

A   B   C

D

ANOTHER LOOK

Divide.

1. $485 \div 5$ **2.** $298 \div 8$ **3.** $806 \div 3$ **4.** $242 \div 5$

5. $667 \div 4$ **6.** $344 \div 9$ **7.** $572 \div 2$ **8.** $198 \div 4$

Polygons

A. The Pentagon is a famous building in Arlington, Virginia. The outline of the Pentagon forms a polygon.

A **polygon** is a closed figure that has three or more connected line segments.

A polygon is named for its number of sides.

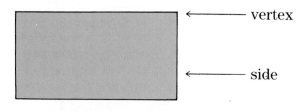

← vertex

← side

quadrilateral
4 sides
4 vertices

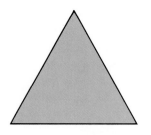 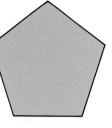 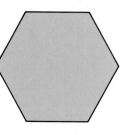 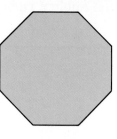

triangle	**pentagon**	**hexagon**	**octagon**
3 sides	5 sides	6 sides	8 sides
3 vertices	5 vertices	6 vertices	8 vertices

B. Some quadrilaterals have special names.

rectangle
4 right angles
4 sides

square
4 right angles
4 sides of equal length

310

Is this figure a polygon? Write *yes* or *no*.

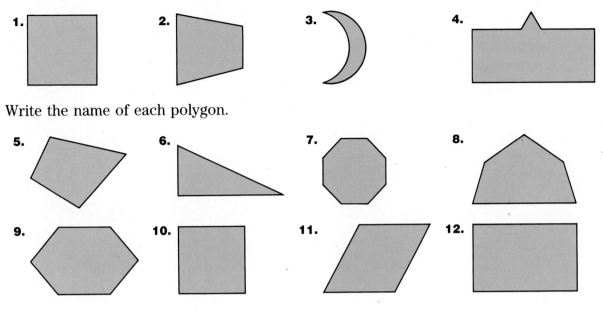

1.

2.

3.

4.

Write the name of each polygon.

5.

6.

7.

8.

9.

10.

11.

12.

Write the number of sides and vertices for each.

13. triangle　　**14.** square　　**15.** pentagon

16. octagon　　**17.** quadrilateral　　**18.** hexagon

Solve.

19. I am a polygon that has 5 sides and 5 vertices. What is my name?

20. I am a polygon that has 6 sides. What is my name?

21. I am a polygon that has 3 sides. What is my name?

22. I am a quadrilateral that has 4 right angles. What is my name?

23. I am a quadrilateral that has 4 equal sides and 4 right angles. What is my name?

24. I am a polygon that has 4 sides and 4 right angles. What is my name?

CHALLENGE

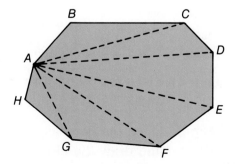

1. Write the name of the figure that is formed by connecting points *GACDEF*.

2. Write the name of the figure that is formed by connecting points *EAHGF*.

Circles

A. The Jefferson Memorial is a building in Washington, D.C. It was built in honor of our third President, Thomas Jefferson. The outline of the main part of the building forms a circle.

A **circle** is made up of points that are the same distance from the center point.

Point W is the center of circle W.

B. There are special names for the parts of a circle.

$\overline{AD}$ is a **radius.**
$\overline{AC}$ and $\overline{AB}$ are also **radii.**

A **radius** is a line segment having one endpoint at the center of the circle and another on the circle.

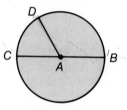

$\overline{CB}$ is a **diameter.**

A **diameter** is a line segment that passes through the center of the circle and connects any two points on the circle. It is twice the length of a radius.

C. You can use a **compass** to draw a circle.

Step 1: Draw a line segment. This will be the radius of the circle.

Step 2: Place the point of the compass on one endpoint of the radius.

Step 3: Open the compass to the length of the radius and draw the circle.

Is the line segment a radius? Write *yes* or *no*.

1. **2.** **3.** **4.**

Is the line segment a diameter? Write *yes* or *no*.

5. **6.** **7.** **8.**

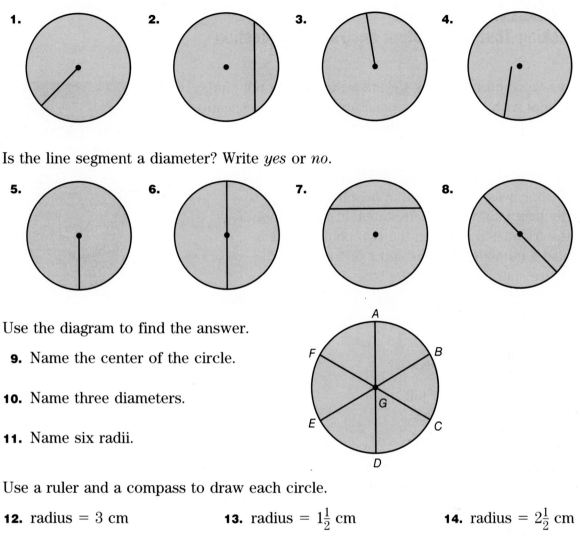

Use the diagram to find the answer.

9. Name the center of the circle.

10. Name three diameters.

11. Name six radii.

Use a ruler and a compass to draw each circle.

12. radius = 3 cm

13. radius = $1\frac{1}{2}$ cm

14. radius = $2\frac{1}{2}$ cm

★**15.** diameter = 5 cm

★**16.** diameter = 3 cm

★**17.** diameter = 6 cm

CHALLENGE

Write how many circles you would have to draw for each.

1. a circle with a radius of 6 inches; a circle with a diameter of 1 foot; a circle with a diameter of $\frac{1}{3}$ yard

★**2.** a circle with a radius of 5 cm; a circle with a diameter of 100 cm; a circle with a radius of 50 mm

PROBLEM SOLVING
Checking That the Solution Answers the Question

Some word problems ask for answers that are not simply numbers with labels. Pay special attention to the question that is asked in a problem. Be sure you answer it.

> The Statue of Liberty, which stands in New York Harbor, was a gift from the people of France to the people of the United States. It is a symbol of the friendship between the two countries. It is also a monument to the spirit of freedom. The entire statue, including the base, is 305 ft tall. The statue alone stands 151 ft tall. Is the statue taller than the base?

Which is the correct answer?

a. The base is 154 ft tall.
b. The statue is taller.
c. No, the base is taller.

Think about what the question asks. You need to compare the height of the statue to the height of the base. Also, you need to subtract to find the height of the base. Choice *a* gives the height of the base, but this is not the answer to the question. Choice *b* also does not answer the question. The correct answer is *c*. If you are not sure why, carefully reread the question that was asked in the problem.

Which sentence answers the question? Write the letter
of the correct answer.

1. The Mount Rushmore National
   Monument in South Dakota is a giant
   monument to four United States
   Presidents. It was begun in 1927 and
   completed in 1941. Was the
   monument completed in 14 years?

   a. Yes, the monument was
      completed in 14 years.
   b. No, the monument took fewer
      than 14 years to complete.
   c. No, the monument took more
      than 14 years to complete.

2. The construction of the Washington
   Monument began in 1848. The
   monument was first opened to the
   public in 1888. Did more than 50
   years pass between the two dates?

   a. Yes, more than 50 years passed
      between the two dates.
   b. No, fewer than 50 years passed
      between the two dates.
   c. No, 50 years passed between the
      two dates.

Solve.

3. The Gateway to the West Arch in St.
   Louis, Missouri, is 630 ft tall. It
   honors the settlers who went west.
   Is the arch twice as tall as the Statue
   of Liberty, including the base?

4. The Smithsonian Institution is in
   Washington, D.C. The National Air
   and Space Museum, an addition to
   the Smithsonian, records air and
   space developments. How old is the
   Air and Space Museum?

5. Some students walked around one
   floor of the Hirshhorn Museum at
   the Smithsonian. They discovered
   that they returned to the point from
   which they started without taking
   any sharp turns. Did their path
   outline a square?

6. The City Hall Tower in Philadelphia,
   including the statue of William Penn
   at the top, is 548 ft tall. The statue is
   37 ft tall. Without the statue, would
   the City Hall Tower still be taller
   than the 519-ft Lincoln Tower in
   Chicago?

7. The Empire State Building is 1,250 ft
   tall. After its completion in the
   1960's, the Sears Tower became the
   world's tallest building. Its height is
   1,454 ft. How many feet taller than
   the Empire State Building is the
   Sears Tower?

Congruence

A. The twin towers of the World Trade Center are the tallest buildings in New York City. Because they have the same size and shape, they are **congruent.**

You can find whether two polygons are congruent by tracing one polygon and placing it on top of the other.

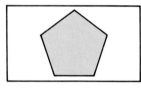

These polygons match exactly. They are congruent.

B. Two line segments of the same length are congruent. Measure $\overline{AB}$ and $\overline{CD}$.

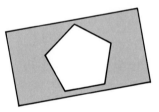

$\overline{AB}$ and $\overline{CD}$ are both 2 cm in length. They are congruent.

C. Polygons of the same shape are **similar.** They can be different sizes.

These triangles are similar.

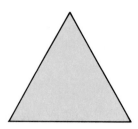

316

Are the polygons congruent? Write *yes* or *no*.

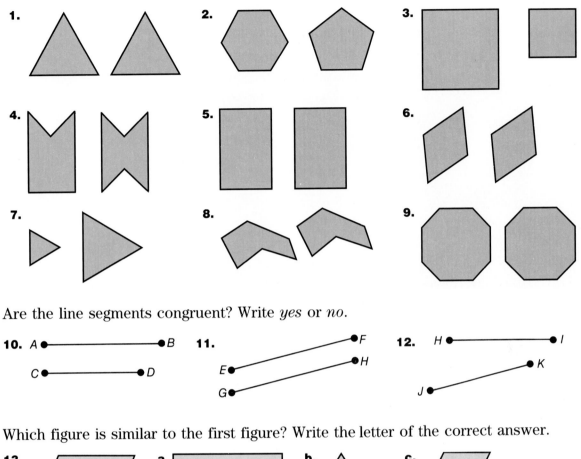

1.

2.

3.

4.

5.

6.

7.

8.

9.

Are the line segments congruent? Write *yes* or *no*.

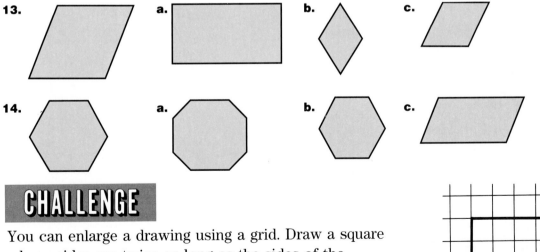

10. A •————————• B

C •———————• D

11. •F

E •

G • •H

12. H •————————• I

J • • K

Which figure is similar to the first figure? Write the letter of the correct answer.

13.

a.

b.

c.

14.

a.

b.

c.

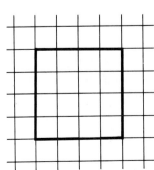

CHALLENGE

You can enlarge a drawing using a grid. Draw a square whose sides are twice as long as the sides of the square at the right. It must be similar to the square shown. How long are the sides?

For a related activity, see *Connecting Math Ideas,* p. 399 .

Symmetry

A. United States senators and representatives work in the Capitol Building in Washington, D.C.

You can fold a picture of the Capitol Building in the middle to see that its two sides are exactly the same. This means that the building is symmetrical.

If a figure can be folded so that its two parts are congruent, the figure is **symmetrical.** The fold is the **line of symmetry.**

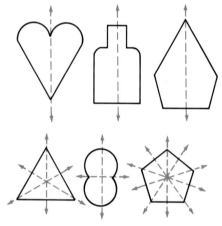

B. Some figures have two or more lines of symmetry.

C. Some figures have no lines of symmetry.

D. Some figures have more lines of symmetry than you can count.

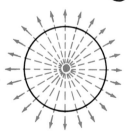

Is each figure symmetrical? Write *yes* or *no*.

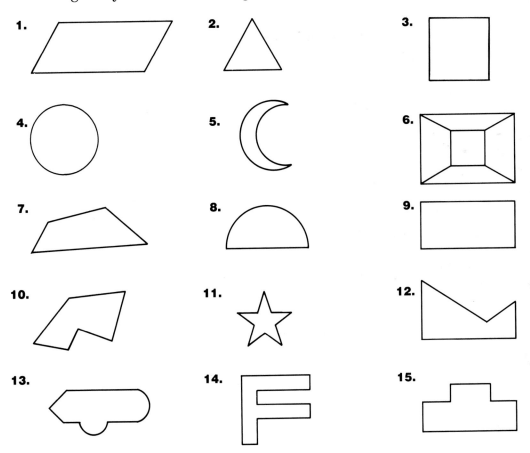

1.

2.

3.

4.

5.

6.

7.

8.

9.

10.

11.

12.

13.

14.

15.

Draw a figure similar to the one shown. You may want
to cut it out and fold it to find lines of symmetry. Write
the number of lines of symmetry for each.

16.

17.

18.

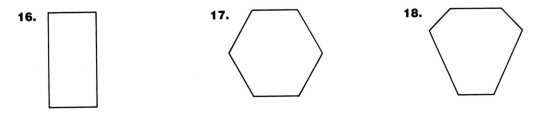

ANOTHER LOOK

Add or subtract. Write the answer in simplest form.

1. $3\frac{1}{3} + 4\frac{1}{3}$ **2.** $6\frac{5}{8} - 4\frac{1}{8}$ **3.** $1\frac{1}{4} + \frac{1}{4}$ **4.** $2\frac{3}{10} - 2\frac{1}{10}$ **5.** $5\frac{7}{8} - 4\frac{3}{8}$

Ordered Pairs

A. You can use a pair of numbers, or **ordered pair,** to name a point on a grid.

What is the point named by the ordered pair (2,5)?

Start at 0.
Move 2 spaces to the right.
Move 5 spaces up.

The ordered pair (2,5) names point A.

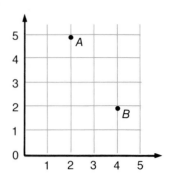

B. You can locate an ordered pair from a point on a grid.

What ordered pair is located by point C?

Start at 0.
Point C is 3 spaces to the right.
Point C is 2 spaces up.

Point C is located by the ordered pair (3,2).

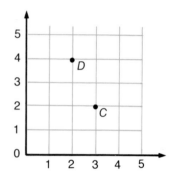

Philadelphia, Pennsylvania, is a city known for its many historic landmarks.

Write an ordered pair to describe the location of each landmark.

1. City Hall

2. Betsy Ross House

3. Academy of Music

4. United States Mint

5. Liberty Bell Pavilion

6. Afro-American Museum

Write the name of the landmark described by the ordered pair.

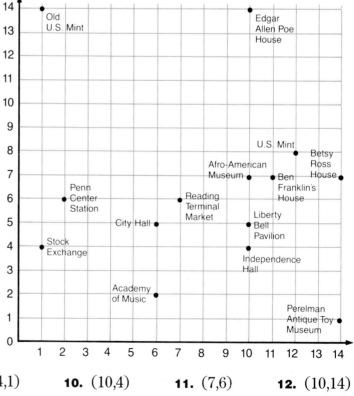

7. (11,7)   **8.** (1,4)   **9.** (14,1)   **10.** (10,4)   **11.** (7,6)   **12.** (10,14)

320

Use graph paper to make a grid. Remember to number
the sides. Then connect the points in order. Write the
name of the figure you have drawn.

★**13.** *A* (4,1), *B* (3,4), *C* (6,6), *D* (9,4), *E* (8,1)

★**14.** *F* (2,2), *G* (9,2), *H* (9,7)

★**15.** *I* (3,4), *J* (4,2), *K* (7,2), *L* (8,4), *M* (7,6), *N* (4,6)

★**16.** *O* (4,8), *P* (2,6), *Q* (2,3), *R* (4,1), *S* (7,1), *T* (9,3), *U* (9,6), *V* (7,8)

For a related activity, see *Connecting Math Ideas,* p. 400

MIDCHAPTER REVIEW

Use the figure at the right to answer these questions.

1. Write the names of three line segments
in the drawing.

2. Write the name of one line.

3. Write the names of three angles in
the drawing.

4. What figure is formed by connecting
points *ABDE*?

5. What is figure *ABCDEF*?

6. Is figure *ABCDEF* symmetrical?

7. Are figures *FABC* and *FCDE*
congruent?

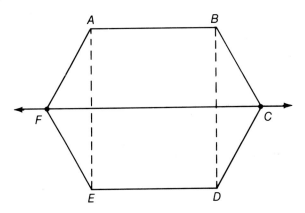

Use the circle at the right to answer
these questions.

8. Write the names of two diameters
in circle *P*.

9. Write the names of three radii in
circle *P*.

10. Are radii $\overline{PC}$ and $\overline{PQ}$ the same length?

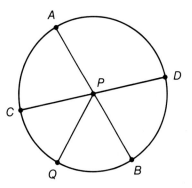

Perimeter

The tallest building in Washington, D.C., is the Washington Monument. It is a white marble tower that was built in honor of George Washington, the first President of the United States.

The base of the monument forms a square. Each side measures about 17 meters. You can find the perimeter of the base of the Washington Monument.

> The **perimeter** of a figure is the distance around it. To find the perimeter, add the measures of its sides.

Add the measures.

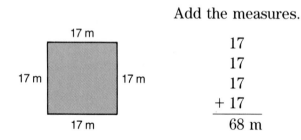

$$17$$
$$17$$
$$17$$
$$+\ 17$$
$$\overline{68\ m}$$

The perimeter of the base of the Washington Monument is about 68 meters.

Other examples:

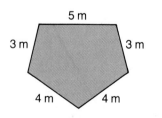

$$5$$
$$3$$
$$4$$
$$4$$
$$+\ 3$$
$$\overline{19\ m}$$

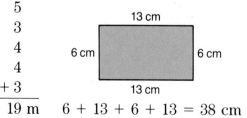

$$6 + 13 + 6 + 13 = 38\ cm$$

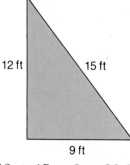

$$12 + 15 + 9 = 36\ ft$$

Find the perimeter.

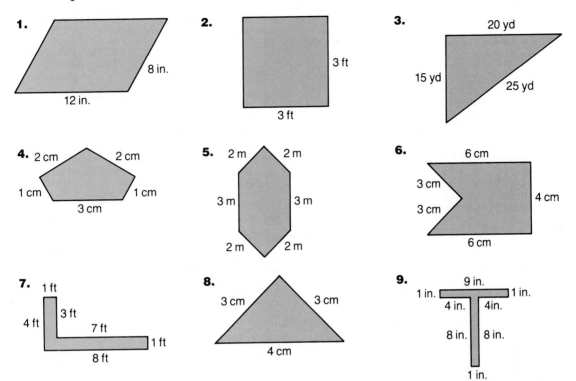

1.
8 in.
12 in.

2.
3 ft
3 ft

3.
20 yd
15 yd
25 yd

4. 2 cm   2 cm
1 cm   1 cm
3 cm

5. 2 m   2 m
3 m   3 m
2 m   2 m

6.
6 cm
3 cm
3 cm
4 cm
6 cm

7. 1 ft
3 ft
4 ft   7 ft
1 ft
8 ft

8.
3 cm   3 cm
4 cm

9. 9 in.
1 in.   1 in.
4 in.   4in.
8 in.   8 in.
1 in.

Solve.

10. A rectangle has a length of 8 in. and a width of 6 in. What is its perimeter?

★11. The perimeter of a square is 16 cm. What is the length of each side?

★12. The sum of the sides of a triangle is 24 in. If the sides are all the same length, what is the length of each side?

FOCUS: REASONING

Look at the diagram.
Five friends wrote their names to show which sports they play.

1. Who plays only soccer and basketball?
2. How many friends don't play any of the sports?
3. What else can you tell from this diagram?

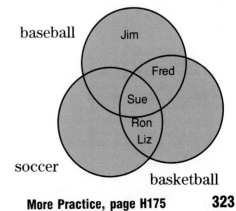

baseball
Jim
Fred
Sue
Ron
Liz
soccer
basketball

Area

A. These activities can help you explore how to find the area of a figure.

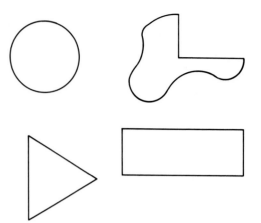

On a sheet of tracing paper, draw large, closed figures like the ones at the right. Lay your drawings on top of a piece of graph paper, and find how many square units each figure contains. This is the **area** of each figure.

Trade drawings with a partner. Use your graph paper to measure the area of each figure.

• In what kind of units would you record the areas?

• Compare your area counts to your partner's. How close are they? Why might they be different?

Thinking as a Team

1. Which kinds of figures did you find it easier to measure?

2. What did you do when your figures did not contain an exact number of squares?

3. Why is it a good idea for everyone to use the same size square when measuring area? What size do you think this square should be? Why?

B. On graph paper, draw a closed figure with all right angles. Find the area according to the square units on the graph paper.

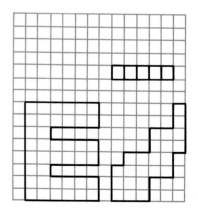

• Why is it helpful to draw figures on graph paper when finding area?

• Look at the E-shaped figure. Find the area of a small part of it. How can this help you find the total area of the figure?

324

C. Drawing only on the lines of a sheet of graph paper, make rectangles with the following areas: 4 square units, 7 square units, 10 square units, 15 square units, and 28 square units. Some of these rectangles can be drawn in more than one way. Copy this chart. For each rectangle you draw, complete the chart. Compare your charts and drawings with those of your teammates.

Length	Width	Area in Square Units
		4
		7
		10
		15
		28

Thinking as a Team

1. Did everyone draw the same rectangle for each area?

2. Which areas can be shown by more than two rectangles? Why? Which area can be shown by only two rectangles? Why?

3. Describe the pattern between the lengths, widths, and areas of the rectangles. Use the pattern to write a rule for finding the area of a rectangle.

4. Use this rule to find the area of a rectangle that has a width of 4 inches and a length of 9 inches.

D. Your school is putting grass seed on its athletic fields. Your team is measuring the areas to find out how much seed to order. You have to find the areas of the football field and the baseball diamond. Each of you has a stopwatch, a yardstick, chalk, and string. Here are some approaches:
- Pace off distances.
- Measure with given lengths of string.
- See how long it takes to walk 25 yards.

Working as a Team

Discuss the best approach for finding the areas. After making all measurements, how could you record your findings? What else would you need to know before you could order the grass seed?

PROBLEM SOLVING
Looking for a Pattern

Sometimes you are given a group of numbers, shapes, or letters, and you are asked to find the ones that come next. If you look closely at these numbers, shapes, or letters, you can often see a pattern.

During a school trip to Yellowstone National Park, Mr. Kelly asked his students to guess the pattern of a set of numbers. Here are the first 5 numbers of the pattern.

1   6   11   16   21

What are the next two numbers in the pattern?

Look at the numbers. The numbers in the pattern increase. You could try adding to find what number is added to the first to find the second number and so on.

Add 5 to 1 to get 6.
Add 5 to 6 to get 11.
Add 5 to 11 to get 16.
Add 5 to 16 to get 21.

The pattern is + 5. So, the next two numbers are 26 and 31.

What are the next two numbers in this pattern?

1   2   6   12   36

You cannot find the pattern by adding. You could try multiplying to find the pattern.

Multiply 1 by 2 to get 2.
Multiply 2 by 3 to get 6.
Multiply 6 by 2 to get 12.
Multiply 12 by 3 to get 36.

The pattern is × 2, × 3, × 2, × 3. So, the next two numbers are 72 and 216.

Find the pattern. Write the two numbers that come next.

1. Carlos is good in math. At his science exhibit, students challenge him by giving him number, shape, and letter patterns to solve. What is this number pattern? What are the next two numbers?

   23   18   19   14   15   10   11   6   7

2. Kirk saw the geysers at Yellowstone National Park. One geyser erupts on a schedule. It erupts at 1:20 P.M., 1:50 P.M., 2:20 P.M., and 2:50 P.M. What is the geyser's schedule for the rest of the day until 5:00 P.M.?

3. The students have a raffle for the Statue of Liberty. The numbers on four tickets are shown below. One ticket is not a winner, because its numbers follow a pattern that differs from the pattern for the other three. Which one is not a winner? What is the pattern of the numbers on the winning tickets?

   a. 2—4—8—10—20
   b. 3—6—12—15—30
   c. 5—7—14—16—32
   d. 1—3—6—8—16

4. Nell tries to stump Carlos. She gives him the following places and asks him to add another one to the pattern.

   New Mexico, Oregon, Nebraska, Arkansas, South Dakota.

   Carlos says that Alaska could be the next place. Is he right? Why or why not? What places could be next in the pattern? HINT: Look at the end of each name as well as the beginning.

Solid Figures

A. The United Nations building is located in New York City. Its shape is a rectangular prism.

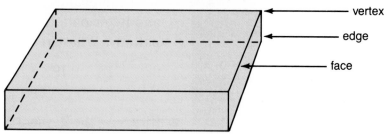

vertex
edge
face

A **rectangular prism** has 6 faces, 8 vertices, and 12 edges.

> A **face** is a flat side of the figure.
> Two faces meet at an **edge.**
> A point where edges meet is a **vertex** of the figure.

B. These are other common solid figures.

triangular prism
5 faces
6 vertices
9 edges

cube
6 faces
8 vertices
12 edges

pyramid
5 faces
5 vertices
8 edges

C. Some solid figures have curved sides and no edges.

cone
1 face

cylinder
2 faces

sphere
0 faces

Name each shape.

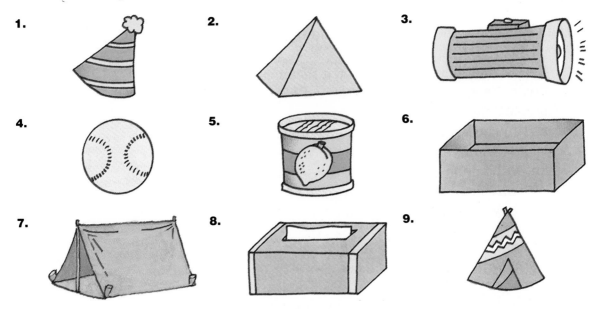

1.

2.

3.

4.

5.

6.

7.

8.

9.

Complete.

Figure	Number of faces	Number of edges	Number of vertices
10.	■	■	8
11.	5	■	■
★12.	■	■	12

For a related activity, see *Connecting Math Ideas*, p. 400.

CHALLENGE

You can make models to help you solve problems.

1. Trace the two pentagons. Put them together to form a new figure that has 6 sides and a perimeter of 32.

2. Trace the triangle and the octagon. Put them together to form a new figure that has 7 sides and a perimeter of 17.

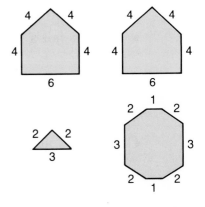

Volume

A. You can explore the volume of a solid figure.

Step 1: Use 12 multilink cubes to form a rectangular prism. Record its length, width, and height. Take it apart. Form as many other rectangular prisms as you can using all 12 cubes. Record the length, width, and height of each. You already know the number of cubic units contained in the solid figure. This is the **volume** of the figure. Volume is measured in cubic units.

- How many different rectangular prisms can you form using all 12 cubes?

- In which ways can you find the volume of a rectangular prism?

Step 2: Work with a partner. Without your partner watching, count out three groups of cubes such as 8, 11, and 23. Then form three different solid figures using the groups of cubes. Show the figures to your partner. Your partner should find the volume of each figure. Then switch roles.

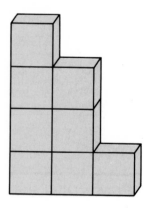

- Could you form more than one figure with each group of cubes?

- If the figure was a prism, how did you find its volume?

- If it was not a prism, how did you find its volume?

- Can you separate every figure that is not a prism into smaller solids that are prisms?

- Suppose you have an object of 18 cubic units. Could there be more than one rectangular prism that has this volume? How can you tell?

330

Thinking as a Team

1. Why is the cube a good shape with which to measure volume?

2. What do you need to know about a rectangular prism in order to calculate its volume?

3. What is a rule for finding the volume of a rectangular prism?

B. Certain solid figures are described in the Infobank on page 405. Use what you have learned with cubes to find their volume in cubic inches.

- Which measurements are given for the solids? In which units are these measurements given?

- Suppose you know the length, width, and volume of a prism. Could you find its height? How?

- You have the measurements of two sides of a prism given in inches. You know the measurement of the third side in feet. Can you find the prism's volume? What steps would you take?

C. Look at the figure at the right. Use a calculator to find its volume in cubic centimeters.

Compare your answers to other students' answers.

- What strategy did you use to find the volume?

- How can you be sure that your answer is reasonable?

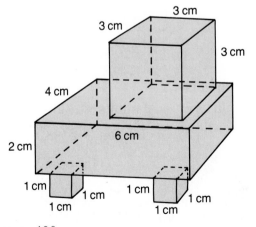

For a related activity, see *Connecting Math Ideas*, p. 400

PROBLEM SOLVING
Using Advertisements

Advertising provides one source of information. Read ads carefully, however, to be sure you understand what they say.

Mr. and Mrs. Galway of Denver, Colorado, are planning to take a trip with their 2 children to Washington, D.C. They have 9 days for their vacation and want to spend 6 days in Washington. The Galways also want to travel in the least expensive way. They look at these three ads.

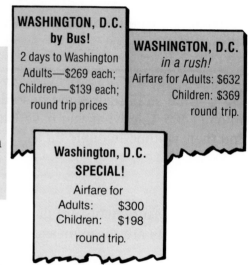

WASHINGTON, D.C. by Bus!
2 days to Washington
Adults—$269 each;
Children—$139 each;
round trip prices

WASHINGTON, D.C. *in a rush!*
Airfare for Adults: $632
Children: $369
round trip.

Washington, D.C. SPECIAL!
Airfare for
Adults: $300
Children: $198
round trip.

Here is how the Galways use the ads to figure out costs.

Step 1: Find the price of each plan.

Bus:
2 adults × $269 = $538
2 children × $139 = + 278
Total cost $816

Regular airfare:
2 adults × $632 = $1,264
2 children × $369 = +   738
Total cost $2,002

Special airfare:
2 adults × $300 = $600
2 children × $198 = + 396
Total cost $996

Step 2: Consider the amount of time each trip takes.

Bus:
2 days going
+ 2 days returning
4 days of travel time

Regular airfare:
$\frac{1}{2}$ day going
+ $\frac{1}{2}$ day returning
1 day of travel time

Special airfare:
$\frac{1}{2}$ day going
+ $\frac{1}{2}$ day returning
1 day of travel time

The Galways can now decide how much time and money they will need for each kind of travel.

Use the ads on page 332 to solve. Write the letter of the correct answer.

1. The Galways decide to spend their entire vacation in Washington. They want to spend no more than a day traveling. But they can't spend more than $1,000 on airfare. Which form of travel should they choose?

   a. bus
   b. regular airfare
   c. special airfare

2. Suppose only Mrs. Galway and one of the children travel to Washington. They want to use the special airfare. How much will their airfare cost them?

   a. between $400 and $450
   b. between $450 and $500
   c. between $500 and $1,000

Use this advertisement to solve each problem.

3. How much money will the Galway family save by taking advantage of the special family rate given by the Denver Mint?

4. Suppose Mr. Galway does not want to visit the mint. Would the rest of the family save money by using the family rate?

5. The family leaves home at noon. They spend 2 hours at the zoo and 2 hours at the art museum. The mint closes at 5:00 P.M. Do they have time to take the tour of the mint?

Making a Bar Graph

The table shows the heights of the tallest waterfalls in Yosemite National Park in California. You can use the information in the table to make a bar graph.

Step 1: Round the numbers in the table to the hundreds place.

Step 2: **a.** Draw a vertical line and a horizontal line.
Write 0 at the point where the two lines meet.
b. Label the left side **Height in Feet** and insert a scale.
For numbers 700 to 1,600, a scale of 200 could be used.
c. Label the bottom of the graph **Waterfalls**. Insert the names.
d. Title the graph.

Step 3: Draw the bars on the graph. Look at the bar for Middle Yosemite Falls. Since its waterfall is 700 feet, which is between 600 feet and 800 feet, the bar is drawn between the two numbers.

TALLEST WATERFALLS IN YOSEMITE NATIONAL PARK

Name of falls	Feet high
Ribbon Falls	1,612
Upper Yosemite Falls	1,430
Silver Strand Falls	1,170
Middle Yosemite Falls	675

$$1,612 \longrightarrow 1,600$$
$$1,430 \longrightarrow 1,400$$
$$1,170 \longrightarrow 1,200$$
$$675 \longrightarrow 700$$

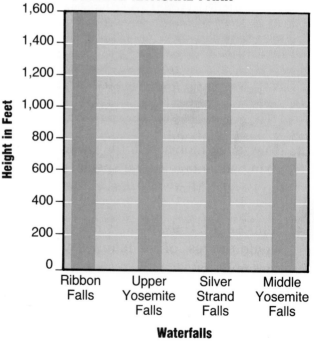

From the graph, you can see the difference in heights of the tallest waterfalls in Yosemite National Park.

334

1. Copy the bar graph. Use the information in the table to complete the graph.

NATIONAL PARK SYSTEM

Type of area	Number of areas
National parks	48
National monuments	78
National historic sites	63
National seashores	10
National recreation areas	17
National battlefields	10

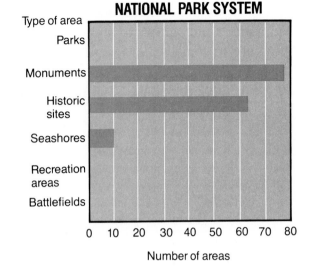

NATIONAL PARK SYSTEM

Use the graph to answer the questions.

2. Which type of area has the largest number of areas?

3. About how many National historic sites are there?

4. Which two types of areas have the same number of areas?

5. Use the information in the table below to make your own bar graph.

STUDENTS WHO HAVE VISITED NATIONAL MONUMENTS

Name of student	Number of monuments visited
Elizabeth	5
David	8
Les	1
Armand	2
Emmy	4
Arthur	7
Rachael	6

Use the graph to answer the questions.

6. Who visited the fewest number of monuments?

7. How many monuments did Emmy visit?

★8. What is the difference between the number of monuments that David visited and the number of monuments that Elizabeth visited?

★9. How many monuments did Arthur, Rachael, and Armand visit altogether?

Making a Pictograph

Pictographs use symbols to show large numbers. You can make a pictograph to show about how many seats there are in some major-league baseball stadiums.

MAJOR-LEAGUE BASEBALL STADIUMS

Stadium	Seating capacity	Rounded amount
Shea Stadium	55,300	55,000
Oakland Coliseum	50,219	50,000
Astrodome	45,000	45,000
Anaheim Stadium	65,158	65,000
Busch Memorial Stadium	50,222	50,000

Step 1: List the stadiums vertically, as shown in the chart.

Step 2: Round the numbers to a reasonable place. In this case, round to the nearest thousand.

Step 3: Choose a symbol to show a number of people.

Step 4: Change the numbers to symbols.

Step 5: Write the title and the meaning of the symbol.

Step 6: Complete the graph.

⚾⚾ = 10,000 people
⚾ = 5,000 people
45,000 = ⚾⚾ ⚾⚾ ⚾⚾ ⚾⚾ ⚾

SEATING CAPACITY OF MAJOR-LEAGUE BASEBALL STADIUMS

Shea Stadium	⚾⚾ ⚾⚾ ⚾⚾ ⚾⚾ ⚾⚾ ⚾
Oakland Coliseum	⚾⚾ ⚾⚾ ⚾⚾ ⚾⚾ ⚾⚾
Astrodome	⚾⚾ ⚾⚾ ⚾⚾ ⚾⚾ ⚾
Anaheim Stadium	⚾⚾ ⚾⚾ ⚾⚾ ⚾⚾ ⚾⚾ ⚾⚾ ⚾
Busch Memorial Stadium	⚾⚾ ⚾⚾ ⚾⚾ ⚾⚾ ⚾⚾

Each ⚾⚾ equals 10,000 people; each ⚾ equals 5,000 people.

1. Copy and complete the table. Then use the information in the table to make a pictograph. Make up your own symbols for the pictograph.

UNITED STATES BRIDGES

Name of bridge	Length in feet	Rounded length
Verrazano-Narrows, New York	4,260	4,000
Tacoma Narrows, Washington	2,800	■
Newport, Rhode Island	1,600	■
Deer Isle, Maine	1,080	■
Transbay, San Francisco	2,310	■

Use the pictograph to answer the questions.

VISITORS TO THE STATUE OF LIBERTY

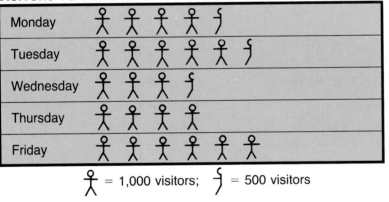

Monday	𝕩 𝕩 𝕩 𝕩 ᔅ
Tuesday	𝕩 𝕩 𝕩 𝕩 𝕩 ᔅ
Wednesday	𝕩 𝕩 𝕩 ᔅ
Thursday	𝕩 𝕩 𝕩 𝕩
Friday	𝕩 𝕩 𝕩 𝕩 𝕩 𝕩

𝕩 = 1,000 visitors; ᔅ = 500 visitors

2. On what day of the week do the greatest number of people visit the Statue of Liberty?

3. On what day of the week do the fewest number of people visit the Statue of Liberty?

4. How many people visit the statue on Wednesday and Thursday combined?

5. How many more people visit the statue on Tuesday than on Monday?

6. Write the days of the week from the least number of visitors to the greatest number of visitors.

7. What is the total number of visitors from Monday through Friday?

CALCULATOR

You can use your calculator to find the perimeter or the area of a rectangle.

For a rectangle with length 70 cm and width 45 cm the perimeter is equal to

$70 + 45 + 70 + 45 = 230$ or $2 \times (70 + 45) = 230$

Press:

The perimeter is 230 cm.

The area of the same rectangle is equal to $70 \times 45 = 3{,}150$. The area is 3,150 square centimeters.

For a rectangle with length 90 cm and width 35 cm,

Perimeter: 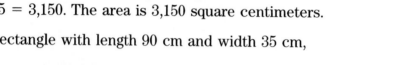 250

The perimeter is 250 cm.

Area:  3,150

The area is 3,150 square centimeters.

Notice that the two rectangles have unequal perimeters, but they have equal areas.

Use your calculator to complete the table.

Rectangle	Length	Width	Perimeter	Area
1.	525 cm	6 cm		
2.	175 cm	18 cm		
3.	105 cm	95 cm		
4.	150 cm	50 cm		
★5.	900 cm		2,200 cm	

6. For the rectangles with area 3,150 square centimeters, which rectangle has the greatest perimeter?

7. For the rectangles with perimeter 400 cm, which rectangle has the greatest area?

GROUP PROJECT

A Winning Flag

The problem: Your school needs a new flag with a different design. A contest is held, and one design is chosen to be made. Can you design the winning flag? Be sure to answer the key questions.

Key Questions

- What do you believe your flag should show about your school?
- What colors should your flag be? Does your school have its own colors? If not, what would each color that you will choose represent?
- What kind of design would you want on your flag? What would the design represent?
- Does your community have something special it is known for? Would you like a symbol of this on your flag?
- Do you want words written on your flag? Would you like the name of your school on the flag?
- How big should the flag be?
- Where do you want your flag displayed?
- How much will the flag cost?

CHAPTER TEST

Use the figure to answer Exercises 1–7. (pages 306 and 308)

1. What is $\overline{FC}$?

2. What is $\overrightarrow{CJ}$?

3. What is $\overleftrightarrow{BD}$?

4. Which two lines are parallel?

5. Name two intersecting lines.

6. Write the name of $\angle CFG$ another way.

7. Is $\angle CGF$ a right angle?

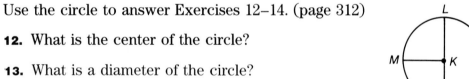

Write the name of each polygon. (page 310)

8.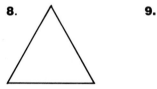

9.

10.

11.

Use the circle to answer Exercises 12–14. (page 312)

12. What is the center of the circle?

13. What is a diameter of the circle?

14. What is a radius of the circle?

Is each pair of figures congruent? Write *yes* or *no*. (page 316)

15.

16.

17.

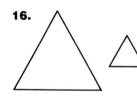

Is each figure symmetrical? Write *yes* or *no*. (page 318)

18.

19.

20.

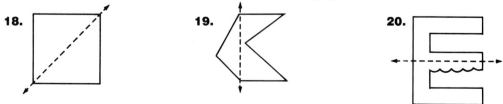

Name each solid figure. Write the number of faces,
edges, and vertices for each. (page 328)

21. 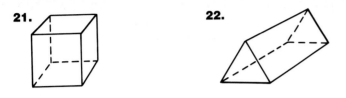   **22.**   **23.**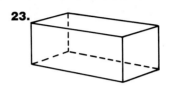

Solve. (pages 322, 324, and 330)

24. What is the perimeter of a
pentagon, each of whose sides
measure 4 cm?

25. What is the perimeter of a
quadrilateral whose sides measure
1 in., 2 in., $2\frac{1}{2}$ in., and $1\frac{1}{2}$ in.?

26. What is the area of a square whose
sides measure 8 ft?

27. What is the area of a rectangle that
is 5 yd long and 3 yd wide?

28. What is the volume of a cube that
measures 7 cm along each edge?

29. What is the volume of a rectangular
prism with a length of 8 in., a width
of 6 in., and a height of 5 in.?

Use the grid to answer questions 30–31. (page 320)

30. Which point is located by the
ordered pair (5,3)?

31. Which ordered pair is named by
point *A*?

Solve. Check that your solution answers the question. (page 314)

32. At Yellowstone National Park, Inez
took pictures of Old Faithful, a
famous geyser. It erupts about once
every hour. Inez took 5 pictures
each time the geyser erupted. About
how many times does Old Faithful
erupt in 3 hours?

33. For the first 3 days that Joe was in
Washington, D.C., he visited 3
famous buildings each day. On the
fourth day, he toured the White
House. On which day did he tour
the White House?

RETEACHING

A. The **area** of a figure is the number of square units it contains. You can find the area of a square or of a rectangle. You multiply its length times its width.

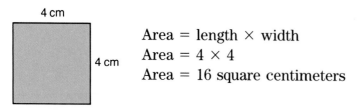

4 cm

4 cm

Area = length × width
Area = 4 × 4
Area = 16 square centimeters

Find the area.

1.

6 ft

2 ft

2.

5 cm

3 cm

3.

6 yd

6 yd

B. The **volume** of a solid figure is the number of cubic units it contains. You can find the volume of a cube or of a rectangular prism. You multiply its length times its width times its height.

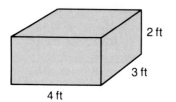

2 ft

3 ft

4 ft

Volume = length × width × height
Volume = 4 × 3 × 2
Volume = 24 cubic feet

Find the volume.

4.

5 cm

5 cm

5 cm

5.

1 yd

4 yd

6 yd

6.

3 ft

2 ft

3 ft

ENRICHMENT

Flips, Slides, and Turns

You can move a figure to a new position by flipping, sliding, or turning the figure.

You can **slide** triangle R across a line of symmetry.

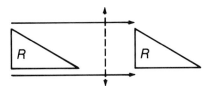

You can **flip** triangle R across a line of symmetry.

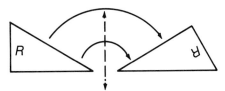

You can **turn** triangle R about a point on a line of symmetry.

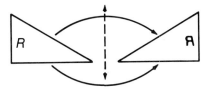

Compare the pair of figures. Write *slide, flip,* or *turn* for the way each figure was moved to a new position.

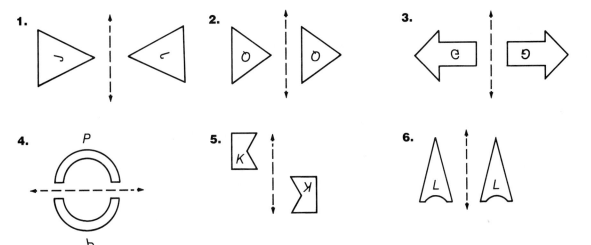

CUMULATIVE REVIEW

Write the letter of the correct answer.

1. 5 m = ▓ cm
   a. 50
   b. 500
   c. 5,000
   d. not given

2. 9,000 g = ▓ kg
   a. 9
   b. 90
   c. 900
   d. not given

3. 4 c = ▓ pt
   a. 2
   b. 8
   c. 16
   d. not given

4. 3 yd = ▓ ft
   a. 6
   b. 12
   c. 36
   d. not given

5. 8,000 lb = ▓ T
   a. 4
   b. 8
   c. 80
   d. not given

6. 14.3 + 12.79
   a. 14.22
   b. 26.09
   c. 27.09
   d. not given

7. Which number sentence is true?
   a. $\frac{3}{4} > \frac{7}{8}$
   b. $\frac{7}{8} > \frac{2}{3}$
   c. $\frac{3}{4} < \frac{2}{3}$
   d. not given

8. $7\frac{3}{4} - 2\frac{1}{4}$
   a. 5
   b. $5\frac{1}{2}$
   c. 10
   d. not given

9. There are 3 apples and 3 oranges in a bag. What is the probability of picking an apple?
   a. 1
   b. $\frac{1}{2}$
   c. $\frac{1}{3}$
   d. not given

10. Find $\frac{1}{3}$ of 18.
    a. 3
    b. 6
    c. 54
    d. not given

11. 6 × 7,842
    a. 42,842
    b. 47,052
    c. 47,842
    d. not given

12. Marge bought 6 pens for $1.20 each and 9 markers for $2.70 each. What was the cost of the 6 pens?
    a. $7.20
    b. $24.30
    c. $31.50
    d. not given

13. Danny sold 32 pt of lemonade. What information do you need to know to find how many gallons of lemonade he sold?
    a. 2 c = 1 pt
    b. 2 pt = 1 qt
    c. 8 pt = 1 gal
    d. not given

Here's a challenge. You have a rope, a ball, and a beanbag. You are to invent a game that can be played with these objects. Will your game be played by teams? How will the players score points, and how many points must they score in order to win? What rules will your game have?

11 MULTIPLICATION: 2-DIGIT MULTIPLIERS

Multiplying Multiples of 10; 100; and 1,000

During his professional football career, Gale Sayers ran for an average of 30 yards for each kickoff return. How many yards would he run if he returned 10 kickoffs?

You can multiply the number of kickoffs by the average number of yards for each kickoff.

Multiply 10 × 30.

You can see a pattern when you multiply multiples of 10.

$$
\begin{array}{ll}
1 \times 3 = 3 & \quad\quad 30 \\
10 \times 3 = 30 & \quad\quad \underline{\times\ 10} \\
10 \times 30 = 300 \quad \textbf{OR} & \quad\quad 300
\end{array}
$$

Gale Sayers would run about 300 yards.

Other examples:

$$
\begin{array}{ll}
5 \times 4 = 20 & \quad\quad 4 \times 8 = 32 \\
50 \times 4 = 200 & \quad\quad 40 \times 8 = 320 \\
50 \times 40 = 2{,}000 & \quad\quad 40 \times 80 = 3{,}200 \\
50 \times 400 = 20{,}000 & \quad\quad 40 \times 800 = 32{,}000 \\
50 \times 4{,}000 = 200{,}000 & \quad\quad 40 \times 8{,}000 = 320{,}000
\end{array}
$$

Checkpoint   Write the letter of the correct answer.

Multiply.

1.   70
    × 30

a. 100
b. 210
c. 1,000
d. 2,100

2.   900
    × 80

a. 980
b. 7,200
c. 72,000
d. 720,000

3.   8,000
    ×   50

a. 4,000
b. 8,050
c. 40,000
d. 400,000

Multiply.

1.	30 $\times$ 30	**2.**	50 $\times$ 10	**3.**	40 $\times$ 60	**4.**	50 $\times$ 20	**5.**	30 $\times$ 60

6.	200 $\times$ 80	**7.**	700 $\times$ 80	**8.**	100 $\times$ 60	**9.**	500 $\times$ 70	**10.**	300 $\times$ 40

11.	8,000 $\times$ 70	**12.**	6,000 $\times$ 20	**13.**	4,000 $\times$ 60	**14.**	3,000 $\times$ 90	**15.**	5,000 $\times$ 40

16.	9,000 $\times$ 20	**17.**	600 $\times$ 80	**18.**	1,000 $\times$ 70	**19.**	80 $\times$ 20	**20.**	700 $\times$ 90

21. 40×100 **22.** 600×20 **23.** $30 \times 8,000$ **24.** 50×50 **25.** 30×700

26. 20×400 **27.** 400×80 **28.** 90×100 **29.** 90×70 **30.** 70×700

31. $60 \times 9,000$ **32.** 90×800 **33.** 10×100 **34.** $80 \times 3,000$ **35.** 20×70

Solve.

36. A pass receiver runs for an average of 10 yards each time he catches the ball. About how many yards would he run if he caught the ball 60 times?

★37. Joe passed the ball 20 times during a game. Half of Joe's passes were caught. Of the passes caught, the average gain was 11 yards. How many yards did his team gain on passes?

CHALLENGE Patterns, Relations, and Functions

Each symbol stands for the same digit in all of the exercises. Write a number sentence for each.

♦ + ♥ + ♣ = ▌♥   is $4 + 5 + 6 = 15$

1. ♦▌ + ♣♥ = ▌★♣   **2.** ▲★ ÷ ♦ = ♥

3. ♣♣♣ × ⊕★ = ♦,♣▲★

Estimating Products

A. A major-league baseball pitcher throws about 135 pitches in a complete nine-inning game. In 1987, Roger Clemens pitched 18 nine-inning games. Estimate the number of pitches he threw in all.

You can estimate the product by rounding each factor to its largest place and then multiplying. Estimate 18×135.

Round each factor to its largest place.		Multiply.

$$135 \longrightarrow 100$$
$$\times\ 18 \longrightarrow \times\ 20$$

Round to the nearest hundred.
Round to the nearest ten.

$$100$$
$$\times\ 20$$
$$\overline{2,000}$$

Roger Clemens threw about 2,000 pitches in all.

B. You can estimate with money in the same way. Estimate $32 \times \$4.99$.

Round each factor to its largest place.

$$32 \times \$4.99$$
$$\downarrow \qquad \downarrow$$
$$30 \times \$5$$

Multiply.

$$30 \times \$5 = \$150$$

Another example:

$$\$0.22 \longrightarrow \$0.20$$
$$\times\ 17 \longrightarrow \times\ 20$$
$$\overline{\$4.00}$$

Estimate.

1. 88×69 **2.** 47×39 **3.** 21×72 **4.** 92×53

5. 29×488 **6.** 18×689 **7.** 31×715 **8.** 42×823

9. $71 \times \$8.15$ **10.** $48 \times \$6.95$ ★**11.** $(3 \times 7) \times 412$ ★**12.** $(8 \times 9) \times 685$

348

Estimate.

13. 650
× 49

14. 212
× 52

15. 395
× 67

16. $4.32
× 84

17. $6.29
× 74

18. 43 × 37 **19.** 77 × 74 **20.** 63 × 321 **21.** 39 × $0.25 **22.** 59 × $7.85

23. 834
× 17

24. 929
× 12

25. 433
× 56

26. $8.32
× 78

27. $0.76
× 82

28. 88 × 42 **29.** 63 × 72 **30.** 408 × 94 **31.** 19 × $3.70 **32.** 56 × $0.36

33. 46 × 21 **34.** 550 × 35 **35.** 277 × 17 **36.** 29 × $0.61 **37.** 17 × $2.77

38. 696 × 55 **39.** 438 × 38 **40.** 46 × 39 **★41.** (3 × 7) × 42

Use the chart to answer the questions below.

Player	Average hits per season	Average home runs per season	Seasons played
Babe Ruth	131	32	22
Lou Gehrig	160	29	17
Ted Williams	140	27	19
Willie Mays	149	30	22

42. Estimate the number of home runs Ted Williams hit during his career.

43. How many more hits per season did Lou Gehrig average than Willie Mays?

44. Babe Ruth hit 60 home runs in 1927. If he had hit 60 home runs each season, would he have hit more than 1,000 home runs in his career?

ANOTHER LOOK

Subtract.

1. 6.3
− 1.78

2. 22.4
− 8.07

3. 186
− 12.83

4. 117
− 22.46

5. 12.3
− 8.34

PROBLEM SOLVING
Choosing a Strategy or Method

Write the strategy or method you choose. Then solve.

1. On the Olympic Bobsled Route, one team's bobsled fell over on Beginner's Turn. About how many yards had the team gone?

2. From Lookout Point to Three Pines Curve, the sun was in the driver's eyes. In which direction was he traveling?

3. Which curve is at about the halfway point of the race?

4. If you wanted to see the bobsleds go around a sharp curve near the end of the race, where would you stand?

5. One of the fastest times run by a 4-person bobsled was 2 minutes, 17.39 seconds. An excellent time for a 2-person bobsled is 3 minutes, 40.40 seconds. What is the difference in times?

6. A bobsled course has to be at least 1,650 yards. If a course is 1,652.7 yards, how much longer is it than the minimum?

7. In polo, each player needs several ponies. If, in one game, every player on 2 teams of 4 players has 3 ponies, how many ponies are there?

Writing a Simpler Problem
Choosing the Operation
Using a Map
Estimation
Identifying Needed Information
Making a Diagram
Making a Model
Writing a Number Sentence
Checking for a Reasonable Answer
Checking that the Solution Answers the Question

OLYMPIC BOBSLED ROUTE

Math Reasoning, page H201

Write the strategy or method you choose. Then solve.

8. In polo, the playing time is 42 minutes. The game is divided into 6 equally long periods called "chukkers." How long is one chukker?

9. Bob Schaffer likes to play alone against 6-member volleyball teams. Since 1963, he has won 2,102 games and lost 3 games. How many more players than 1 play against Schaffer?

10. Rick Mears won the Indianapolis 500 in 1984. He won $2,795,399. In 1983, the winner was Tom Sneva. He won $2,411,450. To the nearest hundred thousand, how much more did Mears win?

11. During one year, a basketball team scored an average of 122.7 points per game. The next year, their average was 127.1. What was the difference in the 2 averages?

12. The longest punt in football history is 294 feet. A football field is 100 yards long. How much longer is a football field than the longest punt?

13. A pitcher threw 140 pitches during a baseball game. If he threw the same number of pitches to each of 14 batters, how many pitches did he throw to each batter?

14. In bobsled racing a team can be either 2 people or 4 people. A 2-person bobsled is 8.9 feet long. A 4-person bobsled is 12.5 feet long. Which bobsled is longer?

15. The winner of a bobsled race is the team with the fastest time. If the United States team finishes in 4 minutes, 9 seconds, and Canada's team finishes in 4 minutes, 27 seconds, who wins the race?

Multiplying Two 2-Digit Factors

A. New floor tile is being laid in the school locker room. The floor is rectangular in shape. It will be 23 tiles in length and 37 tiles in width. How many tiles will the floor contain when finished?

You can use a model to help find the answer. You will need a piece of graph paper.

Step 1: Mark off the length of the floor, 23 tiles, on your graph paper. Now mark off the width, 37 tiles. Complete the floor plan by drawing the other two sides of a rectangle.

You can solve the problem now by counting every square in the rectangle. Describe a faster way.

Step 2: Count off 20 squares along the length, and then draw a line across. Label the lengths of the two segments. Count off 30 squares along the width, and then draw a line down. Label the lengths of the segments. Your rectangle now contains four smaller rectangles. Find the area of each one of these. Then add the areas together.

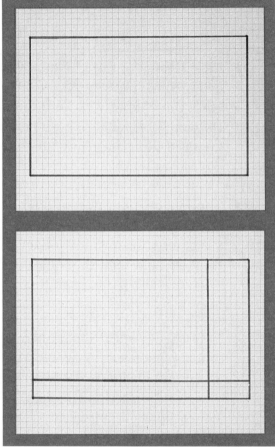

Thinking as a Team

1. How many tiles will the floor contain?

2. Why is it easier to find the area of each smaller rectangle than the area of the whole rectangle?

3. Can mental computation be used to find the smaller areas?

4. Write a multiplication sentence for each smaller area.

B. There are shorter ways of writing what you just did with the model.

$$
\begin{array}{r}
37 \\
\times\,23 \\
\hline
21 \leftarrow (3 \times 7) \\
90 \leftarrow (3 \times 30) \\
140 \leftarrow (20 \times 7) \\
+\,600 \leftarrow (20 \times 30) \\
\hline
851
\end{array}
$$

or

$$
\begin{array}{r}
37 \\
\times\,23 \\
\hline
111 \leftarrow (3 \times 37) \\
+\,740 \leftarrow (20 \times 37) \\
\hline
851
\end{array}
$$

- In the example above, look at the four numbers added together. What part of the model does each number stand for?

- Why are only two numbers added together in the example at the right?

- Compare the two examples. What is the same? What is different?

Work with a partner to model and write other multiplication problems. Discuss how the model and the written problem are related.

C. On the faraway planet of Trululu, all months that end in the letter *r* are very hot. All months that end in *y* are very cold. Other months are mild.

Your team will manage 25 houses for settlers in Trululu. All heating and cooling costs come out of a yearly budget of $15,000. The monthly costs for heating and cooling one house for the year so far are listed at the right.

Cost per House		
January $58		February $56
March $18	April $21	May $60
June $19	July $62	August $12
September $89		October $91

Working as a Team

1. Are the months of November and December hot, cold, or mild? About what would be the average heating or cooling costs per house for these months?

2. Estimate the total cost for all of the houses for the whole year. Will your budget be enough to pay the bills?

More Multiplying Two 2-Digit Factors

Mrs. Martinez is in charge of buying equipment for the city soccer league. She bought 34 boxes of uniforms. Each box contained 36 uniforms. How many uniforms did she buy?

Because each box has the same number of uniforms, you can multiply.

Multiply 34 × 36.

Multiply by ones.	Multiply by tens.	Add.
$$\begin{array}{r} 36 \\ \times\,34 \\ \hline 144 \end{array}$$	$$\begin{array}{r} 36 \\ \times\,34 \\ \hline 144 \\ 1080 \end{array}$$	$$\begin{array}{r} 36 \\ \times\,34 \\ \hline 144 \\ 1080 \\ \hline 1{,}224 \end{array}$$

Mrs. Martinez bought 1,224 uniforms.

Other examples:

$$\begin{array}{r} \$0.98 \\ \times\quad 79 \\ \hline 8\,82 \\ 68\,60 \\ \hline \$77.42 \end{array}$$

Write the dollar sign and the cents point in the answer.

$$\begin{array}{r} 63 \\ \times\,45 \\ \hline 315 \\ 2\,520 \\ \hline 2{,}835 \end{array}$$

Checkpoint   Write the letter of the correct answer.

Multiply.

1. 58 × 67

2. 49 × 83

3. 36 × $0.76

a. 3,536	**a.** 1,079	**a.** $26.06
b. 3,886	**b.** 2,567	**b.** $27.36
c. 4,086	**c.** 3,067	**c.** $29.36
d. 5,436	**d.** 4,067	**d.** 2,736

354

Multiply.

1. 68
× 71

2. 36
× 51

3. 66
× 63

4. 90
× 17

5. 46
× 85

6. 94
× 96

7. 79
× 21

8. 15
× 37

9. 59
× 24

10. 62
× 22

11. 33
× 85

12. 73
× 50

13. $0.49
×   20

14. $0.59
×   13

15. $0.46
×   32

16. $0.32
×   79

17. $0.49
×   84

18. $0.21
×   66

19. 24 × 66

20. 18 × 28

21. 66 × $0.23

22. 59 × 26

23. 47 × $0.83

24. 23 × $0.94

25. 43 × $0.76

26. 50 × $0.19

27. 38 × $0.24

28. 60 × $0.99

29. 27 × 93

30. 89 × $0.55

31. 46 × 21

★32. $(9 \times 8) \times 88$

★33. $(6 \times 7) \times 17$

★34. $(84 - 5) \times \$0.98$

★35. $(2 \times 6) \times \$0.55$

Solve. For Problem 38, use the Infobank.

36. Valerie sold programs at the all-star youth soccer game. She sold 46 programs for $0.55 each. How much did Valerie collect?

37. Pete played 45 min in the first half of the soccer game. He played 39 min in the second half. How many fewer minutes did he play in the second half?

38. Use the information on page 406 to solve. Giorgio ran a distance 36 times as great as the width of the soccer field. How far did he run?

★39. Spike Flannery owns a sporting-goods store. Each year for the last 3 years, he has sold 34 sets of uniforms to each of 6 different teams. How many uniforms has he sold?

MIDCHAPTER REVIEW

Multiply.

1. 60
× 20

2. 800
× 70

3. 7,000
×   40

4. 13
× 22

5. $0.43
×   30

6. $0.52
×   22

7. 69
× 67

8. 94
× 49

9. $0.76
×   47

10. $0.38
×   99

PROBLEM SOLVING
Estimation

Whenever you estimate

- Think about whether you should overestimate or underestimate.

- You may have to find a better estimate or an exact answer if your estimate is close to an amount with which you are comparing it.

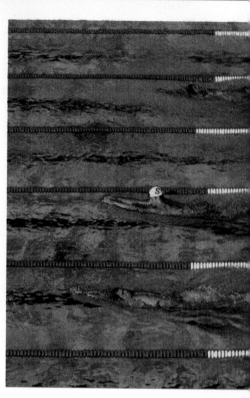

> Public School 321 is holding a swim meet to which 6 teams are invited. Public School 321 has 130 lockers for visitors. Will there be enough lockers?

First, the meet planners have to estimate the number of swimmers. The teams have 10, 18, 16, 18, 17, and 14 swimmers. To be sure that there are enough lockers, the planners overestimate the number of swimmers per team.

   20 estimated number of swimmers per team
$\times$ 6 number of teams invited
 120 overestimated number of visitors   About 120 lockers will be needed.

Because the overestimate—120—is less than the actual 130 lockers, the planners know that they have enough. The next day, the meet planners decide to invite a seventh team that has 18 members. Will 130 lockers still be enough?

   20 estimated number of swimmers per team
$\times$ 7 number of teams invited
 140 estimated number of visitors   About 140 lockers will be needed.

Because 140 is greater than 130, the planners need to find an exact answer.

$10 + 18 + 16 + 18 + 14 + 18 + 17 = 111$ number of visitors

There will be enough lockers for the 7 teams.

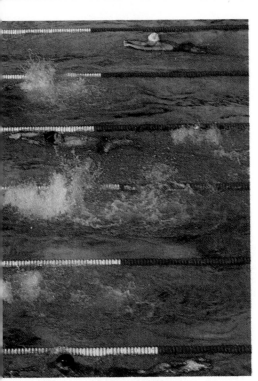

Write the letter of the phrase that completes each sentence.

1. The swim team orders T-shirts. It will earn money by running a car wash. T-shirts cost between $4.95 and $7.95 each. Can the team afford to buy 12 T-shirts? The team members should

   a. overestimate earnings and underestimate costs.
   b. underestimate earnings and overestimate costs.
   c. find the exact answer.

2. The swim team travels 25 mi to the swim meet. How long will it take the team to travel there? To be sure they will be on time, the team members should

   a. underestimate distance and overestimate speed.
   b. underestimate number of people on the team.
   c. overestimate distance and underestimate speed.

Solve. Find an estimate or an exact answer as needed.

3. Ted buys trophies for the meet. They cost between $12 and $15 each. Ted has $172. Is this enough money to buy 12 of the $15 trophies?

4. Rae needs to buy enough juice for 400 servings. One can of juice makes 12 servings. Will 34 cans be enough?

5. To qualify for the finals, a swimmer must finish 3 laps in fewer than 45 seconds. Jan swam 3 laps in 14.5 seconds, 12.3 seconds, and 11.1 seconds. Will she qualify for the finals?

6. Greg has $5.88 with which to buy milk for the swim team. He wants to buy 3 half-gallons for $1.78 each. Does he have enough money to buy this quantity of milk?

★7. After the swim meet, the members of the team eat lunch. It took the team 35 minutes to travel to the meet. Including lunch, how long might the trip home take?

★8. Any student who sells $500 worth of tickets wins a prize. Rick sold 123 adults' tickets for $2.25 each and 281 children's tickets for $1.25 each. Will he win a prize?

Multiplying a 3-Digit Factor

Wayne Gretzky is a famous hockey player. In 1981, he scored 212 points for the Edmonton Oilers. If he scored 212 points per season for 15 seasons, how many points would he score in all?

If the number of points is the same for each season, you can multiply to find the total number of points. Multiply 15 × 212.

Multiply by ones.	Multiply by tens.	Add.
212	212	212
× 15	× 15	× 15
1060	1060	1060
	2120	2120
		3,180

Wayne Gretzky would score a total of 3,180 points in 15 seasons.

Other examples:

413	$4.07	650	700
× 32	× 64	× 76	× 84
826	16 28	3 900	2 800
12 390	244 20	45 500	56 000
13,216	$260.48	49,400	58,800

Checkpoint   Write the letter of the correct answer.

Multiply.

1. 56 × 465

a. 5,115
b. 22,510
c. 26,040
d. 26,140

2. 12 × 601

a. 613
b. 1,803
c. 7,212
d. 7,332

3. 25 × $5.50

a. $125.50
b. $137.50
c. $137.75
d. $147.50

Multiply.

1. 611	**2.** 424	**3.** 133	**4.** 940	**5.** 910
× 66	× 12	× 33	× 20	× 51

Multiply.

6.	100 × 23	**7.**	500 × 30	**8.**	200 × 81	**9.**	624 × 14	**10.**	213 × 39

11.	932 × 62	**12.**	780 × 91	**13.**	840 × 15	**14.**	935 × 24	**15.**	763 × 38

16.	$4.70 × 94	**17.**	$8.23 × 50	**18.**	$5.99 × 36	**19.**	$1.29 × 18	**20.**	$1.95 × 92

21.	$5.98 × 13	**22.**	$3.19 × 40	**23.**	$9.63 × 25	**24.**	$8.52 × 36	**25.**	$7.26 × 42

26. 58 × $9.12 **27.** 33 × 908 **28.** 54 × $5.60 **29.** 700 × 20

30. 16 × 230 **31.** 53 × 732 ★**32.** (40 + 6) × 375 ★**33.** (90 + 8) × $2.73

Solve.

34. The 27 players on Lou's neighborhood hockey team want to earn money to attend a professional hockey game. Each ticket costs $9.50. How much money do they need to earn?

35. During one season, Mike Bossy scored a total of 147 points, and Brian Propp scored 91 points. How many fewer points than Bossy did Propp score that season?

36. Use this information to write and solve your own word problem. Hockey sticks cost $6.00 each. If more than 8 sticks are bought, the cost of each stick is $1.50 less. Sara's hockey team has 27 players.

★**37.** Hockey pucks cost $3.00 each. If more than 12 pucks are bought, the cost of each puck is $0.50 less. Al's coach bought 16 pucks. How much did he spend?

CHALLENGE

Make 2 groups of 4 pennies by moving only 1 penny.

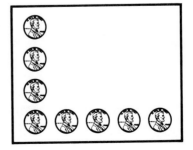

PROBLEM SOLVING
Checking for a Reasonable Answer

Errors in computation can lead to incorrect answers. When you solve a problem, think about the value of your answer. Is it much too great? Is it much too small? You can often spot a wrong answer just by seeing whether it's reasonable or not.

> The North Winds, a hockey team, takes an average of 37 shots on goal per game. There are 29 games in the season. About how many shots on goal would be taken by the end of the season?
>
> **a.** 66 shots   **b.** 1,073 shots   **c.** 64,163 shots

Without finding the answer, you can see that choice *a* is too small and choice *c* is too great. The team would take more than 66 shots on goal in two games. It would have to play more than 1,000 games to take 64,163 shots on goal.

Read each problem. Without finding the exact answer, write the letter of the reasonable answer.

1. José is the star pitcher of the Rayville baseball team. He strikes out an average of 7 batters per game. If he pitched 17 games in a season, about how many strikeouts did he make?

   a. 49 strikeouts
   b. 119 strikeouts
   c. 1,241 strikeouts

2. Candlestick Park, a baseball stadium in San Francisco, California, holds 58,000 people. If the stadium is almost full and each person received a baseball cap, about how many baseball caps were given out?

   a. about 7,000 caps
   b. about 84,000 caps
   c. about 51,000 caps

Read each problem. Without finding the exact answer,
write the letter of the reasonable answer.

3. Phil Esposito, a professional hockey player, once held the record for the most 3-goal games. He scored 3 or more goals in 32 games. What is the minimum number of goals he scored in those 32 games?

a. 25 goals
b. 45 goals
c. 96 goals

4. Lee School needs new basketball uniforms. They plan a teacher-student basketball game to raise money. They charge $3.50 for each ticket and sell 712 tickets. How much money do they raise?

a. $366
b. $2,492
c. $15,321

5. Jan is a gymnast. She decides to practice for 15 hours per week. The first meet is 16 weeks away. For how many hours does Jan practice until the first meet?

a. 89 hours
b. 1,136 hours
c. 240 hours

6. About 30 minutes before a baseball game begins, Randy joins the line to buy a hot dog. He waits for 20 minutes. How many more minutes are there until the game begins?

a. 10 minutes
b. 10 seconds
c. 5 minutes

7. Bob can run 100 meters in 16 seconds. If he can keep up this speed, in how much time will he run 300 meters?

a. 15 seconds
b. 2 minutes 3 seconds
c. 48 seconds

8. Of the 18 members of the Lucky Ducks Little League team, $\frac{1}{6}$ can pitch. How many members can pitch?

a. 3 members
b. 6 members
c. 10 members

9. John played football for an average of 20 minutes per game in a 9-game season. For how many minutes did John play during the season?

a. 18 minutes
b. 180 minutes
c. 300 minutes

★10. Rene buys a baseball mitt for $7.96, a basketball for $5.99, and a team cap for $1.59. How much change does she receive from a $20 bill?

a. $1.29
b. $4.46
c. $11.16

LOGICAL REASONING

You can use *all*, *some*, or *none* to describe
how two sets of objects are related.

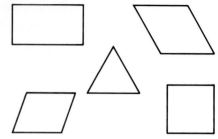

All of the squares are quadrilaterals.
Some of the quadrilaterals are squares.
Some of the quadrilaterals are not squares.
None of the quadrilaterals are triangles.

Notice that a square is always a quadrilateral, but a
quadrilateral is not always a square. A triangle is never
a quadrilateral.

Write *true* or *false*.

1. All of the quadrilaterals are red.

2. Some of the squares are blue.

3. Some of the triangles are not blue.

4. None of the squares are blue.

5. None of the circles are
quadrilaterals.

6. Some of the quadrilaterals are not
rectangles.

7. All of the rectangles are red.

8. None of the triangles are congruent.

Write *always*, *sometimes*, or *never* for ■.

9. January 1 ■ falls on a Monday.

10. A square is ■ a polygon.

11. The month before spring vacation is
■ November.

12. The day before yesterday is ■
tomorrow.

13. The sum of two 2-digit numbers is
■ more than 19.

14. A triangle is ■ a quadrilateral.

GROUP PROJECT

Team Ticktacktoe

The problem: Choose 2 teams of 4 players each. Give each player on one team a sheet of green construction paper, and each player on the other team a sheet of red construction paper. Place 9 chairs in a grid as shown in the picture. Discuss the rules with your classmates. May the best team win.

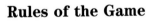

Rules of the Game

- Decide which team will go first.
- Then each team will take turns seating one player at a time.
- The object is to place 3 players from your team in a row.
- Each team must decide its own moves.
- If neither team has 3 in a row when all the players are seated, the teams can begin again.
- If a team needs to plan its moves in secret, the members can leave their construction-paper sheets on their chairs to mark their seats while they talk.
- The first team to place 3 players in a row wins.

CHAPTER TEST

Find the product. (pages 352, 354, and 358)

1. 10×23

2. 16×45

3. $16 \times \$0.53$

4. 87×98

5. 12×241

6. $41 \times \$9.55$

7. 38×677

8. 82×309

9. $86 \times \$3.77$

10. $\begin{array}{r} 66 \\ \times\, 20 \\ \hline \end{array}$

11. $\begin{array}{r} 41 \\ \times\, 67 \\ \hline \end{array}$

12. $\begin{array}{r} 44 \\ \times\, 55 \\ \hline \end{array}$

13. $\begin{array}{r} 52 \\ \times\, 72 \\ \hline \end{array}$

14. $\begin{array}{r} 90 \\ \times\, 86 \\ \hline \end{array}$

15. $\begin{array}{r} 17 \\ \times\, 14 \\ \hline \end{array}$

16. $\begin{array}{r} \$0.71 \\ \times\quad 27 \\ \hline \end{array}$

17. $\begin{array}{r} \$0.44 \\ \times\quad 16 \\ \hline \end{array}$

18. $\begin{array}{r} \$0.33 \\ \times\quad 59 \\ \hline \end{array}$

19. $\begin{array}{r} 789 \\ \times\quad 56 \\ \hline \end{array}$

20. $\begin{array}{r} 457 \\ \times\quad 30 \\ \hline \end{array}$

21. $\begin{array}{r} 703 \\ \times\quad 34 \\ \hline \end{array}$

22. $\begin{array}{r} 209 \\ \times\quad 55 \\ \hline \end{array}$

23. $\begin{array}{r} 810 \\ \times\quad 26 \\ \hline \end{array}$

24. $\begin{array}{r} 478 \\ \times\quad 90 \\ \hline \end{array}$

25. $\begin{array}{r} \$1.19 \\ \times\quad 72 \\ \hline \end{array}$

26. $\begin{array}{r} \$0.17 \\ \times\quad 14 \\ \hline \end{array}$

27. $\begin{array}{r} \$6.19 \\ \times\quad 60 \\ \hline \end{array}$

Estimate. (page 348)

28. $0.88
      × 27

29.   37
      × 42

30. $5.16
      × 24

31.   789
      × 18

Solve. Find an estimate or an exact answer as needed. (page 356)

32. Coach Ryan has $30. She needs to buy wristbands for the 12 members of the gymnastics team. Each set of wristbands costs $2.86. Does she have enough money to buy wristbands for the team? If not, about how much money does she need?

Read the problem. Without finding the exact answer, write the letter of the best answer. (page 360)

33. Brian carries the ball an average of 22 times per football game. Last year, his team played 11 football games. How many times did Brian carry the ball last year?

a. 24 times   **b.** 242 times   **c.** 440 times

BONUS

Each letter stands for a digit. Solve the problems to find the hidden message. (HINT: B stands for the digit 7)

1. $2 \times 4B = 94$

2. $N \times 1B = 136$

3. $3 \times 3N = 11U$

4. $S \times 1B = 51$

5. $1A \times N = 96$

6. $2 \times 1E = S2$

7. $R \times 1A = 10N$

8. $W \times 1R = RW$

9. $U \times SL = LAU$

Now replace each number with its corresponding letter to find the message.

$$\frac{O}{7} \ \frac{}{0} \ \frac{}{8} \ \frac{}{4} \ \frac{}{3} \ \frac{}{6} \ \frac{}{3} \qquad \frac{}{2} \ \frac{}{9} \ \frac{}{6}$$

$$\frac{}{3} \ \frac{}{5} \ \frac{}{6} \ \frac{}{1} \ \frac{}{1}!$$

RETEACHING

You may need to regroup when you multiply by a 2-digit factor.

Find the product of 37×95.

Multiply by the ones.

```
   95
×  37
─────
  665
```

Multiply by the tens.

```
   95
×  37
─────
  665
 2850
```

Add.

```
   95
×  37
──────
  665
 2 850
──────
 3,515
```

Other examples:

```
 $0.77
×   84
──────
  3 08
 61 60
──────
$64.68
```

```
  659
×  52
──────
 1 318
32 950
──────
34,268
```

```
 $8.36
×   79
───────
 75 24
585 20
───────
$660.44
```

Multiply.

1.
```
  67
× 84
────
```

2.
```
  39
× 28
────
```

3.
```
  86
× 38
────
```

4.
```
  97
× 53
────
```

5.
```
  48
× 63
────
```

6.
```
  549
×  53
─────
```

7.
```
  627
×  98
─────
```

8.
```
  932
×  47
─────
```

9.
```
  399
×  85
─────
```

10.
```
  824
×  75
─────
```

11.
```
 $0.85
×   73
──────
```

12.
```
 $0.82
×   39
──────
```

13.
```
 $0.43
×   94
──────
```

14.
```
 $0.65
×   57
──────
```

15.
```
 $0.92
×   33
──────
```

16.
```
 $9.49
×   38
──────
```

17.
```
 $2.75
×   62
──────
```

18.
```
 $8.64
×   49
──────
```

19.
```
 $6.25
×   28
──────
```

20.
```
 $5.16
×   89
──────
```

21. 53×769

22. $89 \times \$0.75$

23. 56×48

24. $74 \times \$9.36$

ENRICHMENT

Casting Out Nines

A. You can cast out nines from 562.

First, add the digits.
If the sum is greater than 9,
add the digits of the sum.
Write the result.

$5 + 6 + 2 = 13$ $\boxed{13 > 9}$

$1 + 3 = 4$

4

B. You can check addition by casting out nines.

Cast out nines from the addends and the sum.

Add the results.
Cast out nines from the sum.

$639 \longrightarrow 6 + 3 + 9 = 18 \longrightarrow 1 + 8 = 9$
$1,330 \longrightarrow 1 + 3 + 3 + 0 = 7$
$+ 3,875 \longrightarrow 3 + 8 + 7 + 5 = 23 \longrightarrow 2 + 3 = 5$
$5,844 \longrightarrow 5 + 8 + 4 + 4 = 21 \longrightarrow 2 + 1 = 3$

$\begin{array}{r} 9 \\ 7 \\ + 5 \\ \hline 21 \end{array} \longrightarrow 2 + 1 = 3$

The results from both sums should be the same.

C. You can check multiplication by casting out nines.

Cast out nines from the factors and the product.

Multiply the results.
Cast out nines from the product.

$476 \longrightarrow 4 + 7 + 6 = 17 \longrightarrow 1 + 7 = 8$
$\times\ 27 \longrightarrow 2 + 7 = 9$
$12,852 \longrightarrow 1 + 2 + 8 + 5 + 2 = 18 \longrightarrow 1 + 8 = 9$

$\begin{array}{r} 8 \\ \times\ 9 \\ \hline 72 \end{array} \longrightarrow 7 + 2 = 9$

The results from both products should be the same.

Check each sum or product by casting out nines.
Write *correct*, or write the correct answer.

1.	4,368	**2.**	3,905	**3.**	25,438	**4.**	6,723	**5.**	9,026
	2,985		12,469		8,575		921		32,166
	+ 1,606		+ 2,251		283		7,477		44,853
	8,859		18,625		+ 4,925		+ 5,354		+ 8,739
					39,221		21,475		94,784

6.	495	**7.**	927	**8.**	674	**9.**	832	**10.**	657
	× 38		× 55		× 76		× 49		× 97
	18,810		50,985		51,324		40,778		62,729

367

CUMULATIVE REVIEW

Write the letter of the correct answer.

Use the figure to answer Exercises 1–5.

1. Which is a line?

    a. $\overrightarrow{AB}$ **b.** $\overleftrightarrow{AF}$

    c. $\overline{CG}$ **d.** not given

2. Which is a right angle?

    a. $\angle GCD$ **b.** $\angle GCF$

    c. $\angle GFC$ **d.** not given

3. What is figure *CDEG?*

    a. quadrilateral   **b.** pentagon

    c. triangle   **d.** not given

4. What is the perimeter of *CDEF?*

    a. 6 cm   **b.** 8 cm

    c. 10 cm   **d.** not given

5. What is the area of *CDEF?*

    a. 5 square   **b.** 10 square
        centimeters   centimeters

    c. 12 square   **d.** not given
        centimeters

6. 6,000 mL = ▦ L

    a. 6   **b.** 60

    c. 600   **d.** not given

7. $\frac{4}{5} + \frac{7}{10}$

    a. $\frac{11}{15}$ **b.** $1\frac{1}{10}$

    c. $1\frac{1}{2}$ **d.** not given

8. $\frac{2}{3} = \frac{▦}{12}$

    a. 4   **b.** 8

    c. 9   **d.** not given

9. 764 + 299

    a. 953   **b.** 1,153

    c. 1,063   **d.** not given

10. Maria exercises for 5 min on Monday, 10 min on Tuesday, 20 min on Wednesday, and 40 min on Thursday. For how many minutes would you expect her to exercise on Friday?

    a. 50 min

    b. 75 min

    c. 80 min

    d. not given

11. Mr. Lee grows 62 plants. He sells an equal number of plants to 8 people. At most, how many plants does each person buy?

    a. 7 plants

    b. 7 R6 plants

    c. 8 plants

    d. not given

Your class has decided to raise $600 to buy a computer. How would you go about earning the money? Maybe you could sell T-shirts or hold a secondhand-book sale. How many items would you have to sell? What price would you charge for each item?

12 DIVISION: 2-DIGIT DIVISORS

Mental Computation: Dividing Tens and Hundreds

A. The Eastern Cannery packs 3,500 cans of tuna every 5 days. If it packs the same number of cans per day, how many cans of tuna does the cannery pack each day?

You can mentally divide $5\overline{)3,500}$.

Think: $5\overline{)35}$.

Divide to find the first digit of the quotient.	Write 0's for the other digits.	Check by multiplying.
$\dfrac{7}{5\overline{)3,500}}$	$\dfrac{700}{5\overline{)3,500}}$	$700 \times 5 = 3,500$

The cannery packs 700 cans of tuna each day.

B. You can divide mentally by multiples of 10.

Divide $30\overline{)1,800}$.

Think: $3\overline{)18}$.

$\dfrac{6}{30\overline{)1,800}}$ So, $30\overline{)1,800}$. $60 \times 30 = 1,800$ | Check. |

Checkpoint   Write the letter of the correct answer.

Divide mentally.

1. $280 \div 7$

a. 4
b. 40
c. 400
d. 4,000

2. $50\overline{)4,000}$

a. 8
b. 80
c. 800
d. 8,000

3. $20\overline{)12,000}$

a. 6
b. 60
c. 600
d. 6,000

Divide mentally.

1. $6\overline{)240}$ **2.** $3\overline{)150}$ **3.** $5\overline{)400}$ **4.** $9\overline{)450}$ **5.** $8\overline{)480}$

6. $3\overline{)2,700}$ **7.** $4\overline{)3,600}$ **8.** $2\overline{)1,800}$ **9.** $3\overline{)2,100}$ **10.** $9\overline{)3,600}$

11. $40\overline{)280}$ **12.** $50\overline{)250}$ **13.** $30\overline{)120}$ **14.** $70\overline{)420}$ **15.** $20\overline{)160}$

16. $50\overline{)1,500}$ **17.** $60\overline{)2,400}$ **18.** $40\overline{)3,200}$ **19.** $90\overline{)8,100}$ **20.** $90\overline{)3,600}$

21. $20\overline{)10,000}$ **22.** $40\overline{)20,000}$ **23.** $30\overline{)15,000}$ **★24.** $50\overline{)80,000}$

25. $3,600 \div 4$ **26.** $5,400 \div 6$ **27.** $450 \div 5$ **28.** $1,200 \div 3$

29. $1,000 \div 20$ **30.** $560 \div 8$ **31.** $3,200 \div 80$ **32.** $4,500 \div 50$

Solve.

33. At one cannery, 7 machines label a total of 5,600 cans per day. If each machine labels an equal number of cans, how many cans does each machine label per day?

★34. Each week 2 tons of fish arrive at the cannery. How many pounds of fish is this?

NUMBER SENSE

It may be easier to divide by multiples of 10 if you write the division problem as a fraction.

Divide $360 \div 90$.

Write $360 \div 90$ as a fraction.

$\dfrac{360}{90}$

Cross out the same number of 0's in the numerator and in the denominator.

$\dfrac{36\cancel{0}}{9\cancel{0}}$

Divide.

$\dfrac{36}{9} = 4$

Find the quotient.

1. $450 \div 90$ **2.** $240 \div 60$ **3.** $420 \div 60$ **4.** $720 \div 80$

5. $180 \div 20$ **6.** $350 \div 50$ **★7.** $2,100 \div 70$ **★8.** $4,800 \div 60$

PROBLEM SOLVING
Writing a Number Sentence

You have learned the steps to take to write a number sentence to solve a problem. Try to write a number sentence for the problem below. Then check it.

> Harriet sells products made by the Unique Manufacturing Company. One day, she sells 6 pairs of sunglasses that have automatic windshield wipers for $5 per pair. What was the total cost of the sunglasses?

1. List what you know and what you need to find.

Know	Harriet sold 6 pairs of sunglasses. The sunglasses cost $5 per pair.

Find	How much did all 6 pairs cost?

2. What does your list tell you about whether to +, −, ×, or ÷? Write a number sentence about this problem. Use n to stand for the number you need to find.

$$6 \times \$5 = n$$
number of   price of   total
pairs   each pair   cost

3. Solve. Write the answer.

$$6 \times \$5 = n$$
$$6 \times \$5 = \$30$$
$$n = \$30$$

The total cost was $30.

Write the letter of the correct number sentence.

1. A worker completes 8 gas-powered pogo sticks every hour. How many hours will it take her to complete 32 sticks?

  a. $8 \times 32 = n$ **b.** $32 \div 8 = n$
  c. $32 - 8 = n$

2. Gene packages rubber boots for dogs. He puts 4 boots into each box. Each crate holds 36 boxes. How many boots are there in a crate?

  a. $4 \times 36 = n$ **b.** $36 \div 4 = n$
  c. $36 - 4 = n$

Math Reasoning, page H203

Write a number sentence. Solve.

3. The Batty Bat Company sells 28 bats to Little League teams. If it sells 4 bats to each team, how many teams does the Little League have?

4. The Surf Company makes *Sea Tunes*, a waterproof radio. The company sells 42 *Sea Tunes* to Stereo Sounds Stores for $12 each. How much did all the radios sell for?

5. Joanne bought 32 boxes of invisible-ink pens and 69 boxes of chattering teeth for her new toy store. How many boxes did she buy in all?

6. Craig makes automatic homework machines. It takes him 9 days to complete one machine. How many machines can he complete in 117 days?

7. Lynn makes sunglasses for dogs at the Bow Wow Company. She earns $350 per week. If she works 35 hours per week, how much does she earn per hour?

8. Hats for Hounds makes fashionable headgear for dogs. The company sells 25 hats to a department store for $2 per hat. How much will the company earn if it sells all 25 hats?

9. The Addams Pet Store orders 48 parrots through the mail. The post office calls to say that 19 squawking parrots are loose in the office. The rest have flown the coop. How many parrots have flown the coop?

10. Mark invents a glow-in-the-dark baseball. He gives each of 5 friends a baseball for batting practice. Mark's friends get a total of 65 hits. Each friend hits his baseball an equal number of times. How many times is each baseball hit?

Dividing by Multiples of 10

A. You can use base-10 blocks to explore dividing by multiples of 10.

Step 1: Use the ones blocks to model 4. Separate the blocks into groups of 2.

- How many groups are there?

- Write a number sentence to show what you did.

Step 2: Use the tens blocks to model 40. Separate the blocks into groups with 2 tens in each group.

- What number does each group stand for?

- How many groups are there?

- Write a number sentence to show what you did.

Step 3: Model 400. Separate it into groups of 20.

- How did you have to change your model of 400 to separate it into groups?

- How many groups are there?

- Write a number sentence to show what you did.

What do you notice about all of the answers?

Use base-10 blocks to explore other related problems, such as

$$3\overline{)9} \qquad 30\overline{)90} \qquad 30\overline{)900}$$

Thinking as a Team _____

1. What patterns do you see in the problems you have solved?

2. How can you use mental math to help you divide by multiples of 10?

B. You can use what you have discovered to explore how to divide other numbers by multiples of 10.

Model 122 using base-10 blocks. Separate your model into groups of 40.

Describe how you did this.

- How many groups of 40 are there?

- Are there any blocks remaining?
  If so, how many?

- Write a number sentence to show what you did.

- How can you use mental math to check whether your answer is reasonable?

Use base-10 blocks to solve other problems.

$20\overline{)86}$ $10\overline{)99}$ $60\overline{)127}$ $79 \div 30$ $191 \div 70$

Working as a Team

Work with a partner. Each partner takes four index cards and writes a division problem on each, such as

$60\overline{)420}$ $20\overline{)100}$ $50\overline{)255}$ $40\overline{)340}$

On the back of the cards, write the quotients.

Decide who goes first. Hold up each index card in turn for your partner, asking a question such as

- Is there a 6 in the quotient?

- Does the answer have a remainder?

- How many digits are there in the quotient?

Your partner calculates mentally to answer.

Make up other sets of division problems and questions. Can you make up other games to play using the cards? How can you score right and wrong answers? Trade your cards and rules with other teams.

Dividing with 2-Digit Divisors

A publisher sent samples of 96 children's magazines to the school librarian. If the librarian gives an equal number of the magazines to each of 21 teachers, how many magazines will each teacher receive? How many magazines will be left?

Find the quotient of $21\overline{)96}$.

Divide the tens.   Think: $21\overline{)9}$. Not enough tens.
Divide the ones.   Think: $21\overline{)96}$, or $2\overline{)9}$.

Estimate 4.   Check.

$$\begin{array}{r} 4 \text{ R12} \\ 21\overline{)96} \\ 84 \\ \hline 12 \end{array}$$

Multiply.
Subtract and compare.
Write the remainder.

$$\begin{array}{r} 21 \\ \times\ 4 \\ \hline 84 \\ +12 \\ \hline 96 \end{array}$$

Each teacher will receive 4 magazines. There will be 12 magazines left.

Checkpoint   Write the letter of the correct answer.

Divide.

1. $21\overline{)84}$ **a.** 3 R21   **b.** 4   **c.** 4 R4   **d.** 40

2. $95 \div 31$ **a.** 2 R33   **b.** 3   **c.** 3 R2   **d.** 3 R5

3. $44\overline{)99}$ **a.** 2 R11   **b.** 2 R19   **c.** 20 R11   **d.** 211

Divide.

1. $31\overline{)93}$ 2. $46\overline{)92}$ 3. $32\overline{)64}$ 4. $24\overline{)96}$ 5. $28\overline{)56}$

6. $38\overline{)76}$ 7. $22\overline{)88}$ 8. $13\overline{)26}$ 9. $12\overline{)48}$ 10. $11\overline{)33}$

11. $26\overline{)58}$ 12. $74\overline{)90}$ 13. $37\overline{)42}$ 14. $31\overline{)79}$ 15. $25\overline{)26}$

16. $24\overline{)75}$ 17. $38\overline{)87}$ 18. $12\overline{)29}$ 19. $31\overline{)65}$ 20. $23\overline{)99}$

Divide.

21. $12\overline{)48}$ **22.** $31\overline{)96}$ **23.** $53\overline{)75}$ **24.** $32\overline{)96}$ **25.** $11\overline{)16}$

26. $42\overline{)88}$ **27.** $13\overline{)39}$ **28.** $21\overline{)66}$ **29.** $33\overline{)84}$ **30.** $26\overline{)53}$

31. $55 \div 11$ **32.** $44 \div 22$ **33.** $50 \div 25$ **34.** $99 \div 33$ **35.** $90 \div 45$

36. $29 \div 14$ **37.** $93 \div 52$ **38.** $92 \div 23$ **39.** $76 \div 67$ **40.** $64 \div 32$

41. $76 \div 32$ **42.** $94 \div 46$ **43.** $58 \div 29$ **44.** $86 \div 42$ **45.** $76 \div 21$

46. $59 \div 43$ **47.** $77 \div 36$ **48.** $91 \div 22$ **49.** $64 \div 31$ **50.** $87 \div 21$

Solve. For Problem 53, use the Infobank.

51. The newsstand on Dewey Street orders 75 copies of a magazine. The magazine is shipped in bundles of 24. How many bundles does the newsstand receive? How many loose magazines does it receive?

★52. A company publishes 12 issues of its magazine each year. This year, it published 24 short stories and 48 poems. If every issue contained the same number of stories and the same number of poems, how many of each were there in each issue?

53. Use the information on page 406 to solve. If each newsstand receives the same number of copies, how many copies of *Universe* does each receive? How many copies of *Animals* does each receive?

54. A puzzle publisher sold 46,605 copies of its magazine in January; 52,198 copies in February; and 48,037 copies in March. How many copies were sold in those three months?

Find the divisor.

1. $\blacksquare\overline{)63}$ ^{7} **2.** $\blacksquare\overline{)100}$ ^{25} **3.** $\blacksquare\overline{)43}$ $^{6\,R1}$ **4.** $\blacksquare\overline{)53}$ $^{8\,R5}$ **5.** $\blacksquare\overline{)72}$ $^{10\,R2}$

Correcting Estimates

Evelyn paints billboards in Chicago. The billboard for the city zoo had to be done in a rush; so, Evelyn worked 13 hours per day. If the job took 49 hours, how many full 13-hour days did Evelyn work? For how many hours did she work on the next day?

Divide 49 ÷ 13.

Divide the tens.   Think: $13\overline{)4}$. Not enough tens.
Divide the ones.   Think: $13\overline{)49}$, or $1\overline{)4}$.

Estimate 4.

$$\begin{array}{r} 4 \\ 13\overline{)49} \\ 52 \\ \hline \end{array}$$ Multiply.
Too great.

You need to correct the estimate.

Try 3.

$$\begin{array}{r} 3 \ \textbf{R10} \\ 13\overline{)49} \\ 39 \\ \hline 10 \end{array}$$ Multiply.
Subtract and compare.
Write the remainder.

She worked 3 full 13-hour days. She worked for 10 hours on the fourth day.

Another example:

Divide 81 ÷ 28.

Estimate 4.
$$\begin{array}{r} 4 \\ 28\overline{)81} \\ 112 \end{array}$$ Multiply.
Too great.

Try 3.
$$\begin{array}{r} 3 \\ 28\overline{)81} \\ 84 \end{array}$$ Multiply.
Too great.

Try 2.
$$\begin{array}{r} 2 \ \text{R25} \\ 28\overline{)81} \\ 56 \\ \hline 25 \end{array}$$ Multiply.
Subtract and compare.
Write the remainder.

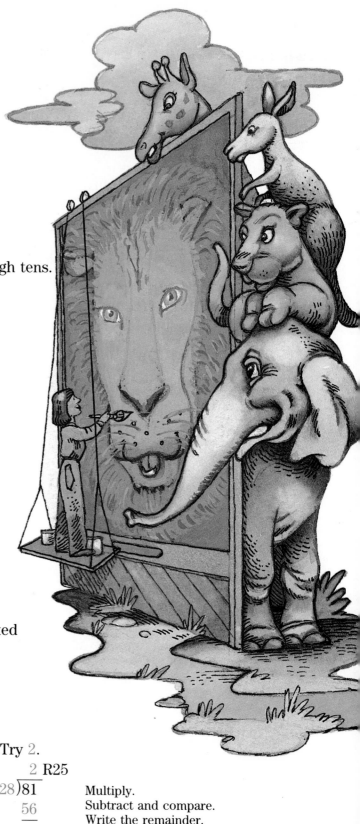

378

Divide.

1. $17\overline{)51}$ 2. $23\overline{)92}$ 3. $27\overline{)81}$ 4. $24\overline{)96}$ 5. $19\overline{)76}$ 6. $25\overline{)75}$

7. $18\overline{)42}$ 8. $35\overline{)40}$ 9. $12\overline{)50}$ 10. $49\overline{)99}$ 11. $27\overline{)53}$ 12. $12\overline{)92}$

13. $42\overline{)81}$ 14. $14\overline{)40}$ 15. $43\overline{)82}$ 16. $28\overline{)52}$ 17. $45\overline{)88}$ 18. $28\overline{)82}$

19. $13\overline{)46}$ 20. $15\overline{)71}$ 21. $35\overline{)67}$ 22. $38\overline{)91}$ 23. $47\overline{)86}$ 24. $15\overline{)46}$

25. $46\overline{)91}$ 26. $18\overline{)90}$ 27. $38\overline{)74}$ 28. $39\overline{)78}$ 29. $17\overline{)52}$ 30. $47\overline{)88}$

31. $18\overline{)56}$ 32. $29\overline{)87}$ 33. $19\overline{)56}$ 34. $44\overline{)81}$ 35. $28\overline{)66}$ 36. $14\overline{)99}$

37. $73 \div 38$ 38. $49 \div 15$ 39. $46 \div 19$ 40. $51 \div 26$ 41. $37 \div 13$

42. $75 \div 27$ 43. $83 \div 18$ 44. $81 \div 26$ 45. $62 \div 24$ 46. $67 \div 15$

Solve.

47. Louise sells advertising space for a newspaper. During a 28-day period, a customer bought 84 pages of advertising space, buying the same amount each day. How many pages were bought each day?

48. A television commercial is shown 14 times per week for 12 weeks. What is the total number of times it is shown?

★49. In a TV ad, 40 toys are held by 19 children. One child holds 4 toys. If the rest of the toys are divided equally among the other 18 children, how many toys does each of those children hold?

50. Use the following information to write and solve your own word problem. On a very hot day, 24 actors are filming a commercial for beachwear. The director of the commercial brings the actors 72 glasses of juice during a rest period.

MIDCHAPTER REVIEW

Divide.

1. $20\overline{)95}$ 2. $80\overline{)240}$ 3. $20\overline{)1,000}$ 4. $60\overline{)247}$ 5. $70\overline{)222}$ 6. $90\overline{)646}$

7. $46\overline{)92}$ 8. $21\overline{)95}$ 9. $25\overline{)74}$ 10. $27\overline{)89}$ 11. $38\overline{)97}$ 12. $29\overline{)62}$

PROBLEM SOLVING
Choosing a Strategy or Method

Write the strategy or method you use. Then solve.

> Making an Organized List
> Making a Table
> Guessing and Checking
> Making a Diagram
> Choosing the Operation
> Acting It Out
> Estimation

1. On one day, the Betsy Ross Company produces 3 United States flags for every 5 state flags. How many state flags are made if the company produces 30 United States flags?

2. Joggers, Inc., makes running outfits. Its tops are made in green, orange, or purple. Its sweatpants are made in green, orange, purple, or white. How many combinations of tops and sweatpants are there?

3. There are 6 new children's books at the bookstore. Veronica can choose 2 of the books for her birthday. From how many combinations can Veronica choose?

4. Mr. Bliss buys a new suit and a new topcoat at the Gentleman's Apparel Shop. The total cost of both items is $275. The topcoat costs $85 less than the suit. What is the cost of each item?

5. Barry packs 12 rolls of flag stickers in each box. If he packs 24 boxes in 1 hour, how many rolls of stickers has he packed?

6. For each record player in a home in the United States, there are 2 televisions. For every television, there are 3 radios. There are 4 record players in an apartment building. About how many televisions and radios are there?

7. A new kind of running shoes cost $100 per pair. A customer pays for a pair of the shoes with one $20 bill and a combination of $10, $5, and $1 bills. He gives the clerk at least one of each of the bills and no more than five of any bill. With what combination of bills does he pay the clerk?

8. Edward Stratemeyer wrote children's books in three different series. The series were *The Rover Boys*, *The Bobbsey Twins*, and *Tom Swift*. Suppose you own 2 of his books. Each of your books is from a different series. What combinations could your books represent?

9. A company wants a new trademark. It plans to use a circle, a square, or a triangle. On the trademark, the company will show a design with its initials, an animal, a torch, or a star. How many different combinations of shapes and designs could appear on the trademark?

10. A record store found that it sold 4 single records for every 3 albums. For every 3 albums, it sold 1 cassette. One day, the store sold 36 albums. About how many single records and cassettes did it sell that day?

11. Mary sells flags in her store. She pays $12.75 for each flag. She has $200 in her budget to buy more flags. Is this enough to buy 12 new flags?

12. From this lesson, choose one problem that you have already solved. Show how it can be solved by using a different strategy or method from the one you used originally.

1-Digit Quotients

Lori is a florist. For Valentine Day, she orders 186 red roses. What is the greatest number of red roses she can sell to each of her 22 customers? How many red roses will Lori have left after she sells them to her customers?

Divide 186 ÷ 22.

Divide the hundreds.
Think: $22\overline{)1}$. Not enough hundreds.
Divide the tens. Think: $22\overline{)18}$. Not enough tens.
Divide the ones. Think: $22\overline{)186}$, or $2\overline{)18}$.

Estimate 9.

$$\begin{array}{r} 9 \\ 22\overline{)186} \\ \underline{198} \end{array}$$

Multiply.
Too great.

You need to correct the estimate.

Try 8.

$$\begin{array}{r} 8 \text{ R10} \\ 22\overline{)186} \\ \underline{176} \\ 10 \end{array}$$

Multiply.
Subtract and compare.
Write the remainder.

Check your answer.

$$\begin{array}{r} 22 \\ \times\ 8 \\ \hline 176 \\ +\ 10 \\ \hline 186 \end{array}$$

The greatest number of red roses that Lori can sell to each of her 22 customers is 8. She will have 10 left.

Checkpoint Write the letter of the correct answer.

Divide.

1. 198 ÷ 33   **a.** 60 R10   **b.** 6   **c.** 6 R10   **d.** 60

2. $41\overline{)336}$ **a.** 8   **b.** 8 R8   **c.** 8 R16   **d.** 88

3. 320 ÷ 69   **a.** 4 R54   **b.** 4 R44   **c.** 4 R8   **d.** 40 R44

4. $31\overline{)193}$ **a.** 5 R38   **b.** 6 R7   **c.** 162   **d.** 224

Divide.

1. $62\overline{)310}$ 2. $31\overline{)124}$ 3. $41\overline{)164}$ 4. $91\overline{)546}$ 5. $53\overline{)159}$

6. $14\overline{)126}$ 7. $45\overline{)360}$ 8. $42\overline{)168}$ 9. $28\overline{)168}$ 10. $91\overline{)637}$

11. $42\overline{)227}$ 12. $73\overline{)106}$ 13. $81\overline{)669}$ 14. $42\overline{)298}$ 15. $23\overline{)147}$

16. $49\overline{)168}$ 17. $76\overline{)726}$ 18. $38\overline{)364}$ 19. $96\overline{)456}$ 20. $76\overline{)712}$

21. $65\overline{)349}$ 22. $66\overline{)726}$ 23. $26\overline{)235}$ 24. $59\overline{)356}$ 25. $91\overline{)717}$

26. $456 \div 93$ 27. $482 \div 76$ 28. $405 \div 45$ 29. $605 \div 74$ 30. $324 \div 81$

31. $568 \div 91$ 32. $160 \div 40$ 33. $273 \div 29$ 34. $120 \div 13$ 35. $628 \div 66$

36. $249 \div 64$ 37. $555 \div 91$ 38. $145 \div 70$ 39. $126 \div 14$ 40. $183 \div 61$

41. $118 \div 41$ 42. $249 \div 31$ 43. $215 \div 53$ 44. $637 \div 91$ 45. $482 \div 80$

Solve.

46. The Flower Basket Shop must make 34 identical corsages for a wedding. If the shop has 132 roses for the corsages, what is the greatest number of roses that there can be in each corsage?

47. A group of florists join to form a flower delivery service. They have a total of 28 vans. In one day they must make 275 deliveries. The driver of each van tries to make the same number of deliveries. Use this information to write and solve your own word problem.

CHOOSING THE METHOD

Decide whether you would use mental math, pencil and paper, or a calculator to solve each. Explain your answer, then solve.

1. $94.08 + 8.94$ 2. $1.95 - 0.85$ 3. $\$9.86 \times 14$

4. $3,525 \div 5$ 5. 989×7 6. $30,000 \div 30$

2-Digit Quotients

The Snow-Scene Company makes 695 pairs of racing skis to deliver to 32 stores. If the same number of pairs of skis are shipped to each store, how many pairs of skis will each store receive? How many pairs will be left?

Divide 695 ÷ 32.

Divide the hundreds.   Think: $32\overline{)6}$. Not enough hundreds.

Divide the tens.   Think: $32\overline{)695}$, or $3\overline{)6}$.

Estimate 2.

$$\begin{array}{r} 2 \\ 32\overline{)695} \\ 64 \\ \hline 5 \end{array}$$

Multiply.
Subtract and compare.

Divide the ones.   Think: $32\overline{)55}$, or $3\overline{)5}$.

Estimate 1.

$$\begin{array}{r} 21 \ \text{R23} \\ 32\overline{)695} \\ 64\downarrow \\ \hline 55 \\ 32 \\ \hline 23 \end{array}$$

Multiply.
Subtract and compare.
Write the remainder.

Each store will receive 21 pairs of skis. There will be 23 pairs left.

Checkpoint   Write the letter of the correct answer.
Divide.

1. $42\overline{)840}$ 2. $255 \div 21$ 3. $30\overline{)627}$ 4. $908 \div 48$

a. 2	**b.** 20	**a.** 10 R45	**b.** 12	**a.** 19 R31	**b.** 20	**a.** 10 R8	**b.** 18
c. 21	**d.** 22	**c.** 12 R3	**d.** 15	**c.** 20 R27	**d.** 24 R7	**c.** 18 R44	**d.** 19

Divide.

1. $20\overline{)480}$ 2. $70\overline{)910}$ 3. $60\overline{)780}$ 4. $30\overline{)690}$ 5. $40\overline{)880}$

6. $31\overline{)961}$ 7. $42\overline{)882}$ 8. $63\overline{)945}$ 9. $72\overline{)792}$ 10. $53\overline{)689}$

11. $34\overline{)702}$ 12. $15\overline{)955}$ 13. $11\overline{)508}$ 14. $59\overline{)620}$ 15. $39\overline{)534}$

16. $903 \div 32$ 17. $801 \div 49$ 18. $643 \div 14$ 19. $785 \div 18$ 20. $981 \div 46$

21. $176 \div 17$ 22. $995 \div 28$ 23. $430 \div 12$ 24. $954 \div 40$ 25. $271 \div 21$

26. $930 \div 62$ 27. $877 \div 80$ 28. $800 \div 42$ 29. $360 \div 18$ 30. $489 \div 26$

31. $772 \div 61$ 32. $495 \div 99$ 33. $358 \div 30$ 34. $784 \div 50$ 35. $319 \div 29$

Solve.

36. A factory uses 682 feet of webbing to make 62 snowshoes daily. The same amount of webbing is used in each shoe. How much webbing is used for each shoe?

★37. During January, a store sold 26 hats each day. If the store was open every day, how many hats were sold in January?

38. Use the information in the chart to write and solve your own word problem.

WINTER EQUIPMENT

Type	Number ordered	Average sold each week
Volleyballs	144	18
Basketballs	260	26
Soccer balls	121	11

ANOTHER LOOK

Add. Write your answer as a whole number or as a mixed number in simplest form.

1. $\frac{1}{2} + \frac{4}{6}$ 2. $\frac{1}{3} + \frac{8}{12}$ 3. $\frac{4}{5} + \frac{3}{10}$ 4. $\frac{2}{3} + \frac{5}{6}$ 5. $\frac{7}{8} + \frac{3}{4}$

Dividing Money

A. The Custom Design Furniture Company pays $8.45 for 65 feet of trimming. How much does each foot of trimming cost?

Find the quotient of $8.45 ÷ 65.
To divide amounts of money, think of the amounts as whole numbers.

$$65\overline{)\$8.45}$$

Think: $65\overline{)845}$.

$$\begin{array}{r} \$0.1\,3 \\ 65\overline{)\$8.4\,5} \\ 6\,5 \\ \hline 1\,9\,5 \\ 1\,9\,5 \\ \hline 0 \end{array}$$

This 0 should be written.

Remember to write the dollar sign and the cents point.

Check.

$$\begin{array}{r} \$0.1\,3 \\ \times6\,5 \\ \hline 6\,5 \\ 7\,8\,0 \\ \hline \$8.4\,5 \end{array}$$

Each foot of trimming costs $0.13.

B. You need to write a zero to the right of the cents point when the quotient is less than $0.10. Find the quotient of $2.25 ÷ 25.

$$25\overline{)\$2.25}$$

Think: $25\overline{)225}$.

$$\begin{array}{r} \$0.0\,9 \\ 25\overline{)\$2.2\,5} \\ 2\,2\,5 \\ \hline 0 \end{array}$$

This 0 must be written.

Remember to write the dollar sign and the cents point.

Check.

$$\begin{array}{r} \$0.0\,9 \\ \times2\,5 \\ \hline 4\,5 \\ 1\,8\,0 \\ \hline \$2.2\,5 \end{array}$$

Checkpoint   Write the letter of the correct answer.

Divide.

1. $42\overline{)\$0.84}$ **a.** $0.002   **b.** $0.02   **c.** $0.20   **d.** 2

2. $8.12 ÷ 28   **a.** $0.21 R3   **b.** $0.29   **c.** $2.90   **d.** 29

Divide.

1. $0.64 \div 16$
2. $0.74 \div 37$
3. $2.28 \div 19$
4. $6.90 \div 46$

5. $5.72 \div 26$
6. $4.35 \div 29$
7. $7.28 \div 26$
8. $4.25 \div 25$

9. $84\overline{)\$5.88}$
10. $23\overline{)\$1.84}$
11. $78\overline{)\$5.46}$
12. $24\overline{)\$2.16}$
13. $61\overline{)\$1.22}$

14. $18\overline{)\$1.62}$
15. $52\overline{)\$4.16}$
16. $72\overline{)\$3.60}$
17. $36\overline{)\$3.24}$
18. $22\overline{)\$1.54}$

19. $39\overline{)\$1.17}$
20. $64\overline{)\$8.32}$
21. $89\overline{)\$8.90}$
22. $19\overline{)\$4.75}$
23. $13\overline{)\$5.33}$

24. $23\overline{)\$8.97}$
25. $12\overline{)\$5.04}$
26. $75\overline{)\$6.00}$
27. $15\overline{)\$6.30}$
28. $25\overline{)\$6.50}$

29. $28\overline{)\$8.96}$
30. $15\overline{)\$7.65}$
31. $79\overline{)\$5.53}$
32. $45\overline{)\$4.95}$
33. $51\overline{)\$8.16}$

34. $21\overline{)\$6.09}$
35. $27\overline{)\$9.99}$
36. $12\overline{)\$9.60}$
37. $69\overline{)\$2.76}$
38. $11\overline{)\$3.30}$

Solve.

39. A cabinetmaker pays $6.65 for a gallon of stain. If a gallon covers 35 cabinet doors, how much does it cost him to stain 1 door?

40. A cabinetmaker spends $3.25 for 25 feet of lumber. What is the cost of 1 foot of lumber?

41. A dining-room table costs $329.00. The chairs cost $245.00, and a china cabinet costs $399.99. How much does the whole set cost?

★42. A furniture company wants to print a color catalog of its products. One printer charges $4.41 for 49 pages. Another printer charges $5.44 for 68 pages. Which do you think is the better buy? Why?

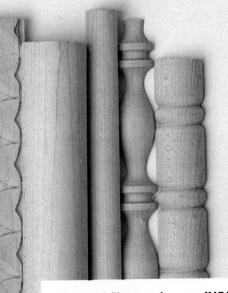

CALCULATOR

Use your calculator to find the better buy.

1. $5.28 for 16 feet of molding, or $6.67 for 23 feet of molding

2. $9.36 for 12 pounds of tacks, or $8.68 for 14 pounds of tacks

PROBLEM SOLVING
Estimation

When you make plans, you may not have exact information. In order to complete plans, you may have to supply estimated amounts.

A Taney School fourth-grade class is planning a trip. Before they leave, Mr. Valente, the teacher, wants to make breakfast for the class. The bus will leave at 8:00 A.M. How much time should Mr. Valente allow for preparing and eating breakfast?

Mr. Valente does not know exactly how much time breakfast will take. But he can make an estimate based on this information:

1. Mr. Valente is serving bran muffins, orange juice, milk, and fresh fruit.

2. The muffins should bake for 20 minutes.

3. The muffins will be baked in the school's cafeteria oven.

4. Muffins can be eaten after they are out of the oven for 5 minutes.

Which estimate of the time it will take to prepare and eat the breakfast is the most reasonable?

a. 20 min to prepare; 5 min to eat

b. 25 min to prepare; 5 min to eat

c. 30 min to prepare; 2 min to eat

d. 45 min to prepare; 30 min to eat

Mr. Valente estimates that it will take 75 minutes to prepare and eat the breakfast. He decides to overestimate to be sure that the class is on time for the trip.

At what time should he tell student volunteers to come in to prepare the breakfast?

a. 6:30 A.M.   **b.** 7:30 A.M.   **c.** 9:00 A.M.

Students should come in at 6:30 A.M.

Mr. Valente has to decide how much money the students should carry on the trip. Decide whether each question needs to be answered. Write *needs no answer*, *needs an exact answer*, or *estimate only*.

5. How much does the bus rental cost per student?

6. How much money is needed for snacks?

7. How much is each student going to spend on souvenirs?

8. How much does the lunch that each student brings from home cost?

9. How much allowance does each student receive?

10. How much will the PTA give to the class for the trip?

Use the information given to finish the schedule and to answer each question.

11. At what time will the bus arrive back at the school from the factory?

12. At what time should Mr. Valente tell parents to meet the class at school?

13. What is the earliest movie that Ralph, one of Mr. Valente's students, and his family can see?

Schedule

8:00 – 10:00 Travel
10:00 – 12:00 Tour
12:00 – ■ Lunch

Information

- The bus leaves at 8:00 A.M.

- The round trip takes about 4 hours.

- The tour takes about $2\frac{1}{2}$ to $3\frac{1}{2}$ hours, depending on the number of questions students ask.

- Lunch takes from 30 to 45 minutes and starts at noon, after 2 hours of the tour.

- Snacks and souvenir shopping take from 15 to 30 minutes.

- The movie will be shown at the following times:
  1:00 P.M.   3:30 P.M.   5:00 P.M.
  6:30 P.M.   8:00 P.M.

- Ralph and his family can eat dinner any time between 5:00 P.M. and 7:00 P.M.

- Ralph lives 5 blocks from school and 3 blocks from the theater.

CALCULATOR

You can use the calculator to divide amounts of money. Look at your calculator. Find the cents point on the keyboard. When you divide money on your calculator, you need to press the cents point.

To divide $45\overline{)\$31.05}$ think of the problem as

$\$31.05 \div 45 = \blacksquare$

Press the keys in order. You don't have to press a dollar sign key. You do have to press the cents point.

The answer is 0.69. You write $0.69.

Solve using a calculator.

1. $22\overline{)\$5.50}$ **2.** $8\overline{)\$21.36}$ **3.** $58\overline{)\$3.48}$ **4.** $9\overline{)\$77.31}$

5. $5\overline{)\$6.25}$ **6.** $39\overline{)\$10.14}$ **7.** $14\overline{)\$5.60}$ **8.** $69\overline{)\$86.25}$

Sometimes you need to round the answer shown by the calculator.

Use the calculator to find $32\overline{)\$8.52}$.

The screen shows 0.26625. You should round the answer to the nearest cent to get a useful answer. Look at the digit to the right of the cents place.

0.26625 becomes $0.27

Divide. Round answers to the nearest cent.

9. $45\overline{)\$7.32}$ **10.** $12\overline{)\$0.56}$ **11.** $26\overline{)\$1.02}$ **12.** $39\overline{)\$7.77}$

13. $62\overline{)\$3.65}$ **14.** $28\overline{)\$1.45}$ **15.** $19\overline{)\$0.39}$ **16.** $54\overline{)\$0.89}$

GROUP PROJECT

Boating for Play and Profit

The problem: You live in a small town on a lake. You own a large boat. You want to earn your spending money during the summer with the boat. How can you earn enough money?

The Options: You could use the boat for fishing and sell your catch or rent it out for fishing or recreation. Consider the Key Facts before making your choice.

Key Facts

Fishing Business

- The lake has a large number of fish in it. You have caught as many as 8 fish in a single day. Each fish weighs 3 to 5 pounds.
- The markets in your town need to buy fresh fish daily. They will pay about $1 per pound.
- There are many other fishers who have boats in your town.
- You will have to find a way to market the fish.
- You will have to find out how much money you can earn weekly.
- You might need someone to help you with the business.

Rental Business

- Many people come to the lake for vacation.
- Tourists will want to go boating for fun.
- The tourist season lasts for only three months.
- You will have to determine a price to charge per hour to rent the boat.
- You will have to figure out for how many hours per day you would rent the boat.
- You will have to advertise.
- You will have to find out how much time it will take to clean and maintain the boat.

CHAPTER TEST

Divide. (pages 376, 378, 382, 384, and 386)

1. $87 \div 23$

2. $65 \div 14$

3. $423 \div 47$

4. $219 \div 36$

5. $468 \div 26$

6. $693 \div 51$

7. $\$5.60 \div 10$

8. $\$1.53 \div 17$

9. $\$2.40 \div 16$

10. $11\overline{)65}$

11. $15\overline{)96}$

12. $50\overline{)89}$

13. $23\overline{)69}$

14. $78\overline{)91}$

15. $29\overline{)65}$

16. $34\overline{)203}$

17. $50\overline{)400}$

18. $62\overline{)396}$

19. $18\overline{)855}$

20. $56\overline{)500}$

21. $23\overline{)574}$

22. $29\overline{)199}$

23. $12\overline{)468}$

24. $30\overline{)495}$

25. $31\overline{)961}$

26. $28\overline{)854}$

27. $19\overline{)304}$

28. $41\overline{)\$0.82}$

29. $39\overline{)\$6.24}$

30. $32\overline{)\$9.92}$

Write the letter of the best estimate. Then solve. (page 388)

31. The Four Seasons Nursery grew 770 dogwood trees. They delivered the same number of dogwood trees to each of 22 plant stores. How many trees did they deliver to each plant store?

   a. 3 dogwood trees
   b. 30 dogwood trees
   c. 300 dogwood trees

Write a number sentence. Then solve. (page 372)

32. Janine's Garden Stand sells trays of tomato plants. There are 12 plants in each tray. One day, Janine's sold 300 tomato plants. How many trays did Janine's sell?

33. Janine's Garden Stand sells trays of squash plants. There are 12 squash plants in each tray. One weekend, Janine's sold 144 trays of squash plants. How many squash plants did Janine's sell?

BONUS

Divide.

1. $23\overline{)4,669}$ **2.** $37\overline{)6,901}$ **3.** $59\overline{)1,234}$ **4.** $22\overline{)5,436}$

RETEACHING

You may need to correct your estimate when you divide.

Divide $48\overline{)831}$.

Divide the hundreds. Think: $48\overline{)8}$. Not enough hundreds.

Divide the tens.
 Think: $48\overline{)83}$, or $4\overline{)8}$.
 Estimate 2.

$$\begin{array}{r} 2 \\ 48\overline{)831} \\ 96 \end{array}$$

Multiply. Too great.

You need to correct the estimate.

Divide the ones.
 Think: $48\overline{)351}$, or $4\overline{)35}$.
 Estimate 8.

$$\begin{array}{r} 18 \\ 48\overline{)831} \\ 48\downarrow \\ \overline{351} \\ 384 \end{array}$$

Multiply. Too great.

You need to correct the estimate.

Try 1.

$$\begin{array}{r} 1 \\ 48\overline{)831} \\ 48 \\ \overline{35} \end{array}$$

Multiply.

Subtract.

Compare.

Try 7.

$$\begin{array}{r} 17\,\text{R}15 \\ 48\overline{)831} \\ 48\downarrow \\ \overline{351} \\ 336 \\ \overline{15} \end{array}$$

Multiply.

Subtract.

Compare.

Other examples:

$$\begin{array}{r} 2\,\text{R}16 \\ 38\overline{)92} \\ 76 \\ \overline{16} \end{array} \qquad \begin{array}{r} 3\,\text{R}18 \\ 29\overline{)105} \\ 87 \\ \overline{18} \end{array}$$

Divide.

1. $47\overline{)81}$ **2.** $29\overline{)65}$ **3.** $32\overline{)91}$ **4.** $36\overline{)63}$ **5.** $28\overline{)45}$

6. $28\overline{)115}$ **7.** $35\overline{)102}$ **8.** $46\overline{)125}$ **9.** $55\overline{)209}$ **10.** $68\overline{)315}$

11. $29\overline{)432}$ **12.** $35\overline{)622}$ **13.** $17\overline{)311}$ **14.** $26\overline{)617}$ **15.** $18\overline{)421}$

16. $27\overline{)602}$ **17.** $12\overline{)451}$ **18.** $48\overline{)856}$ **19.** $39\overline{)922}$ **20.** $13\overline{)754}$

21. $345 \div 13$ **22.** $101 \div 29$ **23.** $43 \div 19$ **24.** $219 \div 28$

394

ENRICHMENT

Time Cards

Mr. Lee is paid $7.25 per hour. To keep a record of how much he earns each week, he fills out a time card.

The time card shows Mr. Lee's name and the days of the week. *In* and *Out* show the times he begins work and the times he finishes work.

Name M. Lee	In	Out	Day's total	Wages earned
Monday	8:00 A.M.	5:00 P.M.	9 h	$65.25
Tuesday	9:00 A.M.		8 h	
Wednesday		4:30 P.M.		
Thursday	8:30 A.M.	4:30 P.M.		
Friday		6:15 P.M.		$72.50
			Total weekly earnings	

On Monday, Mr. Lee worked from 8:00 A.M. to 5:00 P.M. From 8:00 A.M. to 5:00 P.M., 9 hours have passed. So, he wrote 9 h under *Day's total.*

To find how much he earned on Monday, he multiplies his hourly wage by his day's total. Since 9 × $7.25 = $65.25 he wrote $65.25 under *Wages earned* for Monday.

Use the time card to solve.

1. For how many hours did Mr. Lee work on Thursday? How much did he earn that day?

2. At what time did Mr. Lee leave work on Tuesday? How much did he earn that day?

3. For how many hours did Mr. Lee work on Friday? At what time did he begin work that day?

4. On Wednesday, Mr. Lee began work 1 h 30 min later than on Monday. For how many hours did he work on Wednesday? How much did he earn?

5. How much were Mr. Lee's *Total weekly earnings?*

CUMULATIVE REVIEW

Write the letter of the correct answer.

1. 30×500

    a. 150   **b.** 1,500
    c. 15,000   **d.** not given

2. Estimate 22×496.

    a. 8,000   **b.** 9,920
    c. 10,000   **d.** 20,000

3. 22×34

    a. 136   **b.** 748
    c. 6,868   **d.** not given

4. $47 \times \$0.93$

    a. \$42.51   **b.** \$45.71
    c. 4,371   **d.** not given

5. 36×597

    a. 5,373   **b.** 18,752
    c. 21,492   **d.** not given

6. $52 \times \$4.68$

    a. \$32.76   **b.** \$213.36
    c. \$243.36   **d.** not given

7. 85×123

    a. 1,599   **b.** 9,145
    c. 10,455   **d.** not given

8. $21\overline{)85}$

    a. 4
    b. 4 R1
    c. 4 R5
    d. not given

9. $129 \div 47$

    a. 2   **b.** 2 R35
    c. 3 R9   **d.** not given

10. $17\overline{)578}$

    a. 3 R7   **b.** 33 R17
    c. 34   **d.** not given

11. $24\overline{)892}$

    a. 3 R17   **b.** 37
    c. 37 R4   **d.** not given

12. $\$4.96 \div 62$

    a. \$0.08   **b.** \$0.80
    c. 8   **d.** not given

13. $43\overline{)\$9.46}$

    a. \$0.20 R8   **b.** \$0.22
    c. 22   **d.** not given

14. In a toy factory, Bill packs 895 game boxes per week. About how many boxes does he pack in 52 weeks?

    a. 40,000 boxes   **b.** 45,000 boxes
    c. 54,000 boxes   **d.** 60,000 boxes

15. Eve has 252 flowers to put equally in 12 vases. Which number sentence would you write to find how many flowers are in each vase?

    a. $252 \div 12 = n$ **b.** $252 + 12 = n$
    c. $12 \times 252 = n$ **d.** not given

Connecting Math Ideas

Page 87 Exploring Patterns in Operations with Odd and Even Numbers

Copy and complete each table.

1. The rule is add 3.

3	9	25
6		

2. The rule is add 5.

4	10	28
9		

3. The rule is subtract 6.

9	11	21
3		

Write *even* or *odd* to complete each statement. Use the tables to help you.

4. even number + even number = ▓ number

5. odd number + odd number = ▓ number

6. odd number + even number = ▓ number

7. even number − odd number = ▓ number

Page 95 Finding Elapsed Time

Use a calendar to solve.

1. If today is Wednesday, what day of the week was 6 days before the day after tomorrow?

2. If the first day of the month is Monday, what will be the day of the week and the date 4 weeks later?

Page 113 Constructing a Line Graph

The professional basketball player was not always 7 feet tall. He was only 2 feet at birth. Use the table to complete the line graph.

Birth	2 feet
3 years	3 feet
5 years	4 feet
12 years	5 feet
15 years	6 feet
21 years	7 feet

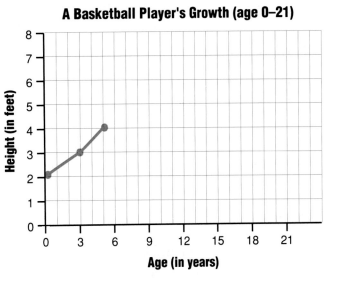

A Basketball Player's Growth (age 0–21)

1. At what age was the basketball player shorter than 6 feet and taller than 5 feet?

2. How much taller was the basketball player at age 21 than at birth?

Page 243 Identifying Patterns on the Multiplication Table and
Using Patterns of Factor Pairs to Identify Prime Numbers

Copy and complete the multiplication table. Multiply each number at the side by each number at the top.

1. What properties of multiplication can you use to fill in the first two rows and columns?

2. What pattern do you see on the multiplication table that is made by the products of the doubles facts? (1×1, 2×2, 3×3 and so on)

3. After you complete the table, circle all of the prime numbers.
Remember: A prime number has only two factors: itself and 1.

Example: $2 \times 9 = 18$

×	0	1	2	3	4	5	6	7	8	9
0										
1		1	2	3	4	5	6	7		
2		2	4							
3		3	6		12		18	21	24	27
4		4	8		16		24	28		36
5		5	10		20		30	35	40	45
6			12	18	24		36			54
7		7	14	21	28		42	49	56	63
8		8	16	24	32	40	48	56	64	72
9		9	18	27	36					

Page 247 Using Physical Models to Represent Mixed Numbers

Solve.

1. Brian had a pizza party. He and his friends ate 19 slices of pizza. Write a mixed number to show the amount of pizza they ate.

2. Draw a picture of pizza to show each mixed number.
a. $2\frac{1}{6}$ **b.** $1\frac{3}{8}$ **c.** $3\frac{1}{4}$

Page 277 Measuring Length Using Nonstandard Units

Use a paper clip to measure the length of the following objects.
Express your answer using paper clips as the unit.

1. length and width of this book

2. height from the floor to the top of your desk

3. length of your index finger

4. distance from the tip of your index finger to your elbow

Page 293   Estimating and Measuring the Capacity of a Container

Copy and complete the table. Choose the unit to measure each object: *cup*, *pint*, *quart*, or *gallon*. Estimate the capacity of each object and then measure to find the actual capacity.

Object	Unit	Estimate	Actual Measure
1. mixing bowl			
2. water pitcher			
3. sink			

Page 309   Comparing Angles in Relationship to Right Angles

1. Angle BAC is a right angle. Write the names of the angles that are smaller than a right angle.

2. Write the names of the angles that are larger than a right angle.

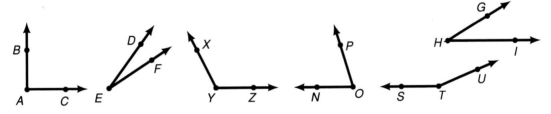

Page 317   Flips, Turns, and Slides Using Concrete Models

Design your own pattern. Move the figure on graph paper by sliding, flipping, and turning it to make a pattern.

Example:

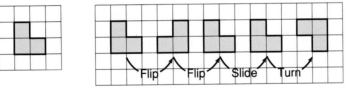

Use graph paper to make a pattern using each figure. Repeat the pattern at least twice.

1.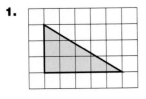

2.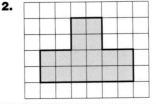

3.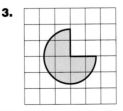

Page 321 Plotting Points on the Coordinate Plane That Represent Ordered Pairs of Whole Numbers

Use graph paper. Plot the points for each ordered pair. Start at A and connect the points in alphabetical order. What figure did you draw?

1. A (2, 3)
2. B (8, 9)
3. C (7, 1)
4. D (2, 9)
5. E (11, 5)

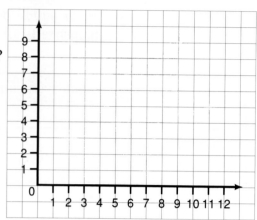

Page 329 Exploring Patterns Made by Changing Shapes

The pictures below all show the same block, but seen from a different view each time.

What design is on the opposite side of each of these sides?

Page 331 Exploring the Volume of a Rectangular Solid as a Geometric Model for Multiplication of Three Factors

The volume of a solid figure is the number of cubic units that will fit inside the figure.

How many cubic units will fit into this figure?

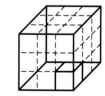

1 cubic unit

length: 3 units
width: 3 units
height: 3 units

You can also multiply to find the volume.
Volume = length × width × height

Find the volume. Express your answer in cubic units.

1. length: 6 units
   width: 4 units
   height: 5 units

2. length: 8 units
   width: 7 units
   height: 3 units

3. length: 10 units
   width: 6 units
   height: 7 units

Infobank

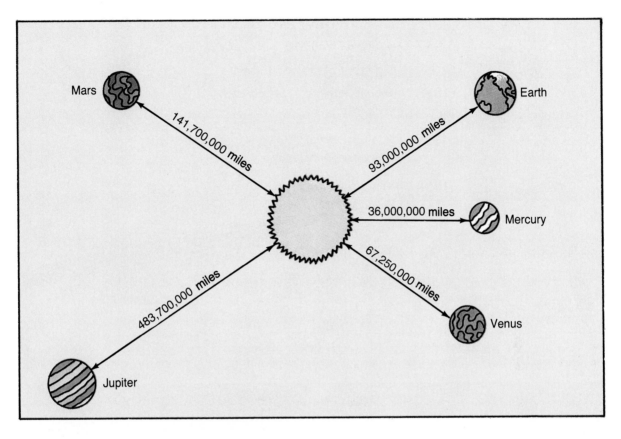

JERRY'S GREAT CLAMBAKES

	Nantucket	Fire Island	Rhode Island
Corn	3,875 ears	4,075 ears	5,622 ears
Lobsters	2,004	2,721	2,973
Clams	6,259	8,134	9,025

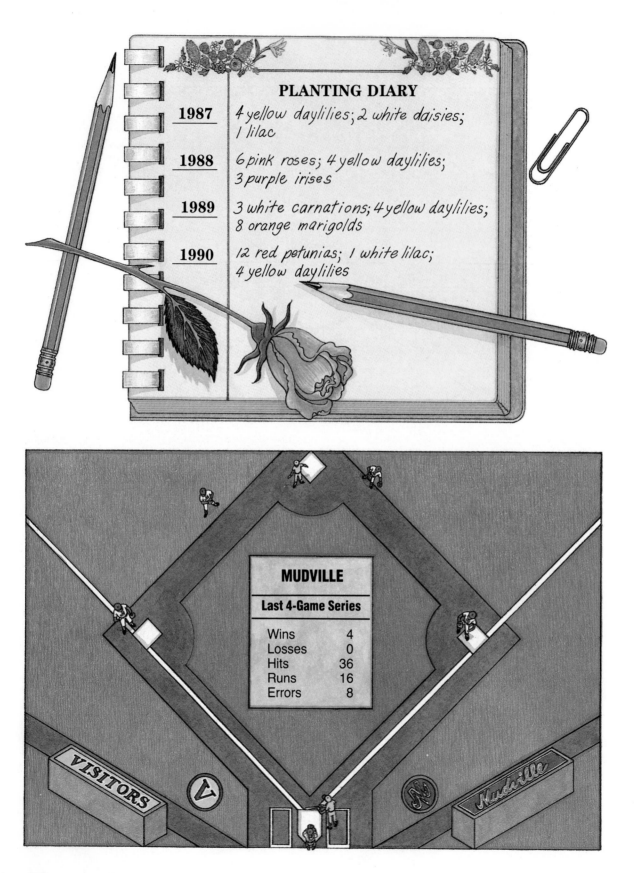

PLANTING DIARY

1987 *4 yellow daylilies; 2 white daisies; 1 lilac*

1988 *6 pink roses; 4 yellow daylilies; 3 purple irises*

1989 *3 white carnations; 4 yellow daylilies; 8 orange marigolds*

1990 *12 red petunias; 1 white lilac; 4 yellow daylilies*

MUDVILLE

Last 4-Game Series

Wins	4
Losses	0
Hits	36
Runs	16
Errors	8

VISITORS

Mudville

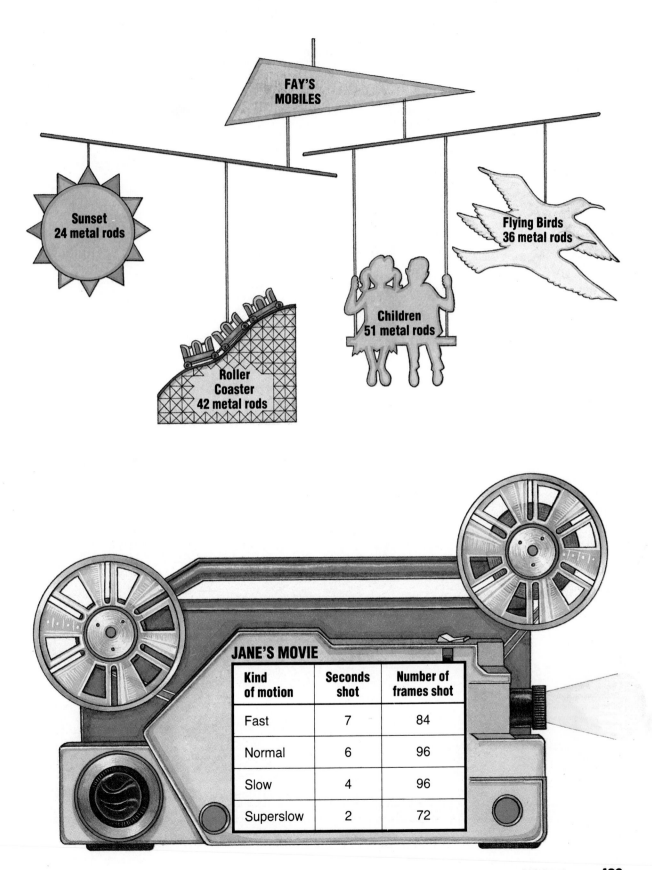

FAY'S MOBILES

Sunset
24 metal rods

Flying Birds
36 metal rods

Roller
Coaster
42 metal rods

Children
51 metal rods

JANE'S MOVIE

Kind of motion	Seconds shot	Number of frames shot
Fast	7	84
Normal	6	96
Slow	4	96
Superslow	2	72

DEANA'S HEALTH CLUB

Day	New members
Monday	卌 |||
Tuesday	卌 卌
Wednesday	卌 卌
Thursday	卌 卌 ||
Friday	卌 卌 ||||

CARLA'S TRAVELS

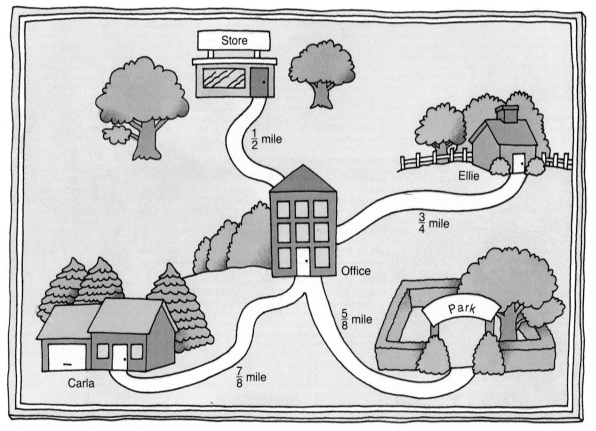

RAY'S GROWTH

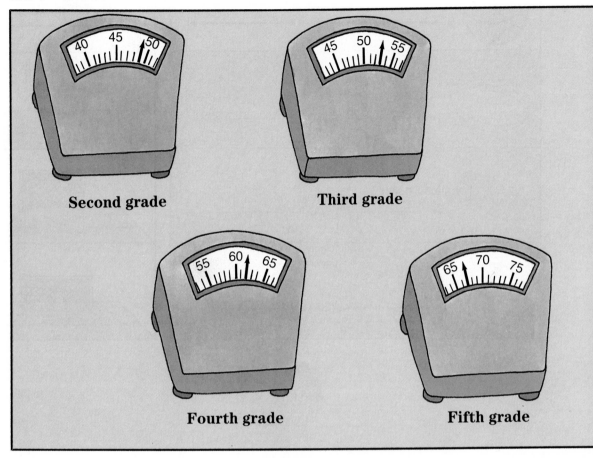

Second grade

Third grade

Fourth grade

Fifth grade

MEASUREMENT IN INCHES

	Length	Width	Height
Figure *A*	3	1	2
Figure *B*	4	3	1
Figure *C*	3	2	3

Length of Playing Area

	Basketball	26 m
	Football	360 ft
	Ice Hockey	200 ft
	Soccer	120 yd

Width of Playing Area

15 m
160 ft
85 ft
75 yd

	VOYAGE	NATURE	Animals	UNIVERSE
Number of newsstands	36	21	12	32
Number of copies	985	672	96	288

STUDENT HANDBOOK

1 CLASSWORK/
HOMEWORK
H1–H155

2 MORE
PRACTICE
H157–H180

3 MATH
REASONING
H181–H204

4 TABLE OF MEASURES
AND SYMBOLS
H205

5 GLOSSARY
H207–H210

Write each in standard form.

	Hundreds	Tens	Ones	
Example:	2	7	8	278
1.	1	0	1	
2.	9	3	5	
3.			9	
4.	3	6	0	
5.	7	4	2	

6. 500 + 30 + 6 _____

7. 800 + 20 + 3 _____

8. three hundred forty-five _____

9. nine hundred fifty-two _____

10. two hundred thirty-eight _____

11. eight hundred six _____

Write the digit that is in the tens place.

12. 992 _____ **13.** 66 _____ **14.** 313 _____ **15.** 27 _____

Write the digit that is in the hundreds place.

16. 692 _____ **17.** 103 _____ **18.** 335 _____ **19.** 296 _____

Write the value of the underlined digit.

20. 65<u>9</u> _____ **21.** 8<u>7</u>7 _____ **22.** <u>9</u>91 _____

23. 32<u>7</u> _____ **24.** <u>2</u>11 _____ **25.** <u>1</u>96 _____

Write in expanded form. **Example: 317 = 300 + 10 + 7**

26. 97 _____

27. 73 _____

28. 138 _____

29. 201 _____

Write each in standard form.

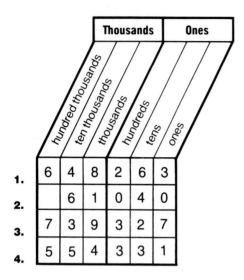

hundred thousands	ten thousands	thousands	hundreds	tens	ones
6	4	8	2	6	3
	6	1	0	4	0
7	3	9	3	2	7
5	5	4	3	3	1

1. (row 1)
2. (row 2)
3. (row 3)
4. (row 4)

5. six hundred thirty-one thousand, two hundred one

6. thirty-two thousand, four hundred sixty-seven

Write the digit for each place in the number 896,423.

7. hundred thousands   tens   hundreds

ones   thousands   ten thousands

Write each number in expanded form.

8. 763,724

9. 299,448

10. 94,562

Write the value of the underlined digit.

11. 1<u>3</u>6,963   **12.** 872,1<u>1</u>1   **13.** 445,<u>8</u>76

14. 975,577   **15.** 1<u>3</u>1,674   **16.** <u>7</u>66,223

Use the Four-Step Plan to solve each problem. Use the table to find the information you need.

- State the problem in your own words.
- Tell which tools you will use.
- Solve the problem.
- Check your solution.

JOURNEY OF THE SEARCHER

Day	Distance (mi)
Monday	157,624
Tuesday	460,533
Wednesday	398,721
Thursday	574,009
Friday	513,218

1. What was the total distance traveled by Searcher?

2. How far did Searcher travel during its first hour of flight on Monday?

3. The 3 sections of Searcher each weigh 2,801 pounds. How much does Searcher weigh?

4. How many more miles did Searcher travel on Thursday than on Tuesday?

5. On which day did Searcher travel the farthest?

6. Searcher traveled a distance which had the same digit in the tens place and the ten thousands place. On which day did this happen?

7. At one point during its mission, Searcher traveled nearly 3 times as far as it had the day before. On which day did this happen?

8. On which days did the Searcher travel a distance of more than a half million miles?

Write in order from the least to the greatest.

1. 343, 434, 216, 316

2. 1,234; 1,334; 2,234; 1,244

Compare. Write = or ≠.

3. 6,313 ◯ 6,230

4. 932 ◯ 932

5. 31,004 ◯ 31,400

6. 236 ◯ 623

7. 10,514 ◯ 10,514

8. 5,621 ◯ 5,621

Compare. Write >, <, or =.

9. 865 ◯ 942

10. 14,672 ◯ 17,672

11. 5,105 ◯ 5,100

12. 254 ◯ 243

13. 2,089 ◯ 2,089

14. 1,001 ◯ 2,001

15. 8,993 ◯ 8,003

16. 34,081 ◯ 43,018

17. 81,623 ◯ 83,623

18. 811 ◯ 811

19. 1,510 ◯ 2,009

20. 20,126 ◯ 19,847

Use the map for Exercises 21–23.

Write > or <.

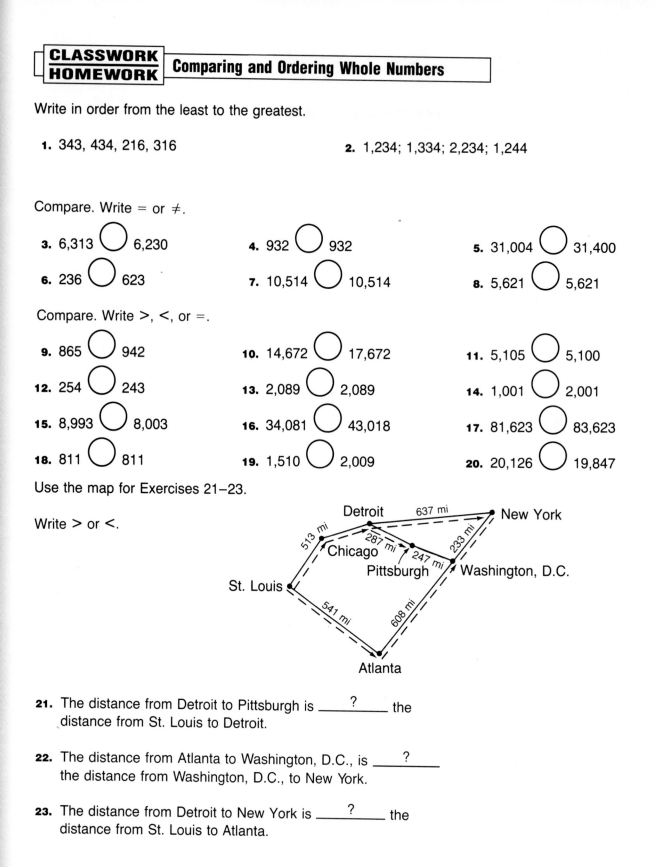

21. The distance from Detroit to Pittsburgh is ____?____ the distance from St. Louis to Detroit.

22. The distance from Atlanta to Washington, D.C., is ____?____ the distance from Washington, D.C., to New York.

23. The distance from Detroit to New York is ____?____ the distance from St. Louis to Atlanta.

Write the amount. Use the dollar sign and the cents point.

1. five dollars and twenty-two cents

2. nineteen dollars and six cents

3. two cents

4. thirteen dollars and thirteen cents

Count the money. Write each amount. Use the dollar sign and the cents point.

5. **6.**

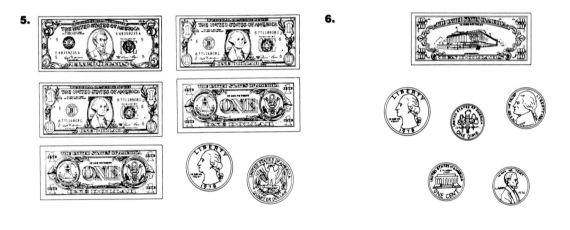

7. **8.**

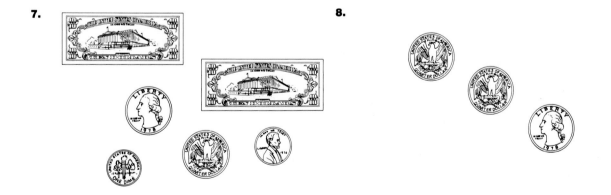

Write each in standard form.

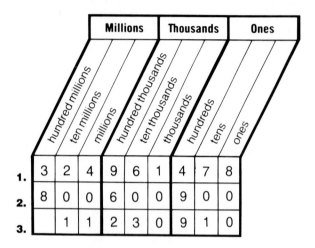

	hundred millions	ten millions	millions	hundred thousands	ten thousands	thousands	hundreds	tens	ones
1.	3	2	4	9	6	1	4	7	8
2.	8	0	0	6	0	0	9	0	0
3.		1	1	2	3	0	9	1	0

Write the digit for each place value in the number 482,631,975.

4. ten millions

5. thousands

6. hundreds

7. ones

8. hundred millions

9. tens

10. ten thousands

11. millions

Write the value of the underlined digit.

12. 3̲42,816,431

13. 8̲,742,111

14. 42̲6,583,727

15. 27̲,041,033

16. 179̲,400,908

17. 111,22̲2,333

Round to the nearest ten.

1. 12

2. 37

3. 61

4. 153

5. 379

6. 86

7. 22

8. 97

Round to the nearest hundred or the nearest dollar.

9. 316

10. $1.29

11. $41.60

12. 989

13. 1,121

14. $3.44

15. $23.62

16. 4,320

17. 349

18. 501

19. 7,824

20. 672

Round to the nearest thousand. Write the correct answer.

21.   8,726

9,000   8,000
   W   I

22.   10,112

11,000   10,000
    F   O

23.   3,750

4,000   3,000
   N   A

24.   1,126

1,000   2,000
   D   C

25.   26,212

27,000   26,000
    B   E

26.   81,989

82,000   81,000
    R   S

27.   6,925

6,000   7,000
   T   F

28.   5,555

5,000   6,000
   A   U

29.   4,026

4,000   5,000
   L   E

30. Write the letter of each answer to solve the puzzle.

Read each question. You may use any reference source to find the answer. Solve.

1. How many people can attend a game in Candlestick Park in San Francisco, California?

2. Can more people sit in the Orange Bowl in Miami, Florida, than in Candlestick Park?

3. In what year was the first Winter Olympics held in Chamonix, France?

4. How many Army–Navy football games has Army won since 1962?

5. What was the Army–Navy game score in 1973?

6. How many gold medals did the United States win in the Winter Olympics in 1984?

7. Which country won the most medals at the Summer Olympics in 1984?

8. How many times was Lou Gehrig at bat in his baseball career?

9. To the nearest thousand, how many times did Gehrig get a hit?

Add.

1. 8 + 7

   7 + 8

2. 6 + 4

   4 + 6

3. 3 + 9

   9 + 3

4. 0 + 6

   6 + 0

5. 4 + 8

   8 + 4

6. 7 + 6

   6 + 7

7. $\begin{array}{r} 8 \\ +\ 7 \\ \hline \end{array}$

8. $\begin{array}{r} 7 \\ +\ 2 \\ \hline \end{array}$

9. $\begin{array}{r} 9 \\ +\ 3 \\ \hline \end{array}$

10. $\begin{array}{r} 3 \\ +\ 9 \\ \hline \end{array}$

11. $\begin{array}{r} 6 \\ +\ 0 \\ \hline \end{array}$

12. $\begin{array}{r} 8 \\ +\ 1 \\ \hline \end{array}$

13. $\begin{array}{r} 5 \\ +\ 7 \\ \hline \end{array}$

14. $\begin{array}{r} 8 \\ +\ 2 \\ \hline \end{array}$

15. $\begin{array}{r} 6 \\ +\ 5 \\ \hline \end{array}$

16. $\begin{array}{r} 5 \\ +\ 6 \\ \hline \end{array}$

17. $\begin{array}{r} 5 \\ +\ 4 \\ \hline \end{array}$

18. $\begin{array}{r} 8 \\ +\ 0 \\ \hline \end{array}$

19. $\begin{array}{r} 9 \\ +\ 9 \\ \hline \end{array}$

20. $\begin{array}{r} 0 \\ +\ 5 \\ \hline \end{array}$

21. $\begin{array}{r} 7 \\ +\ 7 \\ \hline \end{array}$

22. $\begin{array}{r} 6 \\ +\ 1 \\ \hline \end{array}$

23. $\begin{array}{r} 3 \\ +\ 4 \\ \hline \end{array}$

24. $\begin{array}{r} 4 \\ +\ 3 \\ \hline \end{array}$

25. (4 + 3) + 8

26. 5 + (4 + 0)

27. (3 + 5) + 6

28. (1 + 3) + 6

29. (3 + 4) + 9

   9 + (4 + 3)

30. (5 + 4) + 6

   6 + (5 + 4)

Solve.

31. Vera collects rocks. On a family trip to the Grand Canyon, she found 3 quartz rocks, 2 feldspar rocks, and 2 agate rocks. How many rocks did she add to her collection?

32. Vera's brother, Jim, went fishing in the Colorado River. He caught 4 trout, 3 bass, and 1 catfish. How many fish did he catch?

Subtract.

1. 8 − 0	**2.** 13 − 9	**3.** 16 − 8	**4.** 6 − 6	**5.** 4 − 2	**6.** 14 − 7
7. 12 − 4	**8.** 5 − 0	**9.** 13 − 7	**10.** 18 − 9	**11.** 7 − 0	**12.** 14 − 9
13. 15 − 8	**14.** 13 − 4	**15.** 7 − 2	**16.** 5 − 5	**17.** 15 − 6	**18.** 12 − 5
19. 17 − 9	**20.** 8 − 1	**21.** 8 − 6	**22.** 17 − 8	**23.** 16 − 8	**24.** 7 − 6

25. 6 − 6   **26.** 7 − 0   **27.** 12 − 5

28. 15 − 7   **29.** 9 − 9   **30.** 11 − 8

31. 7 − 7   **32.** 16 − 9   **33.** 9 − 5

34. 14 − 8   **35.** 13 − 5   **36.** 11 − 6

Copy and complete each subtraction table.

37.

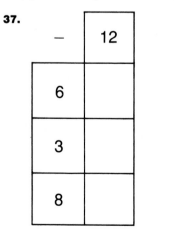

38.

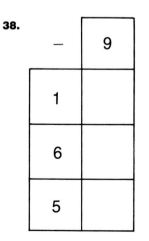

Complete each family of facts.

1. 7 − 3 = 4

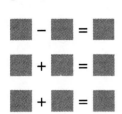

2. 8 + 5 = 13

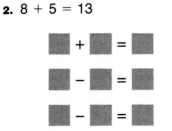

3. 9 + 2 = 11

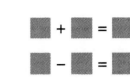

Write a family of facts for each group.

4. 3, 9, 12

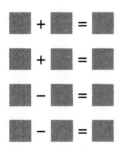

5. 7, 6, 13

6. 7, 4, 11

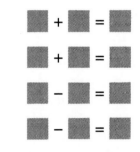

Write the missing addend. Write the letter of each answer to solve the riddle at the bottom of the page.

7. 6 + _____ 7 _____ = 13
I

8. 4 + _____ ? _____ = 12
T

9. _____ ? _____ + 9 = 15
N

10. 6 + _____ ? _____ = 10
D

11. _____ ? _____ + 9 = 11
C

12. 5 + _____ ? _____ = 6
O

13. 8 + _____ ? _____ = 17
A

14. 8 + _____ ? _____ = 13
R

15. 7 + _____ ? _____ = 10
Y

Where does Friday come before Thursday?

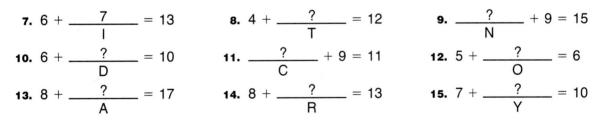

$$\frac{I}{7} \quad \frac{?}{6} \quad \quad \frac{?}{9}$$

$$\frac{?}{4} \quad \frac{I}{7} \quad \frac{?}{2} \quad \frac{?}{8} \quad \frac{I}{7} \quad \frac{?}{1} \quad \frac{?}{6} \quad \frac{?}{9} \quad \frac{?}{5} \quad \frac{?}{3} \; !$$

Decide whether to add or subtract. Then, solve.

1. Baseball has a National League. This league has 2 groups. There are 6 teams in the Eastern group. There are 6 teams in the Western group. How many teams are in the National League?

2. There are 14 baseball teams in the American League. The Eastern group has 7 teams. How many teams are there in the Western group?

3. Babe Ruth hit only 2 home runs in 1917. He hit 9 more home runs in 1918 than he did in 1917. How many home runs did he hit in 1918?

4. Tom Seaver got 10 strikeouts in a row in one game in 1970. Don Drysdale got 6 strikeouts in a row in one game in 1968. How many more strikeouts did Seaver get than Drysdale?

5. The major leagues play an All-Star game every year. In 1949, the game was held in Brooklyn. The National League won with 11 runs. The American League had 4 fewer runs. How many runs did the American League have?

6. There was an All-Star game in 1965. The National League scored 6 runs. The American League scored 5 runs. How many runs were scored in the 1965 game?

7. There are 2 home-run champions every year. In 1905, the 2 champions hit 17 home runs altogether. Harry Davis of the American League hit 8 of these home runs. How many home runs did Fred Odwell of the National League hit?

8. Harry Davis was the home-run champion of the American League for 4 years in a row. In 1905, he hit 8 home runs. He hit 4 more home runs in 1906 than he hit in 1905. How many home runs did he hit in 1906?

9. In 1916, Wally Pipp was home-run champion of the American League. He hit 12 home runs. In 1917, he was champion again with 9 home runs. How many more home runs did he hit in 1916 than he hit in 1917?

10. In 1880, there were 2 National League home-run champions. Each man hit 6 home runs. How many home runs were hit by both National League champions in 1880?

Add.

1. 67 + 31

2. 43 + 13

3. $0.11 + $0.65

4. 52 + 19

5. $0.14 + $0.78

6. 45 + 51

7. $0.11 + $0.41

8. 8 + 27

9. 41 + 43

10. 13 + 73

11. $0.24 + $0.75

12. 17 + 65

13. $0.27 + $0.26

14. 42 + 54

15. 29 + 45

16.   17
     + 72

17. $0.43
     + 0.28

18.   31
     + 53

19.   58
     + 7

20. $0.23
     + 0.49

21.   29
     + 59

22.   28
     + 16

23. $0.46
     + 0.19

24. $0.18
     + 0.14

25.   34
     + 8

26. $0.73
     + 0.25

27. $0.25
     + 0.65

28.   78
     + 6

29.   33
     + 39

30.   64
     + 15

31.   48
     + 22

32. $0.39
     + 0.14

33. $0.85
     + 0.03

34. $0.19
     + 0.47

35.   32
     + 49

Solve.

36. Anne is working on costumes for the school play. She bought 28 bow ties and 13 top hats. How many items did she buy?

Add.

1.	68 + 49	**2.**	31 + 48	**3.**	76 + 83	**4.**	64 + 12	**5.**	45 + 64
6.	54 + 62	**7.**	44 + 15	**8.**	62 + 36	**9.**	47 + 48	**10.**	66 + 38
11.	27 + 15	**12.**	77 + 34	**13.**	83 + 99	**14.**	46 + 46	**15.**	63 + 9
16.	$0.45 + 0.90	**17.**	91 + 49	**18.**	89 + 16	**19.**	$0.28 + 0.93	**20.**	$0.48 + 0.83
21.	64 + 8	**22.**	96 + 7	**23.**	66 + 95	**24.**	27 + 83	**25.**	45 + 99

Solve.

26. Jason has $1.00. Add the prices of each set of items. Write the items in the sets that Jason can buy.

List pairs of numbers that, when added together, make about 100.

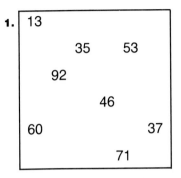

1.
```
13
        35      53
    92
           46
60                    37
           71
```

List pairs of numbers that, when added together, make about 1,000.

2.
```
620                    911
        440
            319
    715
                    180
    589
            848
```

Estimate. Add the front digits. Then adjust the estimate.

3. 133 + 255 + 311 =

4. 371 + 296 + 257 =

5. 362 + 424 + 168 =

6. 249 + 363 + 427 =

7.
```
  21
  32
+ 47
```

8.
```
  332
+ 967
```

9.
```
  476
+ 901
```

10.
```
  6,124
  8,527
+ 3,010
```

11.
```
  9,762
  9,100
+ 9,321
```

12.
```
  732
+ 861
```

13.
```
  1,976
  6,312
+ 1,400
```

14.
```
  4,213
  5,672
+ 8,999
```

15.
```
  10
  89
+ 65
```

16.
```
  1,976
  2,437
+ 2,634
```

Write the information you would need to solve each problem.

1. North Dakota and South Dakota are divided into counties. There are 67 counties in South Dakota. There are not as many counties in North Dakota. How many counties are there in both states?

2. New Jersey became a state on December 18, 1787. New Hampshire became a state on June 21, 1788. It was the ninth state. How many states joined the Union after New Jersey and before New Hampshire?

3. There are 8 state forests in California. Delaware is a much smaller state. It also has state forests. How many fewer state forests are there in Delaware?

4. Colorado has many large cities. Denver is the capital city. Boulder has a population of 76,685. Arvada is another big city. Which city is larger: Boulder or Arvada?

5. Maryland is proud of its natural beauty. It has 42 state parks. It also has many state forests. How many state parks and forests does Maryland have?

6. Many state mottoes are written in Latin. The motto of Alabama has 4 Latin words. It means "We defend our rights." The motto of Maine, also written in Latin, means "I direct." How many fewer Latin words are in the motto of Maine than are in the motto of Alabama?

Add.

1. $2.12
   + 9.41

2. $4.58
   + 1.41

3. $2.13
   + 7.34

4. $6.56
   + 0.85

5. $5.83
   + 6.14

6. $2.30
   + 9.00

7. $9.19
   + 3.34

8. $3.17
   + 2.68

9. $4.00
   + 2.33

10. $2.46
    + 7.23

11. $4.30
    + 8.43

12. $7.37
    + 6.63

13. $2.02
    + 5.63

14. $6.56
    + 4.80

15. $5.26
    + 3.21

16. $5.86
    + 2.25

17. $3.28
    + 4.30

18. $5.73
    + 8.54

19. $2.25
    + 8.00

20. $7.16
    + 5.28

21. $5.82
    + 5.42

22. $2.52
    + 5.41

23. $3.96
    + 8.98

24. $3.80
    + 7.36

25. $8.49
    + 4.11

26. $4.24
    + 7.57

27. $5.36
    + 3.25

28. $4.78
    + 1.80

29. $6.09
    + 1.60

30. $3.51
    + 7.99

Solve.

31. Jackie is planning a surprise party. She will serve tacos and fruit punch. The tacos will cost $9.48, and the fruit punch will cost $3.25. How much money will Jackie spend?

Add.

1. 2,658
+ 302

2. 7,315
+ 1,744

3. 4,326
+ 3,065

4. 3,652
+ 2,171

5. $15.48
+ 6.25

6. 6,482
+ 5,517

7. 58,504
+ 21,387

8. $46.89
+ 5.01

9. $13.75
+ 11.50

10. $372.25
+ 350.80

11. $29.25
+ 10.80

12. $81.74
+ 10.23

13. 3,698
+ 1,253

14. 9,750
+ 492

15. 8,645
+ 2,759

16. 8,705
+ 4,310

17. 9,028
+ 3,796

18. $199.98
+ 26.40

19. 23,496
+ 603

20. 6,487
+ 5,578

21. 72,361
+ 4,922

22. $450.25
+ 19.47

23. 27,369
+ 15,458

24. $626.26
+ 598.77

25. 77,593
+ 45,619

26. 4,367 + 290

27. 88,207 + 20,574

28. $35.19 + $26.37

29. 23,962 + 981

30. 4,798 + 958

31. $110.80 + $91.20

32. Glen Ferris raises cattle on his ranch. One week, the cattle ate 33,649 pounds of hay. The next week, they ate even more—41,824 pounds of hay! How many pounds of hay did they eat in all?

33. One year, Mr. Ferris sold 1,565 head of cattle. The next year, 1,780 head of cattle were sold. How many head of cattle did Mr. Ferris sell in the two years?

Use with pages 46–47.

Add. Check by adding up.

1.   10,127
    4,617
+ 11,294

2.   639
    1,421
+ 42,304

3.   42,961
  11,372
+ 22,986

4.   21,169
  33,333
+ 46,319

5.   48,911
    2,634
+ 11,195

6.   32,117
  11,112
+ 28,916

7.   10,101
    4,976
+ 11,001

8. $472.00
  111.11
+   241.98

9.   1,242
  3,428
  6,972
+ 1,133

10.   2,648
  7,921
  1,043
+ 3,210

11.   1,100
  3,200
  6,320
+ 1,400

12. $21.32
  37.50
  29.98
+   52.70

13.   6,702
    340
  2,100
+   999

14.   1,000
    900
  8,000
+   99

15. $99.99
  1.00
  0.11
+   10.00

16.   4,123
  3,124
  5,432
+ 1,234

17. 12,119 + 2,987 + 46,232

18. 479 + 334 + 81

19. $101.92 + $328.47 + $28.28

20. 1,605 + 22,493 + 738

21. $263.47 + $93.17 + $111.99

22. 196 + 98 + 78

Add the numbers from START to FINISH.

23.

24.

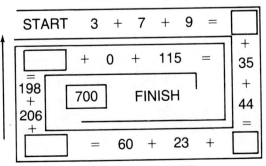

Estimate by rounding to the largest place.

1. 36 + 12 + 59

2. 44 + 29 + 36

3. $0.67 + $0.42 + $0.29

4. 94 + 56 + 32

5. $0.89 + $0.19 + $0.95

6. 61 + 50 + 77

7.
```
  $17.28
   26.95
+  15.18
```

8.
```
   6,512
   4,480
+  1,986
```

9.
```
  $0.67
   0.31
+  0.45
```

10.
```
   7,361
   4,700
+  3,299
```

11.
```
   961
   916
+  219
```

12.
```
  $1.29
   4.56
+  3.98
```

13.
```
   1,892
   1,942
+  2,010
```

14.
```
   6,400
   7,500
+  3,659
```

15.
```
  $9.87
   6.57
+  5.31
```

16.
```
   185
   251
+  816
```

17.
```
  $77.17
+  32.86
```

18.
```
   1,652
+  2,289
```

19.
```
  $0.29
   0.59
+  0.77
```

20.
```
   652
   126
+  275
```

21.
```
  $34.19
   43.99
+  15.79
```

22.
```
   9,861
   3,346
+  1,719
```

23.
```
   333
   276
+  810
```

24.
```
  $4.16
   1.87
+  1.23
```

25.
```
   4,217
   3,460
+  2,815
```

26.
```
   1,327
+  4,866
```

Estimate. Write the letter of the correct answer.

27. 44 + 26 + 11   **a.** 70   **b.** 80   **c.** 90

28. $0.13 + $0.58 + $0.86   **a.** $1.60   **b.** $1.70   **c.** $1.80

29. 5,271 + 6,563   **a.** 10,000   **b.** 12,000   **c.** 14,000

30. $33.27 + $77.54   **a.** $10.00   **b.** $100.00   **c.** $110.00

31. 624 + 491 + 119   **a.** 1,100   **b.** 1,200   **c.** 1,300

Estimate to solve each problem. Find the exact answer if your estimate is too close.

1. Cathy is helping to plan the class picnic. She counts the seats on the school vans and buses. These are her results: 19 seats, 12 seats, 48 seats. She knows 80 students will go to the picnic. She wants to be sure there are enough seats. Should she estimate or get the exact answer?

2. Bud and the school cook are baking muffins for the picnic. They use four school muffin pans. These are the number of muffins each pan holds: 12 muffins, 24 muffins, 30 muffins, 20 muffins. Bud needs to bring 80 muffins to the picnic. Do Bud and the cook need to use another muffin pan?

3. Ron is getting cups for the picnic. There are several packages that he can use. He counts the cups in each package. These are his results: 12 cups, 25 cups, 48 cups, 35 cups. Ron needs 100 cups. Write the numbers Ron should use to see if there are enough cups in the packages.

4. Linda is packing songbooks to be used at the picnic. She counts the songbooks on each shelf in the school storage closet. Here is her count: 12 songbooks, 23 songbooks, 31 songbooks, 17 songbooks. Linda wants to bring 80 songbooks in all. Are there enough songbooks in the storage closet?

5. May is getting paper for tablecloths. She needs 138 feet of paper. She looks at these rolls of paper in the school storage closet: a. 81 ft, b. 65 ft, c. 38 ft, d. 94 ft. May wants to take no more than 2 rolls. Which two rolls will come closest to the amount of paper she needs?

6. Greg is bringing the school camera. He plans to take pictures for the school yearbook. He has 3 rolls of film. This list shows how many pictures can be taken on the 3 rolls: 12 pictures, 24 pictures, 36 pictures. Greg plans to take about 75 pictures during the picnic. Will he have enough film? Should he estimate or get the exact answer?

Subtract.

1. 59 − 24

2. 82 − 61

3. 98 − 11

4. 64 − 27

5. $0.76 − $0.24

6. 81 − 69

7. 73 − 10

8. 87 − 24

9. $0.84 − $0.11

10.　82
　− 61

11.　98
　− 11

12.　64
　− 27

13.　$0.34
　− 0.15

14.　67
　− 33

15.　94
　− 16

16.　$0.95
　− 0.74

17.　87
　− 19

18.　73
　− 67

19.　85
　− 7

20.　93
　− 18

21.　$0.99
　− 0.75

22.　62
　− 10

23.　98
　− 6

24.　$0.67
　− 0.39

25.　77
　− 51

26.　$0.33
　− 0.20

27.　$0.69
　− 0.39

28.　80
　− 25

29.　70
　− 40

30. Kim is putting his finishing touches on his model of the clipper ship *Flying Cloud*. He has carefully put on 12 of the ship's 28 sails. How many more sails must he add before the ship is finished?

Estimate.

1. $\begin{array}{r} 57 \\ -\ 27 \\ \hline \end{array}$	**2.** $\begin{array}{r} 976 \\ -\ 328 \\ \hline \end{array}$	**3.** $\begin{array}{r} \$0.88 \\ -\ 0.59 \\ \hline \end{array}$	**4.** $\begin{array}{r} 861 \\ -\ 723 \\ \hline \end{array}$	**5.** $\begin{array}{r} \$0.92 \\ -\ 0.24 \\ \hline \end{array}$
6. $\begin{array}{r} \$89.98 \\ -\ 56.79 \\ \hline \end{array}$	**7.** $\begin{array}{r} 3,010 \\ -\ 1,156 \\ \hline \end{array}$	**8.** $\begin{array}{r} 8,527 \\ -\ 3,108 \\ \hline \end{array}$	**9.** $\begin{array}{r} 8,036 \\ -\ 3,112 \\ \hline \end{array}$	**10.** $\begin{array}{r} \$67.23 \\ -\ 37.98 \\ \hline \end{array}$
11. $\begin{array}{r} 7,642 \\ -\ 1,115 \\ \hline \end{array}$	**12.** $\begin{array}{r} 8,761 \\ -\ 3,764 \\ \hline \end{array}$	**13.** $\begin{array}{r} 4,163 \\ -\ 1,821 \\ \hline \end{array}$	**14.** $\begin{array}{r} 758 \\ -\ 349 \\ \hline \end{array}$	**15.** $\begin{array}{r} \$6.41 \\ -\ 3.95 \\ \hline \end{array}$
16. $\begin{array}{r} 3,826 \\ -\ 2,554 \\ \hline \end{array}$	**17.** $\begin{array}{r} \$8.15 \\ -\ 2.99 \\ \hline \end{array}$	**18.** $\begin{array}{r} 42 \\ -\ 28 \\ \hline \end{array}$	**19.** $\begin{array}{r} \$79.10 \\ -\ 33.46 \\ \hline \end{array}$	**20.** $\begin{array}{r} \$55.34 \\ -\ 42.97 \\ \hline \end{array}$

21. $56.72 − $31.45

22. 87 − 69

23. 9,226 − 4,715

24. 3,100 − 1,999

25. 721 − 436

26. 79 − 67

27. $0.41 − $0.29

28. 4,702 − 1,360

29. The Watchyer Stepp Handrail Company sold 2,326 handrails last month. This month they sold 2,981 handrails. About how many more handrails did they sell this month than last month?

30. The Watchyer Stepp Handrail Company received 755 orders. Of these orders, 286 have been filled. About how many orders are left to be filled?

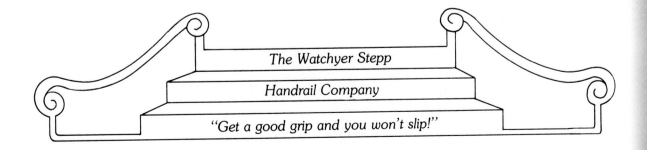

The Watchyer Stepp

Handrail Company

"Get a good grip and you won't slip!"

Subtract.

1. 871 − 652

2. 756 − 157

3. 575 − 483

4. 785 − 93

5. 561 − 488

6. 127 − 39

7. 725 − 512

8. 253 − 136

9. 776 − 321

10.
```
  593
− 473
```

11.
```
  867
− 326
```

12.
```
  764
− 107
```

13.
```
  738
− 563
```

14.
```
  $9.71
−  2.39
```

15.
```
  $8.75
−  5.46
```

16.
```
  868
− 749
```

17.
```
  765
−  32
```

18.
```
  989
− 839
```

19.
```
  $5.15
−  2.12
```

20.
```
  326
− 285
```

21.
```
  $8.16
−  2.99
```

22.
```
  614
− 309
```

23.
```
  746
−  98
```

24.
```
  $8.39
−  1.50
```

25.
```
  456
− 321
```

26.
```
  328
− 276
```

27.
```
  $7.45
−  2.57
```

28.
```
  833
− 452
```

29.
```
  721
−  65
```

30.
```
  943
− 512
```

31.
```
  575
− 258
```

32.
```
  $8.23
−  6.79
```

33.
```
  311
− 287
```

34.
```
  619
− 435
```

35. The Lee Key Shipyard manufactures canoes. One month, out of 844 canoes, only 681 could actually float. The others were sent to the first-aid dock for repairs. How many were sent for repairs?

36. A sporting-goods store ordered 164 paddles and 45 canoes. How many more paddles than canoes were ordered?

Subtract.

1. 8,723 − 4,196

2. 98,222 − 9,333

3. $76.92 − $38.85

4. 58,269 − 9,999

5.   5,689
  − 4,352
	6. 3,646
	  − 1,144
		7. 1,271
		  − 174
			8. 89,966
			  − 9,832
				9. $217.36
				 − 15.30

10.   4,397
  − 1,149
	11. 36,984
	  − 4,322
		12. $389.21
		 − 291.30
			13. 8,885
			  − 6,501
				14. $388.72
				 − 197.50

15. 26,723 − 18,391	16. $46.86 − 32.36	17. 45,219 − 6,147	18. 98,716 − 29,821	19. $329.64 − 286.72
20. 32,941 − 19,327	21. $389.71 − 299.64	22. 45,971 − 23,239	23. $428.40 − 389.51	24. 6,738 − 4,563

25.   5,483
  − 4,192
	26. 69,813
	  − 3,207
		27. $753.14
		 − 630.62
			28. 9,635
			 − 5,814
				29. $859.63
				 − 467.40

Copy and complete. Subtract across and down to find the missing numbers.

30.

98,797	45,311	
36,432		
	23,211	

Subtract.

1. 803 − 46

2. 7,008 − 268

3. 50,000 − 14,652

4. $6.09 − $5.48

5. $460.03 − $285.14

6. 350 − 167

Subtract. Write the letter of each answer to solve the riddle at the bottom of the page.

7.
```
  906
−  57
```
B

8.
```
  700
− 598
```
C

9.
```
  8,300
− 5,127
```
E

10.
```
  8,006
− 2,307
```
A

11.
```
  2,005
− 1,326
```
U

12.
```
  9,100
−  867
```
S

13.
```
  77,003
− 69,875
```
I

14.
```
  58,000
− 39,607
```
W

15.
```
  50,800
−   992
```
T

16.
```
  20,000
− 13,762
```
O

17.
```
  82,008
− 19,825
```
L

18.
```
  91,000
−  8,926
```
D

19.
```
  60,050
− 42,824
```
F

Why can't a rabbit's nose be 12 inches long?

?	?	?	?	?	?	?
849	3,173	102	5,699	679	8,233	3,173

?	?	?	?	?	?	?
7,128	49,808	18,393	6,238	679	62,183	82,074

?	?	?	?	?	?	?	
849	3,173	5,699	17,226	6,238	6,238	49,808	!

Write a number sentence for each problem. Then solve the number sentence.

1. A *province* is another name for a state. Canada has 10 provinces. There are also 2 territories in Canada. How many more provinces are there than territories?

2. There are 106 museums in the province of Quebec. There are 293 museums in the province of Ontario. How many museums are there in the 2 provinces?

3. British Columbia is close to the Pacific Ocean. It has 356 parks. Ontario is north of the Great Lakes. It has 138 parks. How many more parks are in British Columbia?

4. Mount Logan is the highest point in Canada. Mount Logan is in the Yukon Territory. Mount Columbia in Alberta, Canada, is 12,294 feet high. Mount Logan is 7,556 feet higher than Mount Columbia. How high is Mount Logan?

5. A plane flies from Montreal to Toronto. It travels 326 air miles. The plane then flies 2,118 miles from Toronto to Vancouver. How far did the plane fly?

6. The tallest building in Canada is the CN Tower in Toronto. It is 1,821 feet high. The second-tallest building is 952 feet high. How much higher is the CN Tower?

7. The Peace River is 1,195 miles long. The Mackenzie River is 1,440 miles longer than the Peace River. How long is the Mackenzie River?

Multiply.

1. 2 ×8	**2.** 2 ×5	**3.** 3 ×3	**4.** 3 ×1	**5.** 2 ×9	**6.** 2 ×6
7. 3 ×6	**8.** 2 ×7	**9.** 2 ×9	**10.** 3 ×8	**11.** 5 ×3	**12.** 2 ×1
13. 3 ×6	**14.** 2 ×5	**15.** 2 ×2	**16.** 3 ×9	**17.** 2 ×8	**18.** 2 ×4
19. 3 ×7	**20.** 3 ×2	**21.** 3 ×3	**22.** 2 ×3	**23.** 3 ×4	**24.** 3 ×5

25. 6 × 2 **26.** 4 × 3 **27.** 4 × 2

28. 8 × 3 **29.** 7 × 2 **30.** 7 × 3

31. 1 × 3 **32.** 9 × 3 **33.** 2 × 1

34. 3 × 3 **35.** 1 × 2 **36.** 9 × 2

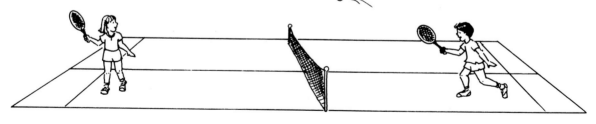

Solve.

37. Janice plays tennis on her school team. She must practice 2 hours a day, 4 days each week. How many hours does she practice in a week?

38. After each practice, Janice runs 3 laps around the school track. How many laps will she have run after 8 practices?

Multiply.

1. 2×4

2. 9×4

3. 3×5

4. 8×5

5. 3×4

6. 9×4

7. 6×5

8. 1×5

9. 7×5

10.
$$\begin{array}{r} 5 \\ \times\, 9 \\ \hline \end{array}$$

11.
$$\begin{array}{r} 4 \\ \times\, 6 \\ \hline \end{array}$$

12.
$$\begin{array}{r} 4 \\ \times\, 3 \\ \hline \end{array}$$

13.
$$\begin{array}{r} 5 \\ \times\, 5 \\ \hline \end{array}$$

14.
$$\begin{array}{r} 5 \\ \times\, 8 \\ \hline \end{array}$$

15.
$$\begin{array}{r} 5 \\ \times\, 4 \\ \hline \end{array}$$

16.
$$\begin{array}{r} 4 \\ \times\, 7 \\ \hline \end{array}$$

17.
$$\begin{array}{r} 4 \\ \times\, 6 \\ \hline \end{array}$$

18.
$$\begin{array}{r} 4 \\ \times\, 5 \\ \hline \end{array}$$

19.
$$\begin{array}{r} 5 \\ \times\, 2 \\ \hline \end{array}$$

20.
$$\begin{array}{r} 5 \\ \times\, 9 \\ \hline \end{array}$$

21.
$$\begin{array}{r} 5 \\ \times\, 7 \\ \hline \end{array}$$

22.
$$\begin{array}{r} 4 \\ \times\, 5 \\ \hline \end{array}$$

23.
$$\begin{array}{r} 4 \\ \times\, 7 \\ \hline \end{array}$$

24.
$$\begin{array}{r} 4 \\ \times\, 8 \\ \hline \end{array}$$

25.
$$\begin{array}{r} 4 \\ \times\, 1 \\ \hline \end{array}$$

26.
$$\begin{array}{r} 4 \\ \times\, 4 \\ \hline \end{array}$$

27.
$$\begin{array}{r} 5 \\ \times\, 2 \\ \hline \end{array}$$

28.
$$\begin{array}{r} 4 \\ \times\, 1 \\ \hline \end{array}$$

29.
$$\begin{array}{r} 5 \\ \times\, 3 \\ \hline \end{array}$$

30.
$$\begin{array}{r} 5 \\ \times\, 6 \\ \hline \end{array}$$

31.
$$\begin{array}{r} 4 \\ \times\, 6 \\ \hline \end{array}$$

32.
$$\begin{array}{r} 5 \\ \times\, 9 \\ \hline \end{array}$$

33.
$$\begin{array}{r} 5 \\ \times\, 7 \\ \hline \end{array}$$

Copy and complete the table. Multiply each number on the side by each number at the top.

X	1	2	3	4	5	6	7	8
4	4							
5	5							

Multiply.

1.	2.	3.	4.	5.
1	1	0	3	2
$\times 7$	$\times 9$	$\times 8$	$\times 0$	$\times 4$

6.	7.	8.	9.	10.
4	5	1	0	1
$\times 3$	$\times 0$	$\times 4$	$\times 0$	$\times 1$

11.	12.	13.	14.	15.
3	0	1	3	4
$\times 9$	$\times 9$	$\times 6$	$\times 4$	$\times 9$

16. 2×1 17. 1×0 18. 1×3

19. 7×0 20. 9×5 21. 8×2

22. 5×5 23. 6×3 24. 5×1

25. 6×0 26. 8×1 27. 5×3

Write the missing factor.

28. $7 \times 2 = \underline{\quad ? \quad} \times 7$ 29. $6 \times 5 = 5 \times \underline{\quad ? \quad}$

30. $6 \times 3 = 3 \times \underline{\quad ? \quad}$ 31. $9 \times 5 = 5 \times \underline{\quad ? \quad}$

Group the factors another way and multiply.

32. $7 \times (1 \times 3)$ 33. $2 \times (4 \times 5)$ 34. $(6 \times 2) \times 2$

35. $2 \times (3 \times 4)$ 36. $(8 \times 1) \times 4$ 37. $0 \times (7 \times 3)$

Decide how to solve each problem. Then, solve.

1. The earth has several layers. The center, or *core*, is 1,050 miles thick. The *mantle* covers the core. It is 1,800 miles thick. How thick are both layers?

2. The *crust* is the outside layer of the earth. At its thinnest, it is 5 miles deep. It is 5 times as deep in other places. How many miles deep is it at these other places?

3. Suppose we could drill from the North Pole to the South Pole. We would have to drill for 7,900 miles. We would have to drill 27 more miles through the earth at the equator. How many miles thick is the earth at the equator?

4. There are many planets that revolve around the sun. Earth is among the 3 planets closest to the sun. There are 3 times that many planets. How many planets revolve around the sun?

5. A regular earth year is 365 days long. An earth leap year is 366 days long. How many days long are these 2 years together?

6. Earth has only 1 moon. Mars has 2 times as many moons as Earth has. How many moons does Mars have?

7. Uranus is a planet far from the sun. It moves at 4 miles per second. Jupiter is another planet. Jupiter moves 2 times as fast as Uranus. How many miles per second does Jupiter travel?

8. Saturn is the sixth planet from the sun. It is surrounded by beautiful rings. Saturn moves 6 miles every second. How many miles does Saturn move in 3 seconds?

9. A trip around Earth's moon at its widest is about 6,782 miles. A trip around Earth at its widest is about 18,119 miles farther than a trip around the moon. How many miles is the trip around Earth?

10. Pluto is the farthest planet from the sun. Pluto rotates completely every 6 days. The sun turns completely in 4 times as many days. How many days does it take the sun to turn around completely?

Multiply.

1. $\begin{array}{r} 7 \\ \times\,6 \\ \hline \end{array}$	2. $\begin{array}{r} 6 \\ \times\,8 \\ \hline \end{array}$	3. $\begin{array}{r} 7 \\ \times\,9 \\ \hline \end{array}$	4. $\begin{array}{r} 7 \\ \times\,4 \\ \hline \end{array}$	5. $\begin{array}{r} 6 \\ \times\,9 \\ \hline \end{array}$	6. $\begin{array}{r} 6 \\ \times\,1 \\ \hline \end{array}$
7. $\begin{array}{r} 7 \\ \times\,4 \\ \hline \end{array}$	8. $\begin{array}{r} 6 \\ \times\,8 \\ \hline \end{array}$	9. $\begin{array}{r} 7 \\ \times\,3 \\ \hline \end{array}$	10. $\begin{array}{r} 6 \\ \times\,6 \\ \hline \end{array}$	11. $\begin{array}{r} 7 \\ \times\,1 \\ \hline \end{array}$	12. $\begin{array}{r} 7 \\ \times\,5 \\ \hline \end{array}$
13. $\begin{array}{r} 6 \\ \times\,5 \\ \hline \end{array}$	14. $\begin{array}{r} 7 \\ \times\,6 \\ \hline \end{array}$	15. $\begin{array}{r} 7 \\ \times\,2 \\ \hline \end{array}$	16. $\begin{array}{r} 6 \\ \times\,4 \\ \hline \end{array}$	17. $\begin{array}{r} 6 \\ \times\,2 \\ \hline \end{array}$	18. $\begin{array}{r} 7 \\ \times\,8 \\ \hline \end{array}$
19. $\begin{array}{r} 6 \\ \times\,9 \\ \hline \end{array}$	20. $\begin{array}{r} 6 \\ \times\,2 \\ \hline \end{array}$	21. $\begin{array}{r} 6 \\ \times\,3 \\ \hline \end{array}$	22. $\begin{array}{r} 6 \\ \times\,1 \\ \hline \end{array}$	23. $\begin{array}{r} 6 \\ \times\,6 \\ \hline \end{array}$	24. $\begin{array}{r} 7 \\ \times\,5 \\ \hline \end{array}$

25. 8×7

26. 3×7

27. 7×7

28. 5×6

29. 9×7

30. 6×7

31. 1×7

32. 4×6

33. 3×6

Solve.

34. When Seth paints, he uses a set of 6 different-size brushes. He keeps 5 sets of brushes in his studio. How many brushes does he have?

35. Seth buys paints at a nearby art store. There are 7 jars of paint in one set. He bought 3 sets of paint. How many jars did he buy?

Multiply.

1. 2×9

2. 1×8

3. 4×8

4. 7×9

5. 6×3

6. 5×4

7. $\begin{array}{r} 8 \\ \times\, 8 \\ \hline \end{array}$

8. $\begin{array}{r} 9 \\ \times\, 4 \\ \hline \end{array}$

9. $\begin{array}{r} 7 \\ \times\, 3 \\ \hline \end{array}$

10. $\begin{array}{r} 9 \\ \times\, 5 \\ \hline \end{array}$

11. $\begin{array}{r} 8 \\ \times\, 6 \\ \hline \end{array}$

12. $\begin{array}{r} 6 \\ \times\, 4 \\ \hline \end{array}$

13. $\begin{array}{r} 9 \\ \times\, 1 \\ \hline \end{array}$

14. $\begin{array}{r} 8 \\ \times\, 7 \\ \hline \end{array}$

15. $\begin{array}{r} 5 \\ \times\, 7 \\ \hline \end{array}$

16. $\begin{array}{r} 3 \\ \times\, 4 \\ \hline \end{array}$

17. $\begin{array}{r} 8 \\ \times\, 3 \\ \hline \end{array}$

18. $\begin{array}{r} 9 \\ \times\, 9 \\ \hline \end{array}$

19. $\begin{array}{r} 8 \\ \times\, 2 \\ \hline \end{array}$

20. $\begin{array}{r} 9 \\ \times\, 8 \\ \hline \end{array}$

21. $\begin{array}{r} 7 \\ \times\, 6 \\ \hline \end{array}$

22. $\begin{array}{r} 9 \\ \times\, 6 \\ \hline \end{array}$

23. $\begin{array}{r} 7 \\ \times\, 8 \\ \hline \end{array}$

24. $\begin{array}{r} 9 \\ \times\, 0 \\ \hline \end{array}$

25. $\begin{array}{r} 6 \\ \times\, 6 \\ \hline \end{array}$

26. $\begin{array}{r} 2 \\ \times\, 6 \\ \hline \end{array}$

27. $\begin{array}{r} 8 \\ \times\, 5 \\ \hline \end{array}$

28. $\begin{array}{r} 5 \\ \times\, 6 \\ \hline \end{array}$

29. $\begin{array}{r} 8 \\ \times\, 4 \\ \hline \end{array}$

30. $\begin{array}{r} 3 \\ \times\, 8 \\ \hline \end{array}$

31. $\begin{array}{r} 9 \\ \times\, 3 \\ \hline \end{array}$

32. $\begin{array}{r} 8 \\ \times\, 0 \\ \hline \end{array}$

33. $\begin{array}{r} 7 \\ \times\, 7 \\ \hline \end{array}$

34. $\begin{array}{r} 4 \\ \times\, 7 \\ \hline \end{array}$

35. $\begin{array}{r} 6 \\ \times\, 9 \\ \hline \end{array}$

36. $\begin{array}{r} 6 \\ \times\, 8 \\ \hline \end{array}$

Solve.

37. The product of two numbers is 63. One of the factors is 9. What is the other factor?

38. The product of two numbers is 48. One of the factors is 6. What is the other factor?

Write *even* or *odd* for each number.

1. 15   **2.** 8   **3.** 36   **4.** 181

5. 242   **6.** 867   **7.** 29   **8.** 654

Is the number a multiple of 3? Write *yes* or *no*.

9. 36   **10.** 24   **11.** 32   **12.** 12   **13.** 9   **14.** 23

15. Complete. Skip-count by 5's.

5, 10, 15, __?__, __?__, __?__, __?__, __?__, __?__

16. Complete. Skip-count by 10's.

10, 20, 30, __?__, __?__, __?__, __?__, __?__, __?__, __?__

17. Complete. Skip-count by 2's.

8, 10, 12, __?__, __?__, __?__, __?__, __?__, __?__

Copy and complete the table to find the multiples.

		1	2	3	4	5	6	7	8	9
18.	3x									
19.	4x									

Solve.

20. Alvia works for the Bryte Lyte Reflector Company, counting bicycle reflectors that come 6 to a box. Copy and fill in her tally sheet for the total number of reflectors she counts in all.

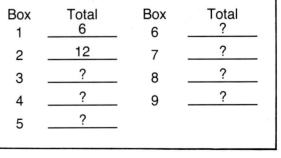

The Bryte Lyte Reflector Company
"*Always* be bright when you ride at night."

Box	Total	Box	Total
1	6	6	?
2	12	7	?
3	?	8	?
4	?	9	?
5	?		

Students at Copley Elementary School are helping arrange the new school library. Make a plan for each problem. Solve.

1. Janice carries 4 dictionaries. Ted carries 2 times as many dictionaries. Lena carries 1 more dictionary than Ted. How many dictionaries does Lena carry?

2. Barry and Eva have to move 17 library tables. They move 5 tables before lunch. They move 2 times as many after lunch. How many must still be moved?

3. There are 6 teachers working with the students. There are 8 times as many students as there are teachers. How many students and teachers are working at the library?

4. Karen fills 3 shelves with books. Annie and Ron fill 2 times as many shelves with books. There are 9 shelves in the bookcase. Have they filled all the shelves in the bookcase?

5. Cara has agreed to type 232 labels for shelves. She types 87 labels before lunch. She types 134 labels after lunch. How many labels must still be typed?

6. Matt and Terry are putting cards into the drawers of the card catalog. Matt put 57 cards into 1 drawer and 108 into another drawer. Terry put 168 cards into some drawers. How many more cards did Terry put into drawers?

7. Ms. Kelly and Mr. Ruiz are putting up posters. Ms. Kelly put up 3 travel posters and 4 times as many posters for books. Mr. Ruiz put up 17 posters. How many more posters did he put up?

8. There are 4 bookcases of biographies. There are 5 times as many bookcases of fiction. How many bookcases hold biographies and fiction?

9. Tammy and Rick are carrying chairs to the new library. They have agreed to move 84 chairs. Rick has moved 32 chairs. Tammy has moved 28 chairs. How many chairs have not been moved?

10. The fourth grade moved 657 books. The fifth grade moved 589 books. The sixth grade moved 48 more books than the fourth grade. How many books were moved by students in all 3 grades?

Write the time for each.

1.

quarter to _____?_____

_____?_____ forty-five

2.

_____?_____ thirty

half past _____?_____

3.

| 1:20 |

_____?_____ minutes after _____?_____

4.

_____?_____ minutes

after _____?_____

5.

_____?_____ fifty-five

6.

_____?_____ forty

7.

_____?_____ minutes

after _____?_____

Complete. Write *seconds, minutes, hours,* or *days.*

8. Parts of an hour are measured in _____?_____ and _____?_____.

9. School recess usually lasts about 15 _____?_____.

10. A major-league baseball game usually lasts at least 2 _____?_____.

11. It takes about 5 _____?_____ to fly from Boston to Los Angeles.

12. There are 60 _____?_____ in one minute.

13. A television commercial often lasts about 30 _____?_____.

14. A school day lasts about 6 _____?_____.

Use the colon (:) and A.M. or P.M. to write each time.

15. five o'clock at night _____?_____

16. four o'clock in the afternoon _____?_____

17. eight o'clock in the morning _____?_____

18. eleven o'clock at night _____?_____

Write the time for each.

1. three-forty-five

2. seven-nineteen

3. quarter to three

4. half past one

5. six-fifty

6. eleven-fifty-nine

Write the amount of time that has passed.

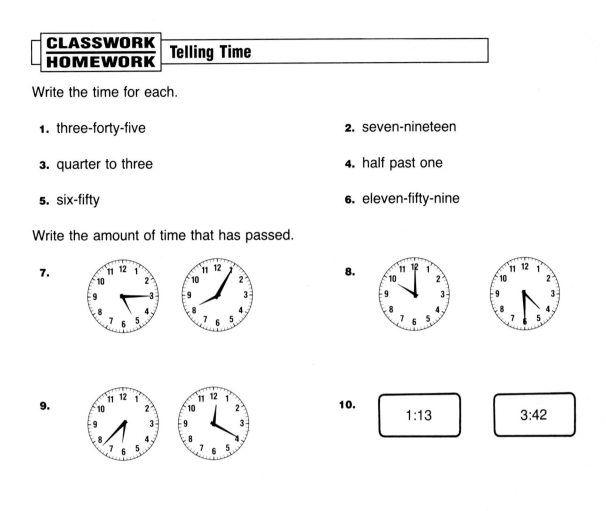

10.

| 1:13 | 3:42 |

Write the letter of the time that best matches the statement.

11. 2 h after 3:00 P.M.

a. 7:00 A.M.

12. 10 h before 6:00 A.M.

b. 5:10 A.M.

13. 5 h 15 min before 8:30 P.M.

c. 8:00 P.M.

14. 9 h after 10:00 P.M.

d. 5:00 P.M.

15. 1 h 30 min before 7:00 A.M.

e. 7:45 P.M.

16. 3 h 45 min after 4:00 P.M.

f. 3:15 P.M.

17. 2 h 10 min after 3:00 A.M.

g. 5:30 A.M.

Use the calendar to complete.

JULY						
Sunday	**Monday**	**Tuesday**	**Wednesday**	**Thursday**	**Friday**	**Saturday**
	1	2	3	4	5	6
7	8	9	10	11	12	13
14	15	16	17	18	19	20
21	22	23	24	25	26	27
28	29	30	31			

1. July 16 is a _____?_____ .

2. There are _____?_____ days in July.

3. July has _____?_____ full weeks.

4. The third Friday in July is the _____?_____ .

5. How many days are there between July 2 and July 9? _____?_____

6. How many Wednesdays are there in July? _____?_____

7. How many days are there between the first and last Tuesday in July? _____?_____

8. The third Tuesday is _____?_____ .

9. Five days from July 23 is _____?_____ .

Write *days, weeks, months,* or *years.*

10. The weekend lasts 2 _____?_____ .

11. Bill's grandfather is 68 _____?_____ old.

12. A school _____?_____ is usually 5 days.

13. The school year is about 9 _____?_____ .

Use the bar graph to answer the questions.

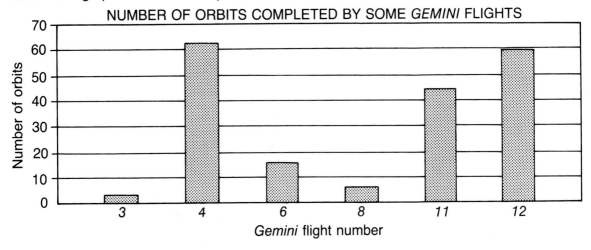

NUMBER OF ORBITS COMPLETED BY SOME *GEMINI* FLIGHTS

Gemini flight number

1. Which Gemini flight completed the fewest orbits?

2. Which Gemini flight completed the most orbits?

3. What is the difference in the number of orbits completed by Gemini 3 and Gemini 12? Is the difference greater or less than the difference between the orbits referred to in problems 1 and 2?

4. Which Gemini flight completed twice as many orbits as Gemini 3?

5. Can you use this bar graph to find how many orbits were made by every Gemini flight?

6. Do you see a pattern: As you read the graph from left to right, do the bars get taller? Do they get shorter? Do they change continuously in any way?

Divide.

1. 2)4 2. 2)10 3. 3)6 4. 2)18 5. 3)15

6. 3)24 7. 2)14 8. 3)18 9. 2)8 10. 2)12

11. 3)27 12. 2)16 13. 3)12 14. 2)6 15. 3)9

16. 21 ÷ 3 17. 16 ÷ 2 18. 10 ÷ 2

19. 27 ÷ 3 20. 6 ÷ 2 21. 14 ÷ 2

22. 18 ÷ 3 23. 8 ÷ 2 24. 12 ÷ 3

25. 24 ÷ 3 26. 15 ÷ 3 27. 12 ÷ 2

28. 4 ÷ 2 29. 9 ÷ 3 30. 6 ÷ 3

Solve.

31. Gary is collecting old newspapers to give to the recycling center. The newspapers must be bundled and put in groups of 2 in front of the recycling center. He collected a total of 12 bundles. How many groups did he make?

32. Melissa is collecting aluminum cans to give to the recycling center. The cans must be put in large trash bags and brought to the center. She can only fit 3 bags into her father's car each trip. She filled 15 bags. How many trips did she make?

Divide.

1. $20 \div 4$ 2. $25 \div 5$ 3. $10 \div 5$

4. $35 \div 5$ 5. $32 \div 4$ 6. $36 \div 4$

7. $12 \div 4$ 8. $24 \div 4$ 9. $40 \div 5$

10. $5\overline{)15}$ 11. $4\overline{)8}$ 12. $5\overline{)10}$ 13. $4\overline{)16}$ 14. $4\overline{)32}$

15. $4\overline{)28}$ 16. $5\overline{)20}$ 17. $4\overline{)20}$ 18. $5\overline{)40}$ 19. $5\overline{)25}$

20. $4\overline{)36}$ 21. $5\overline{)35}$ 22. $5\overline{)30}$ 23. $4\overline{)24}$ 24. $5\overline{)45}$

Solve.

25. What comes after 10 and before blast off?

$45 \div 5$

$40 \div 5$

$35 \div 5$

$30 \div 5$

$20 \div 4$

$16 \div 4$

$12 \div 4$

$8 \div 4$

$4 \div 4$

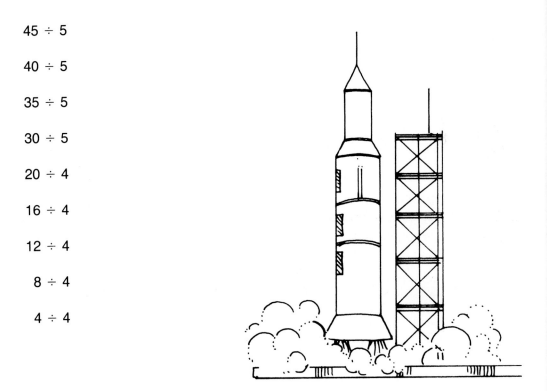

This line graph shows the number of people who lived on farms in the United States. Use the line graph to answer the questions.

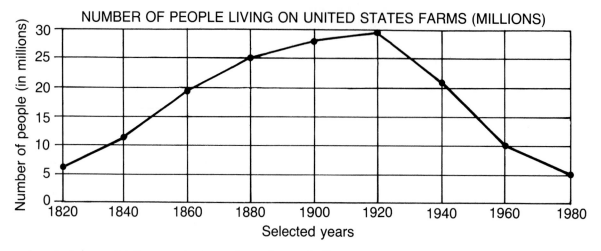

NUMBER OF PEOPLE LIVING ON UNITED STATES FARMS (MILLIONS)

1. In what year did the greatest number of people live on farms?

2. In what year did the least number of people live on farms?

3. During what 20-year period did the number of people living on farms increase the most?

4. During what 20-year period did the number of people on farms decrease the most?

5. How many people lived on farms in 1980? In what year did about 5 times as many people live on farms?

6. Did the number of people living on farms increase or decrease between 1820 and 1900?

7. How has the number of people living on farms changed since 1920?

Complete each family of facts.

1. 28 ÷ 4

   4 × 7

   28 ÷ 7

   7 × 4

2. 3 × 9

   27 ÷ 3

   27 ÷ 9

   9 × 3

3. 4 × 5

   20 ÷ 5

   5 × 4

   20 ÷ 4

Write a family of facts for each set of numbers.

4. 3, 4, 12   5. 16, 4, 4   6. 6, 24, 4   7. 8, 5, 40   8. 7, 21, 3

Write the missing number for each.

9. $5 \times \underline{\quad?\quad} = 30$ 10. $16 \div \underline{\quad?\quad} = 8$ 11. $25 \div \underline{\quad?\quad} = 5$ 12. $4 \times \underline{\quad?\quad} = 32$

13. $\underline{\quad?\quad} \times 3 = 15$ 14. $36 \div \underline{\quad?\quad} = 9$ 15. $\underline{\quad?\quad} \times 5 = 45$ 16. $18 \div \underline{\quad?\quad} = 6$

Copy and complete the cross-number puzzle.

Across

a. 9 × 6

b. 36 ÷ 4

c. 35 ÷ 5

e. 18 ÷ 3

f. 6 × 7

h. 24 ÷ 3

Down

a. 8 × 7

d. 4 × 8

e. 7 × 9

f. 9 × 5

g. 14 ÷ 2

i. 27 ÷ 3

Divide.

1. $7\overline{)7}$

2. $5\overline{)0}$

3. $1\overline{)8}$

4. $2\overline{)2}$

5. $8\overline{)0}$

6. $1\overline{)9}$

7. $6\overline{)0}$

8. $4\overline{)4}$

9. $1\overline{)5}$

10. $3\overline{)3}$

11. $0 \div 4$

12. $0 \div 9$

13. $6 \div 1$

14. $1 \div 1$

15. $0 \div 1$

16. $0 \div 7$

Write the letter of each mailbox that gets mail.

17. She only delivers letters to the boxes that have a quotient of 0.

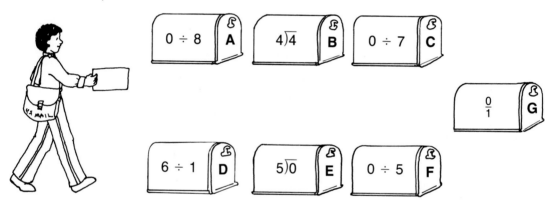

18. He only delivers letters to the boxes that have a quotient of 1.

Copy and complete the table. Then solve each problem.

1. The campers at Camp Pioneer are making beaded necklaces. One camper puts beads on a string in this pattern: 5 red beads and 3 blue beads. How many red beads are on the string when the 18th blue bead is added?

red	5					
blue	3	6				

2. Another camper puts 2 yellow beads on a string. Then, he adds 4 red beads. How many yellow beads are on the string when the 12th red bead is added?

yellow	2	4				
red	4					

3. Another camper puts 2 blue beads on a string. Then, she adds 1 red bead and 1 white bead. She repeats the pattern. How many blue beads are on the string when the 10th white bead is added?

4. One necklace has red, blue, and gold beads. This is the pattern: 2 red, 2 blue, 1 gold. How many red beads are on the string when the 7th gold bead is added?

5. Another necklace shows this pattern: 2 black, 3 red, 2 black, 3 red. How many black beads are on the string when the 15th red bead is added?

6. One necklace has 1 white bead, 5 red beads, and 4 blue beads. How many red beads are on the string when the 28th blue bead is added?

Copy and complete the table. Then solve each problem.

1. The campers at Camp Pioneer have made items for the camp crafts show. One team made 3 belts each day. Another team made 8 pot holders each day. The second team made 64 pot holders. How many belts did the first team make?

holders	8	16	24					
belts	3	6						

2. Team A painted 5 postcards each day. Team B made 3 boxes each day. Team A painted 30 postcards. How many boxes did Team B make?

postcards	5	10				
boxes	3					

3. Team C made 4 kites each day. Team D made 6 bookmarks each day. Team C made 28 kites. How many bookmarks did Team D make?

4. Team A made 3 knapsacks each day. Team C made 9 book covers each day. Team A completed 18 knapsacks. How many book covers did Team C make?

5. Team B made 2 dried-flower arrangements each day. Team D made 7 string-art pictures each day. Team B made 16 dried-flower arrangements. How many string-art pictures did Team D make?

6. There are 2 counselors to help every 3 campers. If there are 27 campers, how many counselors are there?

Find the quotient.

1. 6)12
2. 6)24
3. 7)14
4. 6)42
5. 7)7

6. 6)30
7. 6)36
8. 7)21
9. 6)48
10. 7)28

11. 7)49
12. 6)54
13. 6)6
14. 7)42
15. 7)35

16. 7)35
17. 6)36
18. 6)18
19. 7)42
20. 7)56

21. 54 ÷ 6
22. 42 ÷ 7
23. 63 ÷ 7

24. 56 ÷ 7
25. 18 ÷ 6
26. 49 ÷ 7

27. 24 ÷ 6
28. 6 ÷ 6
29. 28 ÷ 7

Solve.

30. Jan is planting tomatoes in her garden. She has 30 tomato plants. She can fit 6 plants in each row. How many rows of tomatoes will Jan have?

31. Stephanie is helping Jan with her garden. She is planting corn. Each row has 7 stalks. She has 35 stalks to plant. How many rows of corn will Stephanie plant?

Find the quotient.

1. 9)9̄   2. 8)64̄   3. 9)27̄   4. 8)24̄   5. 9)45̄

6. 8)40̄   7. 8)16̄   8. 9)63̄   9. 9)54̄   10. 8)56̄

11. 36 ÷ 9   12. 54 ÷ 9   13. 72 ÷ 8

14. 32 ÷ 8   15. 48 ÷ 8   16. 72 ÷ 9

Write the letter of the quotient that answers the division problem.

17. 9)63̄   a. 0

18. 8)40̄   b. 1

19. 81 ÷ 9   c. 2

20. 8 ÷ 8   d. 3

21. 8)16̄   e. 4

22. 72 ÷ 9   f. 5

23. 0 ÷ 8   g. 6

24. 9)54̄   h. 7

25. 32 ÷ 8   i. 8

26. 27 ÷ 9   j. 9

Write the factors of each number.

1. 4

2. 6

3. 9

4. 12

5. 16

6. 24

7. 14

8. 28

9. 32

10. 42

11. 18

12. 45

13. 36

14. 40

15. 27

16. 35

17. 13

18. 15

Write the factors of each pair of numbers. Then write the common factors.

19. 6

    9

20. 12

    15

21. 24

    36

22. 30

    40

23. 21

    34

24. 56

    20

The factors of 100 are inside the circle.

The factors of 70 are inside the square.

Write the common factors of 100 and 70.

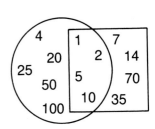

| Solving a Two-Step Problem
Writing a Number Sentence | Choosing the Operation
Using a Line Graph | Estimation
Solving a Multistep Problem /
Making a Plan |

Write the strategy or method you choose. Then solve.

1. The first hot-air balloon was made in 1783. It rose 6,000 feet. The second hot-air balloon rose 1,700 feet and carried animals. How much higher did the first balloon go?

2. One hot-air balloon carried people for 5 miles. Later, a gas balloon carried people 3 times as far. How much farther did the gas balloon go?

3. There were 6 hot-air balloons in one show. There were 3 times as many gas balloons in the show. How many balloons were there altogether?

4. The first hot-air balloon carried no passengers. The second carried 3 animals. There were 2 people in the third balloon. How many animals and people traveled in the first three balloons?

5. In which year were airplane workers paid the most money?

6. How much more per hour were workers paid in 1980 than in 1970?

7. About how many times larger were workers' salaries in 1990 than in 1960?

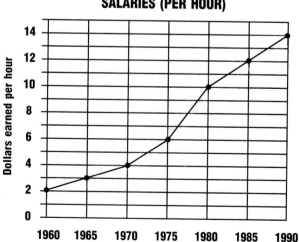

AIRPLANE WORKERS' SALARIES (PER HOUR)

Choosing a Strategy or Method

| Solving a Two-Step Problem | Solving a Multistep Problem | Using a Line Graph |
| Writing a Number Sentence | Using a Bar Graph | Choosing the Operation |

Write the strategy or method you choose. Then solve.

1. Which airport is the busiest?

2. Which airport is used by 33 million passengers?

3. Which airport is busier, Los Angeles or Atlanta?

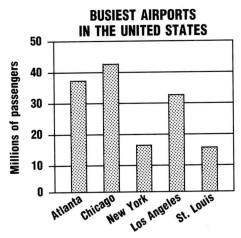

BUSIEST AIRPORTS IN THE UNITED STATES

4. In 1939, a German plane flew at a speed of 439 miles per hour. In 1945, a British plane flew 606 miles per hour. How much faster was the British plane?

5. In 1953, an American plane flew at a speed of 755 miles per hour. In 1955, another American plane flew 67 miles per hour faster. A British plane flew at a speed of 1,132 miles per hour. How much faster did the British plane travel than the fastest American plane?

6. Chris bought a special airplane ticket. The flight from New York to San Francisco cost $319. The return flight cost $285. The regular price of a round-trip ticket is $730. How much did Chris save by buying the special ticket?

7. A French plane flew at an altitude of 44,819 feet in 1933. In the next year, an Italian plane flew 2,533 feet higher. How high did the Italian plane fly?

Multiply.

1. 50
    × 1

2. 400
    × 7

3. 700
    × 2

4. 60
    × 3

5. 90
    × 8

6. 6,000
    × 9

7. 900
    × 5

8. 300
    × 4

9. 9,000
    × 7

10. 200
    × 5

11. 700
    × 5

12. 30
    × 2

13. 800
    × 4

14. 50
    × 6

15. 20
    × 7

16. 2,000
    × 9

17. 10
    × 1

18. 40
    × 4

19. 600
    × 7

20. 80
    × 9

21. 9 × 600

22. 3 × 40

23. 6 × 60

24. 3 × 3,000

25. 6 × 200

26. 5 × 50

27. 4 × 500

28. 9 × 4,000

29. 1 × 300

30. 8 × 90

31. 7 × 40

32. 2 × 700

Estimate by rounding to the largest place.

1. 7 × 48

2. 8 × 67

3. 5 × 97

4. 5 × $1.98

5. 3 × $7.89

6. 2 × $14.98

7. 7 × 789

8. 3 × 697

9. 5 × 4,982

10. 4 × $1.79

11. 5 × $10.29

12. 3 × $2.48

13. 2 × 187

14. 4 × $12.25

15. 8 × 423

16. 4,496
     ×   6

17. 6,701
     ×   5

18. $50.39
     ×   4

19. $68.21
     ×   8

Estimate.

20. 4 × 832

21. 5 × $2.88

22. 8 × $7.49

23. 6 × $47.11

24. 9 × $87.74

25. 3 × $11.42

Estimate. Then write the correct answer.

26. If you have $5.00 and want to buy 3 toys that cost $1.98 each, will you have enough money?

    a. yes   **b.** no

27. If you have $10.00 and want to buy 2 posters that cost $4.75 each, will you have enough money?

    a. yes   **b.** no

Multiply.

1. $\begin{array}{r} 23 \\ \times\ 3 \\ \hline \end{array}$	**2.** $\begin{array}{r} 34 \\ \times\ 2 \\ \hline \end{array}$	**3.** $\begin{array}{r} 31 \\ \times\ 3 \\ \hline \end{array}$	**4.** $\begin{array}{r} \$22 \\ \times\ 4 \\ \hline \end{array}$	**5.** $\begin{array}{r} 51 \\ \times\ 8 \\ \hline \end{array}$	**6.** $\begin{array}{r} 18 \\ \times\ 5 \\ \hline \end{array}$
7. $\begin{array}{r} 14 \\ \times\ 6 \\ \hline \end{array}$	**8.** $\begin{array}{r} 34 \\ \times\ 2 \\ \hline \end{array}$	**9.** $\begin{array}{r} 28 \\ \times\ 3 \\ \hline \end{array}$	**10.** $\begin{array}{r} 17 \\ \times\ 5 \\ \hline \end{array}$	**11.** $\begin{array}{r} 32 \\ \times\ 3 \\ \hline \end{array}$	**12.** $\begin{array}{r} 41 \\ \times\ 2 \\ \hline \end{array}$
13. $\begin{array}{r} 39 \\ \times\ 2 \\ \hline \end{array}$	**14.** $\begin{array}{r} 16 \\ \times\ 6 \\ \hline \end{array}$	**15.** $\begin{array}{r} 25 \\ \times\ 3 \\ \hline \end{array}$	**16.** $\begin{array}{r} 11 \\ \times\ 9 \\ \hline \end{array}$	**17.** $\begin{array}{r} 13 \\ \times\ 7 \\ \hline \end{array}$	**18.** $\begin{array}{r} 27 \\ \times\ 3 \\ \hline \end{array}$

19. 3×31 **20.** 4×18 **21.** 5×11

22. 2×49 **23.** 3×26 **24.** 6×15

25. 7×14 **26.** 2×43 **27.** 5×19

Solve.

28. Rhonda needs 28 tiles to cover a tray. How many tiles does she need to cover 3 trays?

29. The art class uses 18 jars of paint each week. How many jars of paint are used in 4 weeks?

30. Yukio teaches a ceramics class of 36 students. Each student must make 6 large vases. How many vases are there in all?

31. Matthew has 32 students in his art class. Each student must have 4 paint brushes. How many should he order from the store?

Multiply.

1. $\begin{array}{r} 68 \\ \times\ 8 \\ \hline \end{array}$	2. $\begin{array}{r} 39 \\ \times\ 4 \\ \hline \end{array}$	3. $\begin{array}{r} 85 \\ \times\ 2 \\ \hline \end{array}$	4. $\begin{array}{r} 24 \\ \times\ 5 \\ \hline \end{array}$	5. $\begin{array}{r} 93 \\ \times\ 5 \\ \hline \end{array}$
6. $\begin{array}{r} 92 \\ \times\ 5 \\ \hline \end{array}$	7. $\begin{array}{r} 48 \\ \times\ 7 \\ \hline \end{array}$	8. $\begin{array}{r} 18 \\ \times\ 7 \\ \hline \end{array}$	9. $\begin{array}{r} 68 \\ \times\ 5 \\ \hline \end{array}$	10. $\begin{array}{r} 64 \\ \times\ 6 \\ \hline \end{array}$
11. $\begin{array}{r} 35 \\ \times\ 9 \\ \hline \end{array}$	12. $\begin{array}{r} 43 \\ \times\ 5 \\ \hline \end{array}$	13. $\begin{array}{r} 39 \\ \times\ 7 \\ \hline \end{array}$	14. $\begin{array}{r} 15 \\ \times\ 8 \\ \hline \end{array}$	15. $\begin{array}{r} 57 \\ \times\ 5 \\ \hline \end{array}$
16. $\begin{array}{r} 72 \\ \times\ 8 \\ \hline \end{array}$	17. $\begin{array}{r} 45 \\ \times\ 4 \\ \hline \end{array}$	18. $\begin{array}{r} 33 \\ \times\ 6 \\ \hline \end{array}$	19. $\begin{array}{r} 48 \\ \times\ 3 \\ \hline \end{array}$	20. $\begin{array}{r} 54 \\ \times\ 6 \\ \hline \end{array}$
21. $\begin{array}{r} 84 \\ \times\ 7 \\ \hline \end{array}$	22. $\begin{array}{r} 79 \\ \times\ 3 \\ \hline \end{array}$	23. $\begin{array}{r} 29 \\ \times\ 8 \\ \hline \end{array}$	24. $\begin{array}{r} 13 \\ \times\ 9 \\ \hline \end{array}$	25. $\begin{array}{r} 32 \\ \times\ 9 \\ \hline \end{array}$

Find the product.

26. $(4 \times 7) \times 6$

27. $(3 \times 9) \times 8$

28. $3 \times (5 \times 7)$

29. $5 \times (5 \times 5)$

30. $(8 \times 2) \times 4$

31. $6 \times (7 \times 8)$

The sign below shows the price list of a hardware store. Use the price list to answer each question. Write *overestimate* or *underestimate* to tell how you got your answer.

HAPPY HARDWARE

Item	Price	Item	Price
handsaw	$9.95	box of nails	$3.55
hammer	$3.95	sandpaper	$0.75
pliers	$2.15	wrench	$11.25
screwdriver	$2.98	chisel	$2.79

1. Stella wants to buy a hammer and a box of nails. She has $8.00. Does she have enough money?

2. Tommy works at the hardware store. He is paid to run errands. He wants to buy a handsaw. He has saved $3.35. He will earn $6.05 by Friday. Can he buy the handsaw on Friday?

3. Joe needs to buy sandpaper, a hammer, and a wrench. He has $15.00. Does he have enough money to buy all these tools?

4. Sally must buy at least $25.00 worth of items to receive a free watch. She has bought a box of nails, a screwdriver, a wrench, and a hammer. Will she receive a free watch?

5. Terry earns between $2.50 and $5.50 a day. He wants to buy a saw. He figures it will take 5 days to earn the money to buy the saw. How much money can he count on having in 5 days?

Use with pages 146–147.

Multiply.

1. 203
   × 3

2. 112
   × 4

3. 414
   × 2

4. 300
   × 3

5. 789
   × 1

6. 222
   × 4

7. 101
   × 5

8. 310
   × 2

9. 121
   × 4

10. 302
    × 3

11. 334
    × 2

12. 968
    × 1

13. 122
    × 3

14. 211
    × 4

15. 100
    × 8

16. 8 × 111

17. 3 × 313

18. 4 × 200

19. 3 × 302

20. 9 × 100

21. 2 × 324

22. 7 × 101

23. 5 × 110

24. 1 × 798

Solve.

25. The museum has 3 rooms for modern art. Each room has 121 paintings in it. How many paintings are there in all?

26. On Saturday and Sunday, there were 210 people at the museum each day. How many people went to the museum?

27. The toy store manager dropped 5 open boxes of jigsaw puzzles on the floor. Each box has 198 pieces. How many pieces fell in all?

28. The owners of an art gallery are having an exhibit. They are expecting 324 people. They want to give two posters to each person. How many posters should they make?

Find the product.

1.	423	2.	209	3.	436	4.	147	5.	382
	× 5		× 2		× 3		× 4		× 5

6.	542	7.	592	8.	165	9.	368	10.	400
	× 6		× 7		× 6		× 8		× 9

11.	295	12.	167	13.	718	14.	503	15.	506
	× 5		× 7		× 8		× 4		× 5

16.	359	17.	615	18.	398	19.	125	20.	372
	× 3		× 7		× 6		× 5		× 3

21. 9 × 194   **22.** 3 × 167   **23.** 9 × 318

24. 9 × 426   **25.** 2 × 395   **26.** 4 × 703

27. 6 × 658   **28.** 7 × 509   **29.** 9 × 999

Solve.

30. An art book has 245 pictures in color. How many pictures in color would 5 books have?

31. The bookstore has 7 tables of art books. There are 238 books on each table. How many art books does the bookstore have?

32. The pet store has 157 fish tanks. Each tank has 9 fish in it. How many fish are there in all?

33. The grocery store has 8 rows of shelves. Each row holds 304 cans. How many cans are on the shelves in the store?

Use with pages 150–151.

Multiply.

1. $\begin{array}{r} 3,102 \\ \times\ \ \ \ 2 \\ \hline \end{array}$	**2.** $\begin{array}{r} 4,513 \\ \times\ \ \ \ 3 \\ \hline \end{array}$	**3.** $\begin{array}{r} 6,366 \\ \times\ \ \ \ 8 \\ \hline \end{array}$	**4.** $\begin{array}{r} 5,724 \\ \times\ \ \ \ 4 \\ \hline \end{array}$
5. $\begin{array}{r} 9,389 \\ \times\ \ \ \ 9 \\ \hline \end{array}$	**6.** $\begin{array}{r} 1,525 \\ \times\ \ \ \ 5 \\ \hline \end{array}$	**7.** $\begin{array}{r} 9,405 \\ \times\ \ \ \ 8 \\ \hline \end{array}$	**8.** $\begin{array}{r} 5,193 \\ \times\ \ \ \ 7 \\ \hline \end{array}$
9. $\begin{array}{r} 6,342 \\ \times\ \ \ \ 6 \\ \hline \end{array}$	**10.** $\begin{array}{r} 7,984 \\ \times\ \ \ \ 7 \\ \hline \end{array}$	**11.** $\begin{array}{r} 7,196 \\ \times\ \ \ \ 6 \\ \hline \end{array}$	**12.** $\begin{array}{r} 5,640 \\ \times\ \ \ \ 9 \\ \hline \end{array}$
13. $\begin{array}{r} 2,005 \\ \times\ \ \ \ 6 \\ \hline \end{array}$	**14.** $\begin{array}{r} 4,010 \\ \times\ \ \ \ 9 \\ \hline \end{array}$	**15.** $\begin{array}{r} 9,898 \\ \times\ \ \ \ 2 \\ \hline \end{array}$	**16.** $\begin{array}{r} 7,286 \\ \times\ \ \ \ 7 \\ \hline \end{array}$
17. $\begin{array}{r} 8,345 \\ \times\ \ \ \ 4 \\ \hline \end{array}$	**18.** $\begin{array}{r} 4,153 \\ \times\ \ \ \ 5 \\ \hline \end{array}$	**19.** $\begin{array}{r} 6,903 \\ \times\ \ \ \ 7 \\ \hline \end{array}$	**20.** $\begin{array}{r} 3,471 \\ \times\ \ \ \ 9 \\ \hline \end{array}$
21. $\begin{array}{r} 1,728 \\ \times\ \ \ \ 2 \\ \hline \end{array}$	**22.** $\begin{array}{r} 4,468 \\ \times\ \ \ \ 7 \\ \hline \end{array}$	**23.** $\begin{array}{r} 3,532 \\ \times\ \ \ \ 8 \\ \hline \end{array}$	**24.** $\begin{array}{r} 9,536 \\ \times\ \ \ \ 6 \\ \hline \end{array}$

Write the letter of the product that is the answer to the
multiplication problem. One answer is extra.

25. $8 \times 1,879$

26. $4 \times 6,781$

27. $7 \times 4,582$

28. $9 \times 2,297$

29. $3 \times 6,721$

30. $6 \times 3,875$

a. 27,124

b. 20,163

c. 18,460

d. 15,032

e. 23,250

f. 32,074

g. 20,673

Make 3 Tic-Tac-Toe diagrams on a separate sheet of paper.
Play Tic-Tac-Toe. Multiply. Put an X in the spaces in which
the product is greater than $20.00. Put an O in the spaces in
which the product is less than $20.00.

$6.21 × 3	$7.89 × 5	$9.98 × 6
$8.33 × 3	$5.98 × 2	$1.25 × 2
$8.26 × 7	$704 × 6	$3.08 × 4

The winner

is

$2.13 × 6	$926 × 6	$7.45 × 3
$505 × 5	$4.68 × 3	$6.32 × 8
$2.87 × 2	$4.31 × 7	$3.46 × 9

The winner

is

$7.37 × 6	$6.06 × 3	$8.42 × 2
$321 × 2	$4.87 × 5	$7.09 × 5
$8.79 × 1	$5.33 × 2	$9.01 × 7

The winner

is

Write any facts you do not need to solve the problems. Then, solve.

1. Katherine Lee Bates wrote the words for "America the Beautiful." She was born in Massachusetts in 1859. She was a college professor from 1891 to 1925. She died in 1929. How old was she when she died?

_____

2. Clara Barton founded the American Red Cross. She was born in 1821 in Massachusetts. The Red Cross was founded in 1880. She was president until 1904. For how many years did she serve as president?

_____

3. Mary Garden was a famous American singer. She became the director of the Chicago Opera in 1920. She studied in France for 11 years. Then, she lectured for 3 times as many years. For how many years did she lecture?

_____

4. Ellen Glasgow was an American writer. She was born in Virginia in 1874. She wrote six books. She was elected to the Academy of Arts and Letters in 1938. She died 7 years later. In what year did she die?

_____

5. Edith Hamilton was an American writer. She studied Greek and Roman stories. She was born in 1867. She wrote 2 books of stories. She was 96 years old when she died. In what year did she die?

_____

6. Katharine Hepburn is an American actress. She was born in 1909. Several actors have won 2 Oscars. Hepburn has won 2 times as many Oscars. How many Oscars has she won?

_____

7. "Grandma" Moses was a famous American painter. She was born in 1860. She died in 1961. She was 101 years old! She started to paint when she was 78 years old. In what year did she begin to paint?

_____

8. Margaret Chase Smith was an American politician. She served in Congress for 9 years. She was a U.S. senator for 12 years. She served 2 terms as senator. For how many years did each of her terms last?

_____

Decide how to solve each problem. Then, solve.

1. There are 2 senators from every state in the United States Senate. There are 50 states. How many senators are there in all?

2. The U.S. House of Representatives has 435 members. California has 45 representatives. This number is 9 times as many as Kansas has. How many representatives does Kansas have?

3. Wisconsin has 9 representatives. Texas has 3 times as many representatives as Wisconsin has. How many representatives does Texas have?

4. Ohio has 21 representatives. This is 3 times as many as Alabama has. How many representatives does Alabama have?

5. There are 435 representatives. Florida has 19 representatives. How many representatives are *not* from Florida?

6. The largest groups of representatives come from California, New York, and Texas. You know how many come from Texas and California. New York has 34. How many representatives come from these 3 states?

7. The leader of the House of Representatives is called the Speaker. Henry Clay was the Speaker of the House 5 times. Sam Rayburn was the Speaker twice as many times. How many times was Rayburn the Speaker?

8. Wyoming was the first state to let women vote. This happened in 1869. In 1925, Wyoming had the first woman governor. How many years apart were these 2 events?

9. North Dakota and South Dakota each have 1 representative. Virginia has 5 times as many representatives as both Dakotas have. How many representatives does Virginia have?

10. Connecticut has 2 women representatives. It has 2 times as many men who serve as representatives. How many of its representatives are men?

Divide.

1. $5\overline{)16}$ **2.** $3\overline{)25}$ **3.** $9\overline{)60}$ **4.** $6\overline{)30}$ **5.** $7\overline{)47}$

6. $5\overline{)48}$ **7.** $6\overline{)39}$ **8.** $7\overline{)40}$ **9.** $9\overline{)66}$ **10.** $8\overline{)32}$

11. $3\overline{)29}$ **12.** $2\overline{)17}$ **13.** $8\overline{)74}$ **14.** $2\overline{)11}$ **15.** $3\overline{)24}$

16. $26 \div 5$ **17.** $54 \div 7$ **18.** $36 \div 6$ **19.** $85 \div 9$

20. $13 \div 2$ **21.** $58 \div 8$ **22.** $12 \div 3$ **23.** $17 \div 7$

24. $38 \div 4$ **25.** $20 \div 6$ **26.** $32 \div 5$ **27.** $21 \div 9$

Solve.

28. Leslie uses 8 beads to make a bracelet. How many bracelets can she make from 50 beads? How many beads will be left?

29. Leslie also uses 7 inches of wire for each bracelet. How many bracelets can she make from a piece of wire 45 inches long? How much wire will be left?

30. Kevin buys 60 nails to make small boxes. He uses 11 nails for each box. How many boxes can he make? How many nails are left?

31. Sammy is making baskets of fruit. He bought 91 apples. How many baskets can he make if he puts 8 apples in each basket? How many are left?

How many digits will the quotient contain?

1. $3\overline{)226}$ **2.** $7\overline{)2,861}$ **3.** $4\overline{)397}$ **4.** $2\overline{)763}$ **5.** $6\overline{)1,592}$

6. $5\overline{)4,921}$ **7.** $8\overline{)767}$ **8.** $9\overline{)835}$ **9.** $4\overline{)5,171}$ **10.** $5\overline{)3,784}$

Estimate the quotient.

11. $6\overline{)752}$ **12.** $5\overline{)299}$ **13.** $3\overline{)461}$ **14.** $4\overline{)718}$ **15.** $2\overline{)735}$

16. $7\overline{)811}$ **17.** $9\overline{)476}$ **18.** $4\overline{)476}$ **19.** $7\overline{)111}$ **20.** $5\overline{)482}$

21. $3\overline{)1,986}$ **22.** $5\overline{)7,113}$ **23.** $4\overline{)1,117}$ **24.** $2\overline{)1,908}$

25. $8\overline{)3,117}$ **26.** $9\overline{)9,304}$ **27.** $6\overline{)5,777}$ **28.** $8\overline{)4,853}$

29. $2,615 \div 3$ **30.** $1,327 \div 6$ **31.** $651 \div 7$

32. $313 \div 2$ **33.** $419 \div 8$ **34.** $644 \div 9$

35. $131 \div 4$ **36.** $3,068 \div 7$ **37.** $8,619 \div 5$

38. $9,347 \div 9$ **39.** $2,154 \div 6$ **40.** $1,179 \div 5$

41. $237 \div 4$ **42.** $567 \div 9$ **43.** $391 \div 5$

44. $4,263 \div 6$ **45.** $6,705 \div 7$ **46.** $5,091 \div 7$

Use with pages 170–171.

Divide.

1. $77 \div 5$ 2. $96 \div 8$ 3. $86 \div 8$

4. $79 \div 6$ 5. $37 \div 2$ 6. $59 \div 3$

7. $63 \div 5$ 8. $89 \div 8$ 9. $67 \div 5$

10. $81 \div 4$ 11. $78 \div 6$ 12. $98 \div 6$

13. $3\overline{)45}$ 14. $2\overline{)91}$ 15. $4\overline{)86}$ 16. $3\overline{)96}$ 17. $5\overline{)69}$

18. $7\overline{)99}$ 19. $6\overline{)84}$ 20. $8\overline{)91}$ 21. $7\overline{)86}$ 22. $6\overline{)95}$

23. $3\overline{)38}$ 24. $4\overline{)75}$ 25. $6\overline{)90}$ 26. $7\overline{)95}$ 27. $9\overline{)99}$

Solve.

28. Bob has 75 photographs from his vacation. He puts 6 photographs on each page in his album. How many pages does he fill? How many photographs will there be on the page he does not fill?

29. Yumi took 51 photographs when she was at the seashore. She was away for 3 days and took the same number of photographs each day. How many photographs did she take each day?

Solve each problem. Decide what to do with the quotient and the remainder. Write the solution.

Once upon a time, there was a very rude dragon. It blew smoke on the clothes on clotheslines. It squashed gardens. It made loud noises, even at night when people wanted to sleep.

1. One day, the dragon decided to squash some gardens. It planned to squash 4 gardens each day. There were 38 gardens in the village. How many days would the dragon need to squash all the village gardens?

2. People did not like having their gardens squashed. So, 74 people went to the king to complain. There were 8 chairs in the king's complaint room. He talked only to complete groups of 8. How many people did not get to complain to the king?

3. The king had 53 knights. He formed "Dragon Discipline" teams. He put 6 knights on each team. The extra knights kept track of the teams. How many teams were there?

4. The knights had no luck. Then, 2 children told the people to go to the dragon to complain. So, 27 people marched in rows. Each row had 4 people. The extra people marched in the last row. How many rows were there?

5. The dragon was very surprised! Then, it felt ashamed. It cried 46 great dragon tears. The tears fell in puddles. There were 7 tears in each full puddle. How many full puddles were there?

6. The dragon felt awful! It wrote 40 letters (38 "I'm sorry" letters and 2 "thank you" notes to the children). The dragon wanted to save stamps. So, it put 6 letters into each envelope. How many envelopes did it use for all the letters?

7. The people in the village had a picnic. They invited the dragon. There were 93 people at the picnic. Each table seated 8 people. The extra people sat with the dragon. How many people sat with the dragon?

8. The dragon gave rides to the children at the picnic. There were 74 children. The dragon's tail held 5 children at a time. How many rides did the dragon give to all the children?

Divide.

1. 3)298

2. 2)170

3. 4)272

4. 3)299

5. 6)558

6. 4)216

7. 3)285

8. 7)482

9. 6)477

10. 5)490

11. 5)497

12. 8)610

13. 7)327

14. 9)199

15. 6)535

16. 320 ÷ 5

17. 522 ÷ 8

18. 738 ÷ 9

19. 333 ÷ 4

20. 128 ÷ 3

21. 193 ÷ 2

22. 654 ÷ 7

23. 176 ÷ 8

24. 316 ÷ 5

25. 225 ÷ 9

26. 402 ÷ 6

27. 498 ÷ 7

28. 521 ÷ 8

29. 377 ÷ 7

30. 242 ÷ 9

31. 187 ÷ 6

32. 754 ÷ 8

33. 446 ÷ 6

34. 360 ÷ 5

35. 195 ÷ 7

Divide.

1. $6\overline{)898}$
2. $3\overline{)468}$
3. $4\overline{)459}$
4. $3\overline{)949}$
5. $6\overline{)3,874}$

6. $9\overline{)8,811}$
7. $5\overline{)3,763}$
8. $8\overline{)3,546}$
9. $3\overline{)2,775}$
10. $8\overline{)6,926}$

11. $5\overline{)2,674}$
12. $9\overline{)4,332}$
13. $7\overline{)3,584}$
14. $2\overline{)1,855}$
15. $4\overline{)2,692}$

16. $2,646 \div 7$
17. $1,055 \div 5$
18. $1,265 \div 2$

19. $3,074 \div 9$
20. $4,527 \div 6$
21. $1,018 \div 8$

22. $1,676 \div 4$
23. $1,695 \div 2$
24. $826 \div 3$

25. $3,508 \div 4$
26. $4,792 \div 7$
27. $3,987 \div 5$

28. $1,030 \div 3$
29. $1,002 \div 4$
30. $2,113 \div 6$

31. $2,446 \div 5$
32. $4,691 \div 6$
33. $1,489 \div 7$

Find the average.

1. 32, 48

2. 55, 61, 70

3. 525, 311

4. 148, 222, 296

5. 19, 29, 39, 49

6. 101, 202, 303

7. 55, 82, 91, 80

8. 251, 371, 197

9. 365, 472, 805, 766

10. 419, 246, 378, 213

Use the chart to solve.

Student	NUMBER OF SIT-UPS		
	Monday	Wednesday	Friday
Marsha	38	39	40
Tony	41	38	44
Louise	37	38	33
Juan	44	37	39

11. What was Marsha's average number of sit-ups?

12. What was Juan's average number of sit-ups?

13. Which student had the highest average for the 3 days?

14. How much higher was Marsha's average than Louise's average?

15. What was the average number of sit-ups done by all the students on Friday?

16. On which day was the average for all the students the highest?

Solving Two-Step Problems	Writing a Number Sentence	Making a Model
Choosing the Operation	Estimation	

Write the strategy or method you choose. Then solve.

1. Yellowstone National Park is in Wyoming, Idaho, and Montana. One of its roads is called the Grand Loop. It is 143 miles long. There are 157 more miles of road in the park. How many miles of road are there in the park?

2. Eagle Peak is the highest place in the park. It is 11,353 feet high. Mount Washburn is the second highest. It is 10,243 feet high. How much taller is Eagle Peak?

3. Laura camped at Yellowstone. She hiked 12 miles in 4 hours. Then she ate lunch for 1 hour. She returned to the camp 2 hours after she finished lunch. How many hours was Laura gone from the campsite?

4. There is a train ride to the top of Snow Queen Mountain. It costs $1.00 for children and $2.50 for adults. One train carried 5 adults and 10 children. How much did their tickets cost?

Write the information you will need to solve each problem.

5. The Yellowstone River runs through a canyon. It forms 2 waterfalls. The lower falls are 308 feet high. The upper falls are much shorter than the lower falls. What is the difference in the heights of the two falls?

6. In 1872, Congress created Yellowstone Park. The Army ran the park after 1886. The National Park Service took over later. How many years passed between 1886 and the date on which the National Park Service took over the park?

Solving Two-Step Problems	Writing a Number Sentence	Making a Model
Choosing the Operation	Estimation	

Write the strategy or method you choose. Then solve.

1. At Yosemite Park, there are several tall mountains. Clouds Rest is 5,964 feet high. Half Dome is 1,072 feet lower. How high is Half Dome?

2. Niagara Falls is 170 feet high. Yosemite Falls is more than 9 times as high. About how high is Yosemite Falls?

3. Mammoth Cave is 100 miles south of Louisville, Kentucky. It was discovered in 1809. It became a park in 1936. How many years passed before Mammoth Cave became a park?

4. Carlsbad Caverns are the world's largest caves. The largest room in the caverns is 4,000 feet long and 625 feet wide. The largest room in Mammoth Cave is 450 feet long and 130 feet wide. How much longer is the room at Carlsbad?

Write what information you would need to solve each problem.

5. The Niagara River connects Lake Erie and Lake Ontario. The river is 326 feet lower at Lake Ontario than at Lake Erie. How high is the river at Lake Ontario?

6. In 1954, hundreds of tons of rock fell at Niagara Falls. Scientists have learned that Niagara Falls moves west about 5 feet each year. In how many years will it reach Lake Erie?

Divide. The Mystery Quotient will appear several times on this page. Look for it!

1. 6)626

2. 2)415

3. 4)832

4. 5)527

5. 4)827

6. 5)3,025

7. 9)1,857

8. 5)1,033

9. 8)6,470

10. 4)2,832

11. 8)1,651

12. 7)2,163

13. 6)3,014

14. 7)1,445

15. 3)1,227

16. 6)1,239

17. 4,443 ÷ 8

18. 4,329 ÷ 9

19. 621 ÷ 3

20. 3,739 ÷ 7

21. 4,522 ÷ 9

22. 4,311 ÷ 8

23. 1,307 ÷ 5

24. 5,001 ÷ 7

25. What is the Mystery Quotient?

26. How many times does it appear?

Divide.

1. $3.00 ÷ 6

2. $11.70 ÷ 2

3. $29.40 ÷ 3

4. $66.48 ÷ 8

5. $21.28 ÷ 7

6. $17.55 ÷ 5

7. $18.00 ÷ 5

8. $14.07 ÷ 7

9. $6.21 ÷ 3

10. $4\overline{)\$1.20}$

11. $9\overline{)\$3.69}$

12. $8\overline{)\$1.20}$

13. $3\overline{)\$12.66}$

14. $6\overline{)\$18.24}$

15. $7\overline{)\$43.47}$

16. $2\overline{)\$7.50}$

17. $9\overline{)\$64.80}$

18. $3\overline{)\$14.55}$

19. $8\overline{)\$74.48}$

20. $4\overline{)\$2.72}$

21. $2\overline{)\$19.70}$

22. $4\overline{)\$8.24}$

23. $6\overline{)\$25.38}$

24. $2\overline{)\$18.90}$

25. $7\overline{)\$11.83}$

America has many tall-tale heroes. Read each problem. Write a number sentence. Then solve your number sentence.

1. Paul Bunyan was a famous logger. A blue ox was his pet. He dug the Grand Canyon with his pick. Most loggers are about 6 feet tall. Paul Bunyan was 3 times as tall. How tall was Paul Bunyan?

2. Johnny Appleseed planted the same number of apple trees each day. Pioneers in Ohio and the Midwest got apples from his trees. Suppose he planted 63 trees in 7 days. How many trees did he plant each day?

3. Pecos Bill was a famous cowboy. Once, he roped a wind storm called a twister. The twister dragged Bill for 1,595 miles. Then, Bill climbed onto the twister. He rode for 988 miles. How far did Bill and the twister go in all?

4. Betsy Ross is believed to have sewed the first American flag. She made 13 stars. Each star had 5 points. How many points were there on all 13 stars?

5. John Henry was a railroad hero. He pounded large nails called spikes. Once, he had a race with a machine. The machine pounded 978 spikes in one day. John Henry pounded 1,253 spikes that day. How many more spikes did John Henry pound?

6. Zorro was a California hero. He once found 56 gold coins. He gave the coins to 4 poor families. Each family got the same number of coins. How many coins did each family get?

Write the fraction for the shaded part.

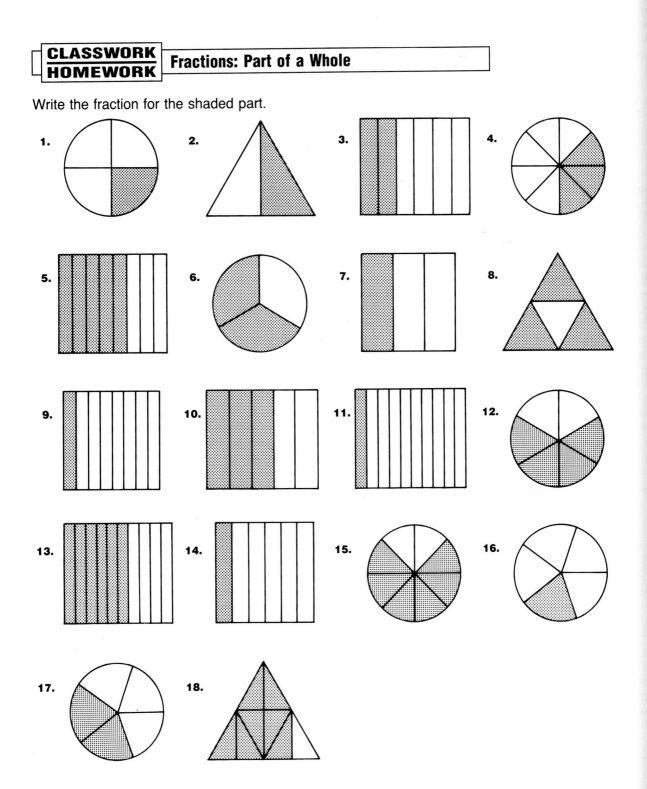

1.

2.

3.

4.

5.

6.

7.

8.

9.

10.

11.

12.

13.

14.

15.

16.

17.

18.

Write the fraction for the shaded part of each set.

1.

2.

3.

4.

5.

6.

7.

8.

9.

Draw the items. Then shade the correct number to show the fraction of each set.

10. $\frac{3}{4}$

11. $\frac{1}{10}$

12. $\frac{4}{5}$

Write the missing number.

1.

$\frac{1}{2}$ of 4

2.

$\frac{2}{3}$ of 6

3.

$\frac{3}{4}$ of 8

Write the part of each set.

4. $\frac{1}{2}$ of 10

5. $\frac{1}{6}$ of 12

6. $\frac{1}{3}$ of 9

7. $\frac{3}{4}$ of 16

8. $\frac{2}{5}$ of 10

9. $\frac{3}{8}$ of 8

10. $\frac{1}{4}$ of 12

11. $\frac{2}{3}$ of 15

12. $\frac{1}{8}$ of 16

13. $\frac{1}{6}$ of 18

14. $\frac{5}{6}$ of 24

15. $\frac{1}{5}$ of 25

16. $\frac{3}{4}$ of 40

17. $\frac{4}{5}$ of 20

18. $\frac{2}{3}$ of 30

Solve.

19. The hiking club has 18 members. Of the members, $\frac{2}{3}$ are on the mountain. How many members are there on the mountain?

20. The store has 30 tents. Of the tents, $\frac{5}{6}$ are waterproof. How many tents are waterproof?

Write the equivalent fraction.

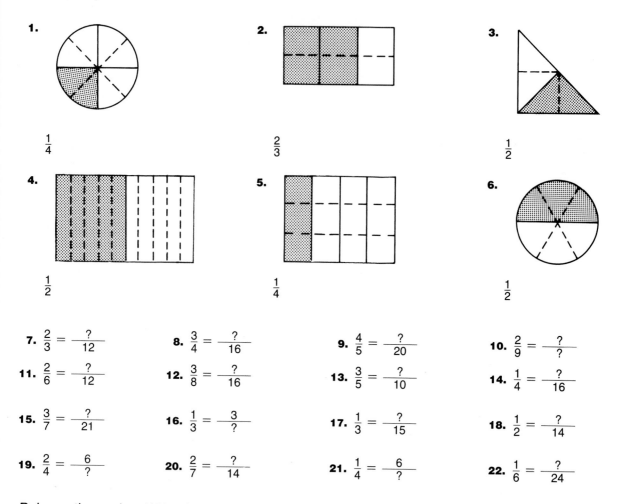

1. $\frac{1}{4}$

2. $\frac{2}{3}$

3. $\frac{1}{2}$

4. $\frac{1}{2}$

5. $\frac{1}{4}$

6. $\frac{1}{2}$

7. $\frac{2}{3} = \frac{?}{12}$

8. $\frac{3}{4} = \frac{?}{16}$

9. $\frac{4}{5} = \frac{?}{20}$

10. $\frac{2}{9} = \frac{?}{?}$

11. $\frac{2}{6} = \frac{?}{12}$

12. $\frac{3}{8} = \frac{?}{16}$

13. $\frac{3}{5} = \frac{?}{10}$

14. $\frac{1}{4} = \frac{?}{16}$

15. $\frac{3}{7} = \frac{?}{21}$

16. $\frac{1}{3} = \frac{3}{?}$

17. $\frac{1}{3} = \frac{?}{15}$

18. $\frac{1}{2} = \frac{?}{14}$

19. $\frac{2}{4} = \frac{6}{?}$

20. $\frac{2}{7} = \frac{?}{14}$

21. $\frac{1}{4} = \frac{6}{?}$

22. $\frac{1}{6} = \frac{?}{24}$

Balance the scales. Write the equivalent fraction.

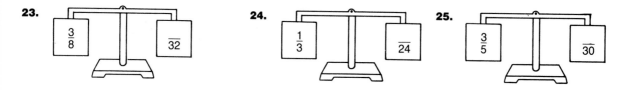

23. $\frac{3}{8}$ $\frac{}{32}$

24. $\frac{1}{3}$ $\frac{}{24}$

25. $\frac{3}{5}$ $\frac{}{30}$

Write the equivalent fraction.

1. $\dfrac{16}{24} = \dfrac{?}{3}$

2. $\dfrac{8}{10} = \dfrac{4}{?}$

3. $\dfrac{30}{40} = \dfrac{3}{?}$

4. $\dfrac{7}{14} = \dfrac{1}{?}$

5. $\dfrac{8}{12} = \dfrac{?}{3}$

6. $\dfrac{10}{30} = \dfrac{?}{3}$

7. $\dfrac{9}{18} = \dfrac{1}{?}$

8. $\dfrac{2}{4} = \dfrac{?}{2}$

9. $\dfrac{5}{15} = \dfrac{1}{?}$

10. $\dfrac{12}{48} = \dfrac{?}{4}$

11. $\dfrac{8}{16} = \dfrac{?}{2}$

12. $\dfrac{6}{9} = \dfrac{?}{3}$

Write each fraction in simplest form.

13. $\dfrac{?}{18}$

14. $\dfrac{18}{?}$

15. $\dfrac{4}{?}$

16. $\dfrac{?}{15}$

17. $\dfrac{2}{?}$

18. $\dfrac{?}{5}$

Climb down the staircase. Write equivalent fractions.

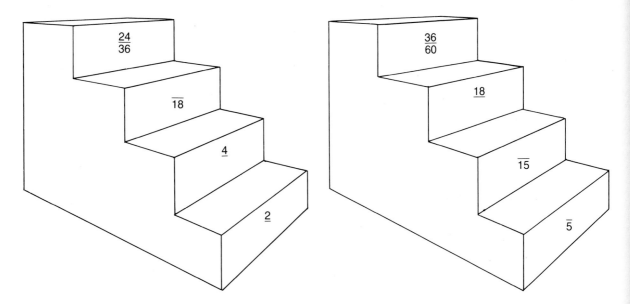

$\dfrac{24}{36}$ $\dfrac{36}{60}$

$\dfrac{}{18}$ $\dfrac{18}{}$

$\dfrac{4}{}$ $\dfrac{}{15}$

$\dfrac{2}{}$ $\dfrac{}{5}$

Use the circle graph to answer the questions.

1. How many fruit juices are there in the fruit punch?

2. What fraction of fruit punch is water?

3. Which ingredient is used in the smallest amount?

$\frac{1}{12}$
Orange juice

$\frac{1}{6}$
Cherry juice

$\frac{1}{6}$
Cranberry juice

$\frac{1}{4}$
Apple juice

$\frac{1}{3}$
Water

INGREDIENTS IN FRUIT PUNCH

4. Arrange the ingredients in order from the smallest to the largest.

5. Which 2 ingredients are used in the same amount?

6. Which ingredient is $\frac{1}{4}$ of the fruit punch?

7. What fraction of the fruit punch would be apple juice if you doubled the recipe?

8. Which ingredient plus cherry juice makes $\frac{1}{2}$ the fruit punch?

9. After you have read this graph, will you know all the ingredients in fruit punch? Explain your answer.

Write a whole number or a mixed number in simplest form for each shaded part.

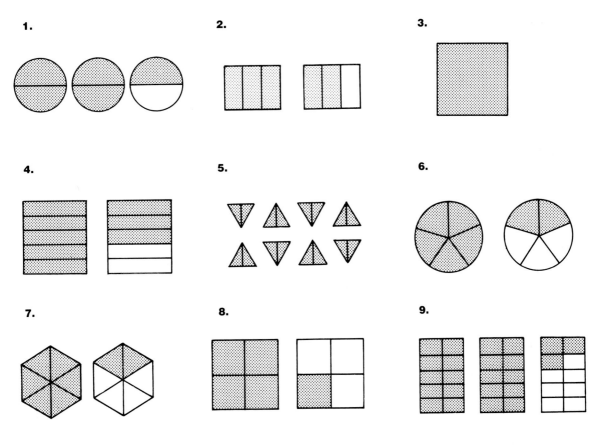

1.

2.

3.

4.

5.

6.

7.

8.

9.

Write a whole number or a mixed number for each fraction.

10. $\frac{12}{4}$ **11.** $\frac{17}{5}$ **12.** $\frac{13}{6}$ **13.** $\frac{9}{8}$ **14.** $\frac{11}{4}$

15. $\frac{8}{3}$ **16.** $\frac{18}{7}$ **17.** $\frac{15}{2}$ **18.** $\frac{10}{6}$ **19.** $\frac{14}{5}$

Solve.

20. Renee used $\frac{10}{4}$ cups of flour to make bread. Write this as a mixed number in simplest form.

21. Brian used $\frac{12}{3}$ cups of raisins to make bran muffins. Write this as a mixed number in simplest form.

Comparing Fractions and Mixed Numbers

Compare. Write >, <, or =. Then write the letter that is next to the correct answer to solve the riddle at the bottom of the page.

1. $\frac{1}{4}$ < Y   > I $2\frac{2}{4}$ = B

2. $\frac{5}{6}$ < T   > O $\frac{4}{6}$ = T

3. $\frac{3}{5}$ < U   > P $\frac{4}{5}$ = S

4. $\frac{2}{3}$ < F   > L $\frac{2}{3}$ = A

5. $\frac{1}{4}$ < R   > T $2\frac{1}{4}$ = W

6. $3\frac{1}{8}$ < T   > E $1\frac{1}{8}$ = M

7. $2\frac{1}{4}$ < Q   > Y $2\frac{1}{4}$ = A

8. $\frac{7}{6}$ < R   > E $1\frac{1}{6}$ = C

9. $\frac{12}{7}$ < B   > A $1\frac{8}{14}$ = C

10. $\frac{2}{3}$ < L   > V $\frac{4}{6}$ = P

11. $\frac{5}{10}$ < W   > A $\frac{2}{5}$ = X

12. $\frac{2}{3}$ < B   > I $\frac{3}{4}$ = L

13. $4\frac{1}{2}$ < L   > I $4\frac{3}{4}$ = T

14. $1\frac{1}{5}$ < E   > F $1\frac{3}{10}$ = T

15. $\frac{3}{8}$ < S   > T $\frac{1}{2}$ = P

16. $\frac{8}{16}$ < T   > L $\frac{3}{4}$ = M

17. $3\frac{4}{8}$ < U   > M $3\frac{5}{8}$ = A

18. $\frac{8}{9}$ < R   > D $\frac{2}{3}$ = K

19. $\frac{1}{3}$ < E   > A $\frac{5}{12}$ = S

20. $2\frac{1}{4}$ < N   > K $2\frac{1}{2}$ = E

21. $6\frac{1}{5}$ < T   > W $6\frac{7}{10}$ = I

22. $\frac{1}{16}$ < S   > J $\frac{2}{32}$ = I

23. $\frac{1}{4}$ < U   > N $\frac{1}{16}$ = S

24. $\frac{3}{2}$ < G   > R $\frac{6}{4}$ = D

25. $\frac{3}{9}$ < E   > A $\frac{2}{3}$ = T

26. $\frac{4}{16}$ < E   > N $\frac{2}{4}$ = P

27. $1\frac{1}{2}$ < L   > D $\frac{10}{8}$ = F

28. $\frac{1}{3}$ < !   > . $\frac{2}{4}$ = ?

$\frac{?}{1}$ $\frac{?}{2}$ $\frac{?}{3}$ $\frac{?}{4}$ $\frac{?}{5}$ $\frac{?}{6}$ $\frac{?}{7}$ $\frac{?}{8}$ $\frac{?}{9}$ $\frac{?}{10}$ $\frac{?}{11}$ $\frac{?}{12}$ $\frac{?}{13}$ $\frac{?}{14}$

$\frac{?}{15}$ $\frac{?}{16}$ $\frac{?}{17}$ $\frac{?}{18}$ $\frac{?}{19}$ $\frac{?}{20}$ $\frac{?}{21}$ $\frac{?}{22}$ $\frac{?}{23}$ $\frac{?}{24}$ $\frac{?}{25}$ $\frac{?}{26}$ $\frac{?}{27}$ $\frac{?}{28}$

Work backward to solve each problem.

1. On Saturday, Penny went on an all-day bird-watching hike. She saw 5 more cardinals than doves. She saw 15 fewer doves than blue jays. Penny saw 37 blue jays.

   a. How many doves did Penny see?

   b. How many cardinals did she see?

2. Foresters counted 3 times as many trees in Overlook Park as in Windsor Park. They counted only half as many trees in Franklin Park as in Overlook Park. They counted 550 trees in Windsor Park.

   a. How many trees are in Overlook Park?

   b. How many trees are in Franklin Park?

3. Before he went on vacation, Miguel bought several things to take with him. He paid $5.95 more for the T-shirt than for the sunglasses. He paid $4.35 less for the guidebook than for the T-shirt. He paid $11.45 for the sunglasses.

   a. How much did Miguel pay for the T-shirt?

   b. How much did Miguel pay for the guidebook?

4. Rob, Marcia, and Randy went cross-country skiing. Rob went 3 times as far as Randy. Marcia went $\frac{1}{2}$ as far as Rob. Randy went 16 kilometers.

   a. How far did Rob ski?

   b. How far did Marcia ski?

5. This fall, 425 students enrolled in Collins School. Walker School has $\frac{3}{5}$ as many students as Collins School. Vineland School has 112 more students than Walker School.

   a. How many students are enrolled in Walker School?

   b. How many students are enrolled in Vineland School?

6. Mr. Young assigned 12 more problems for math homework on Monday then he did on Tuesday. He assigned 15 fewer problems on Wednesday than he did on Monday. He assigned 25 problems on Tuesday.

   a. How many problems did Mr. Young assign on Monday?

   b. How many problems did he assign on Wednesday?

Write the probability of picking one of the shapes.

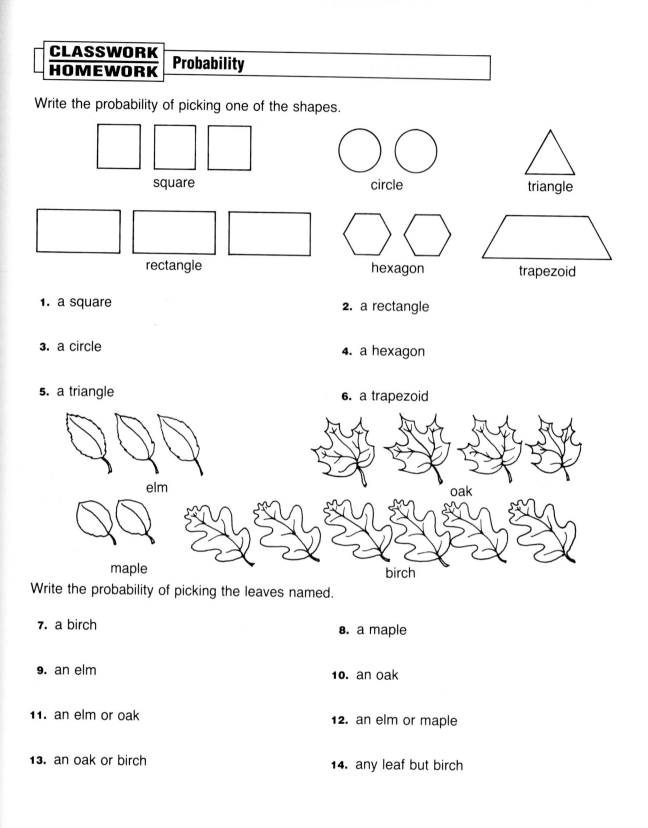

square   circle   triangle

rectangle   hexagon   trapezoid

1. a square

2. a rectangle

3. a circle

4. a hexagon

5. a triangle

6. a trapezoid

elm   oak

maple   birch

Write the probability of picking the leaves named.

7. a birch

8. a maple

9. an elm

10. an oak

11. an elm or oak

12. an elm or maple

13. an oak or birch

14. any leaf but birch

Use the tables to solve.

1. There were several different-color golf tees in a box. Some of the tees were wood and some were plastic. Frank chose one of the tees from the box. Predict if Frank was more likely to pick a wooden tee or a plastic tee.

Golf tees	Color of tees
Wood	White
	Black
	Yellow
Plastic	Green
	Red
	Orange
	Blue

2. Four friends—Suzanna, Lucien, Dennis, and Mary—played 1 round of golf. Frank predicted that Suzanna would lose the most golf balls during the round. Complete the table to find out how many golf balls each player lost. Was Frank's prediction correct?

Players	Tally of lost golf balls	Total
Suzanna	̶H̶H̶ l	
Lucien	̶H̶H̶ lll	
Dennis	̶H̶H̶	
Mary	̶H̶H̶ ll	

3. Five schools entered the Evergreen Golf Tournament. The golf coach at Pine Tree Junior High predicted that his school would have the most players in the tournament. Complete the table to find out how many golfers from each school entered the tournament. Was the golf coach's prediction correct?

School	Tally of players	Total
Pine Tree Junior High	̶H̶H̶ llll	
Ellis Middle School	̶H̶H̶ ll	
Washington Junior High	̶H̶H̶ l	
Lincoln Middle School	̶H̶H̶ lll	

Write the fraction to show each ratio.

1.

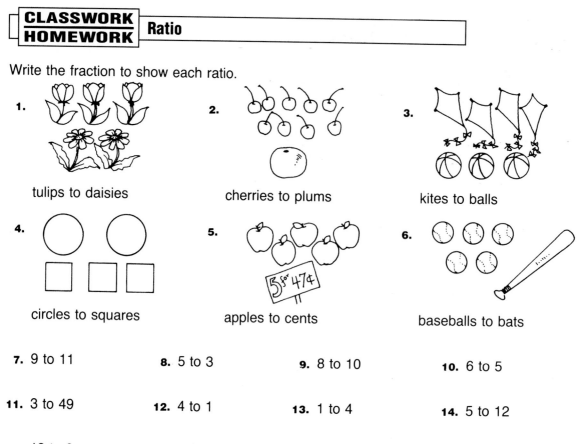

tulips to daisies

2.

cherries to plums

3.

kites to balls

4.

circles to squares

5.

apples to cents

6.

baseballs to bats

7. 9 to 11   **8.** 5 to 3   **9.** 8 to 10   **10.** 6 to 5

11. 3 to 49   **12.** 4 to 1   **13.** 1 to 4   **14.** 5 to 12

15. 13 to 9   **16.** 7 to 8

Look at this picture. Write a fraction showing the ratio of

17. pumpkins to watermelons.

18. baskets of apples to baskets of corn.

19. potted plants to pumpkins.

20. pumpkins to baskets of apples.

21. watermelons to potted plants.

The National Car Company is making plans for next year's cars. Copy and complete the tree diagram. Show the company's choices.

1. National Car is making color choices. Each car can have red, black, or tan seats. Each car can have a red, black, yellow, blue, or white body. How many color choices are there?

   Seat Color   *Body Color*   *Choices*

                   red ——————— red seats/red body

   red ———————— black ————

Make a tree diagram for each problem. Then solve.

2. National Car builds a sports car. It can have a black, tan, white, or gray roof. The body can be black, gray, green, or red. How many color choices are there for the sports model?

3. National's sedan can have a 200- or a 300-horsepower engine. The sedan can also have electric windows, electric locks, or an electric sun roof. What choices are there?

4. National makes a van and a pickup truck. The van and the truck can have green, gray, or blue seats. They can have red, black, or white bodies. How many choices are there?

5. National's seat makers are busy, too. Seats can be leather, vinyl, or cloth. They can be black, tan, green, red, blue, or gray. How many choices are there?

6. National Car has two lists of special features. List A has radio, bench seats, CB, telephone, and travel computer. List B has bucket seats, tape deck, door lights, and automatic locks. You can select one feature from each list. How many combinations of special features are there?

Copy and complete the tree diagram. Answer each question.

1. National Car Company has worker teams. There is a red team, a blue team, and a white team. Each team has a welder, a bolter, a checker, and a tester. How many possible combinations are there for new workers at National Car?

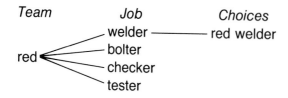

Make a tree diagram for each problem. Then solve.

2. Each worker team participates in the sports program. There are red, white, and blue teams. The teams play baseball, soccer, and volleyball. How many choices are there?

3. Each National Car worker can work on Shift A, Shift B, Shift C, or Shift D. Each worker can be a welder, a bolter, a checker, or a tester. How many combinations of shifts and jobs are there?

4. After National car workers are trained, they are sent to other cities to work. They can go to Seattle, Phoenix, Chicago, Atlanta, or Boston. They can work in the office or in the factory in each city. How many workplace combinations are there?

5. National Car workers are setting up an activity schedule. Activities can take place on Monday, Tuesday, Wednesday, Thursday, or Friday. Activities are sports, school, or hobbies. How many choices are there?

Fourth-grade students at Shipper Elementary School are planning a carnival. They want to raise money for the new school library. They want to sell tickets. They also want to plan the events at the carnival. The students know there will be some expenses. Read each sentence. Then write a question that the students should answer before making a decision.

1. Students want to buy an encyclopedia for the library.

2. Students must decide how much to charge for tickets.

3. Students must decide how much food to prepare.

4. Students must advertise the carnival in town.

5. Students need equipment for games.

6. Students need items for prizes.

7. Students want to charge more to people who bought no tickets before the carnival opened.

8. Students do not want to hold the carnival on the same day that other events will be held in town.

Add. Then ring the sums that are greater than 1.

1. $\frac{2}{7} + \frac{1}{7}$

2. $\frac{3}{8} + \frac{1}{8}$

3. $\frac{3}{10} + \frac{3}{10}$

4. $\frac{3}{5} + \frac{3}{5}$

5. $\frac{3}{8} + \frac{4}{8}$

6. $\frac{3}{4} + \frac{1}{4}$

7. $\frac{1}{6} + \frac{5}{6}$

8. $\frac{2}{5} + \frac{2}{5}$

9. $\frac{2}{3} + \frac{2}{3}$

10. $\frac{1}{6} + \frac{3}{6}$

11. $\frac{2}{8} + \frac{3}{8}$

12. $\frac{8}{9} + \frac{3}{9}$

13. $\begin{array}{r} \frac{3}{7} \\ + \frac{2}{7} \\ \hline \end{array}$

14. $\begin{array}{r} \frac{3}{4} \\ + \frac{3}{4} \\ \hline \end{array}$

15. $\begin{array}{r} \frac{2}{6} \\ + \frac{3}{6} \\ \hline \end{array}$

16. $\begin{array}{r} \frac{6}{10} \\ + \frac{2}{10} \\ \hline \end{array}$

17. $\begin{array}{r} \frac{4}{8} \\ + \frac{7}{8} \\ \hline \end{array}$

18. $\begin{array}{r} \frac{4}{9} \\ + \frac{1}{9} \\ \hline \end{array}$

19. $\begin{array}{r} \frac{4}{5} \\ + \frac{4}{5} \\ \hline \end{array}$

20. $\begin{array}{r} \frac{1}{3} \\ + \frac{2}{3} \\ \hline \end{array}$

21. $\begin{array}{r} \frac{2}{4} \\ + \frac{3}{4} \\ \hline \end{array}$

22. $\begin{array}{r} \frac{3}{5} \\ + \frac{1}{5} \\ \hline \end{array}$

23. $\begin{array}{r} \frac{3}{7} \\ + \frac{6}{7} \\ \hline \end{array}$

24. $\begin{array}{r} \frac{1}{3} \\ + \frac{5}{3} \\ \hline \end{array}$

25. $\begin{array}{r} \frac{1}{4} \\ + \frac{1}{4} \\ \hline \end{array}$

26. $\begin{array}{r} \frac{2}{5} \\ + \frac{4}{5} \\ \hline \end{array}$

27. $\begin{array}{r} \frac{2}{8} \\ + \frac{1}{8} \\ \hline \end{array}$

28. $\begin{array}{r} \frac{1}{4} \\ + \frac{2}{4} \\ \hline \end{array}$

29. $\begin{array}{r} \frac{1}{8} \\ + \frac{6}{8} \\ \hline \end{array}$

30. $\begin{array}{r} \frac{3}{5} \\ + \frac{4}{5} \\ \hline \end{array}$

31. $\begin{array}{r} \frac{5}{10} \\ + \frac{4}{10} \\ \hline \end{array}$

32. $\begin{array}{r} \frac{7}{8} \\ + \frac{6}{8} \\ \hline \end{array}$

Add. Write the sum in simplest form.

1. $\frac{2}{12}$
$+\frac{1}{2}$

2. $\frac{1}{2}$
$+\frac{4}{10}$

3. $\frac{7}{9}$
$+\frac{2}{3}$

4. $\frac{1}{6}$
$+\frac{1}{3}$

5. $\frac{2}{5}$
$+\frac{4}{15}$

6. $\frac{1}{2}$
$+\frac{5}{6}$

7. $\frac{3}{5}$
$+\frac{5}{10}$

8. $\frac{1}{5}$
$+\frac{9}{10}$

9. $\frac{1}{15}$
$+\frac{2}{3}$

10. $\frac{3}{4}$
$+\frac{16}{20}$

11. $\frac{1}{2}$
$+\frac{1}{8}$

12. $\frac{2}{3}$
$+\frac{5}{6}$

13. $\frac{1}{5}$
$+\frac{7}{20}$

14. $\frac{1}{2}$
$+\frac{4}{8}$

15. $\frac{7}{8}$
$+\frac{3}{4}$

16. $\frac{1}{5} + \frac{7}{10}$

17. $\frac{1}{4} + \frac{7}{8}$

18. $\frac{1}{2} + \frac{1}{6}$

19. $\frac{1}{3} + \frac{4}{9}$

20. $\frac{1}{4} + \frac{3}{8}$

21. $\frac{1}{3} + \frac{1}{9}$

22. $\frac{5}{8} + \frac{1}{4}$

23. $\frac{1}{2} + \frac{5}{8}$

24. $\frac{1}{10} + \frac{1}{5}$

25. $\frac{4}{5} + \frac{1}{15}$

26. $\frac{4}{6} + \frac{2}{3}$

27. $\frac{2}{3} + \frac{2}{9}$

28. $\frac{1}{2} + \frac{6}{12}$

29. $\frac{5}{6} + \frac{10}{12}$

30. $\frac{4}{5} + \frac{8}{10}$

31. $\frac{7}{9} + \frac{2}{3}$

32. $\frac{7}{15} + \frac{4}{5}$

33. $\frac{15}{20} + \frac{7}{10}$

Writing a Number Sentence	Interpreting the Quotient	Making a Diagram
Making an Organized List	and the Remainder	Choosing the Operation
	Using a Graph	Guessing and Checking

Write the strategy or method you choose. Then solve.

1. The Ridley School is putting on a play. The students have sold tickets to 975 people. There will be 3 shows. The same number of people are expected to come to each show. How many people are expected to come to each show?

2. Each ticket for the play costs $2.75. Mr. Loring bought 5 tickets for his family. How much did he pay for the tickets?

MONEY SPENT TO PUT ON A PLAY

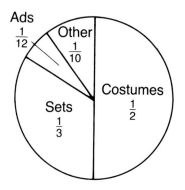

3. Which two items shown on the graph cost about the same amount of money?

4. Write the expenses in order from the greatest to the least.

5. A boy and a girl in the chorus will wear a tree costume, a bird costume, or a flower costume. How many possible combinations are there?

6. Sam, Deb, Jay, and Lee are members of the chorus. Each can play a tree, a bird, or a flower. How many possible combinations are there?

7. Students will set up chairs for the audience. There are 375 chairs. The students will put 8 chairs in each row. How many complete rows will there be?

8. When the students have set up all the rows, how many chairs will be left over?

Writing a Number Sentence	Using a Graph	Choosing the Operation
Interpreting the Quotient and the Remainder	Making a Diagram	Guessing and Checking

Write the strategy or method you choose. Then solve.

1. Mrs. Post's class is making puppets. They are working on giraffe puppets. Each giraffe puppet is made of 2 cardboard tubes. How many cardboard tubes are needed for a herd of 14 giraffe puppets?

2. Some of the students are using brown yarn to make lion manes. It takes 18 yards of yarn to make 9 manes. How much yarn is needed to make the mane of 1 lion?

3. Did the students use more yarn or more ribbon in making the puppets?

4. List the materials for the puppets in order from the least to the greatest.

MATERIALS USED TO MAKE PUPPETS

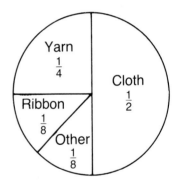

5. The monkey puppets can be gray, black, or gold. They can have blue eyes, brown eyes, or black eyes. How many possible combinations are there?

6. The alligator puppets can be either green or brown. They can have silver teeth or gold teeth. How many possible combinations are there?

7. The class has 22 inches of rope for monkey tails. It takes 7 inches to make each tail. How many tails can be made from the rope?

8. After the tails have been cut from the rope, how much rope is left?

Subtract. Write the difference in simplest form.

1. $\frac{5}{7} - \frac{2}{7}$

2. $\frac{3}{4} - \frac{1}{4}$

3. $\frac{9}{10} - \frac{2}{10}$

4. $\frac{2}{3} - \frac{1}{3}$

5. $\frac{4}{6} - \frac{2}{6}$

6. $\frac{3}{5} - \frac{1}{5}$

7. $\frac{7}{9} - \frac{1}{9}$

8. $\frac{3}{7} - \frac{3}{7}$

9. $\frac{4}{10} - \frac{2}{10}$

10. $\frac{8}{9} - \frac{3}{9}$

11. $\frac{2}{6} - \frac{1}{6}$

12. $\frac{3}{5} - \frac{2}{5}$

13. $\frac{1}{3}$ $-\frac{1}{3}$

14. $\frac{7}{10}$ $-\frac{1}{10}$

15. $\frac{6}{8}$ $-\frac{2}{8}$

16. $\frac{5}{9}$ $-\frac{3}{9}$

17. $\frac{3}{4}$ $-\frac{2}{4}$

18. $\frac{3}{7}$ $-\frac{1}{7}$

19. $\frac{2}{6}$ $-\frac{2}{6}$

20. $\frac{6}{10}$ $-\frac{5}{10}$

21. $\frac{7}{8}$ $-\frac{6}{8}$

22. $\frac{7}{12}$ $-\frac{5}{12}$

23. $\frac{9}{9}$ $-\frac{7}{9}$

24. $\frac{6}{6}$ $-\frac{5}{6}$

25. $\frac{4}{10}$ $-\frac{3}{10}$

26. $\frac{9}{10}$ $-\frac{6}{10}$

27. $\frac{6}{8}$ $-\frac{3}{8}$

28. $\frac{4}{7}$ $-\frac{2}{7}$

29. $\frac{4}{5}$ $-\frac{2}{5}$

30. $\frac{8}{9}$ $-\frac{2}{9}$

31. $\frac{4}{5}$ $-\frac{3}{5}$

32. $\frac{6}{7}$ $-\frac{3}{7}$

Solve.

33. Larry grew $\frac{7}{8}$ inch in height and Bob grew $\frac{5}{8}$ inch in height. How much more did Larry grow?

34. Albert grew $\frac{3}{4}$ inch in height and Lucky grew $\frac{1}{4}$ inch in height. How much more did Albert grow?

Subtract. Write the difference in simplest form.

1. $\frac{2}{3} - \frac{2}{9}$ **2.** $\frac{4}{5} - \frac{3}{10}$ **3.** $\frac{3}{4} - \frac{3}{8}$

4. $\frac{5}{6} - \frac{1}{12}$ **5.** $\frac{7}{10} - \frac{3}{5}$ **6.** $\frac{8}{20} - \frac{4}{10}$

7. $\frac{7}{10} - \frac{1}{5}$ **8.** $\frac{1}{2} - \frac{3}{12}$ **9.** $\frac{5}{9} - \frac{1}{3}$

10. $\frac{3}{4} - \frac{1}{8}$ **11.** $\frac{5}{6} - \frac{2}{3}$ **12.** $\frac{5}{6} - \frac{3}{12}$

13. $\begin{array}{r} \frac{5}{6} \\ -\frac{1}{3} \\ \hline \end{array}$ **14.** $\begin{array}{r} \frac{9}{10} \\ -\frac{1}{2} \\ \hline \end{array}$ **15.** $\begin{array}{r} \frac{7}{8} \\ -\frac{3}{4} \\ \hline \end{array}$ **16.** $\begin{array}{r} \frac{2}{3} \\ -\frac{1}{9} \\ \hline \end{array}$ **17.** $\begin{array}{r} \frac{3}{5} \\ -\frac{1}{10} \\ \hline \end{array}$

18. $\begin{array}{r} \frac{5}{6} \\ -\frac{1}{2} \\ \hline \end{array}$ **19.** $\begin{array}{r} \frac{5}{10} \\ -\frac{2}{5} \\ \hline \end{array}$ **20.** $\begin{array}{r} \frac{6}{8} \\ -\frac{3}{4} \\ \hline \end{array}$ **21.** $\begin{array}{r} \frac{5}{6} \\ -\frac{1}{2} \\ \hline \end{array}$ **22.** $\begin{array}{r} \frac{1}{3} \\ -\frac{3}{9} \\ \hline \end{array}$

23. $\begin{array}{r} \frac{8}{10} \\ -\frac{1}{2} \\ \hline \end{array}$ **24.** $\begin{array}{r} \frac{3}{4} \\ -\frac{1}{2} \\ \hline \end{array}$ **25.** $\begin{array}{r} \frac{2}{3} \\ -\frac{3}{9} \\ \hline \end{array}$ **26.** $\begin{array}{r} \frac{2}{3} \\ -\frac{4}{9} \\ \hline \end{array}$ **27.** $\begin{array}{r} \frac{5}{10} \\ -\frac{1}{5} \\ \hline \end{array}$

28. $\begin{array}{r} \frac{4}{6} \\ -\frac{1}{2} \\ \hline \end{array}$ **29.** $\begin{array}{r} \frac{6}{9} \\ -\frac{2}{3} \\ \hline \end{array}$ **30.** $\begin{array}{r} \frac{1}{2} \\ -\frac{2}{8} \\ \hline \end{array}$ **31.** $\begin{array}{r} \frac{2}{3} \\ -\frac{5}{12} \\ \hline \end{array}$ **32.** $\begin{array}{r} \frac{16}{20} \\ -\frac{1}{5} \\ \hline \end{array}$

Solve.

33. Maria's dog, Sobrina, loves pizza. One day, Maria brought home a Pepperoni Special cut in 10 slices. She ate $\frac{1}{10}$ of the pizza. When she went to get a napkin, Sobrina gobbled up $\frac{2}{5}$ of the pizza. How much of the pizza was left?

Add or subtract. Write the answer in simplest form.

1. $3\frac{3}{7} + 6\frac{2}{7}$

2. $10\frac{2}{5} + 9\frac{1}{5}$

3. $5\frac{3}{10} + 3\frac{4}{10}$

4. $14\frac{2}{4} + 7\frac{1}{4}$

5. $6\frac{3}{4} + 7\frac{1}{4}$

6. $4\frac{8}{10} + 2\frac{1}{10}$

7. $3\frac{2}{8} - 3\frac{1}{8}$

8. $7\frac{3}{4} - 5\frac{1}{4}$

9. $14\frac{2}{3} - 3\frac{1}{3}$

10. $6\frac{7}{8} - 6\frac{7}{8}$

11. $8\frac{1}{4} - 4\frac{1}{4}$

12. $9\frac{2}{3} - 6\frac{1}{3}$

13. $4\frac{2}{5}$
$+ 8\frac{3}{5}$

14. $16\frac{3}{4}$
$+ 12\frac{1}{4}$

15. $9\frac{3}{9}$
$+ 5\frac{2}{9}$

16. $6\frac{5}{6}$
$+ 5\frac{1}{3}$

17. $3\frac{1}{5}$
$+ 2\frac{3}{5}$

18. $9\frac{5}{6}$
$- 7\frac{1}{6}$

19. $18\frac{5}{8}$
$- 10\frac{3}{8}$

20. $15\frac{8}{9}$
$- 6\frac{6}{9}$

21. $7\frac{3}{4}$
$- 4\frac{1}{4}$

22. $6\frac{6}{7}$
$- 2\frac{4}{7}$

23. $6\frac{5}{8}$
$- 2\frac{2}{8}$

24. $7\frac{5}{6}$
$+ 7\frac{1}{6}$

25. $14\frac{5}{6}$
$- 8\frac{2}{6}$

26. $12\frac{5}{10}$
$+ 5\frac{3}{10}$

27. $9\frac{2}{3}$
$- 4\frac{2}{3}$

28. $10\frac{2}{4}$
$+ 2\frac{1}{4}$

29. $6\frac{8}{9}$
$- 4\frac{2}{9}$

30. $3\frac{7}{20}$
$+ 6\frac{13}{20}$

31. $11\frac{4}{7}$
$- 3\frac{1}{7}$

32. $7\frac{2}{8}$
$+ 2\frac{2}{8}$

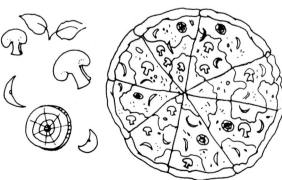
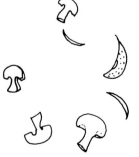

Make a list, and solve.

1. A group of tourists is visiting Paris. They can visit 2 places each day. The tourists can go to a museum, a store, a park, or a theater. How many different combinations of 2 events are there?

2. The Louvre is a famous French museum. The group can visit 2 displays before lunch. They can see statues, paintings, drawings, furniture, or coins. How many combinations of 2 displays are there?

3. The group goes to a store. One man realizes he has enough money to buy only 3 items. He can buy a tie, a shirt, a hat, or socks. How many combinations of items can he buy?

4. The Luxembourg Gardens is a famous park in Paris. One woman sees a fruit stand in the park. She can buy apples, bananas, pears, peaches, oranges, or grapes. She decides to buy 3 kinds of fruit. How many combinations of 3 kinds of fruit can she buy?

5. The group goes to the theater. They can buy tickets for sections A, B, C, D, or E. They buy tickets for 3 of the sections. How many combinations of tickets could they have bought?

6. One tourist has collected 7 different French stamps. She takes 3 of the stamps from her purse. How many combinations of stamps could she have taken from her purse?

Make a list and solve.

1. The tourists plan to show slides, films, and photographs. Their friends will have time to see only 2 of them. How many possible combinations are there?

2. One man has collected 6 travel posters. He will place 2 posters in the hall. How many possible combinations of posters can he show in the hall?

3. The tourists bought postcards in France. There are 4 different postcards about France. 2 postcards cost a quarter. How many combinations of different postcards are there?

4. The tourists also bought packages of French wildflower seeds. There are 8 different kinds of wildflower seeds. 2 packets of seeds cost a quarter. How many possible combinations of seeds could they have bought?

5. One tourist bought 6 different packages of seeds. She plans to give 3 packages to each of 2 friends. From how many possible combinations did she select the packages of seeds?

6. A tourist bought 2 different photographs. He chose from the Eiffel Tower, the Louvre, the Seine River, and the Arc de Triomphe. How many possible combinations could he have selected?

7. Copies of 6 of the slides used in the show can be purchased. You can buy 2 of the same slide or 2 different slides. 2 slides cost $1.00. How many possible combinations of slides could be bought for $1.00?

Write a decimal for the picture.

1.

2.

3.

Write a decimal for each.

4. $4\frac{2}{10}$

5. $\frac{7}{10}$

6. $12\frac{1}{10}$

7. $38\frac{9}{10}$

8. $83\frac{4}{10}$

9. $72\frac{6}{10}$

10. $19\frac{2}{10}$

11. $\frac{8}{10}$

12. $17\frac{3}{10}$

Write in words.

13. 1.2

14. 24.3

15. 5.1

16. 31.9

17. 10.8

18. 0.1

19. 6.2

20. 16.8

Use the number lines to help solve the riddle. Match the letter under the numbers on the number lines to the numbers at the bottom of the page.

1.0	1.1	1.2	1.3	1.4	1.5	1.6	1.7	1.8	1.9	2.0
A	B	C	D	E	F	G	H	I	J	K

6.0	6.1	6.2	6.3	6.4	6.5	6.6	6.7	6.8	6.9	7.0
L	M	N	O	P	Q	R	S	T	U	V

What has a mouth and a fork but never eats?

?	?	?	?	?	?
1.0	6.6	1.8	7.0	1.4	6.6

Write a decimal for the picture.

1.

2.

Write a decimal for each.

3. $2\frac{18}{100}$

4. $13\frac{64}{100}$

5. $\frac{25}{100}$

6. $4\frac{6}{100}$

7. $\frac{39}{100}$

8. $11\frac{9}{100}$

Write in words.

9. 2.36

10. 0.71

11. 1.07

12. 11.44

13. 0.03

14. 0.12

Write each decimal named in the place-value chart.

Hundreds	Tens	Ones	Tenths	Hundredths
		4	5	6
1	0	0	2	9
	3	3	3	3
2	6	5	0	2

15. 4.56   30.33   10.29   127.31

16. 45.6   3.333   26.502   100.29

17. 33.33   0.456   1.29   26.52

18. 10.29   265.02   333.33   45.06

Compare. Write >, <, or = .

1. 0.25 ◯ 2.5

2. 12.1 ◯ 0.67

3. 0.3 ◯ 0.30

4. 6.40 ◯ 6.04

5. 0.75 ◯ 0.38

6. 8.2 ◯ 8.20

7. 1.1 ◯ 1.11

8. 5.3 ◯ 3.97

9. 7.08 ◯ 7.12

Write in order from the greatest to the least.

10. 6.4, 6.41, 6.04

11. 38.5, 3.85, 8.35

Write in order from the least to the greatest.

12. 31.10, 13.01, 3.10, 31.01

13. 0.25, 0.05, 0.30, 2.25

Write the numbers from Group A from the least to the
greatest up the mountain. Write the numbers from Group B
from the greatest to the least down the mountain.

Group A: 1.06, 0.07, 3.69, 0.12, 0.25, 1.55, 3.8

Group B: 40.50, 41.77, 44.38, 40.05, 43.99, 42.01, 40.88

Group A _____ ? _____ ? _____ Group B

? ?

? ?

? ?

? ?

? ?

? ?

LODGE

Round to the nearest whole number.

1. 7.51   **2.** 16.3   **3.** 3.8   **4.** 4.47

5. 98.6   **6.** 3.12   **7.** 0.91   **8.** 5.01

Estimate.

9.   1.25
     + 6.78

10.   31.2
     + 8.8

11. $46.01
     + 29.91

12.   12.4
     + 6.9

13. $22.03
     + 11.90

14.   2.65
     + 8.32

15. $7.68
     + 6.95

16. $20.01
     + 32.22

17.   49.7
     + 3.0

18. $37.65
     +   2.10

19.   9.82
     − 6.47

20.   73.5
     − 42.1

21. $7.88
     − 5.30

22.   4.33
     − 1.58

23. $6.72
     − 3.49

24. $4.74
     − 2.49

25.   11.2
     − 8.9

26.   3.69
     − 2.25

27.   11.11
     − 9.02

28. $33.01
     − 20.90

Solve.

Franny Frugal kept a record of the gasoline she put in her car during the week.

29. Estimate how much it cost Franny for gasoline that week.

	Gallons	Cost
Monday	12.8	$17.66
Thursday	14.3	$19.31

30. Estimate how much more gasoline Franny put in the car on Thursday than on Monday.

Add.

1. 1.43
    + 2.12

2. $0.82
    + 0.62

3. 0.34
    + 2.45

4. 11.01
    + 29.30

5. $15.30
    + 3.24

6. 1.12
    + 0.57

7. $56.98
    + 22.83

8. 37.01
    + 9.90

9. 12.9
    + 48.6

10. 37.23
    + 0.36

11. 4.3
    + 7.3

12. 18.52
    + 61.14

13. 1.01
    + 0.06

14. 29.9
    + 21.6

15. 32.38
    + 27.17

16. $47.82
    + 64.22

17. 25.29
    + 46.69

18. 11.43
    + 11.62

19. 23.05
    + 13.69

20. 9.52
    + 4.31

21. 45.73
    + 19.58

22. 36.04
    + 9.09

23. 2.95
    + 14.86

24. 75.44
    + 6.87

25. 94.02
    +   .09

26. 3.88
    + 11.87

27. 19.99
    + 8.55

28. 23.08
    + 16.78

29. 55.44
    + 3.99

30. 3.79
    + 11.38

31. $44.89
    + 12.35

32. 35.60
    + 14.33

33. 67.06
    + 8.97

34. 13.45
    + 33.48

35. $17.38
    + 25.79

Subtract.

| 1. | $35.60 − 23.12 | 2. | 69.00 − 5.98 | 3. | 29.12 − 15.47 | 4. | $77.05 − 9.86 | 5. | 8.94 − 2.66 |

| 6. | 32.99 − 20.14 | 7. | 34.03 − 9.28 | 8. | 6.92 − 1.04 | 9. | $12.50 − 1.00 | 10. | 5.2 − 3.1 |

| 11. | 76.98 − 11.84 | 12. | 8.3 − 1.75 | 13. | 12.05 − 9.99 | 14. | $70.81 − 12.99 | 15. | 26.04 − 2.98 |

| 16. | 0.81 − 0.27 | 17. | 0.98 − 0.09 | 18. | 11.26 − 5.78 | 19. | $27.60 − 3.81 | 20. | 5.6 − 4.93 |

21. $26.97 − $10.00

22. 56.1 − 2.37

23. $4.29 − $0.87

24. 86.54 − 29.99

25. 47.29 − 3.03

26. $37.50 − $9.85

27. 9.4 − 1.77

28. 5.8 − 0.96

Solve.

29. The Commen Geddit Lunch Wagon is raising the price of its Banana Savanna Yogurt Shakes. At the old price, the wagon made $75.25 each week selling shakes. Now they will make $98.50 each week. How much more money will they make each week?

30. Tyrone buys lunch at the Commen Geddit Lunch Wagon. His lunch costs $3.85. How much change does he receive from $5.00?

Banana Savanna Yogurt

Use simpler numbers to write a number sentence. Then, use the numbers in the problem, and solve.

1. Terry has $123.46 in his savings account. He wants to buy a bicycle for $98.95. How much will be left in his account?

2. Terry's father offers to pay $14.95 for a special mirror and $21.95 for a horn. How much will the bike cost with all these extra items?

3. Terry and his friends plan to take a bike trip. They will leave on July 28. They will be gone for 14 days. On what date will they return?

4. Terry will have to buy his own food for 8 days of the trip. He figures that lunch will cost about $3.75 each day. Dinner will cost about $5.75 each day. About how much will he spend for lunch and dinner for 8 days?

5. Terry wants to buy postage stamps so he can mail postcards to his friends. A postcard stamp costs $0.14. How much will 9 postcard stamps cost?

6. Terry gives the clerk $2.00 to pay for the 9 postcard stamps. How much change will he get?

7. Terry figures that he travels about one mile every 5 minutes on his bike. How many miles will Terry travel in 1 hour if he travels at the same rate of speed?

Measure to the nearest centimeter.

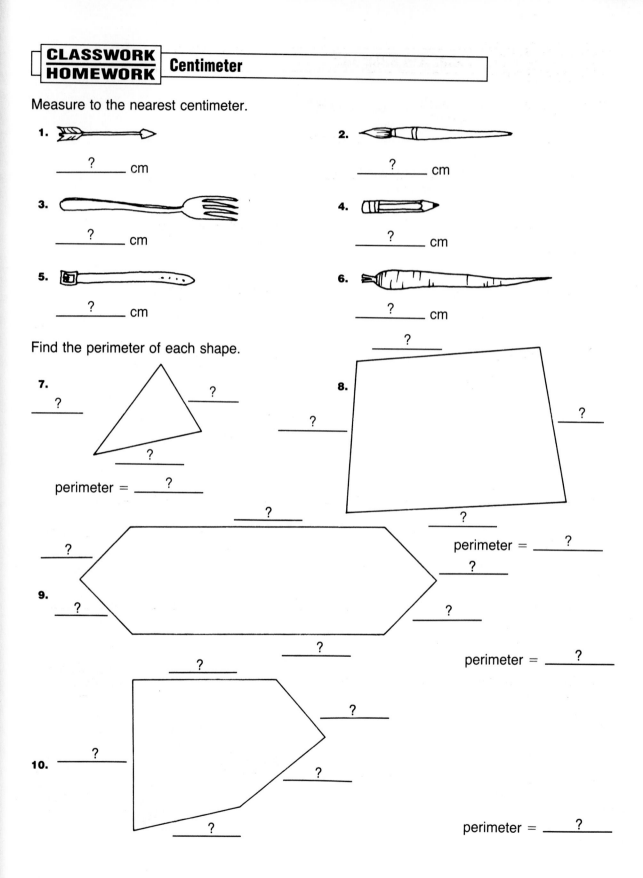

1. _____?_____ cm

2. _____?_____ cm

3. _____?_____ cm

4. _____?_____ cm

5. _____?_____ cm

6. _____?_____ cm

Find the perimeter of each shape.

7. perimeter = _____?_____

8. perimeter = _____?_____

9. perimeter = _____?_____

10. perimeter = _____?_____

Write the abbreviation for each.

1. kilometer

2. centimeter

3. meter

Write *cm*, *m*, or *km* for the unit you would use to measure each.

4. the length of a pair of scissors

5. the width of notebook paper

6. the distance across the United States

7. the height of a stove

8. the height of a telephone pole

9. the length of a fork

10. the length of a car

11. the distance across the Pacific Ocean

Complete.

12. 6 m = ___?___ cm

13. 6 km = ___?___ m

14. 4 km = ___?___ m

15. 100 cm = ___?___ m

16. 9,000 m = ___?___ km

17. 800 cm = ___?___ m

18. 3,000 m = ___?___ km

19. 15,000 m = ___?___ km

20. 2 m = ___?___ cm

21. 27 m = ___?___ cm

22. 20 km = ___?___ m

23. 48,000 m = ___?___ km

Solve.

24. Lynn travels from home to school. Then she goes to the park. How many kilometers does Lynn travel?

25. How many meters is it from the park to Lynn's house?

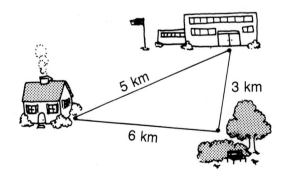

5 km

3 km

6 km

Write *mL* or *L* for the unit you would use to measure each.

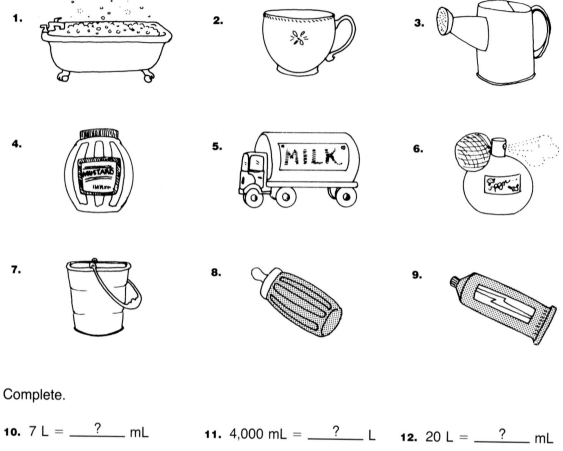

1.   2.   3.

4.   5.   6.

7.   8.   9.

Complete.

10. 7 L = _____?_____ mL   **11.** 4,000 mL = _____?_____ L   **12.** 20 L = _____?_____ mL

13. 11,000 mL = _____?_____ L   **14.** 3 L = _____?_____ mL   **15.** 55,000 mL = _____?_____ L

16. 1 L = _____?_____ mL   **17.** 10 L = _____?_____ mL   **18.** 35,000 mL = _____?_____ L

19. 2,000 mL = _____?_____ L   **20.** 8,000 mL = _____?_____ L   **21.** 9 L = _____?_____ mL

22. 5 L = _____?_____ mL   **23.** 12,000 mL = _____?_____ L   **24.** 50 L = _____?_____ mL

25. 1,000 mL = _____?_____ L   **26.** 17 L = _____?_____ mL   **27.** 100 L = _____?_____ mL

28. 10 L = _____?_____ mL   **29.** 20,000 mL = _____?_____ L   **30.** 6 L = _____?_____ mL

Write *g* or *kg* for the unit you would use to measure each.

1.   **2.**   **3.**

4.   **5.**   **6.**

7. a chair   **8.** a paper bag   **9.** a dictionary

10. a cracker   **11.** a pony   **12.** a mouse

13. a cup   **14.** a postage stamp   **15.** a dump truck

Complete.

16. 7,000 g = ___?___ kg   **17.** 37 kg = ___?___ g   **18.** 2,000 g = ___?___ kg

19. 6 kg = ___?___ g   **20.** 9,000 g = ___?___ kg   **21.** 6,000 g = ___?___ kg

22. 23 kg = ___?___ g   **23.** 7 kg = ___?___ g   **24.** 3 kg = ___?___ g

25. 14 kg = ___?___ g   **26.** 15,000 g = ___?___ kg   **27.** 4 kg = ___?___ g

28. 18 kg = ___?___ g   **29.** 1 kg = ___?___ g   **30.** 10 kg = ___?___ g

Draw a picture or make a model to solve each problem.

1. Orlando is giving his friend Rudy directions to his house. Orlando tells Rudy to turn left from Rudy's front door and go 3 blocks, turn right and go 5 blocks more, and then turn left again. Then he should go two blocks to Orlando's house. How many blocks is it from Rudy's house to Orlando's house?

2. Marty and his father are planning to put wood paneling along one wall of Marty's room. The wall is 10 feet long and 8 feet tall. The paneling comes in 4-feet by 8-feet sheets.

   a. How many pieces of paneling will Marty and his father need to buy?

   b. How much of the paneling will they actually use?

3. Mario is taller than Andrew and shorter than Rebecca. Rebecca is taller than Jill. Who is the tallest?

4. Gina was watching the circus parade. She saw the lions after the giraffes. She saw the clowns after the lions and before the elephants. What did Gina see first?

5. Phil made his bed before he ate breakfast. He picked up his toys after he put on his shoes but before he made his bed. What did Phil do first?

6. Shelly is putting away her little brother's alphabet blocks. The tray that holds the blocks is 14 inches long and 8 inches wide. Each block is 2 inches long and 2 inches wide. How many blocks will fit in the tray?

7. Mr. Wendell's class planted a garden for a science project. They planted more carrots than beans. They planted fewer peas than carrots, but more peas than squash. They planted fewer squash plants than beans. Of which vegetable did they plant the most?

8. Jennifer is putting her books in her new bookcase. The top 2 shelves of the bookcase hold 9 books each. The other 3 shelves hold 12 books each. How many books will her new bookcase hold?

Make a guess and check your work to solve each problem.

1. Carla is in the fourth grade. She multiplies her age times itself 3 times. Her final answer is 729. How old is she?

2. Her friend, Jeb, multiplies his age times itself 4 times. His final answer is 4,096. How old is Jeb?

3. Jerry is 9 years older than his sister, Fay. In 3 years, he will be twice as old as his sister. How old are Jerry and Fay right now?

4. Right now, Alan's mother is 4 times older than he is. In 4 years, she will be 3 times older than he is. How old are Alan and his mother right now?

5. Kim is using a list of his friends' ages. He adds two of his friends' ages and gets 17. He multiplies the ages and gets 72. How old are his two friends?

6. Kim adds two more friends' ages and gets 21. He multiplies the ages and gets 108. How old are his two friends?

7. Today, Lena's dog is 3 times as old as her cat. In three years, the dog will be two years older than the cat. How old will the dog and the cat be in 3 years?

Ten students decided to make art projects using the letters in their names. Use the list of students' names to solve each problem.

Jo Ruiz	Jenny Meyer
Tom Brown	Sam Dodd
Ricky Montrose	Juan Ramirez
Ricardo Corrios	Hu Lee
Marcus Danver	Maria Rosa

1. Two of the students made a poster using the letters in their names. The sum of the letters is 23. The product is 130. Which students made the poster?

2. Two of the students made a macrame hanging using the letters in their names. The sum is 18, and the product is 72. Which students made the macrame hanging?

3. Two of the students made a mobile using the letters in their names. The sum is 14, the product is 45. Which students made the mobile?

4. Two of the students hooked a rug using the letters in their names. The sum of the letters is 21, and the product is 98. Which students made the rug?

5. Two of the students made a fabric hanging using the letters in their names. The sum is 19, and the product is 88. Which students made the fabric hanging?

Measure each length.

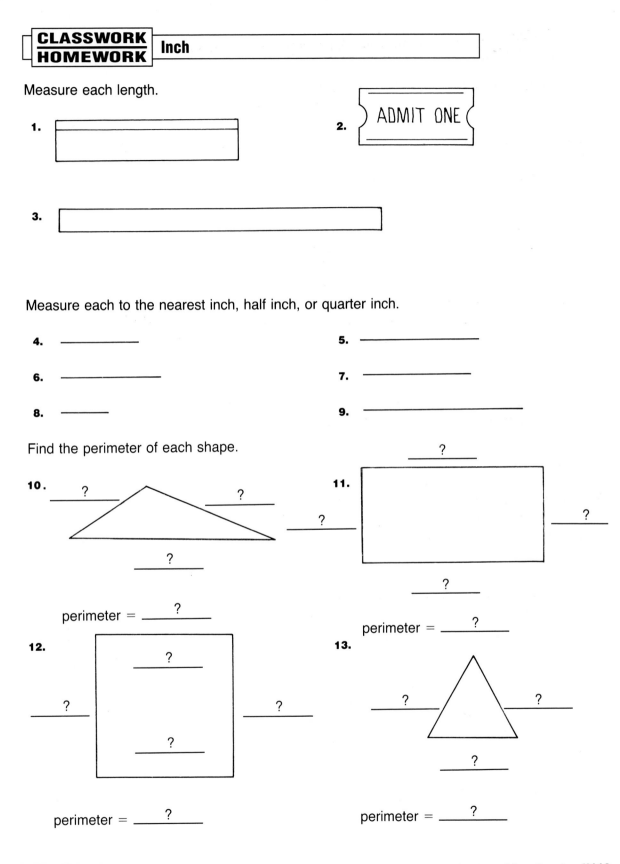

1.

2.) ADMIT ONE (

3.

Measure each to the nearest inch, half inch, or quarter inch.

4. _____

5. _____

6. _____

7. _____

8. ____

9. _____

Find the perimeter of each shape.

10.
?
?
?
?

perimeter = ___?___

11.
?
?
?
?

perimeter = ___?___

12.
?
?
?
?

perimeter = ___?___

13.
?
?
?

perimeter = ___?___

Write *in.*, *ft*, *yd*, or *mi* for the unit you would use to measure each.

1. the height of a swing set

2. the length of the highway

3. the distance across a pond

4. the height of a flower

5. the length of a hiking trail

6. the length of a park bench

7. the distance between the park and the city

8. the length of a bird's nest

Complete.

9. 24 in. = _____?_____ ft

10. 1 yd = _____?_____ ft

11. 1,760 yd = _____?_____ mi

12. 1 mi = _____?_____ ft

13. 3 ft = _____?_____ in.

14. 4 yd = _____?_____ ft

15. 15 ft = _____?_____ yd

16. 50 yd = _____?_____ ft

17. 36 in. = _____?_____ ft

18. 5,280 ft = _____?_____ mi

19. 7 ft = _____?_____ in.

20. 6 yd = _____?_____ ft

Solve.

21. Cynthia kicks a football 15 yards. How many feet is this?

22. Jason throws a football 21 feet. How many yards is this?

Write *oz*, *lb*, or *T* for the unit you would use to measure each.

1. a pair of glasses

2. a train engine

3. a large bag of flour

4. a chair

5. a garbage truck

6. a tomato

Complete.

7. 4 T = ____?____ lb

8. 4 lb = ____?____ oz

9. 48 oz = ____?____ lb

10. 1 T = ____?____ lb

11. 16 oz = ____?____ lb

12. 2,000 lb = ____?____ T

13. 8 lb = ____?____ oz

14. 6 lb = ____?____ oz

15. 2 T = ____?____ lb

16. 112 oz = ____?____ lb

Write *oz*, *lb*, or *T* to tell which unit you would use to measure.

17.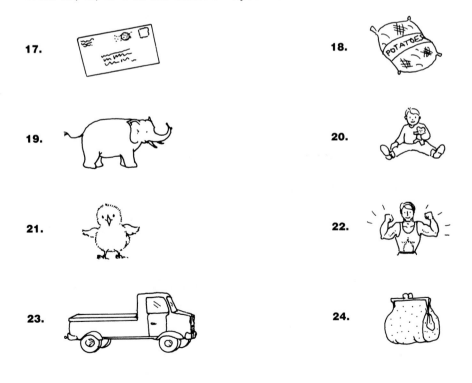

18.

19.

20.

21.

22.

23.

24.

Write the unit you would use to measure the capacity of each.

1. large container of milk   cup   or   gallon

2. small amount of ice cream   pint   or   quart

3. can of oil for a car   quart   or   pint

4. tank of gas for a truck   gallon   or   cup

5. amount of water in a glass   cup   or   quart

Complete.

6. 5 qt = ___?___ pt

7. 2 gal = ___?___ qt

8. 3 pt = ___?___ c

9. 10 pt = ___?___ c

10. 8 qt = ___?___ pt

11. 7 gal = ___?___ qt

12. 6 c = ___?___ pt

13. 8 pt = ___?___ qt

14. 16 c = ___?___ pt

15. 4 gal = ___?___ qt

16. 28 qt = ___?___ gal

17. 12 pt = ___?___ qt

18. 8 c = ___?___ pt

19. 10 gal = ___?___ qt

20. 32 qt = ___?___ gal

Write the letter of the equivalent measure.

21. 1 gal	a. 2 gal	28. 1 qt	h. 4 qt
22. 1 pt	b. 3 pt	29. 16 c	i. 3 qt
23. 6 c	c. 3 qt	30. 3 gal	j. 5 pt
24. 8 qt	d. 4 c	31. 6 pt	k. 2 pt
25. 6 pt	e. 4 qt	32. 16 c	l. 12 qt
26. 5 qt	f. 2 c	33. 10 c	m. 1 qt
27. 2 pt	g. 10 pt	34. 2 pt	n. 1 gal

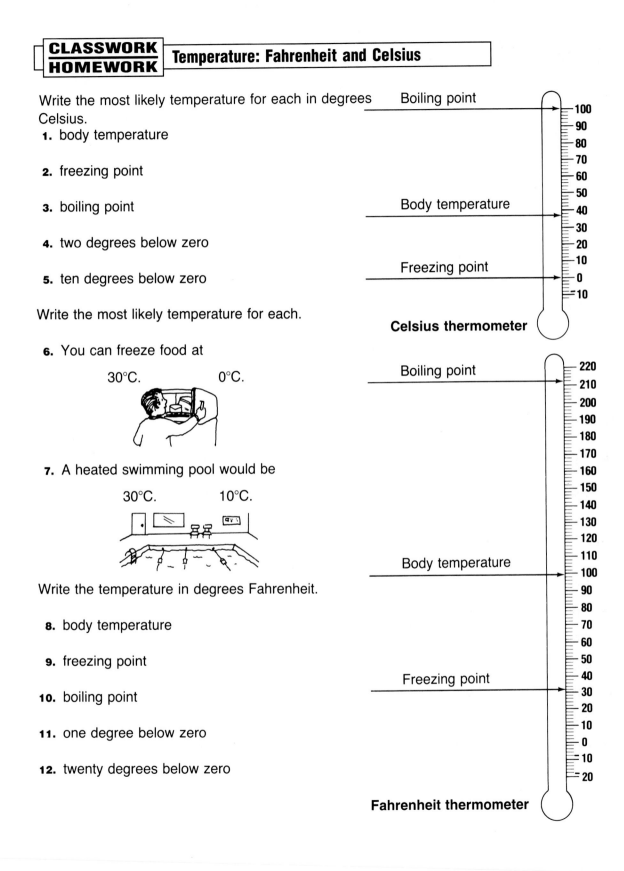

Write the most likely temperature for each in degrees Celsius.

1. body temperature

2. freezing point

3. boiling point

4. two degrees below zero

5. ten degrees below zero

Write the most likely temperature for each.

6. You can freeze food at

      30°C.   0°C.

7. A heated swimming pool would be

      30°C.   10°C.

Write the temperature in degrees Fahrenheit.

8. body temperature

9. freezing point

10. boiling point

11. one degree below zero

12. twenty degrees below zero

Boiling point — 100
— 90
— 80
— 70
— 60
— 50
Body temperature — 40
— 30
— 20
— 10
Freezing point — 0
— 10

Celsius thermometer

Boiling point — 220
— 210
— 200
— 190
— 180
— 170
— 160
— 150
— 140
— 130
— 120
— 110
Body temperature — 100
— 90
— 80
— 70
— 60
— 50
Freezing point — 40
— 30
— 20
— 10
— 0
— 10
— 20

Fahrenheit thermometer

Write the letter of the information you need to solve the problem. Use the information to solve the problem.

1. Mr. Hendrix brought 9 feet of rags to school. His class was going to make a rag rug. How many inches of rags did he bring?

2. Justin can braid 1 foot of rug in 1 hour. How long will it take him to braid 2 yards?

3. It takes Lisa 25 minutes to braid 5 yards of the rug. How many minutes did it take her to braid 3 feet?

a. 12 items = 1 dozen
b. 24 hours = 1 day
c. 12 inches = 1 foot
d. 3 feet = 1 yard
e. 60 seconds = 1 minute
f. 60 minutes = 1 hour
g. 8 ounces = 1 cup
h. 4 quarts = 1 gallon
i. 2 pints = 1 quart
j. 16 ounces = 1 pound
k. 144 items = 1 gross

4. Jeb brought 3 pounds of health bread for his friends to eat while they work. How many ounces of health bread is that?

5. Tina made fruit punch for the class. She made 12 quarts of punch. How many gallons did she make?

6. Mr. Hendrix sliced 3 pounds of health bread. He gave each student 6 ounces of bread. To how many students did he give bread?

7. Andy brought a gross of pins to school to use before the rug was sewn. How many pins did he bring?

8. Students popped popcorn to eat while they worked. They used 4 ounces of kernels. This made 2 quarts of popcorn. How many ounces would they need to make 1 gallon?

9. Rhea worked for 4 hours, gathering and sorting rags for the rug. How many minutes did she work?

Name each line segment two ways.

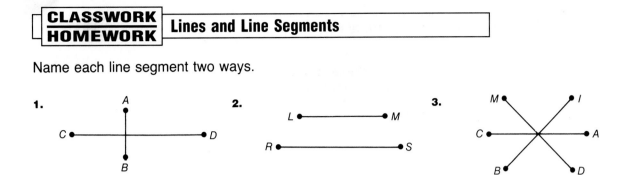

1. **2.** **3.**

Write *parallel* or *intersecting* to describe each pair of lines.

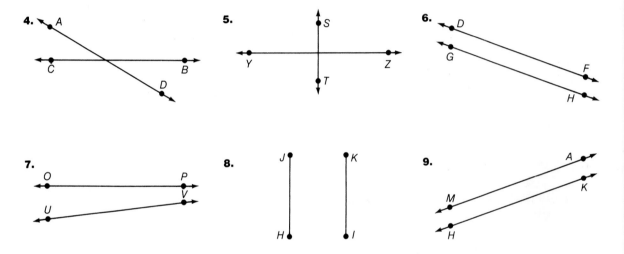

4. **5.** **6.**

7. **8.** **9.**

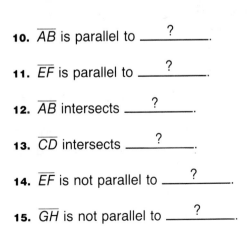

Use the drawing to find each answer.

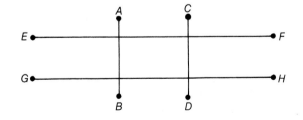

10. $\overline{AB}$ is parallel to ____?____.

11. $\overline{EF}$ is parallel to ____?____.

12. $\overline{AB}$ intersects ____?____.

13. $\overline{CD}$ intersects ____?____.

14. $\overline{EF}$ is not parallel to ____?____.

15. $\overline{GH}$ is not parallel to ____?____.

Write the name of each ray.

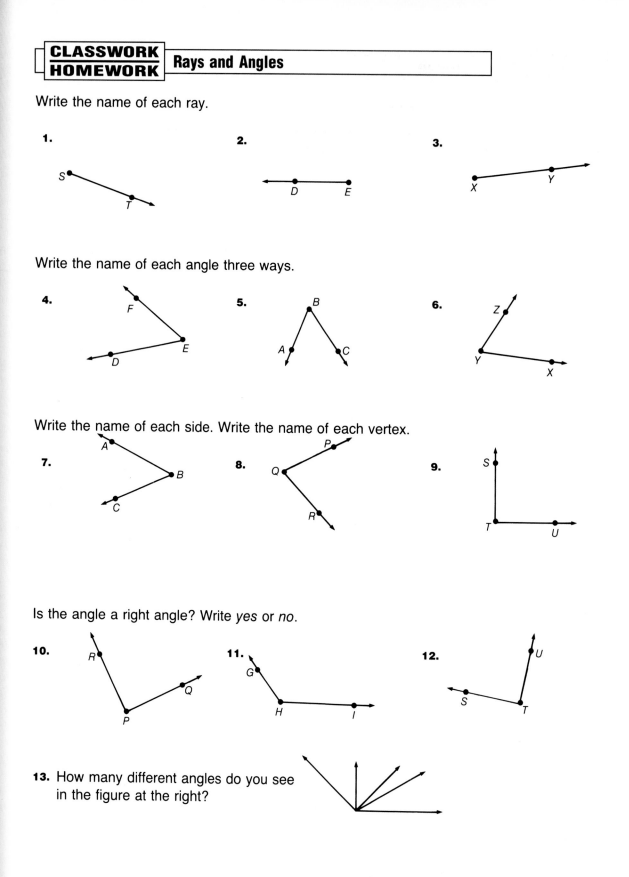

1.

2.

3.

Write the name of each angle three ways.

4.

5.

6.

Write the name of each side. Write the name of each vertex.

7.

8.

9.

Is the angle a right angle? Write *yes* or *no*.

10.

11.

12.

13. How many different angles do you see in the figure at the right?

Write a word from the box to name each shape.

triangle	pentagon	hexagon	octagon
square	rectangle	quadrilateral	

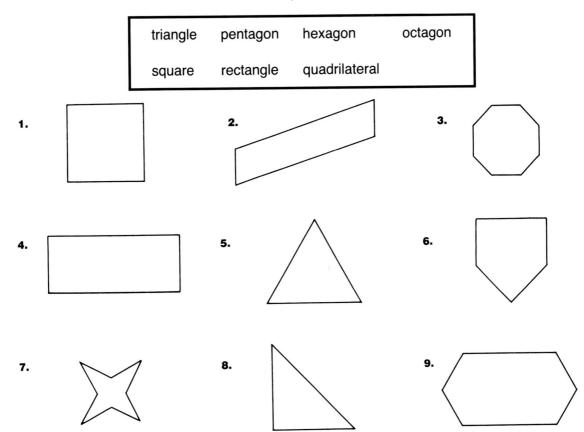

1.

2.

3.

4.

5.

6.

7.

8.

9.

Write the number of sides and vertices for each.

10. hexagon

sides: ___?___

vertices: ___?___

11. octagon

sides: ___?___

vertices: ___?___

12. square

sides: ___?___

vertices: ___?___

Look carefully at the figure on the right.

13. How many triangles do you see?

14. How many squares do you see?

Write a word from the box that describes the part shown.

| radius diameter center |

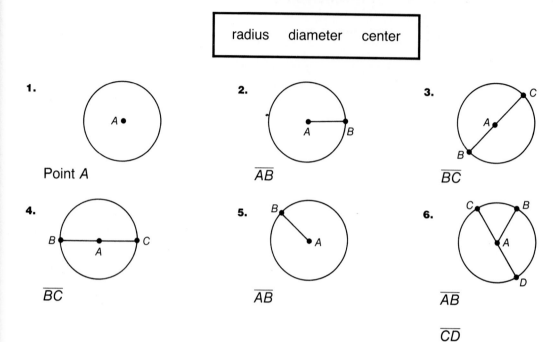

1.

Point A

2.

$\overline{AB}$

3.

$\overline{BC}$

4.

$\overline{BC}$

5.

$\overline{AB}$

6.

$\overline{AB}$

$\overline{CD}$

7. Use a ruler and a compass. Draw a circle with a 1-inch radius. Use point A as the center. Draw radius $\overline{AB}$ and diameter $\overline{CD}$.

A •

8. You can draw a *Compass Rose*. Set your compass at a $\frac{1}{2}$-inch radius. Trace the points. Draw a circle at each point.

Solve each problem. Be sure you have answered the
question.

1. The first state to enter the Union was
Delaware in 1788. The forty-eighth state
was Arizona in 1912. Hawaii was the
fiftieth state in 1959. The greatest
number of years passed between the
statehood of which two states mentioned
in this problem?

2. Hawaii was discovered by Europeans in
1778. It became a state on August 21,
1959. Alaska became a state on January
3, 1959. Did more than 6 months pass
between the entry of the 2 states?

3. The area of New Jersey is 7,836 square
miles. The area of New Mexico is
121,666 square miles. The area of
Nevada is 110,540 square miles. Which
2 states are close in size?

4. Louisiana has 4,438,000 people. They
live in 64 parishes, or counties. Ohio has
10,746,000 people. They live in 88
counties. How many more counties are
there in Ohio?

5. Rhode Island is the smallest state. It
measures 1,055 square miles. Delaware
is the next largest state. It measures
1,932 square miles. Is Delaware twice as
large as Rhode Island?

6. Colorado entered the Union in 1876. Its
state flower is the columbine. The
columbine was chosen in 1899. The
state bird is the lark bunting. It was
chosen in 1931. How old was the state of
Colorado when the state bird was
chosen?

7. There were 33,426 Alaskans in 1880.
Then, 30,000 people went to Alaska
during the Gold Rush of 1898. Today,
there are 479,000 people in Alaska. How
many more people are in Alaska today
than were there in 1880?

8. North Carolina became a state on
November 21, 1789. It has 100 counties.
South Carolina became a state on May
23, 1788. It has 46 counties. Does North
Carolina have more than twice as many
counties?

Are these segments and polygons congruent? Write *yes* or *no*.

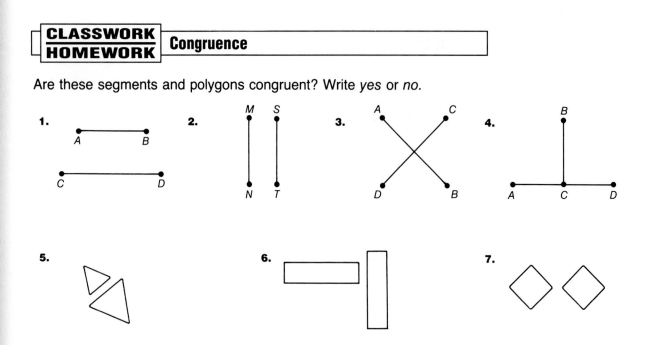

1.

2.

3.

4.

5.

6.

7.

Write *similar* or *congruent*. Some figures may be both.

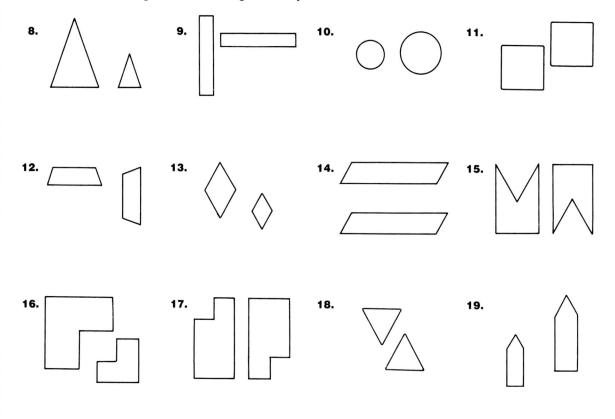

8.

9.

10.

11.

12.

13.

14.

15.

16.

17.

18.

19.

Is the figure symmetrical? Write *yes* or *no*.

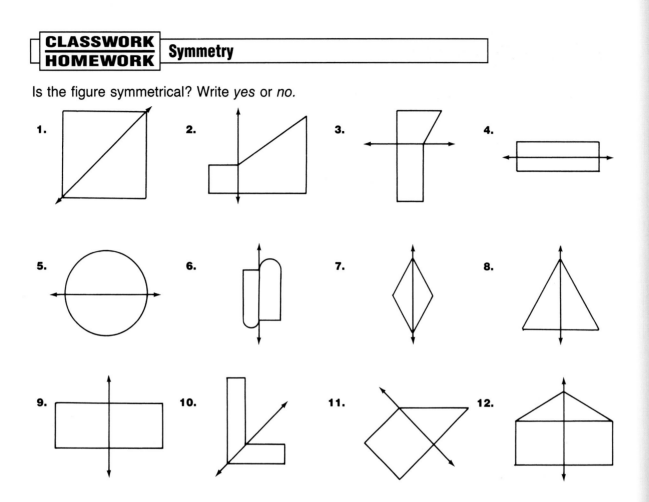

1. 2. 3. 4.

5. 6. 7. 8.

9. 10. 11. 12.

Are the lines drawn through the figures lines of symmetry? Write
yes or *no*.

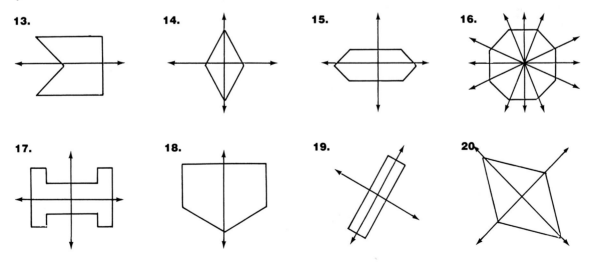

13. 14. 15. 16.

17. 18. 19. 20.

Write the ordered pair for each letter.

1.

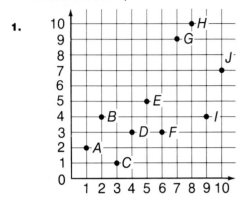

A (____?____)   F (____?____)

B (____?____)   G (____?____)

C (____?____)   H (____?____)

D (____?____)   I (____?____)

E (____?____)   J (____?____)

2. Write the ordered pair for each point on the square.

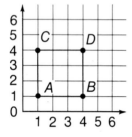

A (____?____)

B (____?____)

C (____?____)

D (____?____)

3. Copy and complete. Graph the points and letters for each ordered pair. Start at A and connect the points in alphabetical order. What figure have you drawn?

C (7,7)   G (5,1)   F (7,1)
H (5,3)   J (5,7)   E (7,3)
K (4,7)   A (6,10)   D (10,3)
B (8,7)   I (2,3)

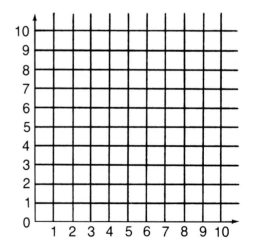

Find the perimeter.

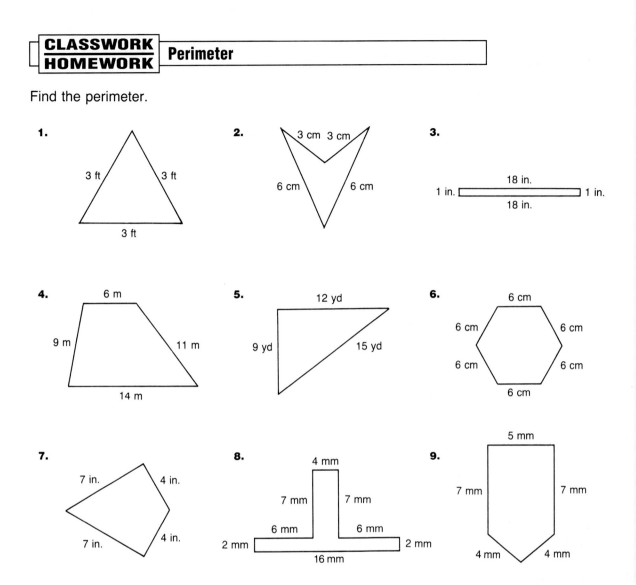

1.

3 ft   3 ft

3 ft

2.

3 cm 3 cm

6 cm   6 cm

3.

18 in.

1 in. [   ] 1 in.

18 in.

4.

6 m

9 m   11 m

14 m

5.

12 yd

9 yd   15 yd

6.

6 cm

6 cm   6 cm

6 cm   6 cm

6 cm

7.

7 in.   4 in.

7 in.   4 in.

8.

4 mm

7 mm   7 mm

6 mm   6 mm

2 mm   2 mm

16 mm

9.

5 mm

7 mm   7 mm

4 mm   4 mm

Solve.

10. The perimeter of a square is 36 m. What is the length of each side?

11. The perimeter of a quadrilateral is 51 cm. The lengths of three of the sides are 6 cm, 12 cm, and 15 cm. What is the length of the fourth side?

Count. Write the area in square units. ☐ = 1 square unit.

1.

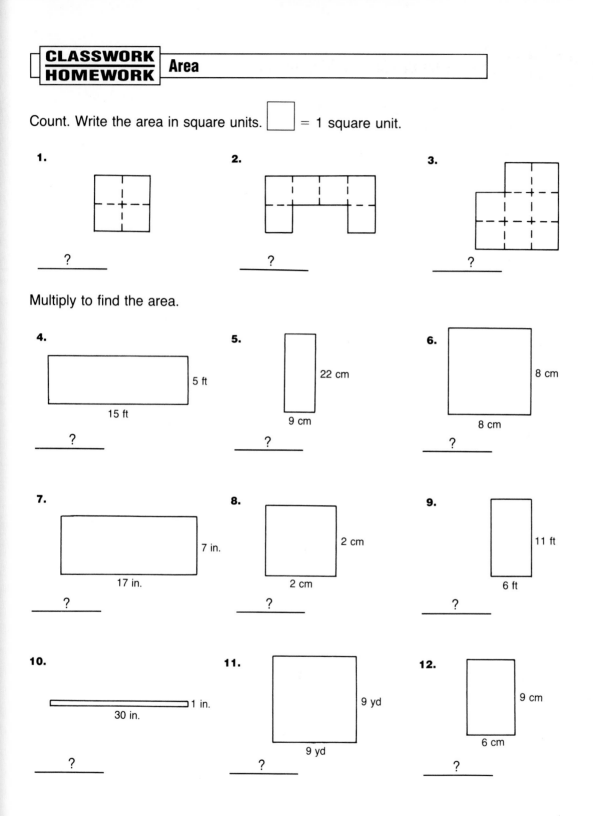

_____?_____

2.

_____?_____

3.

_____?_____

Multiply to find the area.

4.

5 ft

15 ft

_____?_____

5.

22 cm

9 cm

_____?_____

6.

8 cm

8 cm

_____?_____

7.

7 in.

17 in.

_____?_____

8.

2 cm

2 cm

_____?_____

9.

11 ft

6 ft

_____?_____

10.

1 in.

30 in.

_____?_____

11.

9 yd

9 yd

_____?_____

12.

9 cm

6 cm

_____?_____

Use with pages 324–325.

Jenny and her friends are playing a pattern game. Write the missing item or items in each pattern.

1. Jack wrote these numbers on the chalkboard. What are the next two numbers in Jack's pattern?

12 9 18 15 30

2. Linda wrote these names on the chalkboard:

Alice Bill Carla David Emily
Should *Fred* or *Fay* be the next name? Explain your answer.

3. Jerry writes these words on the chalkboard. Suggest two more animals in the pattern. Explain your answer.

duck kangaroo opossum mouse

4. Elena wrote these words on the chalkboard. Write two more words that might appear in Elena's pattern.

I my the five stand

5. Marc wrote these words on the chalkboard.

pink tulip purple heather lavender
Should *violets* or *daffodils* be the next in the pattern?

Explain your answer.

6. Jill wrote this pattern on the chalkboard. Suggest two more numbers in the pattern. Explain your answer.

3 9 11 33 35 105 107

Welcome to the new television game show, TEST PATTERNS! You must find the pattern to win. Good Luck!

1. The host of the show turns the number cards over. Look at the cards. What are the next 4 numbers?

3	6	12	W	I	E	R

2. The cards are collected and turned over again. Write the next 2 numbers in the pattern.

2	6	7	21	22	N	N

3. The cards are collected and turned over again. Write the next 3 numbers in the pattern.

2	8	5	11	R	A	E

4. The cards are collected and turned over again. Write the next 3 numbers in the pattern.

2	4	3	5	Y	U	O

5. Write the numbers in your answers in order from the smallest to the largest. Then write the letters in the answer boxes under the matching numbers. Did you win or lose?

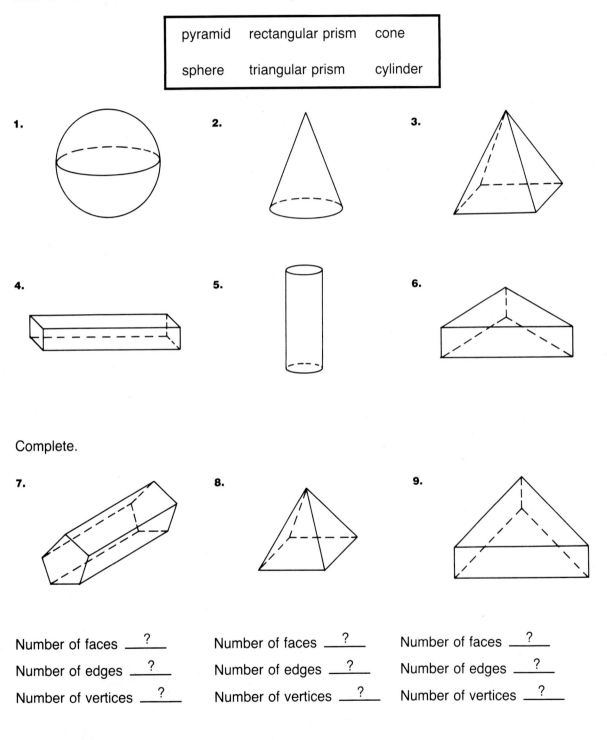

Write a word from the box to name each shape.

pyramid	rectangular prism	cone
sphere	triangular prism	cylinder

1.

2.

3.

4.

5.

6.

Complete.

7.

Number of faces ___?___

Number of edges ___?___

Number of vertices ___?___

8.

Number of faces ___?___

Number of edges ___?___

Number of vertices ___?___

9.

Number of faces ___?___

Number of edges ___?___

Number of vertices ___?___

Find the volume. 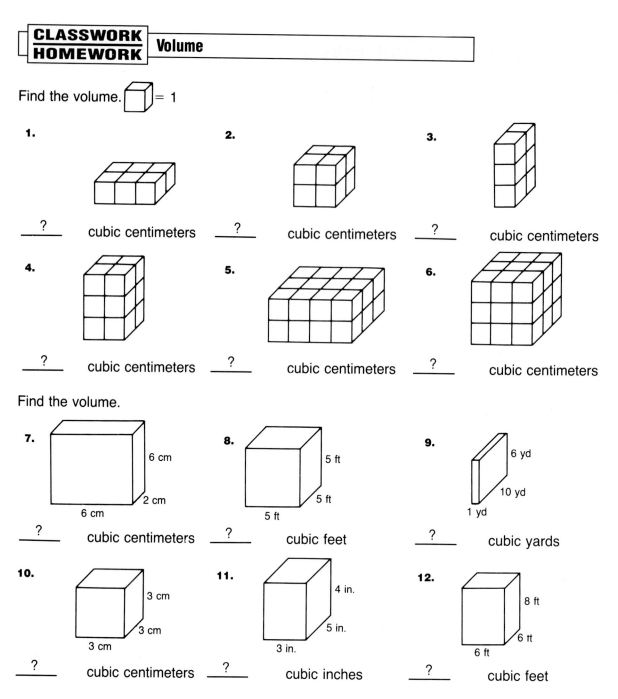 = 1

1.

_____?_____ cubic centimeters

2.

_____?_____ cubic centimeters

3.

_____?_____ cubic centimeters

4.

_____?_____ cubic centimeters

5.

_____?_____ cubic centimeters

6.

_____?_____ cubic centimeters

Find the volume.

7.

6 cm
2 cm
6 cm

_____?_____ cubic centimeters

8.

5 ft
5 ft
5 ft

_____?_____ cubic feet

9.

6 yd
10 yd
1 yd

_____?_____ cubic yards

10.

3 cm
3 cm
3 cm

_____?_____ cubic centimeters

11.

4 in.
5 in.
3 in.

_____?_____ cubic inches

12.

8 ft
6 ft
6 ft

_____?_____ cubic feet

Solve.

13. Apples were shipped in rectangular boxes to the Best Buy Market. Each box was 3 ft long, 2 ft wide, and 2 ft high. Find the volume of each box.

14. A cereal box at the market is 10 in. long, 4 in. wide, and 9 in. high. Find the volume of the cereal box.

The Sunshine Gardens flower farm printed this ad. Use the
information in the ad to solve the problem.

SUNSHINE GARDENS COMPANY

Special Combination of Spring Bulbs

25 Emperor   20 King Alfred   10 Daffodils
  Tulips   Daffodils   Variety
Mixed Colors   Mixture

20 Dutch Iris   25 Crocus   20 Anemones
3-Color Mixture 4-Color Mixture   Mixture

10 Dutch   20 Grape
Hyacinths   Hyacinths
3-Color Mixture   Blue

150 bulbs	REGULAR PRICE	$22.50
add 15% shipping charge		3.38
THE REGULAR COST TO YOU		$25.88
OUR SPECIAL PRICE IN THIS OFFER and this includes		$22.00

the shipping charge! We can ship this order only until
December 20.

---

1. What is the difference between the
regular total cost and the special price?

2. What is the last date on which bulbs can
be shipped?

3. How many hyacinth bulbs are included in
the special offer?

4. How many more iris or anemone bulbs
are there than daffodil bulbs?

5. There are 5 kinds of daffodils in the
variety mixture. The mixture costs $2.00.
How much does each kind of daffodil
cost?

6. Suppose you wanted to buy only King
Alfred daffodils. 20 King Alfred bulbs cost
$3.50. You want to buy 100 of these
bulbs. What would 100 bulbs cost?

1. Copy the bar graph on a separate sheet of paper. Use the following information to complete the bar graph.

   Approximate lengths of six long tunnels in the world:

   Northern Line (England)—17 mi   Apennine (Italy)—12 mi
   Simplon I, II (Switzerland/Italy)—13 mi   Gotthard (Switzerland)—10 mi
   Shin Kanmon (Japan)—12 mi   Rokko (Japan)—10 mi

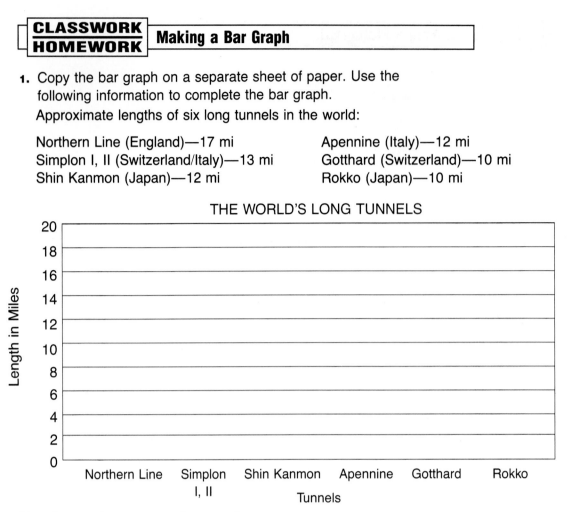

THE WORLD'S LONG TUNNELS

Use the graph to answer the questions.

2. Which tunnels are about the same length?

3. Which tunnel is the *second* longest tunnel?

   How long is it?

4. How much longer is the Shin Kanmon Tunnel than the

   Gotthard Tunnel?

5. Which tunnels are longer than Shin Kanmon?

Joel has collected baseball cards every year for five years.
The list shows how many he has collected each year.

1986—53 cards
1987—89 cards
1988—101 cards
1989—85 cards
1990—10 cards

1. Round the number of cards to the nearest ten. Copy the pictograph on a separate sheet of paper. Use the information above to complete the pictograph.

JOEL'S BASEBALL CARD COLLECTION

Year	Number of cards collected
1986	
1987	
1988	
1989	
1990	

Each ☐ = 10 cards.

Use the pictograph to answer each question.

2. About how many more cards did Joel collect in 1987 than in 1986?

3. About how many cards in all did Joel collect in 1989 and 1990?

4. In which two years did Joel collect nearly equal amounts of cards?

5. In which year did Joel collect the most cards, 1987 or 1988?

6. What is the total number of baseball cards that Joel collected in the five years?

Multiply.

1.	30 × 10	2.	700 × 20	3.	50 × 10	4.	400 × 30	5.	60 × 40
6.	90 × 90	7.	200 × 80	8.	1,000 × 90	9.	6,000 × 50	10.	80 × 70
11.	9,000 × 40	12.	300 × 60	13.	4,000 × 50	14.	200 × 80	15.	7,000 × 40
16.	5,000 × 70	17.	300 × 60	18.	80 × 90	19.	2,000 × 40	20.	600 × 90

21. 30×20

22. 60×20

23. $70 \times 5{,}000$

24. 400×30

25. $60 \times 7{,}000$

26. 40×600

27. 800×10

28. 60×70

29. $90 \times 4{,}400$

30. 600×50

Solve.

31. The Bumbly Company produces three items:
Fidders which are sold in boxes of 10,
Snookers which are sold in boxes of 100,
Hornwogs which are sold in boxes of 1,000.

The Packway Department Store is having a sale and
wants to place an order for extra goods. They order:
50 boxes of Fidders, 30 boxes of Snookers, 60 boxes of Hornwogs.
How many of each item did they order?

_____?_____ Fidders _____?_____ Snookers _____?_____ Hornwogs

Estimate.

1. $0.23 × 18	**2.** 116 × 77	**3.** 329 × 46	**4.** $4.76 × 37	**5.** $9.91 × 26
6. $7.22 × 48	**7.** 901 × 33	**8.** 352 × 64	**9.** $9.68 × 16	**10.** 386 × 62
11. 462 × 86	**12.** 631 × 90	**13.** $6.15 × 29	**14.** 874 × 61	**15.** 226 × 47
16. 386 × 62	**17.** $9.47 × 12	**18.** 505 × 55	**19.** $1.32 × 14	**20.** 37 × 52

Round the measurement and the dollar amount. Then estimate.

144 square inches = 1 square foot
9 square feet = 1 square yard
640 acres = 1 square mile

21. In Palukaville, 1 square inch of land costs $6.95. Estimate how much 1 square foot would cost.

22. In Frapp Falls, 1 square foot of land costs $5.42. Estimate how much 1 square yard would cost.

23. In Hittsville, 1 acre of land costs $5.42. Estimate how much 1 square mile would cost.

24. In Appleton, 1 acre of land costs $9.03. Estimate how much 1 square mile would cost.

FOR SALE
10 acres

Choosing the Operation	Identifying Needed Information	Writing a Number Sentence
Estimation	Checking for a Reasonable	Using a Graph
Using a Map	Answer	Checking That the Solution Answers the Question

Write the strategy or method you choose. Then solve.

1. Alaska is our biggest state. It has the smallest population. At one time, there were 401,851 people in Alaska. Of these, 174,431 lived in the city of Anchorage. How many Alaskans did not live in Anchorage?

2. Juneau is the capital of Alaska. There are 19,528 people in Juneau. Fairbanks has 22,645 people. Ketchikan has 7,198 people. Sitka has 7,803 people. How many people live in these four cities?

3. Alaska's first census was taken in 1880. There were 33,426 Alaskans. Only 430 of these people were not native Alaskans. Were there more or fewer native Alaskans than non-native Alaskans?

4. Alaska had a gold rush in 1898. About 2,500 people arrived each month. More than 30,000 people arrived in all. Did more than 10,000 people arrive in 6 months?

5. Ron is reading a map of Alaska. The scale is 200 miles to the inch. Juneau is $\frac{1}{2}$ inch from Sitka. About how many miles is Juneau from Sitka?

6. The Terrys drive from Fairbanks to Whitehorse, Canada. The map scale shows 25 miles to the inch. The distance they must travel to reach Whitehorse is shown as 8 inches on the map. About how far is Whitehorse from Fairbanks?

Choosing the Operation	Using a Map	Writing a Number Sentence
Estimation	Identifying Needed Information	Using a Graph

Write the strategy or method you choose. Then solve.

1. There were 769,913 people living in Hawaii in 1970. There were 964,691 living in Hawaii in 1980. How much larger was the population of Hawaii in 1980?

2. In 1900, Hawaii's population was about 154,000. It was 3 times as large by 1950. How many people lived in Hawaii in 1950?

3. Honolulu, the capital of Hawaii, became a city in 1907. In what year will Honolulu celebrate its 150th birthday as a city?

4. Honolulu has 5,279 acres of parks. Jacksonville, Florida has 1,522 acres of parks. Does Honolulu have more than twice as much parkland as Jacksonville?

5. Tom is sitting in a park, looking at a map of Hawaii. The scale is 5 miles to the inch. Tom wants to go back to his hotel. The hotel is 3 inches away from the park on the map. How many miles is Tom from his hotel?

6. On one map, Hawaii is 21 inches from San Francisco, California. If the scale of this map is 100 miles to the inch, how far is San Francisco from Hawaii?

Write the information needed to solve the problem.

7. Mauna Kea is the highest mountain in Hawaii. It stands 13,796 feet high. Mauna Loa is also in Hawaii. It is the highest volcano on Earth. How much taller is Mauna Kea than Mauna Loa?

8. Kilauea is another Hawaiian volcano. It is 4,090 feet high. It has been active several times in this century. It was last active in 1983. How many years passed between Kilauea's last eruption and its next-to-last eruption?

Multiply.

1. 35
    × 11

2. 23
    × 13

3. 40
    × 21

4. $0.52
    ×   15

5. 78
    × 32

6. 91
    × 63

7. $0.76
    ×   51

8. 38
    × 25

9. 80
    × 57

10. 60
     × 49

11. 94
     × 73

12. 64
     × 64

13. $0.50
     ×   25

14. 82
     × 16

15. 58
     × 30

16. $0.71
     ×   17

17. 65
     × 22

18. 90
     × 81

19. 75
     × 25

20. 80
     × 79

21. 70
     × 63

22. 94
     × 49

23. $0.69
     ×   27

24. 60
     × 50

25. 97
     × 48

26. $0.26
     ×   49

27. $0.92
     ×   21

28. 80
     × 22

Multiply.

1. $0.93
   × 16

2. 28
   × 36

3. $0.84
   × 45

4. 16
   × 25

5. 64
   × 27

6. 22
   × 46

7. $0.71
   × 11

8. 34
   × 33

9. $0.61
   × 19

10. 38
    × 20

Multiply. Find your answer under one of the lines below.
Write the code letter for your answer. When all the letters
are written, you will know a tall tale! Then add the answers.
Write the sum to finish the sentence.

11. 88
    × 42 T

12. 65
    × 44 E

13. 56
    × 65 E

14. 63
    × 76 S

15. 75
    × 50 T

16. 67
    × 53 E

17. 27
    × 98 V

18. 69
    × 59 R

M ____?____ .
   3,696

?	?	?	?	?	?	?
2,860	2,646	3,640	4,071	3,551	4,788	3,750

is the highest mountain in the world at ____?____ feet above
sea level.

Write *overestimate, underestimate,* or *exact* to describe how you would get the answer to each problem.

1. Tanya is selling tickets to an art show. The tickets cost $3.25 each. Tanya will win a prize when she sells $50 of tickets. She has sold 17 tickets. Has she won a prize? Look at the ticket price.

   overestimate   underestimate   exact

2. Sally wants to buy tickets for each person in her family. There are 5 people in the family. Each ticket costs $3.25. Sally has $15.75. Does she have enough money for the tickets? Look at the price of each ticket.

   overestimate   underestimate   exact

3. Cary needs to frame 113 drawings for the show. He frames 15 drawings each day. The show will open in 12 days. Will he have all the drawings framed in time? Look at the number of drawings framed each day.

   overestimate   underestimate   exact

4. Glenda will buy 4 trophies for the art show. Each trophy costs $28. Glenda has $115 to spend for the trophies. Can she buy all the trophies? Look at the cost of each trophy.

   overestimate   underestimate   exact

5. Fred will buy ribbons for the winners of the show. He needs to buy 16 ribbons. Each ribbon costs $1.65. Fred has $20.00. Does he have enough money? Look at the price of each ribbon.

   overestimate   underestimate   exact

6. Celia is lettering labels for the art show. She makes 23 labels each evening. She needs to make 156 labels in 8 days. Will she finish all the labels in time? Look at the number of labels finished each evening.

   overestimate   underestimate   exact

Multiply.

1. 230
   × 32

2. 501
   × 15

3. 704
   × 64

4. $3.06
   × 40

5. $7.21
   × 63

6. 418
   × 23

7. 674
   × 30

8. $9.05
   × 71

9. 413
   × 29

10. 578
    × 42

11. $1.87
    × 26

12. 808
    × 90

13. $6.15
    × 34

14. $2.04
    × 62

15. $5.49
    × 21

16. $7.95
    × 47

17. 350
    × 15

18. 999
    × 99

19. $4.91
    × 78

20. $6.09
    × 70

21. 938
    × 86

22. $6.01
    × 20

23. $2.18
    × 31

24. 800
    × 24

25. $4.90
    × 60

26. 979
    × 10

27. 589
    × 99

28. 342
    × 76

Read each problem. Do not figure the exact answer. Write the letter of the most reasonable answer.

1. According to one story, a man lived 969 years. The oldest tree on Earth is about 5 times older. How old is this tree?

   a. 500 years   **b.** 5,000 years   **c.** 50,000 years

2. A cheetah can go from a standstill position to 45 miles per hour in 2 seconds. About how many miles per hour does its speed increase in the third second?

   a. $22\frac{1}{2}$ mph   **b.** 45 mph   **c.** 90 mph

3. A bamboo plant can grow as much as 4 feet in 24 hours. In how many hours will a bamboo plant grow 1 foot?

   a. 6 hours   **b.** 12 hours   **c.** 48 hours

4. There are no more elephant birds in Africa. These birds stood 10 feet tall and weighed 1,000 pounds. How many pounds did two elephant birds weigh?

   a. 100 pounds   **b.** 500 pounds   **c.** 2,000 pounds

5. A blue whale can weigh as much as 130 tons. It needs 4 horsepower for each ton. How many horsepower does it need for 130 tons?

   a. 32.5   **b.** 52   **c.** 520

6. A centipede can travel 24 miles per day. This is about 19.6 inches each second. About how many feet can it travel in 2 seconds?

   a. 3 feet   **b.** 40 feet   **c.** 0.4 feet

7. Elephants are the only animals that cannot jump. They are also the only animals that have 4 knees. If you counted 156 elephant knees in an elephant herd, how many elephants would you have counted?

   a. 160 elephants   **b.** 39 elephants   **c.** 624 elephants

Divide mentally.

1. $7\overline{)280}$

2. $4\overline{)160}$

3. $8\overline{)640}$

4. $9\overline{)450}$

5. $6\overline{)360}$

6. $5\overline{)3,000}$

7. $6\overline{)4,200}$

8. $3\overline{)2,700}$

9. $7\overline{)4,900}$

10. $9\overline{)8,100}$

11. $20\overline{)400}$

12. $80\overline{)560}$

13. $40\overline{)240}$

14. $50\overline{)350}$

15. $60\overline{)540}$

16. $30\overline{)1,800}$

17. $70\overline{)3,500}$

18. $50\overline{)4,500}$

19. $90\overline{)7,200}$

20. $40\overline{)3,600}$

21. $50\overline{)40,000}$

22. $60\overline{)48,000}$

23. $80\overline{)24,000}$

24. $30\overline{)12,000}$

25. $2,000 \div 5$

26. $800 \div 20$

27. $2,700 \div 9$

28. $3,000 \div 60$

29. $4,800 \div 8$

30. $7,200 \div 80$

31. $6,300 \div 90$

32. $5,000 \div 50$

33. $8,100 \div 9$

Solve.

34. A flower market received 2,400 roses. The workers made 30 bunches. Each bunch had the same number of roses. How many roses are there in each bunch?

35. The flower market has 180 geranium plants. The plants are displayed in rows of 20. How many rows of plants are there?

Write a number sentence to solve each problem. Then, solve.

1. The flag of Liberia is the only flag in the world that was designed by women. This flag has 11 stripes. Each stripe stands for one signer of the Liberian Declaration of Independence. The flag was designed by 7 Liberian women. How many more signers were there than designers?

2. There are symbols on many world flags. The most common symbol is the star. There are 41 flags that have stars. The next most common symbol is the half-moon. There are 9 flags that have half-moons. How many flags have either stars or half-moons?

3. The largest American flag was made in 1980. It is 411 feet long and 210 feet wide. What is the perimeter of this flag?

4. Denmark has the oldest flag in the world. It was first used in 1219. The American flag was first used in 1776. How much older is Denmark's flag?

5. There are 8 stars on the flag of Alaska. There are 3 times as many stars on the flag of Missouri. How many stars are there on Missouri's flag?

6. Norway once belonged to Denmark. In 1814, Norway became part of Sweden. Norway became independent in 1905. For how many years did Norway use Sweden's flag?

7. The ancient Chinese flag had a yellow background and a four-footed dragon. The dragon on the emperor's flag had 5 claws on each foot. How many claws did the emperor's dragon have?

8. Chinese nobles also used a flag. Their flag had a four-footed dragon as well. The nobles' dragon had only 16 claws. How many claws were on each foot of the dragon on the nobles' flag?

9. The American flag has a star for each state. There were 15 stars on the American flag in 1795. By 1896, there were 3 times as many stars on the flag. How many states were there in 1896?

10. There are 50 states and 51 state flags! Minnesota has 2 state flags. The Ohio flag is shaped like a triangle. There are 3 times as many state flags as there are stars on the Ohio flag. How many stars are there on the Ohio flag?

Divide.

1. $50\overline{)400}$ 2. $30\overline{)173}$ 3. $80\overline{)532}$ 4. $20\overline{)143}$ 5. $30\overline{)290}$

6. $70\overline{)601}$ 7. $40\overline{)360}$ 8. $60\overline{)361}$ 9. $90\overline{)533}$ 10. $80\overline{)160}$

11. $20\overline{)140}$ 12. $90\overline{)632}$ 13. $50\overline{)435}$ 14. $70\overline{)667}$ 15. $80\overline{)480}$

16. $216 \div 70$ 17. $300 \div 60$ 18. $676 \div 70$

19. $320 \div 80$ 20. $531 \div 90$ 21. $437 \div 60$

22. $460 \div 40$ 23. $270 \div 30$ 24. $320 \div 80$

25. $265 \div 50$ 26. $300 \div 20$ 27. $751 \div 90$

Divide.

1. $18\overline{)20}$

2. $72\overline{)95}$

3. $30\overline{)90}$

4. $48\overline{)58}$

5. $15\overline{)85}$

6. $22\overline{)92}$

7. $39\overline{)78}$

8. $21\overline{)73}$

9. $11\overline{)36}$

10. $54\overline{)62}$

11. $13\overline{)91}$

12. $10\overline{)95}$

13. $32\overline{)64}$

14. $47\overline{)53}$

15. $20\overline{)80}$

16. $12\overline{)28}$

17. $33\overline{)75}$

18. $14\overline{)28}$

19. $25\overline{)75}$

20. $44\overline{)95}$

Solve.

21. Juan the baker made 96 rolls in the morning. He packaged the rolls in "baker's dozens." There are 13 units in a baker's dozen. How many packages did he have? How many rolls were left?

22. Mr. B. Dough orders 45 baking pans for his bakery. The pans come in boxes of 15 each. How many boxes of baking pans does Mr. Dough receive?

Use with pages 376–377.

Divide.

1. $37\overline{)83}$ 2. $26\overline{)67}$ 3. $12\overline{)85}$ 4. $10\overline{)43}$ 5. $59\overline{)95}$

6. $16\overline{)90}$ 7. $48\overline{)65}$ 8. $14\overline{)57}$ 9. $11\overline{)68}$ 10. $36\overline{)80}$

11. $25\overline{)87}$ 12. $11\overline{)53}$ 13. $23\overline{)75}$ 14. $15\overline{)90}$ 15. $12\overline{)99}$

16. $36\overline{)91}$ 17. $26\overline{)64}$ 18. $13\overline{)51}$ 19. $46\overline{)81}$ 20. $22\overline{)41}$

21. $42\overline{)84}$ 22. $12\overline{)66}$ 23. $39\overline{)88}$ 24. $24\overline{)52}$ 25. $10\overline{)67}$

26. $18\overline{)81}$ 27. $16\overline{)80}$ 28. $32\overline{)66}$ 29. $12\overline{)98}$ 30. $15\overline{)75}$

Making an Organized List	Guessing and Checking	Estimation
Making a Diagram	Choosing the Operation	

Write the strategy or method you choose. Then solve.

1. Farmer Grey put 2 pigs in the first pen, 5 goats in the second pen, and 3 cows in the third pen. He put 2 horses in the fourth pen, 5 sheep in the fifth pen, and 3 ducks in the sixth pen. In the seventh pen, he put 2 chickens. How many geese should he put in the eighth pen? How many rabbits should he put in the ninth pen?

2. Mrs. Rand is looking at coats. She can buy a leather, vinyl, or cloth coat. She can choose a blue, red, brown, or black coat. How many different choices does Mrs. Rand have?

3. There are 6 animals in the petting zoo: a chicken, a goat, a camel, a lamb, a llama, and a pony. The zookeeper wants to put 2 of the animals in one pen. How many combinations of animals can he put in the pen?

4. Maria is trying to guess what two secret numbers are. She knows that the product of the two numbers is 117. She also knows that both numbers are odd and that their sum is 22. What are the two secret numbers?

5. Shawn has given names to each of his pets. His guinea pig is named Zeke. His cat is named Yolanda, his goldfish is names Xanthe, his dog is named Walter, and his canary is named Vinnie. Shawn just got a new turtle. Should he name it Anna or Una?

| Making a Table | Guessing and Checking | Acting it Out |
| Making a Diagram | Choosing the Operation | |

Write the strategy or method you choose. Then solve.

1. Two friends are dividing money. Each person will get the same amount of money. Ellen takes the pennies. Donna takes the nickels. Each time Ellen takes 10 pennies, Donna takes 2 nickels. Ellen took 50 pennies. How many nickels did Donna take?

2. Bud is packing his coin collection. He can put his coins in bags, envelopes, or boxes. The holders are white, blue, or yellow. How many choices does Bud have?

3. Elana has four coins from the year she was born. She has a penny, a nickel, a dime, and a quarter. She wants to display 2 of the coins in a frame in her room. How many combinations of coins are there?

4. Perry has divided his coin collection into 2 stacks. If you multiply the number of coins in one stack by the number of coins in the other stack, the product would be 70. There are a total of 37 coins in both stacks. How many coins are in each stack?

5. Tim is organizing his coin collection. He plans to display each coin on a separate page. He has 57 different coins in his collection. Each display book has 20 pages in it. How many display books does Tim need for his collection?

Divide.

1. $46\overline{)122}$ 2. $65\overline{)108}$ 3. $90\overline{)722}$ 4. $21\overline{)168}$ 5. $80\overline{)746}$

6. $16\overline{)120}$ 7. $30\overline{)240}$ 8. $91\overline{)829}$ 9. $55\overline{)250}$ 10. $18\overline{)123}$

11. $12\overline{)114}$ 12. $40\overline{)320}$ 13. $99\overline{)198}$ 14. $31\overline{)166}$ 15. $53\overline{)371}$

16. $42\overline{)252}$ 17. $80\overline{)120}$ 18. $29\overline{)203}$ 19. $90\overline{)186}$ 20. $32\overline{)160}$

Copy the circle and the numbers on a separate sheet of paper. Then divide each number by the one in the center circle. Write the quotients that belong in the outer circle.

21.   22.

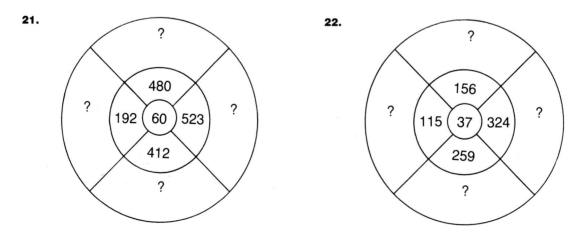

Divide.

1. 35)700

2. 22)382

3. 16)640

4. 24)432

5. 65)743

6. 15)320

7. 13)689

8. 18)810

9. 70)543

10. 48)576

11. 14)420

12. 60)745

13. 11)660

14. 31)293

15. 16)407

16. 35)426

17. 80)800

18. 20)185

19. 25)350

20. 35)630

21. 50)590

22. 31)620

23. 22)475

24. 15)210

25. 19)380

Solve.

26. The Bridgewood train can carry 960 passengers. Each car can hold a maximum of 60 passengers. How many cars are there in the train?

Divide.

1. $32\overline{)\$3.52}$ 2. $20\overline{)\$2.40}$ 3. $44\overline{)\$0.88}$ 4. $50\overline{)\$1.50}$ 5. $74\overline{)\$2.22}$

6. $80\overline{)\$7.20}$ 7. $25\overline{)\$6.75}$ 8. $20\overline{)\$3.40}$ 9. $32\overline{)\$4.80}$ 10. $11\overline{)\$9.13}$

11. $15\overline{)\$5.40}$ 12. $16\overline{)\$9.76}$ 13. $13\overline{)\$2.60}$ 14. $16\overline{)\$6.40}$ 15. $31\overline{)\$7.13}$

16. $75\overline{)\$8.25}$ 17. $12\overline{)\$8.40}$ 18. $11\overline{)\$5.72}$ 19. $10\overline{)\$0.10}$ 20. $33\overline{)\$7.59}$

21. $24\overline{)\$2.64}$ 22. $14\overline{)\$9.52}$ 23. $20\overline{)\$9.40}$ 24. $36\overline{)\$8.28}$ 25. $44\overline{)\$7.48}$

26. $25\overline{)\$1.50}$ 27. $15\overline{)\$3.75}$ 28. $22\overline{)\$9.24}$ 29. $19\overline{)\$6.84}$ 30. $55\overline{)\$2.75}$

Imagine that you have invited 5 friends to lunch. Think about each problem. Answer each question. Then, write a sentence explaining your answer.

1. You plan to make sandwiches for lunch. You want to give 2 sandwiches to each person. You have cut 1 loaf of bread into 20 slices. Are there enough slices?

2. You have made a salad to serve at lunch. You have made 14 ounces of salad. A typical portion of salad is 2 ounces. Have you made enough salad?

3. You are serving fruit juice at lunch. There are 24 ice cubes in the freezer. You want to put 4 ice cubes in each person's glass. Are there enough ice cubes?

4. You have bought cherries for lunch. You bought 2 pounds of cherries. Each pound will serve 4 people. Have you bought enough?

5. Your guests will be arriving at noon. You plan to start preparing the food at 11:00 A.M. It takes you 45 minutes to make the sandwiches, 15 minutes to make the salad, and 8 minutes to make the juice. (Hint: There are 60 minutes in an hour.) Is there enough time to prepare the food?

6. Your friends' parents will pick them up. You have told their parents to pick them up at 3:00 P.M. Is this enough time to eat your lunch?

MORE PRACTICE

Chapter 1, Page 9

Write in order from the least to the greatest.

1. 4,764; 4,647; 4,746; 7,416
2. 6,940; 9,729; 9,149; 8,149
3. 8,725; 3,875; 4,195; 8,875
4. 3,966; 3,963; 3,369; 369

Write in order from the greatest to the least.

5. 212; 957; 912; 297
6. 8,149; 9,149; 6,940; 9,729
7. 5,118; 5,011; 5,918; 5,919
8. 2,907; 2,917; 2,948; 4,849

Chapter 1, Page 11

Write each amount. Use the dollar sign and the cents point.

1. three quarters, one dime, and two pennies
2. seventy-five dollars and two cents
3. thirteen dollars and eighteen cents
4. six dimes, one nickel, and one penny
5. four dollars and twenty-five cents
6. eleven quarters and one nickel
7. eighteen dimes and eighteen cents
8. two dollars and forty-five cents
9. one dollar and one cent
10. eighty-one dollars

Chapter 1, Page 13

Write each in standard form.

1. two hundred eight million, three hundred twenty-two thousand, two
2. seventeen million, fifty-two thousand, one hundred forty-six
3. 743 million, 638 thousand, 569
4. 24 million, 391 thousand, 453

Write the digit that is in the given place.

5. 473,652,180 (millions place)
6. 715,942,386 (hundred millions place)

Write the value of the blue digit.

7. 929,860,123
8. 257,804,310
9. 773,294,921
10. 148,801,211
11. 486,374,950
12. 367,521,894
13. 501,298,847
14. 69,572,758

Chapter 1, Page 15

Round to the nearest ten or to the nearest ten cents.

1. 39 **2.** $5.01 **3.** 62 **4.** 85¢ **5.** 28 **6.** 634

7. 239 **8.** 57 **9.** 275 **10.** $7.84 **11.** 97 **12.** 83¢

Round to the nearest hundred or to the nearest dollar.

13. 520 **14.** 201 **15.** $29.22 **16.** 5,288 **17.** $9.10

18. $6.58 **19.** 7,492 **20.** 809 **21.** $5.37 **22.** 3,295

Round to the nearest thousand or to the nearest ten dollars.

23. $638.99 **24.** 4,232 **25.** 71,904 **26.** $66.14 **27.** 52,379

Chapter 1, Page 19

Add.

1. $7 + 2$
$2 + 7$

2. $4 + 3$
$3 + 4$

3. $8 + 9$
$9 + 8$

4. $5 + 9$
$9 + 5$

5. $3 + 2$
$2 + 3$

6. 9
$+ 2$

7. 5
$+ 8$

8. 6
$+ 4$

9. 7
$+ 3$

10. 1
$+ 0$

11. 4
$+ 5$

12. 8
$+ 6$

13. $3 + 3$ **14.** $2 + 8$ **15.** $0 + 5$ **16.** $1 + 7$ **17.** $9 + 7$

18. $(8 + 1) + 1$ **19.** $2 + (5 + 1)$ **20.** $(4 + 2) + 2$ **21.** $3 + (4 + 2)$

Chapter 1, Page 21

Subtract.

1. 5
$- 1$

2. 7
$- 4$

3. 4
$- 4$

4. 8
$- 6$

5. 6
$- 3$

6. 3
$- 0$

7. 9
$- 2$

8. 9
$- 8$

9. 2
$- 2$

10. 6
$- 5$

11. 8
$- 4$

12. 5
$- 4$

13. 9
$- 7$

14. 7
$- 3$

15. $7 - 6$ **16.** $4 - 2$ **17.** $1 - 0$ **18.** $3 - 2$ **19.** $7 - 5$

20. $9 - 4$ **21.** $6 - 6$ **22.** $8 - 0$ **23.** $5 - 3$ **24.** $2 - 1$

Add.

1. 49 + 59	**2.** 78 + 73	**3.** 97 + 8	**4.** 39 + 79	**5.** 88 + 9	**6.** 11 + 99
7. $0.62 + 0.39	**8.** 15 + 65	**9.** $0.57 + 0.76	**10.** 83 + 29	**11.** $0.49 + 0.81	
12. $0.56 + 0.90	**13.** $0.77 + 0.65	**14.** $0.26 + 0.09	**15.** $0.87 + 0.42	**16.** $0.92 + 0.19	

Add.

1. 372 + 496	**2.** 857 + 89	**3.** $7.98 + 5.25	**4.** 129 + 985	**5.** 349 + 104
6. 1,649 + 3,872	**7.** 4,399 + 7,833	**8.** $29.95 + 72.09	**9.** 21,394 + 68,731	**10.** 78,912 + 39,456

11. 8,924 + 765   **12.** 42,909 + 55,086   **13.** 52,192 + 9,384

Add.

1. 497 365 + 514	**2.** $7.89 0.60 + 1.14	**3.** 5,678 29 + 351	**4.** $0.56 2.07 + 0.94	**5.** 4,985 3,654 + 197
6. 29 381 2,771 + 56	**7.** $95.01 1.99 0.76 + 8.12	**8.** 7,444 9 108 + 1,006	**9.** $78.09 1.21 9.00 + 0.16	**10.** 137 2,006 989 + 16

11. 467 + 1,239 + 12   **12.** 78 + 8,634 + 33   **13.** 7,889 + 234 + 82 + 976

Chapter 2, Page 55

Subtract.

1. 55
− 16

2. 39
− 28

3. 27
− 9

4. $0.40
− 0.17

5. $0.87
− 0.63

6. $0.18
− 0.10

7. 36
− 23

8. 22
− 5

9. 80
− 45

10. $0.82
− 0.67

11. $0.79
− 0.69

12. $0.72
− 0.15

13. 56 − 11

14. $0.30 − $0.15

15. 16 − 12

16. $0.84 − $0.75

Chapter 2, Page 61

Subtract.

1. 8,276
− 1,564

2. $95.88
− 29.71

3. 51,281
− 22,379

4. $883.74
− 703.07

5. $262.71
− 126.26

6. 94,145
− 19,438

7. 6,339
− 5,822

8. $78.16
− 20.98

9. 6,979
− 3,359

10. $817.73
− 698.98

11. $445.47
− 267.84

12. $96.94
− 17.75

13. 7,115
− 4,263

14. 5,455
− 1,086

15. $81.91
− 46.37

16. 72,418 − 47,736

17. $968.81 − $168.62

18. 7,896 − 4,265

Chapter 2, Page 63

Subtract.

1. 9,600
− 3,511

2. 30,000
− 17,342

3. $39.07
− 3.25

4. 9,000
− 3,256

5. $960.60
− 725.41

6. 6,309
− 5,171

7. 85,080
− 4,421

8. 93,803
− 51,422

9. $80.67
− 41.43

10. $82.09
− 61.41

11. 68,070 − 36,521

12. $600.00 − $217.15

13. 6,350 − 424

14. 8,500 − 2,431

15. $980.25 − $42.21

16. 89,000 − 67,716

Chapter 3, Page 75

Multiply.

1. 3×2
2. 2×7
3. 3×5
4. 2×4
5. 3×8
6. 2×2
7. 2×6

8. 3×3
9. 3×6
10. 2×3
11. 3×1
12. 2×5
13. 3×9
14. 3×4

15. 4×2
16. 7×3
17. 6×2
18. 9×2
19. 1×2

20. 3×3
21. 5×2
22. 6×3
23. 2×2
24. 9×3

Chapter 3, Page 77

Multiply.

1. 4×6
2. 5×6
3. 4×3
4. 5×8
5. 4×7
6. 5×2
7. 5×9

8. 4×4
9. 5×4
10. 4×1
11. 4×8
12. 5×3
13. 5×7
14. 4×2

15. 5×5
16. 5×4
17. 9×4
18. 1×5
19. 3×4

20. 2×4
21. 9×5
22. 1×4
23. 3×5
24. 8×5

Chapter 3, Page 83

Multiply.

1. 7×1
2. 7×8
3. 6×2
4. 7×5
5. 6×1
6. 6×6
7. 7×4

8. 7×3
9. 6×7
10. 7×2
11. 6×8
12. 6×5
13. 7×7
14. 6×3

15. 3×6
16. 0×6
17. 9×7
18. 6×7
19. 4×7

20. 3×7
21. 4×6
22. 0×7
23. 9×6
24. 7×6

Multiply.

1. $\begin{array}{r} 8 \\ \times\,1 \\ \hline \end{array}$	**2.** $\begin{array}{r} 8 \\ \times\,7 \\ \hline \end{array}$	**3.** $\begin{array}{r} 9 \\ \times\,1 \\ \hline \end{array}$	**4.** $\begin{array}{r} 8 \\ \times\,5 \\ \hline \end{array}$	**5.** $\begin{array}{r} 9 \\ \times\,7 \\ \hline \end{array}$	**6.** $\begin{array}{r} 9 \\ \times\,3 \\ \hline \end{array}$	**7.** $\begin{array}{r} 8 \\ \times\,2 \\ \hline \end{array}$

8. 2×9 **9.** 0×8 **10.** 8×8 **11.** 6×8 **12.** 9×9

13. 4×9 **14.** 6×9 **15.** 8×9 **16.** 3×8 **17.** 4×8

18. 5×9 **19.** 2×8 **20.** 0×9 **21.** 1×8 **22.** 7×9

Write *even* or *odd* for each number.

1. 3   **2.** 95   **3.** 7   **4.** 128   **5.** 61   **6.** 6   **7.** 19

8. 5   **9.** 38   **10.** 934   **11.** 647   **12.** 48   **13.** 50   **14.** 656

Copy and complete to find the multiples.

		1	2	3	4	5	6	7	8	9
15.	2 ×									
16.	4 ×									
17.	5 ×									
18.	7 ×									

Write the amount of time that has passed

1. from 12:23 to 4:25.   **2.** from 7:06 to 4:40.

3. from 6:45 to 7:15.   **4.** from 5:19 to 2:30.

5. from five-twenty-nine A.M. to eleven-forty A.M.

6. from two-forty P.M. to one-forty A.M.

7. from five past six P.M. to quarter after eight P.M.

8. from quarter to three P.M. to midnight.

9. from seven-twelve A.M. to eight-fifty-seven A.M.

Divide.

1. $2\overline{)4}$ 2. $3\overline{)9}$ 3. $2\overline{)12}$ 4. $3\overline{)15}$ 5. $2\overline{)10}$

6. $3\overline{)18}$ 7. $3\overline{)12}$ 8. $2\overline{)16}$ 9. $3\overline{)6}$ 10. $2\overline{)8}$

11. $14 \div 2$ 12. $24 \div 3$ 13. $6 \div 2$ 14. $27 \div 3$ 15. $18 \div 2$

16. $10 \div 2$ 17. $12 \div 2$ 18. $6 \div 3$ 19. $8 \div 2$ 20. $24 \div 3$

21. $21 \div 3$ 22. $16 \div 2$ 23. $15 \div 3$ 24. $4 \div 2$ 25. $9 \div 3$

Divide.

1. $5\overline{)25}$ 2. $4\overline{)16}$ 3. $5\overline{)45}$ 4. $4\overline{)8}$ 5. $5\overline{)10}$

6. $4\overline{)28}$ 7. $4\overline{)32}$ 8. $5\overline{)35}$ 9. $4\overline{)12}$ 10. $5\overline{)40}$

11. $30 \div 5$ 12. $20 \div 4$ 13. $25 \div 5$ 14. $20 \div 5$ 15. $24 \div 4$

16. $45 \div 5$ 17. $12 \div 4$ 18. $35 \div 5$ 19. $16 \div 4$ 20. $40 \div 5$

21. $36 \div 4$ 22. $15 \div 5$ 23. $28 \div 4$ 24. $32 \div 4$ 25. $10 \div 5$

Copy and complete each family of facts.

1. $6 \times 4 = \blacksquare$
    $4 \times 6 = \blacksquare$
    $24 \div 4 = \blacksquare$
    $24 \div 6 = \blacksquare$

2. $5 \times 9 = \blacksquare$
    $9 \times 5 = \blacksquare$
    $45 \div 9 = \blacksquare$
    $45 \div 5 = \blacksquare$

3. $4 \times 7 = \blacksquare$
    $7 \times 4 = \blacksquare$
    $28 \div 7 = \blacksquare$
    $28 \div 4 = \blacksquare$

4. $7 \times 3 = \blacksquare$
    $3 \times 7 = \blacksquare$
    $21 \div 3 = \blacksquare$
    $21 \div 7 = \blacksquare$

Write the value of $\blacksquare$ for each.

5. $2 \times \blacksquare = 16$ 6. $4 \times 3 = \blacksquare$ 7. $5 \times \blacksquare = 10$ 8. $\blacksquare \times 4 = 32$

9. $\blacksquare \times 3 = 6$ 10. $7 \times \blacksquare = 14$ 11. $3 \times 3 = \blacksquare$ 12. $\blacksquare \times 5 = 35$

13. $9 \times 5 = \blacksquare$ 14. $\blacksquare \times 8 = 40$ 15. $6 \times \blacksquare = 18$ 16. $\blacksquare \times 7 = 21$

Write a family of facts for each set of numbers.

17. $3, 4, 12$ 18. $15, 3, 5$ 19. $3, 3, 9$ 20. $30, 6, 5$ 21. $8, 32, 4$

Divide.

1. $6\overline{)48}$
2. $7\overline{)49}$
3. $6\overline{)24}$
4. $7\overline{)63}$
5. $6\overline{)36}$

6. $7\overline{)42}$
7. $6\overline{)30}$
8. $6\overline{)12}$
9. $7\overline{)21}$
10. $6\overline{)54}$

11. $7\overline{)35}$
12. $6\overline{)18}$
13. $7\overline{)28}$
14. $7\overline{)56}$
15. $6\overline{)0}$

16. $6 \div 6$
17. $49 \div 7$
18. $30 \div 6$
19. $18 \div 6$
20. $21 \div 7$

21. $14 \div 7$
22. $54 \div 6$
23. $35 \div 7$
24. $48 \div 6$
25. $7 \div 7$

Divide.

1. $9\overline{)0}$
2. $8\overline{)24}$
3. $9\overline{)45}$
4. $8\overline{)32}$
5. $9\overline{)63}$

6. $8\overline{)40}$
7. $9\overline{)36}$
8. $8\overline{)56}$
9. $9\overline{)81}$
10. $9\overline{)27}$

11. $8\overline{)64}$
12. $8\overline{)16}$
13. $9\overline{)54}$
14. $8\overline{)8}$
15. $9\overline{)72}$

16. $18 \div 9$
17. $48 \div 8$
18. $9 \div 9$
19. $40 \div 8$
20. $72 \div 8$

21. $56 \div 8$
22. $54 \div 9$
23. $27 \div 9$
24. $0 \div 8$
25. $45 \div 9$

List the factors of each number.

1. 12
2. 2
3. 15
4. 24
5. 14

6. 6
7. 18
8. 20
9. 17
10. 4

11. 9
12. 16
13. 27
14. 13
15. 10

Find the common factors of each set of numbers.

16. 24, 6
17. 19, 3
18. 9, 18
19. 10, 24
20. 15, 25

21. 12, 21
22. 35, 28
23. 2, 14
24. 11, 5
25. 18, 24

Multiply.

1. $\begin{array}{r} 16 \\ \times\ 3 \\ \hline \end{array}$	**2.** $\begin{array}{r} 24 \\ \times\ 2 \\ \hline \end{array}$	**3.** $\begin{array}{r} 12 \\ \times\ 8 \\ \hline \end{array}$	**4.** $\begin{array}{r} 19 \\ \times\ 5 \\ \hline \end{array}$	**5.** $\begin{array}{r} 27 \\ \times\ 3 \\ \hline \end{array}$	**6.** $\begin{array}{r} 49 \\ \times\ 2 \\ \hline \end{array}$
7. $\begin{array}{r} 11 \\ \times\ 8 \\ \hline \end{array}$	**8.** $\begin{array}{r} 21 \\ \times\ 4 \\ \hline \end{array}$	**9.** $\begin{array}{r} 23 \\ \times\ 3 \\ \hline \end{array}$	**10.** $\begin{array}{r} 17 \\ \times\ 5 \\ \hline \end{array}$	**11.** $\begin{array}{r} 32 \\ \times\ 2 \\ \hline \end{array}$	**12.** $\begin{array}{r} 16 \\ \times\ 6 \\ \hline \end{array}$

13. 4×17 **14.** 2×36 **15.** 1×49 **16.** 3×14 **17.** 6×15

18. 3×25 **19.** 6×10 **20.** 7×13 **21.** 3×33 **22.** 4×22

Multiply.

1. $\begin{array}{r} 36 \\ \times\ 5 \\ \hline \end{array}$	**2.** $\begin{array}{r} 44 \\ \times\ 7 \\ \hline \end{array}$	**3.** $\begin{array}{r} 29 \\ \times\ 8 \\ \hline \end{array}$	**4.** $\begin{array}{r} 37 \\ \times\ 3 \\ \hline \end{array}$	**5.** $\begin{array}{r} 25 \\ \times\ 6 \\ \hline \end{array}$	**6.** $\begin{array}{r} 47 \\ \times\ 7 \\ \hline \end{array}$
7. $\begin{array}{r} 51 \\ \times\ 2 \\ \hline \end{array}$	**8.** $\begin{array}{r} 72 \\ \times\ 3 \\ \hline \end{array}$	**9.** $\begin{array}{r} 49 \\ \times\ 4 \\ \hline \end{array}$	**10.** $\begin{array}{r} 37 \\ \times\ 6 \\ \hline \end{array}$	**11.** $\begin{array}{r} 74 \\ \times\ 3 \\ \hline \end{array}$	**12.** $\begin{array}{r} 70 \\ \times\ 5 \\ \hline \end{array}$

13. 9×62 **14.** 8×44 **15.** 3×49 **16.** 4×26 **17.** 9×12

18. $8 \times (3 \times 7)$ **19.** $(5 \times 7) \times 9$ **20.** $4 \times (6 \times 8)$ **21.** $(8 \times 7) \times 2$

Find the product.

1. $\begin{array}{r} 242 \\ \times\ \ 2 \\ \hline \end{array}$	**2.** $\begin{array}{r} 421 \\ \times\ \ 2 \\ \hline \end{array}$	**3.** $\begin{array}{r} 301 \\ \times\ \ 3 \\ \hline \end{array}$	**4.** $\begin{array}{r} 402 \\ \times\ \ 2 \\ \hline \end{array}$	**5.** $\begin{array}{r} 111 \\ \times\ \ 7 \\ \hline \end{array}$
6. $\begin{array}{r} 102 \\ \times\ \ 3 \\ \hline \end{array}$	**7.** $\begin{array}{r} 221 \\ \times\ \ 4 \\ \hline \end{array}$	**8.** $\begin{array}{r} 107 \\ \times\ \ 1 \\ \hline \end{array}$	**9.** $\begin{array}{r} 110 \\ \times\ \ 5 \\ \hline \end{array}$	**10.** $\begin{array}{r} 211 \\ \times\ \ 4 \\ \hline \end{array}$
11. $\begin{array}{r} 144 \\ \times\ \ 2 \\ \hline \end{array}$	**12.** $\begin{array}{r} 233 \\ \times\ \ 3 \\ \hline \end{array}$	**13.** $\begin{array}{r} 403 \\ \times\ \ 2 \\ \hline \end{array}$	**14.** $\begin{array}{r} 102 \\ \times\ \ 4 \\ \hline \end{array}$	**15.** $\begin{array}{r} 610 \\ \times\ \ 1 \\ \hline \end{array}$

16. 4×201 **17.** 2×440 **18.** 3×120 **19.** 9×111 **20.** 8×101

Find the product.

1. $\begin{array}{r} 983 \\ \times\ \ 3 \\ \hline \end{array}$ 2. $\begin{array}{r} 416 \\ \times\ \ 9 \\ \hline \end{array}$ 3. $\begin{array}{r} 132 \\ \times\ \ 4 \\ \hline \end{array}$ 4. $\begin{array}{r} 506 \\ \times\ \ 5 \\ \hline \end{array}$ 5. $\begin{array}{r} 711 \\ \times\ \ 6 \\ \hline \end{array}$

6. $\begin{array}{r} 207 \\ \times\ \ 5 \\ \hline \end{array}$ 7. $\begin{array}{r} 300 \\ \times\ \ 4 \\ \hline \end{array}$ 8. $\begin{array}{r} 619 \\ \times\ \ 3 \\ \hline \end{array}$ 9. $\begin{array}{r} 147 \\ \times\ \ 2 \\ \hline \end{array}$ 10. $\begin{array}{r} 101 \\ \times\ \ 9 \\ \hline \end{array}$

11. 3×902 12. 8×165 13. 7×407 14. 6×112 15. 5×402

16. 3×497 17. 8×201 18. 5×409 19. 7×113 20. 6×333

Multiply.

1. $\begin{array}{r} 4{,}012 \\ \times\ \ 3 \\ \hline \end{array}$ 2. $\begin{array}{r} 6{,}709 \\ \times\ \ 7 \\ \hline \end{array}$ 3. $\begin{array}{r} 3{,}110 \\ \times\ \ 2 \\ \hline \end{array}$ 4. $\begin{array}{r} 5{,}513 \\ \times\ \ 6 \\ \hline \end{array}$ 5. $\begin{array}{r} 7{,}006 \\ \times\ \ 5 \\ \hline \end{array}$

6. $\begin{array}{r} 9{,}111 \\ \times\ \ 4 \\ \hline \end{array}$ 7. $\begin{array}{r} 4{,}603 \\ \times\ \ 5 \\ \hline \end{array}$ 8. $\begin{array}{r} 3{,}221 \\ \times\ \ 3 \\ \hline \end{array}$ 9. $\begin{array}{r} 1{,}090 \\ \times\ \ 7 \\ \hline \end{array}$ 10. $\begin{array}{r} 2{,}113 \\ \times\ \ 8 \\ \hline \end{array}$

11. $6 \times 5{,}995$ 12. $5 \times 4{,}985$ 13. $7 \times 9{,}669$ 14. $3 \times 5{,}111$

15. $4 \times 8{,}339$ 16. $6 \times 5{,}410$ 17. $3 \times 8{,}000$ 18. $9 \times 9{,}009$

Multiply.

1. $\begin{array}{r} \$3.33 \\ \times\ \ 4 \\ \hline \end{array}$ 2. $\begin{array}{r} \$0.97 \\ \times\ \ 6 \\ \hline \end{array}$ 3. $\begin{array}{r} \$46.07 \\ \times\ \ 3 \\ \hline \end{array}$ 4. $\begin{array}{r} \$1.10 \\ \times\ \ 5 \\ \hline \end{array}$ 5. $\begin{array}{r} \$7.65 \\ \times\ \ 8 \\ \hline \end{array}$

6. $\begin{array}{r} \$10.90 \\ \times\ \ 7 \\ \hline \end{array}$ 7. $\begin{array}{r} \$4.17 \\ \times\ \ 9 \\ \hline \end{array}$ 8. $\begin{array}{r} \$6.54 \\ \times\ \ 6 \\ \hline \end{array}$ 9. $\begin{array}{r} \$15.32 \\ \times\ \ 8 \\ \hline \end{array}$ 10. $\begin{array}{r} \$0.79 \\ \times\ \ 4 \\ \hline \end{array}$

11. $6 \times \$5.16$ 12. $8 \times \$49.09$ 13. $4 \times \$5.55$ 14. $2 \times \$81.73$

15. $4 \times \$18.39$ 16. $8 \times \$6.60$ 17. $7 \times \$72.00$ 18. $5 \times \$1.09$

Chapter 6, Page 169

Divide.

1. $5\overline{)32}$ 2. $6\overline{)41}$ 3. $4\overline{)29}$ 4. $7\overline{)39}$ 5. $6\overline{)39}$

6. $4\overline{)17}$ 7. $5\overline{)23}$ 8. $9\overline{)16}$ 9. $2\overline{)13}$ 10. $7\overline{)26}$

11. $3\overline{)28}$ 12. $4\overline{)38}$ 13. $9\overline{)42}$ 14. $8\overline{)77}$ 15. $5\overline{)43}$

16. $59 \div 8$ 17. $85 \div 9$ 18. $21 \div 5$ 19. $23 \div 6$ 20. $16 \div 5$

21. $16 \div 6$ 22. $50 \div 9$ 23. $48 \div 5$ 24. $37 \div 6$ 25. $50 \div 8$

Chapter 6, Page 173

Divide.

1. $5\overline{)54}$ 2. $3\overline{)49}$ 3. $2\overline{)67}$ 4. $4\overline{)86}$ 5. $8\overline{)99}$

6. $7\overline{)89}$ 7. $4\overline{)57}$ 8. $6\overline{)71}$ 9. $9\overline{)92}$ 10. $5\overline{)61}$

11. $2\overline{)99}$ 12. $6\overline{)79}$ 13. $5\overline{)67}$ 14. $5\overline{)55}$ 15. $3\overline{)94}$

16. $83 \div 7$ 17. $94 \div 6$ 18. $59 \div 4$ 19. $66 \div 6$ 20. $79 \div 5$

21. $40 \div 3$ 22. $79 \div 2$ 23. $17 \div 1$ 24. $59 \div 3$ 25. $80 \div 5$

Chapter 6, Page 177

Divide.

1. $3\overline{)133}$ 2. $4\overline{)341}$ 3. $7\overline{)373}$ 4. $9\overline{)617}$ 5. $8\overline{)249}$

6. $5\overline{)416}$ 7. $2\overline{)198}$ 8. $4\overline{)250}$ 9. $7\overline{)529}$ 10. $6\overline{)433}$

11. $7\overline{)577}$ 12. $9\overline{)241}$ 13. $8\overline{)666}$ 14. $6\overline{)411}$ 15. $7\overline{)209}$

16. $394 \div 4$ 17. $556 \div 6$ 18. $498 \div 7$ 19. $335 \div 5$ 20. $819 \div 9$

21. $677 \div 7$ 22. $311 \div 5$ 23. $798 \div 8$ 24. $355 \div 4$ 25. $419 \div 6$

Divide.

1. $7\overline{)918}$ 2. $3\overline{)694}$ 3. $8\overline{)7,120}$ 4. $5\overline{)674}$ 5. $3\overline{)937}$

6. $4\overline{)851}$ 7. $7\overline{)6,978}$ 8. $4\overline{)698}$ 9. $3\overline{)876}$ 10. $6\overline{)5,691}$

11. $3\overline{)497}$ 12. $3\overline{)689}$ 13. $2\overline{)1,096}$ 14. $5\overline{)3,857}$ 15. $4\overline{)894}$

16. $839 \div 6$ 17. $493 \div 2$ 18. $1,764 \div 2$ 19. $367 \div 3$ 20. $4,379 \div 6$

21. $611 \div 4$ 22. $937 \div 7$ 23. $2,865 \div 5$ 24. $876 \div 5$ 25. $1,092 \div 3$

Divide.

1. $6\overline{)612}$ 2. $3\overline{)1,521}$ 3. $7\overline{)755}$ 4. $6\overline{)3,654}$ 5. $7\overline{)739}$

6. $5\overline{)750}$ 7. $3\overline{)1,200}$ 8. $6\overline{)960}$ 9. $7\overline{)1,421}$ 10. $5\overline{)3,600}$

11. $7\overline{)916}$ 12. $5\overline{)1,045}$ 13. $9\overline{)911}$ 14. $8\overline{)1,625}$ 15. $9\overline{)1,881}$

16. $4,567 \div 8$ 17. $2,835 \div 7$ 18. $452 \div 3$ 19. $816 \div 4$ 20. $2,121 \div 7$

21. $624 \div 3$ 22. $1,813 \div 2$ 23. $2,104 \div 7$ 24. $1,859 \div 6$ 25. $615 \div 2$

Find the quotient.

1. $3\overline{)\$2.07}$ 2. $5\overline{)\$1.25}$ 3. $8\overline{)\$71.76}$ 4. $5\overline{)\$6.55}$ 5. $2\overline{)\$1.32}$

6. $9\overline{)\$41.67}$ 7. $8\overline{)\$30.96}$ 8. $5\overline{)\$6.75}$ 9. $9\overline{)\$81.45}$ 10. $6\overline{)\$37.02}$

11. $7\overline{)\$6.58}$ 12. $8\overline{)\$3.28}$ 13. $4\overline{)\$24.08}$ 14. $7\overline{)\$35.77}$ 15. $3\overline{)\$3.27}$

16. $\$7.64 \div 4$ 17. $\$76.65 \div 5$ 18. $\$54.00 \div 9$ 19. $\$8.72 \div 8$ 20. $\$6.30 \div 9$

Write a fraction for the shaded part.

1. **2.** **3.** **4.**

Write a fraction for each.

5. three sixths

6. seven eighths

7. one tenth

8. two thirds

9. four fifths

10. five sixths

11. one half

12. nine tenths

Write each fraction in words.

13. $\frac{3}{8}$

14. $\frac{7}{10}$

15. $\frac{2}{5}$

16. $\frac{6}{8}$

17. $\frac{4}{6}$

18. $\frac{5}{10}$

Find the part of each set.

1. $\frac{1}{2}$ of 4

2. $\frac{2}{5}$ of 10

3. $\frac{3}{10}$ of 10

4. $\frac{1}{2}$ of 16

5. $\frac{2}{3}$ of 15

6. $\frac{1}{2}$ of 18

7. $\frac{7}{8}$ of 16

8. $\frac{7}{10}$ of 30

9. $\frac{3}{4}$ of 16

10. $\frac{3}{8}$ of 8

11. $\frac{5}{8}$ of 24

12. $\frac{3}{5}$ of 20

Find the equivalent fraction.

1. $\frac{4}{8} = \frac{4 \times 2}{8 \times 2} = \frac{\blacksquare}{\blacksquare}$

2. $\frac{3}{5} = \frac{3 \times 5}{5 \times 5} = \frac{\blacksquare}{\blacksquare}$

3. $\frac{1}{3} = \frac{1 \times 6}{3 \times 6} = \frac{\blacksquare}{\blacksquare}$

4. $\frac{5}{6} = \frac{\blacksquare}{18}$

5. $\frac{2}{8} = \frac{8}{\blacksquare}$

6. $\frac{1}{5} = \frac{3}{\blacksquare}$

7. $\frac{3}{10} = \frac{\blacksquare}{50}$

8. $\frac{3}{4} = \frac{12}{\blacksquare}$

9. $\frac{4}{5} = \frac{20}{\blacksquare}$

10. $\frac{6}{8} = \frac{\blacksquare}{24}$

11. $\frac{1}{2} = \frac{\blacksquare}{14}$

12. $\frac{6}{10} = \frac{\blacksquare}{40}$

13. $\frac{2}{6} = \frac{12}{\blacksquare}$

14. $\frac{7}{8} = \frac{\blacksquare}{32}$

15. $\frac{4}{6} = \frac{16}{\blacksquare}$

Find the equivalent fraction.

1. $\dfrac{6}{12} = \dfrac{6 \div 2}{12 \div 2} = \dfrac{\blacksquare}{\blacksquare}$

2. $\dfrac{12}{21} = \dfrac{12 \div 3}{21 \div 3} = \dfrac{\blacksquare}{\blacksquare}$

3. $\dfrac{16}{28} = \dfrac{16 \div 4}{28 \div 4} = \dfrac{\blacksquare}{\blacksquare}$

4. $\dfrac{15}{27} = \dfrac{\blacksquare}{9}$

5. $\dfrac{13}{26} = \dfrac{\blacksquare}{2}$

6. $\dfrac{6}{10} = \dfrac{3}{\blacksquare}$

7. $\dfrac{4}{12} = \dfrac{1}{\blacksquare}$

8. $\dfrac{10}{12} = \dfrac{5}{\blacksquare}$

9. $\dfrac{3}{18} = \dfrac{\blacksquare}{6}$

10. $\dfrac{8}{14} = \dfrac{4}{\blacksquare}$

11. $\dfrac{15}{24} = \dfrac{\blacksquare}{8}$

Write each fraction in simplest form.

12. $\dfrac{15}{35}$

13. $\dfrac{4}{6}$

14. $\dfrac{9}{12}$

15. $\dfrac{5}{25}$

16. $\dfrac{3}{9}$

17. $\dfrac{8}{32}$

18. $\dfrac{2}{14}$

19. $\dfrac{6}{8}$

20. $\dfrac{14}{21}$

21. $\dfrac{12}{30}$

22. $\dfrac{8}{10}$

23. $\dfrac{12}{18}$

Write a whole number or a mixed number in simplest form for each shaded part.

1.   **2.**   **3.**

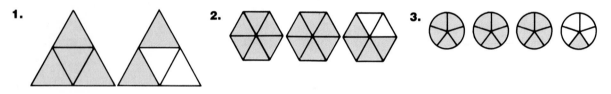

Write a whole number or a mixed number for each fraction.

4. $\dfrac{5}{2}$

5. $\dfrac{16}{4}$

6. $\dfrac{4}{3}$

7. $\dfrac{10}{8}$

8. $\dfrac{13}{13}$

9. $\dfrac{15}{5}$

10. $\dfrac{9}{7}$

11. $\dfrac{8}{8}$

12. $\dfrac{32}{16}$

13. $\dfrac{17}{10}$

14. $\dfrac{8}{5}$

15. $\dfrac{14}{4}$

16. $\dfrac{30}{9}$

17. $\dfrac{25}{3}$

Compare. Write $>$, $<$, or $=$ for $\bullet$.

1. $\dfrac{4}{5} \bullet \dfrac{2}{5}$

2. $1\dfrac{6}{12} \bullet 1\dfrac{3}{4}$

3. $\dfrac{9}{10} \bullet \dfrac{9}{9}$

4. $\dfrac{7}{21} \bullet \dfrac{2}{3}$

5. $5\dfrac{6}{8} \bullet 2\dfrac{4}{8}$

6. $5\dfrac{1}{4} \bullet 4\dfrac{1}{2}$

7. $\dfrac{5}{5} \bullet \dfrac{6}{6}$

8. $4\dfrac{4}{10} \bullet 4\dfrac{1}{5}$

9. $\dfrac{18}{5} \bullet \dfrac{13}{5}$

10. $\dfrac{16}{32} \bullet \dfrac{15}{32}$

11. $\dfrac{12}{9} \bullet \dfrac{7}{3}$

12. $\dfrac{25}{3} \bullet \dfrac{3}{1}$

13. $\dfrac{7}{14} \bullet \dfrac{4}{7}$

14. $6\dfrac{4}{8} \bullet 6\dfrac{6}{12}$

15. $1\dfrac{1}{3} \bullet 1\dfrac{3}{15}$

Add. Write the sum in simplest form.

1. $\frac{1}{2} + \frac{5}{10}$ **2.** $\frac{3}{4} + \frac{7}{8}$ **3.** $\frac{1}{3} + \frac{5}{6}$ **4.** $\frac{3}{4} + \frac{5}{8}$ **5.** $\frac{5}{6} + \frac{7}{12}$

6. $\frac{2}{4} + \frac{3}{8}$ **7.** $\frac{2}{6} + \frac{2}{3}$ **8.** $\frac{2}{10} + \frac{1}{2}$ **9.** $\frac{1}{8} + \frac{2}{4}$ **10.** $\frac{1}{2} + \frac{3}{6}$

11. $\frac{7}{10} + \frac{2}{5}$ **12.** $\frac{2}{3} + \frac{3}{6}$ **13.** $\frac{1}{3} + \frac{4}{9}$ **14.** $\frac{6}{12} + \frac{1}{3}$ **15.** $\frac{1}{4} + \frac{5}{8}$

16. $\begin{array}{r} \frac{3}{12} \\ + \frac{1}{4} \\ \hline \end{array}$ **17.** $\begin{array}{r} \frac{4}{8} \\ + \frac{1}{2} \\ \hline \end{array}$ **18.** $\begin{array}{r} \frac{2}{3} \\ + \frac{1}{6} \\ \hline \end{array}$ **19.** $\begin{array}{r} \frac{6}{8} \\ + \frac{1}{4} \\ \hline \end{array}$ **20.** $\begin{array}{r} \frac{4}{6} \\ + \frac{1}{3} \\ \hline \end{array}$ **21.** $\begin{array}{r} \frac{5}{8} \\ + \frac{1}{2} \\ \hline \end{array}$ **22.** $\begin{array}{r} \frac{6}{10} \\ + \frac{3}{5} \\ \hline \end{array}$

Subtract. Write the difference in simplest form.

1. $\frac{3}{4} - \frac{1}{2}$ **2.** $\frac{5}{6} - \frac{1}{3}$ **3.** $\frac{8}{10} - \frac{2}{5}$ **4.** $\frac{7}{8} - \frac{1}{4}$ **5.** $\frac{4}{5} - \frac{1}{10}$

6. $\frac{7}{10} - \frac{1}{2}$ **7.** $\frac{1}{2} - \frac{1}{4}$ **8.** $\frac{4}{9} - \frac{1}{3}$ **9.** $\frac{1}{2} - \frac{1}{6}$ **10.** $\frac{6}{8} - \frac{1}{2}$

11. $\frac{9}{12} - \frac{1}{3}$ **12.** $\frac{9}{10} - \frac{1}{5}$ **13.** $\frac{7}{8} - \frac{3}{4}$ **14.** $\frac{4}{10} - \frac{1}{5}$ **15.** $\frac{5}{8} - \frac{1}{2}$

16. $\begin{array}{r} \frac{9}{10} \\ - \frac{1}{2} \\ \hline \end{array}$ **17.** $\begin{array}{r} \frac{1}{2} \\ - \frac{2}{6} \\ \hline \end{array}$ **18.** $\begin{array}{r} \frac{7}{12} \\ - \frac{1}{2} \\ \hline \end{array}$ **19.** $\begin{array}{r} \frac{5}{6} \\ - \frac{2}{3} \\ \hline \end{array}$ **20.** $\begin{array}{r} \frac{6}{9} \\ - \frac{1}{3} \\ \hline \end{array}$ **21.** $\begin{array}{r} \frac{3}{6} \\ - \frac{1}{2} \\ \hline \end{array}$ **22.** $\begin{array}{r} \frac{8}{10} \\ - \frac{2}{5} \\ \hline \end{array}$

Add or subtract. Write the answer in simplest form.

1. $1\frac{1}{5} + 2\frac{1}{5}$ **2.** $2\frac{1}{2} + 3\frac{1}{2}$ **3.** $4\frac{5}{6} - 3\frac{2}{6}$ **4.** $2\frac{3}{4} - 1\frac{2}{4}$ **5.** $2\frac{2}{5} + 3\frac{2}{5}$

6. $1\frac{1}{8} + 3\frac{5}{8}$ **7.** $4\frac{4}{9} - 4\frac{1}{9}$ **8.** $3\frac{2}{3} + 4\frac{1}{3}$ **9.** $6\frac{7}{10} - 5\frac{4}{10}$ **10.** $3\frac{1}{3} + 1\frac{2}{3}$

11. $7\frac{1}{4} + 1\frac{2}{4}$ **12.** $6\frac{4}{6} - 3\frac{3}{6}$ **13.** $4\frac{1}{2} + 1\frac{1}{2}$ **14.** $7\frac{6}{10} - 3\frac{2}{10}$ **15.** $6\frac{1}{3} + 1\frac{2}{3}$

16. $\begin{array}{r} 4\frac{5}{10} \\ - 3\frac{1}{10} \\ \hline \end{array}$ **17.** $\begin{array}{r} 6\frac{2}{3} \\ + 7\frac{1}{3} \\ \hline \end{array}$ **18.** $\begin{array}{r} 4\frac{5}{9} \\ - 3\frac{2}{9} \\ \hline \end{array}$ **19.** $\begin{array}{r} 6\frac{1}{3} \\ + 2\frac{2}{3} \\ \hline \end{array}$ **20.** $\begin{array}{r} 4\frac{3}{8} \\ + 3\frac{3}{8} \\ \hline \end{array}$ **21.** $\begin{array}{r} 9\frac{7}{8} \\ - 2\frac{5}{8} \\ \hline \end{array}$

Chapter 8, Page 255

Compare. Write >, <, or = for ●.

1. 4.6 ● 4.06   **2.** 3.79 ● 3.87   **3.** 7.9 ● 7.90   **4.** 14.5 ● 1.45

5. 5.25 ● 5.52   **6.** 25.9 ● 2.59   **7.** 46.9 ● 49.6   **8.** 3.0 ● 2.99

Write in order from the least to the greatest.

9. 7.9, 9.7, 7.09   **10.** 45.6, 6.54, 5.86   **11.** 9.33, 38.9, 7.09

Write in order from the greatest to the least.

12. 19.3, 9.13, 31.9   **13.** 7.03, 3.79, 91.0   **14.** 37.41, 473.1, 4.17

Chapter 8, Page 259

Add.

1. 4.31 + 1.7   **2.** 61.9 + 7.32   **3.** 4.25 + 6.73   **4.** $10.17 + 0.43   **5.** 61.99 + 3.7

6. 41.41 + 7.37   **7.** $46.71 + 30.70   **8.** 9.37 + 0.09   **9.** $16.05 + 3.50   **10.** 49.1 + 3.17

11. 17.39 + 4.03   **12.** $6.30 + $0.91   **13.** 40.01 + 4.1   **14.** 6.74 + 4.09

15. 37.9 + 9.75   **16.** 0.91 + 1.7   **17.** 41.76 + 0.3   **18.** 9.9 + 54.37

Chapter 8, Page 261

Subtract.

1. 4.73 − 3.07   **2.** 16.96 − 3.8   **3.** $45.16 − 31.15   **4.** 7.2 − 5.11   **5.** 33.91 − 29.39

6. 7.6 − 4.51   **7.** 37.94 − 6.34   **8.** 6.4 − 3.21   **9.** $7.94 − 3.76   **10.** 61.59 − 15.51

11. 43.91 − 23.79   **12.** 4.79 − 3.08   **13.** $17.97 − $3.65   **14.** 9.89 − 0.9

15. 7.8 − 5.19   **16.** 3.84 − 0.97   **17.** 54.3 − 24.43   **18.** 71.6 − 3.51

Copy and complete.

1. 900 cm = ▓ m   **2.** 5 km = ▓ m   **3.** 1,400 cm = ▓ m

4. 21 m = ▓ cm   **5.** 8 m = ▓ cm   **6.** 16 km = ▓ m

7. 84,000 m = ▓ km   **8.** 2,400 cm = ▓ m   **9.** 52 m = ▓ cm

Write *cm*, *m*, or *km* for the unit you would use to measure each.

10. the height of your teacher   **11.** the length of a road

12. the width of a chair   **13.** the depth of a puddle

Copy and complete.

1. 6 L = ▓ mL   **2.** 57,000 mL = ▓ L   **3.** 8,000 mL = ▓ L

4. 28,000 mL = ▓ L   **5.** 17 L = ▓ mL   **6.** 99 L = ▓ mL

7. 24 L = ▓ mL   **8.** 3,000 mL = ▓ L   **9.** 7 L = ▓ mL

Write *mL* or *L* for the unit you would use to measure each.

10. a bucket of water   **11.** a glass of milk   **12.** a spoonful of water

13. a barrel of oil   **14.** a lake   **15.** a bowl of soup

Copy and complete.

1. 40 kg = ▓ g   **2.** 9,000 g = ▓ kg   **3.** 15,000 g = ▓ kg

4. 8,000 g = ▓ kg   **5.** 21 kg = ▓ g   **6.** 47,000 g = ▓ kg

Write *g* or *kg* for the unit you would use to measure each.

7. a banana   **8.** a big dog   **9.** a television set

10. yourself   **11.** a ladybug   **12.** a rhinoceros

Chapter 9, Page 289

Write *in.*, *ft*, *yd*, or *mi* for the unit you would use to measure each.

1. the height of a mountain

2. the length of an umbrella

3. the width of a basketball court

4. the width of a ruler

Copy and complete.

5. 36 in. = ■ ft

6. 5 mi = ■ yd

7. 15 ft = ■ yd

8. 5,280 yd = ■ mi

9. 72 in. = ■ ft

10. 9 yd = ■ ft

11. 8 ft = ■ in.

12. 3 ft = ■ in.

13. 60 in. = ■ ft

Chapter 9, Page 291

Write *oz*, *lb*, or *T* for the unit you would use to measure each.

1. a small twig

2. a bulldozer

3. a whale

4. a watermelon

5. a record album

6. a pig

Copy and complete.

7. 12,000 lb = ■ T

8. 64 oz = ■ lb

9. 10 lb = ■ oz

10. 7 T = ■ lb

11. 9 lb = ■ oz

12. 6,000 lb = ■ T

13. 128 oz = ■ lb

14. 5 T = ■ lb

15. 5 lb = ■ oz

Chapter 9, Page 293

Copy and complete.

1. 5 gal = ■ qt

2. 18 pt = ■ qt

3. 40 c = ■ pt

4. 14 qt = ■ pt

5. 28 qt = ■ gal

6. 24 pt = ■ c

7. 2 gal = ■ qt

8. 50 c = ■ pt

9. 20 pt = ■ qt

10. 6 qt = ■ pt

11. 6 gal = ■ qt

12. 12 pt = ■ qt

13. 3 gal = ■ qt

14. 8 c = ■ pt

15. 10 qt = ■ pt

Write the name of each polygon.

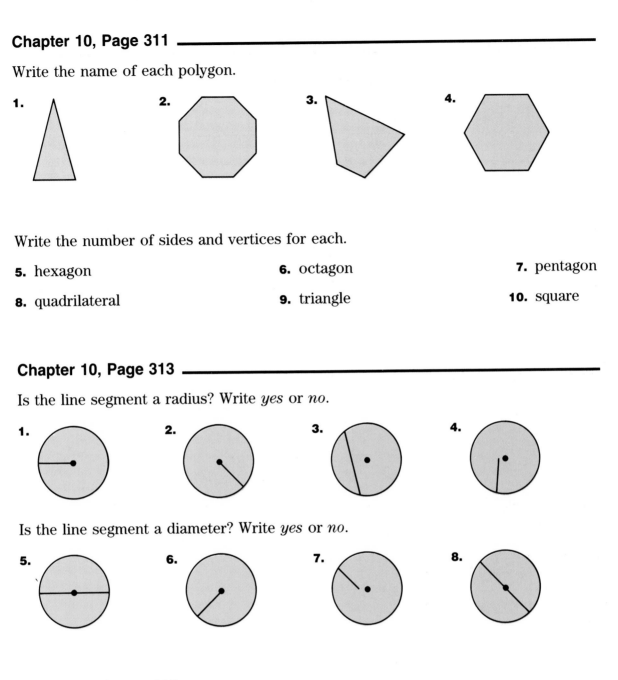

1.

2.

3.

4.

Write the number of sides and vertices for each.

5. hexagon

6. octagon

7. pentagon

8. quadrilateral

9. triangle

10. square

Chapter 10, Page 313

Is the line segment a radius? Write *yes* or *no*.

1.

2.

3.

4.

Is the line segment a diameter? Write *yes* or *no*.

5.

6.

7.

8.

Chapter 10, Page 323

Solve.

1. What is the perimeter of a rectangle that is 9 in. long and 2 in. wide?

2. What is the perimeter of a triangle if each side measures 5 in. long?

3. What is the perimeter of a pentagon that is 3 in. long on two sides and 4 in. long on three sides?

4. What is the perimeter of a hexagon that is 3 in. long on four sides and 4 in. long on two sides?

Count to find the area in square centimeters.

1. 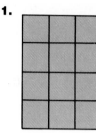 **2.** 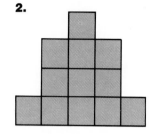 **3.** **4.**

Solve.

5. What is the area of a rectangle that is 4 in. long and 3 in. wide?

6. What is the area of a square that measures 6 in. on each side?

Chapter 10, Page 329

Copy and complete the table.

	1.	**2.**	**3.**
Name of figure			
Number of faces			
Number of edges			
Number of vertices			

Chapter 10, Page 331

Solve.

1. What is the volume of a rectangular prism that is 5 ft long, 3 ft wide, and 2 ft high?

2. What is the volume of a rectangular prism that is 6 m long, 3 m wide, and 8 m high?

3. What is the volume of a rectangular prism that is 7 cm long, 4 cm wide, and 12 cm high?

4. What is the volume of a rectangular prism that is 4 yd long, 4 yd wide, and 4 yd high?

Chapter 11, Page 347

Multiply.

1. $\begin{array}{r} 40 \\ \times 50 \\ \hline \end{array}$
2. $\begin{array}{r} 700 \\ \times 30 \\ \hline \end{array}$
3. $\begin{array}{r} 1,000 \\ \times \quad 90 \\ \hline \end{array}$
4. $\begin{array}{r} 500 \\ \times 40 \\ \hline \end{array}$
5. $\begin{array}{r} 7,000 \\ \times \quad 50 \\ \hline \end{array}$

6. 60×500
7. $40 \times 8,000$
8. 60×900
9. 30×200

10. $80 \times 3,000$
11. 90×500
12. 60×700
13. $90 \times 9,000$

14. 70×900
15. 40×60
16. 90×30
17. $30 \times 4,000$

Chapter 11, Page 349

Estimate by rounding.

1. $\begin{array}{r} 498 \\ \times \quad 32 \\ \hline \end{array}$
2. $\begin{array}{r} 314 \\ \times \quad 76 \\ \hline \end{array}$
3. $\begin{array}{r} \$5.95 \\ \times \quad 46 \\ \hline \end{array}$
4. $\begin{array}{r} 711 \\ \times \quad 91 \\ \hline \end{array}$
5. $\begin{array}{r} \$5.30 \\ \times \quad 57 \\ \hline \end{array}$

6. $\begin{array}{r} 609 \\ \times \quad 38 \\ \hline \end{array}$
7. $\begin{array}{r} 215 \\ \times \quad 46 \\ \hline \end{array}$
8. $\begin{array}{r} \$1.98 \\ \times \quad 27 \\ \hline \end{array}$
9. $\begin{array}{r} 649 \\ \times \quad 35 \\ \hline \end{array}$
10. $\begin{array}{r} \$0.83 \\ \times \quad 88 \\ \hline \end{array}$

11. $\begin{array}{r} \$2.34 \\ \times \quad 37 \\ \hline \end{array}$
12. $\begin{array}{r} 597 \\ \times \quad 84 \\ \hline \end{array}$
13. $\begin{array}{r} \$6.19 \\ \times \quad 76 \\ \hline \end{array}$
14. $\begin{array}{r} 599 \\ \times \quad 28 \\ \hline \end{array}$
15. $\begin{array}{r} \$0.90 \\ \times \quad 13 \\ \hline \end{array}$

16. 56×739
17. $81 \times \$4.17$
18. 64×390
19. $25 \times \$5.78$

Chapter 11, Page 353

Multiply.

1. $\begin{array}{r} 34 \\ \times 11 \\ \hline \end{array}$
2. $\begin{array}{r} 45 \\ \times 20 \\ \hline \end{array}$
3. $\begin{array}{r} 32 \\ \times 22 \\ \hline \end{array}$
4. $\begin{array}{r} 25 \\ \times 32 \\ \hline \end{array}$
5. $\begin{array}{r} 16 \\ \times 52 \\ \hline \end{array}$

6. $\begin{array}{r} 28 \\ \times 32 \\ \hline \end{array}$
7. $\begin{array}{r} 31 \\ \times 62 \\ \hline \end{array}$
8. $\begin{array}{r} 43 \\ \times 23 \\ \hline \end{array}$
9. $\begin{array}{r} 82 \\ \times 32 \\ \hline \end{array}$
10. $\begin{array}{r} 36 \\ \times 12 \\ \hline \end{array}$

11. 18×31
12. 84×22
13. 17×13
14. 40×34

15. 21×36
16. 15×15
17. 27×12
18. 11×52

Multiply.

1. 95
× 36

2. 38
× 74

3. $0.64
× 49

4. 52
× 46

5. $0.89
× 33

6. 67
× 52

7. 84
× 39

8. $0.57
× 44

9. 63
× 75

10. $0.74
× 24

11. 47
× 66

12. 68
× 54

13. $0.59
× 27

14. 27
× 65

15. $0.99
× 36

16. 56
× 23

17. 84
× 56

18. $0.78
× 45

19. 53
× 76

20. $0.46
× 47

21. 48 × $0.39

22. 37 × 46

23. 55 × 39

24. 69 × 35

25. 84 × 14

26. 29 × $0.73

27. 54 × 69

28. 45 × $0.76

Multiply.

1. 409
× 21

2. 569
× 14

3. 865
× 37

4. $9.32
× 48

5. 586
× 17

6. 657
× 36

7. $7.89
× 20

8. 450
× 36

9. 599
× 35

10. 600
× 53

11. 852
× 20

12. 485
× 13

13. $9.81
× 31

14. 479
× 46

15. $7.65
× 36

16. 468
× 20

17. 380
× 35

18. $6.46
× 91

19. 784
× 84

20. 495
× 43

21. 58 × $8.76

22. 60 × 948

23. 22 × 459

24. 11 × $3.46

25. 67 × 369

26. 16 × $7.47

27. 50 × 632

28. 65 × 954

Chapter 12, Page 375

Divide.

1. $40\overline{)80}$ 2. $10\overline{)700}$ 3. $50\overline{)250}$ 4. $60\overline{)320}$ 5. $40\overline{)210}$

6. $20\overline{)75}$ 7. $50\overline{)465}$ 8. $60\overline{)390}$ 9. $30\overline{)180}$ 10. $70\overline{)427}$

11. $90\overline{)270}$ 12. $80\overline{)656}$ 13. $20\overline{)83}$ 14. $50\overline{)221}$ 15. $10\overline{)99}$

16. $40\overline{)260}$ 17. $60\overline{)352}$ 18. $20\overline{)107}$ 19. $30\overline{)219}$ 20. $50\overline{)444}$

Chapter 12, Page 377

Divide.

1. $23\overline{)99}$ 2. $31\overline{)85}$ 3. $52\overline{)93}$ 4. $22\overline{)88}$ 5. $68\overline{)85}$

6. $42\overline{)97}$ 7. $12\overline{)49}$ 8. $21\overline{)68}$ 9. $33\overline{)85}$ 10. $41\overline{)82}$

11. $11\overline{)48}$ 12. $32\overline{)68}$ 13. $63\overline{)89}$ 14. $24\overline{)98}$ 15. $12\overline{)38}$

16. $31\overline{)75}$ 17. $25\overline{)78}$ 18. $11\overline{)57}$ 19. $43\overline{)87}$ 20. $37\overline{)89}$

21. $90 \div 22$ 22. $57 \div 43$ 23. $98 \div 31$ 24. $85 \div 21$

Chapter 12, Page 379

Divide.

1. $12\overline{)86}$ 2. $28\overline{)62}$ 3. $37\overline{)90}$ 4. $17\overline{)77}$ 5. $47\overline{)93}$

6. $26\overline{)48}$ 7. $37\overline{)60}$ 8. $13\overline{)43}$ 9. $38\overline{)65}$ 10. $45\overline{)88}$

11. $19\overline{)75}$ 12. $47\overline{)82}$ 13. $29\overline{)73}$ 14. $15\overline{)39}$ 15. $36\overline{)64}$

16. $43\overline{)81}$ 17. $18\overline{)39}$ 18. $22\overline{)60}$ 19. $35\overline{)69}$ 20. $19\overline{)93}$

Chapter 12, Page 383

Divide.

1. $67\overline{)455}$ 2. $32\overline{)281}$ 3. $78\overline{)253}$ 4. $84\overline{)334}$ 5. $65\overline{)340}$

6. $27\overline{)241}$ 7. $43\overline{)119}$ 8. $58\overline{)362}$ 9. $93\overline{)487}$ 10. $81\overline{)626}$

11. $66\overline{)492}$ 12. $73\overline{)393}$ 13. $25\overline{)115}$ 14. $56\overline{)425}$ 15. $44\overline{)254}$

16. $35\overline{)109}$ 17. $93\overline{)555}$ 18. $87\overline{)627}$ 19. $71\overline{)537}$ 20. $81\overline{)774}$

Chapter 12, Page 385

Divide.

1. $21\overline{)465}$ 2. $38\overline{)830}$ 3. $27\overline{)922}$ 4. $45\overline{)699}$ 5. $17\overline{)832}$

6. $54\overline{)842}$ 7. $78\overline{)921}$ 8. $52\overline{)875}$ 9. $35\overline{)753}$ 10. $24\overline{)836}$

11. $46\overline{)942}$ 12. $42\overline{)834}$ 13. $18\overline{)738}$ 14. $25\overline{)250}$ 15. $64\overline{)999}$

16. $81\overline{)973}$ 17. $52\overline{)795}$ 18. $36\overline{)946}$ 19. $13\overline{)579}$ 20. $33\overline{)894}$

21. $493 \div 15$ 22. $878 \div 65$ 23. $628 \div 31$ 24. $495 \div 28$

Chapter 12, Page 387

Divide.

1. $32\overline{)\$4.80}$ 2. $22\overline{)\$5.72}$ 3. $96\overline{)\$5.76}$ 4. $12\overline{)\$7.44}$ 5. $23\overline{)\$7.82}$

6. $23\overline{)\$9.43}$ 7. $95\overline{)\$7.60}$ 8. $17\overline{)\$4.25}$ 9. $42\overline{)\$7.56}$ 10. $15\overline{)\$5.85}$

11. $58\overline{)\$3.48}$ 12. $42\overline{)\$8.82}$ 13. $95\overline{)\$3.80}$ 14. $17\overline{)\$4.42}$ 15. $12\overline{)\$6.12}$

16. $62\overline{)\$8.06}$ 17. $87\overline{)\$5.22}$ 18. $39\overline{)\$8.97}$ 19. $11\overline{)\$9.79}$ 20. $64\overline{)\$1.92}$

MATH REASONING

Chapter 1

Logical Reasoning, pages 2–3

I am a 3-digit number. My tens digit is 2. My ones digit is 4 more than the tens digit. My hundreds digit is 4 times the tens digit. What number am I ?

Visual Thinking, pages 8–9

1. Find the number of people flying to each of the four cities.

2. List the cities in order from the one with the greatest number of people flying to it, to the one with the fewest number of people flying to it.

PEOPLE FLYING TO FOUR CITIES

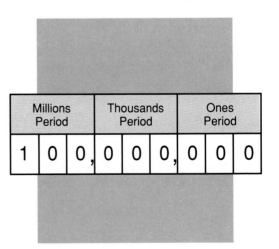

Each 🧑 stands for 50 people.

Logical Reasoning, pages 12–13

1. What is the largest number you can make with the digits 2, 8, 0, 1, 6, 2, 5?

2. Lucy is thinking of a 9-digit number. The millions period is 469. The thousands period is 625. Each of the other digits is 1. What is Lucy's number?

Millions Period			Thousands Period			Ones Period		
1	0	0,	0	0	0,	0	0	0

Math Reasoning

Chapter 1

Challenge, pages 14–15

Estimating money amounts is helpful when you are shopping.

Example: Joe went to the pet store. He bought 3 fish for $2.77, fish food for $1.07, and a fishbowl for $4.95. He paid with a $20.00 bill.

1. Did Joe spend more than or less than $10.00? How do you know?

2. Find the exact answer. You may wish to use a calculator. Was your estimate less than or greater than the exact answer? Why?

3. About how many dollars did Joe get in change?

Challenge, pages 18–19

Sal used five darts to make a score of 2 + 3 + 5 + 2 + 2 for a total of 14 points. Write a number sentence to show how he could score 14 points with

1. three darts.   2. six darts.

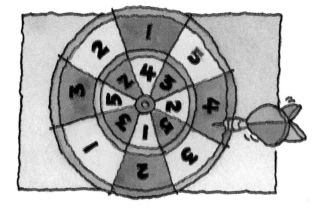

Challenge, pages 20–21

For each group of numbers, write as many addition sentences with two addends and as many subtraction sentences as you can. You may use a number more than one time.

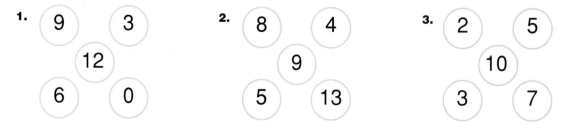

1. 9   3
      12
    6   0

2. 8   4
      9
    5   13

3. 2   5
      10
    3   7

Chapter 2

Logical Reasoning, pages 36–37

Find the missing digits.

1.
```
  6■
+ ■4
─────
  9 3
```

2.
```
  ■6
+ 7■
─────
 1 1 4
```

3.
```
  5 3
+ 5■
─────
 1■2
```

Challenge, pages 44–45

You can solve a problem by using mental math, paper and pencil, or a calculator. For Exercises 1–3, choose a method and solve each problem. Explain your choice.

1. Find the sum of 40, 20, and 50.

2. Find the total of $2.13 + $0.79 + $4.59.

3. Find the sum of 24,167 + 3,904 + 4,001.

4. Write a word problem that can best be solved by using a calculator. Exchange with a classmate and solve.

Challenge, pages 46–47

Kevin bought a remote-control car that was on sale for $80 and later sold it for $90. He bought it back for $100 and sold it again for $110. How much money did he make or lose in buying and selling the remote control car?

Chapter 2

Logical Reasoning, pages 48–49

Write <, >, or = for ●.

1. 52 + 98 + 107 ● 60 + 89 + 108

2. 452 + 690 + 7,182 ● 543 + 788 + 6,985

3. 708 + 888 + 2,007 ● 777 + 807 + 7,002

Visual Thinking, pages 54–55

Write the letter of the correct number sentence.

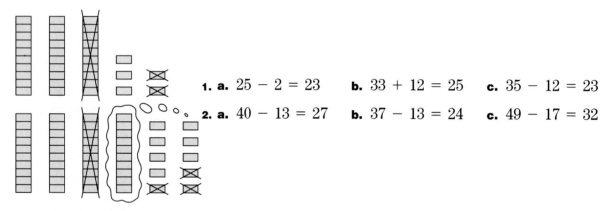

1. a. 25 − 2 = 23   **b.** 33 + 12 = 25   **c.** 35 − 12 = 23

2. a. 40 − 13 = 27   **b.** 37 − 13 = 24   **c.** 49 − 17 = 32

Logical Reasoning, pages 62–63

Find the missing digits.

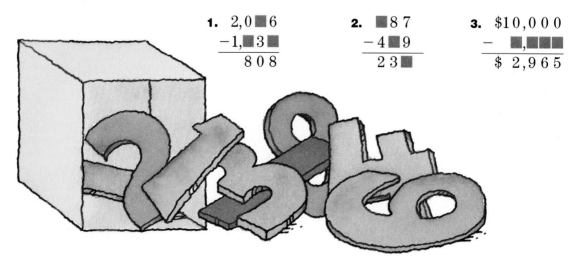

1.
$$\begin{array}{r} 2,0\blacksquare6 \\ -\,1,\blacksquare3\blacksquare \\ \hline 808 \end{array}$$

2.
$$\begin{array}{r} \blacksquare87 \\ -\,4\blacksquare9 \\ \hline 23\blacksquare \end{array}$$

3.
$$\begin{array}{r} \$10,000 \\ -\ \ \blacksquare,\blacksquare\blacksquare\blacksquare \\ \hline \$\,2,965 \end{array}$$

Math Reasoning

Chapter 3

Visual Thinking, pages 76–77

You can show a multiplication number sentence with a number line.

Example: Each arrow shows how many miles Mack rides to and from school in one day.

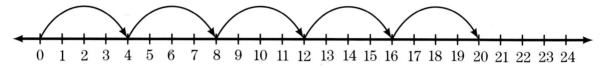

1. How many miles does Mack ride each day?

2. How many miles does Mack ride in 3 days?

3. How many miles does Mack ride in 5 days?

Challenge, pages 76–77

A grocery store has a sale on bottles of grape and orange juice. The bottles are arranged in a display on the store shelves.

1. Write a multiplication number sentence to show how many bottles are in the display.

2. Write a multiplication number sentence to find how many bottles of grape juice are on the shelves.

3. How can you find the number of bottles of orange juice on the shelves?

Logical Reasoning, pages 80–81

Complete the pattern.

1. 26, 38, 50, 62, 74, 86, ■, ■

2. 88, 77, 66, 55, 44, 33, ■, ■

3. 3, 2, 4, 3, 6, 5, 10, ■, ■

Chapter 3

Logical Reasoning, pages 82–83

1. The rule is: Multiply by 6. Find the output.

Input	3	4	5	6	7	8
Output	■	■	■	■	■	■

What is the rule?

Input	4	5	6	7	8	9
Output	28	35	42	49	56	63

Visual Thinking, pages 90–91

Use the clock to answer Exercises 1–3.

1. Write the time that is two and one-half hours later than 6:15 A.M.

2. Write the time that is 4 hours and 15 minutes earlier than 6:15 A.M.

3. How many minutes are there from a quarter after six to half past six?

Challenge, pages 94–95

Simone is a member of the Nature Club. The club meets every other Tuesday in January, February, March, and April, beginning the first Tuesday in January. On the last Saturday in April, the club will go on a camping trip. Use the calendar.

1. List the dates that the club meets.

2. What is the date of the club camping trip?

JANUARY							FEBRUARY						
S	M	T	W	T	F	S	S	M	T	W	T	F	S
					1	2		1	2	3	4	5	6
3	4	5	6	7	8	9	7	8	9	10	11	12	13
10	11	12	13	14	15	16	14	15	16	17	18	19	20
17	18	19	20	21	22	23	21	22	23	24	25	26	27
24	25	26	27	28	29	30	28	29					
31													

MARCH							APRIL						
S	M	T	W	T	F	S	S	M	T	W	T	F	S
		1	2	3	4	5						1	2
6	7	8	9	10	11	12	3	4	5	6	7	8	9
13	14	15	16	17	18	19	10	11	12	13	14	15	16
20	21	22	23	24	25	26	17	18	19	20	21	22	23
27	28	29	30	31			24	25	26	27	28	29	30

Math Reasoning

Chapter 4

Logical Reasoning, pages 108–109

Chuck has a number puzzle for the class to solve. He starts with a 2-digit number. He adds 13 and then divides by 9. He ends up with 3. What was the number that Chuck started with?

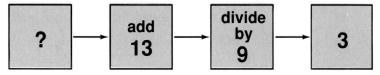

Challenge, pages 110–111

You can use toothpicks to make calculator display digits.

Example: It takes five toothpicks to make a 5.

1. Which digit takes the fewest toothpicks?

2. Which digit takes the most toothpicks?

3. Name three other digits that take five toothpicks.

Challenge, pages 114–115

Write number sentences using the fact family 5, 9, and 45.

1. Write one number sentence with a missing factor.

2. Write one number sentence with a missing product.

3. Write one number sentence with a missing divisor.

4. Write one number sentence with a missing quotient.

5. Exchange your number sentences with a classmate. Solve.

Chapter 4

Visual Thinking, pages 116–117

Solve the riddle.

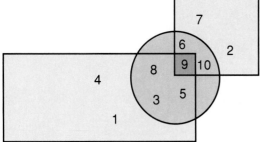

I am a 1-digit number. I am inside the circle and the square. I am not in the rectangle. When I am divided by 3, the quotient is 2. What number am I?

Logical Reasoning, pages 122–123

Find the missing digits. Complete the key.

1. ▲ × ▲ = 9, so ▲ = ■

2. ■ ÷ 4 = 2, so ■ = ■

3. (● × ●) − 9 = 40, so ● = ■

4. (⧗ × ⧗) = 4 × 9, so ⧗ = ■

Key

▲	= ■
■	= ■
●	= ■
⧗	= ■

Logical Reasoning, pages 124–125

This is a factor tree for 8.

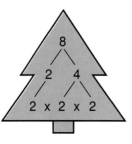

Copy and complete each factor tree.

1.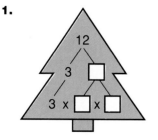

2.

3.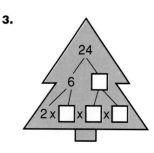

4. Draw a different factor tree for 8, 12, and 24.

Math Reasoning

Chapter 5

Challenge, pages 138–139

a. 360 **b.** 500 **c.** 800 **d.** 900 **e.** 2,000 **f.** 8,000

Estimate the product. Write the letter of the best estimate.

1. $2 \times 4 \times 997 = $

2. $3 \times 1 \times 3 \times 114 = $ ▨

3. $1 \times 2 \times 3 \times 89 = $ ▨

4. $62 \times 3 \times 2 = $ ▨

5. $1 \times 389 \times 2 \times 3 = $ ▨

6. $773 \times 1 \times 2 \times 5 = $ ▨

 Challenge, pages 142–143

Use a calculator to solve.

What number times itself equals each of the following products?

1. 729

2. 1,296

3. 2,809

4. 5,184

Think:
    same   same
    number   number
    ▨ $\times$ ▨ $= 729$

HINT: Use *Guess and Check.*

Challenge, pages 144–145

Copy the crossnumber puzzle.
Solve each problem to complete.

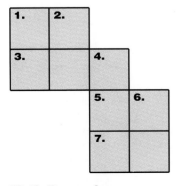

Across
1. $(49 \div 7) \times 8 + 12$
3. $(5 \times 7) \times 9$
5. $(4 \times 8) - (3 \times 6)$
7. $(2 \times 6) \times 2 + 1$

Down
1. $(3 + 4) \times 9$
2. $(9 \times 3) \times 3$
4. $(72 \div 9) \times 60 + 32$
6. $(34 \times 5) - (5 \times 25)$

Math Reasoning

Chapter 5

Challenge, pages 150–151

Use the key to solve each problem.

Key
J = 3
K = 4
L = 5

1. JLK
× L

2. LLL
× J

3. KJL
× K

4. LKJ
× K

5. JKL
× J

6. KLJ
× L

Challenge, pages 154–155

Copy and complete the store receipt to find the amount that was spent on each group of items. Then find the total amount of the sale plus tax.

MAPLE CITY SCHOOL SUPPLY STORE

Item	Quantity	Price for each item	Total
Box of Markers	3	$1.25	■
Pencil	9	$0.39	■
Notebook	4	$1.19	■
		Tax	$0.62
	Total amount of sale		■

Logical Reasoning, pages 156–157

Misty bought a video at the video store. At 9:30 A.M. she bought a compact disc at the music store. Misty left her video at Julia's house. The video store opened at 10:00 A.M..

1. Did Misty have her video at the music store?

2. Did Misty buy the compact disc before going to Julia's house?

3. Did Misty reach Julia's house before or after 9:30 A.M.?

Math Reasoning

Chapter 6

Logical Reasoning, pages 168–169

1. What two numbers have a quotient of 9 and a difference of 56?

2. What two numbers have a quotient of 8 and a difference of 49?

3. What two numbers have a quotient of 7 and a sum of 40?

4. What two numbers have a quotient of 6 and a sum of 28?

Logical Reasoning, pages 170–171

Write = or ≠ to make the number sentence true.

1. $3,000 \div 3 \bullet 10 \times 10,000$

2. $4,200 \div 7 \bullet 6 \times 100$

3. $1,200 \div 4 \bullet 40 \times 40$

4. $800 \div 8 \bullet 8 \times 10$

Challenge, pages 176–177

FEBRUARY MILEAGE

	Miles	Gallons Used	Miles per Gallon
Week 1	208	8	■
Week 2	216	9	■
Week 3	234	9	■
Week 4	196	7	■

Mr. Nelson keeps a record of the miles he travels and the gas he uses each week. Then he divides the number of miles by the number of gallons used. The quotient tells how far Mr. Nelson's car can travel on one gallon of gas. This number is called *miles per gallon*. Copy and complete the table to find the miles per gallon that Mr. Nelson's car got each week.

Chapter 6

Logical Reasoning, pages 178–179

Find the missing digits.

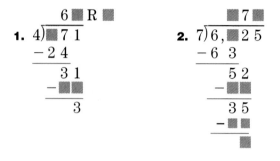

1.
```
       6 ■ R ■
   4)■ 7 1
    −2 4
     ─────
      3 1
    −■■
     ─────
        3
```

2.
```
      ■ 7 ■
  7)6,■ 2 5
   −6 3
    ─────
     5 2
   −■■
    ─────
     3 5
   −■■
    ─────
      ■
```

3.
```
          6,5 ■■ R ■
   ■)3 9,2 8 0
    −■■
     ─────
      3 2
     −3 0
      ─────
       ■ 8
      −■■
       ─────
        4 0
       −■■
        ─────
         ■
```

Challenge, pages 180–181

This table shows the spelling test grades in Ms. Bateman's class for this semester. The first student's average has been calculated.

1. Copy and complete the table.

2. What is the class average for this semester?

SPELLING TEST GRADES

Student's names	1	2	3	4	5	Avg.
Amy	100	95	80	100	90	93
Bobby	65	75	75	80	85	■
Carol	90	90	95	85	90	■
Emilio	80	75	70	90	95	■
Gary	60	70	65	80	80	■
Joan	75	75	80	85	85	■
Kim	95	95	100	90	100	■
					Class average	■

Beth   Olga   Nick   Carmen   Marty   Emily

Visual Thinking, pages 182–183

1. Name the character who is taller than Marty and who is wearing shorts.

2. Name the character who is wearing sunglasses, has curly hair, and plays tennis.

3. Name the character who is shorter than Emily, is barefoot, and isn't playing baseball today.

4. Name the character who is shorter than Emily, is wearing shorts, and plays tennis.

Math Reasoning

Chapter 7

Challenge, pages 198–199

MELINDA'S DAY

Activity	Hours	Fraction
Sleeping	10	▨
Eating	2	▨
Entertainment	4	▨
Chores	3	▨
School	7	▨

1. There are 24 hours in one day. Each hour is $\frac{1}{24}$ of one day. Copy and complete the chart.

2. List three different activities that together would take up at least half a day.

Logical Reasoning, pages 200–201

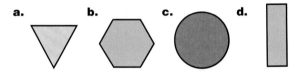

a.   b.   c.   d.   e.   f.   g.   h.

1. Write the letters of the shapes that are red *and* round.

2. Write the letters of the shapes that are green *or* triangular.

Challenge, pages 202–203

Solve.

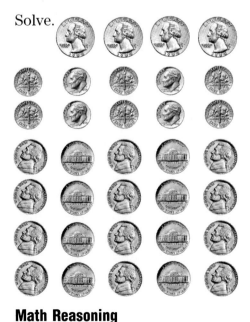

1. Since 1 quarter is $\frac{1}{4}$ of a dollar, what fraction of a dollar is three quarters?

2. Since 1 nickel is $\frac{1}{20}$ of a dollar, what fraction of a dollar is 8 nickels?

3. Since 1 dime is $\frac{1}{10}$ of a dollar, what fraction of a dollar is 5 dimes?

4. Since there are 100 pennies in a dollar, what fraction of a dollar is 23 pennies?

Math Reasoning

Chapter 7

Visual Thinking, pages 212–213

Tell whether each figure has more blue or more yellow.
Write *blue* or *yellow*.

1. **2.** 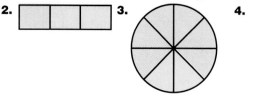 **3.** **4.** 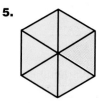 **5.**

Logical Reasoning, pages 216–217

Libby is arranging books on a shelf. She chooses each book from a box of books. Inside the box are 3 science books, 5 history books, 2 craft books, and 1 dictionary. All of the books are the same size. What is the probability that Libby will choose

1. a craft book?

2. a dictionary?

3. a history book or a science book?

4. a math book?

Logical Reasoning, pages 218–219

Look at the pencils. If you choose a pencil without looking, what is the probability of picking

1. a red pencil?

2. a blue pencil?

3. a yellow or a green pencil?

4. a ballpoint pen?

Math Reasoning

Chapter 8

Challenge, pages 238–239

Use the map to answer Exercises 1–5. Follow the roads on the map.

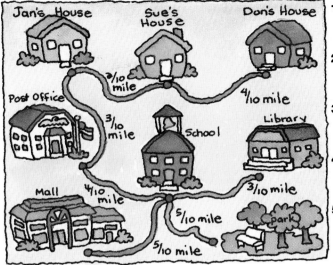

1. How far is it from Don's house to Jan's house?

2. How far is it from the park to the library?

3. How far it from Sue's house to school?

4. How far is it from the post office to the mall?

5. Find two locations that are $\frac{9}{10}$ of a mile apart.

Challenge, pages 244–245

The pizza is divided into 8 equal pieces. This graph shows what fraction of the pizza each person ate. Use the graph to solve Exercises 1–2.

1. Write the fraction that shows how much more pizza Joe ate than Sue.

2. Write the fraction that shows how much more pizza Ellen ate than Sue and Joe.

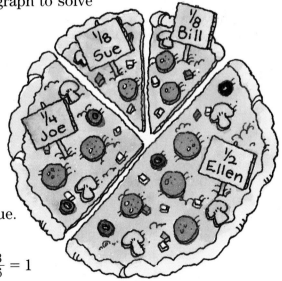

Logical Reasoning, pages 246–247

Write + or − to make the number sentence true. Write the answer in simplest form.

1. $1\frac{2}{8} \bullet 2\frac{1}{8} \bullet \frac{3}{8} = 3$

2. $3\frac{5}{6} \bullet 2\frac{2}{6} \bullet \frac{3}{6} = 1$

3. $4\frac{2}{6} \bullet \frac{2}{6} \bullet 2\frac{4}{6} = 6\frac{2}{3}$

4. $2\frac{2}{10} \bullet 3\frac{4}{10} \bullet 3\frac{2}{10} = 2\frac{2}{5}$

Chapter 8

Visual Thinking, pages 250–251

Write a fraction and a decimal for the blue part of each figure.

1.   **2.**   **3.**

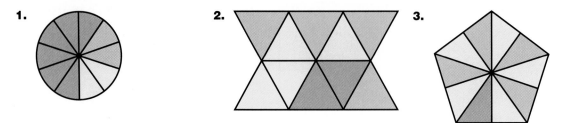

Challenge, pages 254–255

Write each decimal and its letter in order from the least to the greatest. If you are correct, you will find the name of the Sunshine State.

O	D	F	I	A	L	R
1.17	3.05	0.01	2.31	3.13	0.07	1.20

Logical Reasoning, pages 260–261

Solve the riddle.

1. The sum of two fractions is $\frac{8}{9}$. Their difference is $\frac{2}{9}$. They have the same denominator. What are the two fractions?

2. The sum of two decimals is 0.67. Their difference is 0.01. What are the two decimals?

Math Reasoning

Chapter 9

Visual Thinking, pages 274–275

Estimate the length to the nearest centimeter.

1.

2.

3.

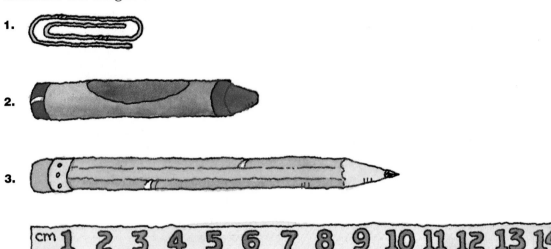

4. Find three things in your desk. Estimate the length of each to the nearest centimeter, and then measure to find the actual length. Record your measurements.

Challenge, pages 276–277

Use the map to answer Exercises 1–4.

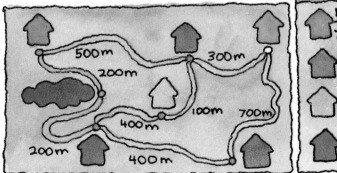

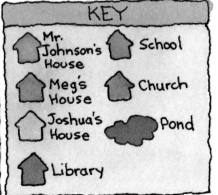

1. What is the shortest distance Mr. Johnson can travel to the library?

2. How far is it from Meg's house to the church if she goes to the library first?

3. Which two paths are the same length?

4. How far is it from the library to the school?

Chapter 9

Logical Reasoning, pages 280–281

Use the graph to solve.

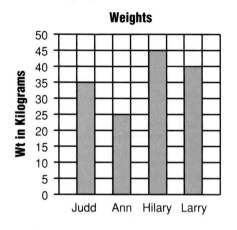

Weights

1. Lane weighs an odd number of kilograms. Her weight is between Hilary's weight and Larry's weight. It is closer to Hilary's weight. How much does Lane weigh?

2. Gary weighs 6 kilograms less than Judd. Together they weigh 64 kilograms. How much does Gary weigh?

3. Jerry weighs 13 kilograms less than twice Ann's weight. How much does Jerry weigh?

Logical Reasoning, pages 288–289

Copy and complete the tables.

feet	1	2	4	6	8	10
inches	12	24	▪	▪	▪	▪

yards	1	2	4	6	8	10
feet	3	6	▪	▪	▪	▪

Challenge, pages 290–291

Use the key to complete each number sentence.

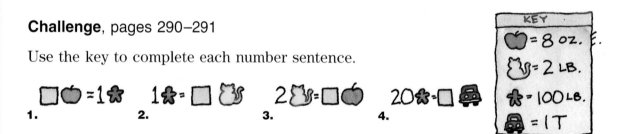

1. □🍎 =1🐿

2. 1🍪= □ 🐿

3. 2🐿=□🍎

4. 20🍪=□🚗

KEY
🍎 = 8 OZ.
🐿 = 2 LB.
🍪 = 100 LB.
🚗 = 1 T

Logical Reasoning, pages 292–293

Use the recipe to solve.

1. Will 1 recipe of punch make more than 1 gallon of punch?

2. How much pineapple juice do you use in the punch to make 24 servings?

3. How much lemon juice is needed to make half a recipe of punch?

Citrus Punch
Makes 12 servings.
4 cups of pineapple juice
4 cups of orange juice
1 cup of lemon juice
3 cups of cranberry juice
1 fresh orange, sliced
Mix the juices. Pour into large pitcher. Chill. Add orange slices.

Math Reasoning

Chapter 10

Challenge, pages 308–309

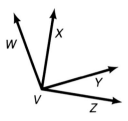

1. Name all the rays in this figure.

2. Name all the angles in this figure.

Visual Thinking, pages 310–311

A polygon that has all sides congruent and all angles the same measure is called a **regular polygon.**

Write the number of the regular quadrilateral, the regular hexagon, and the regular pentagon hidden in the puzzle.

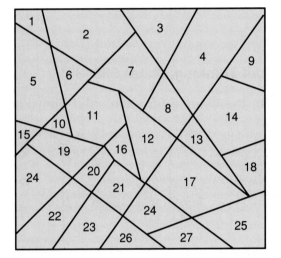

Logical Reasoning, pages 316–317

Copy each figure. Then draw one congruent figure and one similar figure. Use graph paper.

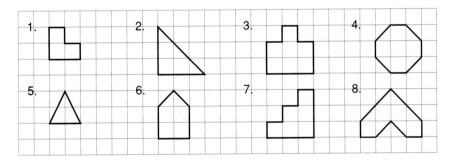

Chapter 10

Visual Thinking, pages 324–325

Write the perimeter and area for each figure. Label the perimeter in units and the area in square units.

1.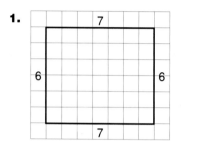

2.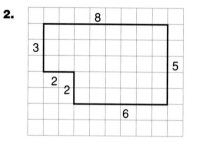

3.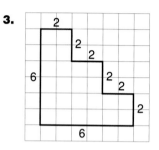

Visual Thinking, pages 330–331

Write the volume for each solid figure in cubic units.

1.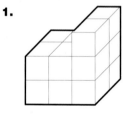

2.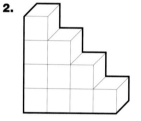

3.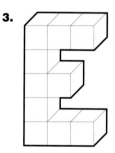

Challenge, pages 336–337

Use the pictograph to answer Exercises 1–4.

NUMBER OF HOUSES

Street	Houses
Oak	🏠 🏠
Maple	🏠 🏠 🏠
Birch	🏠 🏠 🏠
Pine	🏠 🏠 🏠 🏠 🏠

Each 🏠 = 10 houses

1. How many houses are on Birch Street?

2. How many more houses are on Pine Street than on Oak Street?

3. How many houses altogether are on Oak, Maple, and Birch streets?

4. Suppose each 🏠 was equal to 25. How many houses would there be in all?

Math Reasoning

Chapter 11

Logical Reasoning, pages 346–347

Write the correct sign ($+$, $-$, $\times$, or $\div$) in the▲.

1. 50 ▲ 4 = 10 ▲ 20

2. 210 ▲ 14 = 16 ▲ 14

3. 40 ▲ 800 = 30,000 ▲ 2,000

4. 580 ▲ 230 = 10 ▲ 35

5. 64 ▲ 8 = 126 ▲ 70

6. 420 ▲ 7 = 201 ▲ 141

Logical Reasoning, pages 348–349

Write as many different multiplication problems as you can using the digits 3, 4, and 5 in each problem. Solve.

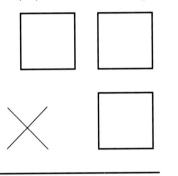

1. How many different products can you make?

2. What is the largest product you can make?

3. What is the smallest product you can make?

Logical Reasoning, pages 350–351

Carl scored 14 points for the Bay Vista basketball team. Billy scored half as many points as Craig. Brock scored 6 more points than Billy. Craig scored 10 more points than Carl. Matthew's score was the same as the average score of the other four players.

1. What was Matthew's score?

2. What was the team's total score?

3. What was the average number of points per player?

Chapter 11

Visual Thinking, pages 352–353

Choose the correct number sentence for each figure. Solve.

1.

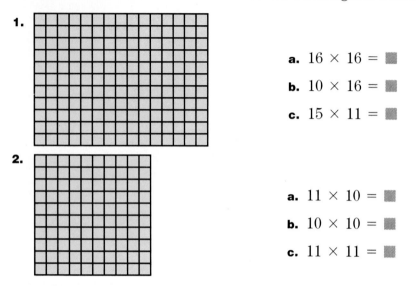

   a. $16 \times 16 = $ ■

   b. $10 \times 16 = $ ■

   c. $15 \times 11 = $ ■

2.

   a. $11 \times 10 = $ ■

   b. $10 \times 10 = $ ■

   c. $11 \times 11 = $ ■

Challenge, pages 354–355

In a contest sponsored by the Athletic Club, students sold stadium blankets. Aaron sold four times as many as Brent. Conrad sold twice as many as Aaron. Conrad said that the number of blankets he sold rounded to 30. Exactly how many stadium blankets did each boy sell?

Logical Reasoning, pages 356–357

Use the picture to solve.

1. How much money will the team spend if they buy 18 pairs of pants and 20 shirts?

2. How much will the team save if they buy 24 caps on sale?

3. How much will the team spend on 3 dozen pairs of socks at the sale price?

4. How much will the team spend for the pants, shirts, caps, and socks?

Math Reasoning

Chapter 12

Logical Reasoning, pages 370–371

Complete the pattern.

120 ÷ 30	4
160 ÷ 40	4
200 ÷ 50	4
1.	
2.	
3.	
4.	

1,600 ÷ 40	40
2,500 ÷ 50	50
3,600 ÷ 60	60
5.	
6.	
7.	
8.	

Logical Reasoning, pages 372–373

Write a number sentence to solve the problem.

Rochelle had $12.00 in her purse. On the way to the mall, her aunt gave her another $12.00. Rochelle bought a cassette tape for $10.96. When she returned home, she put half the money that was left over in her piggy bank. How much money remained in her purse?

Challenge, pages 380–381

Bart is loading bicycle and tricycle frames and their wheels on a delivery truck. There are 12 wheels in all.

1. How many wheels belong on the bicycles?

2. How many wheels belong on the tricycles?

Chapter 12

Logical Reasoning, pages 382–383

Find the missing digits.

     9 R17   3 R31   ■ R19   7 R71

1. 3 9)3 ■ ■   **2.** 4 ■)157   **3.** 2 5)2 1 ■   **4.** 7 6)6 ■ 3

Challenge, pages 384–385

Write the year in which you were born. _____

Write your age today. _____

Now, use a calculator and follow the directions below.

a. Enter the year you were born.
b. Multiply it by 5.
c. Now add 25.
d. Multiply by 20.
e. Add your age.
f. Then add 365.
g. Subtract 865.

Write the answer that appears on your calculator.

What do you notice about the answer?

Logical Reasoning, pages 386–387

Use the grocery store ad to find the cost of

1. two pounds of onions.

2. five pounds of potatoes.

3. ten pounds of apples.

4. fifteen pounds of lemons.

TABLE OF MEASURES

TIME

1 minute (min) = 60 seconds (s)
1 hour (h) = 60 minutes
1 day (d) = 24 hours

METRIC UNITS

LENGTH
1 meter (m) = 100 centimeters (cm)
1 kilometer (km) = 1,000 meters

MASS
1 kilogram (kg) = 1,000 grams (g)

CAPACITY
1 liter (L) = 1,000 milliliters (mL)

TEMPERATURE
0° Celsius (C) . . . . Water freezes
100° Celsius (C) . . . . Water boils

CUSTOMARY UNITS

LENGTH
1 foot (ft) = 12 inches (in.)
1 yard (yd) = 36 inches
1 yard = 3 feet
1 mile (mi) = 5,280 feet
1 mile = 1,760 yards

WEIGHT
1 pound (lb) = 16 ounces (oz)
1 ton (T) = 2,000 pounds

CAPACITY
1 pint (pt) = 2 cups (c)
1 quart (qt) = 2 pints
1 quart = 4 cups
1 gallon (gal) = 4 quarts

TEMPERATURE
32° Fahrenheit (F) . . . . . . Water freezes
212° Fahrenheit (F) . . . . . . Water boils

SYMBOLS

$<$	is less than	°	degree	$\overline{AB}$	line segment AB
$>$	is greater than	•A	point A	$\angle ABC$	angle ABC
$\neq$	is not equal to	$\overleftrightarrow{AB}$	line AB	(5,3)	the ordered pair 5,3
$4 \div 2$	4 divided by 2	$\overrightarrow{AB}$	ray AB		

GLOSSARY

Addends Numbers that are added. 4 + 5 = 9
                                                  ↑   ↑
                                               addends

Angle An angle is formed when two rays have a common endpoint. This is angle *ABC*, angle *CBA*, or ∠*B*.

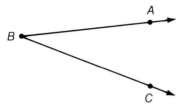

Area The number of square units a figure contains.

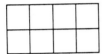

Average The average of a set of numbers is the number found by adding the set of numbers and dividing by the total number of addends.

Bar graph A graph that shows number information by using bars of different lengths.

BASIC BASIC is a computer language. It stands for "Beginner's All-purpose Symbolic Instructional Code."

Circle A closed figure made up of points that are the same distance from the center point.

Common factor A number that is a factor of two or more numbers.

Example: 6 is a factor of 12 and 18.

Composite Number A number that has more than two factors.

Example: 6 is a composite number. Its factors are 1, 2, 3, and 6.

Cone A solid figure that has a circular bottom.

Congruent Line segments or figures that have the same size and shape are congruent.

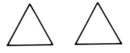

Cube A solid figure that has six square faces.

Cubic unit The measure used for finding the volume or the number of cubes that will fit inside a figure.

Cylinder A solid figure that has two faces that are circles.

Debug To fix the problems in a computer program so that it will do what you want it to do.

Decimal A number that uses place value and a decimal point to show tenths, hundredths, thousandths, and so on.

Examples: 1.7, 0.46, 39.70

Degree A unit used to measure temperature.

Denominator In $\frac{7}{8}$, 8 is the denominator.

Diameter A line segment that passes through the center of a circle and connects any two points on the circle.

Difference The answer in subtraction.

Digit Any of the ten symbols used to write numerals: 0, 1, 2, 3, 4, 5, 6, 7, 8, 9.

Dividend The number that another number is divided into.

Example:

$$9\overline{)45} \quad \frac{5}{}$$

dividend $\longrightarrow$ 45 ÷ 9 = 5

Divisible A number is divisible by another if it can be divided by that number with no remainder.

Example: 14 ÷ 7 = 2

Divisor The number that another number is divided by.

Example:

$$8\overline{)48} \quad \frac{6}{} \text{ or } 48 \div 8 = 6$$

divisor

Edge An edge is the place where two faces of a solid figure meet.

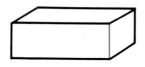

Equation A number sentence that uses the equal sign.

Example: 7 + 5 = 12, or 36 ÷ 9 = 4

Equivalent fractions Two or more fractions that name the same number.

Example: $\frac{1}{3} = \frac{2}{6}$

Even number A number that has 0, 2, 4, 6, or 8 in the ones place.

Expanded form A way to show a number as the sum of the value of its digits.

Example: 526 = 500 + 20 + 6

Face The flat side of a solid figure.

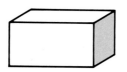

Factors Numbers that are multiplied.

Example: 4 × 3 = 12
$\qquad\quad\uparrow\quad\uparrow$
$\qquad\quad$ factors

Fraction A number used to name parts of a whole or parts of a group.

Examples: $\frac{2}{3}, \frac{3}{4}, \frac{7}{8}$

Graph Information shown by use of pictures, lines, or bars.

Grouping property for addition If you change the way addends are grouped, the sum is always the same.

Example: (6 + 6) + 1 = 6 + (6 + 1)

Grouping property for multiplication If you change the way the factors are grouped, the product is always the same.

Example: (2 × 3) × 1 = 2 × (3 × 1)

Intersecting lines Two or more lines that meet at a common point.

Line A straight path that goes forever in both directions.

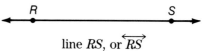

line RS, or $\overleftrightarrow{RS}$

Line of symmetry A line of folding so that the two halves of a figure match.

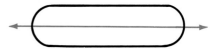

Line segment A straight path that has two endpoints.

line segment CD, or $\overline{CD}$

Mixed number A number that is made up of a whole number and a fraction.

Example: $2\frac{2}{5}$

Multiple The product of a number and any other whole number.

Example: $3 \times 4 = 12$. 12 is a multiple of 3.

Number sentence An equation or inequality.

Examples: $5 + 9 = 14$; $17 - 9 > 6$

Numerator In $\frac{3}{8}$, 3 is the numerator.

Odd number A number that has 1, 3, 5, 7, or 9 in the ones place.

Order Property for Addition If you change the order of the addends, the sum is always the same.

Example: $2 + 4 = 4 + 2$

Order Property for Multiplication If you change the order of the factors, the product is always the same.

Example: $2 \times 9 = 9 \times 2$

Ordered pairs A pair of numbers used to locate a point on a graph.

Parallel lines Lines that never meet.

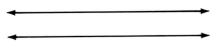

Perimeter The distance around a geometric figure, found by adding the measures of its sides. The perimeter of this figure is 20 cm.

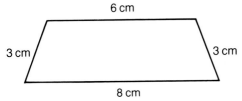

Pictograph A graph that uses pictures to show information.

Place value The value of a digit depends on its position within a number. In 4,578 the 5 stands for 500, while in 56 the 5 stands for 50.

Point An exact location in space.

Polygon A closed figure formed by three or more line segments.

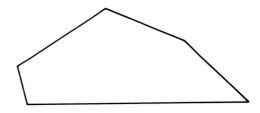

Prime number A number that has exactly two factors, itself and 1. 7 is a prime number.

PRINT A command that tells a computer to print on a screen.

Probability A number, written as a fraction, that tells how likely it is for an event to occur.

Product The answer in multiplication.

Example: $4 \times 3 = 12$.
↑
product

Quotient The answer in division.

Example: $24 \div 6 = 4$ ←——— quotient

Radius A line segment that has one endpoint at the center of the circle and another on the circle.

Ray A portion of a line that extends forever in one direction only.

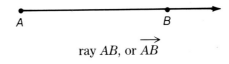

ray AB, or $\overrightarrow{AB}$

Rectangle A quadrilateral that has four right angles.

Rectangular prism A figure that has six faces, each of which is a rectangle.

Related sentences Related sentences use the same numbers and the same or opposite operations.

Examples: 6 + 5 = 11
                    5 + 6 = 11
                   11 − 6 = 5
                   11 − 5 = 6
                    4 × 7 = 28
                    7 × 4 = 28
                   28 ÷ 7 = 4
                   28 ÷ 4 = 7

Remainder In the division 19 ÷ 4, 4 is the quotient and 3 is the remainder.

Example:
$$
\begin{array}{r}
4\ \text{R}3 \\
4\overline{)19} \\
16 \\
\hline
3 \leftarrow \text{remainder}
\end{array}
$$

Right angle An angle that forms a square corner.

Similar figures Figures that have the same shape but are of different sizes.

Simplest form A fraction is in simplest form if its numerator and denominator have no common factor greater than 1.

Example: $\frac{5}{10}$ in simplest form is $\frac{1}{2}$.

Sphere A figure in space of this shape.

Square A figure that has four right angles and four sides of equal length.

Standard form The usual way of writing a number. In standard form, *fifteen* is written 15.

Sum The answer in addition.

Symmetrical If the parts match when a figure is folded on a line, the figure is symmetrical.

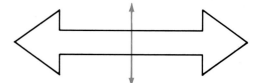

Triangle A polygon that has three sides.

Vertex The common endpoint of the sides of an angle or two sides of a polygon.

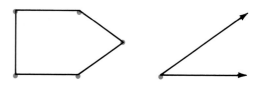

Volume The number of cubic units a solid figure contains. This figure has a volume of 4 cubic units.

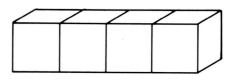

Whole numbers Any of the numbers such as 0, 1, 2, 3, ...

Index

A

Addend, 18
  missing, 22–23
Addition
  annexing zeros, 258–259
  column, 48–49
  with decimals, 258–259
  estimation in, 41, 50–51,
    256–257
  facts, 18–19
  with fractions, 236–239, 268
  of larger numbers, 44–45
  with mixed numbers,
    246–247
  with money, 36–39, 46–49
  properties, 18–19
  related to subtraction,
    22–23
  of three-digit numbers,
    44–45
  of two-digit numbers,
    36–39
  of whole numbers, 18–19,
    36–39, 41, 44–51
Algebra
  graphs of ordered pairs,
    320–321
  missing addends, 22–23
  missing factors, 114–115
  order of operations, 165
  ordered pairs, 320–321
  properties, 18–19, 78–79
  rules of division, 116–117
  variables, 64–65, 188–189,
    372–373
A.M., 90–91
Angle, 308–309
  right, 308–309, 399
Another Look. (*See*
  Maintenance)
Area, 324–325, 338, 342
Associative Property. (*See*
  Grouping Property)
Average, 180–181

B

BK (back), 32
Bar graph. (*See* Graph)
BASIC, 134

C

Calculator. (*See* Technology)
Calendar, 94–95, 397, H186
Capacity
  customary, 292–293
  estimating, 278–279,
    292–293, 399
  metric, 278–279
Casting out nines, 367
Celsius, degree, 295
Center of a circle, 312–313
Centimeter, 274–277
Challenge, 11, 19, 21, 39, 75,
  79, 123, 143, 149, 153, 171,
  185, 199, 201, 217, 221, 243,
  253, 255, 289, 291, 293, 311,
  313, 317, 329, 347, 359, 377
Checkpoint. (*See* Error
  diagnosis)
Choosing the Method, 187, 383
Circle, 312–313
Circle graph. (*See* Graph)
Combinations, 222–223,
  240–241, 248–249, 380–381
Common factors, 124–125
Communication, 26, 128, 226
Commutative Property. (*See*
  Order Property)
Comparing and ordering
  with decimals, 254–255
  with fractions, 212–213
  with mixed numbers,
    212–213
  of whole numbers, 8–9, 30
Compass, 312–313
Composite numbers, 133
Computer. (*See* Technology)
Cone, 328–329
Congruent figures, 316–317,
  399, H199
Connecting Math Ideas,
  397–400
  reference to, 87, 95, 113,
    243, 247, 277, 293, 309,
    317, 321, 329, 331
Consumer
  better buy, 111, 155, 245,
    387
  bills and coins, 10–11, 381
  calorie chart, 299
  change, 71, 89, 263, 361
  comparing costs, 46–47,
    155, 215
  comparing ingredient

    amounts, 208–209
  cost per serving, 187
  elapsed time, 92–95, 102
  estimating costs, 53, 57,
    141, 146–147, 155,
    182–183, 353, 357
  finding costs, 37, 47, 53, 57,
    59, 61, 65, 77, 119,
    154–155, 157, 187, 215,
    245, 262–263, 355, 359,
    361, 380–381, 387
  hourly wage, 373, 395
  mileage chart, 191
  money, 10–11
  raising money, 154–155
  reading a map, 282–283, 351
  reading a recipe, 63, 303,
    H198
  salary, 395
  sales trends, 112–113
  time cards, 395
  time zones, 231
  unit price, 186, 386–387
  using advertisements,
    154–155, 332–333, H204
Coordinate geometry,
  320–321, 400
Cube, 328–329
  volume of, 330–331, 342
Cubic units, 330–331, 342
Cumulative Review. (*See*
  Maintenance)
Cup, 292–293, 399
Customary system
  units of area, 324–325, 342
  units of capacity, 292–293
  units of length, 286–289,
    H195, H198
  units of volume, 330–331,
    342
  units of weight, 290–291
Cylinder, 328–329

D

Data, arranging of, 218–219,
  334–337
Data Sources. (*See* Problem
  Solving—Data Sources;
  Skills Applications—Data
  Sources)
Day, 90–91, 94–95
Decimals
  addition, 258–259

comparing and ordering, 254–255
  skills applications, 255
equivalent, 254–255
estimation, 256–257
  skills applications, 257
and fractions, 250–253, 269
  skills applications, 251, 253, H196
multiplication, 253
and percents, 269
place value, 250–253
reading and writing, 250–253, H196
  skills applications, 251, 253
rounding, 256–257
subtraction, 260–261
Degree, 294–295
Denominator, 198–199
Diameter, 312–313
Difference, 20–21
  even and odd, 103
Digit(s), 4–5, 12–13
Dividend, 108–109
Divisibility, 195
Division
  basic facts
    common factors, 124–125
    dividend, 108–109
    divisor, 108–109
    by eight and nine, 122–123
    factors, 124–125
    by four and five, 110–111
    meaning of, 108–109
    quotient, 108–109
    related to multiplication, 114–115
    rules for, 116–117
    by six and seven, 120–121
    by two and three, 108–109
    zero and one in, 116–117
  by one-digit divisors
    estimating quotients, 170–171
    finding averages, 180–181, H192, H201
    four-digit dividends, 178–179
    with money, 186–187

    with remainders, 168–169
    three-digit dividends, 176–179, H191
    two-digit dividends, 168–169, 172–173
    zero in the quotient, 184–185, 194, H204
  by two-digit divisors
    correcting estimates, 378–379, 394
    mental computation, 370–371, H191
    with money, 386–387
    by multiples of ten, 374–375
    three-digit dividends, 382–385, H192, H204
    two-digit dividends, 376–379
Divisor, 108–109

E

Edge, 328–329
Elapsed time, 92–95, 102
END, 32
Endpoint, 306–307
Enrichment, 31, 71, 103, 133, 165, 195, 231, 269, 303, 343, 367, 395
Equivalent fractions, 204–207, 230
Error diagnosis
  addition
    with fractions, 238
    of whole numbers, 36, 38, 48
  averages, 180
  division, 170, 172, 176, 178, 184, 186, 370, 376, 382, 384
  equivalent forms
    decimals, 250, 252
    fractions, 198, 200, 206
    mixed numbers, 210
  measurement, 278, 280
  money, 36, 38, 48, 58, 60, 62, 186, 386
  multiplication, 138, 142, 144, 148, 150, 152, 346, 354, 358
  Number Sense, 55, 115, 179, 207, 257, 275

  numeration
    decimals, 250, 252
    ratio, 220
  subtraction
    fractions, 242, 244
    whole numbers, 58, 60, 62
Estimation. (*See* Problem Solving—Estimation)
  addition
    with decimals, 256–257, 259
    of whole numbers, 41, 44–45, 50–51, 115
  area, 324–325
  division, 170–171, 179
  fractions, 207, 261
  by front-end, 41, 55
  measures, 275, 276–281, 288–293
  money, 47, 50–51, 56–57, 155
  multiplication, 140–141, 179, 348–349, 353, H189
  by rounding, 50–51, 115, 140–141
  skills applications, 45, 57, 141, 171, 281, 349
  subtraction
    with decimals, 256–257
    of whole numbers, 55, 56–57, 115
Even
  differences, 103
  numbers, 86–87, 397
  products, 103
  sums, 103
Even and odd sums, differences, and products, 103
Expanded form, 4–5

F

Face, 328–329
Factor, 74–75
Factor trees, 133, H188
Factorization, prime, 133, 398
Factors, 124–125
  common, 124–125
  missing, 114–115, H188

Facts, families of
  in addition and
    subtraction, 22–23, H182
  in multiplication and
    division, 114–115, H187
Fahrenheit, degree, 294
Flips, slides, and turns, 343,
  399
Foot, 288–289
FD (forward), 32
Fractions
  addition, 236–239, 268
    skills applications, 239,
      H195, H196
  comparing and ordering,
    212–213
    skills applications, 213
  and decimals, 250–253
  denominator, 198–199
  equal to one, 210–211
  equivalent, 204–207, 230
    skills applications, 205,
      207
  finding part of a set with,
    202–203, 230
  greater than one, 210–211
    skills applications, 211
  on a number line, 212–213
  numerator, 198–199
  part of a set, 200–201
    skills applications, 201
  part of a whole, 198–199
    skills applications, 199,
      H193, H194
  as percents, 269
  as ratios, 220–221, 269
    skills applications, 221
  simplest form, 206–207, 230
    skills applications, 207,
      H195
  subtraction, 242–245, 268
    skills applications, 243,
      245, H195
Functions. (*See* Patterns,
  relations, and functions)

G

Gallon, 292–293, 399
Geometry
  angles, 308–309, 399, H199
  area, 324–325, 342, 352–353
  circles, 312–313
  congruence, 316–317, H199
  enlarging drawings, 317

line segments, 306–307
lines, 306–307
perimeter, 274–275,
  286–287, 322–323
points, 306–307
polygons, 310–311, H199
rays, 308–309, H199
similarity, 316–317
solid figures, 328–329, 400
symmetry, 318–319
transformations, 343, 399
volume, 330–331
Glossary, H207–H210
Gram, 280–281
Graph(s)
  bar
    making, 334–335
    using, 96–97, 126, H198
  circle, 208–209, 240, H195
  enlarging drawings using
    grids, 317
  line
    using and making,
      112–113, 127, 397
  of ordered pairs, 320–321,
    400
  pictograph, 336–337, H181,
    H200
Group Project, 27, 67, 99,
  129, 161, 191, 227, 265, 299,
  339, 363, 391
Grouping Property
  in addition, 18–19
  in multiplication, 78–79

H

Height, 330–331
Hexagon, 310–311
Hour, 90–91

I

Identity Property. (*See* Property of one; Zero Property)
Inch, 286–287
Infobank, 401–406
  how to use, 16–17
  reference to, 13, 49, 77,
    111, 145, 173, 219, 239,
    291, 331, 355, 377

K

Kilogram, 280–281
Kilometer, 276–277

L

LT (left), 32
Length
  customary units of,
    286–289
  estimating, 277, 289
  metric units of, 274–277
LET, 233
Line(s)
  intersecting, 306–307
  parallel, 306–307
  of symmetry, 318–319
Line graph. (*See* Graph)
Line number, 135
Line segments
  congruent, 316–317
  endpoints of, 306–307
Liter, 278–279
Logic, 2–3, 23, 44–45, 86–87,
  109, 125, 160, 199, 219, 255,
  264, 323, 352–353, 362
Logical Reasoning. (*See*
  Logic)
LOGO, 32

M

Maintenance
  Another Look, 37, 63, 83,
    121, 139, 141, 211, 239,
    251, 277, 309, 319, 349,
    385
  Choosing a strategy or
    method, 126–127,
    182–183, 240–241,
    350–351, 380–381
  Cumulative Review, 34, 72,
    106, 136, 166, 196, 234,
    272, 304, 344, 368, 396
  Midchapter Review, 15, 51,
    91, 117, 145, 181, 213,
    247, 279, 321, 355, 379
  Reteaching, 30, 70, 102,
    132, 164, 194, 230, 268,
    302, 342, 366, 394
Manipulatives
  using, 2–3, 154–155,
    168–169, 202–203,
    204–205, 207, 213,
    236–237, 255, 258–259,
    260, 274–275, 279, 283,
    286–287, 300, 302,

312–313, 321, 324–325, 329, 330–331, 352, 374–375

Mass, 280–281

Math Reasoning. (*See* Reasoning)

Measurement, 2–3, 90–95, 102, 236–237, 260–261, 274–281, 286–295, 302, 303, 322–325, 330–331, 342

Measures
area, 324–325, 342
capacity, 278–279, 292–293, 399
Customary system of. (*See* Customary system)
equivalent, 276–281, 288–293
estimating, 276–281, 288–293, H197
length, 274–277, 286–289, 398
mass, 280–281
Metric system of. (*See* Metric system)
perimeter, 274–275, 286–287, 322–323, H200
temperature, 294–295
time, 90–95, 102
time zones, 231
volume, 330–331, 342, H200
weight, 290–291

Mental math, 5, 9, 49, 59, 77, 111, 151, 173, 245, 287, 371

Meter, 276–277

Metric system
units of area, 324–325
units of capacity, 278–279
units of length, 274–277, H197
units of mass, 280–281
units of volume, 330–331, 342

Midchapter Review. (*See* Maintenance)

Mile, 288–289

Milliliter, 278–279

Minute, 90–91

Missing
addends, 22–23
factors, 114–115

Mixed number(s)
addition, 246–247
skills applications, 247

comparing and ordering, 212–213
skills applications, 213
concept of, 210–211, 398
and decimals, 250–253
skills applications, 251, 253
subtraction, 246–247
skills applications, 247

Money, 10–11
addition, 36–39, 45–49, H182
change, making and counting, 71, H182
division, 186–187, 386–387
estimation, 50–51, 56–57, 140–141, 256–257, 348–349, H182
as hundredths of a dollar, 252–253, H193
multiplication, 154–155, 352–355, 358–359
problem solving. (*See* Problem Solving— Applications)
rounding, 14–15
skills applications, 11, 37, 57, 59, 61, 141, 155, 177, 187, 245, 355, 359, 387, H190
skip-counting, 10–11
subtraction, 54–55, 58–63, 70, H182
word names for, 10–11

Month, 94–95

More Practice, H157–H180

Multiples, 86–87, 397, H191

Multiplication
basic facts
with eight and nine, 84–85
factor, 74–75
finding patterns, 397
with four and five, 76–77, H185
missing factors, 114–115, H188
multiples, 86–87
product, 74–75
properties of, 78–79, 398
related to division, 114–115
with six and seven, 82–83, H186

with two and three, 74–75
by one-digit multipliers
decimals, 253
estimation, 140–141
four-digit numbers, 152–153, 164
money, 154–155, 164
multiples of ten, one hundred, and one thousand, 138–139
three one-digit numbers, 144–145
three-digit numbers, 148–151, 164, H190
two-digit numbers, 142–145, 164, H201
table, 398
by two-digit multipliers
estimation, 348–349
money, 352–355, 358–359, 366, H202
multiples of ten, one hundred, and one thousand, 346–347
three-digit numbers, 358–359, 366
two-digit numbers, 352–355, 366, H202

N

Negative number, in temperature, 294–295

Number(s)
comparing and ordering, 8–9, 212–213, 254–255
decimals. (*See* Decimals)
fractions. (*See* Fractions)
expanded form, 4–5
mixed. (*See* Mixed number)
place value, 4–5, 12–13, 250–253
prime, 133, 243, 398
Roman numerals, 31
rounding, 14–15, 256–257
standard form, 4–5, 12–13
whole. (*See* Whole number)

Number line, 8, 14, 30, 212, 254, H185

Number sense, 2–3, 40, 44–45, 236–237, 258–259 (*See also* Estimation *and* Mental Math)
Number sentence, 22–23, 64–65, 114–115, 188–189, 372–373, H203
Number sequence, 79
Number theory
  divisibility, 195
  even numbers, 86–87, 397
  expanded form, 4–5
  factors, 124–125
  multiples, 86–87
  odd numbers, 86–87, 397
  prime factorization, 133, 398
  prime number, 133, 243, 398
  short word name, 4–5, 12–13
  standard form, 4–5, 12–13
Numerator, 198–199

O

Octagon, 310–311
Odd
  differences, 103
  numbers, 86–87, 397
  products, 103
  sums, 103
Operations, order of, 165
Order Property
  in addition, 18–19
  in multiplication, 78–79
Ordered pairs, 320–321, 400
Ordering. (*See* Comparing and ordering)
Ordinal numbers, H181
Ounce, 290–291
Outcomes, possible, 216–217

P

Parallel lines, 306–307
Patterns, relations, and functions, 46–47, 79, 86–87, 138–139, 168–169, 185, 199, 255, 276–281, 288–293, 324–325, 346–347, 352–353, 374–375, 398, 400, H185,

H203
PD (pendown), 32
Pentagon, 310–311
PU (penup), 32
Percent, 269
Perimeter, 274–275, 286–287, 322–323, 338
Pictograph. (*See* Graph)
Pint, 292–293, 399
Place value
  decimals, 250–253
  whole numbers, 4–5, 12–13, 181
P.M., 90–91
Point, 306–307
Polygon, 310–311
  congruent, 316–317
  line(s) of symmetry, 318–319
  perimeter, 322–323
  side, 310–311
  similar, 316–317
Pound, 290–291
Predicting outcomes, 218–219
Prime factorization, 133, 398
Prime numbers, 133, 243, 398
PRINT, 134
Prism, 328–329, 330–331
Probability, 216–219, 229, H194
  making predictions, 218–219
Problem formulation, 21, 57, 83, 95, 109, 123, 139, 177, 185, 255, 289, 359, 379, 383, 385
Problem Solving
  Choosing a strategy or method, 126–127, 182–183, 240–241, 350–351, 380–381
  Organized approach, A Four-Step Plan, 6–7
Problem Solving—Applications
  addition, 24–25, 46–47, 64–65, 80–81, 88–89, 126–127, 182–183, 260–261, 262–263
  algebra, 64–65, 126–127, 158–159, 188–189, 240–241, 350–351, 372–373

comparing and ordering, 17, 126–127, 214–215
division, 158–159, 168–169, 174–175, 182–183, 188–189, 214–215, 240–241, 350–351, 372–373
functions and patterns, 118–119, 326–327, 380–381
logic, 46–47, 222–223, 240–241, 248–249, 380–381
measurement, 296–297, 324–325
money, 46–47, 52–53, 64–65, 146–147, 154–157, 182–183, 214–215, 262–263, 352–353, 356–357, 372–373
multiplication, 80–81, 88–89, 154–159, 182–183, 188–189, 214–215, 222–223, 240–241, 262–263, 296–297, 352–353, 372–373
organized approach, 6–7
statistics and probability, 96–97, 112–113, 208–209
subtraction, 24–25, 88–89, 96–97, 112–113, 126–127, 156–157, 260–263, 314–315, 350–351, 372–373
Problem Solving—Data Sources
  advertisement, 147, 332–333
  bar graph, 96–97, 126
  circle graph, 208–209, 240–241
  Infobank, 401–406
  line graph, 112–113, 126–127, 397
  map, 350–351
Problem Solving—Estimation, 52–53, 146–147, 356–357, 388–389
Problem Solving—Strategies and Skills
  acting it out, 240–241, 363
  checking for a reasonable answer, 360–361

checking that the solution answers the question, 314–315

choosing the operation, 24–25, 80–81, 158–159

choosing a strategy or method, 126–127, 182–183, 240–241, 350–351, 380–381

choosing/writing a sensible question, 224–225

drawing a picture, 282–283

guessing and checking, 284–285

identifying extra information, 156–157

identifying needed information, 42–43, 296–297

interpreting the quotient and the remainder, 174–175

looking for a pattern, 326–327

making a diagram, 222–223

making a diagram, chart, or graph, 222–223, 334–335, 397

making a model, 282–283, 352

making an organized list, 248–249

making a table to find a pattern, 118–119

solving two-step problems/ making a plan, 88–89

using outside sources including the Infobank, 16–17

working backward, 214–215, H187

writing a number sentence, 64–65, 188–189, 372–373, H182, H184

writing a simpler problem, 262–263

Procedure, 32

Product, 74–75

even and odd, 103

Program, 135

Programming languages. (See BASIC; LOGO)

Projects. (See Group Project)

Property

Associative. (See Grouping Property)

Commutative. (See Order Property)

Grouping, 18–19, 78–79

Identity

for addition, 18–19

for multiplication, 78–79

Order, 18–19, 78–79

Zero

in addition, 18–19

in multiplication, 78–79, 398

Property of one, 78–79, 398

Pyramid, 328–329

Q—————————————

Quadrilateral, 310–311

Quart, 292–293, 399

Quotient, 108–109

zero in, 184–185, 194

R—————————————

Radius, 312–313

Ratio, 220–221

and fractions, 220–221, 269

and percents, 269

Ray, 308–309

Reasonableness, 2–3, 44–45, 46–47, 154–155, 258–259, 260–261, 330–331

Reasoning

Challenge, H182, H183, H185, H186, H187, H189, H190, H191, H192, H193, H195, H196, H197, H198, H199, H200, H202, H203, H204

Logical Reasoning, H181, H183, H184, H185, H186, H187, H188, H190, H191, H192, H193, H194, H195, H196, H198, H199, H201, H202, H203, H204

Visual Thinking, H181, H184, H185, H186, H188, H192, H194, H196, H197, H199, H200, H202

Recipe, following a, 303

Rectangle, 310–311

area, 324–325

perimeter, 322–323

Rectangular prism, 328–329

volume, 330–331, 342, 400

Relations. (See also Patterns, relations, and functions)

Remainder, 168–169

REPEAT, 104

Reteaching. (See Maintenance)

Right angle, 308–309

Roman numerals, 31

Rounding, 14–15, 50–51, 56–57, 140–141, 256–257, 348–349

RT (right), 32

Rules of division, 116–117

RUN, 135

S—————————————

Second, 90–91

Side

of an angle, 308–309

of a polygon, 310–311

Similarity, 316–317

Skills Applications—Data Sources

advertisement, 187

charts, 21, 23, 75, 79, 117, 121, 153, 181, 217, 218, 219, 349, 385

graphs, 334–335, 336–337

recipe, 63

sign, 37

spinners, 216–217, 219

tables, 23, 61, 85, 141

tables of equivalent measures, 276, 278, 280, 288, 290, 292

Skip-counting, 10–11, 92–93

Slides, 343, 399

Solid figures, 328–329, 400

Sphere, 328–329

Square, 310–311

area, 324–325, 342

perimeter, 322–323

Square units, 324–325

Standard form, 4–5, 12–13

Statistics and probability, 2–3, 168–169, 324–325, 330–331

data sources, 216–219
graphs
  bar, 334–335
  pictograph, 336–337
  tally, 218–219
Subtraction
  annexing zeros, 260–261
  checking, 54–55
  with decimals, 260–261
  estimation in, 55, 56–57, 256–257
  facts, 20–21, 397
  with fractions, 242–243
  of larger numbers, 60–61, H184
  with mixed numbers, 246–247
  with money, 54–55, 58–59, 60–63, 70
  related to addition, 22–23
  of three-digit numbers, 58–59
  of two-digit numbers, 54–55
  of whole numbers, 20–21, 54–55, 58–63, 70
  with zeros, 62–63, 70
Sum(s), 18–19
  even and odd, 103, 397
Symmetry, 318–319

T

Tables of measures and symbols, H205
Tally, 218–219
Technology
  Calculator, 13, 44–45, 57, 61, 66, 86–87, 98, 154–155, 168–169, 177, 187, 190, 258–259, 298, 330–331, 338, 387, 390, H182, H183, H187, H189, H204
  Computer, 32–33, 104–105, 134–135, 232–233, 270–271
Temperature, 294–295
Tests
  chapter, 28–29, 68–69, 100–101, 130–131, 162–163, 192–193,

228–229, 266–267, 300–301, 340–341, 364–365, 392–393
  cumulative, 34, 72, 106, 136, 166, 196, 234, 272, 304, 344, 368, 396
Thermometer, 294–295
Time
  elapsed, 92–95, 397, H186
  telling, 92–93
  units of, 90–91, 94–95
Time card, 395
Time zones, 231
Ton, 290–291
Transformations, 343, 399
Triangle, 310–311
Triangular prism, 328–329
Turns, 343, 399
Turtle, 32

U

Units
  of area, 324–325, 342
  of volume, 330–331, 342

V

Venn diagram, 323
Vertex (vertices)
  of an angle, 308–309
  of a polygon, 310–311
  of a solid figure, 328–329
Volume, 330–331, 342, 400

W

Weight, customary units of, 290–291
Whole number(s)
  addition, 18–19, 36–39, 44–51
    skills applications, 19, 37, 39, 49
  comparing and ordering, 8–9, 30
  division, 108–111, 116–117, 120–123, 168–169, 172–173, 176–181, 184–185, 194, 370–371,

374–379, 382–385, 394
    skills applications, 109, 111, 117, 121, 123, 173, 177, 179, 185, 371, 377, 379, 383, 385
  estimation, 41, 50–51, 55, 56–57, 140–141, 170–171, 348–349
    skills applications, 51, 57, 141, 349
  finding a fraction of, 202–203
  multiplication, 74–77, 82–85, 138–139, 142–145, 148–153, 164, 346–347, 352–355, 358–359, 366, 367
    skills applications, 75, 77, 83, 139, 143, 145, 149, 151, 153, 347, 353, 355, 359
  place value, 4–5, 12–13
    skills applications, 3, 5, 13
  rounding, 14–15
  subtraction, 20–21, 54–55, 58–63, 70
    skills applications, 21, 55, 59, 61, 63
Width, 330–331
Word names for numbers
  decimals, 250–253
  fractions, 198–201
  money, 10–11
  whole numbers, 4–5, 12–13

Y

Yard, 288–289
Year, 90–91

Z

Zero(s)
  annexing, 258–261
  in division, 116–117, 184–185, 194
  in multiplication, 346–347, 354–355, 358–359
  in subtraction, 62–63, 70
Zero Property
  in addition, 18–19
  in multiplication, 78–79

Learning Resources

The Learning Resources can be traced, colored, and cut out. These resources can be used as tools to help you understand math concepts and solve problems.

Multiplication Table

×	0	1	2	3	4	5	6	7	8	9
0	0	0	0	0	0	0	0	0	0	0
1	0	1	2	3	4	5	6	7	8	9
2	0	2	4	6	8	10	12	14	16	18
3	0	3	6	9	12	15	18	21	24	27
4	0	4	8	12	16	20	24	28	32	36
5	0	5	10	15	20	25	30	35	40	45
6	0	6	12	18	24	30	36	42	48	54
7	0	7	14	21	28	35	42	49	56	63
8	0	8	16	24	32	40	48	56	64	72
9	0	9	18	27	36	45	54	63	72	81

Number Lines

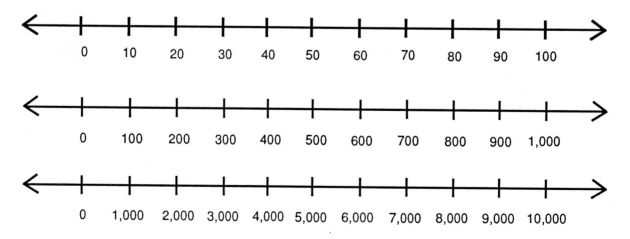

Fraction Circles

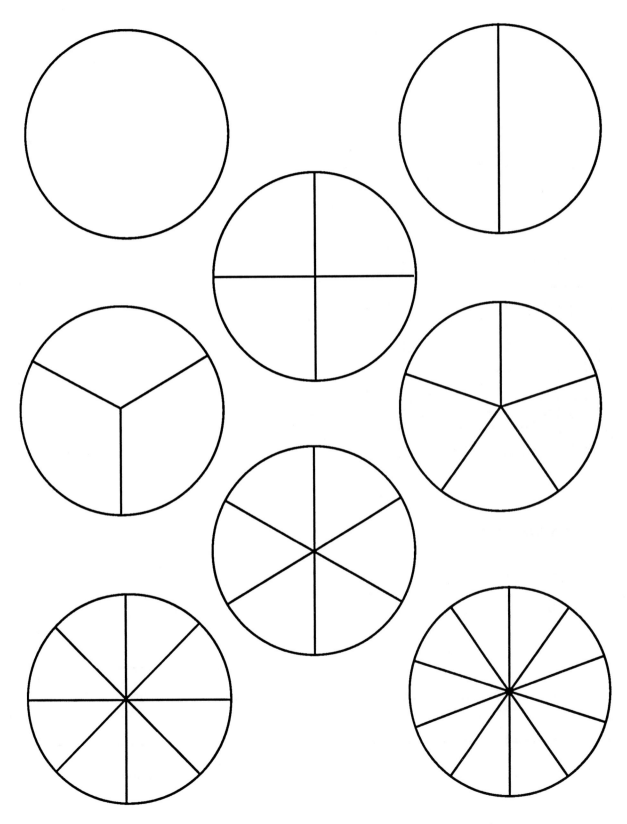

Fraction Bars

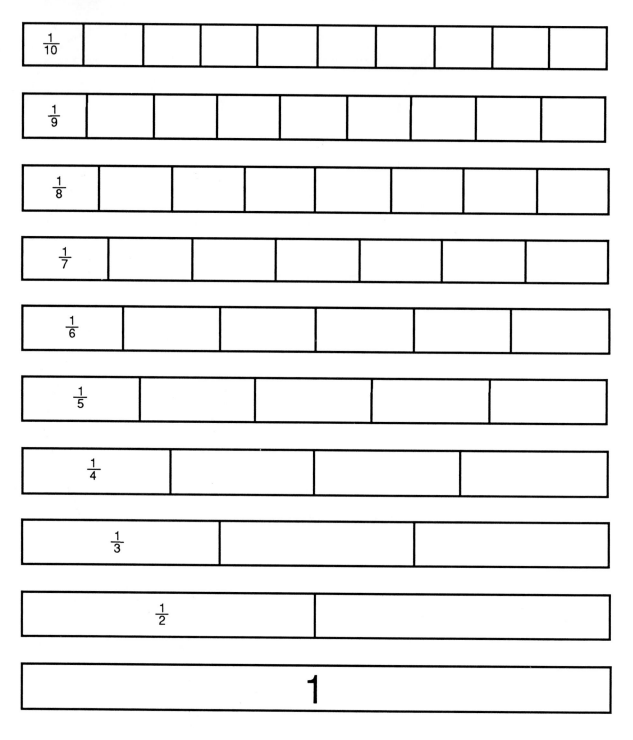

Plane Geometric Shapes

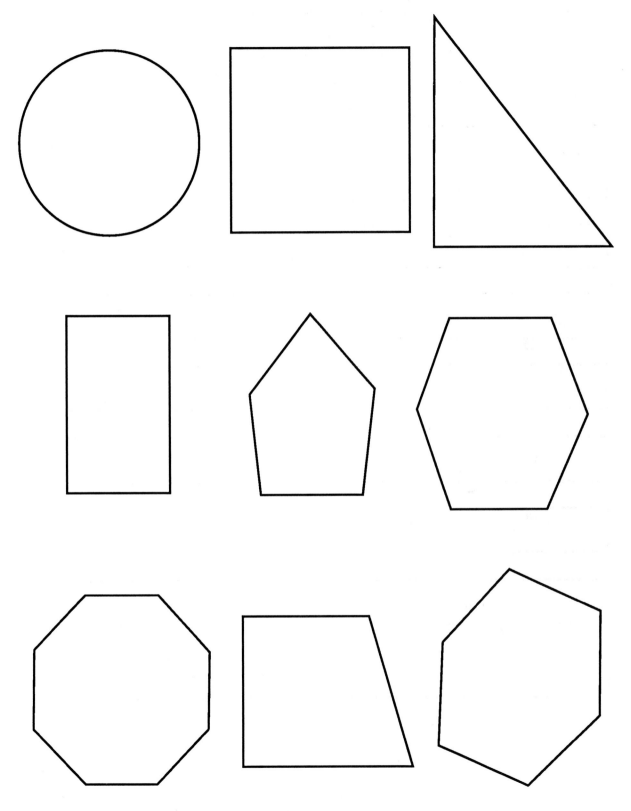

Solid Geometric Shapes

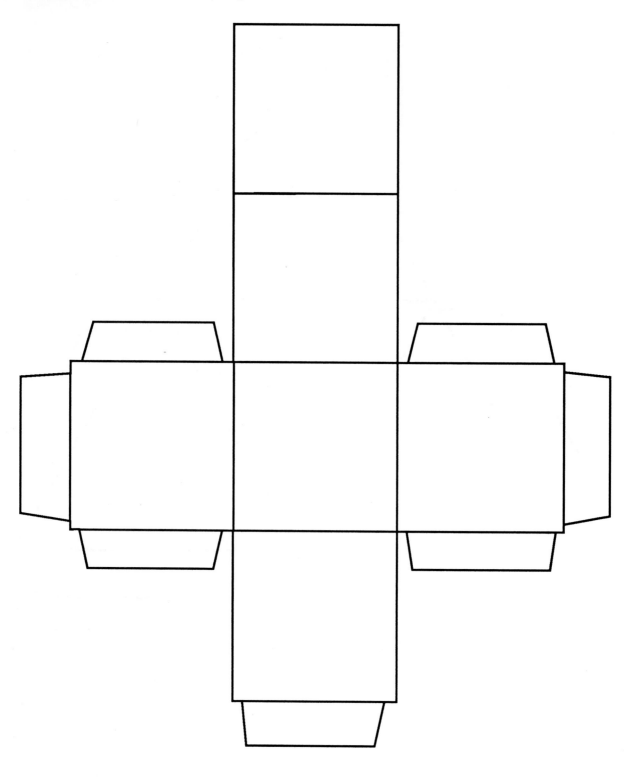

Solid Geometric Shapes

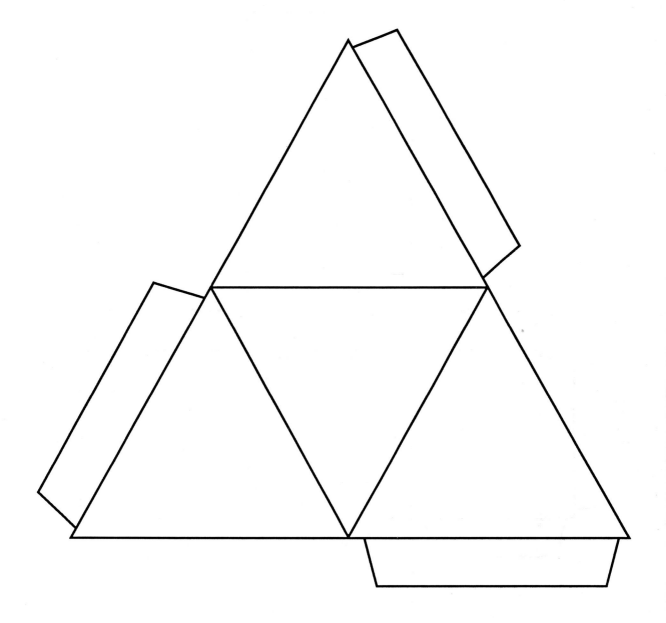

Solid Geometric Shapes

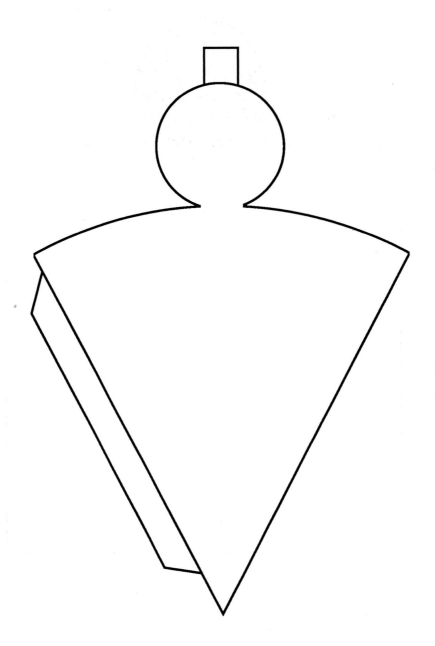

Solid Geometric Shapes

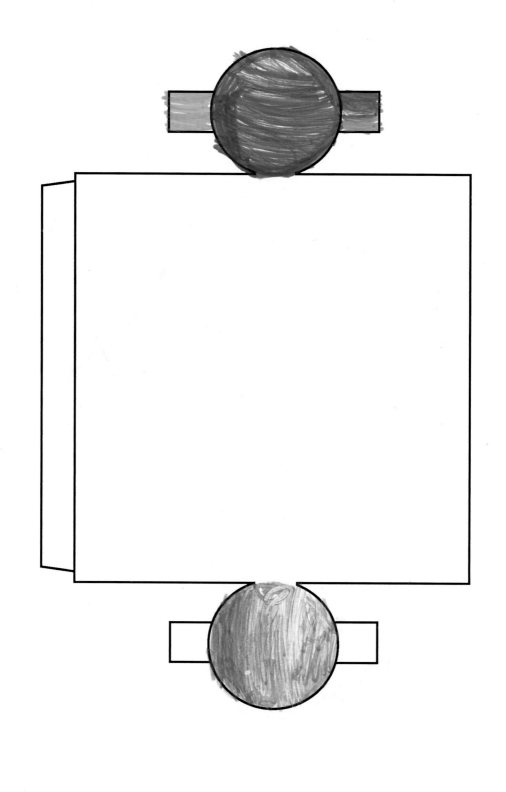

Tangram

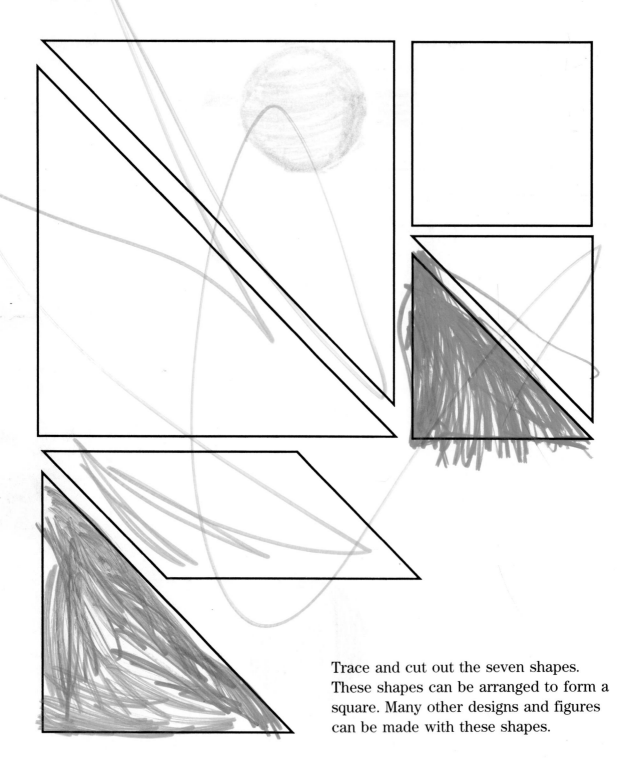

Trace and cut out the seven shapes. These shapes can be arranged to form a square. Many other designs and figures can be made with these shapes.